Lecture Notes in Computer Science 6760

Commenced Publication in 1973
Founding and Former Series Editors:
Gerhard Goos, Juris Hartmanis, and Jan van Leeuwen

Editorial Board

David Hutchison
  Lancaster University, UK
Takeo Kanade
  Carnegie Mellon University, Pittsburgh, PA, USA
Josef Kittler
  University of Surrey, Guildford, UK
Jon M. Kleinberg
  Cornell University, Ithaca, NY, USA
Friedemann Mattern
  ETH Zurich, Switzerland
John C. Mitchell
  Stanford University, CA, USA
Moni Naor
  Weizmann Institute of Science, Rehovot, Israel
Oscar Nierstrasz
  University of Bern, Switzerland
C. Pandu Rangan
  Indian Institute of Technology, Madras, India
Bernhard Steffen
  TU Dortmund University, Germany
Madhu Sudan
  Microsoft Research, Cambridge, MA, USA
Demetri Terzopoulos
  University of California, Los Angeles, CA, USA
Doug Tygar
  University of California, Berkeley, CA, USA
Moshe Y. Vardi
  Rice University, Houston, TX, USA
Gerhard Weikum
  Max Planck Institute for Informatics, Saarbruecken, Germany

W0192963

Per Stenström (Ed.)

Transactions on High-Performance Embedded Architectures and Compilers IV

 Springer

Volume Editor

Per Stenström
Chalmers University of Technology
Department of Computer Science and Engineering
412 96 Gothenburg, Sweden
E-mail: per.stenstrom@chalmers.se

ISSN 0302-9743 (LNCS)   e-ISSN 1611-3349 (LNCS)
ISSN 1864-306X (THIPEAC)   e-ISSN 1864-3078 (THIPEAC)
ISBN 978-3-642-24567-1   e-ISBN 978-3-642-24568-8
DOI 10.1007/978-3-642-24568-8
Springer Heidelberg Dordrecht London New York

Library of Congress Control Number: 2011940725

CR Subject Classification (1998): B.2, C.1, D.3.4, B.5, C.2, D.4

© Springer-Verlag Berlin Heidelberg 2011
This work is subject to copyright. All rights are reserved, whether the whole or part of the material is
concerned, specifically the rights of translation, reprinting, re-use of illustrations, recitation, broadcasting,
reproduction on microfilms or in any other way, and storage in data banks. Duplication of this publication
or parts thereof is permitted only under the provisions of the German Copyright Law of September 9, 1965,
in ist current version, and permission for use must always be obtained from Springer. Violations are liable
to prosecution under the German Copyright Law.
The use of general descriptive names, registered names, trademarks, etc. in this publication does not imply,
even in the absence of a specific statement, that such names are exempt from the relevant protective laws
and regulations and therefore free for general use.

Typesetting: Camera-ready by author, data conversion by Scientific Publishing Services, Chennai, India

Printed on acid-free paper

Springer is part of Springer Science+Business Media (www.springer.com)

Editor-in-Chief's Message

It is my pleasure to introduce you to the fourth volume of *Transactions on High-Performance Embedded Architectures and Compilers*. This journal was created as an archive for scientific articles in the converging fields of high-performance and embedded computer architectures and compiler systems. Design considerations in both general-purpose and embedded systems are increasingly being based on similar scientific insights. For example, a state-of-the-art game console today consists of a powerful parallel computer whose building blocks are the same as those found in computational clusters for high-performance computing. Moreover, keeping power/energy consumption at a low level for high-performance general-purpose systems as well as in, for example, mobile embedded systems is equally important in order to either keep heat dissipation at a manageable level or to maintain a long operating time despite the limited battery capacity. It is clear that similar scientific issues have to be solved to build competitive systems in both segments. Additionally, for high-performance systems to be realized – be it embedded or general-purpose – a holistic design approach has to be taken by factoring in the impact of applications as well as the underlying technology when making design trade-offs. The main topics of this journal reflect this development and include (among others):

- Processor architecture, e.g., network and security architectures, application-specific processors and accelerators, and reconfigurable architectures
- Memory system design
- Power-, temperature-, performance-, and reliability-constrained designs
- Evaluation methodologies, program characterization, and analysis techniques
- Compiler techniques for embedded systems, e.g, feedback-directed optimization, dynamic compilation, adaptive execution, continuous profiling/optimization, back-end code generation, and binary translation/optimization
- Code size/memory footprint optimizations

This volume contains 21 papers divided into four sections. The first section contains five regular papers. The second section is a special one containing the top four papers from the 4th International Conference on High-Performance and Embedded Architectures and Compilers - HiPEAC. I would like to thank Michael O'Boyle (University of Edinburgh) and Margaret Martonosi (Princeton University) for acting as guest editors of that section. The contributions in this section deal with issues related to exploiting parallelism and to reducing power consumption in emerging multicore architectures.

The third section contains a set of six papers providing a snap-shot from the Workshop on Software and Hardware Challenges of Many-Core Platforms (SHCMP 2008). I am indebted to Albert Cohen (INRIA), Xinmin Tian (Intel) and Wenguang Chen (Tsinghua University) for putting together this special section.

Finally, the fourth section provides a snap-shot of six papers from the 8th IEEE International Symposium on Systems, Architectures, Modeling and Simulation, 2008 (SAMOS VIII). I am very much indebted to Nikitas Dimopoulos (University of Victoria), Walid Najjar (UC Riverside), Mladen Berekovic (Technical University of Braunschweig), and Stephan Wong (Delft University of Technology) for their effort in putting together this special section.

In the third volume of *Transactions of HiPEAC*, one of the papers entitled "Software-Level Instruction-Cache Leakage Reduction Using Value-Dependence of SRAM Leakage in Nanometer Technologies" by Maziar Goudarzi et al. was incorrectly listed as belonging to the special issue on the MULTIPROG workshop. This paper was indeed a regular paper and should have been listed accordingly.

In closing, I would like to mention that the editorial board has worked diligently to handle the papers for the journal. I would like to thank all the contributing authors, editors, and reviewers for their excellent work.

Per Stenström, Chalmers University of Technology
Editor-in-Chief
Transactions on HiPEAC

4th International Conference on High-Performance and Embedded Architectures and Compilers (HiPEAC)

Selected Papers

In January 2009 the 4th International Conference on High-Performance Embedded Architectures was held in the beautiful city of Paphos, Cyprus. We were fortunate to attract 97 submissions of which 27 were selected for presentation at the conference. After the conference and in consultation with the Program Committee, we selected four of the most highly-rated and best-received papers to be invited for inclusion in this volume. The authors have prepared extended versions, which are included here.

The first paper by Azevedo et al. addresses the problem of application scaling on multi-core systems. It develops a new algorithm to exploit inter-frame parallelism in the widely-used video decoder H.264. Combining this with existing intra-frame parallelism leads to a new technique that gives scalable performance on a greater number of processors than existing techniques.

In the second paper by Muralidhara and Kandemir, multi-core utilization is again the subject of study. This paper addresses the energy cost of within-chip communication. The authors develop a new Markov-based approach that predicts when links can be powered down. This accurate scheme is able to deliver significant power reduction without incurring excessive performance impact.

The third paper, by Vandeputte and Eeckhout, tackles the issue of workload selection for design and evaluation of computer systems. Using representative sampling, they propose a technique that can automatically select benchmarks that stretch a processor's capabilities. Using threshold clustering they can find stress patterns significantly faster than standard approaches.

Finally, the fourth paper combines the issues of application behavior and power reduction. Here, Henry and Nazhandali tackle the widely used FFT algorithm and investigate the use of partitioning a hardware implementation of the algorithm into two different circuit technologies. They show that the correct partition can deliver a large energy reduction, significantly increasing battery life.

Michael F.P. O'Boyle
Margaret Martonosi

Workshop on Software and Hardware Challenges of Many-Core Platforms (SHCMP)

Selected Papers

Processors built with two or more on-chip cores are already shipping in volume. Soon, most mainstream computers could be configured with many-core processors built with eight or more on-chip cores and possibly on-chip heterogeneous many-cores. This shift to an increasing number of cores places new burdens on mainstream software and will require new software tools for developing systems. Meanwhile, parallel programming and computing has come a long way boosting the performance for numerical scientific applications. However, today, mainstream application programmers are challenged by the daunting task of parallelizing general non-numerical applications and must have reasonable knowledge of architecture, compilers, threading libraries and multithreading. It is time to explore new technologies so that general programs can be multithreaded efficiently and effectively for many-core platforms.

In this context, a workshop on Software and Hardware Challenges of Many-Core Platforms (SHCMP 2008) was held together with the 35th International Symposium on Computer Architecture (ISCA 2008). It provided a forum for the presentation and discussion of research on all aspects of software and hardware for developing applications on many-core platforms.

We received 23 submissions in response to a call for papers, and each submission was evaluated by three reviewers. Based on feedback received, the Program Committee accepted 13 papers which were presented in the SHCMP 2008 workshop held on June 22, 2008. Of the 13 accepted papers, the 8 papers ranked at the top were selected by the SHCMP 2008 Program Committee. We invited the authors of these eight papers to submit a revised version to be considered for publication in this special issue. Authors of seven out of eight invited papers accepted the invitation and submitted their revised journal version. The revised papers were reviewed by the same reviewers again to ensure the authors addressed the issues raised in the first round of review. Finally, of the eight papers, six were accepted for inclusion in this Special Section.

We are deeply grateful to the Program Committee members. The Program Committee was working under a tight schedule. We wish to thank all Program Committee members for their assistance in organizing the SHCMP 2008 program and determining the paper selection guidelines. Without the solid work and dedication of these committee members, the success of the program and the workshop itself would not have been possible. We appreciate the contribution of Wenguang Chen's local team at Tsinghua University Beijing who organized and handled the workshop website for paper submission and review.

We would also like express our gratitude for the support and sponsorship we received from the Steering Committee and the 35th International Symposium on Computer Architecture (ISCA 2008) Organizing Committee for their support in this endeavor. Finally, we are grateful to the HiPEAC network, and Per Stenstrom in particular, for making this special issue possible.

Albert Cohen
Xinmin Tian
Wenguang Chen

8th IEEE International Symposium on Systems, Architectures, Modeling and Simulation (SAMOS VIII)

Selected Papers

It is our pleasure to introduce this special issue that includes selected papers from the International Symposium on Systems, Architectures, Modeling and Simulation 2008 (SAMOS VIII). The International Symposium on Embedded Computer Systems: Architectures, Modeling, and Simulation (SAMOS) is an annual gathering of highly qualified researchers from academia and industry, sharing a three-day lively discussion on the quiet and inspiring northern mountainside of the Mediterranean island of Samos. The symposium is unique in the sense that not only solved research problems are presented and discussed, but also (partly) unsolved problems and in-depth topical reviews can be unleashed in the scientific arena. It comprises two co-located events: The International SAMOS Conference and the SAMOS Workshop. In 2008, more than 200 papers were submitted for these two events. After a very competitive selection process only about 30% of these papers were selected for presentation. According to the symposium's ranked results and the results of a second stage review process of all presentations from the SAMOS workshop and conference, ten papers were invited to this special issue, out of which the following seven papers were selected for publication in this special issue. These works address a broad spectrum of issues in embedded systems architecture and design and range from design space exploration environments to networking.

The paper by Beiu et al. presents an interesting use of Rent's rule to compare the connectivity of a variety of networks. The authors further utilize Rent's rule to also compare the connectivity of the brain and show through their analysis that two-layer hierarchical networks mimic the brain's connectivity, and that particular combinations of parameters produce global networks with significantly reduced complexity.

The paper by Llorente et al. presents two novel packet segmentation algorithms targeting network processors. These algorithms aim to achieve increased system throughput by balancing the number of segments per packet to the memory efficiency.

The paper by Osborne et al. presents a method of developing energy-efficient run-time reconfigurable designs. The authors propose to deactivate part of the design by restricting the accuracy of the computations (i.e., optimizing the word length) and then select the most optimal reconfiguration strategy. The authors have developed a model through which they determine the conditions that establish when the bitstream reconfiguration method is more efficient than multiplexing. They have applied their approach to various case studies including ray tracing, vector multiplication B-Splines etc.

The paper by Rullman and Merker develops a cost model for reconfigurable architectures. Based on a general module transition model (MTM), the authors develop two metrics that estimate the reconfiguration time and reconfiguration size. These two quantities constitute the reconfiguration cost. The model is then applied to analyze costs at different levels of abstraction. Benchmark results show the efficacy of the method in lowering the reconfiguration costs.

The paper by Plishker et al. presents a new dataflow approach that enables the description of heterogeneous applications utilizing multiple forms of dataflow. Existing dataflow models are translated to the new dataflow formalism. A simulation environment allows designers to model and verify the designs. The paper provides a design example based on polynomial evaluation. A programmable polynomial evaluation accelerator (PEA) is presented, as well as a design employing two PEAs each targeting a different polynomial function (hence the heterogeneity).

The paper by Cope et al. presents a design exploration tool that is capable of exploring the customization options for a homogeneous multiprocessor (HoMP). The impact of architectural parameters on the performance of a variety of algorithms is explored and this is used to suggest post-fabrication optimizations where reconfigurable logic (RL) can be used to optimize the architecture as suggested during the exploration. The examples taken are from the domain of video processing utilizing graphics processing units; however, the tool is general enough to be applicable to a larger range of architectures.

The paper by Jaddoe et al. focuses on the problem of calibrating the analytical performance models used in system-level simulation environments. To accomplish this goal, the authors use the notion of separation of concerns (i.e., the decoupling of the computational requirements of an application from the capabilities of the architecture). The computational requirements of an application are described as signatures, i.e., vectors of instruction counts from an abstract instruction set (AIS) that expresses the application. The architectural capabilities are then expressed as the clock cycles required for an application (or operation) to run on a particular architecture. The signatures of several applications (operations) from a training set are then used to derive a best fit estimate of cycles per (AIS) instruction. These processor signatures can now be used to estimate the time (in terms of cycles) an application would require to run on a particular architecture. The paper presents experimental results of the application of the said approach in the mapping of a motion-JPEG encoder to an MP-Soc.

We would like to thank all the authors who submitted manuscripts for this special issue. Special thanks go to all the reviewers for their valuable comments, criticism, and suggestions. The investment of their time and insight is very much appreciated and helped to generate this selection of high-quality technical papers. We also appreciate the support from the editor-in-chief and publisher of the *Transactions on HiPEAC* for organizing this special issue.

Nikitas Dimopoulos
Walid Najjar
Mladen Berekovic
Stephan Wong

Editorial Board

Per Stenström is a professor of computer engineering at Chalmers University of Technology. His research interests are devoted to design principles for high-performance computer systems and he has made multiple contributions to high-performance memory systems in particular. He has authored or co-authored three textbooks and more than 100 publications in international journals and conferences. He regularly serves Program Committees of major conferences in the computer architecture field. He is also an associate editor of *IEEE Transactions on Parallel and Distributed Processing Systems*, a subject-area editor of the *Journal of Parallel and Distributed Computing*, an associate editor of the *IEEE TCCA Computer Architecture Letters*, and the founding Editor-in-Chief of *Transactions on High-Performance Embedded Architectures and Compilers*. He co-founded the HiPEAC Network of Excellence funded by the European Commission. He has acted as General and Program Chair for a large number of conferences including the ACM/IEEE International Symposium on Computer Architecture, the IEEE High-Performance Computer Architecture Symposium, and the IEEE International Parallel and Distributed Processing Symposium. He is a Fellow of the ACM and the IEEE and a member of Academia Europaea and the Royal Swedish Academy of Engineering Sciences.

Koen De Bosschere obtained his PhD from Ghent University in 1992. He is a professor in the ELIS Department at the Universiteit Gent where he teaches courses on computer architecture and operating systems. His current research interests include: computer architecture, system software, code optimization. He has co-authored 150 contributions in the domain of optimization, performance modeling, microarchitecture, and debugging. He is the coordinator of the ACACES research network and of the European HiPEAC2 network. Contact him at Koen.DeBosschere@elis.UGent.be.

Jose Duato is Professor in the Department of Computer Engineering (DISCA) at UPV, Spain. His research interests include interconnection networks and multiprocessor architectures. He has published over 340 papers. His research results have been used in the design of the Alpha 21364 microprocessor, and the Cray T3E, IBM BlueGene/L, and Cray Black Widow supercomputers. Dr. Duato is the first author of the book *Interconnection Networks: An Engineering Approach*. He served as associate editor of IEEE TPDS and IEEE TC. He was General Co-chair of ICPP 2001, Program Chair of HPCA-10, and Program Co-chair of ICPP 2005. Also, he served as Co-chair, Steering Committee member, Vice-Chair, or Program Committee member in more than 55 conferences, including HPCA, ISCA, IPPS/SPDP, IPDPS, ICPP, ICDCS, Europar, and HiPC.

Manolis Katevenis received the PhD degree from U.C. Berkeley in 1983 and the ACM Doctoral Dissertation Award in 1984 for his thesis on "Reduced Instruction Set Computer Architectures for VLSI." After a brief term on the faculty of Computer Science at Stanford University, he is now in Greece, and has been with the University of Crete and with FORTH since 1986. After RISC, his research has been on interconnection networks and interprocessor communication. In packet switch architectures, his contributions since 1987 have been mostly in per-flow queueing, credit-based flow control, congestion management, weighted round-robin scheduling, buffered crossbars, and non-blocking switching fabrics. In multiprocessing and clustering, his contributions since 1993 have been on remote-write-based, protected, user-level communication.

His home URL is http://archvlsi.ics.forth.gr/~kateveni.

Michael O'Boyle is a professor in the School of Informatics at the University of Edinburgh and an EPSRC Advanced Research Fellow. He received his PhD in Computer Science from the University of Manchester in 1992. He was formerly an SERC Postdoctoral Research Fellow, a Visiting Research Scientist at IRISA/INRIA Rennes, a Visiting Research Fellow at the University of Vienna and a Visiting Scholar at Stanford University. More recently he was a Visiting Professor at UPC, Barcelona.

Dr. O'Boyle's main research interests are in adaptive compilation, formal program transformation representations, the compiler impact on embedded systems, compiler-directed low-power optimization and automatic compilation for parallel single-address space architectures. He has published over 50 papers in international journals and conferences in this area and manages the Compiler and Architecture Design group consisting of 18 members.

Cosimo Antonio Prete is full professor of Computer Systems at the University of Pisa, Italy, and faculty member of the PhD School in Computer Science and Engineering (IMT), Italy. He is coordinator of the graduate degree program in Computer Engineering and Rector's Adviser for Innovative Training Technologies at the University of Pisa. His research interests are focused on multiprocessor architectures, cache memory, performance evaluation and embedded systems. He is an author of more than 100 papers published in international journals and conference proceedings. He has been project manager for several research projects, including: the SPP project, OMI, Esprit IV; the CCO project, supported by VLSI Technology, Sophia Antipolis; the ChArm project, supported by VLSI Technology, San Jose, and the Esprit III Tracs project.

André Seznec is "directeur de recherches" at IRISA/INRIA. Since 1994, he has been the head of the CAPS (Compiler Architecture for Superscalar and Special-purpose Processors) research team. He has been conducting research on computer architecture for more than 20 years. His research topics have included memory hierarchy, pipeline organization, simultaneous multithreading and branch prediction. In 1999–2000, he spent a sabbatical with the Alpha Group at Compaq.

Olivier Temam obtained a PhD in computer science from the University of Rennes in 1993. He was assistant professor at University of Versailles from 1994 to 1999, and then professor at University of Paris Sud until 2004. Since then, he is a senior researcher at INRIA Futurs in Paris, where he heads the Alchemy group. His research interests include program optimization, processor architecture, and emerging technologies, with a general emphasis on long-term research.

Theo Ungerer is Chair of Systems and Networking at the University of Augsburg, Germany, and Scientific Director of the Computing Center of the University of Augsburg. He received a Diploma in Mathematics at the Technical University of Berlin in 1981, a Doctoral Degree at the University of Augsburg in 1986, and a second Doctoral Degree (Habilitation) at the University of Augsburg in 1992. Before his current position he was scientific assistant at the University of Augsburg (1982-89 and 1990-92), visiting assistant professor at the University of California, Irvine (1989-90), professor of computer architecture at the University of Jena (1992-1993) and the Technical University of Karlsruhe (1993-2001). He is Steering Committee member of HiPEAC and of the German Science Foundation's priority programme on "Organic Computing." His current research interests are in the areas of embedded processor architectures, embedded real-time systems, organic, bionic and ubiquitous systems.

Mateo Valero obtained his PhD at UPC in 1980. He is a professor in the Computer Architecture Department at UPC. His research interests focus on high-performance architectures. He has published approximately 400 papers on these topics. He is the director of the Barcelona Supercomputing Center, the National Center of Supercomputing in Spain. Dr. Valero has been honored with several awards, including the King Jaime I by the Generalitat Valenciana, and the Spanish national award "Julio Rey Pastor" for his research on IT technologies. In 2001, he was appointed Fellow of the IEEE, in 2002 Intel Distinguished Research Fellow and since 2003 he has been a Fellow of the ACM. Since 1994, he has been a foundational member of the Royal Spanish Academy of Engineering. In 2005 he was elected Correspondant Academic of the Spanish Royal Academy of Sciences, and his native town of Alfamén named their Public College after him.

Georgi Gaydadjiev is a professor in the computer engineering laboratory of the Technical University of Delft, The Netherlands. His research interests focus on many aspects of embedded systems design with an emphasis on reconfigurable computing. He has published about 50 papers on these topics in international refereed journals and conferences. He has acted as Program Committee member of many conferences and is subject area editor for the *Journal of Systems Architecture*.

Table of Contents

Workshop on Software and Hardware Challenges of Many-core Platforms – SHCMP (Selected Papers)

8th IEEE International Symposium on Systems, Architectures, Modeling and Simulation – SAMOS VIII (Selected Papers)

A High Performance Adaptive Miss Handling Architecture for Chip Multiprocessors*

Magnus Jahre and Lasse Natvig

Norwegian University of Science and Technology
HiPEAC European Network of Excellence
{jahre,lasse}@idi.ntnu.no

Abstract. Chip Multiprocessors (CMPs) mainly base their performance gains on exploiting thread-level parallelism. Consequently, powerful memory systems are needed to support an increasing number of concurrent threads. Conventional CMP memory systems do not account for thread interference which can result in reduced overall system performance. Therefore, conventional high bandwidth Miss Handling Architectures (MHAs) are not well suited to CMPs because they can create severe memory bus congestion. However, high miss bandwidth is desirable when sufficient bus bandwidth is available. This paper presents a novel, CMP-specific technique called the Adaptive Miss Handling Architecture (AMHA). If the memory bus is congested, AMHA improves performance by dynamically reducing the maximum allowed number of concurrent L1 cache misses of a processor core if this creates a significant speedup for the other processors. Compared to a 16-wide conventional MHA, AMHA improves performance by 12% on average for one of the workload collections used in this work.

1 Introduction

Chip multiprocessors (CMPs) are now in widespread use and all major processor vendors currently sell CMPs. CMPs alleviate three important problems associated with modern superscalar microprocessors: diminishing returns from techniques that exploit instruction level parallelism (ILP), high power consumption and large design complexity. However, much of the internal structures in these multi-core processors are reused from single-core designs, and it is unclear if reusing these well-known solutions is the best way to design a CMP.

The performance gap between the processor and main memory has been growing since the early 80s [1]. Caches efficiently circumvent this problem because most programs exhibit spatial and temporal locality. However, adding more processors on one chip increases the demand for data from memory. Furthermore, latency hiding techniques will become more important and these tend to increase bandwidth demand [2].

---

* This work was supported by the Norwegian Metacenter for Computational Science (NOTUR).

P. Stenström (Ed.): Transactions on HiPEAC IV, LNCS 6760, pp. 1–20, 2011.
© Springer-Verlag Berlin Heidelberg 2011

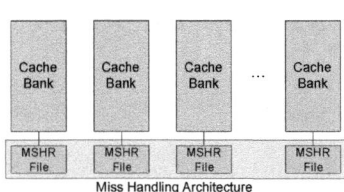
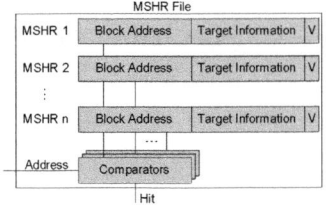

Fig. 1. Miss Handling Architecture (MHA) [4]   **Fig. 2.** A Generic MSHR File

A straightforward way of providing more bandwidth is to increase the clock frequency and width of the memory bus. Unfortunately, the number of pins on a chip is subject to economic as well as technological constraints and is expected to grow at a slow rate in the future [3]. In addition, the off-chip clock frequency is limited by the electronic characteristics of the circuit board. The effect of these trends is that off-chip bandwidth is a scarce resource that future CMPs must use efficiently. If the combined bandwidth demand exceeds the off-chip bandwidth capacity, the result is memory bus congestion which increases the average latency of all memory accesses. If the out-of-order processor core logic is not able to fully hide this latency, the result is a reduced instruction commit rate and lower performance.

It is critical for performance that the processor cores are able to continue processing at the same time as a long-latency operation like a memory or L2 cache access is in progress. Consequently, the caches should be able to service requests while misses are processed further down in the memory hierarchy. Caches with this ability are known as *non-blocking* or *lockup-free* and were first introduced by Kroft [5].

Within the cache, the Miss Handling Architecture (MHA) is responsible for keeping track of the outstanding misses. Figure 1 shows an MHA for a cache with multiple banks [4]. The main hardware structure within an MHA is called a *Miss Information/Status Holding Register (MSHR)*. This structure contains the information necessary to successfully return the requested data when the miss completes. If an additional request for a cache block arrives, the information regarding this new request is stored but no request is sent to the next memory hierarchy level. In other words, multiple requests for the same cache block are combined into a single memory access.

In this work, we investigate the performance impact of non-blocking caches in shared-cache CMPs and introduce a novel Miss Handling Architecture called *Adaptive MHA (AMHA)*. AMHA is based on the observation that the available miss bandwidth should be adjusted according to the utilization of the memory bus at runtime. Memory bus congestion can significantly increase the average memory access latency and result in increased lock-up time in the on-chip caches. If the processor core is not able to hide this increased latency, it directly affects its performance. Memory bus congestion reduces the performance of some programs more than others since the ability to hide the memory latency varies between programs. AMHA exploits this property by reducing the available miss bandwidth for the latency insensitive threads. Since these programs are good at hiding latency, the reduction in miss bandwidth only slightly reduces their performance. However, the memory latency experienced by the congestion sensitive programs is reduced which results in a large performance improvement. For our *Amplified Congestion Probability Workload* collection, AMHA improves the single program oriented Harmonic Mean of Speedups (HMoS) metric by 12% on average.

The paper has the following outline: First, we discuss previous work in Section 2 before we introduce our multiprogrammed workload collections and discuss system performance metrics in Section 3. Then, our new AMHA technique is presented in Section 4. Section 5 describes our experimental methodology, and Section 6 discusses the results from our evaluation of both conventional and adaptive MHAs. Finally, Section 7 discusses future technology trends and possible extensions of AMHA before Section 8 concludes the paper.

2   Related Work

2.1   Miss Handling Architecture Background

A generic Miss Status/Information Holding Register (MSHR) file is shown in Figure 2. This structure consists of n MSHRs which contain space to store the cache block address of the miss, some target information and a valid bit. The cache can handle as many misses to *different cache block addresses* as there are MSHRs without blocking. Each MSHR has its own comparator and the MSHR file can be described as a small fully associative cache. For each miss, the information required for the cache to answer the processor's request is stored in the *Target Information* field. However, the exact *Target Information* content of an MSHR is implementation dependent. The *Valid (V)* bit is set when the MSHR is in use, and the cache must block when all valid bits are set. A blocked cache cannot service any requests.

Another MHA design option regards the number of misses to the *same cache block address* that can be handled without blocking. We refer to this aspect of the MHA implementation as *target storage*, and this determines the structure of the *Target Information* field in Figure 2. Kroft used *implicit* target storage in the original non-blocking cache proposal [5]. Here, storage is dedicated to each processor word in a cache block. Consequently, additional misses to a given cache block can be handled as long as they go to a *different processor word*. The main advantage of this target storage scheme is its low hardware overhead.

Farkas and Jouppi [6] proposed explicitly addressed MSHRs which improves on the implicit scheme by making it possible for any miss to use any target storage location. Consequently, it is possible to handle multiple misses to *the same processor word*. We refer to the number of misses to the same cache block that can be handled without blocking as the number of targets. This improvement increases hardware cost as the offset of the requested processor word within the cache block must be stored explicitly. In this paper, we use explicitly addressed MSHRs because they provide low lock-up time for a reasonable hardware cost.

Tuck et al. [4] extended the explicitly addressed MSHR scheme to write-back caches. If the miss is a write, it is helpful to buffer the data until the miss completes which adds to the hardware overhead of the scheme. To reduce this overhead, Tuck et al. evaluated MSHRs where only a subset of the target entries has a write buffer. In addition, they extended the implicitly addressed MSHR scheme by adding a write buffer and a write mask which simplify data forwarding for reads and reduce the area cost. The target storage implementations of Tuck et al. can all be used in our AMHA scheme to provide a more fine-grained area/performance trade-off. In this paper, we opt for the simple option of having a write buffer available to all target storage locations as this is likely to give the best performance.

In addition, Tuck et al. proposed the Hierarchical MHA [4]. This MHA provides a large amount of Memory Level Parallelism (MLP) and is primarily aimed at processors that provide very high numbers of in-flight instructions. In a CMP, providing too much MLP can create congestion in shared resources which may result in reduced performance.

Farkas and Jouppi [6] proposed the inverted MSHR organization which can support as many outstanding requests as there are destinations in the machine. Furthermore, Franklin and Sohi [7] observed that a cache line that is waiting to be filled can be used to store MSHR information. These MHAs are extremes of the area/performance trade-off and we choose to focus on less extreme MHAs. In addition, researchers have looked into which number of MSHRs gives the best performance for conventional architectures [7,8].

2.2   Related Work on Bus Scheduling, Shared Caches and Feedback

Mutlu and Moscibroda [9], Nesbit et al. [10] and Rafique et al. [11] are examples of recent work that use the memory bus scheduler to improve Quality of Service (QoS). These works differ from AMHA in that they issue memory requests in a thread-fair manner while AMHA dynamically changes the bandwidth demand to utilize the shared bus efficiently. Furthermore, memory controller scheduling techniques that improve DRAM throughput are complementary to AMHA (e.g. [12,13]).

Other researchers have focused on techniques that use shared cache partitioning to increase performance (e.g. [14,15]). These techniques optimize for the same goal as AMHA, but are complementary since AMHA's only impact on cache partitioning is due to a reduced cache access frequency for the most frequent bus user.

Recently, a large number of researchers have focused on providing shared cache QoS. Some schemes enforce QoS primarily in hardware (e.g. [16]) while others make the OS scheduler cooperate with hardware resource monitoring and control to achieve QoS (e.g. [17]). It is difficult to compare these techniques to AMHA as improving performance is not their primary aim.

Table 1. Randomly Generated Multiprogrammed Workloads (RW)

ID	Benchmarks	ID	Benchmarks	ID	Benchmarks	ID	Benchmarks	ID	Benchmarks
1	perlbmk, ammp, parser, mgrid	9	vortex1, apsi, fma3d, sixtrack	17	perlbmk, parser, applu, apsi	25	facerec, parser, applu, gap	33	gzip, galgel, lucas, equake
2	mcf, gcc, lucas, twolf	10	ammp, bzip, parser, equake	18	perlbmk, gzip, mgrid, mgrid	26	mcf, ammp, apsi, twolf	34	facerec, facerec, gcc, apsi
3	facerec, mesa, eon, eon	11	twolf, eon, applu, vpr	19	mcf, gcc, apsi, sixtrack	27	swim, ammp, sixtrack, applu	35	swim, mcf, mesa, sixtrack
4	ammp, vortex1, galgel, equake	12	swim, galgel, mgrid, crafty	20	ammp, gcc, art, mesa	28	swim, fma3d, parser, art	36	mesa, bzip, sixtrack, equake
5	gcc, apsi, galgel, crafty	13	twolf, galgel, fma3d, vpr	21	perlbmk, apsi, lucas, equake	29	twolf, gcc, apsi, vortex1	37	mcf, gcc, vortex1, gap
6	facerec, art, applu, equake	14	bzip, bzip, equake, vpr	22	mcf, crafty, vpr, vpr	30	gzip, apsi, mgrid, equake	38	facerec, mcf, parser, lucas
7	gcc, parser, applu, gap	15	swim, galgel, crafty, vpr	23	gzip, mesa, mgrid, equake	31	mgrid, eon, equake, vpr	39	twolf, mesa, eon, eon
8	swim, twolf, mesa, gap	16	mcf, mesa, mesa, wupwise	24	facerec, fma3d, applu, lucas	32	facerec, twolf, gap, wupwise	40	mcf, apsi, apsi, equake

Unpredictable interactions between processors may result in performance degradation in multiprocessor systems. Feedback control schemes can be used to alleviate such bottlenecks if the reduction is due to inadequate knowledge of the state of shared structures. For instance, Scott and Sohi [18] used feedback to avoid tree saturation in multistage networks. Thottethodi et al. [19] used source throttling to avoid network saturation and controlled their policy by a feedback-based adaptive mechanism. In addition, Martin et al. [20] used feedback to adaptively choose between a directory-based and a snooping-based cache coherence protocol. AMHA further extends the use of feedback control by using memory bus and performance measurements to guide miss bandwidth allocations.

3   Multiprogrammed Workload Selection and Performance Metrics

To thouroughly evaluate Miss Handling Architectures in a CMP context, we create 40 multiprogrammed workloads consisting of 4 SPEC CPU2000 benchmarks [21] as shown in Table 1. We picked benchmarks at random from the full SPEC CPU2000 benchmark suite, and each processor core is dedicated to one benchmark. The only requirement given to the random selection process was that each SPEC benchmark had to be represented in at least one workload. We refer to these workloads as *Random Workloads (RW)*. To avoid unrealistic interference when more than a single instance of a benchmark is part of a workload, the benchmarks are fast-forwarded a different number of clock cycles if the same benchmark is run on more than one core. If there is only one instance of a benchmark in a workload, it is fast-forwarded for 1 billion clock cycles. The

Table 2. Amplified Congestion Probability Workloads (ACPW)

ID	Benchmarks	ID	Benchmarks	ID	Benchmarks	ID	Benchmarks	ID	Benchmarks
1	mcf, apsi, applu, wupwise	9	galgel, apsi, art, gcc	17	wupwise, vortex1, apsi, gap	25	gzip, mesa, apsi, gcc	33	wupwise, apsi, art, gap
2	gzip, mcf, art, gap	10	mcf, mesa, vortex1, wupwise	18	mcf, mesa, vortex1, gcc	26	galgel, apsi, art, gcc	34	art, apsi, mgrid, gap
3	gzip, mesa, galgel, applu	11	facerec, mcf, gcc, sixtrack	19	mcf, galgel, vortex1, applu	27	facerec, vortex1, art, gap	35	swim, mesa, mgrid, wupwise
4	gzip, galgel, mesa, sixtrack	12	gzip, mcf, mesa, applu	20	mesa, applu, sixtrack, gap	28	vortex1, mcf, mesa, applu	36	facerec, mcf, art, sixtrack
5	facerec, galgel, mgrid, vortex1	13	galgel, apsi, applu, sixtrack	21	swim, mesa, art, sixtrack	29	swim, gcc, vortex1, gap	37	facerec, gzip, gcc, gap
6	gzip, mcf, mesa, art	14	swim, vortex1, apsi, art	22	swim, mcf, gcc, wupwise	30	swim, gzip, galgel, art	38	facerec, mcf, gcc, sixtrack
7	swim, apsi, sixtrack, applu	15	swim, gzip, mesa, applu	23	mesa, apsi, vortex1, sixtrack	31	swim, gzip, galgel, wupwise	39	facerec, swim, vortex1, gzip
8	facerec, swim, art, sixtrack	16	vortex1, galgel, mesa, sixtrack	24	art, galgel, mgrid, gap	32	gzip, mcf, mesa, wupwise	40	facerec, mcf, mgrid, sixtrack

Table 3. System Performance Metrics

Metric	Formula
Harmonic Mean of Speedups (HMoS) [22]	$\dfrac{1}{\sum_{i=1}^{P} \frac{IPC_i^{\text{baseline}}}{IPC_i^{\text{shared}}}}$
System Throughput (STP) [23]	$\sum_{i=1}^{P} \dfrac{IPC_i^{\text{shared}}}{IPC_i^{\text{baseline}}}$

second time a benchmark appears in the workload, we increase the number of fast-forward clock cycles for this instance to 1.02 billion. Then, measurements are collected for 100 million clock cycles.

To investigate the performance of AMHA in the situation it is designed for, we create 40 additional workloads where this situation is more likely than in the randomly generated workload. Here, we randomly select two workloads from the 7 SPEC2000 benchmarks that has an average memory queue latency of more than 1000 processor clock cycles when running alone in the CMP. In our simulations, these benchmarks (*mcf, gap, apsi, facerec, galgel, mesa* and *swim*) have average queue latencies of between 1116 and 3724 clock cycles. The two remaining benchmarks are randomly chosen from the 8 benchmarks that have an average memory queue latency of between 100 and 1000 clock cycles (i.e. *wupwise, vortex1, sixtrack, gcc, art, gzip, mgrid, applu*). We also require that a benchmark is only used once in one workload. We refer to these workloads as *Amplified Congestion Probability Workloads (ACPW)* and they are shown in Table 2.

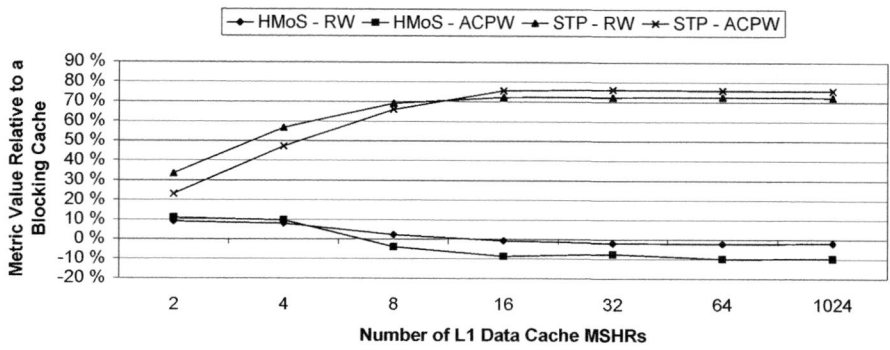

Fig. 3. Average MHA Throughput (Aggregate IPC)

Eyerman and Eeckhout [24] recently showed that the *System Throughput (STP)* and *Harmonic Mean of Speedups (HMoS)* metrics are able to represent workload performance at the system level. The STP metric is a system-oriented performance metric, and the HMoS metric is a user-oriented performance metric. Both metrics require a performance baseline where all programs receive equal access to shared resources. In this work, we give each process exactly a $\frac{1}{P}$ share of the shared cache and at least a $\frac{1}{P}$ share of the available memory bus bandwidth where P is the number of processors. To divide memory bandwidth fairly between threads, we use Rafique et al.'s Network Fair Queueing technique [11] with a starvation prevention threshold of 1. Consequently, access to the memory bus is allocated in a round-robin fashion if all processors have at least one waiting request. The formulae used to compute the HMoS and STP metrics are shown in Table 3. The HMoS metric was originally proposed by Luo et al. [22] and the STP metric is the same as the weighted speedup metric originally proposed by Snavely and Tullsen [23].

4 The Adaptive Miss Handling Architecture (AMHA)

4.1 Motivation

Our Adaptive MHA technique is based on the observation that it is possible to drastically improve the performance of certain programs by carefully distributing miss bandwidth between threads when the memory bus is congested. This differs from earlier research on MHAs where the aim has been to provide as much miss bandwidth as possible in an area-efficient manner. Unfortunately, our results show that following this strategy can create severe congestion in the memory bus which heavily reduces the performance of some benchmarks while hardly affecting others. Figure 3 shows the performance of a conventional MHA in a 4-core CMP plotted relative to the throughput with a blocking cache. To reduce the search space, we only modify the number of MSHRs in the L1 data cache. The 1024 MSHR architecture is very expensive and is used to estimate the performance of a very large MHA.

Figure 3 shows that a large conventional MHA is able to provide high throughput as measured by the STP metric. Furthermore, throughput increases with more MSHRs up to 8 MSHRs for the RW collection and up to 16 MSHRs with the ACPW collection. The reason for this difference is that there are more memory intensive benchmarks in the ACPW collection which perform better when more miss parallelism is available. Consequently, we can conclude that throughput is improved by adding more MSHRs up to 16.

The trend with the HMoS metric in Figure 3 is very different. Here, the best values are achieved with 2 or 4 MSHRs while adding 16 or more MSHRs reduces the HMoS value below that of a blocking cache for both workload collections. The reason for this trend is that memory bus congestion does not affect all programs equally. For a memory intensive program, an increase in latency due to congestion will not create a large performance degradation. The reason is that these programs already spend a lot of their time waiting for memory. However, less memory intensive programs can hide the most of the access latency and make good progress as long as the memory latencies are reasonably low. When the memory bus is congested, the memory latencies become to large to be hidden which result in a considerable performance degradation. By carefully reallocating the available miss bandwidth, AMHA improves the performance of these latency sensitive benchmarks by reducing the available miss parallelism of the latency insensitive ones.

Figure 3 also offers some insights into why choosing a small number of MSHRs to avoid congestion results in a considerable throughput loss. When both metrics are taken into account, the MHA with 4 MSHRs seems like the best choice. However, this results in an average throughput loss of 9% for the RW collection and 16% for the ACPW collection. In other words, simply reducing the likelyhood of congestion carries with it a significant throughput cost and an adaptive approach is needed.

4.2   AMHA Implementation

AMHA exploits the observation that throughput can be improved by adapting the available miss parallelism to the current memory bus utilization. Figure 4 shows a 4-core CMP which uses AMHA. Implementing AMHA requires only small changes to the existing CMP design. First, an *Adaptive MHA Engine* is added which monitors the memory bus traffic. At regular intervals, the AMHA Engine uses run time measurements to modify the number of available MSHRs in the L1 data cache of each core. Furthermore, the MHAs of the L1 data caches are modified such that the number of available MSHRs can be changed at runtime.

The AMHA Engine. Figure 5 shows the internals of the AMHA Engine. It consists of a control unit and a set of registers called *Performance Registers*. These registers are used to measure the performance impact of an AMHA

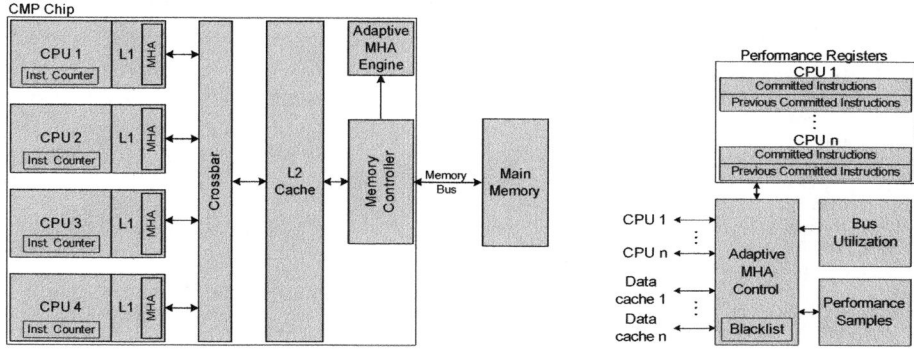

Fig. 4. General Architecture with Adaptive MHA   **Fig. 5.** Adaptive MHA Engine

decision on all threads. In addition, the AMHA Engine stores the average bus utilization during the last sample. Here, the memory controller increments a counter each time it schedules a memory operation. The value of this counter is proportional to the actual bus utilization because each memory request occupies the data bus for a fixed number of cycles and the time between each AMHA evaluation is constant. For clarity, we will refer to this quantity as bus utilization even if AMHA uses the counter value internally. Lastly, the AMHA Engine uses a bit vector called the *blacklist* and a set of registers called *performance samples*. The blacklist is used to mark configurations that should not be tested again, and the performance samples are used to store the performance measurements for certain MHA configurations.

The performance registers store the number of committed instructions in the current and previous MHA samples. Since the number of clock cycles between each AMHA decision is constant, this quantity is proportional to IPC. These values are collected from performance counters inside each processor core when the current MHA is evaluated. By comparing these values, it is possible to estimate the performance impact of a given AMHA decision. This is necessary because it is difficult to determine the consequences of an MHA change from locally measurable variables like average queueing delays or bus utilization. The reason is that the performance with a given MHA is a result of a complex trade-off between an application's ability to hide memory latencies and its congestion sensitivity.

Evaluating the Current MHA. Every 500000 clock cycles, the current MHA is evaluated using the information stored in the *Performance Registers*. This evaluation is carried out by the control unit and follows the pseudocode outlined in Algorithm 1. We refer to the time between each evaluation as one MHA *sample*.

To adapt to phase changes, AMHA returns all data caches to their maximum number of MSHRs at regular intervals. We refer to the time between two such resets as an *AMHA period*. After a reset, we run all data caches with their

---

Algorithm 1. Adaptive MHA Main Algorithm

```
 1: procedure EVALUATEMHA
 2:     if RunCount == PERIODSIZE then
 3:         Reset all MHAs to their original configuration, set phase = 1 and useAMHA = true
 4:         return
 5:     end if
 6:     if First time in a period and no congestion then
 7:         Disable AMHA in this period (useAMHA = false)
 8:     end if
 9:     Retrieve the current number of committed instruction from the performance counters
10:     if phase == 1 and useAMHA then                                       ▷ Search Phase 1
11:         if Symmetric MHAs remaining then
12:             Reduce the MSHRs of all L1 data caches to the nearest power of 2
13:         else
14:             Choose the best performing symmetric MHA and enter Phase 2
15:         end if
16:     else if phase == 2 and useAMHA then                                  ▷ Search Phase 2
17:         if Performance improvement of last AMHA decision not acceptable and useAMHA then
18:             Roll back previous decision and add processor to the blacklist
19:         end if
20:         Find the processor with the largest MHA performance impact that is not blacklisted
21:         if Processor found then
22:             Reduce or increase the number of MSHR to the nearest power of 2
23:         else
24:             All processors are blacklisted, keep current configuration for the rest of this period
25:         end if
26:     end if
27:     Increment RunCount
28:     Move current committed instructions to previous committed instructions
29: end procedure
```

---

maximum number of MSHRs in one sample to gather performance statistics. If the bus utilization is lower than a configurable threshold in this sample, AMHA decides that the memory bus is not congested and turns itself off in this AMHA period. We refer to this threshold as the *Congestion Threshold*. The AMHA search procedure has a small performance impact, so we want to be reasonably certain that it is possible to find a better MHA for it to be invoked.

AMHA has now established that the memory bus is most likely congested, and it starts to search for an MHA with better performance. This search consists of two phases. In the first phase, AMHA looks for the best performing *symmetric* MHA. A symmetric MHA has the same number of MSHRs in all L1 data caches. Here, AMHA starts with the largest possible MHA and then tries all symmetric MHAs where the number of MSHRs is a power of two. At the end of each sample, AMHA stores the performance with this MHA in a *Performance Samples* register and tries the next symmetric MHA. When AMHA has tried all symmetric MHAs, the *Performance Samples* registers are analyzed and the best performing MHA is chosen. Since the performance measurements might not be representable for the whole period, we require that a smaller MHA must outperform the largest MHA by a certain percentage called the *Acceptance Threshold*. For each symmetric configuration, we also store the number of committed instructions for each processor. This information is used in search phase 2.

In search phase 2, AMHA attempts to improve performance by searching for an *asymmetric* MHA. Here, we adjust the MHA of one processor each time the MHA is evaluated. Since a new MHA might have been chosen in phase 1, the bus may or may not be congested. Therefore, we need to choose between increasing or decreasing the number of MSHRs in this phase. If the bus utilization is larger than the *Congestion Threshold*, AMHA assumes that the bus is congested and decreases the number of MSHRs to the nearest power of two. If not, the number of MSHRs is increased to the nearest power of two. At the end of the sample, the performance impact is computed and the MHA is either kept or rolled back. If the MHA is not accepted, the processor is blacklisted and phase 2 finishes when all processors have been added to the blacklist. To maximize the performance benefit, we start with the processor where the symmetric MHA had the largest performance impact and process them in descending order.

We use a heuristic to accept or reject an MHA change in search phase 2. If the last operation was a decrease, we sum the speedups of all processors that did not have their MSHRs reduced and compare this to the degradation experienced by the reduced processor. If the difference between the sum of speedups and the degradation is larger than the configurable *Acceptance Threshold*, the new MHA is kept. For simplicity, we use the same acceptance threshold in both search phases. If the memory bus is severely congested, reducing the number of MSHRs of a processor can actually increase its performance. In this case, we set the degradation to 0. In addition, we reject any performance degradations of processors that have not had its number of MSHRs reduced as measurement errors. If the last operation increased the number of MSHRs, we sum the performance degradations of the other processors and weigh this against the performance improvement of the processor that got its number of MSHRs increased. Again, the difference must be larger than the *Acceptance Threshold* to keep the new MHA.

For each AMHA evaluation, we need to carry out P divisions in phase 1 and P divisions in phase two where P is the number of processors. The reason is that AMHA's decisions are based on relative performance improvements or degradations and not the number of committed instructions. Since there are no hard limits to when the AMHA decision needs to be ready, it can be feasible to use a single division unit for this purpose. For simplicity, we assume that the AMHA Engine analysis can be carried out within 1 clock cycle in this work. Since we need relatively large samples for the performance measurements to be accurate, it is unlikely that this assumption will influence the results. We leave investigating area-efficient AMHA Engine implementations and refining the experiments with accurate timings as further work.

MHA Reconfiguration. An MHA which includes the features needed to support AMHA is shown in Figure 6. This MHA is changed slightly compared to the generic MHA in Figure 2. The main difference is the addition of a *Usable (U)* bit to each MSHR. If this is set, the MSHR can be used to store miss data. By manipulating these bits, it is possible to change the number of available MSHRs at runtime. The maximum number of MSHRs is determined by the number of physical registers and decided at implementation time. As in the conventional MSHR file, the *Valid (V)* bit is set if the MSHR contains valid miss data.

The other addition needed to support AMHA is *Mask Control*. This control unit manipulates the values of the U bits subject to the commands given by the

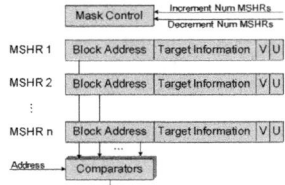

Fig. 6. The New MHA Implementation

AMHA Engine. For instance, if the *AMHA Engine* decides that the number of MSHRs in cache *A* should be reduced, cache *A*'s *Mask Control* sets the *U* bits for some MSHRs to 0. In the current implementation, the number of available MSHRs is increased or decreased to the nearest power of two.

When the number of MSHRs is decreased, it is possible that some registers that contain valid miss data are taken out of use. Consequently, these registers must be searched when a response is received from the next memory hierarchy level. However, the cache should block immediately to reflect the decision of the *AMHA Engine.* This problem is solved by taking both the *V* and *U* bits into account on a cache miss and for the blocking decision. Furthermore, all registers that contain valid data (i.e. have their *V* bit set) are searched when a response is received.

We have chosen to restrict the adaptivity to the number of available MSHRs, but it is also possible to change the amount of target storage available. In other words, it is possible to manipulate the number of simultaneous misses to the same cache block that can be handled without blocking. This will increase the implementation complexity of AMHA considerably. Furthermore, it is only a different way to reduce the number of requests injected into the memory system. The reason is that the cache is blocked for a shorter amount of time with more targets which indirectly increases the bandwidth demand. For these reasons, AMHA keeps the amount of target storage per MSHR constant.

AMHA only requires slightly more area than a conventional MHA with the same maximum number of MSHRs as each MSHR only needs to be extended with one additional bit. Furthermore, the AMHA Engine needs a few registers and logic to compute and compare application speedups. In addition, the control functions in both the AMHA Engine and the reconfigurable MHAs require a small amount of logic.

5   Experimental Setup

We use the system call emulation mode of the cycle-accurate M5 simulator [25] to evaluate the conventional MHAs and AMHA. The processor architecture parameters for the simulated 4-core CMP are shown in Table 4, and Table 5 contains the baseline memory system parameters. We have extended M5 with an AMHA implementation, a crossbar interconnect and a detailed DDR2-800 memory bus and SDRAM model [26]. The DDR2-800 memory bus is a split transaction bus

Table 5. Memory System Parameters

Parameter	Value
Level 1 Data Cache	64 KB 8-way set associative, 64B blocks, 3 cycles latency
Level 1 Instruction Cache	64 KB 8-way set associative, 64B blocks, 16 MSHRs, 8 targets per MSHR, 1 cycle latency
Level 2 Unified Shared Cache	4 MB 8-way set associative, 64B blocks, 14 cycles latency, 16 MSHRs per bank, 8 targets per MSHR, 4 banks
L1 to L2 Interconnection Network	Crossbar topology, 8 cycles latency, 64B wide transmission channel
Memory Bus and DRAM	DDR2-800, 4-4-4-12 timing, 64 entry read queue, 64 entry write queue, 1 KB pages, 8 banks, FR-FCFS scheduling [13], closed page policy

Table 4. Processor Core Parameters

Parameter	Value
Clock frequency	4 GHz
Reorder Buffer	128 entries
Store Buffer	32 entries
Instruction Queue	64 instructions
Instruction Fetch Queue	32 entries
Load/Store Queue	32 instructions
Issue Width	8 instructions/cycle
Functional Units	4 Integer ALUs, 2 Integer Multipy/Divide, 4 FP ALUs, 2 FP Multiply/Divide
Branch Predictor	Hybrid, 2048 local history registers, 2-way 2048 entry BTB

which accurately models overlapping of requests to different banks, burst mode transfer as well as activation and precharging of memory pages. When a memory page has been activated, subsequent requests are serviced at a much lower latency (page hit). We refer the reader to Cuppu et al. [27] for more details on modern memory bus interfaces. The DDR2 memory controller uses Rixner et al.'s First Ready - First Come First Served (FR-FCFS) scheduling policy [13] and reorders memory requests to achieve higher page hit rates.

6   Results

6.1   Conventional MHA Performance in CMPs

In Section 4.1, we established that increasing the number of MSHRs improves throughput but reduces HMoS performance. However, the cause of this trend was not explained in detail. In this section, we shed some light on this issue by thoroughly analyzing the performance of the RW12 workload. This workload consists of the benchmarks *swim*, *mgrid*, *crafty* and *galgel* which are responsible for 53%, 39%, 5% and 3% of the memory bus requests with 16 MSHRs, respectively.

Figure 7(a) shows the speedups relative to the equal allocation baseline plotted relative to the benchmark's speedup with a blocking cache configuration. In addition, the figure shows the performance trend for the system performance

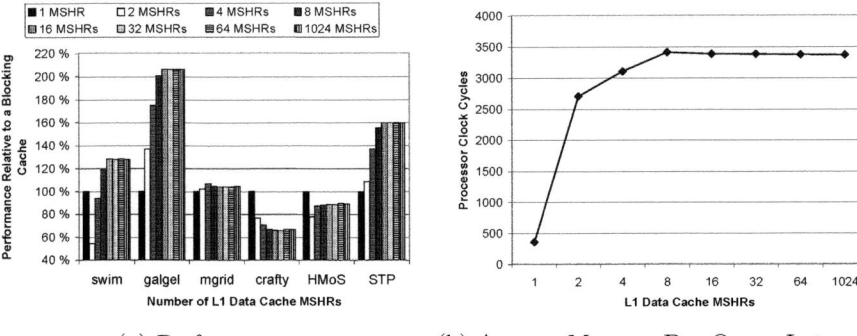

(a) Performance   (b) Average Memory Bus Queue Latencies

Fig. 7. MHA Performance with RW12

metrics HMoS and STP. The only benchmark that experiences a performance improvement with every increase in MHA size is *galgel*. For the other benchmarks, memory bus congestion causes more complex performance trends.

For *crafty*, performance is reduced substantially when the number of MSHRs is increased to 2. Performance is further reduced until the MHA contains 8 MSHRs before it stabilizes. Figure 7(b) shows the average memory bus queue latency as a function of the number of MSHRs. By comparing the performance trend of *crafty* with the average queue latency, we can see that for every increase in average queue latency there is a decrease in *crafty*'s performance. Since the HMoS metric is dominated by the program with the lowest performance, the HMoS metric has its highest value with the 1 MSHR MHA. However, the STP metric hides this effect and reports a throughput improvement with every increase in MHA size.

When *galgel* is provided with more MSHRs, its ability to hide the memory latencies improves enough to remove the effects of bus congestion which result in a net performance improvement. *Swim* needs a lager number of MSHRs to experience a performance improvement, but otherwise the performance trend is similar to that of *galgel*. The 2 and 4 MSHR MHAs both result in a performance reduction for *swim* because they provide to little miss parallelism to hide the long memory latencies. However, adding more MSHRs improve *swim*'s ability to hide the memory latency and result in a performance improvement. Changes in MHA size has a small performance impact on *mgrid*, and the performance difference between its best and worst MHA is only 6%.

Our study of workload RW12 has identified three properties that an adaptive MHA should be aware of. Firstly, programs with fewer memory requests are more sensitive to MHA size than memory intensive programs. Consequently, the MHA size of the memory intensive programs can be reduced to speed up the congestion sensitive programs without creating an unnecessarily large throughput degradation. Secondly, the impact of bus congestion on program performance is application dependent. Therefore, we can only rely on memory bus measurements to detect congestion while performance measurements are needed to determine the effects of an MHA change. Finally, the performance impact on an application

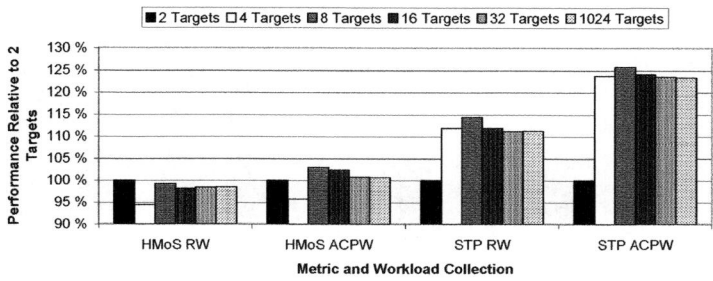

Fig. 8. Target Performance with 16 MSHRs

from a change in MHA size depends on the relationship between the program's ability to hide memory latencies and the combined load the workload puts on the memory bus.

6.2   The Performance Impact of the Number of Targets Per MSHR

Figure 8 shows the results from varying the number of outstanding misses to the same cache block address that can be handled without blocking (i.e. the number of targets). We investigated the performance impact of varying this parameter for L1 caches with 2, 4, 8 and 16 L1 data cache MSHRs, but only report the results for the 16 MSHR case because the performance trends are very similar. The main difference is that the performance impact of adding more targets is larger with more MSHRs. If there is one target per MSHR, the cache has to block on the first miss, and this is equivalent to a blocking cache.

For both workload collections, throughput is maximized with 8 targets per MSHR. The reason is that this creates a good compromise between latency tolerance and memory bus congestion. Unfortunately, the area cost of adding 8 targets is high. Consequently, the MHA with 4 targets is probably a better choice given the small performance benefit of increasing the number of targets beyond 4. The performance impact from adding more targets is larger for the ACPW collection because its workloads contain a larger number of memory intensive benchmarks by design. In other words, a greater number of benchmarks are memory intensive enough to benefit from increased miss parallelism. On the HMoS metric, adding more targets only slightly affects performance. Although the performance with 4 targets is the worst out of the examined target counts, the large increase in throughput and reasonable hardware cost makes a compelling argument for choosing this number of targets.

6.3   Adaptive MHA Performance

In this section, we report the results from our evaluation of the Adaptive MHA. For the experiments in this section, AMHA has a maximum of 16 MSHRs available in the L1 data cache. Therefore, the area overhead of this configuration is comparable to the conventional MHA with 16 MSHRs. AMHA only changes the

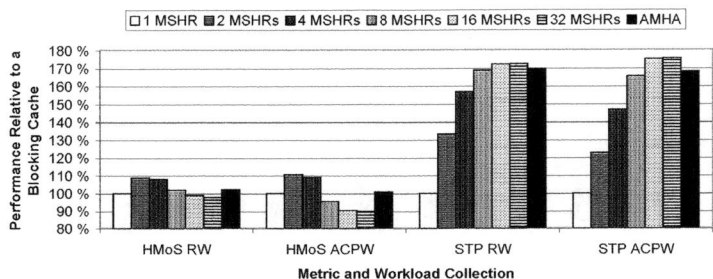

Fig. 9. AMHA Average Performance

number of available MSHRs in the L1 data cache for each core, and we keep the number of MSHRs in the L1 instruction caches constant at 16 for all conventional and adaptive configurations. The number of targets is 4 in all MSHRs.

AMHA aims at improving the performance of the applications that are victims of memory bus bandwidth overuse by other programs. Consequently, we expect an improvement on the HMoS metric with a reasonable reduction in system throughput. Figure 9 shows AMHA's average performance compared to various conventional MHAs. For the RW collection, the performance impact by running AMHA is small on average, since AMHA only has a significant performance impact on 4 workloads. This is necessary for AMHA to give stable performance because reducing the number of available MSHRs can drastically reduce performance if the memory bus is not sufficiently congested. RW35 is the workload where AMHA has the largest impact with an HMoS improvement of 193% compared to a 16 MSHR MHA. If we only consider the 4 workloads where AMHA has a HMoS impact of more than 5% (both improvement and degradation), the result is an average HMoS improvement by 72% and a 3% average improvement in throughput. Consequently, we can conclude that with randomly generated workloads, AMHA has a large performance impact when it is needed and effectively turns itself off when it is not.

In the ACPW collection, the impact of AMHA is much larger since memory bus congestion is more likely for these workloads. Figure 10 shows the performance of AMHA relative to that of a conventional 16 MSHR MHA for the workloads where AMHA has a larger HMoS impact (both improvement and degradation) of more than 10%. Again, AMHA has a large HMoS impact when it is needed and improves HMoS by 52% on average and as much as 324%. In some cases AMHA also improve STP, but the common case is a small STP degradation. Since AMHA reduces the miss bandwidth of the memory bus intensive programs, it is likely that their performance is reduced which is shown in our measurements as a throughput reduction.

For ACPW36 (*facerec, mcf, art* and *sixtrack*), AMHA reduces both HMoS and STP. Here, bus utilization is low enough for AMHA to be turned off in most periods. However, there are two periods of bus congestion where AMHA's performance measurements indicate a large speed-up by significantly reducing

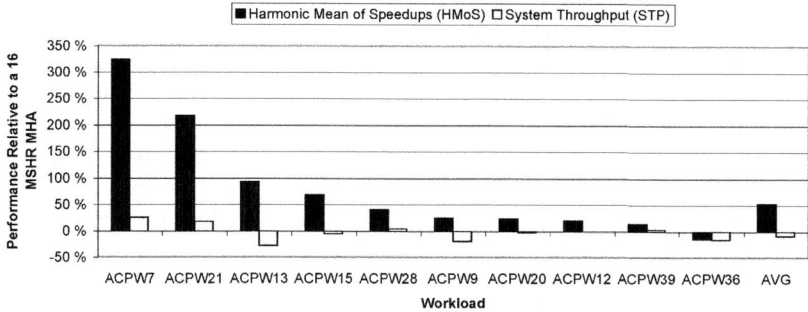

Fig. 10. AMHA Performance with High-Impact Workloads from ACPW

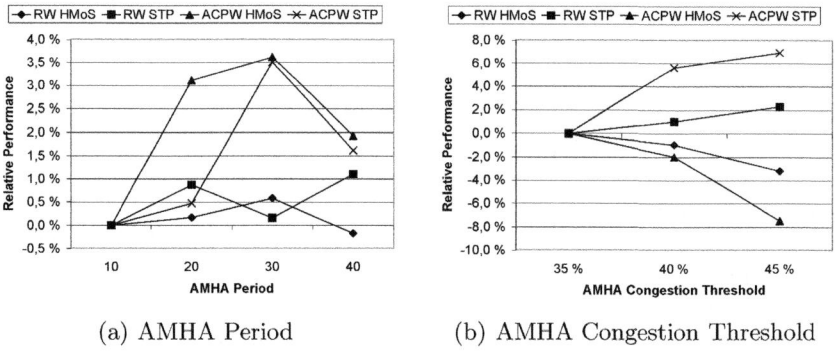

| (a) AMHA Period | (b) AMHA Congestion Threshold |

Fig. 11. AMHA Settings

sixtrack's number of MSHRs. Although this is correct when the measurements are taken, AMHA keeps this configuration also after the brief period of congestion has passed. Consequently, the available miss parallelism is reduced more than necessary which results in a performance degradation on both metrics.

6.4   Choosing AMHA Implementation Constants

Up to now, we have used an AMHA implementation with a period of 30, a congestion threshold of 40% and an acceptance threshold of 10%. These values have been determined through extensive simulation of possible AMHA implementations. Figure 11(a) shows the performance impact of varying the AMHA period setting. Here, the value must be chosen such that the cost of searching for a good MHA is amortized over a sufficiently long period as well as that a new search is carried our before the findings from the last search becomes obsolete. Figure 11(b) shows the parameter space for the congestion threshold setting which adjusts the bus utilization necessary to conduct an MHA search. Here, STP is maximized with a high threshold value and HMoS is maximized with a low threshold value. Since we in this work aim at increasing HMoS while tolerating a small STP reduction, the middle value of 40% is a good choice. However, choosing 45% as the threshold is appropriate if a more throughput friendly AMHA is desired.

Finally, AMHA also needs an acceptance threshold which determines how large the difference between the performance benefit and performance cost of a sample MHA must be for the sample MHA to be used for the remainder of the AMHA period. Here, we investigated values in the 2% to 10% range and found that 10% gave the best results. For the RW collection this parameter had nearly no impact while for the ACPW collection both HMoS and STP was maximized by choosing 10%. In general, the acceptance threshold must be large enough to filter out reduction operations that are not justified and small enough to carry out the MHA reductions when they are needed.

7   Discussion

AMHA works well for the CMP architecture used in this paper. However, it is important that it will also work well in future CMP architectures. Since AMHA improves performance when there is congestion in the memory bus, the performance gains are closely tied to the amount of congestion. The width of the memory bus and the clock frequency are both subject to technological constraints [3]. Consequently, it is unlikely that bus bandwidth can be improved sufficiently to match the expected increase in the number of processing cores [28]. Unless a revolutionary new memory interface solution is discovered, off-chip bandwidth is likely to become an even more constrained resource in the future [29]. Consequently, techniques like AMHA will become more important.

Currently, AMHA does not support multithreaded applications or processor cores with SMT. To support multithreaded applications, we need to treat multiple processor cores as a single entity when allocating miss bandwidth. This can be accomplished by letting the operating system provide some simplified process IDs as discussed by Zaho et al. [30] and communicate this to the Adaptive MHA Engine. Furthermore, some logic must be added to keep instructions committed in busy wait loops out of AMHA's performance measurements. Introducing SMT further complicates matters as each core now supports more than one hardware thread. Here, we need to further extend the MHA to allocate a different number of L1 MSHRs to each hardware thread. We leave the exact implementation and evaluation of such extensions as further work.

By targeting the victims of memory bus congestion and improving their performance, one might argue that AMHA is a fairness technique. However, AMHA only target unfairness in one situation, namely when the memory bus is severely congested. Furthermore, AMHA makes no guarantees of how much miss bandwidth each processor is given. Therefore, it is better to view AMHA as a simple performance optimization that can be applied when certain conditions are met.

8   Conclusion

When designing Miss Handling Architectures (MHAs), the aim has been to support as many outstanding misses as possible in an area efficient manner. Unfortunately, applying this strategy to a CMP will not realize its performance potential. The reason is that allowing too much miss parallelism creates congestion in the off-chip memory bus.

The first contribution of this paper is a thorough investigation of conventional MHA performance in a CMP. The main result of this investigation was that a majority of applications need large miss parallelism. However, this must be provided in a way that avoids memory bus congestion. Our Adaptive MHA (AMHA) scheme serves this purpose and is the second contribution in this paper. AMHA increases CMP performance by dynamically adapting the allowed number of outstanding misses in the private L1 data caches to the current memory bus utilization.

References

1. Hennessy, J.L., Patterson, D.A.: Computer Architecture - A Quantitative Approach, 4th edn. Morgan Kaufmann Publishers, San Francisco (2007)
2. Burger, D., Goodman, J.R., Kgi, A.: Memory Bandwidth Limitations of Future Microprocessors. In: ISCA 1996: Proc. of the 23rd An. Int. Symp. on Comp. Arch. (1996)
3. ITRS: Int. Tech. Roadmap for Semiconductors (2006), http://www.itrs.net/
4. Tuck, J., Ceze, L., Torrellas, J.: Scalable Cache Miss Handling for High Memory-Level Parallelism. In: MICRO 39: Proc. of the 39th An. IEEE/ACM Int. Symp. on Microarchitecture, pp. 409–422 (2006)
5. Kroft, D.: Lockup-free Instruction Fetch/Prefetch Cache Organization. In: ISCA 1981: Proc. of the 8th An. Symp. on Comp. Arch., pp. 81–87 (1981)
6. Farkas, K.I., Jouppi, N.P.: Complexity/Performance Tradeoffs with Non-Blocking Loads. In: ISCA 1994: Proc. of the 21st An. Int. Symp. on Comp. Arch., pp. 211–222 (1994)
7. Sohi, G.S., Franklin, M.: High-bandwidth Data Memory Systems for Superscalar Processors. In: ASPLOS-IV: Proc. of the Fourth Int. Conf. on Architectural Support for Programming Languages and Operating Systems, pp. 53–62 (1991)
8. Belayneh, S., Kaeli, D.R.: A Discussion on Non-Blocking/Lockup-Free Caches. SIGARCH Comp. Arch. News 24(3), 18–25 (1996)
9. Mutlu, O., Moscibroda, T.: Stall-Time Fair Memory Access Scheduling for Chip Multiprocessors. In: MICRO 40: Proc. of the 40th An. IEEE/ACM Int. Symp. on Microarchitecture (2007)
10. Nesbit, K.J., Aggarwal, N.: L., J., Smith, J.E.: Fair Queuing Memory Systems. In: MICRO 39: Proc. of the 39th An. IEEE/ACM Int. Symp. on Microarchitecture, pp. 208–222 (2006)
11. Rafique, N., Lim, W.T., Thottethodi, M.: Effective Management of DRAM Bandwidth in Multicore Processors. In: PACT 2007: Proc. of the 16th Int. Conf. on Parallel Architecture and Compilation Techniques, pp. 245–258 (2007)
12. Shao, J., Davis, B.: A Burst Scheduling Access Reordering Mechanism. In: HPCA 2007: Proc. of the 13th Int. Symp. on High-Performance Comp. Arch. (2007)

13. Rixner, S., Dally, W.J., Kapasi, U.J., Mattson, P., Owens, J.D.: Memory Access Scheduling. In: ISCA 2000: Proc. of the 27th An. Int. Symp. on Comp. Arch., pp. 128–138 (2000)
14. Qureshi, M.K., Patt, Y.N.: Utility-Based Cache Partitioning: A Low-Overhead, High-Performance, Runtime Mechanism to Partition Shared Caches. In: MICRO 39: Proc. of the 39th An. IEEE/ACM Int. Symp. on Microarch., pp. 423–432 (2006)
15. Dybdahl, H., Stenstrm, P.: An Adaptive Shared/Private NUCA Cache Partitioning Scheme for Chip Multiprocessors. In: HPCA 2007: Proc. of the 13th Int. Symp. on High-Performance Comp. Arch. (2007)
16. Nesbit, K.J., Laudon, J., Smith, J.E.: Virtual Private Caches. In: ISCA 2007: Proc. of the 34th An. Int. Symp. on Comp. Arch., pp. 57–68 (2007)
17. Chang, J., Sohi, G.S.: Cooperative Cache Partitioning for Chip Multiprocessors. In: ICS 2007: Proc. of the 21st An. Int. Conf. on Supercomputing, pp. 242–252 (2007)
18. Scott, S.L., Sohi, G.S.: The Use of Feedback in Multiprocessors and Its Application to Tree Saturation Control. IEEE Trans. Parallel Distrib. Syst., 385–398 (1990)
19. Thottethodi, M., Lebeck, A., Mukherjee, S.: Exploiting Global Knowledge to achieve Self-tuned Congestion Control for k-ary n-cube Networks. IEEE Trans. on Parallel and Distributed Systems, 257–272 (2004)
20. Martin, M., Sorin, D., Hill, M., Wood, D.: Bandwidth Adaptive Snooping. In: HPCA 2002: Proc. of the 8th Int. Symp. on High-Performance Comp. Arch., p. 251 (2002)
21. SPEC: SPEC CPU 2000 Web Page, http://www.spec.org/cpu2000/
22. Luo, K., Gummaraju, J., Franklin, M.: Balancing Throughput and Fairness in SMT Processors. In: ISPASS (2001)
23. Snavely, A., Tullsen, D.M.: Symbiotic Jobscheduling for a Simultaneous Multi-threading Processor. In: Arch. Support for Programming Languages and Operating Systems, pp. 234–244 (2000)
24. Eyerman, S., Eeckhout, L.: System-Level Performance Metrics for Multiprogram Workloads. IEEE Micro 28(3), 42–53 (2008)
25. Binkert, N.L., Dreslinski, R.G., Hsu, L.R., Lim, K.T., Saidi, A.G., Reinhardt, S.K.: The M5 Simulator: Modeling Networked Systems. IEEE Micro 26(4), 52–60 (2006)
26. JEDEC Solid State Technology Association: DDR2 SDRAM Specification (May 2006)
27. Cuppu, V., Jacob, B., Davis, B., Mudge, T.: A Performance Comparison of Contemporary DRAM Architectures. In: Proc. of the 26th Inter. Symp. on Comp. Arch., pp. 222–233 (1999)
28. Asanovic, K., et al.: The Landscape of Parallel Computing Research: A View from Berkeley. Technical Report UCB/EECS-2006-183, EECS Department, University of California at Berkeley (December 2006)
29. Huh, J., Burger, D., Keckler, S.W.: Exploring the Design Space of Future CMPs. In: Malyshkin, V.E. (ed.) PaCT 2001. LNCS, vol. 2127, pp. 199–210. Springer, Heidelberg (2001)
30. Zhao, L., Iyer, R., Illikkal, R., Moses, J., Makineni, S., Newell, D.: CacheScouts: Fine-Grain Monitoring of Shared Caches in CMP Platforms. In: PACT 2007: Proc. of the 16th Int. Conf. on Parallel Architecture and Compilation Techniques, pp. 339–352 (2007)

Characterizing Time-Varying Program Behavior Using Phase Complexity Surfaces*

Frederik Vandeputte and Lieven Eeckhout

ELIS Department, Ghent University
Sint-Pietersnieuwstraat 41, B-9000 Gent, Belgium
{fgvdeput,leeckhou}@elis.UGent.be

Abstract. It is well known that a program exhibits time-varying execution behavior, i.e., a program typically goes through a number of phases during its execution exhibiting relatively homogeneous behavior within a phase and distinct behavior across phases. In fact, several recent research studies have been exploiting this time-varying behavior for various purposes such as simulation acceleration, code optimization, hardware adaptation for reducing energy consumption, etc.

This paper proposes phase complexity surfaces to characterize a computer program's phase behavior across various time scales in an intuitive manner. The phase complexity surfaces incorporate metrics that characterize phase behavior in terms of the number of phases, their predictability, the degree of variability within and across phases, and the phase behavior's dependence on the time scale granularity. Leveraging phase complexity surfaces, the paper then characterizes the phase behavior of the SPEC CPU benchmarks across multiple platforms (Alpha and IA-32) and across two CPU benchmark suite generations (CPU2000 and CPU2006).

1 Introduction

Understanding program behavior is at the foundation of computer system design and optimization. Deep insight into inherent program properties drives software and hardware research and development. A program property that has gained increased interest over the past few years, is time-varying program behavior. Time-varying program behavior refers to the observation that a computer program typically goes through a number of phases at run-time with relatively homogeneous behavior within a phase and distinct behavior across phases. Various research studies have been done towards exploiting program phase behavior, for example for simulation acceleration [1,2], hardware adaptation for energy consumption reduction [3,4,5,6], program profiling and optimization [7,8], etc.

---

* This paper extends the paper 'Phase Complexity Surfaces: Characterizing Time-Varying Program Behavior' by F. Vandeputte and L. Eeckhout published at the HiPEAC conference in January 2008. This journal submission extends the conference version by presenting more results and analyses. In particular, it presents more phase complexity surface graphs; it analyzes the phase behavior in SPEC CPU2000 in more detail; it compares the phase behavior across platforms; and it compares the phase behavior across SPEC CPU2000 and CPU2006.

P. Stenström (Ed.): Transactions on HiPEAC IV, LNCS 6760, pp. 21–41, 2011.
© Springer-Verlag Berlin Heidelberg 2011

This paper concerns characterizing a program's phase behavior. To identify phases, we divide a program execution into non-overlapping intervals. An *interval* is a contiguous sequence of instructions from a program's dynamic instruction stream. A *phase* is a set of intervals within a program execution that exhibit similar behavior irrespective of temporal adjacency, i.e., a program may go through the same phase multiple times at different points in time during its execution.

Basically, there are four properties that characterize a program's phase behavior.

- The first property is the *time scale* at which time-varying program behavior is being observed. Some programs exhibit phase behavior at a small time scale granularity while other programs only exhibit phase behavior at a coarse granularity; and yet other programs may exhibit phase behavior across various time scales, and the phase behavior may be hierarchical, i.e., a phase at one time scale may consist of multiple phases at a finer time scale.
- The second property is the *number of phases* a program goes through at run-time. Some programs repeatedly stay in the same phase, for example when executing the same piece of code over and over again; other programs may go through many distinct phases.
- The third property concerns the *variability* within phases versus the variability across phases. The premise of phase behavior is that there is less variability within a phase than across phases, i.e., the variability in behavior for intervals belonging to a given phase is fairly small compared to intervals belonging to different phases.
- The fourth and final property relates to the *predictability* of the program phase behavior. For some programs, the time-varying behavior may be very regular and by consequence very predictable. For other programs on the other hand, the time-varying behavior may be complex, irregular and hard to predict.

Obviously, all four properties are related to each other. More in particular, the time scale determines the number of phases to be found with a given degree of homogeneity within each phase; the phases found, in their turn, affect the predictability of the phase behavior. By consequence, getting a good understanding of a program's phase behavior requires all four properties to be characterized simultaneously.

This paper presents *phase complexity surfaces* as a way to characterize program phase behavior. The important benefit over prior work in characterizing program phase behavior is that phase complexity surfaces capture *all* of the four properties mentioned above in a unified and intuitive way while enabling the reasoning in terms of these four properties individually.

As a subsequent step, we use phase complexity surfaces to characterize and classify the SPEC CPU2000 and CPU2006 programs in terms of their phase behavior. We provide a number of example phase complexity surfaces in this paper and refer the interested reader to the following website for the phase complexity surfaces of all benchmarks: http://www.elis.ugent.be/PCS/. Within SPEC CPU2000 and CPU2006 we identify a number of prominent groups of benchmarks with similar phase behavior. Researchers can use this classification to select benchmarks for their studies in exploiting program phase behavior. In addition, we find that the phase complexity surfaces computed on different platforms (Alpha and IA-32 with respective compilers in this paper) are very similar. Finally, we compare the phase behavior in SPEC CPU2000 against CPU2006, and we find that CPU2006 exhibits more complex time-varying behavior than CPU2000.

2   Related Work

There exists a large body of related work on program phase behavior. In this section, we only discuss the issues covered in prior work that relate most closely to this paper.

Granularity. The granularity at which time-varying behavior is studied and exploited varies widely. Some researchers look for program phase behavior at the 100K instruction interval size [3,4,5]; others look for program phase behavior at the 1M or 10M instruction interval granularity [9]; and yet others identify phase behavior at yet a larger granularity of 100M or even 1B instructions [2,10]. The granularity chosen obviously depends on the purpose of the phase-level optimization. The advantage of a small time scale is that the optimization can potentially achieve better performance because the optimization can be applied more aggressively. A larger time scale on the other hand has the advantage that the overhead of exploiting the phase behavior can be amortized more easily.

Some researchers study phase behavior at different time scales simultaneously. Wavelets for example provide a natural way of characterizing phase behavior at various time scales [11,12,13], and Lau et al. [14] identify a hierarchy of phase behavior.

Fixed-Length versus Variable-Length Phases. Various researchers detect phase behavior by looking into fixed-length instruction intervals [3,4,5]. The potential problem with the fixed-length interval approach though is that in some cases it may be hard to identify phase behavior because of a dissonance effect between the fixed-length interval size and the natural period of the phase behavior: in case the length of a fixed-length interval is slightly smaller or bigger than the period of the phase behavior, the observation made will be out of sync with the natural phase behavior. To address this issue, some researchers advocate identifying phases using variable-length intervals. Lau et al. [14] use pattern matching to find variable-length intervals, and in their follow-on work [15] they identify program phases by looking into a program's control flow structure consisting of loops, and method calls and returns. Huang et al. [16] detect (variable-length) phases at method entry and exit points by tracking method calls via the call stack.

Microarchitecture-Dependent versus Microarchitecture-Independent Characterization. Identifying phases can be done in a number of ways. Some identify program phase behavior by inspecting microarchitecture-dependent program behavior, i.e., they infer phase behavior by inspecting time-varying microarchitecture performance numbers. For example, Balasubramonian et al. [3] collect CPI and cache miss rates. Duesterwald et al. [17] collect IPC numbers, cache miss rates and branch misprediction rates. Isci and Martonosi [18] infer phase behavior from power vectors. A concern with microarchitecture-dependent based phase detection is that once phase behavior is being exploited, it may affect the microarchitecture-dependent metrics being measured; this potentially leads to the problem where it is unclear whether the observed time-varying behavior is a result of natural program behavior or is a consequence of exploiting the observed phase behavior.

An alternative approach is to measure microarchitecture-independent metrics to infer phase behavior. Dhodapkar and Smith [4,5] for example keep track of a program's working set; when the working set changes, they infer that the program transitions to another phase. Sherwood et al. [2] use Basic Block Vectors (BBVs) to keep track of the basic blocks executed — BBVs are shown to correlate well with performance in [19]. Other microarchitecture-independent metrics are for example memory addresses [12] and data reuse distances [13], a program's control flow structure such as loops and methods [7,15,16], a collection of program characteristics such as instruction mix, ILP, memory access patterns, etc. [1,20].

Phase Classification. Different researchers have come up with different approaches to partitioning instruction intervals into phases. Some use threshold clustering [4,5,6,18]; others use k-means clustering [2], or pattern matching [13,14]; yet others use frequency analysis through wavelets [11,12,13,21].

Phase Prediction. An important aspect to exploiting phase behavior is the ability to predict and anticipate future phase behavior. Sherwood et al. [6] proposed last phase, RLE and Markov phase predictors. In their follow-on work [22], they added confidence counters to the phase predictors. Vandeputte et al. [23] proposed conditional update, which only updates the phase predictor at the lowest confidence level.

Relation to this Paper. In this paper, we characterize program phase behavior at different time scale granularities. To this end, we consider fixed-length intervals, use BBVs to identify phase behavior, use threshold clustering for phase classification, and use a theoretical predictor to study phase predictability. We will go in more detail about our phase characterization approach in the next section.

The important difference between this paper compared to prior work is that the explicit goal of this paper is to *characterize* the complexity of a program's phase behavior in an intuitively understandable way. Most of the prior work on the other hand was concerned with *identifying* and *exploiting* program phase behavior. The work most closely related to this paper is the work done by Cho and Li [11,21]. They use wavelets to characterize the complexity of a program's phase behavior by looking at different time scales. This complexity measure intermingles the four phase behavior properties mentioned in the introduction; phase complexity surfaces on the other hand provide a more intuitive view on a program's phase behavior by teasing apart all four properties.

3   Phase Complexity Surfaces

As mentioned in the introduction, there are four properties that characterize a program's overall phase behavior: (i) the time scale, (ii) the number of phases, (iii) the within and across phase variability, and (iv) phase sequence and transition predictability. The phase behavior characterization surfaces proposed in this paper capture all four properties in a unified way. There are three forms of surfaces: the phase count surface, the phase predictability surface and the phase complexity surface. This section discusses all three surfaces which give an overall view of the complexity of a program's time-varying behavior. Before doing so, we first need to define a Basic Block Vector (BBV) and discuss how to classify instruction intervals into phases.

3.1   Basic Block Vector (BBV)

In this paper, we use the Basic Block Vector (BBV) proposed by Sherwood et al. [24] to capture a program's time-varying behavior. A basic block is a linear sequence of instructions with one entry and one exit point. A Basic Block Vector (BBV) is a one-dimensional array with one element per static basic block in the program binary. Each BBV element captures how many times its corresponding basic block has been executed. This is done on an interval basis, i.e., we compute one BBV per interval. Each BBV element is also multiplied by the number of instructions in the corresponding basic block. This gives a higher weight to basic blocks containing more instructions. A BBV thus provides a picture of what portions of code are executed and also how frequently those portions of code are executed.

We use a BBV to identify a program's time-varying behavior because it is a micro-architecture-independent metric and by consequence gives an accurate picture of a program's time-varying behavior across microarchitectures. Previous work by Lau et al. [19] has shown that there exists a strong correlation between the code being executed — this is what a BBV captures — and actual performance. The intuition is that if two instruction intervals execute roughly the same code, and if the frequency of the portions of code executed is roughly the same, these two intervals should exhibit roughly the same performance.

3.2   Phase Classification

Once we have a BBV per instruction interval, we now need to classify intervals into phases. As suggested above, and intuitively speaking, this is done by comparing BBVs to find similarities. Intervals with similar BBVs are considered to belong to the same program phase.

Classifying instruction intervals into phases can be done in a number of ways. We view it as a clustering problem and the resulting clusters then represent the various phases. There exist a number of clustering algorithms, such as linkage clustering, k-means clustering, threshold clustering, and many others. In this paper, we use threshold clustering because it provides a natural way of bounding the variability within a phase: by construction, the variability within a phase (in terms of its BBV behavior) is limited by a threshold θ — the θ threshold is expressed as a percentage of the maximum possible Manhattan distance between two instruction intervals. Classifying intervals into phases using threshold clustering works in an iterative way. It selects an instruction interval as a cluster center and then computes the distance with all the other instruction intervals. If the distance measure is smaller than a given threshold θ, the instruction interval is considered to be part of the same cluster/phase. Out of all remaining instruction intervals (not part of previously formed clusters), another interval is selected as a cluster center and the above process is repeated. This iterative process continues until all instruction intervals are assigned to a cluster/phase. In this work, we use a variant of this clustering approach (for speed reasons) which performs a linear scan of the instruction intervals from the beginning until the end of the dynamic instruction stream. Threshold clustering has a time complexity of $O(kN)$ with N the number of instruction intervals and k clusters ($k \ll N$).

We use the Manhattan distance as our distance metric between two BBVs:

$$d = \sum_{i=1}^{D} |A_i - B_i|,$$

with A and B being two BBVs and A_i being the i-th element of BBV A; the dimensionality of the BBV, i.e., the number of basic blocks in the program binary, equals D. The advantage of the Manhattan distance over the Euclidean distance is that it weighs differences more heavily. Assuming that the BBVs are normalized — the sum over all BBV elements equals one — the Manhattan distance varies between 0 (both BBVs are identical) and 2 (maximum possible difference between two BBVs).

Having applied threshold clustering, there are typically a number of clusters that represent only a small fraction of the total program execution, i.e., clusters with a small number of cluster members. We group all the smallest clusters to form a single cluster, the so called transition phase [22]. The transition phase accounts for no more than 5% of the total program execution.

3.3   Phase Count Surfaces

Having discussed how to measure behavioral similarity across instruction intervals using BBVs and how to group similar instruction intervals into phases through threshold clustering, we can now describe what a phase count surface looks like. A *phase count surface* shows the number of program phases (on the vertical Z-axis) as a function of intra-phase variability (X-axis) across different time scales (Y-axis), i.e., each point on a phase count surface shows the number of program phases at a given time scale at a given intra-phase variability threshold. The time scale is represented as the instruction interval length, and the per-phase variability is represented by θ used to drive the threshold clustering.

3.4   Phase Predictability Surfaces

As a result of the threshold clustering step discussed in the previous section, we can now assign phase IDs to all the instruction intervals. In other words, the dynamic instruction stream can be represented as a sequence of phase IDs with one phase ID per instruction interval in the dynamic instruction stream. We are now concerned with the predictability of the phase ID sequence. This is what a phase predictability surface characterizes.

Prediction by Partial Matching. We use the Prediction by Partial Matching (PPM) technique proposed by Chen et al. [25] to characterize phase predictability. The reason for choosing the PPM predictor is that it is a universal compression/prediction technique which presents a theoretical basis for phase prediction, and is not tied to a particular implementation.

A PPM predictor is built on the notion of a Markov predictor. A Markov predictor of order k predicts the next phase ID based upon k preceding phase IDs. Each entry in the Markov predictor records the number of phase IDs for the given history. To predict the next phase ID, the Markov predictor outputs the most likely phase ID for the given k-length history. An m-order PPM predictor consists of $(m+1)$ Markov predictors of orders 0 up to m. The PPM predictor uses the m-length history to index the mth order Markov predictor. If the search succeeds, i.e., the history of phase IDs occurred previously, the PPM predictor outputs the prediction by the mth order Markov predictor. If the search does not succeed, the PPM predictor uses the $(m-1)$-length history to index the $(m-1)$th order Markov predictor. In case the search misses again, the PPM predictor indexes the $(m-2)$th order Markov predictor, etc. Updating the PPM predictor is done by updating the Markov predictor that makes the prediction and all its higher order Markov predictors. In our setup, we consider a 32-order PPM phase predictor.

Predictability Surfaces. A *phase predictability surface* shows the relationship between phase predictability and intra-phase variability across different time scales. Each point on a phase predictability surface shows the phase predictability as a function of time scale (quantified by the instruction interval granularity) and intra-phase variability (quantified by the θ parameter used during threshold clustering). Phase predictability itself is measured through the PPM predictor, i.e., for a given θ threshold and a given time scale, we report the prediction accuracy by the PPM predictor to predict phase IDs.

3.5 Phase Complexity Surfaces

Having discussed both the phase count surface and the phase predictability surface, we can now combine both surfaces to form a so called *phase complexity surface*. A phase complexity surface shows phase count versus phase predictability across different time scales. A phase complexity surface is easily derived from the phase count and predictability surfaces by factoring out the θ threshold. In other words, each point on the phase complexity surface corresponds to a particular θ threshold which determines phase count and predictability at a given time scale. The motivation for the phase complexity surface is to represent an easy-to-grasp intuitive view on a program's phase behavior through a single graph.

Time Complexity. The time complexity for computing phase complexity surfaces is linear as all of the four steps show a linear time complexity. The first step computes the BBVs at the smallest interval granularity of interest. This requires a functional simulation or instrumentation run of the complete benchmark execution; its cost is linear. The second step computes BBVs at larger interval granularities by aggregating the BBVs from the previous step. This step is linear in the number of smallest-granularity intervals. The third step applies threshold clustering at all interval granularities, which involves a linear scan over the BBVs. Once the phase IDs are determined through the clustering step, the fourth step then determines the phase predictability by predicting next phase IDs — this again has a linear time complexity.

Applications. The phase complexity surfaces provide a number of potential applications. First, it provides an easy-to-grasp, qualitative tool for characterizing the time-varying behavior of program executions across time scales. Second, workload designers and analysts can use the surfaces for comparing workloads in terms of their phase behavior. In particular, the surfaces can be used to select representative benchmarks for performance analysis based on their inherent program phase behavior. A set of benchmarks that represent diverse phase behaviors can capture a representative picture of the benchmark suite's phase behavior; this will be illustrated further in Section 6. Third, phase complexity surfaces are also useful for phase-based optimizations. For example, reducing energy consumption can be done by downscaling hardware resources on a per-phase basis [3,4,5,6]. An important criterion for good energy saving and limited performance penalty, is to limit the number of phases (in order to limit the training time at run time of finding a good per-phase hardware setting) and to achieve good phase predictability (in order to limit the number of phase mispredictions which may be costly in terms of missed energy saving opportunities and/or performance penalty). A phase complexity surface can help determine an appropriate interval size for optimization that provides a good trade-off between the number of phases and their predictability.

4   Experimental Setup

We use all the SPEC CPU2000 and CPU2006 integer and floating-point benchmarks and all of their reference inputs. And we run all benchmarks to completion. We consider Alpha binaries as well as IA-32 (x86) binaries. The Alpha binaries, which are aggressively optimized with the Alpha `cc` compiler, were taken from the SimpleScalar website; the IA-32 binaries were compiled using the Intel `icc` compiler v9.1 with the `-O2` optimization flag. We use the SimpleScalar Tool Set [26] for collecting BBVs on an interval basis for the Alpha binaries, and we use Diota [27], a dynamic binary instrumentation tool, for collecting BBVs for the IA-32 binaries.

5   Program Phase Characterization

Due to space constraints, it is impossible to present phase complexity curves for all benchmarks. Instead we present and discuss typical example phase complexity surfaces that we observed during our study for SPEC CPU2000 using the Alpha binaries — we will be discussing the IA-32 binaries and CPU2006 later — and refer the interested reader to http://www.elis.ugent.be/PCS/ for phase complexity surfaces for all benchmarks. Example surfaces are shown in Figures 1 and 2: Figure 1 shows phase count and predictability surfaces for gcc-scilab, gzip-program, eon-kajiya and equake; Figure 2 shows surfaces for bzip2-graphic, lucas, fma3d and gap. As mentioned before, a phase count surface shows the (logarithm of the) number of phases on the vertical axis versus the clustering threshold θ (which is a measure for intra-phase variability) and the interval size (which is a measure of the time scale granularity) on the horizontal axes; the phase predictability surface shows

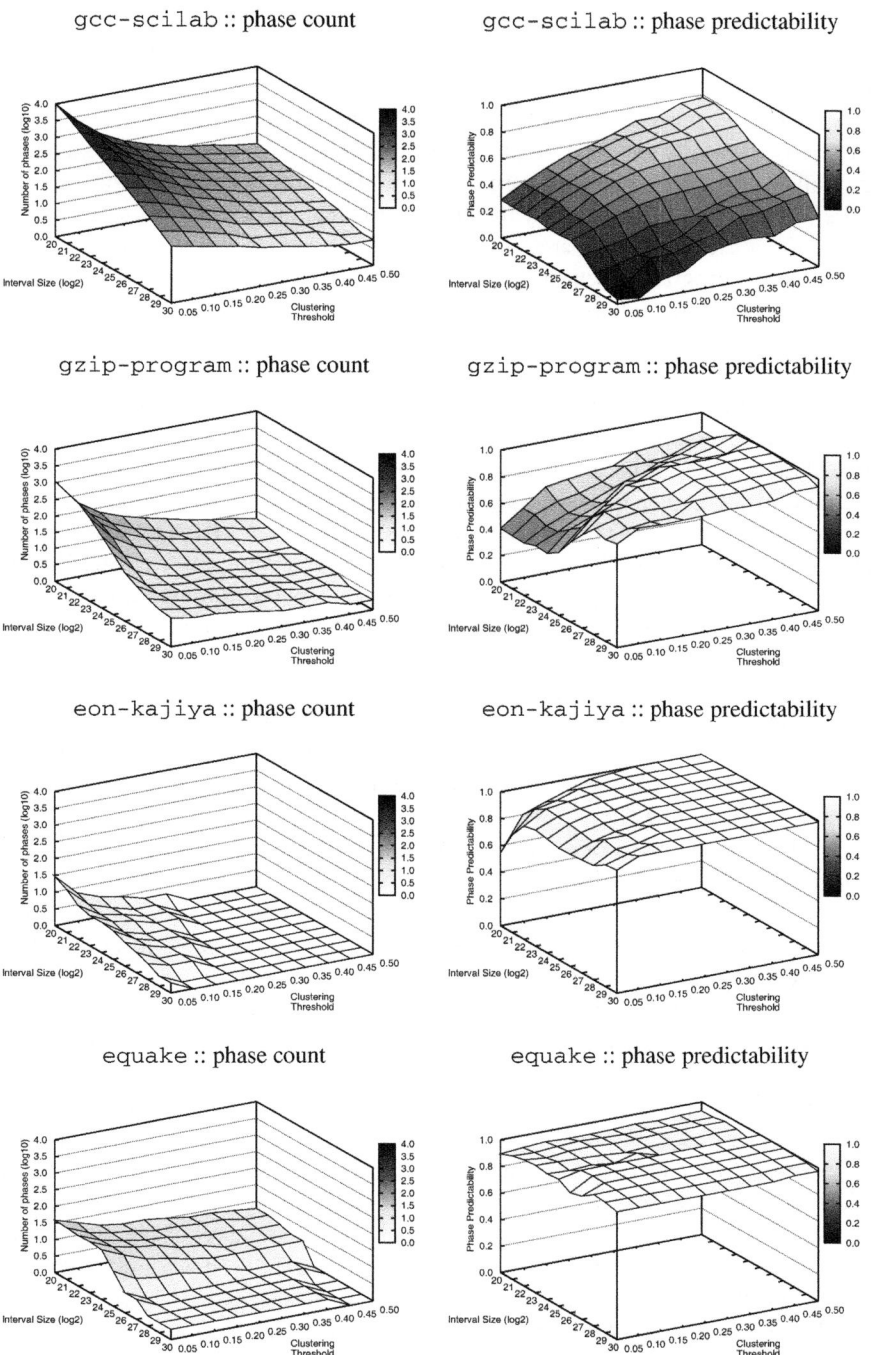

Fig. 1. Phase count surfaces (left column) and phase predictability surfaces (right column) for (from top to bottom) gcc-scilab, gzip-program, eon-kajiya and equake

phase predictability (on the vertical axis) versus clustering threshold and interval size. The θ clustering threshold is varied from 0.05 up to 0.5 in 0.05 increments — the smaller the threshold, the smaller the intra-phase variability; interval size is varied from 1M up to 1G — note the labels are shown as log_2 of the interval size.

There are basically two types of phase count surfaces. The first type shows a decreasing number of program phases at larger time granularities, see the examples shown in Figure 1. This can be explained by the observation that phase behavior at a small time granularity gets averaged out at a larger time granularity. As a result, more and more portions of the program execution start looking similar which is reflected in a decreasing number of program phases.

The second type shows an increasing number of program phases at moderate time granularities and a decreasing number of program phases at a yet larger time granularity, see the examples in Figure 2. This behavior appears for programs with obvious phase behavior, however, this obvious phase behavior seems to be difficult to capture over a range of time scales. This can occur in case the period of the inherent phase behavior is not a multiple of a given time scale granularity. For the purpose of illustration, consider the following example of a phase ID sequence: 'AAABBAAABBAAABB...' with 'A' and 'B' being phase IDs. The number of phases at time granularity 1 equals 2, namely 'A' and 'B'. At the time granularity of 2, there are 3 phases observed, namely 'AA', 'AB' (or 'BA') and 'BB'. At the time granularity of 4, there are only 2 phases observed: 'AAAB' and 'AABB'. In some sense this could be viewed of as a consequence of our choice for fixed-length intervals in our phase-level characterization, however, we observe the large number of phases across a range of time granularities. This seems to suggest that this phase behavior has a fairly long period, and that variable-length intervals (which are tied to some notion of time granularity as well) may not completely solve the problem either.

It is also interesting to observe that for both types of phase count surfaces, phase predictability can be either high or low. For example, the predictability is low for gcc-scilab, gzip-program and gap, and is very high for equake and fma3d. For some benchmarks, phase predictability correlates inversely with the number of phases, see for example gzip-program: the higher the number of phases, the lower their predictability. For other benchmarks on the other hand, the opposite seems to be true: phase predictability decreases with a decreasing number of phases, see for example gcc-scilab.

The phase count and predictability surfaces can now be combined into phase complexity surfaces, see Figure 3 for examples for gcc-scilab, eon-kajiya, gzip-program and gap. The annotation in the gcc-scilab graph (top left in Figure 3) illustrates how these surfaces should be read: there are lines showing $\theta = 0.05$, $\theta = 0.25$ and $\theta = 0.50$, i.e., interval size, the number of phases and phase predictability are shown explicitly whereas the θ threshold is shown implicitly. These examples clearly show distinct phase behaviors. The phase behavior for eon-kajiya is much less complex than for gcc-scilab: eon-kajiya has fewer program phases and shows very good phase predictability; gcc-scilab on the other hand, exhibits a large number of phases and in addition, phase predictability is very poor.

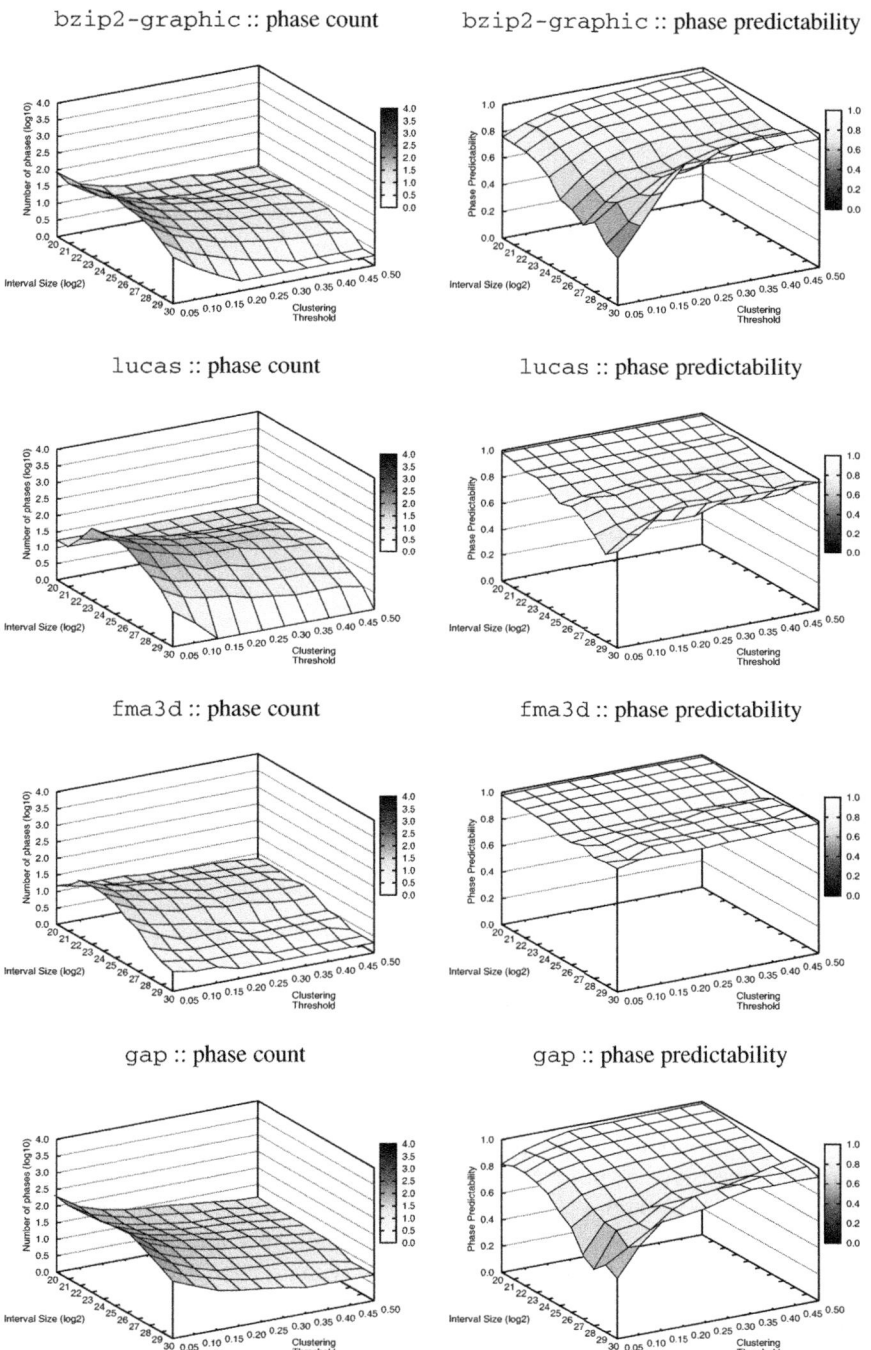

Fig. 2. Phase count surfaces (left column) and phase predictability surfaces (right column) for (from top to bottom) bzip2-graphic, lucas, fma3d and gap

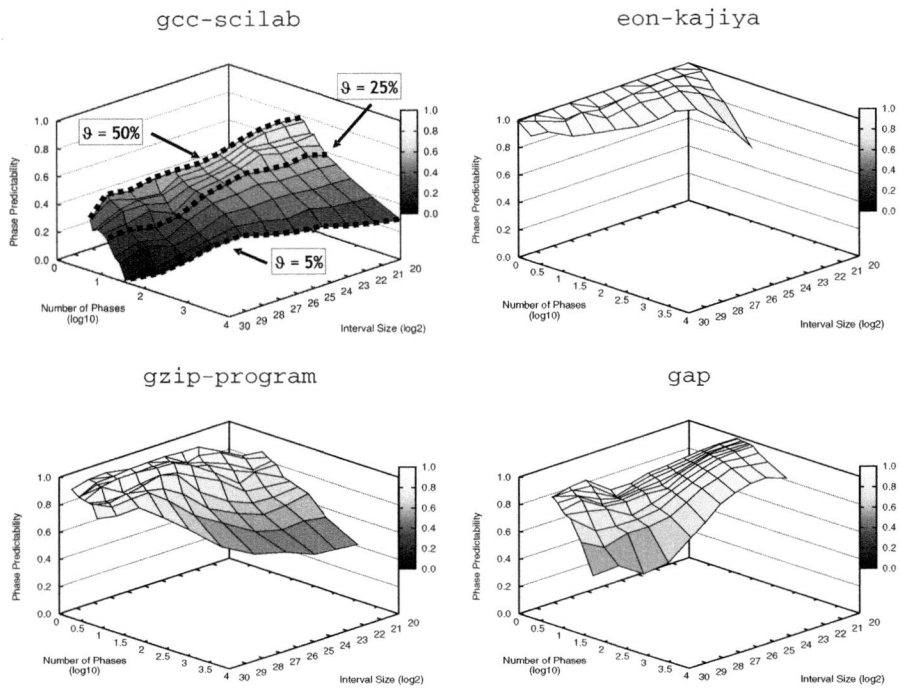

Fig. 3. Phase complexity surfaces for gcc-scilab (top left), eon-kajiya (top right), gzip-program (bottom left) and gap (bottom right)

6   Classifying Benchmarks

Having characterized all the SPEC CPU2000 benchmarks in terms of their phase behavior using phase complexity surfaces, we can now categorize these benchmarks according to their phase behavior. To this end we employ the methodology proposed by Eeckhout et al. [28] to find similarities across benchmarks.

6.1   Methodology

As input to this methodology we provide a number of characteristics per benchmark: we provide phase predictability and (the logarithm of) the number of phases at three threshold values ($\theta = 0.05$, $\theta = 0.15$ and $\theta = 0.25$) at four time scales (1M, 8M, 64M and 512M) — there are 24 characteristics in total. Intuitively speaking, we sample the phase complexity surface. This yields a data matrix with the rows being the benchmarks and the columns being the 24 phase characteristics.

This data matrix serves as input to Principal Components Analysis (PCA) [29] — the goal of PCA is (i) to remove correlation from the data set and (ii) to reduce the dimensionality. PCA computes new dimensions, called *principal components*, which are *linear combinations* of the original phase characteristics. In other words, PCA tranforms the $p = 24$ phase characteristics $X_1, X_2, \ldots, X_p$ into p principal components

$Z_1, Z_2, \ldots, Z_p$ with $Z_i = \sum_{j=1}^{p} a_{ij} X_j$. This transformation has the properties (i) $Var[Z_1] \geq Var[Z_2] \geq \ldots \geq Var[Z_p]$ — this means Z_1 contains the most information and Z_p the least; and (ii) $Cov[Z_i, Z_j] = 0, \forall i \neq j$ — this means there is no information overlap between the principal components. Some principal components have a higher variance than others. By removing the principal components with the lowest variance from the analysis, we reduce the dimensionality of the data set while controlling the amount of information that is thrown away. On our data set we retain three principal components that collectively explain 87.4% of the total variance in the original data set. Note that prior to PCA we normalize the data matrix (the columns have a zero mean and a variance of one) to put all characteristics on a common scale; also after PCA, we normalize the principal components to give equal weight to the underlying mechanisms extracted by PCA.

We now have a reduced data matrix, i.e., we are left with three principal component values for all benchmarks. This reduced data set now serves as input to cluster analysis which groups benchmarks that exhibit similar phase behavior. We use linkage clustering here because it allows for visualizing the clustering through a dendrogram. Linkage clustering starts with a matrix of distances between the benchmarks. As a starting point for the algorithm, each benchmark is considered a group. In each iteration of the algorithm, groups that are closest to each other are merged and groups are gradually merged until we are left with a single group. This can be represented in a so called *dendrogram*, which graphically represents the linkage distance for each group merge at each iteration of the algorithm. Having obtained a dendrogram, it is up to the user to decide how many clusters to take. This decision can be made based on the linkage distance. Indeed, small linkage distances imply strong clustering while large linkage distances imply weak clustering. There exist several methods for calculating the distance between clusters. In this paper we use the weighted pair-group average method which computes the distance between two clusters as the weighted average distance between all pairs of benchmarks in the two different clusters. The weighting of the average is done by considering the cluster size, i.e., the number of benchmarks in the cluster.

6.2 Results

We can now plot the benchmarks in terms of the three principal components obtained after PCA. This is shown in Figure 5 displaying two graphs, PC_1 versus PC_2, and PC_1 versus PC_3. These graphs visualize the similarity across the benchmarks in terms of their phase behavior. To help interpreting these graphs, we refer to Figure 4 which represents the factor loadings for the three principal components; the factor loadings are the coefficients a_{ij} defining the principal components $Z_i = \sum_{j=1}^{p} a_{ij} X_j$. Interpreting the factor loadings helps understanding the meaning of the principal components and helps understanding the phase behavior of a program in terms of these principal components. For example, the higher the value along the first principal component for a given program, the more phases it has and the lower its phase predictability. The programs having a low value along the first principal component exhibit few phases and high predictability. A program having a high score along the second principal component

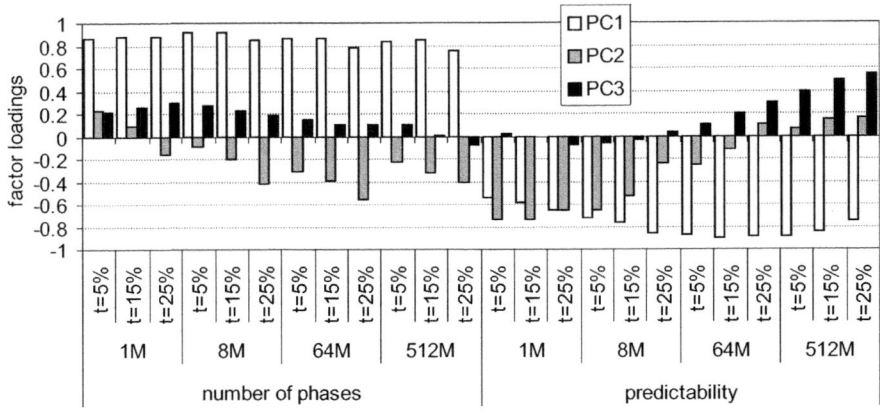

Fig. 4. Factor loadings for the three principal components

exhibits low phase predictability at a small time granularity, and relatively few phases at a large time granularity. The third principal component weighs the number of phases at a small time granularity and the predictability at a large time granularity.

As a next step, we can now apply cluster analysis within this space obtained after PCA. Figure 6 shows the dendrogram obtained from clustering the benchmarks based on their phase behavior. Classifying the benchmarks using this dendrogram with a critical threshold of 2.5, results in four major clusters representing the most diverse phase behaviors across the SPEC CPU2000 benchmarks. Note that in case a more fine-grained distinction needs to be made among the benchmarks in terms of their phase behavior, the critical threshold should be made smaller; this will result in more fine-grained types of phase behavior. We observe the following key phase characteristics in each of the four major clusters:

- cluster 1 :: very poor phase predictability and a very large number of phases;
- cluster 2 :: very small number of phases and very good phase predictability;
- cluster 3 :: a relatively poor predictability and a high number of phases at small time granularities, in combination with relatively better predictability and relatively fewer phases at large time granularities;
- cluster 4 :: a moderate number of phases across all time granularities, and mostly good to excellent predictability.

In summary, cluster 2 exhibits the simplest phase behavior. Clusters 3 and 4 show moderately complex phase behaviors, with cluster 3 showing poorer phase predictability at small time granularities. Cluster 1 represents the most complex phase behaviors observed across the SPEC CPU2000 benchmark suite. Referring back to Figure 3, the phase complexity surfaces shown represent an example benchmark from each of these groups: eon-kajiya as an example for the simple phase behavior in cluster 2; gzip-program and gap as examples for the moderately complex phase behaviors in clusters 3 and 4, respectively; and gcc-scilab as an example for the very complex phase behavior in cluster 1.

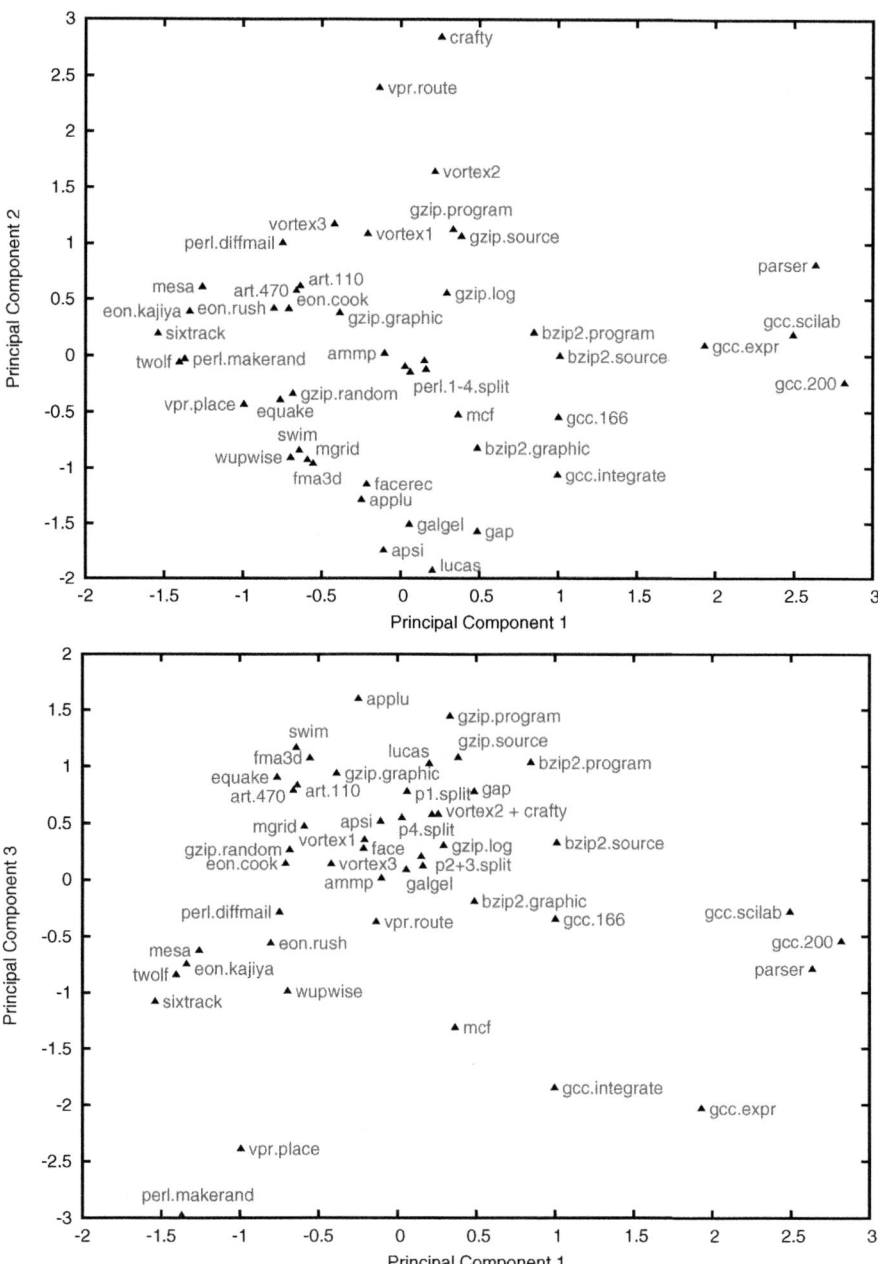

Fig. 5. Plotting the SPEC CPU2000 benchmarks in the PCA space: PC_1 vs PC_2 (top graph), and PC_1 vs PC_3 (bottom graph)

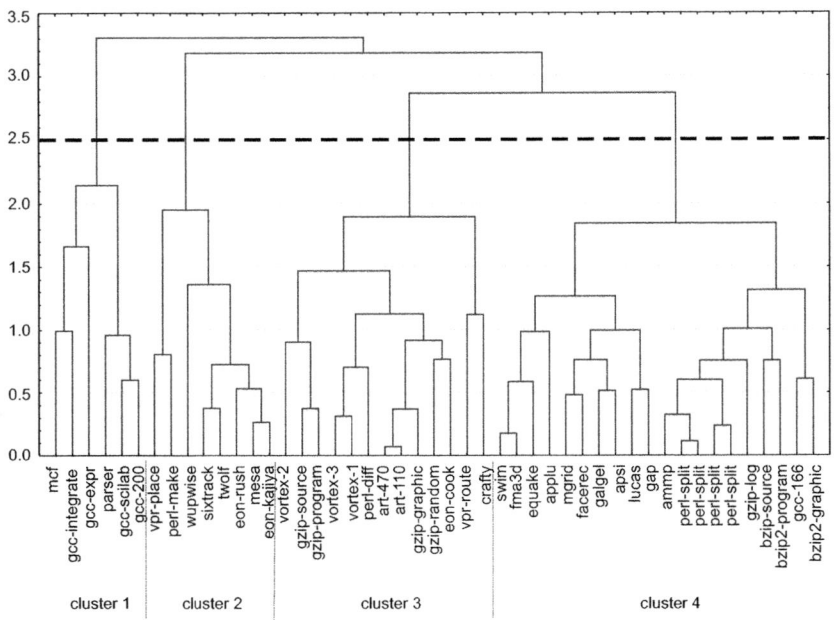

Fig. 6. Dendrogram visualizing the clustering for the Alpha SPEC CPU2000 benchmark suite

Researchers exploiting program phase behavior can use this classification to select benchmarks for their experiments. A performance analyst should pick benchmarks from all groups in order to have a representative set of program phase behaviors.

7   Are Phase Complexity Surfaces Platform-Specific?

So far, we considered the Alpha binaries of the SPEC CPU2000 benchmarks. A relevant question however is whether the phase complexity surfaces computed for one platform are transferable to another platform, i.e., can we use the insights obtained from phase complexity surfaces across platforms? Or in other words, is similar phase behavior being observed across platforms with different ISAs and compilers? To answer this question we now consider the SPEC CPU2000 Alpha and IA-32 binaries and compare their phase complexity surfaces. The Alpha ISA, which is a RISC ISA, is very different from the IA-32 ISA, which is a CISC ISA; in addition, the respective compilers are also very different.

To answer the above question, we set up the following experiment. We first compute phase complexity surfaces for all the Alpha and IA-32 binaries, and subsequently sample those surfaces as described in the previous section. We then apply cluster analysis on this Alpha plus IA-32 data set. Figure 7 shows the resulting dendrogram; the Alpha binaries are marked with an 'a', and the IA-32 binaries are marked with an 'i'. The key observation from this dendrogram is that the Alpha and IA-32 binaries lie very close to each other in the dendrogram (their linkage distance is very small) which

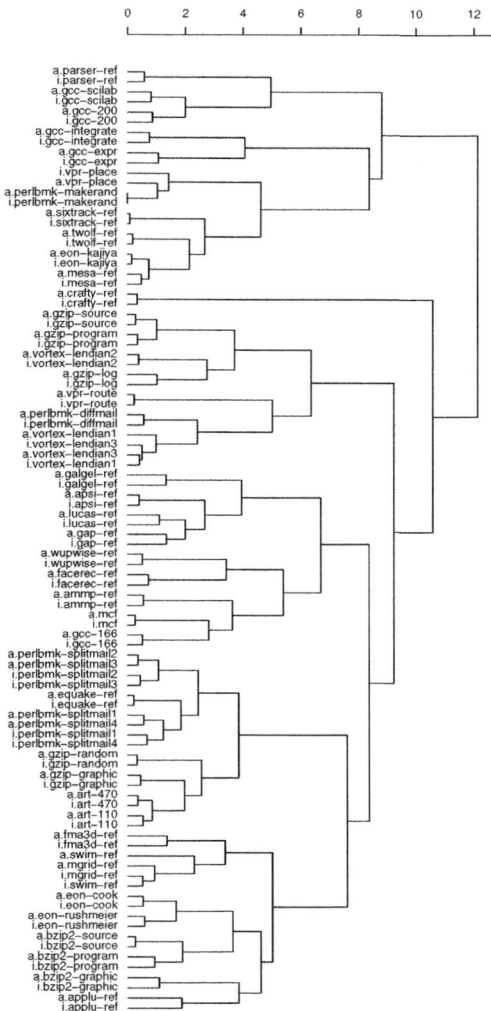

Fig. 7. Dendrogram visualizing the clustering for the SPEC CPU2000 benchmark suite and two platforms: Alpha (denoted as 'a') versus IA-32 (denoted as 'i')

means that they have very similar phase complexity surfaces. We thus conclude that phase complexity surfaces are transferable across platforms, i.e., similar complexity of a program's phase behavior is observed across ISAs and compilers.

8 Multiple Generations of SPEC CPU

SPEC provides new generations of its benchmark suites to reflect new workload demands over time. The two most recent CPU benchmark suites are CPU2000 and

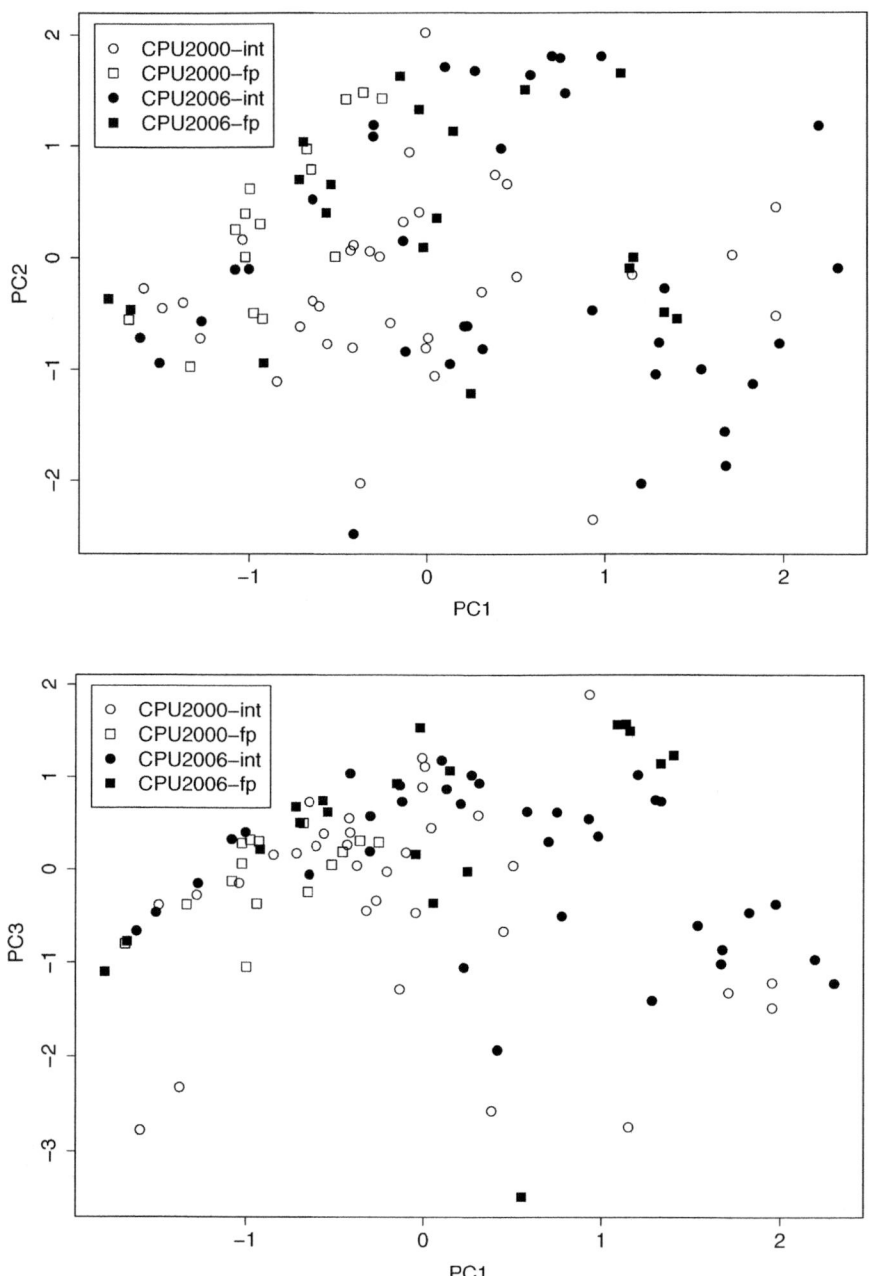

Fig. 8. Plotting the SPEC CPU2000 and CPU2006 benchmarks in the PCA space: PC_1 vs PC_2 (top graph), and PC_1 vs PC_3 (bottom graph)

CPU2006. We now compare CPU2000 versus CPU2006 in terms of their phase behavior, see Figure 8. There are several interesting observations to be made here. First, the time-varying program behavior tends to be more diverse for the floating-point benchmarks in SPEC CPU2006 compared to CPU2000, as the CPU2006 floating-point benchmarks are spread over a larger area of the workload space that the CPU2000 floating-point benchmarks. Second, the integer benchmarks in CPU2006 tend to have higher values along the first principal component than the integer CPU2000 benchmarks: this means the integer benchmarks in CPU2006 exhibit more phases and poorer phase predictability than in CPU2000. In summary, SPEC CPU2006 shows more diverse and more complex time-varying behavior than CPU2000.

9   Conclusion

Program phase behavior is a well-known program characteristic that is subject to many optimizations both in software and hardware. In order to get a good understanding of a program's phase behavior, it is important to have a way of characterizing a program's time-varying behavior. This paper proposed phase complexity surfaces which characterize a program's phase behavior in terms of its four key properties: time scale, number of phases, phase predictability and intra- versus inter-phase predictability. Phase complexity surfaces provide an intuitive and unified view of a program's phase behavior. These complexity surfaces can be used to classify benchmarks in terms of their inherent phase behavior. We computed phase complexity surfaces for the SPEC CPU2000 and CPU2006 benchmark suites and conclude that (i) the observed phase behavior differs widely across benchmarks, (ii) phase complexity surfaces are transferable across platforms (ISAs and respective compilers), and (iii) CPU2006 exhibits more complex and more diverse time-varying program behavior than CPU2000.

Acknowledgements

We would like to thank the reviewers for their valuable comments. Frederik Vandeputte and Lieven Eeckhout are supported by the Fund for Scientific Research in Flanders (Belgium) (FWO-Vlaanderen). Additional support is provided by the FWO projects G.0160.02 and G.0255.08, and the UGent-BOF project 01J14407, as well as the HiPEAC FP7 EU Network-of-Excellence.

References

1. Eeckhout, L., Sampson, J., Calder, B.: Exploiting program microarchitecture independent characteristics and phase behavior for reduced benchmark suite simulation. In: Proceedings of the 2005 IEEE International Symposium on Workload Characterization (IISWC), pp. 2–12 (2005)
2. Sherwood, T., Perelman, E., Hamerly, G., Calder, B.: Automatically characterizing large scale program behavior. In: Proceedings of the International Conference on Architectural Support for Programming Languages and Operating Systems (ASPLOS), pp. 45–57 (2002)

3. Balasubramonian, R., Albonesi, D., Buyuktosunoglu, A., Dwarkadas, S.: Memory hierarchy reconfiguration for energy and performance in general-purpose processor architectures. In: Proceedings of the 33th Annual International Symposium on Microarchitecture (MICRO), pp. 245–257 (2000)
4. Dhodapkar, A., Smith, J.E.: Dynamic microarchitecture adaptation via co-designed virtual machines. In: International Solid State Circuits Conference (2002)
5. Dhodapkar, A., Smith, J.E.: Managing multi-configuration hardware via dynamic working set analysis. In: Proceedings of the 29th Annual International Symposium on Computer Architecture (ISCA), pp. 233–244 (2002)
6. Sherwood, T., Sair, S., Calder, B.: Phase tracking and prediction. In: Proceedings of the 30th Annual International Symposium on Computer Architecture (ISCA), pp. 336–347 (2003)
7. Georges, A., Buytaert, D., Eeckhout, L., De Bosschere, K.: Method-level phase behavior in Java workloads. In: Proceedings of the 19th Annual ACM SIGPLAN Conference on Object-Oriented Programming, Languages, Applications and Systems (OOPSLA), pp. 270–287 (2004)
8. Nagpurkar, P., Krintz, C., Sherwood, T.: Phase-aware remote profiling. In: Proceedings of the International Conference on Code Generation and Optimization (CGO), pp. 191–202 (2005)
9. Perelman, E., Hamerly, G., Calder, B.: Picking statistically valid and early simulation points. In: Proceedings of the 12th International Conference on Parallel Architectures and Compilation Techniques (PACT), pp. 244–256 (2003)
10. Patil, H., Cohn. R., Charney, M., Kapoor, R., Sun, A., Karunanidhi, A.: Pinpointing representative portions of large Intel Itanium programs with dynamic instrumentation. In: Proceedings of the 37th Annual International Symposium on Microarchitecture (MICRO), pp. 81–93 (2004)
11. Cho, C.B., Li, T.: Complexity-based program phase analysis and classification. In: Proceedings of the 15th International Conference on Parallel Architectures and Compilation Techniques (PACT), pp. 105–113 (2006)
12. Huffmire, T., Sherwood, T.: Wavelet-based phase classification. In: Proceedings of the 15th International Conference on Parallel Architectures and Compilation Techniques (PACT), pp. 95–104 (2006)
13. Shen, X., Zhong, Y., Ding, C.: Locality phase prediction. In: International Conference on Architectural Support for Programming Languages and Operating Systems (ASPLOS), pp. 165–176 (2004)
14. Lau, J., Perelman, E., Hamerly, G., Sherwood, T., Calder, B.: Motivation for variable length intervals and hierarchical phase behavior. In: Proceedings of the International Symposium on Performance Analysis of Systems and Software (ISPASS), pp. 135–146 (2005)
15. Lau, J., Perelman, E., Calder, B.: Selecting software phase markers with code structure analysis. In: Proceedings of the International Conference on Code Generation and Optimization (CGO), pp. 135–146 (2006)
16. Huang, M., Renau, J., Torrellas, J.: Positional adaptation of processors: Application to energy reduction. In: Proceedings of the 30th Annual International Symposium on Computer Architecture (ISCA), pp. 157–168 (2003)
17. Duesterwald, E., Cascaval, C., Dwarkadas, S.: Characterizing and predicting program behavior and its variability. In: Proceedings of the International Conference on Parallel Architectures and Compilation Techniques (PACT), pp. 220–231 (2003)
18. Isci, C., Martonosi, M.: Identifying program power phase behavior using power vectors. In: Proceedings of the Sixth Annual IEEE International Workshop on Workload Characterization, WWC (2003)
19. Lau, J., Sampson, J., Perelman, E., Hamerly, G., Calder, B.: The strong correlation between code signatures and performance. In: Proceedings of the International Symposium on Performance Analysis of Systems and Software (ISPASS), pp. 236–247 (2005)

20. Lau, J., Schoenmackers, S., Calder, B.: Structures for phase classification. In: Proceedings of the 2004 International Symposium on Performance Analysis of Systems and Software (ISPASS), pp. 57–67 (2004)
21. Cho, C.B., Li, T.: Using wavelet domain workload execution characteristics to improve accuracy, scalability and robustness in program phase analysis. In: Proceedings of the International Symposium on Performance Analysis of Systems and Software, ISPASS (2007)
22. Lau, J., Schoenmackers, S., Calder, B.: Transition phase classification and prediction. In: Proceedings of the 11th International Symposium on High Performance Computer Architecture (HPCA), pp. 278–289 (2005)
23. Vandeputte, F., Eeckhout, L., De Bosschere, K.: A detailed study on phase predictors. In: Proceedings of the 11th International Euro-Par Conference, pp. 571–581 (2005)
24. Sherwood, T., Perelman, E., Calder, B.: Basic block distribution analysis to find periodic behavior and simulation points in applications. In: Proceedings of the International Conference on Parallel Architectures and Compilation Techniques (PACT), pp. 3–14 (2001)
25. Chen, I.K., Coffey, J.T., Mudge, T.N.: Analysis of branch prediction via data compression. In: Proceedings of the 7th International Conference on Architectural Support for Programming Languages and Operating Systems (ASPLOS), pp. 128–137 (1996)
26. Burger, D.C., Austin, T.M.: The SimpleScalar Tool Set. Computer Architecture News (1997), http://www.simplescalar.com
27. Maebe, J., Ronsse, M., De Bosschere, K.: DIOTA: Dynamic instrumentation, optimization and transformation of applications. In: Compendium of Workshops and Tutorials Held in Conjunction with PACT 2002: International Conference on Parallel Architectures and Compilation Techniques (2002)
28. Eeckhout, L., Vandierendonck, H., De Bosschere, K.: Workload design: Selecting representative program-input pairs. In: Proceedings of the International Conference on Parallel Architectures and Compilation Techniques (PACT), pp. 83–94 (2002)
29. Johnson, R.A., Wichern, D.W.: Applied Multivariate Statistical Analysis, 5th edn. Prentice Hall, Englewood Cliffs (2002)

Compiler Directed Issue Queue
Energy Reduction

Timothy M. Jones[1], Michael F.P. O'Boyle[3],
Jaume Abella[2], and Antonio González[4]

[1] Member of HiPEAC, Computer Laboratory
University of Cambridge, UK
timothy.jones@cl.cam.ac.uk
[2] Barcelona Supercomputing Center (BSC-CNS)
Barcelona, Spain
jaume.abella@bsc.es
[3] Member of HiPEAC, School of Informatics
University of Edinburgh, UK
mob@inf.ed.ac.uk
[4] Intel Barcelona Research Center, Intel Labs - UPC,
Barcelona, Spain
antonio.gonzalez@intel.com

Abstract. The issue logic of a superscalar processor consumes a large
amount of static and dynamic energy. Furthermore, its power density
makes it a hot-spot requiring expensive cooling systems and additional
packaging. This paper presents a novel approach to energy reduction
that uses compiler analysis communicated to the hardware, allowing the
processor to dynamically resize the issue queue, fitting it to the available
ILP without slowing down the critical path. Limiting the entries available
reduces the quantity of instructions dispatched, leading to energy savings
in the banked issue queue without adversely affecting performance.

Compared with a recently proposed hardware scheme, our approach
is faster, simpler and saves more energy. A simplistic scheme achieves
31% dynamic and 33% static energy savings in the issue queue with a
7.2% performance loss. Using more sophisticated compiler analysis we
then show that the performance loss can be reduced to less than 0.6%
with 24% dynamic and 30% static energy savings and an EDD product
of 0.96, outperforming two current state-of-the-art hardware approaches.

1 Introduction

Superscalar processors contain complex logic to hold instructions and information as they pass through the pipeline. Unfortunately, extracting sufficient instruction level parallelism (ILP) and performing out-of-order execution consumes
a large amount of energy, with important implications for future processors.

With up to 27% of the total processor energy consumption being consumed by
the issue logic [1], this is one of the main sources of power dissipation in current
superscalar processors [2]. Furthermore, this logic is one of the components with

P. Stenström (Ed.): Transactions on HiPEAC IV, LNCS 6760, pp. 42–62, 2011.
© Springer-Verlag Berlin Heidelberg 2011

the highest power density and is a hot-spot. Reducing its power dissipation is therefore more important than for other structures. Consequently there has been much work in developing hardware schemes to reduce this energy cost by turning off unused entries and adapting the issue queue to the available ILP [1, 3, 4]. Unfortunately, there is an inevitable delay in sensing rapid phase changes and adjusting accordingly. Furthermore, these mechanisms are based on past program behaviour, rather than knowledge of the future. This leads to either a loss of IPC due to too small an issue queue or excessive power dissipation due to too large an issue queue.

This paper proposes an entirely different approach - software directed issue queue control. In essence, the compiler knows which parts of the program are to be executed in the near future and can resize the queue accordingly. It reduces the number of instructions in the queue without delaying the critical path of the program. Reducing the number of instructions in the issue queue reduces the number of non-ready operands woken up each cycle and hence saves energy. We evaluate the energy savings for the issue queue using a simplistic scheme in section 6 and with more sophisticated compiler analysis in section 7.

1.1 Related Work

Saving energy by turning off unused parts of the processor has been the focus of much previous work. Bahar and Manne [5] introduce *pipeline balancing* which changes the issue width of the processor depending on the issue IPC over a fixed window size. Other papers [6, 7] propose shutting down parts of the processor in a similar manner with comparable results.

Considering the issue queue alone, Folegnani and González [1] reduce useless activity by gating off the precharge signal for tag comparisons to empty or ready operands. They then suggest ways to take advantage of the empty entries by dynamically resizing the queue. Buyuktosunoglu et al. [3] propose a similar resizing scheme, using banks which can be turned off for static energy savings. Abella and González [4] use heuristics to limit the number of instructions in the issue queue, as in [1]. They decrease the size of the queue when the heuristic determines potential energy savings. Buyuktosunoglu et al. [8] use fetch gating to control the number of instructions entering the issue queue and combine this with heuristics to limit the issue queue too. However, for both these schemes, limiting the issue queue comes at the price of a non-negligible performance loss.

There have been proposals for an issue queue without wakeups which works by tracking the dependences between instructions [9]. Huang et al. [10] use direct-mapped structures to track dependences and allow more than one consumer per result by adding extra bits. Önder and Gupta [11] implement many consumers to one producer by linking consumers together. Canal and González [9] allow set-associativity in their dependence structure for the same goal. FIFO queues are used by Palacharla et al. [12] into which instructions are dispatched in dependence chains. This means only the oldest instruction in each queue needs to be

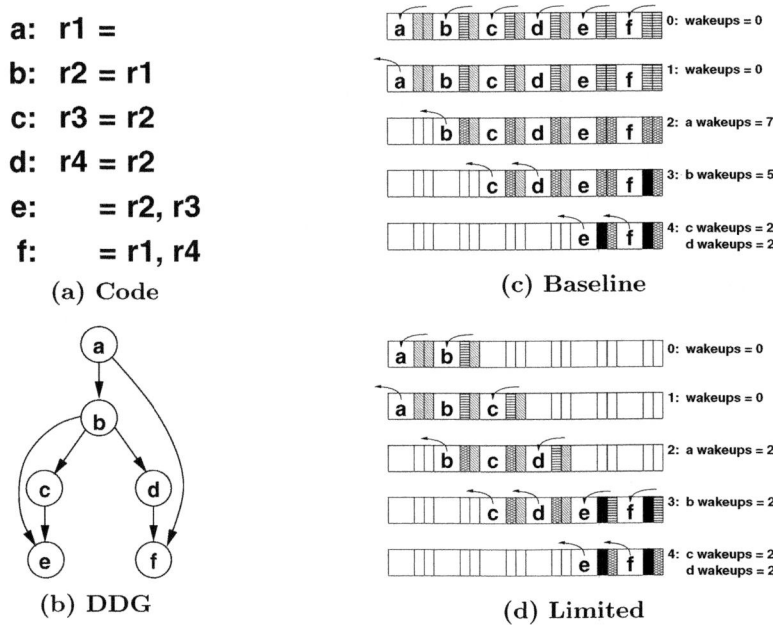

a: r1 =

b: r2 = r1

c: r3 = r2

d: r4 = r2

e: = r2, r3

f: = r1, r4

(a) Code

(b) DDG

(c) Baseline

(d) Limited

Fig. 1. Issue queue energy savings. 1(a) shows a basic block and 1(b) shows its DDG. In 1(c) it takes 5 cycles and causes 16 wakeups. Limiting the queue to 2 entries in 1(d) means it still takes 5 cycles but only causes 8 wakeups.

monitored for potential issue. Abella and González [13] extend this technique so that floating-point queues do not cause a high performance loss. Other schemes have also been recently proposed [14, 15].

The majority of compiler directed approaches to energy reduction have focused on embedded processors. VLIW instruction scheduling has been studied [16–19] whereas others have considered dynamic voltage scaling techniques [20] and the use of compiler controlled caches for frequently executed code [21]. For superscalar processors, most contributions have considered dynamic voltage scaling techniques [20, 22]. Other schemes have targeted the register file, deallocating registers early for energy savings or performance gains [23, 24]. In [25] a compiler-based technique that performs fine-grained issue queue throttling is presented. This paper performs an extensive exploration of the compiler design space, showing the improvements available through both coarse-grained and fine-grained issue queue limiting.

1.2   Contribution and Structure

This paper presents a novel approach to dynamically resizing the issue queue with compiler support. To the best of our knowledge, this is the first paper to develop compiler directed analysis of issue queue size based on critical path analysis. It can be applied to any superscalar organisation and is not tuned to any hardware configuration. The rest of this paper is structured as follows. Section 2 presents an example showing how energy savings can be achieved in the issue queue. Section 3 describes the microarchitecture we use and the small changes we have made. This is followed by section 4 where we outline the compiler analysis performed on different structures in a program. Section 5 briefly describes our experimental setup. Sections 6 and 7 describe two different limiting schemes with their results and they are followed by section 8 which concludes this paper.

2   Motivation

This section describes minimising the issue queue size without affecting the critical path. For the sake of this example, only data dependences that affect the critical path are considered.

Figure 1 shows a basic block where all instructions belong to at least one critical path. To aid readability, instructions are written using pseudo-code. A fragment of assembly code is shown in figure 1(a) and its data dependence graph (DDG) is shown in figure 1(b). There is no need for instructions b, c, d, e and f to be in the issue queue at the same time as a as they are dependent on it and so cannot issue at the same time as it. Likewise, instructions c, d, e and f do not need to be in the issue queue at the same time as b. In fact, instructions e and f do not need to enter the issue queue until c and d leave. Limiting the issue queue to only 2 instructions means the code will execute in the same number of cycles, but fewer wakeups will occur and so energy will be saved.

Figures 1(c) and 1(d) show the issue queue in the baseline and limited cases respectively. A dispatch width of 8 instructions is assumed with each instruction taking one cycle to execute. It is also assumed instruction a has no other input dependences and can therefore issue the cycle after it dispatches. Finally, as in Folegnani and González [1], it is assumed that empty and ready operands do not get woken. Arrows denote whether an instruction is dispatched into the issue queue or issued from it. A white rectangle next to an instruction indicates an empty operand with an empty entry while a rectangle with diagonal lines denotes an operand that is not needed. A rectangle with horizontal lines shows an operand yet to arrive and one that is crossed diagonally shows a wakeup on that operand. Finally, a black rectangle indicates an operand already obtained.

In the baseline case, figure 1(c), all six instructions dispatch in cycle 0. Instruction a issues in cycle 1, completing in cycle 2. It causes seven wakeups and allows b to issue. In cycle 3, b finishes causing five wakeups, allowing instructions c and d to issue. They cause four wakeups in cycle 4 and finally e and f can issue. They write back in cycle 5 and there are sixteen wakeups in total.

Now consider figure 1(d) with the same initial assumptions, but with the constraint that only two instructions can be in the issue queue at any one time. Instruction c must wait unitl cycle 1 to dispatch, d until cycle 2, and instructions e and f must wait until cycle 3. There is no slowdown and only eight wakeups occur, a saving of 50%. In practice the dependence graphs are more complex and resource constraints must be considered, yet this example illustrates the basic principle of the technique.

3   Microarchitecture

This section describes the hardware changes needed to support the limiting of the issue queue. The compiler has to pass information to the processor about the number of issue queue entries needed. Throughout this paper, two methods of accomplishing this are evaluated: special no-ops and instruction tagging.

The special no-ops consist of an opcode and some unused bits, in which the issue queue size is encoded. The special no-ops do nothing to the semantics of the program and are not executed, but are stripped out of the instruction stream in the final decode stage before dispatch. Tagging assumes there are a number of unused bits within each instruction which can be used to encode the issue queue size needed. Instructions are executed as normal, but the information they contain is extracted during decode and used at dispatch. Tagging overcomes the side-effects caused by special no-ops, such increased instruction cache misses.

We have analysed the free bits within the Alpha ISA and found that many instruction have three unused bits in their encoding. One example is the operate format which is used for all register-to-register operations and contains unused function codes. For memory and branch format instructions, we can shorten the displacement field with little impact. Our analysis shows that shortening by 3 bits would affect only 2% of these instructions.

3.1   Issue Queue

A multiple-banked issue queue is assumed where instructions are placed in sequential order. We assume that the queue is non-collapsible as in [1, 3, 4]. Having a compaction scheme would cause a significant amount of extra energy to be used each cycle. The queue is similar to [3] where a simple scheme is used to turn off the CAM and RAM arrays at a bank granularity at the same time. The selection logic is always on but it consumes much lower energy than the wakeup logic [12]. Empty and ready entries within the queue are prevented from being woken by gating off the precharge signal to the CAM cells, as proposed by Folegnani and González [1]. The baseline simulator performs no gating and all issue queue banks are permanently on. The schemes presented in this paper limit the number of issue queue entries allowed to contain instructions. The changes required are explained with the approaches in sections 6 and 7.

3.2   Fetch Queue

Each cycle the dispatch logic selects a number of instructions to move from the head of the fetch queue to the issue queue. The selection logic has to take into account the dispatch width of the processor, availability of issue queue entries and number of free registers, amongst other criteria. When our schemes use special no-ops to pass information from the compiler to the processor, it is removed from the instruction stream and its value used as the new issue queue limit. Although these instructions are not dispatched, their dispatch slots cannot be used by other instructions. Tagged instructions are not removed from the stream but the limiting value they contain is decoded and used as before.

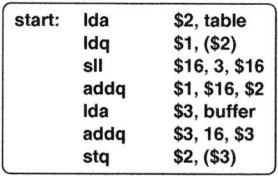

```
start:  lda     $2, table
        ldq     $1, ($2)
        sll     $16, 3, $16
        addq    $1, $16, $2
        lda     $3, buffer
        addq    $3, 16, $3
        stq     $2, ($3)
```

(a) Code

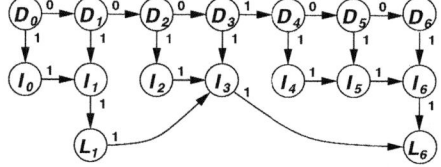

(b) Dependence graph

Fig. 2. An example piece of assembly code and its dependence graph. Edges are weighted with the latency (in cycles) taken to resolve the dependence. A D node with latency 0 on its incoming edge can dispatch at the same time as its predecessor, whereas a D node with latency 1 must be dispatched a cycle after its predecessor. In this example, all operations are assumed to take just one cycle.

4   Compiler Analysis

This section describes the compiler analysis performed to determine the number of issue queue entries needed by each program region. It is used in sections 6 and 7 for coarse-grained and fine-grained issue queue throttling and is based on simple methods to find the critical path of a program taking into consideration data dependences and resources.

4.1   Program Representation

The compiler considers each procedure individually, first building the control flow graph (CFG) using basic blocks as nodes and the flow of control between them as the edges. Analysis is specialised for loops because instructions from different iterations are executed in parallel when the loop is run. Hence, new CFGs are created (as explained below) and their backward edges removed in the original to preserve the dependences between instructions within each loop and those following. The two program structures created are DAGs and loops.

4.2   Critical Path Model

The critical path is modelled as a dependence graph, similar to those proposed by Tullsen and Calder [26] and Fields et al. [27]. This is because it provides an accurate representation of the events that occur to instructions as they are dispatched and issued. However, we compute our model statically within the compiler, removing the commit nodes and adding extra nodes for events occurring in the load/store queue.

In our model, each instruction, i, is represented by nodes which correspond to events occurring within the processor. There is a D (dispatch) node for when the instruction is dispatched into the issue queue, an I (issue) node for when the instruction is issued from the queue and an L (load/store) node if the instruction is a load or store, which denotes the instruction leaving the load/store queue.

Table 1. Edges present in the critical path model

Id	Constraint	Edge	Notes
1	In-order dispatch	$D_p \rightarrow D_i$	If p is immediately follows i
2	IQ issue after dispatch	$D_i \rightarrow I_i$	For every instruction
3	LSQ issue after IQ issue	$I_i \rightarrow L_i$	For every load and store
4	No spec load bypass	$I_p \rightarrow L_i$	If i is a load & p is previous store
5	Data dependence	$I_p \rightarrow I_i$	Non-load p defines source reg of i
6	Data dependence	$I_p \rightarrow L_i$	Non-load p defines data reg of store i
7	Store forwarding	$L_p \rightarrow L_i$	Store p has same address as load i
8	Data dependence	$L_p \rightarrow I_i$	Load p defines source reg of i
9	Data dependence	$L_p \rightarrow L_i$	Load p defines data reg of store i

The edges connecting the graph denote dependences between nodes. Each edge is weighted with the minimum number of cycles that the dependence takes to be resolved. Unlike in Fields et al. [27], control dependences between branches are not modelled because it is assumed that all branches will be predicted correctly. Figure 2 shows an example piece of assembly code and the dependence graph that is formed as the critical path model.

The dependences modelled are shown in table 1. The first edge models in-order instruction dispatch. The second represents instruction issue from the issue queue at least one cycle after dispatch. the third is present for loads and stores, representing issue from the load/store queue at least one cycle after issue from the issue queue. Edge 4 models the constraint that loads cannot speculatively bypass older stores in the load/store queue. Edge 7 models the case where a load accesses the same memory address as a previous store so the data can be forwarded in the load/store queue. Finally, edges 5, 6, 8 and 9 model data dependences via registers between different nodes.

When adding edges to the dependence graph, conservative assumptions are made except in the following cases: all branches are assumed to be predicted correctly; all loads are assumed to hit in the first level data cache; and where a load follows a store and it cannot be determined that they access the same memory address, it is assumed that they do not and that the load can issue before the store once both instructions' addresses have been calculated.

A dependence graph is created for each DAG and loop within the procedure. This graph can be used to calculate the issue queue requirements of the program structure being analysed. Section 4.3 describes the analysis for DAGs and then section 4.4 explains its use for loops.

4.3   Specialised DAG Analysis

Once the dependence graph has been formed each DAG is considered separately. We first describe the specialised analysis and then provide an example of its use.

Analysis. Starting with the entry point, we iterate over the DAG's dependence graph to determine the number of issue queue entries needed. We record the set

1. $next\_nodes = \{(D_0, 0)\}$
2. While $next\_nodes \neq \emptyset$
   (a) $issued = 0$
   (b) $oldest_inode = $ oldest I node not in $issue\_set$
   (c) For each functional unit type T
      i. $used(T) = 0$
   (d) For each pair $(N, X) \in next\_nodes$
      i. If $X = 0$
         (1) If $issued < issue\_width$ and $used(FU(N)) < number(FU(N))$
            a. Then $issue\_set = issue\_set \cup N$
            b. $used(FU(N)) = used(FU(N)) + 1$
            c. $issued = issued + 1$
            d. $youngest\_inode = Younger(N, youngest\_inode)$
            e. For each edge with weight W connecting N with successor S
               (i) $next\_nodes = next\_nodes \cup (S, W)$
      ii. Else
         (1) $X = X - 1$
   (e) $entries = MAX(entries, Distance(oldest\_inode, youngest\_inode))$

   where $FU(N)$ is the functional unit type required by node N
   $Younger(M, N)$ returns the younger of nodes M, N
   $Distance(M, N)$ returns the number of entries between nodes M, N

Fig. 3. Algorithm for analysing a DAG

of nodes reached on each iteration in the *issue set*. We traverse the dependence graph along edges from nodes in the issue set to those nodes outside. The edge weights determine the number of iterations to wait after a node has been added to the set before the edge can be traversed and the dependence satisfied.

At this stage of the algorithm we model functional unit contention and a limited processor issue width. To model a finite issue width, we define a maximum number of I and L nodes to be added to the issue set on any given iteration. Functional unit contention is similar, except we define a maximum number of I and L nodes for each type of functional unit.

We repeatedly iterate over the whole graph until all nodes are included in the issue set. The oldest I node not in the issue set at the start of each iteration is recorded, along with the youngest that is added during the iteration. The difference between the two gives the required issue queue size on that iteration to prevent a slowdown of the critical path. The maximum size over all iterations gives the required issue queue size for the whole dependence graph. Figure 3 gives the complete algorithm for DAG analysis.

Example. Figure 4 shows an example of a piece of code, its dependence graph and the analysis applied to it. The initial graph is shown in figure 4(b). On the first iteration, shown in figure 4(c) the D nodes are added to the issue set.

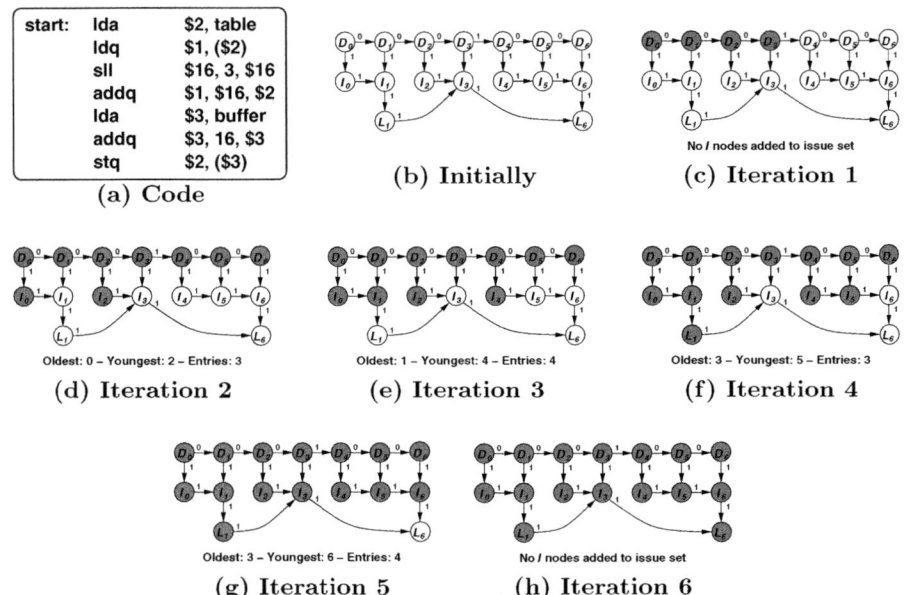

Fig. 4. Example of DAG analysis with a dispatch and issue width of 4 and no limit on the number of functional units. With the issue queue limited to four entries, this DAG would not be slowed down at all.

To indicate this they are coloured grey. However, because the dispatch width allows a maximum of four instructions to enter the pipeline, node D_4 is prevented from being included so the edge $D_3 \rightarrow D_4$ has a weight of 1.

During the second iteration (figure 4(d)), the final three D nodes are added to the issue set along with nodes I_0 and I_2 which have no input dependences. At the start of the iteration I_0 is the oldest I node not in the issue set and the youngest I node to be included is I_2 with a distance of 3 between them. This continues until figure 4(h) when all nodes have been added to the issue set. Over all iterations the maximum number of entries needed in this example is just four which would allow the DAG to issue without slowing down the critical path.

4.4   Specialised Loop Analysis

Out-of order execution of loops allows instructions from different loop iterations to be executed in parallel leading to a pipeline parallel execution of the loop as a whole. The analysis, therefore, has to be adjusted accordingly.

Analysis. Cycles containing I and L nodes in the dependence graph are detected and that with the longest latency chosen. This set of nodes is called the *cyclic dependence set of nodes (CDS)*. The CDS dictates the length of time each loop iteration takes to be completely issued and the next started and it is this set of instructions that is the critical path through the loop.

1. $CDS = Find\_CDS(nodes)$
2. For each node N in $nodes$
    (a) For each immediate predecessor node P in $nodes$
        i. Form equation $N_0 = P_i + Latency(P_i)$
3. While there's a change in the equations and an equation not related to a CDS node
    (a) For each node N in $nodes$
        i. For each equation E of the form $N_i = R_j + X$
            (1) If $\exists$ equation $R_k = C_l + Y$ where $C \in CDS$
                a. Rewrite E as $N_i = C_{l+j-k} + X + Y$
4. For each node N in CDS
    (a) For each equation of the form $L_i = N_j$
        i. $oldest\_inode = Older(L_i, N_j, oldest\_inode)$
        ii. $youngest\_inode = Younger(L_i, N_j, youngest\_inode)$
    (b) $entries = MAX(entries, Distance(oldest\_inode, youngest\_inode))$

> where $Find\_CDS(graph)$ returns the cycle with the highest weight in $graph$
> $Latency(N)$ returns the latency of N
> $Older(M, N, O)$ returns the elder of nodes M, N, O
> $Younger(M, N, O)$ returns the younger of nodes M, N, O
> $Distance(M, N)$ returns the number of entries between nodes M, N

Fig. 5. Algorithm for analysing a loop

Equations are formed for each I and L node in the loop based on the relationships within the dependence graph. The equations express the minimum number of cycles a node must wait to issue after a dependent node has issued. By substitution, these equations can be manipulated to express each I and L node in terms of a node within the CDS, meaning that relationships between CDS nodes and others within the graph are exposed. From these new equations it is possible to determine the nodes (possibly on different loop iterations) that could issue together when the loop is actually executed. The required issue queue size is calculated from the largest distance between any two I nodes issuing together.

Figure 5 summarises the algorithm for analysing a loop. The algorithm is guaranteed to terminate due to the condition in step 3. We do not alter the equations to model a finite issue width or functional unit contention because nodes can execute differently on each loop iteration. Instead, we factor in contention when calculating the required queue size. For example, if the maximum issue width is eight but nine instructions wish to issue then the calculated issue queue size is multiplied by $8/9$.

Example. Figure 6 shows an example of the compiler analysis for loops. The dependence graph for the loop is shown in figure 6(b). In this graph it is easy to see that there is only one candidate cycle for the CDS, containing node I_0 with latency 1. Figure 6(c) shows the initial equations formed for the I and L

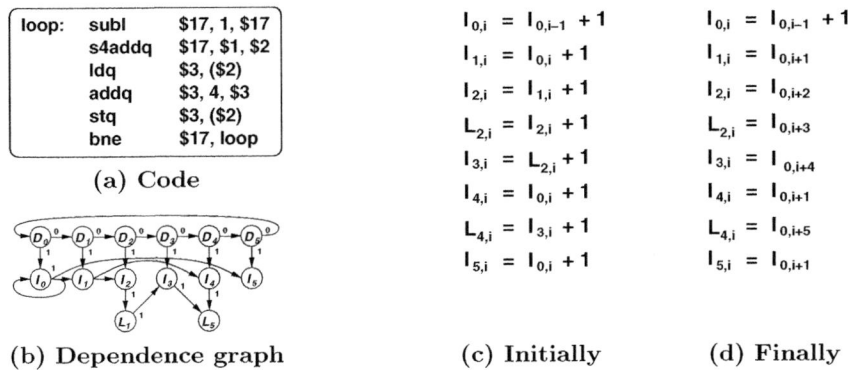

(a) Code

(b) Dependence graph

(c) Initially

(d) Finally

Fig. 6. Example of loop analysis with equations formed for the dependence graph shown. With a dispatch width of 8 and the issue queue limited to 22 entries, the critical path would not be affected.

nodes in the loop. Each equation relates the node on loop iteration i with one of its dependence nodes. Where a node has several dependences then equations are usually maintained for each, however only one is shown here for simplicity.

The equation for node I_0 in figure 6(c) refers to a previous instance of itself, the instance of the node on the previous iteration of the loop. The equation for I_0 means that in iteration i, I_0 can issue one cycle after I_0 from the previous iteration $(i-1)$. Continuing on, I_1 can issue 1 cycle after I_0 from the current iteration, I_2 can issue 1 cycle after I_1 from current iteration, and so on.

Once the equations have been formed they are manipulated to remove constants where possible and, hence, determine which nodes issue at the same time, producing the equations shown in figure 6(d). Considering only the I nodes, it is now trivial to compute the issue queue size needed by the loop. In order that I_0 on iteration $i+4$ can issue at the same time as I_3 on iteration i, they must be in the issue queue at the same time. This would require 22 entries to be available, allowing space for instructions corresponding to I_3, I_4 and I_5 from iteration i, 18 I nodes from iterations $i+1$, $i+2$ and $i+3$ (6 each), and I_0 from loop iteration $i+4$. Providing this many entries would allow parallel execution of this loop without affecting the critical path.

4.5   Interprocedural Analysis

One problem with our current approach is that dependence across procedure boundaries are not considered due to the limitations of our compilation infrastructure. To address this, in section 7.3, we investigate a technique that uses a small amount of extra hand-coded analysis to include these interprocedure dependences. The scheme works by first finding the call sites for each program procedure (which will be at the end of a DAG). Then, a resource list is produced

Table 2. Processor configuration

Component	Configuration
Pipeline	8 instructions wide; 128 entry reorder buffer; 80 entry issue queue (10 banks of 8); 112 integer and FP registers
Branch predictor	Hybrid of 2K gshare and 2K bimodal with a 1K selector; BTB with 2048 entries, 4-way
Caches	64KB, 2-way, 32B line, 1 cycle hit L1 Insn; 64KB, 4-way, 32B line, 2 cycles hit L1 Data; 512KB, 8-way, 64B line, 10/50 cycles hit/miss L2
Functional units	6 ALU (1 cycle), 3 Mul (3 cycles) Integer; 4 ALU (2 cycles), 2 MultDiv (4/12 cycles) FP

for each site which gives the functional unit usage and issue set for each iteration over the DAG. In a second step, the resource lists from all possible call sites are used as initialisation at each procedure start and the analysis updated.

As an example, consider the DAG $I1 \rightarrow I2$, where $I2$ is a function call. The issue set on iteration 1 will be $\{I1\}$ and on iteration 2 it will be $\{I2\}$. Furthermore, consider IALU is busy until iteration 3 and FPALU until iteration 4. This is the first stage of our approach. In the second step, we start analysing the first DAG in the called function. Assuming that this will start in iteration 3, we now know that we cannot schedule anything on FPALU until the following iteration, so we add this constraint into our analysis.

4.6   Summary

Having performed the compiler analysis, identifying the critical path and determining the issue queue requirements that would not slow it down, the information can be communicated to the processor to perform issue queue throttling. Section 6 describes a coarse-grained approach for each DAG or loop. Section 7 then presents a fine-grained scheme for each basic block. First, however, we describe our experimental setup.

5   Experimental Setup

This section describes the compiler, simulator and benchmarks used to evaluate our issue queue throttling schemes. Our processor configuration is shown in table 2 which was implemented in Wattch [28], based on SimpleScalar [29] using the Alpha ISA. We modelled a 70nm technology using Wattch's aggressive conditional clock gating scheme (cc3) which assumes idle resources consume 15% of their full energy. We used the MachineSUIF compiler from Harvard [30] to compile the benchmarks, which is based on the SUIF2 compiler from Stanford [31].

We chose to use the SPEC CPU2000 integer benchmark suite [32] to evaluate our schemes. However, we did not use *eon* because it is written in C++ which SUIF cannot directly compile. Similarly, we did not use any of the floating point benchmarks. Most of them cannot be directly compiled by SUIF because they

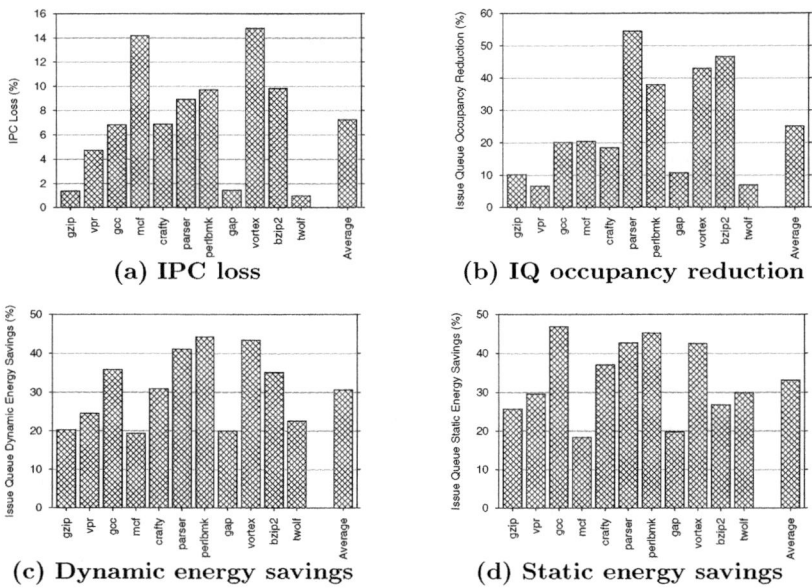

Fig. 7. Performance, issue queue occupancy reductions and issue queue energy savings when limiting using DL no-ops for coarse-grained issue queue throttling

are written in Fortran 90 or contain language extensions. We ran the benchmarks with the *ref* inputs for 100 million instructions after skipping the initialisation part and warming the caches and branch predictor for 100 million instructions.

Throughout this paper we evaluate our schemes in terms of performance and energy savings. For a performance metric we used instructions per cycle (IPC). For energy savings we considered dynamic (i.e. transistor switching activity) and static (i.e. the leakage energy consumed when the transistors are turned on).

6   Coarse-Grained Throttling

This section describes the first use of the analysis presented in section 4 to limit the size of the issue queue for each DAG or loop in its entirety. This is conveyed to the processor through the use of a special no-op or tag at the start of each DAG or loop. In addition a special no-op is also placed after a loop to reset the maximum queue size to the value of the surrounding DAG, allowing the queue to be fit to each structure's requirements.

Section 6.1 next describes the trivial microarchitectural changes to the issue queue, then section 6.2 presents the results from using special no-ops to pass the compiler-inferred queue requirements to the processor. Section 6.3 then evaluates instruction tagging, instead of using the special no-ops.

6.1   Issue Queue

The changes to the issue queue are very minor. The limiting no-op or tag simply indicates the maximum number of entries, both full or empty, that are allowed between the *head* and *tail* pointers in the issue queue. Instructions cannot dispatch if the *tail* pointer would become further than this from the *head*. In certain situations a limiting no-op or tag will be encountered that contains a smaller number of entries than is already allowed. To rectify this, enough instructions must be issued from the *head* for the distance between the two pointers to become less than the new maximum distance before dispatch can start again.

6.2   DL No-ops

The first evaluation of this scheme was performed using special no-ops to communicate the limiting information. We called these *DL no-ops* because of the granularity at which they are placed: at the start of every DAG and loop.

Figure 7(a) shows the effect on the performance of each benchmark in terms of IPC loss. Some benchmarks are badly affected, such as *mcf* and *vortex* which lose over 14% of their performance. Others experience only a small loss, such as *twolf* which has a 1% drop. On average, the performance loss is 7.2% due to a reduction in the dispatch width every time a special no-op is encountered, along with an inability to alter the size of the queue at a fine-enough granularity.

The issue queue occupancy reduction for this scheme is shown in figure 7(b). Although benchmarks that experienced a small performance loss, such as *gzip*, *gap* and *twolf*, also experience a small occupancy reduction, the benchmark that benefits the most is *parser* with a 54% drop. This leads to an average occupancy reduction of 25%. The average issue queue dynamic and static energy savings achieved through this are 31% and 33% respectively (figures 7(c) and 7(d)).

In addition to this, the presence of the DL no-ops in the binary increases the code size and means that more instructions need to be cached and fetched. On the other hand, our scheme throttles the issue queue, reducing the number of mis-speculated instructions that are actually fetched from the cache. The net result is an average reduction of 5% in the number of instruction cache accesses and a 20% increase in the size of each binary, on average.

6.3   Tags

As discussed in section 3.2, DL no-ops take up valuable dispatch resources. To reduce this problem we now consider a scheme where the first instruction in a DAG or loop is tagged with the resizing information, assuming that there were enough redundant bits in the ISA to accommodate the values needed.

The performance loss for each benchmark using these tags is shown in figure 8(a). Most benchmarks benefit to some degree from the removal of the no-ops, *gcc* especially which loses only 2.2% performance with tags compared with 6.8% with no-ops. However, in badly performing benchmarks such as *vortex* and *bzip2*, removal of the no-ops makes little difference. When considering the effects on issue queue occupancy, shown in figure 8(b), dynamic energy (figure 8(c)) and

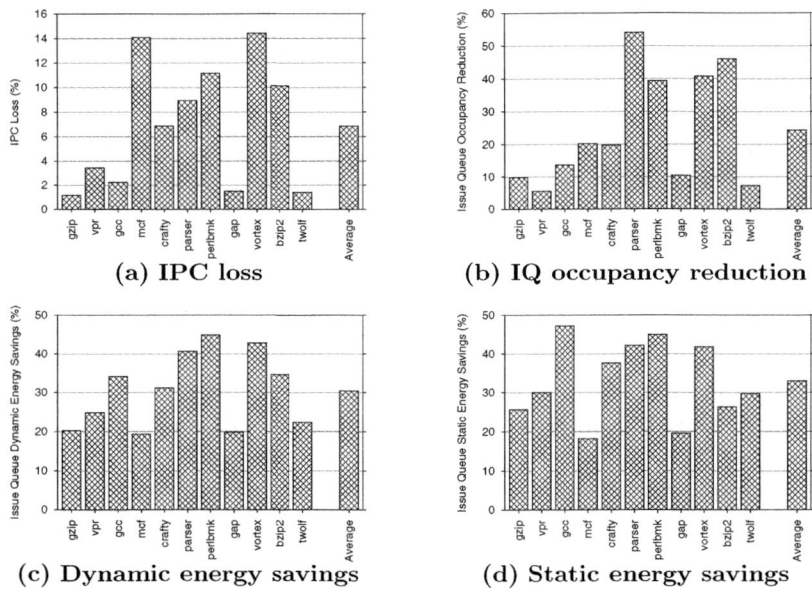

Fig. 8. Performance, issue queue occupancy reductions and issue queue energy savings when limiting using tags for coarse-grained issue queue throttling

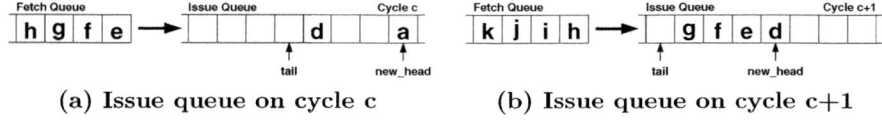

Fig. 9. Operation of *new_head* pointer with a limit of four entries

static energy savings (figure 8(d)) there is also little change when using tagging. This shows that the no-ops have little impact on the behaviour of the issue queue but can have a major impact on performance.

In summary, the two schemes presented in this section that perform coarse-grained analysis of a whole DAG's issue queue requirements can be used to reduce the energy consumption of the queue. However, they incur a non-negligible performance loss. The following section attempts to reduce this by performing the throttling at a much finer granularity.

7   Fine-Grained Throttling

It is clear from section 6 that performing issue queue limiting over a whole DAG is too restrictive and creates significant performance losses for some benchmarks. However, the performance losses are also partly due to the fact that the throttling takes place over the whole issue queue. When the first instructions in a

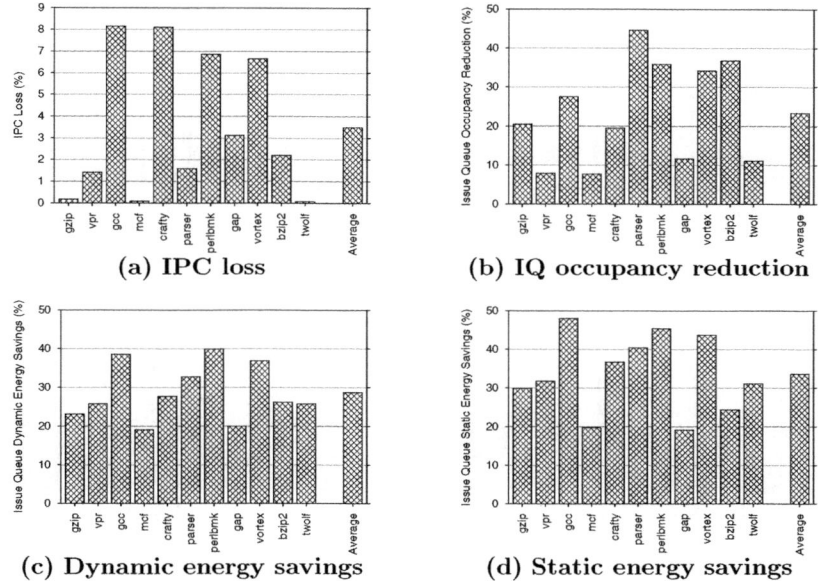

(a) **IPC loss**   (b) **IQ occupancy reduction**

(c) **Dynamic energy savings**   (d) **Static energy savings**

Fig. 10. Performance, issue queue occupancy reductions and issue queue energy savings when limiting using block no-ops for fine-grained issue queue throttling

DAG enter the queue, instructions from a previous DAG will already be there. Without knowing about dependences in the previous DAG, the compiler analysis cannot take into account the issue queue requirements of the older instructions. Any assumptions that underestimate these requirements mean that the older instructions are in the queue longer than the compiler realises and stall the dispatch of the new DAG. Hence, this section restricts the throttling of the issue queue to only the youngest part, allowing older instructions to issue without the compiler needing to know about them and consider them during its analysis.

This section is structured as follows. Section 7.1 describes the changes to the issue queue required so that only the youngest part of the queue is throttled. Section 7.2 presents results obtained using special no-ops to pass the queue size required by the youngest part of the queue. Section 7.3 then presents the same scheme using instruction tags instead of special no-ops. The final approach is also compared to a state-of-the-art hardware scheme.

7.1   Issue Queue

The issue queue requires only minor modifications to allow the new limiting scheme to work. A second *head* pointer, named *new_head*, is introduced which allows compiler control over the youngest entries in the queue. The *new_head* pointer points to a filled entry between the *head* and *tail* pointers. It functions exactly the same as the *head* pointer such that when the instruction it points to is issued it moves towards the *tail* until it reaches a non-empty slot, or becomes the *tail*. New instructions being dispatched are still added to the queue's *tail*.

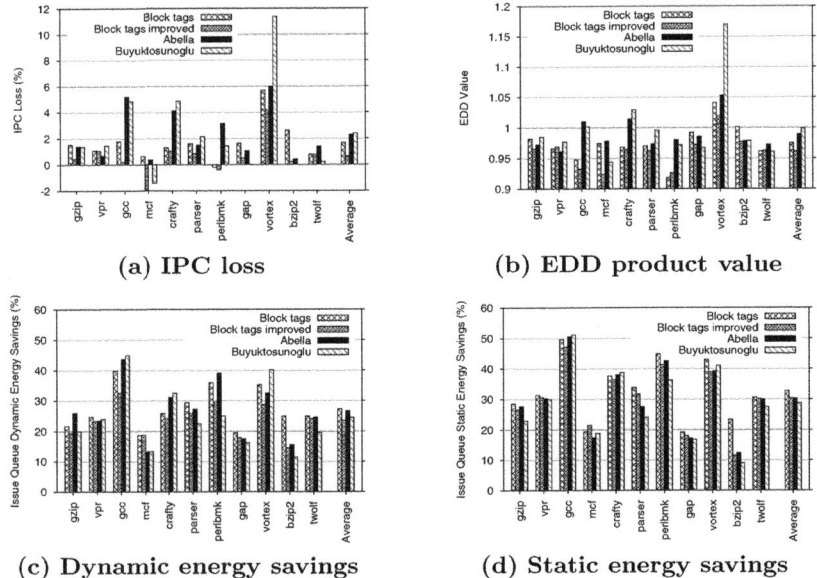

(a) IPC loss   (b) EDD product value

(c) Dynamic energy savings   (d) Static energy savings

Fig. 11. Performance reduction, EDD product values and issue queue energy savings when limiting using tags for fine-grained issue queue throttling

This scheme is based on the fact that it is relatively easy to determine the future additional requirements of a small program region. Where, in the previous approach, the maximum number of entries between *head* and *tail* were limited, in this section the distance between *new_head* and *tail* is restricted. This is so that instructions from previous basic blocks (and previous DAGs) can be present in the queue without affecting the limiting of the youngest part. So, the instructions between *new_head* and *tail* are from the youngest program region whereas the rest of the instructions (between *head* and *new_head*) are from older ones.

The operation of the queue is demonstrated in figure 9. If instruction *a* issues, the *new_head* pointer moves up to the next non-empty instruction, so three slots to *d*. This means that up to three more instructions can be dispatched to keep the number of entries at four or fewer. So, *e*, *f* and *g* can now dispatch as shown in figure 9(b).

7.2   Block No-ops

This section evaluates the new limiting scheme using special no-ops, called block no-ops, inserted into the code. The performance of each benchmark is shown in figure 10(a). In this approach benchmarks are either hardly affected (*gzip*, *mcf* and *twolf* which lose less than 0.2%) or experience large performance losses (e.g. *crafty* at over 8%). On average, however, the loss is only 3.5%.

The issue queue occupancy reduction for this scheme is shown in figure 10(b). Most benchmarks experience around a 20% reduction and *parser* gets an occupancy reduction of 45%, the average being a 23% reduction. This gets converted into dynamic and static energy savings which are shown in figures 10(c) and 10(d). The average dynamic and static energy savings are 29% and 34% respectively. The best savings come from *gcc* which experiences 38% dynamic and 48% static energy savings. All benchmarks achieve 19% dynamic energy savings whilst most see their static energy reduced by at least 30% too.

With this approach there is also an increase in code size of 44% on average. This also increases the number of instructions that need to be fetched but, as described in section 6.2, this is offset by throttling the issue queue. Overall, there is an increase of 1% in the number of instruction cache accesses on average.

7.3 Tags

This section evaluates the use of tags instead of no-ops to convey the limiting information for the youngest part of the issue queue. In each graph three schemes are shown. The first is the approach that simply uses tags instead of no-ops to pass limiting information to the processor. This scheme is called *Block tags*.

The second scheme, called *Block tags improved*, is derived from the *Block tags* technique. By hand, limited extra analysis was applied to all benchmarks to reduce functional unit contention and prevent dispatch stalls causing underutilisation of resources when useful work could be performed. It is described in more detail in section 4.5. This interprocedural analysis would typically be available in a mature industrial compiler but is absent in our SUIF prototype.

For comparison, we implemented two state-of-the-art hardware approaches. The first is from papers published by Abella and González [4, 33], the second from Buyuktosunoglu et al. [8]. We implemented these within the same simulation infrastructure as all other experiments. We compare to the *IqRob64* scheme from [4] as this gave the most energy savings and is henceforth referred to as *Abella*. We call the technique from [8] *Buyuktosunoglu*.

Results. As can be seen from figure 11(a), the compiler schemes lose less performance than *Abella* and *Buyuktosunoglu*, *perlbmk* and *mcf* even gain slightly (0.4% and 1.9% respectively). This is due, in part, to a reduced number of branch mispredictions, but also because young instructions on the critical path are sometimes prevented from executing due to functional unit contention with older, non-critical instructions. With the issue queue throttling scheme here, these older instructions are executed on a different cycle and thus the contention does not occur. All approaches perform badly on *vortex* (especially *Buyuktosunoglu*) but the two hardware schemes cannot cope well with *gcc*, *crafty* or *perlbmk*. The extra analysis performed in *Block tags improved* considerably reduces the performance loss of most benchmarks. On average *Block tags* loses 1.7%, *Block tags improved* 0.6%, *Abella* 2.3% and *Buyuktosunoglu* 2.4% performance.

The energy-delay-squared product for each of the schemes is shown in figure 11(b), where it is assumed that the issue queue consumes 20% of the total processor energy, consistent with the findings of Folegnani and González [1]. We have assumed that leakage accounts for 25% of total energy as described in [34]. The compiler-directed schemes have better EDD products than *Abella* and *Buyuktosunoglu*, with the best, *Block tags improved*, achieving 0.96, compared to 0.99 for both hardware approaches.

These EDD values are achieved through savings in both dynamic and static energy (figures 11(c) and 11(d)). The static energy of the issue queue is completely dependent on the number of banks that are on each cycle whereas the dynamic energy consumption is dependent on the number of instructions waking others and reads and writes to the queue, as well as the occupancy. The average dynamic energy savings of the *Block tags* scheme is the same as *Abella* (27%) whereas it is reduced slightly to 24% in *Block tags improved* and *Buyuktosunoglu*. The static energy reduction is, on average, better than the hardware approaches in both our schemes. The *Block tags* approach reduces it by 33%, *Block tags improved* by 30%, *Abella* by 30% and *Buyuktosunoglu* by 29%.

8   Conclusions

This paper has presented novel techniques to dynamically resize the issue queue using the compiler for support. The compiler analyses and determines the number of issue queue entries needed by each program region and encodes this number in a special no-op or a tag with the instruction. The number is extracted at dispatch and used to limit the number of instructions in the queue. This reduces the issue queue occupancy and thus the amount of energy consumed.

Results from the implementation and evaluation of the proposed schemes show 31% dynamic energy savings with a 7.2% average IPC loss for a basic scheme which attempts to determine the whole queue size needed. By only determining the requirements of the youngest part of the queue, the performance loss can be reduced to just 3.5% when using special no-ops to convey the information. Tagging instructions and using improved analysis reduces this further to just 0.6%, compared with 2.3% and 2.4% for two state-of-the-art hardware schemes [4, 8]. Both compiler and hardware schemes save similar amounts of static and dynamic energy in the issue queue.

Future Work. One of the downsides of our current approach is that it only works on single-threaded processors. On a simultaneous multithreaded (SMT) architecture, the schemes presented in this paper that throttle the issue queue considering only one thread at a time could be detrimental to other processes sharing the resources. Future work will consider issue queue limiting in this type of environment, using compiler analysis of future program requirements and hardware knowledge of the current system state to adapt the issue queue size for the benefit of all executing threads.

Acknowledgements. This work has been partially supported by the Royal Academy of Engineering, EPSRC and the Spanish Ministry of Science and Innovation under grant TIN2007-61763.

References

1. Folegnani, D., González, A.: Energy-effective issue logic. In: ISCA-28 (2001)
2. Emer, J.: Ev8: The post-ultimate alpha. In: Keynote at PACT (2001)
3. Buyuktosunoglu, A., Schuster, S., Brooks, D., Bose, P., Cook, P., Albonesi, D.H.: An adaptive issue queue for reduced power at high performance. In: Falsafi, B., VijayKumar, T.N. (eds.) PACS 2000. LNCS, vol. 2008, p. 25. Springer, Heidelberg (2001)
4. Abella, J., González, A.: Power-aware adaptive issue queue and register file. In: Pinkston, T.M., Prasanna, V.K. (eds.) HiPC 2003. LNCS (LNAI), vol. 2913, pp. 34–43. Springer, Heidelberg (2003)
5. Bahar, R.I., Manne, S.: Power and energy reduction via pipeline balancing. In: ISCA-28 (2001)
6. Maro, R., Bai, Y., Bahar, R.I.: Dynamically reconfiguring processor resources to reduce power consumption in high-performance processors. In: Falsafi, B., VijayKumar, T.N. (eds.) PACS 2000. LNCS, vol. 2008, p. 97. Springer, Heidelberg (2001)
7. Manne, S., Klauser, A., Grunwald, D.: Pipeline gating: Speculation control for energy reduction. In: ISCA-25 (1998)
8. Buyuktosunoglu, A., Karkhanis, T., Albonesi, D.H., Bose, P.: Energy efficient co-adaptive instruction fetch and issue. In: Falsafi, B., VijayKumar, T.N. (eds.) PACS 2000. LNCS, vol. 2008. Springer, Heidelberg (2001)
9. Canal, R., González, A.: Reducing the complexity of the issue logic. In: ICS-15 (2001)
10. Huang, M., Renau, J., Torrellas, J.: Energy-efficient hybrid wakeup logic. In: ISLPED (2002)
11. Önder, S., Gupta, R.: Superscalar execution with dynamic data forwarding. In: PACT (1998)
12. Palacharla, S., Jouppi, N.P., Smith, J.E.: Complexity-effective superscalar processors. In: ISCA-24 (1997)
13. Abella, J., González, A.: Low-complexity distributed issue queue. In: HPCA-10 (2004)
14. Ernst, D., Hamel, A., Austin, T.: Cyclone: A broadcast-free dynamic instruction scheduler with selective replay. In: ISCA-30 (2003)
15. Hu, J.S., Vijaykrishnan, N., Irwin, M.J.: Exploring wakeup-free instruction scheduling. In: HPCA-10 (2004)
16. Lee, C., Lee, J.K., Hwang, T., Tsai, S.-C.: Compiler optimization on instruction scheduling for low power. In: ISSS-13 (2000)
17. Lorenz, M., Leupers, R., Marwedel, P., Dräger, T., Fettweis, G.: Low-energy DSP code generation using a genetic algorithm. In: ICCD-19 (2001)
18. Zhang, W., Vijaykrishnan, N., Kandemir, M., Irwin, M.J., Duarte, D., Tsai, Y.-F.: Exploiting VLIW schedule slacks for dynamic and leakage energy reduction. In: MICRO-34 (2001)
19. Toburen, M.C., Conte, T.M., Reilly, M.: Instruction scheduling for low power dissipation in high performance microprocessors. Technical report, North Carolina State University (1998)
20. Magklis, G., Scott, M.L., Semeraro, G., Albonesi, D.H., Dropsho, S.: Profile-based dynamic voltage and frequency scaling for a multiple clock domain microprocessor. In: ISCA-30 (2003)

21. Bellas, N., Hajj, I., Polychronopoulos, C., Stamoulis, G.: Energy and performance improvements in microprocessor design using a loop cache. In: ICCD-17 (1999)
22. Hsu, C.-H., Kremer, U., Hsiao, M.: Compiler-directed dynamic voltage/frequency scheduling for energy reduction in microprocessors. In: ISLPED (2001)
23. Jones, T.M., O'Boyle, M.F.P., Abella, J., González, A., Ergin, O.: Compiler directed early register release. In: PACT (2005)
24. Lo, J.L., et al.: Software-directed register deallocation for simultaneous multithreaded processors. IEEE TPDS 10(9) (1999)
25. Jones, T.M., O'Boyle, M.F.P., Abella, J., González, A.: Software directed issue queue power reduction. In: HPCA-11 (2005)
26. Tullsen, D.M., Calder, B.: Computing along the critical path. Technical report, University of California, San Diego (1998)
27. Fields, B., Rubin, S., Bodík, R.: Focusing processor policies via critical-path prediction. In: ISCA-28 (2001)
28. Brooks, D., Tiwari, V., Martonosi, M.: Wattch: A framework for architectural-level power analysis and optimizations. In: ISCA-27 (2000)
29. Burger, D., Austin, T.: The simplescalar tool set, version 2.0. Technical Report TR1342, University of Wisconsin-Madison (1997)
30. Smith, M.D., Holloway, G.: The Machine-SUIF documentation set (2000), http://www.eecs.harvard.edu/machsuif/software/software.html
31. The Stanford SUIF Compiler Group: The suif compiler infrastructure, http://suif.stanford.edu/
32. The Standard Performance Evaluation Corporation (SPEC): CPU 2000 (2000), http://www.spec.org/cpu2000/
33. Abella, J., González, A.: Power-aware adaptive instruction queue and rename buffers. Technical Report UPC-DAC-2002-31, UPC (2002)
34. Aygün, K., Hill, M.J., Eilert, K., Radhakrishnan, K., Levin, A.: Power delivery for high-performance microprocessors. Intel Technology Journal 9(4) (2005)

A Systematic Design Space Exploration Approach to Customising Multi-Processor Architectures: Exemplified Using Graphics Processors

Ben Cope[1], Peter Y.K. Cheung[1], Wayne Luk[2], and Lee Howes[2]

[1] Department of Electrical & Electronic Engineering, Imperial College London, UK
[2] Department of Computing, Imperial College London, UK

Abstract. A systematic approach to customising Homogeneous Multi-Processor (HoMP) architectures is described. The approach involves a novel design space exploration tool and a parameterisable system model. Post-fabrication customisation options for using reconfigurable logic with a HoMP are classified. The adoption of the approach in exploring pre- and post-fabrication customisation options to optimise an architecture's critical paths is then described. The approach and steps are demonstrated using the architecture of a graphics processor. We also analyse on-chip and off-chip memory access for systems with one or more processing elements (PEs), and study the impact of the number of threads per PE on the amount of off-chip memory access and the number of cycles for each output. It is shown that post-fabrication customisation of a graphics processor can provide up to four times performance improvement for negligible area cost.

1 Introduction

In this work, the graphics processor architecture is used to demonstrate a systematic approach to exploring the customisation of Homogeneous Multi-Processor (HoMP) architectures for a given application domain. Our approach involves a novel design space exploration tool with a parameterisable system model.

As motivation for the exploration tool presented here, consider the following projections from the Tera Device [1] and HiPEAC [2] road maps:

I. Memory bandwidth and processing element (PE) interconnect restrictions necessitate a revolutionary change in on-chip memory systems [1, 2].
II. It is becoming increasingly important to automate the generation of customisable accelerator architectures from a set of high level descriptors [1, 2].
III. Continuing from II, architecture customisation may be applied at the design, fabrication, computation or runtime stage [1].

The statements above are not mutually exclusive: an answer to statement I may be a customisation from statement II. It is important to note the following key words.

First *customisation*, which represents pre-fabrication (pre-fab) and post-fabrication (post-fab) architectural customisations. Pre-fab customisation is the familiar approach

P. Stenström (Ed.): Transactions on HiPEAC IV, LNCS 6760, pp. 63–83, 2011.
© Springer-Verlag Berlin Heidelberg 2011

to determine 'fixed' architecture components. Post-fab customisation is a choice of re-configurable logic (RL) architectural components (hardware), or a programmable instruction processor (software), to facilitate in-field modifications. Although we refer to RL customisations, the work in this paper is also applicable to instruction processors.

Second, *high-level descriptors*. The increased complexity of the application and architecture domains, necessitate architectural exploration at a suitably high degree of abstraction, with a high-level representation of each domain.

Third, a focus on *interconnect* and *memory systems*. These factors frequent each road map [1, 2]. It is becoming increasingly challenging to present the required input data to, and distribute output data from, processing elements.

It is hoped that the exploration tool presented in this paper can be used to explore the above observations. The aim is to provide significant insight into some of the associated challenges, faced when designing the exploration process and system model.

The example taken in and focus of this work, is to target the graphics processor architecture at the video processing application domain. The approach and model are sufficient to be extended to other architectures and application domains.

The contributions of this work, and the related sections, are as follows:

1. Definition of a classification scheme for the options for post-fab customisation of a HoMP using RL. The scheme is demonstrated by analysing prior art (Section 3).
2. A systematic design space methodology to explore the customisation options for a HoMP. The key feature is the notion of pre- and post-fab options (Section 4).
3. The design space options for a HoMP are presented. A system model is described which implements these options (Section 5).
4. An analysis of the effect of processing pattern on the performance of a model with a single processing element (PE) and a single execution thread (Section 6).
5. Extension of the above single PE analysis, in contribution 4, to a multiple PE and multi-threaded example (Section 7).
6. Case studies including decimation and 2D convolution are used to explore the architectural trends of graphics processors (Section 8).
7. Proposal and exploration of a graphics processor post-fab customisation which is motivated by the results from contributions 4 through 6 (Section 9).

In addition to the above, Section 2 discusses related work; Section 10 considers the impact of our work on other HoMPs; and Section 11 summarises our findings.

This paper is an extended version of [3]. The additional novel contributions to [3] are 1, 4 and 5. There are also technical enhancements to other contribution areas.

2   Related Work

A popular design space exploration approach is the Y-Chart [4]. The Y-Chart combines architecture and application models in 'mapper' and 'simulator' stages to produce performance predictions. In turn, these predictions motivate application and architecture model modifications. A key strength of the Y-Chart is an iterative update of application and architectural choice based on a model of system performance [4, 5].

For this work, a standard Y-Chart approach is insufficient. Two issues are as follows. First, the Y-Chart is too high-level to provide a useful insight into the exploration process. For a constrained design space, a more detailed description is preferable, as is shown in Section 5. Second, the choices of architecture features which support the mapping of application to architecture should be made more explicit than in the Y-Chart. To overcome the second issue, a third design space variable of physical mapping is introduced. This is an overlap of the application and architecture design space, and is the architectural design decisions which support the programming model. For HoMP architectures, the programming model is one of the most challenging parts of the design process. Figure 2(a) is observed to be a suitable adaptation of the Y-Chart approach.

When creating a model for design space exploration one is presented with a tradeoff between a higher level of abstraction, to broaden the design space, and low level architectural detail, to make the results meaningful. Related work on architecture models, Kahn Process Networks and the SystemC library are discussed below.

The following model the low level aspects of the graphics processor architecture.

Moya [6] created a cycle-accurate model of a graphics processor named ATTILA. Long simulation times prohibit its use for broad design space exploration. Also, the fine detail of ATTILA limits its scope to prototyping minor architecture modifications.

QSilver [7] is another fine-grained graphics processor architectural model. One application is to explore thermal management. QSliver is, similarly to [6], too low-level for rapid and straight forward design space exploration.

nVidia provide a graphics shader performance model named nvshaderperf[8]. This is an accurate profile of the computational performance of kernel functions, but provides no information on memory system performance. In the system model in Section 5, nvshaderperf is used to estimate computational cycle count for processing elements.

Govindaraju provides a useful estimate of graphics processor memory system cache arrangement in [9]. For the nVidia GeForce 7800 GTX, Govindaraju estimates cache block size at 8×8 pixels, and cache size at 128 KBytes. The results follow estimates by Moya [6] of a 16 KByte cache with 8×8 pixel cache lines for the older GeForce 6800 GT. A small cache size is well suited to graphics rendering.

In Section 5, a model is presented which provides a tradeoff between the fine-detail in [6, 7], and high-level or feature-specific models in [8, 9]. The advantage of our model is that architectural modifications can be rapidly prototyped, through modelling [noncycle accurate] performance trends. Memory system estimations from [6, 9] are used for model parametrisation to enable results verification in Section 8.

The interconnects between components of the system model in Figure 4 can be interpreted conceptually as a Kahn Process Network (KPN) [10]. Each processing group can be thought of as a KPN 'Process'. The buffer which queues memory accesses between a processing element (PE) and the memory management unit (MMU) is equivalent to an unbounded KPN 'channel'. To ensure that the appropriate latencies are simulated in the system model, flags are passed between process nodes (PEs).

The IEEE 1666-2005 SystemC class library is used to implement the abstract transaction level model (TLM) of the architecture in Section 5. Related work in [7, 11] demonstrates the SystemC class library to be a flexible platform for design space exploration. In [11] Rissa presents the advantages of SystemC over a register transfer level

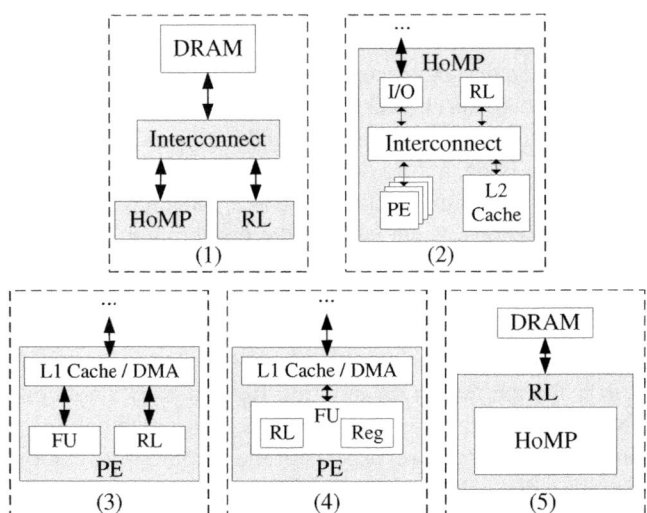

Key: I/O is the input/output interface, FU is the functional unit of a processing element (PE), RL is reconfigurable logic and Reg is a set of local register files

Fig. 1. A classification scheme for the post-fabrication customisation options for a HoMP

(RTL) description in VHDL or Verilog. A simulation time speedup of 360 to 10,000 times is achieved by Rissa for SystemC models over RTL descriptions.

For a comprehensive treatment of the SystemC language and transaction level models the reader is directed to [12].

3 Classification of Customisation Options

In this Section the options for supporting post-fab customisation of a HoMP are classified. This demonstrates the wider applicability of the exploration tool in Section 4. The work is motivated by Todman's hardware-software co-design classification [13], for a single processor coupled in a classified manner to reconfigurable logic fabric. The advantageous factors of the customisation options in Figure 1, are as follows.

In contrast to a traditional HoMP architecture, for example a graphics processor, post-fab customisation enhances an architecture's flexibility. This makes it adaptable to a wider variety of application domains. For example, it is shown in [14] that a small reconfigurable logic block can improve graphics processor memory access performance by an order of magnitude for case study examples.

An advantage over a fully reconfigurable platform (for example, a field programmable gate array (FPGA) from Altera Co. or Xilinx Inc.) is that the architectural design space is bounded. Put another way, the architecture has a clearly defined datapath onto which an algorithm must be mapped. The result is a reduced design time. A fully reconfigurable platform requires the design of a specialised datapath.

The key benefits of post-fab customisation of an HoMP are a constrained application design space alongside support for specialisation to an application domain.

Table 1. A Summary of the Roles for RL within a HoMP

	Role	Effect on Core Type	Level of Integration	'Shared' Memory
1	Off-Chip Co-Processor	Heterogeneous	Low	DRAM
2	On-Chip Co-Processor	Heterogeneous		L2 Cache
3	Local Co-Processor	Homogeneous		L1 Cache
4	Custom Instruction	Homogeneous		Registers
5	Glue Logic	Homogeneous	High	–

In the remainder of this Section the classification of customisation options is explained and prior works are used to exemplify the classified options.

A summary of the qualitative level of integration and lowest level of shared memory for each option in Figure 1 is summarised in Table 1. Key features are discussed below.

For classifications (1) to (4) the level of shared memory is the key identifier. As the level of integration increases, the granularity of the separation of tasks between a RL element becomes finer grained, from a co-processor to a custom instruction. For class (1), different algorithms and video frames may be computed on the RL co-processor and the HoMP. In contrast, in class (4) a single instruction from the assembly code of a processor PE may be accelerated on a RL core.

Class (5) presents an orthogonal use of RL to classes (1)–(4). Instead of performing computation on a part or whole algorithm, RL is used to optimise the architecture in such a manner as to improve HoMP performance for a given algorithm. This is termed as 'glue logic' and is an exciting new area in which the use of RL can thrive.

Prior works which exemplify the options in Figure 1 are now discussed.

The literature contains numerous works promoting multi-chip solutions to using RL (in the form of FPGAs) and a graphics processor as class (1) co-processors [15–18].

Moll [15] presents Sepia, where an FPGA is used to merge outputs from multiple graphics processors. The FPGA performs a subsection of the target 3D visualisation algorithm which makes this a class (1) use of RL.

Manzke [16] combines an FPGA and graphics processor devices on a PCI bus with a shared global memory. The goal is to produce a scalable solution of multiple boards. In Manzke's work the FPGA is master to the graphics processor. For Sepia, the graphics processor output drives the FPGA operation with prompt from a host CPU [15].

An equivalent setup to [15–18] for a Cell BE is proposed by Schleupen [19], this is also an example of a class (1) use of RL.

The work in [15–19] can alternatively be considered as a prototype for a single die solution containing a HoMP, RL and shared memory (class (2)).

Although not fully programmable, the Cell BE DMA engine exemplifies a class 3 use of RL. In a more abstract sense Sun's forthcoming SPARC-family Rock processor is another class 3 example. Although there is no separate hardware, 'scout threads', speculative clones of the primary thread, use the hardware multi-threading support to run ahead of stalls to execute address generation code and pre-fetch data into the cache [20].

Dale [21] proposes small scale reconfiguration within graphics processor functional units. This is a class (4) approach. A functional unit is substituted with a flexible arithmetic unit (FAC) which can be alternately an adder or multiplier. A moderate 4.27%

computational performance speed-up for a 0.2% area increase is achieved. Although the speed-up is small, this demonstrates the potential of the use of reconfiguration in graphics processors at the lowest denomination of the architecture.

Yalamanchili [22] presents two class (5) options. First, a self-tuning cache which matches the memory access requirements to the cache usage heuristic. Second, tuned on-chip interconnects to increase bandwidth for critical paths.

In [14], the authors propose REDA, a reconfigurable engine for data access targeted at graphics processors. REDA is embedded into the graphics processor memory system to optimise its memory access behaviour. This is a class 5 use of RL.

Coarse-grained reconfigurable architectures (CGRA), such as MathStar's Attrix FPOA device [23], are another example of a class (5) use of reconfigurable logic.

There are also a number of prior works which present equivalent solutions, to those shown above, for the case of *heterogeneous* multi-processors.

Chen et al [24] use RL as a controller in a system-on-chip solution. The RL core makes a complex system-on-chip appear as a single co-processor to an external host processor. This is class (5) glue logic.

Verbauwhede [25] presents RINGS. Three locations for RL in a network-on-chip are presented as register mapped (class (4)), memory-mapped (class (3)) and network mapped (class (2)). The terminology describes the hierarchy at which the RL core is implemented and, in similarity to Table 1, the shared memory. Verbauwhede [25] also presents a reconfigurable interconnect arbitration scheme which is a class (5) scenario.

A run-time management scheme for multi-processor systems-on-a-chip is presented by Nollet [26]. It is proposed that RL may be used to implement a flexible hardware management unit. This is also a class (5) use of RL.

It is observed that the scheme in Figure 1 is well suited to classifying a spectrum of uses of RL in HoMPs, with equivalent interpretations for heterogeneous architectures.

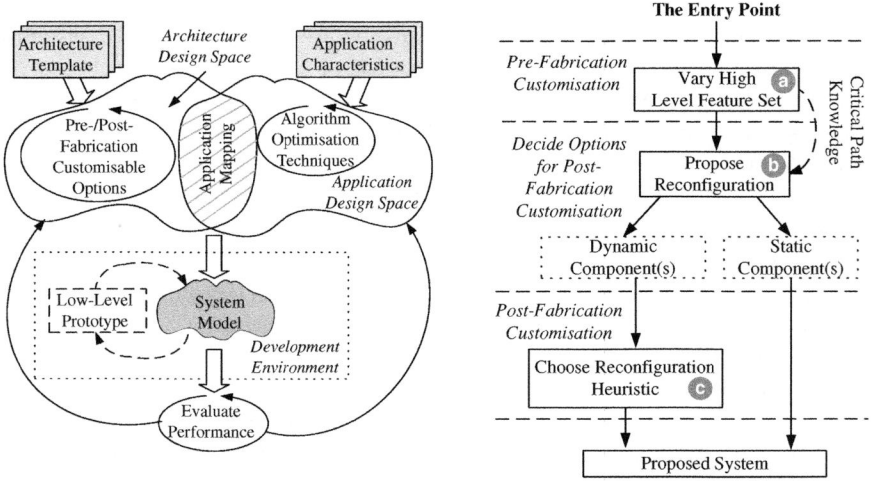

(a) Exploration Method (based on the 'Y-Chart' [4])   (b) Evaluating Customisation Options

Fig. 2. A Systematic Approach to Design Space Exploration

4   Design Space Exploration Approach

This section summarises the proposed approach, which is depicted in Figure 2. An overall picture of the exploration methodology is shown in Figure 2(a) and the process of evaluating customisation options in Figure 2(b). The approach is described as follows.

In Figure 2(a), the entry point to the design space exploration approach is alternative architecture templates and application characteristics. The architecture template and application model described in Section 5 initialise our design space.

The architecture design space is explored through considering the pre- and post-fabrication customisable options. These can be arbitrarily chosen from the features of the template architecture. This process is explained in Figure 2(b).

An application design space is traversed by considering algorithm optimisations.

As described in Section 2, the choice of application and architecture is not mutually exclusive. An application mapping region is defined to depict this. The addition of application mapping is particularly important for HoMPs. This is because the choice of application mapping affects the architecture choice and ultimately the programming model.

Once a set of architecture and application features have been chosen, from the respective design spaces, the options are used to parameterise the system model.

When a reconfigurable logic post-fab customisation option is proposed, the design may require a prototype to determine the area cost, maximum clock speed or power consumption. Alternatively, one may require a HoMP 'test run' to verify a proposal.

The combination of system model and low-level prototyping form the development environment. At progressively later stages in a design process, increased portions of a proposed architecture are prototyped in such a manner.

The output from the development environment is performance figures which are used to evaluate the suitability of the proposed architecture against application requirements. Example requirements in our case are to minimise clock cycle count or number of off-chip memory accesses. The process is iterated to alter application and/or architecture feature choices through educated conjecture after the performance evaluation.

The application of the approach in Figure 2(a) to the evaluation of customisation options is defined in Figure 2(b).

There are three key stages to the evaluation of customisation options. These are summarised below alongside examples of where these stages are employed.

Stage a: The exploration of pre-fab customisation options, which also defines the architecture critical paths (Sections 6, 7 and 8).

Stage b: From the analysis of critical paths post-fab customisation options are proposed (Section 9). The proposal is to supplement current blocks with RL (as chosen pre-fab).

Stage c: A heuristic for blocks supporting post-fab modifications is chosen. This determines the configuration to be applied for a particular algorithm (Section 9).

It is observed that **stage a** is typically the largest part of the exploration process and thus consumes the greatest portion of the work presented here.

A tool flow for the approach is summarised below.

As described in Section 2, SystemC is used to implement the system model. A C++ wrapper encloses the SystemC model to support modification of the two design spaces.

To prototype low level modules the VHDL language is used. Open loop tests may alternatively be implemented on a graphics processor, using for example Cg and the

OpenGL API. This part of the tool set is not used in this work, however, it is used in [14] which is cited in Section 9 as an application of the exploration process.

For visualisation of the performance results the Mathworks MATLAB environment is used. In addition, system trace files record the behaviour of a definable subset of signals. This setup minimises the impact on simulation time.

At present the process is fully user driven, however, it is opportunistically possible to automate **Stage a** in Figure 2(b). An example of how can be found in work by Shen on the automated generation of SystemC transaction level models [27].

5   The System Model

In this section, the design space of HoMP architectures is described alongside a model to explore the graphics processor architecture. The motivation of the model and design space is to support the methodology proposed in Section 4.

As highlighted in Section 4, the 'Y-Chart' [4] is augmented with an application mapping sub-set. The architecture design space is therefore divided into core architectural features and application mapping features, as shown in Figure 3(a). Note that application mapping is grouped with core application features to form the architecture feature set. The core architectural features represent the underlying architecture which is transferrable between different application mappings (and programming models).

In Figure 3(b), the architecture features are presented against an increasing degree of customisation. Regions of the design space represent the customisation options. This work focuses on: number of PEs, on-chip memory type (cache size), and number of threads in Section 8; and processing pattern in Sections 6 and 7.

To explore the design space of the graphics processor for the case study of this work a high-level system model is shown in Figure 4. The astute reader will observe how, with modification, this model may be targeted at alternative HoMPs.

Figure 4(a) shows a one PE example. The pattern generation module supplies each PE with the order in which to process pixels. PE input pixel data is received from off-chip memory through the on-chip memory system (read-only in this example). When

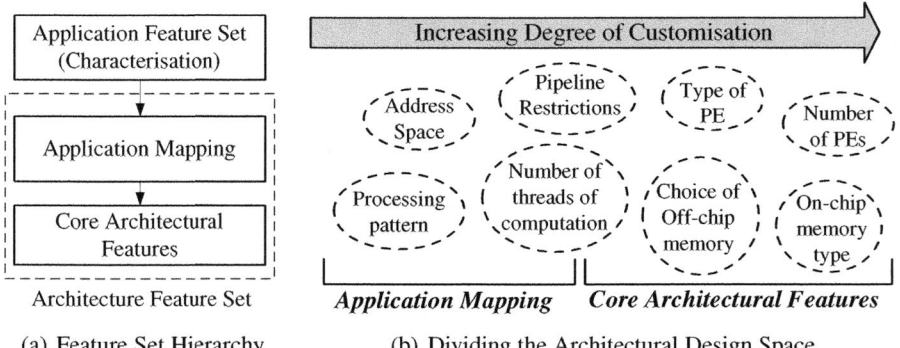

(a) Feature Set Hierarchy   (b) Dividing the Architectural Design Space

Fig. 3. The Architectural Design Space for the HoMP Class of Architectures

Table 2. Symbols used in Formulae

Key	Value
P	Pixel processing pattern order
(x_p, y_p)	General pixel address)
$\widehat{T}$	Thread batch size (thread level parallelism)
n	number of processing elements (PEs)
W	Pattern of accesses for each output (represented as an offset from current output pixel)
C	On-chip memory access pattern (intersection of P and W)
A	Off-chip memory access pattern (C subject to cache behaviour)
n_{conv}	2D convolution kernel dimensionality (symmetric)
N_{in}	Number of input pixels per row of input frame
(s_x, s_y)	Resizing ratio for interpolation / decimation
CPO	Clock cycles per output pixel
$\|\|$	Absolute operator, used to represent size e.g. $|C|$ is total number of off-chip accesses

processing is complete, PE outputs are written to off-chip memory through an output buffer. Figure 4(b) shows the extension to multiple PEs. The PEs are arranged in processing groups, in this example in groups of four. A memory management unit (MMU) arbitrates memory accesses through a given choice of on-chip memory. This setup mimics a graphics processor [6, 28].

The pixel processing pattern P is an arbitrary sequence. This is a simplification of the graphics processor setup where processing order is output from a rasteriser.

A popular video memory storage format and rendering rasterisation ordering is the z-pattern [29]. In general a pixel address $\{x_p, y_p\}$ is calculated as follows. Consider that pixel iterator p is represented as a bit-vector ($p = p_{n-1}...p_2p_1p_0$), where location zero is the least significant bit. Then the x_p and y_p values are the concatenations of even ($x_p = p_{n-2}...p_4p_2p_0$) and odd ($y_p = p_{n-1}...p_5p_3p_1$) bit locations respectively.

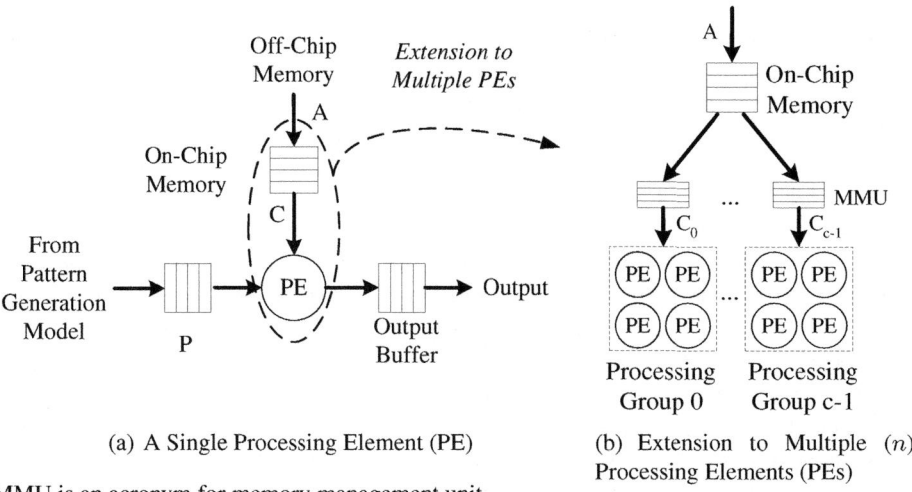

(a) A Single Processing Element (PE)   (b) Extension to Multiple (n) Processing Elements (PEs)

MMU is an acronym for memory management unit

Fig. 4. High Level Representation of the Design Space Exploration Model

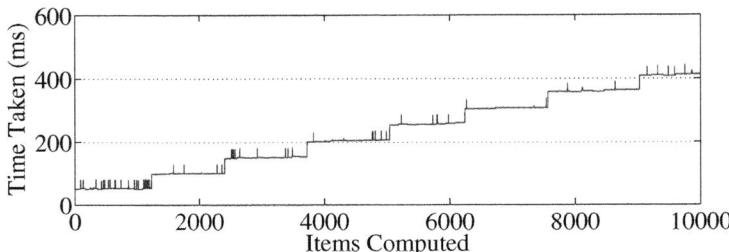

Fig. 5. Concurrent Thread Estimation for the nVidia GeForce 7900 GTX (1300 per batch)

0. Get $\frac{\widehat{T}}{n}$ thread addresses from P
1. For all Accesses $w = 0$ to $W - 1$
2.   For all Threads $i = 0$ to $\frac{\widehat{T}}{n} - 1$
3.   Request Address $f(i, w)$
4.   Wait until All Read Requests Granted
5. Output $\frac{\widehat{T}}{n}$ thread results

Fig. 6. A Model of the Behaviour of a PE

For horizontally raster scanned video an equivalent processing pattern description to that for the z-pattern is $x_p = p_{\frac{n}{2}-1}...p_0$ and $y_p = p_{n-1}...p_{\frac{n}{2}}$. A raster scan or z-pattern can be generated using an n-bit counter and bit rearrangement.

The model is implemented such that $\widehat{T}$ threads can be computed across the n PEs. For simplification $\frac{\widehat{T}}{n}$ threads are live on each PE at any instant. On a graphics processor, a thread may in general be scheduled to different PEs at different points in the computation. However, this arrangement is deemed sufficient.

A graphics processor's thread batch size can be estimated using a computationally intensive kernel to minimise the effect of cache behaviour and to emphasize steps in performance between thread batches. The chosen kernel is the American Put Option financial model [30] which requires 446 computational instructions to one memory access per kernel. Figure 5 shows the performance results for the nVidia GeForce 7900 GTX graphics processor for increasing output frame size from 1 to 10000 pixels.

It is observed that steps in time taken occur at intervals 1300 outputs. This is the predicted thread batch size ($\widehat{T}$).

For the nVidia GeForce 6800 GT steps are observed at intervals of 1500 pixels.

Application Model: The PE application model is a function of computation delay (taken from [8]) and memory access requirements. The pseudo-code for PE memory accesses is shown in Figure 6. A set of $\frac{\widehat{T}}{n}$ output locations is input from the pattern generation block (Line 0). W memory requests per output are iterated over (Line 1). Within this loop (lines 1 to 4), the PE iterates over all threads i (Line 2) issuing a memory access (line 3). The PE waits for accesses for each thread to complete before moving on to the next access w (Line 4). Once all read requests are made, output pixel values are written to an output buffer (Line 5). The code iterates until the end of the processing pattern occurs. Function f is an arbitrary linear or non-linear address mapping.

6   System Model with a Single Processing Element

A system model with one PE, as shown in Figure 4(a), and one execution thread ($\widehat{T} = 1$) is considered in this Section. It is interesting to compare results for a z-pattern and horizontal raster scan processing order. For each scenario the on-chip (C) and off-chip (A) memory access pattern are shown in Figures 7 and 8 respectively.

For the z-pattern processing order the variation in required on and off-chip memory addresses is significantly larger than that for raster scan processing. To quantify this difference, for on-chip reads, consider the convolution case study.

For raster scan the peak distance between reads for each output is n_{conv} rows of an image, where n_{conv} is the convolution size. In Figure 7(a) this equals $\sim 5 \times 256$ pixel locations as shown by the heavy type line. In general the maximum step size is $\sim n_{conv} N_{in}$ pixels, where N_{in} is the number of pixels per row of the input frame.

In contrast, for the z-pattern the peak range of memory accesses for one output is requests in opposing quadrants of the input video frame. This equals $\sim 2 \left(\frac{256}{2}\right)^2$ pixel locations and is demonstrated in Figure 7(a) with variations in excess of $30k$ pixel locations. In general the maximum variation is $\sim 2 \left(\frac{N_{in}}{2}\right)^2$ pixels. This is significantly larger than for raster-scan.

For decimation, Figure 7(b) demonstrates a similar scenario. Input frame size is $s_x^{-1} \times s_y^{-1}$ times larger than for convolution, where s_x and s_y are the horizontal and vertical resizing ratios respectively. The irregular pattern for the z-pattern occurs because input frame dimensions are buffered up to a power of two.

The off-chip memory access patterns (A) for each case study are shown in Figure 8. These patterns approximate the on-chip accesses as expected. A two to three order of magnitude reduction in the number of on-chip ($|C|$) to off-chip ($|A|$) accesses is observed in all cases. This indicates good cache performance. The raster access pattern has the lowest value of $|A|$. This is in fact the optimum value for each case study. For the z-pattern, $|A|$ is within 1.5 times that for a raster scan pattern. The difference is due

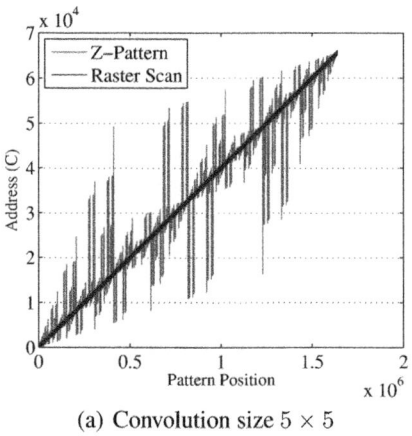

(a) Convolution size 5×5

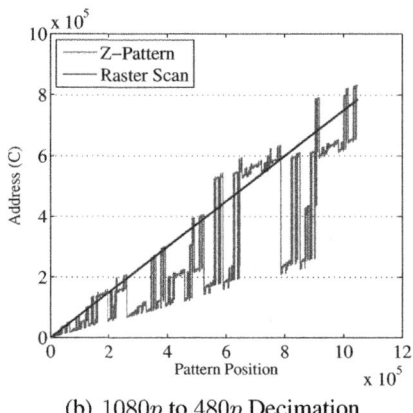

(b) $1080p$ to $480p$ Decimation

Fig. 7. On-chip memory access (C) performance for decimation and 2D convolution for a model with one PE and one execution thread. Output frame size is 256×256 pixels

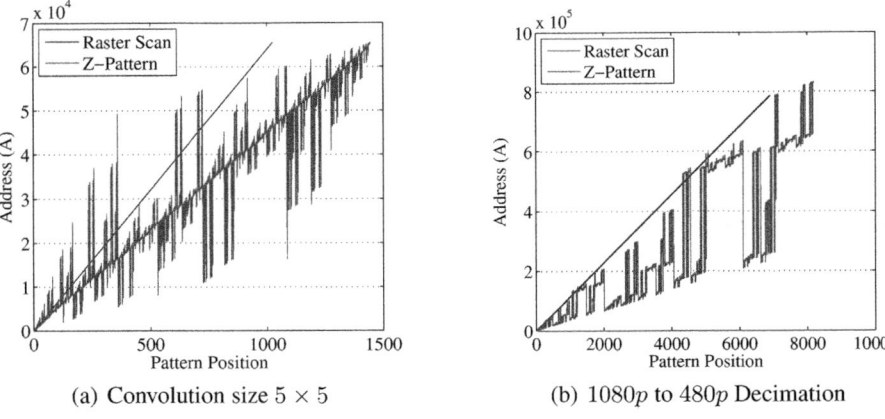

Fig. 8. Off-chip memory access (A) performance for decimation and 2D convolution for a model with one PE and one execution thread. Output frame size is 256×256 pixels.

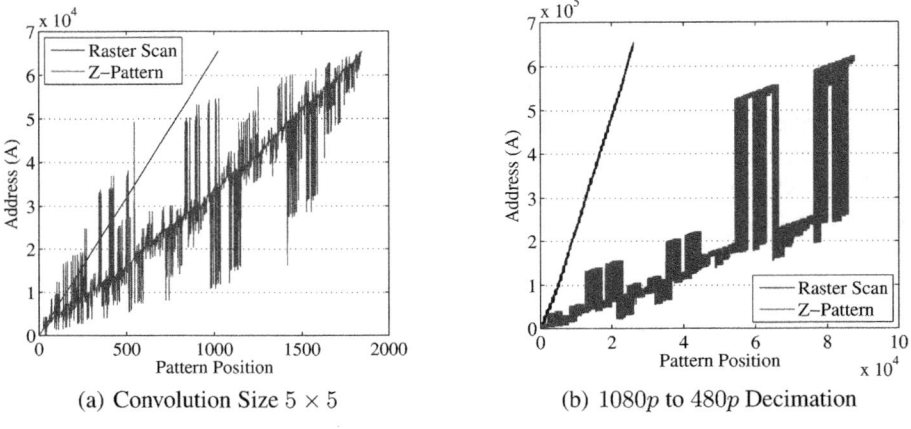

Fig. 9. Off-chip memory access (A) performance for a model with sixteen PEs and $\widehat{T} = 1500$ (equivalent to nVidia GeForce 6800 GT). For an output frame size of 256×256 pixels.

to the larger degree of variance in on-chip accesses (C). A greater variation in memory address location also correlates with a poor DRAM memory access performance [31].

Due to the large reduction between $|C|$ and $|A|$, the performance for each choice of access pattern is not bounded by off-chip memory accesses. The estimated number of clock cycles required is $4.06M$ for decimation and $2.1M$ for 5×5 convolution in both access pattern scenarios. It is interesting to now consider the extension of these issues to a system model for the case of multiple threads ($\widehat{T}$) and PEs.

7   System Model with Multiple Processing Elements

To demonstrate an extended case, off-chip memory access performance for the algorithms from Section 6 and a model with 16 PEs and 1500 threads is shown in Figure 9.

Despite a large degree of multi-threading, the memory access behaviour for 2D convolution in Figure 9(a) is similar to that in Figure 8(a). This is because of the large probability that data will be reused between output pixels. For the raster scan pattern $|A|$ is the optimum value, as was the case in Figure 8(a). For the z-pattern, a small increase in $|A|$ is observed from Figure 8(a) due to memory access conflicts between threads.

A significant change in the pattern of A occurs for the decimation case study in Figure 9(b). For both processing patterns an increased number of off-chip accesses ($|A|$) is required in comparison to Figure 8(b) to satisfy on-chip memory access requirements. The lowest performance is observed for the z-pattern where $|A|$ is only an order of magnitude less than number of on-chip accesses ($|C|$) (approximately that in Figure 7(b)). Three factors influence the increased in $|A|$ for the z-pattern case as explained below.

First, decimation has less potential for pixel reuse (between neighbouring outputs) than convolution. The decimation factor in Figure 9(b) is $s_x = 3, s_y = 2.25$. This translates to a proportion of pixel reuse between two outputs of $\frac{4}{16}$ to $\frac{8}{16}$. In comparison, for convolution size 5×5, the pixel reuse is $\frac{20}{25}$. For decimation a greater number of threads require a different cache line to the previous thread. This increases cache misses.

Second, the variation in C. The choice of a non-power of two resizing ratio is shown to make this pattern irregular in Figure 7(b). This increases conflict cache misses.

Third, the cache replacement policy is also inefficiently utilised due to the non-power of two input frame size.

The increase in $|A|$ in Figure 9 is reflected in the number of clock cycles per output (CPO_m). For convolution CPO_m increase between raster and z-pattern method from 58 to 62. The extra latency for the increased number and variance of A, for the z-pattern method, is mostly hidden through the combination of multi-threading and a large number (5×5 in Figure 9(a)) of spatially local on-chip memory accesses.

For decimation, the change in CPO_m between raster and z-pattern methods is more significant. In this case the raster scan and z-pattern scenarios require 92 and $250 \, CPO_m$ respectively. The z-pattern method is off-chip memory access bound under these conditions. A raster scan processing pattern is advantageous under the case study scenario of low data reuse potential. This is explored further in Section 9.

8 Architecture Trends

In this section the model is used to explore architectural trends for number of PEs, cache size and number of threads. This exemplifies **Stage a** in Figure 2(b).

A summary of the number of off-chip memory accesses ($|A|$) and clock cycles per output (CPO) for changing number of PEs, for four case study algorithms, is shown in Figures 10(a) and 10(b). For all tests the system model setup captures the performance of the GeForce 6800 GT, the number of computational threads is $\widehat{T} = 1500$, and a z-pattern processing order is used throughout. Number of PEs is the variable.

The case study algorithms are bi-cubic decimation, bi-cubic interpolation, 2D convolution and primary colour correction algorithms. The last three are taken from [28].

For primary colour correction, convolution and interpolation CPO remains consistent across all numbers of PEs. Primary colour correction is a computationally bound algorithm so this is as expected, the value of $|A|$ is minimum at 1024.

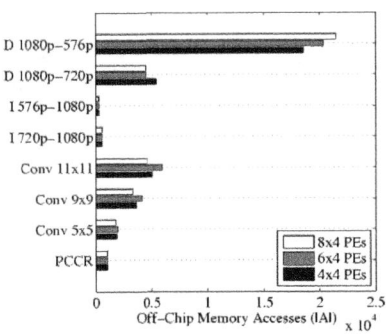
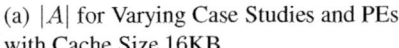

(a) $|A|$ for Varying Case Studies and PEs with Cache Size 16KB

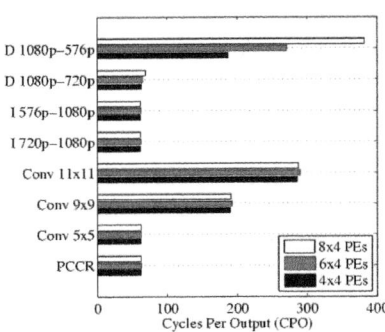

(b) CPO_m for Varying Case Studies and PEs with Cache Size 16KB

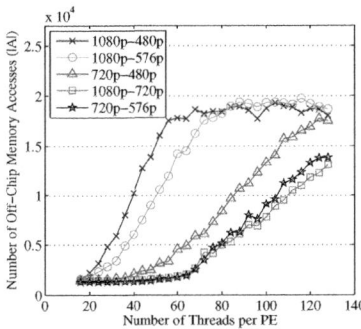

(c) $|A|$ for Varying Decimation Ratios with 4×4 PEs and Cache Size 16KB

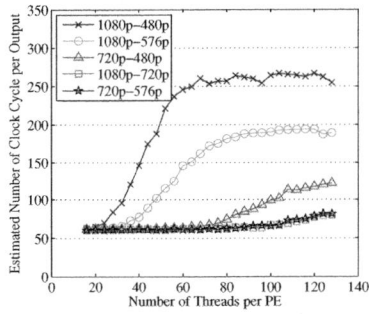

(d) CPO_m for Varying Decimation Ratios with 4×4 PEs and Cache Size 16KB

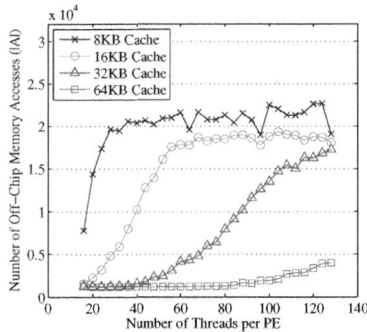

(e) $|A|$ for Varying Cache Size for Decimation $1080p$ to $480p$ and 4×4 PEs

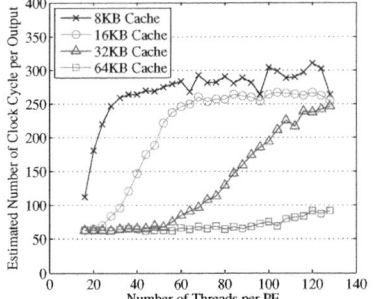

(f) CPO_m for Varying Cache Size for Decimation $1080p$ to $480p$ and 4×4 PEs

Fig. 10. Performance for Varying Design Space Parameters (as Indicated) and Case Studies (with a fixed 256×256 pixel input frame size)

For the setup in Figure 10, each MMU has direct access to on-chip memory. Therefore, the on-chip memory bandwidth scales linearly with the number of PEs. This explains the equal value of CPO for all variants of number of PEs.

A change of up to three times in $|A|$ is observed for 5×5 to 11×11 sized convolutions. In all cases CPO remains unchanged. The increase in $|A|$ is hidden by multi-threading and a large number of on-chip memory accesses.

In contrast to decimation in Section 7, interpolation exhibits a greater potential for data reuse between neighbouring outputs (from $\frac{12}{16}$ to $\frac{16}{16}$) than 2D convolution (fixed at $\frac{(n_{conv}-1)n_{conv}}{n_{conv}^2}$). CPO is therefore also equal for each interpolation ratio. This is despite a difference in $|A|$ of approximately two times. The multi-threaded computation is again successful in hiding off-chip memory access requirements. For convolution and interpolation the critical path is the *on-chip memory bandwidth*.

The most significant variations in $|A|$ and CPO occur for the decimation case study. Whilst $1080p$ to $720p$ decimation has a consistent CPO across all numbers of PEs the $1080p$ to $576p$ case shows more significant variations. This is due to a larger scaling factor for the $1080p$ to $576p$ case. In this scenario $|A|$ (and cache misses) is large enough to make decimation off-chip memory access bound. The performance degradation is proportional to the number of PEs.

Decimation is investigated further in Figures 10(c) to 10(f).

In Figures 10(c) and 10(d) varying decimation ratios are plotted for a setup of 16 PEs and a 16 KByte cache size, which is equivalent to a GeForce 6800 GT. As the number of threads per PE is increased CPO and $|A|$ increase. This effect is most prominent for larger decimation factors. It is observed that as the resizing factor increases, the CPO trend adopts increasing similarity to the $|A|$ trend. This is concurrent with the system being *off-chip memory bandwidth bound*.

For scenarios where the system becomes memory bound there are two choices. First to reduce the number of threads ($\widehat{T}$) or secondly to increase cache size. For the worst performing decimation size ($1080p$ to $480p$) this tradeoff is shown in Figures 10(e) and 10(f). It is observed that as the cache size is increased, $|A|$ (and ultimately CPO) decreases sharply. An approximately linear relationship between CPO and cache size is observed. Ultimately further non-modelled factors affect the performance as cache size is increased, for example, increased cache access latency.

To summarise, the relationship between thread count ($\widehat{T}$) and required memory size (B_{req}) for good cache performance is shown in Equation 1, where R and N_{reads} are the amount of data reuse (exemplified above) and number of reads respectively.

$$B_{req} > N_{reads} + (1 - R)\widehat{T} \tag{1}$$

If B_{req} exceeds on-chip memory size a large value of $|A|$ is expected. As B_{req} approaches the on-chip memory size, $|A|$ increases subject to the choice of reuse heuristic (in this case a 4-way associative cache). This effect is exemplified for increasing $\widehat{T}$ in Figures 10(c) to 10(f). A shift in the graphs is observed for varying cache size as the number of threads and memory size change. For decimation the reuse R is inversely proportional to the resizing factors s_x and s_y in x and y dimensions respectively.

The model performance for the case study algorithms in Figures 10(a) and 10(b) is compared to results for two graphics processors in Table 3.

Table 3. Verification of the Model. CPO is cycles per output for the model (m), nVidia GeForce 6800 GT (gf6) and nVidia GeForce 7900 GTX (gf7)

	$\mathbf{CPO}_{gf6}$	$\mathbf{CPO}_{gf7}$	$\mathbf{CPO}_m$
PCCR	60	43	63
2D Conv (5 × 5)	41	37	62
2D Conv (9 × 9)	162	144	187
2D Conv (11 × 11)	263	230	282
Interp (576p-1080p)	52	47	61
Interp (720p-1080p)	53	48	61
Deci (1080p-576p)	90	84	187
Deci (720p-480p)	78	68	86
Deci (1080p-720p)	69	66	75

Over all case studies the CPO for the model (CPO_m) approximate those for the nVidia GeForce 6800 GT (CPO_{gf6}) and follow the trend for the GeForce 7900 GTX (CPO_{gf7}). Cycle estimates are higher for the model because its architecture is not pipelined to the extent of a graphics processor.

For the GeForce 6800 GT, the number of clock cycles per internal memory access (CPIMA) for 2D convolution is a constant 2.4. The results for the model (CPO_m) range from 290 to 62 cycles per output for convolution size 11×11 and 5×5 respectively. This equals to a value of CPIMA of approximately 2.4 to 2.5. The model mimics the on-chip memory timing of the graphics processor well.

Model implementations of small decimation sizes are well matched to the performance of the graphics processor. A small overhead in number of cycles per output is again observed over equivalent implementations on the GeForce 6800 GT.

An anomaly occurs for decimation size $1080p$ to $576p$ where model results deviate from those for the graphics processors. Four potential reasons for this are as follows.

1. The multi-threaded behaviour is not fully pipelined within the MMU. For the case of large decimation sizes this amplifies memory access cost.
2. The computation model does not fully synchronise the execution of all PEs. This is challenging for algorithms with poor memory access behaviour.
3. The cache size estimate of 16 KBytes for the nVidia GeForce 6800 GT may be incorrect. If a cache size of 32 KBytes is taken CPO_m reduces to 74.
4. Although a latency and delay based model of off-chip DRAM is created, the latency of the entire interface to the DRAM and finer detail of the DRAM is omitted.

Despite the above limitations the model is observed in Table 3 to, under correct parametrisation, correlate well with the performance of two sample graphics processors.

The run time for the system model is between 1 and 5 minutes for all case studies. Although the model is not optimised, it is sufficient for exploration with large input frame sizes. For a frame size of 2048×2048 pixels the simulation time increases to a manageable 25 minutes for the decimation case study.

9   Post-Fabrication Customisable Options

In this Section the results in Sections 6, 7 and 8 are used to reason post-fab customisation options (this exemplifies **Stage b** in Figure 2(b)).

Table 4. Number of Off-Chip Memory Accesses and (Cycles per Output) for Varying Processing Patterns and Decimation

	Z-Pattern			Raster Scan		
	16KB	**32K**	**64K**	**16K**	**32K**	**64K**
A	127319	66984	10223	29828	8910	7596
	(258)	(146)	(63)	(92)	(62)	(62)
B	87671	15387	6084	26133	8112	5138
	(180)	(63)	(62)	(82)	(62)	(62)
C	29144	6481	6481	15779	12473	3591
	(79)	(62)	(62)	(68)	(66)	(62)
D	12756	3124	3124	13835	4332	2695
	(62)	(62)	(62)	(66)	(62)	(62)
E	12347	2770	2770	12967	4783	2568
	(63)	(62)	(62)	(66)	(62)	(62)

A=1080p to 480p, B=1080p to 576p, C=720p to 480p, D=1080p to 720p and E=720p to 576p

First, the off-chip memory system performance is the critical path for large decimation factors. This prompts investigation into ways to improve the memory system for the memory access pattern of decimation. In [14] the authors investigate this option which is an execution of **Stage c** in Figure 2(b) and promotes the exploration tool.

Second, to change the choice of PE in Figure 4. In general a PE may not be a processor and may support reconfiguration. This option is considered by the authors in [28]. An example application is to support local data reuse for a PE to overcome the on-chip memory bandwidth critical path for convolution and interpolation.

Third, a final option not previously considered is to alter the processing pattern. The opportunity for this has been demonstrated in Sections 6 and 7. This option is now used to demonstrate **Stage c** of the approach in this work as outlined below.

To quantify the changing of processing pattern over different cache sizes and decimation factors consider a summary of the performance of a raster and z-pattern as shown in Table 4. In either case the pattern is used for both processing order and memory storage with all else constant. It is observed that for large decimation factors up to a four times reduction, in both number of memory accesses and cycles per output, is achieved from using a raster scan pattern.

As reasoned in Section 7, the justification is that, for the raster scan case, conflict cache misses only occur due to the horizontal resizing factor. For the z-pattern approach, cache misses occur due to both horizontal and vertical resizing factors due to the 2D nature of the z-pattern. As cache size is increased, the benefit of the raster scan approach diminishes. This is because the algorithm becomes on-chip memory access limited under these conditions, for which the access time and latency is fixed. For smaller decimation factors the z-pattern can be beneficial over the raster scan approach. This occurs when the horizontal resizing factor exceeds the vertical factor. A vertical raster pattern could be used to alleviate this issue.

The choice of processing and memory storage pattern is shown to have a significant effect on a subset of algorithms with low data reuse potential. For a graphics application the z-pattern is the optimal choice. This therefore presents an avenue for post-fab customisation to switch between alternative processing patterns depending on the target application domain. The mapping between a z-pattern and raster scan pattern requires bit reordering as explained in Section 5. In the case of two alternative patterns this is implemented with one multiplexor and a configuration bit.

Intentionally, this example is straight forward as a demonstration of the exploration process. It is observed through related work [14, 22, 25] that the exploration of post-fab customisation options can provide even higher performance improvements, of up to an order of magnitude, albeit for a higher area cost than the example here.

As with [14] the example presented above is a class 5 customisation from Figure 1.

10   Implications for Other Graphics Processors and the Cell BE

Whilst the results above are based on the nVidia GeForce 6 and 7 series graphics processors, technology has progressed, examples are considered below.

The architecture template of CUDA (compute unified device architecture) enabled nVidia, starting from GeForce 8 series, graphics processors is fundamentally similar to the model in Figure 4. A large number of PEs are arranged in processing groups and arbitrate through a local MMU to access off-chip memory through shared on-chip memory (cache). The same applies to graphics processors from other venders such as AMD ATI.

One difference for CUDA enabled graphics processors, to the GeForce 6 and 7 series, is that fragment and vertex pipelines are combined in a unified shader. However, the level of abstraction in Figure 4(b) could equally represent a unified shader, in contrast to only the fragment pipeline. For 2D video processing, vertex processing requirements can be disregarded because they are trivially four corner coordinates of the output frame.

The processing elements in the CUDA enabled graphics processors are different from prior GeForce generations. For example, the GeForce 8 contains scalar PEs. An advantage of scalar processors is a reduction in cycle count through increased processor utilisation, over a 4-vector processor performing computation on 3-component video data. This modification is trivial to support in the PE model in Figure 4.

If the implementations from Section 8 were directly ported to a CUDA architecture a similar performance trend would be observed, with variations due to a different trade off of number of PEs, on-chip memory size and number of threads.

AMD ATI and nVidia, in their current generation of graphics processors, have an enhanced and more flexible 'application mapping' which is programmable through the CTM (close to metal) and CUDA programming environments respectively. An immediate advantage is that off-chip memory accesses can be reduced for previously multi-pass algorithms through storage of intermediate results in on-chip memory for later reuse. In addition the contents of on-chip memory can be controlled. This presents an exciting new domain of algorithm optimisations, for example, the ability to control, within limits, the contents of on-chip memory may improve performance for the decimation case study.

The Cell BE presents a shift from the model adopted in Figure 4. In addition to shared global memory a large memory space is local to each processing group. This can be considered as local to the MMU. However, DMA access can be made between MMUs over the EIB^{TM} bus. Processing groups also operate independently which poses further opportunities for algorithm optimisations.

One intriguing possibility is to consider post-fab customisation of the Cell BE DMA engine. In one instance the customisable DMA engine may be used to implement an address mapping function similar to that in [14]. An alternative option is a configurable DMA engine that, on prompt, generate its own addressing patterns.

In general, for alternative HoMPs the core architecture features in Figure 3 are consistent, with minor variations. The key difference is in application mapping characteristics. These include the choice of local, global and control of address space and restrictions on PE execution behaviour.

The results in Sections 6, 7 and 8 show some of the architectural trends for the core architecture features which are present in all HoMPs. However, for each HoMP a different application mapping is chosen. This translates to a new algorithm set of optimisation techniques. Re-parametrisation of the model's application mapping feature set, and choice of algorithm optimisations, is required to support alternative HoMPs.

11 Summary

A novel design space exploration tool has been presented with the application of exploring the customisation options for a Homogeneous Multi-Processor (HoMP). The tool has been demonstrated using the example of an architecture which captures the behaviour of a graphics processor and an application domain of video processing.

To provide a broadened prospective of the work a classification scheme for post-fab options was presented in Section 3. The effectiveness of the classification has been demonstrate through its application to prior art and to classify the proposal in Section 9.

Our exploration tool is divided into a systematic approach to exploring customisation options and a system model. The systematic approach in Section 4 is an adapted version of the well known Y-Chart method. The adaptation is to capture the architectural features which support the programming model. As a part of the approach the customisation options are separated into post- and pre-fabrication options. The associated model, in Section 5, comprises high-level descriptors and is implemented using the SystemC class library and a Kahn process network structure.

Architecture performance is explored using the model. In Section 6, the effect of the processing pattern on a single PE and thread example is analysed. This analysis is extended to the multiple PE and multiple thread case in Section 7. The analysis in both sections promotes the post-fabrication customisation option presented in Section 9.

Architecture trends are explored using four case study examples in Section 8. The options of number of PEs, number of threads and cache size are demonstrated. Alongside these results the model is verified and critiqued against two graphics processors. The behaviour of the graphics processors is shown to be captured by the model.

The architecture trends and analysis from Sections 6 and 7 are used to propose post-fabrication customisation options in Section 9. A positive result is to customise processing pattern which improves performance by four time for a negligible area cost. This is a class 5 'glue logic' use of reconfigurable logic from Section 3.

A grander result of the paper is that the work demonstrates the strengths of the exploration tool and classification in the design of a customised HoMP. We hope that the work will stimulate future research in this area.

In addition to automation as mentioned in Section 4, further work would involve exploring customisation options for other homogeneous multi-processors including the Cell BE and CUDA enabled graphics processors. The Intel Larrabee is a further architecture which may also present exciting opportunities for customisation.

It is also interesting to investigate customising a processor's memory subsystem. In particular customisation of the mapping of off-chip to on-chip memory in a Cell BE DMA engine. Finally, it is also important to study customisation of system interconnects [22] and heterogeneous architectures.

Acknowledgement. We gratefully acknowledge support from Sony Broadcast & Professional Europe and the UK Engineering and Physical Sciences Research Council.

References

1. Vassiliadis, S., et al.: Tera-device computing and beyond: Thematic group 7 (2006), Roadmap
   ftp://ftp.cordis.europa.eu/pub/fp7/ict/docs/fet-proactive/
   masict-01_en.pdf
2. De Bosschere, K., Luk, W., Martorell, X., Navarro, N., O'Boyle, M., Pnevmatikatos, D., Ramírez, A., Sainrat, P., Seznec, A., Stenström, P., Temam, O.: High-performance embedded architecture and compilation roadmap. In: Stenström, P. (ed.) Transactions on High-Performance Embedded Architectures and Compilers I. LNCS, vol. 4050, pp. 5–29. Springer, Heidelberg (2007)
3. Cope, B., Cheung, P.Y.K., Luk, W.: Systematic design space exploration for customisable multi-processor architectures. In: SAMOS, pp. 57–64 (July 2008)
4. Keinhuis, B., et al.: An approach for quantitative analysis of application-specific dataflow architectures. In: ASAP, pp. 338–350 (July 1997)
5. Lieverse, P., et al.: A methodology for architecture exploration of heterogeneous signal processing systems. Journal of VLSI Signal Processing 29(3), 197–207 (2001)
6. Moya, V., Golzalez, C., Roca, J., Fernandez, A.: Shader performance analysis on a modern GPU architecture. In: IEEE/ACM Symposium on Microarchitecture, pp. 355–364 (2005)
7. Sheaffer, J.W., Skadron, K., Luebke, D.P.: Fine-grained graphics architectural simulation with qsilver. In: Computer Graphics and Interactive Techniques (2005)
8. Nvidia: nvidia shaderperf 1.8 performance analysis tool,
   http://developer.nvidia.com/object/nvshaderperf_home.html
9. Govindaraju, N.K., Larsen, S., Gray, J., Manocha, D.: A memory model for scientific algorithms on graphics processors. In: ACM/IEEE Super Computing, pp. 89–98 (2006)
10. Kahn, G.: The semantics of a simple language for parallel programming. In: IFIP Congress (1974)
11. Rissa, T., Donlin, A., Luk, W.: Evaluation of systemc modelling of reconfigurable embedded systems. In: DATE, pp. 253–258 (March 2005)
12. Donlin, A., Braun, A., Rose, A.: SystemC for the design and modeling of programmable systems. In: Becker, J., Platzner, M., Vernalde, S. (eds.) FPL 2004. LNCS, vol. 3203, pp. 811–820. Springer, Heidelberg (2004)

13. Todman, T.J., Constantinides, G.A., Wilton, S.J., Mencer, O., Luk, W., Cheung, P.Y.: Reconfigurable computing: Architectures and design methods. IEE Computers and Digital Techniques 152(2), 193–207 (2005)
14. Cope, B., Cheung, P.Y.K., Luk, W.: Using reconfigurable logic to optimise gpu memory accesses. In: DATE, pp. 44–49 (2008)
15. Moll, L., Heirich, A., Shand, M.: Sepia: Scalable 3d compositing using pci pamette. In: FCCM, pp. 146–155 (April 1999)
16. Manzke, M., Brennan, R., O'Conor, K., Dingliana, J., O'Sullivan, C.: A scalable and reconfigurable shared-memory graphics architecture. In: Computer Graphics and Interactive Techniques (August 2006)
17. Xue, X., Cheryauka, A., Tubbs, D.: Acceleration of fluoro-ct reconstruction for a mobile c-arm on gpu and fpga hardware: A simulation study. In: SPIE Medical Imaging 2006, vol. 6142(1), pp. 1494–1501 (2006)
18. Kelmelis, E., Humphrey, J., Durbano, J., Ortiz, F.: High-performance computing with desktop workstations. WSEAS Transactions on Mathematics 6(1), 54–59 (2007)
19. Schleupen, K., Lekuch, S., Mannion, R., Guo, Z., Najjar, W., Vahid, F.: Dynamic partial fpga reconfiguration in a prototype microprocessor system. In: FPL, pp. 533–536 (August 2007)
20. Tremblay, M., Chaudhry, S.: A third-generation 65nm 16-core 32-thread plus 32-scout-thread cmt sparc processor. In: Proceedings of the IEEE ISSCC, pp. 82–83 (February 2008)
21. Dale, K., et al.: A scalable and reconfigurable shared-memory graphics architecture. In: Bertels, K., Cardoso, J.M.P., Vassiliadis, S. (eds.) ARC 2006. LNCS, vol. 3985, pp. 99–108. Springer, Heidelberg (2006)
22. Yalamanchili, S.: From adaptive to self-tuned systems. In: Symposium on The Future of Computing in memory of Stamatis Vassiliadis (2007)
23. MathStar: Field programmable object arrays: Architecture (2008),
    http://www.mathstar.com/Architecture.php
24. Chen, T.F., Hsu, C.M., Wu, S.R.: Flexible heterogeneous multicore architectures for versatile media processing via customized long instruction words. IEEE Transactions on Circuits and Systems for Video Technology 15(5), 659–672 (2005)
25. Verbauwhede, I., Schaumont, P.: The happy marriage of architecture and application in next-generation reconfigurable systems. In: Computing Frontiers, pp. 363–376 (April 2004)
26. Nollet, V., Verkest, D., Corporaal, H.: A quick safari through the mpsoc run-time management jungle. In: Workshop on Embedded Systems for Real-Time Multimedia, pp. 41–46 (October 2007)
27. Shin, D.: Automatic generation of transaction level models for rapid design space exploration. In: Proceedings of Hardware/Software Codesign and System Synthesis, pp. 64–69 (October 2006)
28. Cope, B., Cheung, P.Y.K., Luk, W.: Bridging the gap between FPGAs and multi-processor architectures: A video processing perspective. In: Application-specific Systems, Architectures and Processors, pp. 308–313 (2007)
29. Priem, C., Solanki, G., Kirk, D.: Texture cache for a computer graphics accelerator. United States Patent No. US 7, 136, 068 B1 (1998)
30. Jin, Q., Thomas, D., Luk, W., Cope, B.: Exploring reconfigurable architectures for financial computation. In: Woods, R., Compton, K., Bouganis, C., Diniz, P.C. (eds.) ARC 2008. LNCS, vol. 4943, pp. 245–255. Springer, Heidelberg (2008)
31. Ahn, J.H., Erez, M., Dally, W.J.: The design space of data-parallel memory systems. In: ACM/IEEE Super Computing, pp. 80–92 (November 2006)

Microvisor: A Runtime Architecture for Thermal Management in Chip Multiprocessors

Omer Khan[1] and Sandip Kundu[2]

[1] University of Massachusetts, Lowell, MA, USA
[2] University of Massachusetts, Amherst, MA, USA
{okhan,kundu}@ecs.umass.edu

Abstract. In today's high performance computing environment, power density issues are at the forefront of design constraints. Many platforms integrate a diverse set of processing cores on the same die to fit small form factors. Due to the design limitations of using expensive cooling solutions, such complex chip multiprocessors require an architectural solution to mitigate thermal problems. Many of the current systems deploy voltage/frequency scaling to address thermal emergencies, either within the operating system or in hardware. These techniques have certain limitations in terms of response lag, scalability, cost and being reactive. In this paper, we present an alternative thermal management system to address these limitations, based on virtual machine concept that uses a runtime layer of software (microvisor) to manage the computational demands of threads to the thermal constraints of cores. Our results show that a predictive, targeted, and localized response to thermal events improves performance by an average of 21% over counterpart operating system and hardware control theoretic implementations.

1 Introduction

Power density problems in today's microprocessors have become a first-order constraint at runtime. Hotspots can lead to circuit malfunction or complete system breakdown. As power density has been increasing with the technology trends, downscaling of supply voltage and innovations in packaging and cooling techniques to dissipate heat have lagged significantly due to technology and design constraints. These problems are further exacerbated for small and restricted form factors.

Ideally, a thermal management solution is expected to push the design to its thermal limits, while delivering optimal system performance. As temperature is well correlated to the application behavior, it is desirable to have insight into application or thread to guide thermal management in addition to physical triggers such as distributed thermal sensors. Avoiding global response to thermal events is another key requirement to ensuring scalable solution for future many cores era. In summary, to tune for best performance at target temperature, a thermal solution needs to deliver predictive and targeted response to thermal events, while keeping the response time and cost overheads low.

In this paper we present a novel system level thermal management architecture based on virtual machine concept. A runtime layer of software (termed as *microvisor*)

P. Stenström (Ed.): Transactions on HiPEAC IV, LNCS 6760, pp. 84–110, 2011.
© Springer-Verlag Berlin Heidelberg 2011

is introduced to manage the computational demands of threads to the thermal constraints of the cores in a chip multiprocessor. We show that system performance losses due handling of thermal events can be mitigated with minimal changes to the hardware and software layers in today's systems. The main features of our proposed scheme are: (i) *Temperature prediction of distributed computational units within cores.* We use past temperature behavior along with a novel phase classification scheme to expose future thermal demands of threads. (ii) *Deploying targeted and localized thermal management actions.* We introduce several fine grain micorarchitecural reconfigurations within the cores as well as a fast and secure thread migration framework. (iii) *Maximized system performance with non-stop thermal management.* Microvisor uses physical thermal triggers along with architectural monitoring mechanisms to tackle thermal management at runtime.

The rest of the paper is organized as follows: In section 2, we provide motivation for our proposed framework. Related work on thermal management is presented in section 3 followed by a discussion of our microvisor based architecture in section 4. Description of our experimental methodology is presented in section 5. Section 6 discusses our program phase classification scheme and section 7 gives a detail account of our temperature prediction mechanism. We discuss thermal management actions in section 8 followed by results and analysis of our experiments in section 9. We conclude in section 6.

2 Background and Motivation

There is an agreed hardware, software framework for power and thermal management through the ACPI framework [1]. When temperature measurements are detected and fed back to the operating system, temporal and spatial thermal aware techniques are engaged to eliminate thermal emergencies. While this has been shown to be effective in many situations, ACPI framework is far from perfect. Following are some of the shortcomings of the ACPI framework:

Current Management techniques are reactive with large response times: On-die droop and thermal sensors are in wide use today. These sensors have inaccuracy problems, which coupled with long system latencies have a detrimental effect on sense-and-react systems. For example, a computer system takes 100s of micro-seconds to adjust clock frequency and power supply voltage [2]. Additionally, a large manufacturer had a product recall for server parts in 2006 due to sensor inaccuracy [3]. As a result, sufficient guard bands must be put in place to prevent errors from creeping in during the response lag. For future technology trend projections by ITRS, as the power density rises, temperature rises will be faster, voltage and frequency response times that are gated by decoupling capacitor size and PLL lock times will remain similar, and therefore, a greater guard band has to be used [4].

Many-core Problems: In a sea-of-core design, thermal management is even more problematic. In POWER6 design, there are 24 temperature sensors [5]. If any of these sensors trigger, the response is global. The problem becomes more challenging when there are 100 or 1000 sensors. In that scenario, it is possible that some sensors trigger with alarming frequency. This will cause a processor to operate mostly at low performance mode. To slow down only one core, it must have its own clock distribution network. A sea-of-cores with each core having its own PLL and a private clock distribution network is a non-trivial design challenge. These are some of the critical challenges for frequency scaling in the future.

If one core is slowed down, the voltage for that core cannot be reduced unless it is in a separate power island. If every core has a separate power island, there will be separate connections between external Voltage Regulator Module (VRM) and the chip, leading to congestion at the board level. Consequently, each core will have its own external decoupling capacitor leading to greater power supply noise inside each core. These issues raise the cost of implementing voltage scaling, while its effectiveness gets reduced. The effectiveness of voltage scaling gets further eroded in 45nm technology, where the power supply voltage is proposed to be 0.9V. For the SRAM bits to work properly, a minimum of 0.7V is needed, reducing the range of supply voltages [4].

In order to address these issues, we propose to unify the thermal monitoring and response management under a common system level framework. Some of the objectives of our proposed architecture are:

Scalable thermal management: Insulating thermal management from the operating system enables a scalable system level solution. This minimizes changes to the operating system as the processor design evolves.

Distributed temperature monitoring: As the chips become larger and feature multiple cores, a targeted response to temperature events become necessary. A global response penalizes all threads across all cores. This is not desired.

Action based on rate of change of temperature: A major benefit of the gradient approach is that thermal emergencies can be intercepted before they occur. This allows a smaller safety margin, also known as temperature guard band. Further, sensors have inaccuracies due to process variation. Multipoint measurements are generally more accurate than single reading. This can potentially alleviate sensor inaccuracy issues.

Application Adaptation: A tight correlation exists between temperature and application behavior. Adapting to each thread's thermal demands can optimize system performance, while keeping the cores thermally saturated.

3   Related Work on Thermal Management

Our approach tackles thermal management in a unified hardware/software framework. One of the first hardware, software co-design approach of dynamic thermal management was presented in the DEETM framework by Huang et al [6]. Borkar identified that thermal packaging costs will increase sharply and estimated that exceeding 35-40W, thermal packaging increases the total cost per chip by $1/W [7]. Dynamic thermal management (DTM) techniques have been proposed to alleviate the thermal packaging costs by enabling the design for temperature less than the peak and use *reactive* DTM to tackle the rare thermal emergencies [8]. The response mechanism initiated by DTM is typically accompanied by degradation in the performance of the chip and persists until normal system operation is resumed. DTM is the philosophy behind Intel, AMD and Transmeta microprocessor's thermal design with support for varying levels of frequency and voltage scaling [9]. Skadron et al

[10] proposed the use of control theory algorithms for DTM, using fetch gating and migrating computation as their action mechanism. Brooks et al [8] proposed several localized reactive mechanisms – I-cache throttling, decode throttling and speculation control. They also identify dynamic (sensors, counters etc) as well as static (compiler optimization) triggers for these mechanisms.

Rohu and Smith [11] present a software technique that allows the operating system to control CPU activity on a per-application basis. Temperature is regularly sampled and when it a reaches dangerous level, the application (or "hot" process) is slowed down. This technique is shown to be superior to throttling as it does not affect slow processes. Srinivasan and Adve [12] proposed a *predictive* DTM algorithm targeted at multimedia applications. They intended to show that predictive combination of architecture adaptation and voltage scaling performs the best across a broad range of applications and thermal limits. Shayesteh et al [13], Powell et al [14], and Michaud et al [15] investigate thread/activity migration via the Operating System as a means of controlling the thermal profile of the chip. They explore the use of swapping applications between multiple cores when a given core exceeds a thermal threshold.

Pure hardware implementation of thermal manager is expensive and lacks flexibility in a typical system. On the other hand, pure software based approach needs instrumentation capabilities to tackle the requirements of managing the low level communication with the hardware platform. Additionally, operating system based implementation lacks flexibility due to strict interface abstractions to the hardware platform. Our preliminary findings show promising results for thermal management using a hardware/software co-design paradigm that is minimally invasive to system abstraction layers [16, 17].

4   Thermal Management Using Microvisor

The central component of our thermal management architecture is *Microvisor*, a layer of implementation-dependent software, co-designed with the hardware. The primary function of microvisor is to manage temperature of the distributed computational structures of the cores within a chip multiprocessor (CMP). Of interest is the detection of temperature, and corresponding actions in terms of thread migration and hardware reconfiguration for thermal control. By their very nature, hardware reconfiguration mechanisms are implementation dependent and cannot be easily managed by conventional software. Conventional software is designed to satisfy a functional interface (Instruction Set Architecture and Application Binary Interface) that is intended to shield the software from implementation details, not reveal them. The microvisor as envisioned in Fig. 1 resides in a region of physical memory that is concealed from all conventional software (including the operating system).

4.1   Microvisor Architecture

Our proposed architecture has both hardware and software components, as shown in Fig. 2. The hardware component consists of thermal sensors strategically distributed throughout the chip and a phase classification unit in each core. Additionally, each core provides hardware reconfiguration capabilities for localized throttling and reduction in capabilities of resources such as queues, buffers and tables, as well as the ability to reduce the width of the major components of the machine such as, fetch, issue and retirement units. Finally, the hardware platform provides support for processor virtualization features like expanded isolation, and mechanisms for quick thread migration.

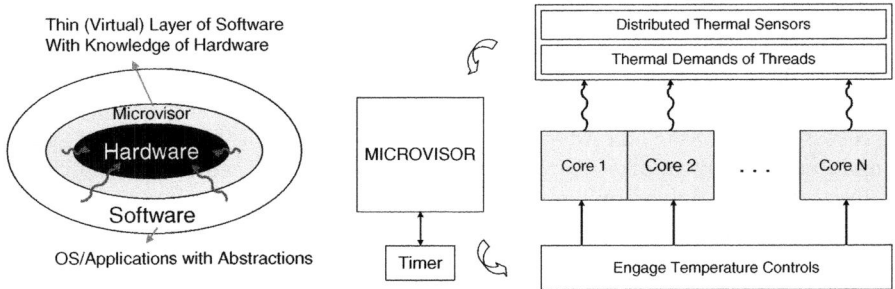

Fig. 1. Microvisor's System View   **Fig. 2.** Microvisor's Interactions within the System

The software component of our scheme is the microvisor's thermal management software that runs natively as a privileged process on the CMP. We assume a thin Virtual Machine Monitor (VMM) running underneath the operating system, which is primarily used to enter and exit, as well as pass specific thread information to the microvisor [18]. Microvisor software maintains several data structures for thermal management. Based on the thread specific thermal demands captured via the phase classification unit, and the past measurements of the distributed thermal sensors, microvisor predicts the thermal mapping for the next epoch of computation. When microvisor predicts a potential for thermal hotspots, it takes a preemptive measure by reconfiguring the hardware platform or migrating threads between the CMP cores. Microvisor considers the performance and thermal tradeoffs, and provides adjustments for sustained performance levels at target temperature.

The microvisor maintains a *timer* that is programmed by the microvisor to periodically interrupt the CMP and transfer control to the microvisor. This timer is set up to adjust its sampling to match the thermal requirements of the threads running on the cores. This is similar in functionality to the timer interrupt used by the operating system. It guarantees that the microvisor can seize control at least at timer intervals.

The distributed thermal sensors periodically log their readings to a memory mapped address space. The microvisor responds to temperature and program phase changes using the timer. Once activated, it has the highest privileged access to the cores. Microvisor examines temperature readings and thermal characteristics of classified phases to determine appropriate thermal management actions. When done, it exits via the VMM and passes control back to the operating system. As a result, our approach delivers a hardware-software co-designed solution that assists the hardware to dynamically adjust to tackle the thermal concerns.

4.2 Related Work on Microvisor

The proposed microvisor is inspired by IBM S/390 system that executes *millicode* for implementing complex ESA/390 instructions [19]. Millicode has access not only to all implemented ESA/390 instructions but also to special instructions used to access specific hardware. Millicode is stored at a fixed location in the real memory and uses a separate set of general purpose and control registers. Unlike millicode, the microvisor is completely hidden from the Operating System leading to greater security, flexibility and portability.

The microvisor is similar in implementation and technology to the hypervisor used in IBM systems that execute millicode held in concealed memory. The main difference is the objective – the hypervisor is directed "upward" at operating system type functions. The microvisor, however, is directed downward at the microarchitecture and implementation dependent aspects of hardware implementation. Thus the microvisor as perceived by us operates beneath the ISA in concealed memory. Therefore, a microvisor can be changed without affecting any other software running above the ISA.

The IBM DAISY project [20] and Transmeta Crusoe processor [21] demonstrated the practicality of using co-designed virtual machines (VMs). Both DAISY and Crusoe used VM technology for runtime binary translation from conventional ISAs (PowerPC and x86 respectively) to propriety VLIW based ISA. Unlike DAISY and Crusoe, we use VM technology for transparent management of processor resources in software – functionality orthogonal to binary translation.

Alpha microprocessors use PALcode [22] to implement low-level hardware support functions such as power-up initialization and TLB fill routines. PALcode aims at hiding low level implementation details from the operating system. Unlike the microvisor, PALcode is part of the architectural specification and accessible through special instructions. The operating system is fully aware and needs to reserve part of the address space for this code.

4.3 Microvisor Software Flow

The main data structures maintained by the microvisor software are Threads to Cores Mapping Table (TCMT), Phase History Table (PHT) and Temperature History Table (THT). TCMT maintains the threads to cores mapping of live threads in the system. The purpose of this table is to keep track of thread mapping, use this information to assist with thread migration and also inform the operating system of such actions. TCMT also ensures a programmable pre-defined time period between thread migrations. This allows enough time for potential thermal imbalance to materialize within the cores.

PHT has an entry for each live thread running in the system. For each thread entry, the PHT maintains the Past Footprints Table (PFT), which is discussed in further detail in section 6. PFT keeps track of classified stable phases within threads along with the runtime characterized thermal behavior and performance characteristics of the phases. When a thread is mapped to a core, the associated PFT is loaded into the core's phase classification unit and updated as the thread executes. Microvisor uses the characterized thermal behavior of the phases to improve temperature prediction and selection of future thermal management actions.

THT constitute several data structures that are used to predict the future temperature for each thermal sensor. THT tracks the rate of change of temperature for each sensor in the system. This is accomplished by sampling the thermal sensors at fixed intervals before the invocation of the microvisor. When microvisor is activated, the temperature readings are captured in the THT. Finally, THT tracks and updates the localized and targeted thermal management actions determined by the microvisor. The high level software flow for the microvisor is presented in Fig. 3.

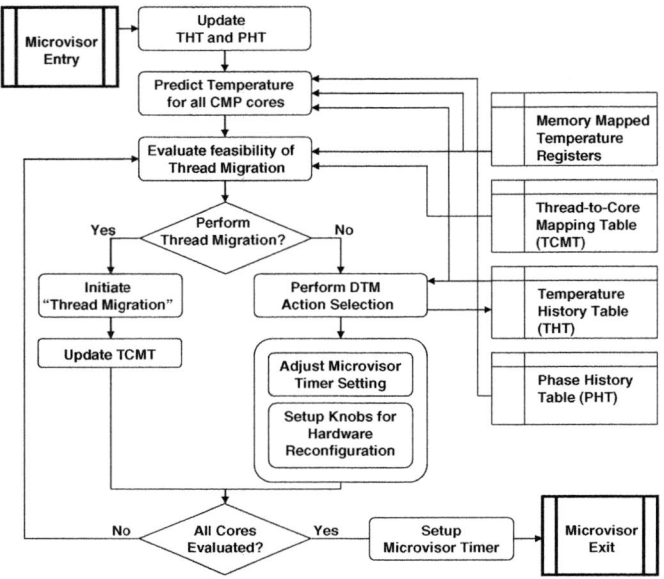

Fig. 3. Microvisor Thermal Management Flow

On each invocation, microvisor first updates the temperature history in the THT and the phase classification unit updates in the PHT using the latest threads to cores mapping. Microvisor then starts the process of determining the next threads to cores mapping and possible thermal management actions via hardware reconfiguration. First temperature is predicted for all thermal sensors in the CMP. Details of the temperature prediction are discussed in sections 6 and 7. Based on the predicted temperature, the final threads to cores mapping is selected based on the following criteria: (1) Largest temperature imbalance exists between two or more cores, and (2) Cores that are not participating in thread migration incur minimum possible performance degradation. This ensures that the CMP will operate at its thermal boundary, while the performance impact of thermal management is minimal.

The predicted temperature delta between thermal sensors on equivalent structures on the logical cores is evaluated for a possible thread migration. If two cores show an imbalance of greater than a pre-defined threshold, thread migration is initiated. In case when thread migration is evaluated to be infeasible, the microvisor takes a fine-grain approach to thermal management. The predicted thermal mapping is fed into an action selection process, which also takes into account the previous action before setting the next action. When the future action is determined for each sensor, a union of these actions is used to setup the knobs for reconfiguring the hardware platform. The next worst case action also appropriately sets the microvisor timer, followed by an update to the TCMT and THT tables. When all cores are successfully evaluated, the microvisor exits and passes control back to the operating system.

5 Experimental Setup

Before diving into the details of our thermal management architecture, we discuss our experimental methodology. We use our modified version of SESC cycle-level MIPS simulator for developing the framework [23]. For modeling dynamic power, SESC implements a version of Wattch [24] and Cacti [25] power estimation tools. We have extended SESC to dynamically invoke HotSpot temperature modeling tool [26]. SESC supports chip multiprocessors within the SMP paradigm. We have extended SESC with thread migration routines to manage and spawn multiple threads dynamically.

We assume a CMP with four cores for our simulations. Each core is an aggressive pipeline with speculation support as shown in Fig. 4. When less than four threads are concurrently run on the CMP, we exclude the additional cores from microvisor management and performance evaluation. We assume a low cost cooling package with a maximum tolerable temperature of 85°C. We assume 65nm technology with chip wide V_{dd} of 1.1V, and frequency of 2.0 GHz. Microvisor's temperature threshold is set at 84°C. We assume that our approach results in better sensor accuracy, as multiple temperature readings used to predict future temperature statistically provides more accurate readings [10]. Therefore, comparison schemes assume higher sensor inaccuracy of ±2°C [2]. Microvisor timer is sampled every 1 to 10 ms, with an estimated entry to exit delay penalty of 2000 clock cycles for each invocation. For each thread migration an additional 20us penalty is assumed for flushing core pipeline and transferring the architecture state. We choose 0.5°C temperature threshold to initiate a thread migration, which yields best results (for our experiments) in terms of temperature imbalance.

Core Parameters	
Fetch, Issue, Retire Width	6, 4, 6 (out-of-order)
L1 Instruction Cache	64KB, 8-way, 1 cycle, LRU
L1 Data Cache	64KB, 8-way, 2 cycles, WB, LRU
Branch Predictor	8K Hybrid 2-level
Branch Target Buffer	4K entries, 4-way
ROB Size	152
Load/Store Buffers	64,48
Last Level Cache	Unified, 2MB, 8-Way, 10 cycles, LRU
Off-chip memory latency	200 cycles (100 ns @ 2 GHz)

Hotspot Parameters	
Ambient Temperature	45°C
Package Thermal Resistance	0.8 K/W
Die Thickness	0.5 mm
Maximum Temperature	85°C
Temperature Sampling Interval	20,000 cycles (@ 2 GHz)

Workload	SPEC2000 Mix	Floating point / Integer	Thermal Behavior (INT/FP)		
			Thread 1	Thread 2	Thread 3
BM1	apsi, applu, ammp	FP-FP-FP	H/M	M/H	M/H
BM2	equake, apsi, applu	FP-FP-FP	C/C	H/M	M/H
BM3	wupwise, ammp, art	FP-FP-FP	M/H	M/H	C/C
BM4	apsi, applu, bzip2	FP-FP-INT	H/M	M/H	H/C
BM5	swim, ammp, gcc	FP-FP-INT	C/C	M/H	H/C
BM6	applu, twolf, bzip2	FP-INT-INT	M/H	M/C	H/C
BM7	vpr, twolf, gcc	INT-INT-INT	M/C	M/C	H/C

Fig. 4. System Parameters   **Fig. 5.** Multithreaded Workloads

5.1 Single Threaded Workloads

To evaluate the proposed phase classification scheme, we use SPEC2000 benchmarks running *reference* input sets. Each benchmark is fast forwarded 5 billion instructions and simulation is run for 50 billion instructions unless identified otherwise.

5.2 Multi Threaded Workloads

We create multithreaded workloads by grouping SPEC2000 benchmarks. Each workload is a combination of Floating point and Integer type benchmarks running *reference* input sets. Before entering performance evaluation mode, each thread is fast forwarded 5 to 6 billion instructions followed by HotSpot initialization. This allows the CMP cores as well as HotSpot and Microvisor tables to get sufficient warm-up. Fig. 5 shows our multithreaded workloads. The thermal characteristics of the threads being evaluated show a diverse mix temperature behavior, thus providing a robust thermal simulation environment. These workloads are used to evaluate our thermal management architecture.

5.3 Performance Metric: CMP Throughput

We use a throughput metric for the CMP to evaluate the performance of our architecture. Each thread runs for 2 billion instructions. Simulation runs until each thread completes at least 2 billion instructions. Performance measurements are only recorded for the first 2 billion instructions of each thread. CMP throughput is defined as the sum of the throughput of all threads. Throughput of a thread is the 2 billion instructions committed divided by its active execution time.

6 Exposing Thermal Demands of Threads

In this section we describe our architecture for detecting and classifying the occurrences of phases in threads. The basic idea is to unlock the thermal demands of an application and classify this information into stable phases. The goal of phase classification is to identify recurring and similar intervals of execution as unique phases. Typical applications incur patterns of recurring behavior with occurrences of stable and unstable phases. We define the stable phase as a series of four or more similar intervals, while the rest of the intervals are categorized as unstable phases. As these phases change during runtime, the thermal demands of threads are characterized and subsequently used to fine tune temperature prediction and management actions. Our scheme uses a simplified Markov model [27] for predicting phase changes. We also compare our proposed scheme to phase classification using Basic Block Vectors [28].

6.1 Related Work on Program Phase Classification

Repetitive and recognizable phases in applications have been observed and exploited by computer architects for decades [29]. There have been several studies on examining and classifying program phase behavior at runtime [30, 31]. Programs exhibit phase behavior in terms of ILP and instruction mix during the course of their execution. It is already well-known that phases may vary significantly across a program [32]. As program phases are rooted in the static structure of a program, using an instruction related model is intuitive. In past researchers have used Page working set, Instruction working set, and Basic Block Vectors to describe program behavior [33, 34, 28]. Taking advantage of this time varying behavior via reconfiguration can enable fine-grain optimizations [35]. To make such phase detection feasible, the implementation has to be low overhead and scalable.

Dhodapakar presented a hardware phase detection scheme based on working set signatures of instructions touched in a fixed interval of time [34]. The instruction working set is hashed into a bit vector, the working set signature. They track phase changes solely upon what code was executed (working set), without weighing the code by its frequency of execution.

Sherwood et al and J. Lau et al also presented a hardware based scheme using Basic Block Vectors (BBV) to track the execution frequencies of basic blocks touched in a particular interval [28, 36]. By examining the proportion of instructions executed from different sections of the code, BBV is used to find the phases that correspond to changes in program behavior. BBV shows best sensitivity and lowest variation in phases because it captures code by frequency of execution in addition to what was executed [37]. Although BBV scheme is shown to be quite effective, it does not reveal any information about the thread's computational requirements.

6.2 Instruction Type Vectors (ITV)

We propose an Instruction Type Vectors based model, which captures the execution frequency of committed instruction types over a profiling interval. Instructions types are classified into eight categories: *iALU, iComplex, iBranch, iLoad, iStore, fpALU, fpMult, fpDiv*. Our implementation independent scheme allows us to capture the application behavior without any dependence on the underlying microarchitecture. This makes the phase classification process a general purpose on-line profiling technique, which is independent of the underlying hardware details, such as capabilities of cores and their memory behavior. Using ITV, rather than prior schemes, allows exposing the computational requirements of a phase in addition to phase classification. The captured instruction type distribution enables the microvisor to characterize the power/thermal requirements at a fine grain granularity of major computational structures within cores.

6.3 Phase Tracking Architecture

Fig. 6 presents a low overhead phase tracking architecture that has both hardware and software components. An Accumulator Table tracks the execution frequencies of the instruction types encountered during an interval. When an instruction type is committed, the corresponding counter is incremented. This accumulator table is compressed into an Instruction Type Vector (ITV) at the end of each interval and cleared to capture the next interval. Each Accumulator Table entry is a saturating counter to capture an instruction type count in a profiling interval. We concatenate all accumulator table counters to form an ITV for an interval.

At the end of each interval the captured ITV is sent to a phase classification unit, which compares the current ITV to the past classified phase information. Past Footprints Table (PFT) is maintained to keep track of stable phases. To keep the hardware overhead low and enable a scalable architecture, we propose to implement the PFT into a multi-level data structure. A 4-entry PFT is maintained as Level 1 PFT1 in hardware, while the Level 2 PFT2 maintains all classified phases for threads running on the CMP. For each thread, PFT2 maintains a data structure to track classified phases and their frequency of occurrence. When a thread is assigned to a core, the top four classified phases are loaded in the core's PFT1. For any subsequent thread migrations, the PFT1 contents are also migrated along with the architected state of the cores. Phase classification unit first attempts to match the current ITV with past phases in PFT1. In the case when none of the PFT1 phases match the current ITV, the microvisor is invoked. Microvisor compares the current ITV against PFT2 entries to find a match. If no match is found in PFT2, the current ITV is categorized as a potentially new phase. If a match is found in the PFT2, the PFT2 entry is replaced by an entry in PFT1 using LRU replacement policy. The matching phase ID is forwarded to the phase change prediction unit.

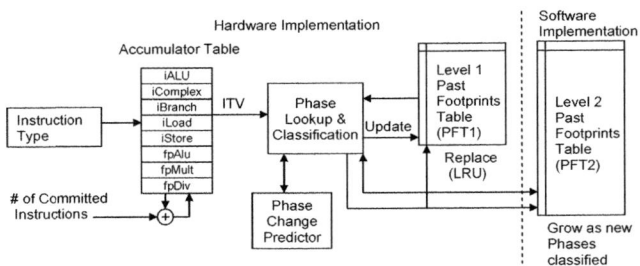

Fig. 6. Phase Tracking Architecture

The goal of phase matching process is to find intervals that have similar instruction distributions. Two ITVs can be considered a match, even if they do not compare exactly. We use Manhattan distance between two ITVs to find and estimated match, which is shown to be an effective differentiator [28]. When the element-wise sum of absolute differences between two ITVs exceeds a pre-defined threshold, it is classified as a new phase. Otherwise, the current ITV is considered a match to a previously classified phase in the PFT table.

Once an ITV is classified, it is not inserted into the PFT1 unless four consecutive ITVs match. This allows us to only classify stable phases into the PFT. When an ITV matches a classified phase in PFT1 or PFT2, we perform an averaging step rather than updating the PFT entry with the latest ITV. This allows the stable phase to drift towards its center. Weight of 10% for new ITV and 90% for original ITV has shown best results for our workloads.

The PFT tracks characterization information when a stable phase is classified for the first time. During the characterization phase, the IPC and temperature rate of change for distributed thermal sensors are captured and stored along with the classified phase ID and the ITV. This information is later used by the microvisor for temperature predictions and thermal management.

6.3.1 Difference Threshold

The ITV information captures intricate details about the computational requirements of a phase, and is found to be highly sensitive to differences between ITVs. Fig. 7 compares several metrics under varying threshold limits, while the phase interval is fixed at 10 million instructions. The data presented here is the average across SPEC2000 benchmarks.

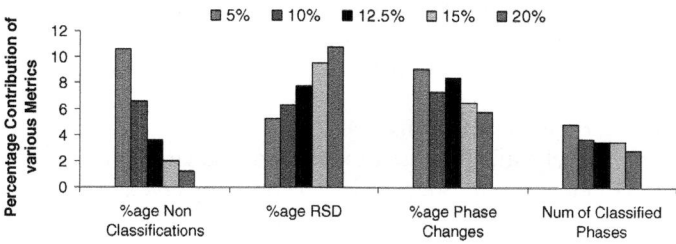

Fig. 7. ITV Difference Threshold

"%age Not Classified" is the percentage of intervals that are not classified in the PFT as a stable phase. "%age RSD" is the percentage relative standard deviation of average IPC for each phase in SPEC2000 benchmarks. This metric evaluates how effectively our scheme classifies performance changes across phases. "%age Phase Changes" is the percentage of intervals that result in phase changes. For a 5% threshold limit, the ITV scheme delivers the best results in terms of classifying phases such that significant performance changes are captured, but it comes at the cost of higher number of phases and especially higher number of phase transitions. Lower thresholds also leave out more intervals from being classified into stable phases. On the other hand, very high threshold limits allow more intervals to be classified into a smaller number of phases. The main drawback is that as the threshold increases, the % RSD goes up significantly.

In order to strike a balance between classifying more intervals into phases that are capable of identifying significant performance changes, we use 12.5% as the threshold for our study.

6.3.2 Profiling Granularity

To capture the runtime phase behavior of programs, our scheme gathers profile information at a sampling interval of 10 million instructions and compares it with information collected over the past intervals. The choice of the sampling interval affects the way phases are resolved. Based on Fig. 8, a 10M instructions granularity provides sufficient resolution of phases.

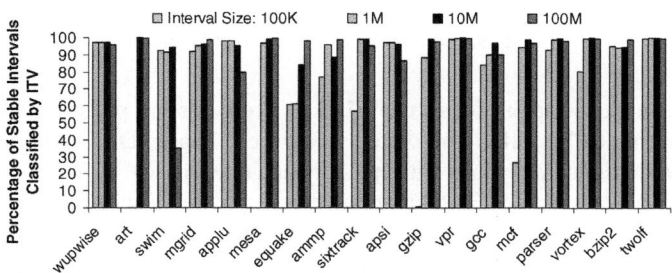

Fig. 8. Interval Granularity

Short intervals (<1M) expose fine grain details and make the phase classification very sensitive to the number of consecutive intervals needed to classify a stable phase. On the other hand, long intervals (>10M) may hide short phases from being classified.

6.3.3 Predicting Phase Transitions

We apply our phase classification unit to detect a change in phase behavior. When a phase change is detected, an interrupt is generated to invoke the microvisor to re-evaluate for a possible thread migration. Sherwood et al. [28] proposed a Run-Length Encoded Markov predictor to detect phase changes. They use the Phase ID and the number of times the Phase ID has occurred in a row, to formulate a state. The next Phase ID is predicted based on the current state. This predictor works well in their implementation where phases are used for fine-grain reconfigurations without any differentiation between stable and unstable phases. As temperature changes slowly at the granularity of several intervals (milliseconds), our goal is to capture coarse grain changes in stable phases.

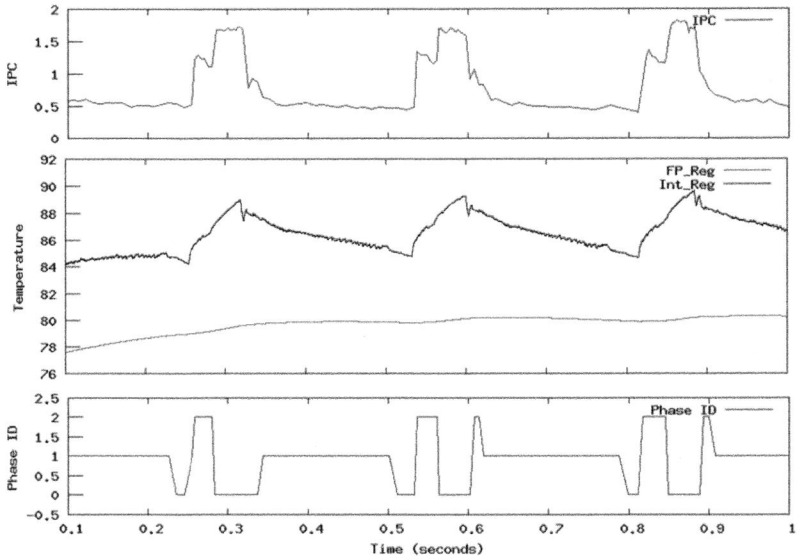

Fig. 9. Capturing *bzip2*'s thermal behavior

We present the simplest form of a Markov predictor for phase change detection, where the current Phase ID is predicted as the next Phase ID. To eliminate some of the false predictions, we apply filtering for unstable phases by masking them from triggering a phase change. Further architecture specific filtering includes instances when microvisor's thermal management software will not result in acting on a particular phase change. For example, if a phase change identifies no thermal imbalance, a thread migration is not initiated between cores. As shown in subsequent sections, IPC may be used as a proxy for thermal behavior of threads. When IPC delta between transitioning phases is below a threshold, we mask out such phase transitions. For our workloads, IPC change threshold of 0.2 shows best results. After applying filtering of unstable phases and insignificant IPC changes, our simple predictor delivers on average better than 90% correct predictions.

6.4 Exposing Thermal Demands Using ITV

In this section we present the applicability of Instruction Type Vectors to enable revealing thermal demands of program phases within threads. Fig. 9 shows an execution snippet of an integer benchmark from SPEC2000 suite. The middle graph shows the temperature behavior of integer and floating point register files without any deployment of thermal management. Inter and intra temperature variations across thermal sensors and benchmarks show the diversity in thermal behavior of threads. We plot the IPC (top graph) and Phase ID (bottom graph) as identified using the ITV phase classification scheme. ITV captures the changing thermal demands as explicit Phase IDs. As these phases recur, the Phase IDs are shown to repeat, enabling runtime thermal optimizations for microvisor. During characterization phase (when a Phase ID is classified for the first time), the rate of change in temperature for each thermal sensor is captured by microvisor. This information is subsequently used to assist in temperature prediction mechanism discussed in section 7.

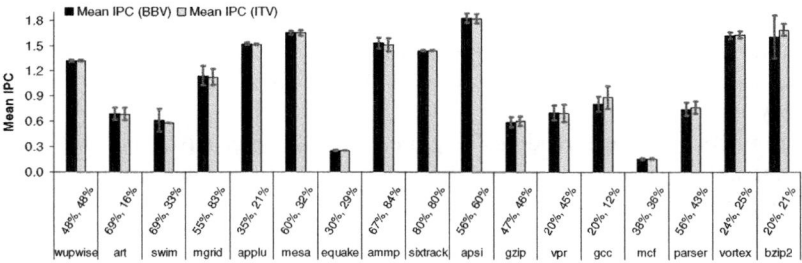

Fig. 10. Comparing BBV versus ITV

6.5 Comparison to Related Work

The main goal of a phase classification scheme is to divide an application into a set of homogeneous phases, where execution intervals with similar behavior are clustered together. We test the performance of our ITV scheme against the BBV scheme based on the criterion of each scheme's capability to differentiate between significant performance changes. To visualize performance changes in a thread, IPC is chosen as the metric of evaluation. Fig. 10 shows the results of this analysis on the BBV and an equivalent ITV implementation with 20 entries for PFT. We show the mean IPC in the graph, although other metrics like memory accesses are shown to perform similar to IPC. For each workload, the top classified phase is shown with its percentage of executed instructions it accounted for (%age number on the x-axis). For benchmarks from SPEC2000, the bar on the left shows the mean IPC and the standard deviation from mean IPC for the BBV, and the bar on the right shows the same for ITV.

When the variability of IPC (shown using the y-axis error bars) within a classified phase is low, an optimization applied for that phase can be effectively reused when the phase recurs. The results show that ITV performs as well as its BBV counterpart across all benchmarks. We can conclude that our ITV scheme is competitive to BBV in terms of accuracy and classification of phases. Additionally, ITV reveals the computational demands of an application by exposing the instruction type distributions within phases.

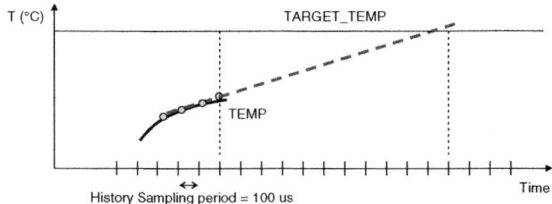

Fig. 11. History based Temperature Prediction

7 Temperature Prediction

Our temperature prediction mechanism relies on past temperature readings to predict future temperature based on past rate of change. Additionally, the characterized thermal demands of phases using the ITV are used to improve the prediction accuracy.

The number of past readings captured by the microvisor is controlled by a programmable register and each reading is taken at 100us interval increments before the scheduled microvisor invocation. The rate of change of temperature for each sensor is calculated using

$$TEMP + ROC * X = TARGET\_TEMP$$

where, ROC is the temperature rate of change calculated using readings separated by 100us samples and ITV based characterization, TEMP is the current temperature status of a particular sensor, and TARGET_TEMP is the temperature threshold for thermal boundary. Finally, X is the unknown variable that determines the number of 100us samples before the temperature is expected to exceed TARGET_TEMP.

Fig. 11 shows a mockup pictorial of the temperature prediction mechanism. The red line shows the projected rate of increase based on the past four readings. The dotted line shows the number of 100us intervals before the projected temperature may exceed the target temperature if thermal management action is not adjusted. Each action is assumed to lower power density at different rates. This determines the severity of action, which is used to setup the microvisor timer for the next invocation. For example, lower severity actions imply that temperature is expected to change slowly; therefore the microvisor invocation lag can be large. This allows us to associate a fixed timer delay for each action. Using the predicted samples and the current action, our temperature predictor associates a discrete rate of change severity level for each thermal sensor. Finally, using this information, microvisor predicts future actions such that the temperature stays below the target.

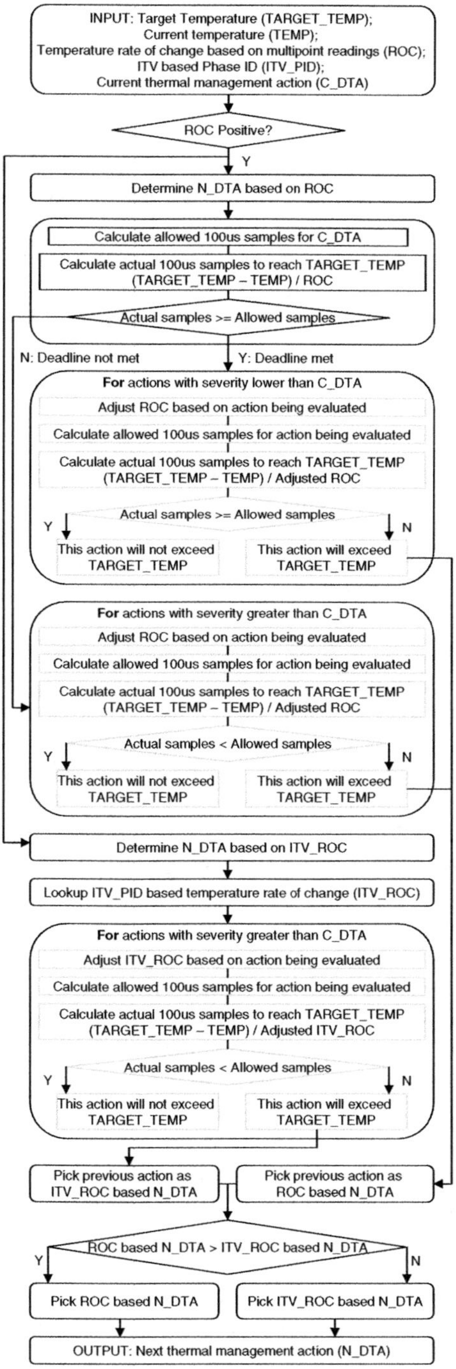

INPUT: Target Temperature (TARGET_TEMP);
Current temperature (TEMP);
Temperature rate of change based on multipoint readings (ROC);
ITV based Phase ID (ITV_PID);
Current thermal management action (C_DTA)
ROC Positive?
Y
Determine N_DTA based on ROC
Calculate allowed 100us samples for C_DTA
Calculate actual 100us samples to reach TARGET_TEMP
(TARGET_TEMP – TEMP) / ROC
Actual samples >= Allowed samples
N: Deadline not met
Y: Deadline met
For actions with severity lower than C_DTA
Adjust ROC based on action being evaluated
Calculate allowed 100us samples for action being evaluated
Calculate actual 100us samples to reach TARGET_TEMP
(TARGET_TEMP – TEMP) / Adjusted ROC
Actual samples >= Allowed samples
Y
N
This action will not exceed TARGET_TEMP
This action will exceed TARGET_TEMP
For actions with severity greater than C_DTA
Adjust ROC based on action being evaluated
Calculate allowed 100us samples for action being evaluated
Calculate actual 100us samples to reach TARGET_TEMP
(TARGET_TEMP – TEMP) / Adjusted ROC
Actual samples < Allowed samples
Y
N
This action will not exceed TARGET_TEMP
This action will exceed TARGET_TEMP
Determine N_DTA based on ITV_ROC
Lookup ITV_PID based temperature rate of change (ITV_ROC)
For actions with severity greater than C_DTA
Adjust ITV_ROC based on action being evaluated
Calculate allowed 100us samples for action being evaluated
Calculate actual 100us samples to reach TARGET_TEMP
(TARGET_TEMP – TEMP) / Adjusted ITV_ROC
Actual samples < Allowed samples
Y
N
This action will not exceed TARGET_TEMP
This action will exceed TARGET_TEMP
Pick previous action as ITV_ROC based N_DTA
Pick previous action as ROC based N_DTA
ROC based N_DTA > ITV_ROC based N_DTA
Y
N
Pick ROC based N_DTA
Pick ITV_ROC based N_DTA
OUTPUT: Next thermal management action (N_DTA)

Fig. 12. Prediction Flow: Temperature rising

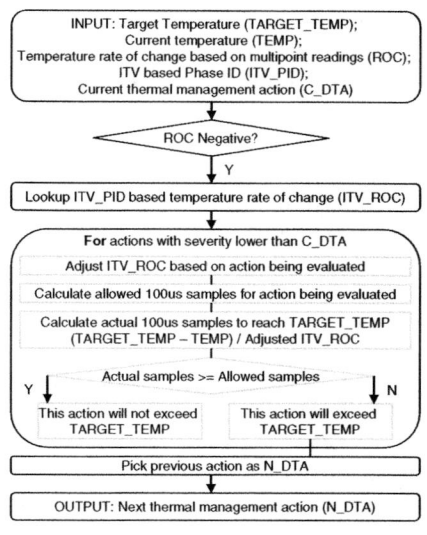

INPUT: Target Temperature (TARGET_TEMP);
Current temperature (TEMP);
Temperature rate of change based on multipoint readings (ROC);
ITV based Phase ID (ITV_PID);
Current thermal management action (C_DTA)
ROC Negative?
Y
Lookup ITV_PID based temperature rate of change (ITV_ROC)
For actions with severity lower than C_DTA
Adjust ITV_ROC based on action being evaluated
Calculate allowed 100us samples for action being evaluated
Calculate actual 100us samples to reach TARGET_TEMP
(TARGET_TEMP – TEMP) / Adjusted ITV_ROC
Actual samples >= Allowed samples
Y
N
This action will not exceed TARGET_TEMP
This action will exceed TARGET_TEMP
Pick previous action as N_DTA
OUTPUT: Next thermal management action (N_DTA)

Fig. 13. Prediction Flow: Temperature decreasing

No ITV
ITV
35%
30%
25%
20%
15%
10%
5%
0%
Percentage of HW Interrupts
84
84.1
84.2
84.3
84.4
Trigger Temperature for HW Interrupt

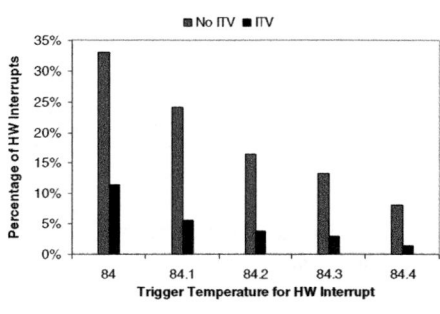

Fig. 14. Prediction Accuracy

Performance of History length
No of HW Interrupts
0.50%
0.30%
0.10%
-0.10%
-0.30%
-0.50%
Perf of History Mechanism relative to Avg_2 @ 83.2
30.00%
15.00%
0.00%
-15.00%
-30.00%
No of HW Interrupts relative to Avg_2 @ 83.2
Avg_4
Avg_8
Weight_2
Weight_4
Weight_8
Temperature History Rate of Change Mechanism

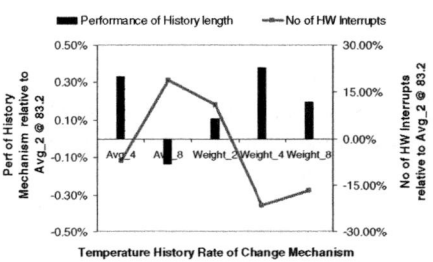

Fig. 15. Impact of history on prediction

Fig. 12 shows the steps taken by the microvisor to determine the next thermal management action (N_DTA) for each thermal sensor in the presence of rising temperature. Microvisor determines the N_DTA based on the past temperature readings as well as ITV based thermal rate of change in temperature. The final N_DTA is selected as the conservative of the two estimates.

Fig. 13 shows the steps taken by microvisor when temperature is decreasing. In this scenario, simply using the past temperature readings to predict the N_DTA is complicated as it is difficult to differentiate between the impact of thermal management action versus the thermal demands of the thread. Microvisor uses the ITV based thermal characterization to predict an optimal N_DTA such that the temperature is not expected to cross the TARGET_TEMP, while the performance loss is minimal.

7.1 Accuracy of Predictions

To avoid thermal emergencies resulting from unforeseen thermal spikes, microvisor uses a hardware interrupt mechanism to invoke re-evaluation of actions. A thermal emergency is triggered when a sensor exceeds a pre-determined temperature, which is set at or above the TARGET_TEMP. We use this special trigger as a proxy to evaluate the effectiveness of our temperature prediction mechanism.

Fig. 14 shows the percentage of hardware interrupts as fraction of microvisor invocations for all the multithreaded workloads. We set the hardware interrupt at increments of 0.1°C from the TARGET_TEMP. The "NoITV" results only rely on multipoint readings to predict future temperature. The results in Fig. 14 show that ITV substantially decreases the number of hardware interrupts, thus highlighting the improvements in prediction accuracy using ITV. We also make the observations that our ITV based temperature prediction mechanism successfully reduces hardware interrupts to less than 5% within a 0.2°C of the TARGET_TEMP. This is a significant reduction from the worst case of 17% at 84.2°C and 32% at 84°C seen by the static counterpart.

We also analyze the impact of varying the length and the rate of change measurement mechanisms of past temperature readings. The effectiveness of the schemes is measured in terms of the performance and the impact on the hardware interrupt count. Fig. 15 shows the data compared to a two reading history length, where the rate of change (ROC) is calculated by averaging the two measurements. We compare against using longer history lengths of four and eight readings, as well as using a weighted function to calculate ROC. The weights are selected such that the temperature rise or fall follows a quadratic function. Apart from Avg_8, other schemes show performance improvements over Avg_2. Avg_8 also shows the most increase in hardware interrupts. This highlights the shortcoming of using averaging function when the actual temperature changes follow a non-linear function. Therefore using linear averaging function is non-optimal and introduces errors. On the other hand, the weighted function delivers best performance and lowest hardware interrupts using four readings. We use 40, 30, 20, and 10% weights for the Weight_4 scheme as the default for this paper.

8   Engaging Temperature Controls

In our proposed architecture, we rank thermal management actions based on their severity level. As shown in Fig. 16, lower ID indicates a lower severity level. In addition the microvisor timer is also set up based on the severity of action being applied. For higher severity, as thermal emergency is imminent, the timer is set to a short interval. To evaluate the microvisor and compare against related work, we present thermal management actions in three broad categories.

Severity ID	Issue Throttle	Issue Width	Retire Width	Speculation	Frequency (GHz)	Voltage (V)	Microvisor Timer	History Samples
0	1/1	4	6	100%	2.00	1.1	10 ms	100
1	1/1	3	4	75%	1.85	1.075	8 ms	80
2	1/1	2	3	75%	1.70	1.5	7 ms	70
3	1/1	1	2	50%	1.55	1.025	6 ms	60
4	1/1	1	1	50%	1.40	1.0	5 ms	50
5	1/2	1	1	25%	1.25	0.975	4 ms	40
6	1/3	1	1	25%	1.10	0.95	3 ms	30
7	1/4	1	1	25%	0.95	0.925	2 ms	20
8	1/5	1	1	25%	0.80	0.9	1 ms	10
10	Thread Migration						10 ms	100

Fig. 16. Thermal Management Actions

8.1   Frequency/Voltage Scaling

Many state of the art systems deploy dynamic voltage and/or frequency scaling to tackle power density problems. To evaluate the efficiency of microvisor based thermal management and compare it against related work, we consider a wide range of frequency and voltage levels. These levels are assumed to be controllable at the chip as well as per core granularity. For voltage scaling (DVFS), we assume a response latency of 100us [2]. However, frequency scaling (DFS) assumes 50us response latency [2].

8.2   Microarchitecture Reconfigurations

Microvisor primarily relies on microarchitecutre based thermal management actions as fine-grain power reduction mechanisms can be architecturally enabled without any dependence on the physical design limitations [38]. Our approach is to initially narrow the processor pipeline to approach a single-issue machine with reduced speculation capabilities and then use issue throttling to further penalize the cores. Issue throttling of x/y indicates that the processor will operate at full capacity for x cycles and after every x cycles, stall for y-x cycles. These reconfigurations are enabled at the chip as well as per core granularity. To enable further fine tuning, we enable microarchitecture reconfigurations at the floating point and integer cluster granularity.

8.3   Thread Migration

Microvisor's thermal management architecture at its heart relies on a fast and reliable thread migration capability. The method has to be fast enough to minimize the performance loss and avoid long system latency issues. Additionally, the state swap

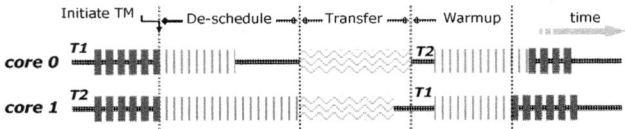

Fig. 17. Thread Migration Flow

must be done in a secure manner without exposing secure processor state to the outside world. Fig. 17 shows the thread migration flow, which is necessary to achieve the stated goals.

When microvisor predicts a thermal imbalance between two cores, thread migration is initiated and the selected cores start de-scheduling the threads mapped to them. When both cores finish de-scheduling, the state transfer mechanism is invoked. At the end of the transfer mechanism, the two threads running on selected cores are swapped and execution is resumed. The only state necessary to swap is the architected state of the cores. This may result in miss-predictions on the caches and branch predictors when the threads are resumed. Therefore, the two cores experience some warm-up penalty before entering full execution of the threads.

8.3.1 Cost of Warm-Up

One of the key costs of thread migration is the warm-up penalty. An option to mitigate warm-up effects is to move speculative state along with the architected state transfer.

Fig. 18 shows the relative CMP performance in the presence of thread migration. For simplicity reasons, the transfer delay is assumed to be ideal. Thread migration frequency is varied to evaluate the impact of warm-up penalties on performance. We choose migration frequencies of 1, 10 and 50 million instructions as they represent the granularity of phase changes in our proposed architecture. The data indicates that the worst performance loss is encountered for Integer benchmarks and is dominated by branch miss-predictions. The loss of performance is at worst 1%. Therefore, we do not propose to transfer any branch state along with the architected state transfer.

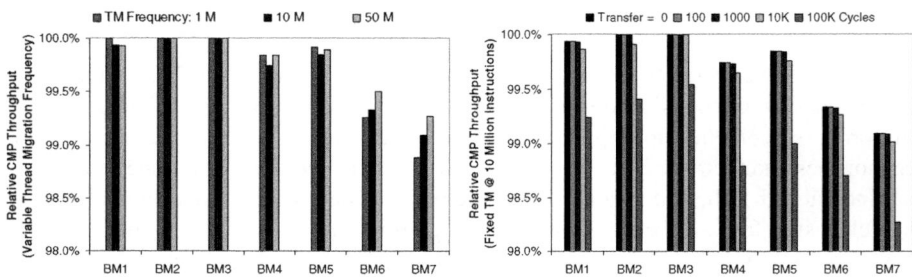

Fig. 18. Cost of Warm-up   **Fig. 19.** Cost of Transfer Delay

8.3.2 Cost of State Transfer Delay

Architected State transfer penalty is a necessary component of thread migration. Fig. 19 shows the impact of transfer penalty on the CMP performance when thread migration is invoked every 10 million instructions. The reported performance loss also includes the cost of warm-up. Best results are achieved when the transfer delay is kept at or below 10,000 cycles. We assume microvisor to support transfer of architected state within 10,000 cycles. We estimate 32K bits of architecture state for a modern RISC architecture. Using 32 bits bus and last level cache or non-core queues as the buffering mechanism, a non-optimized implementation takes 1000 cycles to transfer state. Therefore, our 10,000 cycle assumption is realistic.

9   Results and Analysis

In this section we discuss the simulation results of the microvisor based thermal management. We present analysis of our proposed scheme followed by comparison results using voltage/frequency scaling and microarchitecture reconfigurations. We conclude by presenting some sensitivity analysis of our microvisor based scheme.

All results are compared against a baseline simulation run that assumes no thermal management. The performance metric used is CMP throughput as discussed in section 5.3.

9.1   Analysis of Thermal Behavior

Fig. 20 (top graph) shows the thermal behavior of three threads running on the CMP cores when no thermal management is applied. The temperature is shown for the integer and floating point register file's thermal sensors. The thermal diversity of thermal sensors highlights the need for a distributed sensing and localized management paradigm for thermal management. Fig. 20 (middle graph) shows a hardware thermal management implementation based on a control theoretic PI controller [10]. This scheme uses microarchitecture reconfigurations from Fig. 16 to adjust temperature controls at the core level granularity. Temperature is controlled within 1°C of target temperature. The thermal behavior across the thermal sensors shows that some of the threads underperform due to thermal imbalance, thus resulting in an unnecessary performance loss. As an alternative, our microvisor based scheme as shown in Fig. 20 (bottom graph) introduces thread migration when a temperature imbalance is seen within the cores. For example, if one thread is floating point intensive, while another thread is integer intensive, proactive thread migration between these two threads results in keeping the associated cores free of thermal emergency at minimal performance loss. Additionally, microvisor tracks thermal management actions localized to integer and floating point clusters within the cores, thus resulting in a fine-grain management of threads running on the CMP cores.

Fig. 21 shows the microvisor actions (top) along with the thermal behavior of threads (bottom). Microvisor predicts the future temperature of each thread and takes preemptive actions to keep all cores saturated around the upper temperature threshold. As all cores are running threads with unique thermal profiles, higher actions are deployed for hot threads, while cold threads run full blown. Additionally the hot and cold threads are regularly migrated among cores as the cold thread is used to cool down the hot core, while the hot thread heats up the cooled down core. Microvisor provides an efficient mechanism to combine thread migration with localized actions to keep all cores thermally saturated.

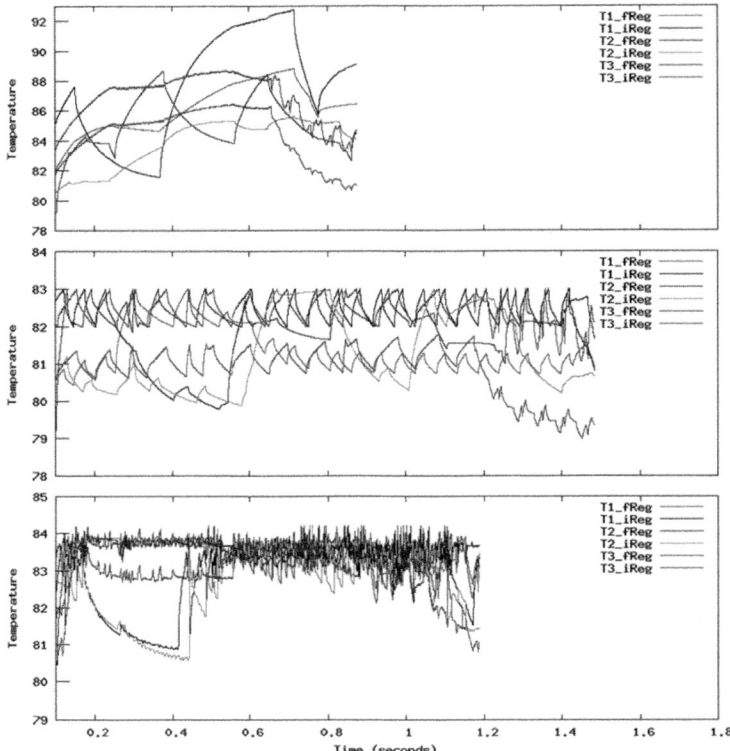

Fig. 20. Microvisor vs. Hardware based control theoretic

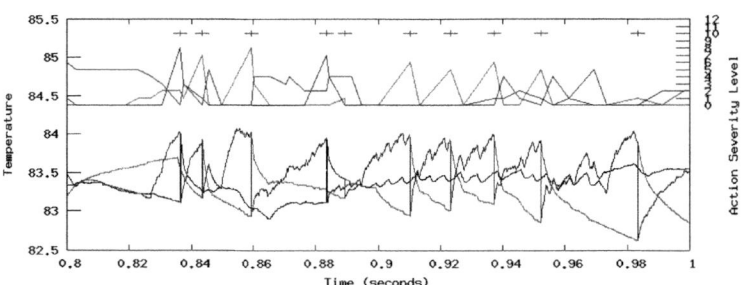

Fig. 21. Microvisor actions and temperature behavior

9.2 Dynamic Frequency Scaling (DFS)

In this section we analyze microvisor implementation with dynamic frequency scaling as the underlying thermal management actions. The frequency settings are used from Fig. 16 where frequency levels are assumed to be available in levels incurring ~10% performance differential. The microvisor manages temperature at per cluster granularity. We compare our results to an operating system and a hardware based implementation. The operating system implementation primarily relies on thread migration based on worst case sensor. This runs on top of a *StopGo* mechanism that halts the machine in presence of thermal emergency and resumes operation when thermal emergency is mitigated (1°C below the target temperature). The hardware based scheme is similar to the one discussed in section 9.1. Both these schemes are implemented at per chip and per core granularities.

Fig. 22 shows the relative performance of these schemes to the baseline implementation with no thermal management. Results indicate that per core outperform per chip implementations for both the operating system and hardware based schemes. Operating system scheme observes an average of 3.5% gain over the chip level management, while the control theoretic hardware scheme outperforms chip level implementation by an average of 21%. The gains are more pronounced in hardware based scheme as the benefits of thread migration are not available and global actions lead to unnecessary performance loss. We note that implementing chip level DFS incurs added design cost of per core clock distribution network in the CMP. The microvisor outperforms the best of operating system and hardware implementations by an average of 18%. These gains are attributed to the predictive, localized and distributed management capabilities in addition to per cluster thread migration.

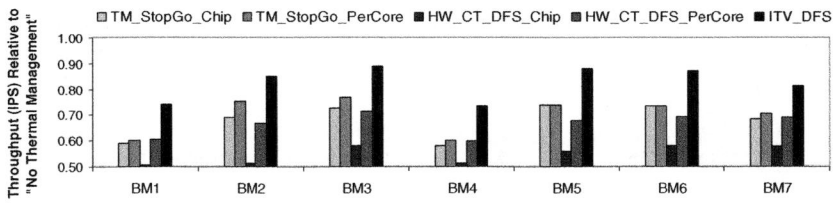

Fig. 22. Thermal management using DFS

9.3 Dynamic Voltage/Frequency Scaling (DVFS)

In this section we analyze microvisor implementation with voltage/frequency scaling as the underlying thermal management actions. The voltage and frequency settings are used from Fig. 16. DVFS delivers cubic reductions in energy, while frequency levels incur ~10% performance differential. The microvisor and the comparison implementations are the same as discussed in section 9.2.

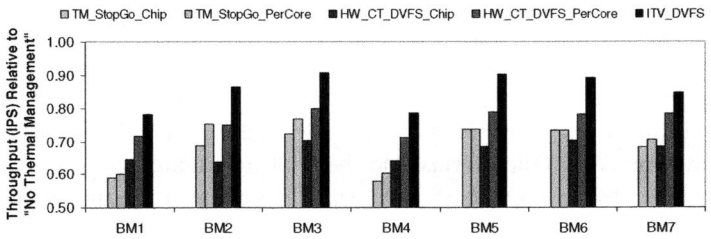

Fig. 23. Thermal management using DVFS

Fig. 23 shows the relative performance of these schemes. Results indicate that per core outperforms per chip implementations for both the operating system and hardware based schemes. The control theoretic hardware scheme outperforms chip level implementation by an average of 13%, which is lower than DFS counterpart due to the extra power savings available due to voltage scaling. Although voltage scaling is quite effective, it comes at the cost of per core power distribution network and is expected to be of limited gains in technologies below 45nm [4]. The microvisor, however, outperforms the best of operating system and hardware implementations by an average of 15%. Under DVFS the hardware based scheme outperforms the operating system scheme, while it was the other way around in DFS implementation. This highlights the tradeoff between an operating system versus a hardware scheme with no thread migration. Microvisor provides an effective management paradigm that intelligently uses thread migration and localized actions to push the performance to its limit under thermal constraints.

9.4 Microarchitecture Reconfigurations

In this section we analyze microvisor implementation with microarchitecture reconfigurations as the underlying thermal management actions. The reconfiguration capabilities are used from Fig. 16 and are assumed to be available down to per cluster granularity. The microvisor and the comparison implementations are the same as discussed in section 9.2.

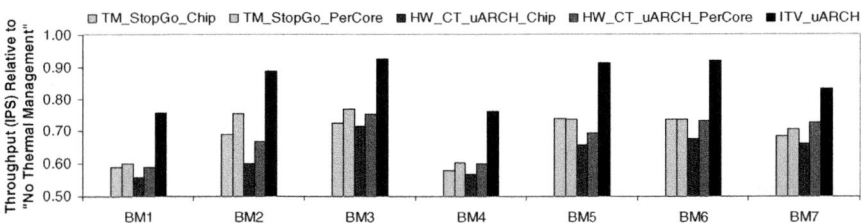

Fig. 24. Thermal management using microarchitecture based actions

Fig. 24 shows the relative performance of these schemes. Results indicate that per core outperform per chip implementations for both the operating system and hardware based schemes. The control theoretic hardware scheme outperforms chip level implementation by an average of 7.5%, which is lower than DFS and DVFS counterparts. This is due to the availability of targeted and localized actions to tackle thermal emergencies. As microarchitecture techniques are independent of physical design constraints, they enable more flexible and scalable implementations. The microvisor, however, outperforms the best of operating system and hardware implementations by an average of 21%. The gains are more prominent compared to the DFS and DVFS counterpart implementations of microvisor.

9.5 Sensitivity Analysis

In this section we discuss the sensitivity analysis of various thermal management actions and components that make up the microvisor framework. Fig. 25 shows per cluster microvisor implementation using ITV to assist in exposing thermal demands of threads. However, the underlying thermal management actions are varied across DFS, DVFS and microarchitecture reconfigurations (MR). DVFS and MR both outperform DFS by an average of 4%.This is attributed to additional power savings using DVFS and localized per cluster actions available using MR. Our result also indicate that per cluster and targeted MR on average performs as well as the DVFS counterpart. The flexibility and scalability of MR in addition to the limitations of future voltage scaling levels make microarchitecture reconfigurations an attractive solution for mitigating power density problems.

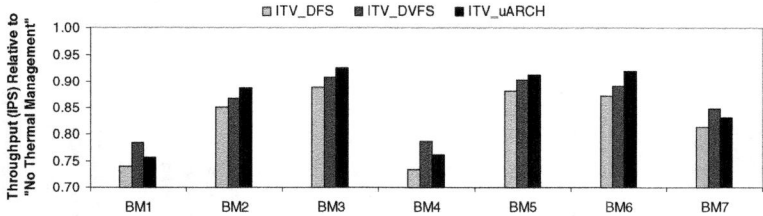

Fig. 25. Comparisons of microvisor actions

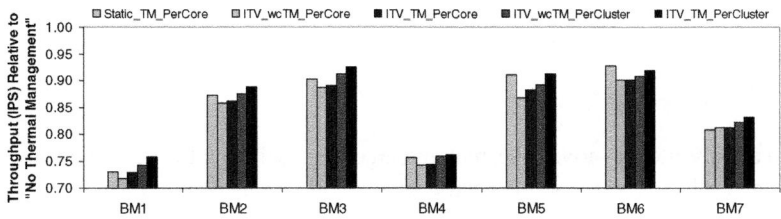

Fig. 26. Breakdown analysis of microvisor

Fig. 26 breaks down the various mechanisms used within the microvisor to keep the CMP thermally saturated, while performance loss is minimal. The Static implementation uses an offline profiling of thread's thermal demands to guide the microvisor temperature prediction mechanism. Additionally, this scheme is implemented with thread migration in presence of worst case thermal imbalance between cores and actions are managed on per core granularity. The static scheme is compared against several runtime ITV based implementations. The thread migration schemes are implemented for worst case imbalance within cores (wcTM) as well as imbalance at per cluster granularity. We also compare implementation of microarchitecture reconfigurations at per core and per cluster granularities.

Fig 26 shows that per cluster implementation of microvisor with ITV outperforms static counterpart by ~2%. This highlights the effectiveness of our ITV based scheme to expose thermal demands for temperature prediction. ITV performs as well an offline profiling of threads. Our data also indicates that per cluster action management improves performance over per core by ~3.5%. This highlights the gains seen by targeted and localized thermal management. In summary, our ITV and microarchitecture reconfigurations based microvisor outperforms static thread profiling as well as DFS and DVFS based implementations.

9.6 Scalability Analysis

Fig. 27 shows the performance gains of microvisor over chip level hardware based implementation using DVFS. We plot the results of varying number of threads running on single, dual and quad core chip multiprocessors. Our data indicates that microvisor's performance improves linearly as the number of threads and cores is increased. This highlights the scalability of using microvisor for thermal management in the many cores, and many threads era.

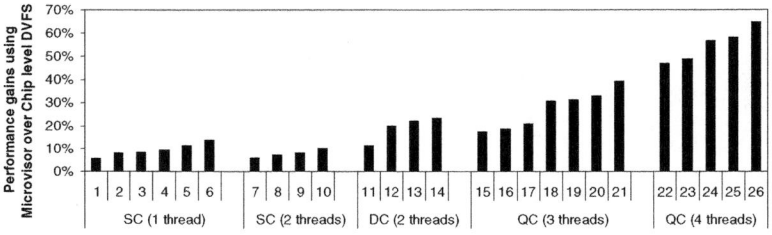

Fig. 27. Scalability as cores and threads increase

10   Conclusions

We have presented a novel thermal management scheme for chip multiprocessors based on hardware/software co-design framework, termed as *microvisor*. The main reason for using virtual machine based microvisor is to enable flexible and scalable thermal management in the presence of changing thermal demands of many core designs and applications. We studied micorvisor as a standalone software scheme with hardware assists such as Instruction Type Vectors based phase classification scheme to expose thermal demands of threads to the microvisor.

Microvisor adapts to each thread to match the thermal demands with the CMP's thermal profile. The microarchitecture reconfigurations enable quick response times as they are not dependent on PLL lock and decoupling capacitor charge/discharge time. Microvisor provides a scalable path to many cores era and is shown to outperform operating system and hardware control theoretic implementations by an average of 21%.

Acknowledgments

This work was supported by a grant from NSF.

References

1. Advanced Configuration and Power Interface (ACPI), http://www.acpi.info/spec.html
2. Naffziger, S., et al.: Power and Temperature Control on a 90nm Itanium®-Family Processor. In: Int'l Solid State Circuit Conf. (2005)
3. Revision Guide for AMD NPT Family 0Fh Processors. AMD Publication # 33610 (October 2006)
4. International Roadmap for Semiconductor (ITRS), Document available at http://www.public.itrs.net/
5. Sanchez, H., et al.: Thermal System Management for high performance PowerPC microprocessors. In: COMPCON (1997)
6. Huang, M., et al.: A Framework for Dynamic Energy Efficiency and Temperature Management. IEEE Micro (2000)
7. Borkar, S.: Design Challenges of Technology Scaling. IEEE Micro (July-August 1999)
8. Brooks, D., Martonosi, M.: Dynamic Thermal Management for High-Performance Microprocessors. In: Int'l Symposium on High Performance Computer Arachitecture (2001)
9. Burd, T.D., et al.: Dynamic Voltage Scaled Microprocessor System. IEEE Journal of Solid-State Circuits (November 2000)
10. Skadron, K., et al.: Temperature-aware computer systems: Opportunities and challenges. IEEE Micro (November-December 2003)
11. Rohou, E., Smith, M.: Dynamically managing processor temperature and power. In: Workshop on Feedback Directed Optimization (November 1999)
12. Srinivasan, J., Adve, S.V.: Predictive Dynamic Thermal Management for Multimedia Applications. In: Int'l Conf. on Supercomputing (June 2003)
13. Kursun, E., et al.: Low-Overhead Core Swapping for Thermal Management. In: Workshop on Power-Aware Computing Systems (2004)
14. Powell, M., Gomma, M., Vijaykumar, T.: Heat-and-run: Leveraging SMT and CMP to Manage Power Density through the Operating System. In: Int'l Conf. on Architectural Support for Programming Languages and Operating Systems (2004)
15. Michaud, P., et al.: A study of thread migration in temperature-constrained multi-cores. ACM Transactions on Architecture and Code Optimization (2007)
16. Khan, O., Kundu, S.: Predictive Thermal Management for Chip Multiprocessors using Co-Designed Virtual Machines. In: Int'l Conf. on High Performance Embedded Architectures & Compilers (2009)
17. Khan, O., Kundu, S.: A Framework for Predictive Dynamic Temperature Management of Microprocessor Systems. In: Int'l Conference on Computer Aided Design (2008)
18. Smith, J., Nair, R.: Virtual Machines: Versatile Platforms for Systems and Processes. Morgan Kaufmann Pub., San Francisco (2005)
19. Heller, L., Farrell, M.: Millicode in an IBM zSeries Processor. IBM Journal of Research and Development, 425–435 (July 2004)
20. Ebcioglu, K., Altman, E.: DAISY: dynamic compilation for 100% architecture compatibility. IBM T. J. Watson Research Center, NY, Research Report RC20538 (1996)
21. Klaiber: The technology behind Crusoe processors. Transmeta White Paper (January 2000)
22. PALcode for Alpha microprocessors system design guide. Digital Equipment Corp. (1996)
23. Renau, J., et al.: SESC Simulator (2005), http://sesc.sourceforge.net
24. Brooks, D., et al.: Wattch: A framework for architectural-level power analysis and optimizations. In: Int'l Symposium on Computer Arachitecture (2000)

25. Shivakumar, P., Jouppi, N.P.: CACTI 3.0: An integrated cache timing, power, and area model. In: WRL, Compaq (2001)
26. Skadron, K., et al.: HotSpot: Techniques for Modeling Thermal Effects at the Processor-Architecture Level. In: THERMINIC (2002)
27. Joseph, D., Grunwald, D.: Prefetching using markov predictors. In: Int'l Symposium on Computer Architecture (1997)
28. Sherwood, T., et al.: Phase Tracking and Prediction. In: Int'l Symposium on Computer Architecture (2003)
29. Denning, P.: The Working Set Model for Program Behavior. Communications of ACM 11(5), 323–333 (1968)
30. Sherwood, T., Calder, B.: Time varying behavior of programs. Technical Report UCSD-CS99-630 (August 1999)
31. Barnes, R.D., et al.: Vacuum packing: Extracting hardware-detected program phases for post-link optimization. IEEE Micro (December 2002)
32. Sherwood, T., et al.: Automatically characterizing large scale program behavior. In: Int'l Conf. on Architectural Support for Programming Languages and Operating Systems (2002)
33. Madison, W., Batson, A.: Characteristics of program localities. Communications of ACM 19, 285–294 (1997)
34. Dhodapakar, A., Smith, J.E.: Managing multi-configuration hardware via dynamic working set analysis. In: Int'l Symposium on Computer Architecture (2002)
35. Isci, C., Buyuktosuniglu, A., Martonosi, M.: Long-Term Workload Phases: Duration Prediction and Applications to DVFS. IEEE Micro (Sepetember-October 2005)
36. Lau, J., et al.: Transition phase classification and prediction. In: Int'l Symp on High Performance Computer Architecture (2005)
37. Dhodapakar, A., Smith, J.E.: Comparing program phase detection techniques. In: Int'l Symp. on Microarchitecture (2003)
38. Ponomarev, D., Kucuk, G., Ghose, K.: Dynamic Resizing of Superscalar Datapath Components for Energy Efficiency. IEEE Transactions on Computers 55(2), 199–213 (2006)

A Highly Scalable Parallel Implementation of H.264[*]

Arnaldo Azevedo[1], Ben Juurlink[1], Cor Meenderinck[1], Andrei Terechko[2],
Jan Hoogerbrugge[3], Mauricio Alvarez[4], Alex Ramirez[4,5], and Mateo Valero[4,5]

[1] Delft University of Technology, Delft, Netherlands
{Azevedo,Benj,Cor}@ce.et.tudelft.nl
[2] Vector Fabrics, Eindhoven, Netherlands
andrei@vectorfabrics.com
[3] NXP, Eindhoven, Netherlands
jan.hoogerbrugge@nxp.com
[4] Technical University of Catalonia (UPC), Barcelona, Spain
{alvarez,mateo}@ac.upc.edu
[5] Barcelona Supercomputing Center (BSC), Barcelona, Spain
alex.ramirez@bsc.es

Abstract. Developing parallel applications that can harness and efficiently use future many-core architectures is the key challenge for scalable computing systems. We contribute to this challenge by presenting a
parallel implementation of H.264 that scales to a large number of cores.
The algorithm exploits the fact that independent macroblocks (MBs) can
be processed in parallel, but whereas a previous approach exploits only
intra-frame MB-level parallelism, our algorithm exploits intra-frame as
well as inter-frame MB-level parallelism. It is based on the observation
that inter-frame dependencies have a limited spatial range. The algorithm has been implemented on a many-core architecture consisting of
NXP TriMedia TM3270 embedded processors. This required to develop
a subscription mechanism, where MBs are subscribed to the *kick-off lists*
associated with the reference MBs. Extensive simulation results show
that the implementation scales very well, achieving a speedup of more
than 54 on a 64-core processor, in which case the previous approach
achieves a speedup of only 23. Potential drawbacks of the 3D-Wave strategy are that the memory requirements increase since there can be many
frames in flight, and that the frame latency might increase. Scheduling
policies to address these drawbacks are also presented. The results show
that these policies combat memory and latency issues with a negligible
effect on the performance scalability. Results analyzing the impact of the
memory latency, L1 cache size, and the synchronization and thread management overhead are also presented. Finally, we present performance
requirements for entropy (CABAC) decoding.

1 Introduction

The demand for computational power increases continuously in the consumer
market as it forecasts new applications such as Ultra High Definition (UHD)

---

[*] This work was performed while the fourth author was with NXP Semiconductors.

P. Stenström (Ed.): Transactions on HiPEAC IV, LNCS 6760, pp. 111–134, 2011.
© Springer-Verlag Berlin Heidelberg 2011

video [1], 3D TV [2], and real-time High Definition (HD) video encoding. In the past this demand was mainly satisfied by increasing the clock frequency and by exploiting more instruction-level parallelism (ILP). Due to the inability to increase the clock frequency much further because of thermal constraints and because it is difficult to exploit more ILP, multicore architectures have appeared on the market.

This new paradigm relies on the existence of sufficient thread-level parallelism (TLP) to exploit the large number of cores. Techniques to extract TLP from applications will be crucial to the success of multicores. This work investigates the exploitation of the TLP available in an H.264 video decoder on an embedded multicore processor. H.264 was chosen due to its high computational demands, wide utilization, and development maturity and the lack of "mature" future applications. Although a 64-core processor is not required to decode a Full High Definition (FHD) video in real-time, real-time encoding remains a problem and decoding is part of encoding. Furthermore, emerging applications such as 3DTV are likely to be based on current video coding methods [2].

In previous work [3] we have proposed the 3D-Wave parallelization strategy for H.264 video decoding. It has been shown that the 3D-Wave strategy potentially scales to a much larger number of cores than previous strategies. However, the results presented there are analytical, analyzing how many macroblocks (MBs) could be processed in parallel assuming infinite resources, no communication delay, infinite bandwidth, and a constant MB decoding time. In other words, our previous work is a limit study.

In this paper, we make the following contributions:

- We present an implementation of the 3D-Wave strategy on an embedded multicore consisting of up to 64 TM3270 processors. Implementing the 3D-Wave turned out to be quite challenging. It required to dynamically identify inter-frame MB dependencies and handle their thread synchronization, in addition to intra-frame dependencies and synchronization. This led to the development of a subscription mechanism where MBs subscribe themselves to a so-called *Kick-off List* (KoL) associated with the MBs they depend on. Only if these MBs have been processed, processing of the dependent MBs can be resumed.
- A potential drawback of the 3D-Wave strategy is that the latency may become unbounded because many frames will be decoded simultaneously. A policy is presented that gives priority to the oldest frame so that newer frames are only decoded when there are idle cores.
- Another potential drawback of the 3D-Wave strategy is that the memory requirements might increase because of large number of frames in flight. To overcome this drawback we present a frame scheduling policy to control the number of frames in flight.
- We analyze the impact of the memory latency and the L1 cache size on the scalability and performance of the 3D-Wave strategy.

- The experimental platform features hardware support for thread management and synchronization, making it relatively light weight to submit/retrieve a task to/from the task pool. We analyze the importance of this hardware support by artificially increasing the time it takes to submit/retrieve a task.
- The 3D-Wave focuses on the MB decoding part of the H.264 decoding and assumes an accelerator for entropy decoding. We analyze the performance requirements of the entropy decoding accelerator not to harm the 3D-Wave scalability.

Parallel implementations of H.264 decoding and encoding have been described in several papers. Rodriguez et al. [4] implemented an H.264 encoder using Group of Pictures (GOP)- (and slice-) level parallelism on a cluster of workstations using MPI. Although real-time operation can be achieved with such an approach, the latency is very high.

Chen et al. [5] presented a parallel implementation that decodes several B frames in parallel. However, even though uncommon, the H.264 standard allows to use B frames as reference frames, in which case they cannot be decoded in parallel. Moreover, usually there are no more than 2 or 3 B frames between P frames. This limits the scalability to a few threads. The 3D-Wave strategy dynamically detects dependencies and automatically exploits the parallelism if B frames are not used as reference frames.

MB-level parallelism has been exploited in previous work. Van der Tol et al. [6] presented the exploitation of intra-frame MB-level parallelism and suggested to combine it with frame-level parallelism. If frame-level parallelism can be exploited is determined statically by the length of the motion vectors, while in our approach it is determined dynamically.

Chen et al. [5] also presented MB-level parallelism combined with frame-level parallelism to parallelize H.264 encoding. In their work, however, the exploitation of frame-level parallelism is limited to two consecutive frames and independent MBs are identified statically. This requires that the encoder limits the motion vector length. The scalability of the implementation is analyzed on a quad-core processor with Hyper-Threading Technology. In our work independent MBs are identified dynamically and we present results for up to 64 cores.

This paper is organized as follows. Section 2 provides an overview of MB parallelization technique for H.264 video decoding and the 3D-Wave technique. Section 3 presents the simulation environment and the experimental methodology to evaluate the 3D-Wave implementation. In Section 4 the implementation of the 3D-Wave on the embedded many-core is detailed. Also a frame scheduling policy to limit the number of frames in flight and a priority policy to reduce latency are presented. Extensive simulation results, analyzing the scalability and performance of the baseline 3D-Wave, the frame scheduling and frame priority policies, as well as the impacts of the memory latency, L1 cache size, parallelization overhead, and entropy decoding, are presented in Section 5. Conclusions are drawn in Section 6.

2   Thread-Level Parallelism in H.264 Video Decoding

Currently, H.264 [7] is one of the best video coding standard, in terms of compression and quality [8]. It has a compression improvement of over two times compared to previous standards such as MPEG-4 ASP, H.262/MPEG-2, etc. The H.264 standard was designed to serve a broad range of application domains ranging from low to high bitrates, from low to high resolutions, and a variety of networks and systems, e.g., internet streams, mobile streams, disc storage, and broadcast.

The coding efficiency gains of advanced video codecs such as H.264 come at the price of increased computational requirements. The computing power demand increases also with the shift towards high definition resolutions. As a result, current high performance uniprocessor architectures are not capable of providing the performance required for real-time processing [9,10]. Therefore, it is necessary to exploit parallelism. The H.264 codec can be parallelized either by a task-level or data-level decomposition.

In a *task-level decomposition* the functional partitions of the application such as vector prediction, motion compensation, and deblocking filter are assigned to different processors. Scalability is a problem because it is limited to the number of tasks, which typically is small. In a *data-level decomposition* the work (data) is divided into smaller parts and each part is assigned to a different processor. Each processor runs the same program but on different (multiple) data elements (SPMD). In H.264 data decomposition can be applied to different levels of the data structure. Only MB-level parallelism is described in this work; a discussion of the other levels can be found in [3].

In H.264, the motion vector prediction, intra prediction, and the deblocking filter kernels use data from neighboring MBs defining the dependencies shown in Fig. 1. Processing MBs in a diagonal wavefront manner satisfies all the dependencies and allows to exploit parallelism between MBs. We refer to this parallelization technique as 2D-Wave, to distinguish it from the 3D-Wave proposed in [3] and for which implementation results are presented in this work.

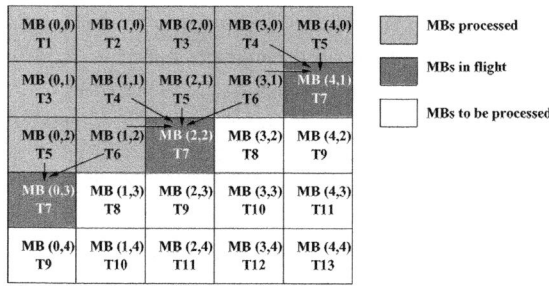

Fig. 1. 2D-Wave approach for exploiting MB parallelism. The arrows indicate dependencies.

Fig. 1 illustrates the 2D-Wave for an image of 5×5 MBs (80×80 pixels). At time slot T7 three independent MBs can be processed: MB(4,1), MB(2,2), and MB(0,3). The number of independent MBs varies over time. At the start it increases with one MB every two time slots, then stabilizes at its maximum, and finally decreases at the same rate it increased. For a low resolution like QCIF there are at most 6 independent MBs during 4 time slots. For Full High Definition (1920×1088) there are 60 independent MBs during 9 time slots.

MB-level parallelism has several advantages over other H.264 parallelization schemes. First, this scheme can have good scalability, since the number of independent MBs increases with the resolution of the image. Second, it is possible to achieve good load balancing if dynamic scheduling is used.

MB-level parallelism also has some disadvantages, however. The first is that entropy decoding can only be parallelized using data-level decomposition at slice-level, since the lowest level of data that can be parsed from the bitstream are slices. Only after entropy decoding has been performed the parallel processing of MBs can start. This disadvantage can be overcome by using special purpose instructions or hardware accelerators for entropy decoding. The second disadvantage is that the number of independent MBs is low at the start and at the end of decoding a frame. Therefore, it is not possible to sustain a certain processing rate during frame decoding.

The 2D-Wave technique, however, does not scale scales to future many-core architectures containing 100 cores or more, unless extremely high resolution frames are used. We have proposed [3] a parallelization strategy that combines intra-frame MB-level parallelism with inter-frame MB-level parallelism and which reveals the large amount of TLP required to harness and effectively use future many-core CMPs. The key points are described below.

In H.264 decoding there is only an inter-frame dependency in the Motion Compensation module. When the reference area has been decoded, it can be used by the referencing frame. Thus it is not necessary to wait until a frame is completely decoded before starting to decode the next frame. The decoding process of the next frame can start after the reference areas of the reference frames have been decoded. Fig. 2 illustrates this strategy called the 3D-Wave.

In our previous study the FFMPEG H.264 decoder [3] was modified to analyze the available parallelism for real movies. The experiments did not consider any practical or implementation issues, but explored the limits to the parallelism

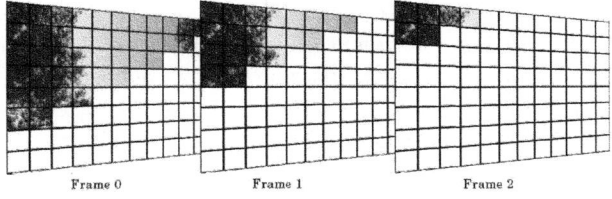

Frame 0   Frame 1   Frame 2

Fig. 2. 3D-Wave strategy: frames can be decoded in parallel because inter-frame dependencies have a limited spatial range

available in the application. The results show that the number of parallel MBs exhibited by the 3D-Wave ranges from 1202 to 1944 MBs for SD resolution (720×576), from 2807 to 4579 MBs for HD (1280×720), and from 4851 to 9169 MBs for FHD (1920×1088). To sustain this amount of parallelism, the number of frames in flight ranges from 93 to 304 depending on the input sequence and the resolution. So, theoretically, the parallelism available on 3D-Wave technique is huge. There are many factors in real systems, however, such as the memory hierarchy and bandwidth, that could limit its scalability. In the next sections the approach to implement the 3D-Wave and exploit this parallelism on an embedded manycore system is presented.

3   Experimental Methodology

In this section the tools and methodology to implement and evaluate the 3D-Wave technique are detailed. Components of the many-core system simulator used to evaluate the technique are also presented.

An NXP proprietary simulator based on SystemC is used to run the application and collect performance data. Computations on the cores are modeled cycle-accurate. The memory system is modeled using average transfer times with channel and bank contention. When channel or bank contention is detected, the traffic latency is increased. NoC contention is supported. The simulator is capable of simulating systems with up to 64 TM3270 cores with shared memory and its cache coherence protocols. The operating system is not simulated.

The TM3270 [11] is a VLIW-based media-processor based on the Trimedia architecture. It addresses the requirements of multi-standard video processing at standard resolution and the associated audio processing requirements for the consumer market. The architecture supports VLIW instructions with five guarded issue slots. The pipeline depth varies from 7 to 12 stages. Address and data words are 32 bits wide. the unified register file has 128 32-bit registers. 2×16-bit and 4×8-bit SIMD instruction are supported. The TM3270 processor can run at up to 350 MHz, but in this work the clock frequency is set to 300 MHz. To produce code for the TM3270 the state-of-the-art highly optimizing NXP TriMedia C/C++ compiler version 5.1 is used.

The modeled system features a shared memory using MESI cache coherence. Each core has its own L1 data cache and can copy data from other L1 caches through 4 channels. The 64Kbyte L1 data cache has 64-byte lines and is 4-way set-associative with LRU replacement and write allocate. The instruction cache is not modeled. The cores share a distributed L2 cache with 8 banks and an average access time of 40 cycles. The average access time takes into account L2 hits, misses, and interconnect delays. L2 bank contention is modeled so two cores cannot access the same bank simultaneously.

The multi-core programming model follows the task pool model. A Task Pool (TP) library implements submissions and requests of tasks to/from the task pool, synchronization mechanisms, and the task pool itself. In this model there is a main core and the other cores of the system act as slaves. Each slave runs a thread by requesting a task from the TP, executing it, and requesting another task. The task execution overhead is low. The time to request a task is less than 2% of the MB decoding time.

The experiments focus on the baseline profile of the H.264 standard. This profile only supports I and P frames and every frame can be used as a reference frame. This feature prevents the exploitation of frame-level parallelization techniques such as the one described in [5]. However, this profile highlights the advantages of the 3D-Wave, since the scalability gains come purely from the application of the 3D-Wave technique. Encoding was done with the X264 encoder [12] using the following options: no B-frames, at most 16 reference frames, weighted prediction, hexagonal motion estimation algorithm with a maximum search range of 24, and one slice per frame. The experiments use all four videos from the HD-VideoBench [13], Blue Sky, Rush Hour, Pedestrian, and Riverbed, in the three available resolutions, SD, HD and FHD.

The 3D-Wave technique focuses on the TLP available in the MB processing kernels of the decoder. The entropy decoder is known to be difficult to parallelize. To avoid the influence of the entropy decoder, its output has been buffered and its decoding time is not taken into account. Although not the main target, the 3D-Wave also eases the entropy decoding challenge. Since entropy decoding dependencies do not cross slice/frame borders, multiple entropy decoders can be used. We analyze the performance requirements of an entropy decoder accelerator in Section 5.7.

4 Implementation

In this work we use the NXP H.264 decoder. The 2D-Wave parallelization strategy has already been implemented in this decoder [14], making it a perfect starting point for the implementation of the 3D-Wave. The NXP H.264 decoder is highly optimized, including both machine-dependent optimizations (e.g. SIMD operations) and machine-independent optimizations (e.g. code restructuring).

The 3D-Wave implementation serves as a proof of concept thus the implementation of all features of H.264 is not necessary. Intra prediction inputs are deblock filtered samples instead of unfiltered samples as specified in the standard. This does not add visual artifacts to the decoded frames or change the MB dependencies.

This section details the 2D-Wave implementation used as the starting point, the 3D-Wave implementation, and the frame scheduling and priority policies.

4.1 2D-Wave Implementation

The MB processing tasks are divided in four kernels: vector prediction (VP), picture prediction (PP), deblocking info (DI), and deblocking filter (DF). VP calculates the motion vectors (MVs) based on the predicted motion vectors of the neighbor MBs and the differential motion vector present in the bitstream. PP performs the reconstruction of the MB based on neighboring pixel information

(Intra Prediction) or on reference frame areas (Motion Compensation). Inverse quantization and the inverse DCT are also part of this kernel. DI calculates the strength of the DF based on MB data, such as the MBs type and MVs. DF smoothes block edges to reduce blocking artifacts.

The 2D-Wave is implemented per kernel. By this we mean that first VP is performed for all MBs in a frame, then PP for all MBs, etc. Each kernel is parallelized as follows. Fig. 1 shows that within a frame each MB depends on at most four MBs. These dependencies are covered by the dependencies from the left MB to the current MB and from the upper-right MB to the current MB, i.e., if these dependencies are satisfied then all dependencies are satisfied. Therefore, each MB is associated with a reference count between 0 and 2 representing the number of MBs it depends on. For example, the upper-left MB has a reference count of 0, the other MBs at the top edge have a reference count of 1, and so do the other MBs at the left edge. When a MB has been processed, the reference counts of the MBs that depend on it are decreased. When one of these counts reaches zero, a thread that will process the associated MB is submitted to the TP. Fig. 3 depicts pseudo C-code for deblocking a frame and for deblocking a MB.

When a core loads a MB in its cache, it also fetches neighboring MBs. Therefore, locality can be improved if the same core also processes the right MB. To increase locality and reduce task submission and acquisition overhead, the

```
int deblock_ready[w][h];          // matrix of reference counts

void deblock_frame() {
    for (x=0; x<w; x++)
        for (y=0; y<h; y++)
            deblock_ready[x][y] = initial reference count; // 0, 1, or 2
    tp_submit(deblock_mb, 0, 0);  // start 1st task MB<0,0>
    tp_wait();
}

void deblock_mb(int x, int y){
    // ... the actual work

    if (x!=0 && y!=h-1){
        new_value = tp_atomic_decrement(&deblock_ready[x-1][y+1], 1);
        if (new_value==0)
            tp_submit(deblock_mb, x-1, y+1);
    }
    if (x!=w-1){
        new_value = tp_atomic_decrement(&deblock_ready[x+1][y], 1);
        if (new_value==0)
            tp_submit(deblock_mb, x+1, y);
    }
}
```

Fig. 3. Pseudo-code for deblocking a frame and a MB

```
void deblock_mb(int x, int y){
again:
    // ... the actual work

    ready1 = x>=1 && y!=h-1 && atomic_dec(&deblock_ready[x-1][y+1])==0;
    ready2 = x!=w-1 && atomic_dec(&deblock_ready[x+1][y])==0;

    if (ready1 && ready2){
        tp_submit(deblock_mb, x-1, y+1);    // submit left-down block
        x++;
        goto again;                          // goto right block
    }
    else if (ready1){
        x--; y++;
        goto again;                          // goto left-down block
    }
    else if (ready2){
        x++;
        goto again;                          // goto right block
    }
}
```

Fig. 4. Tail submit

2D-Wave implementation features an optimization called *tail submit*. After the MB is processed, the reference counts of the MB candidates are checked. If both MB candidates are ready to execute, the core processes the right MB and submits the other one to the task pool. If only one MB is ready, the core starts its processing without submitting or acquiring tasks to/from the TP. In case there is no neighboring MB ready to be processed, the task finishes and the core request another one from the TP. Fig. 4 depicts pseudo-code for MB decoding after the tail submit optimization has been performed. `atomic_dec` atomically decrements the counter and returns its value. If the counter reaches zero, the MB dependencies are met.

4.2   3D-Wave Implementation

In this section the 3D-Wave implementation is described. First we note that the original structure of the decoder is not suitable for the 3D-Wave strategy, because inter-frame dependencies are satisfied only after the DF is applied. To implement the 3D-Wave, it is necessary to develop a version in which the kernels are applied on a MB basis rather than on a slice/frame basis. In other words, we have a function `decode_mb` that applies each kernel to a MB.

Since the 3D-Wave implementation decodes multiple frames concurrently, modifications to the Reference Frame Buffer (RFB) are required. The RFB stores the decoded frames that are going to be used as reference. As it can serve only one frame in flight, the 3D-Wave would require multiple RFBs. In this proof of

```
void decode_mb(int x, int y, int skip, int RMB_start){
    IF (!skip) {
        Vector_Prediction(x,y);
        RMB_List = RMB_Calculation(x,y);
    }
    FOR RMB = RMB_List.table[RMB_start] TO
                            RMB_List.table[RMB_last]{
        IF !RMB.Ready {
            RMB.Subscribe(x, y);
            return;
        }
    }
    Picture_Prediction(x,y);
    Deblocking_Info(x,y);
    Deblocking_Filter(x,y);
    Ready[x][y] = true;

    FOR MB = KoL.start TO KoL.last
        tp_submit(decode_mb, MB.x, MB.y, true, MB.RMB_start);
    //TAIL_SUBMIT
}
```

Fig. 5. Pseudo-code for 3D-Wave

concept implementation, the RFB was modified such that a single instance can serve all frames in flight. In the new RFB all the decoded frames are stored. The mapping of the reference frame index to RFB index was changed accordingly.

Fig. 5 depicts pseudo-code for the decode_mb function. It relies on the ability to test if the reference MBs (RMBs) of the current MB have already been decoded or not. The RMB is defined as the MB in the bottom right corner of the reference area, including the extra samples for fractional motion compensation. To be able to test this, first the RMBs have to be calculated. If an RMB has not been processed yet, a method is needed to resume the execution of this MB after the RMB is ready.

The RMBs can only be calculated after motion vector prediction, which also defines the reference frames. Each MB can be partitioned in up to four 8×8 pixel areas and each one of them can be partitioned in up to four 4×4 pixel blocks The 4×4 blocks in an 8×8 partition share the reference frame. With the MVs and reference frames information, it is possible to calculate the RMB of each MB partition. This is done by adding the MV, the size of the partition, the position of the current MB, and the additional area for fractional motion compensation and by dividing the result by 16, the size of the MB. The RMB results of each partition is added to a list associated with the MB data structure, called the RMB-list. To reduce the number of RMBs to be tested, the reference frame of each RMB is checked. If two RMBs are in the same reference frame, only the one with the larger 2D-Wave decoding order (see Fig. 1) is added to the list.

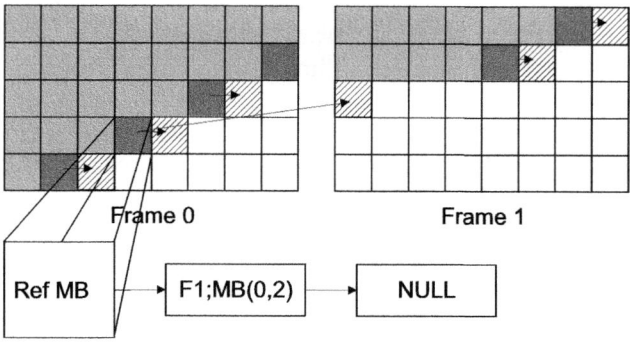

Fig. 6. Illustration of the 3D-Wave and the subscription mechanism

The first time `decode_mb` is called for a specific MB it is called with the parameter `skip` set to `false` and `RMB_start` set to 0. If the decoding of this MB is resumed, it is called with the parameter `skip` set to `true`. Also `RMB_start` carries the position of the MB in the RMB-list to be tested next.

Once the RMB-list of the current MB is computed, it is verified if each RMB in the list has already been decoded or not. Each frame is associated with a MB ready matrix, similar to the `deblock_ready` matrix in Fig. 3. The corresponding MB position in the ready matrix associated with the reference frame is atomically checked. If all RMBs are decoded, the decoding of this MB can continue.

To handle the cases where a RMB is not ready, a RMB subscription technique has been developed. The technique was motivated by the specifics of the TP library, such as low thread creation overhead and no sleep/wake up capabilities. Each MB data structure has a second list called the Kick-off List (KoL) that contains the parameters of the MBs subscribed to this RMB. When a RMB test fails, the current MB subscribes itself to the KoL of the RMB and finishes its execution. Each MB, after finishing its processing, indicates that it is ready in the ready matrix and verifies its KoL. A new task is submitted to the TP for each MB in the KoL. The subscription process is repeated until all RMBs are ready. Finally, the intra-frame MBs that depend on this MB are submitted to the TP using tail submit, identical to Fig. 4.

Fig. 6 illustrates this process. Light gray boxes represent decoded MBs and dark gray boxes MBs that are currently being processed. Hatched boxes represent MBs available to be decoded while white boxes represent MBs whose dependencies have not yet been resolved. In this example MB(0,2) of frame 1 depends on MB(3,3) of frame 0 and is subscribed to the KoL of the latter. When MB(3,3) is decoded it submits MB(0,2) to the task pool.

4.3   Frame Scheduling Policy

To achieve the highest speedup, all frames of the sequence are scheduled to run as soon as their dependencies are met. However, this can lead to a large number of frames in flight and large memory requirements, since every frame must be kept in memory. Mostly it is not necessary to decode a frame as soon as possible to keep all cores busy. A frame scheduling technique was developed to keep the working set to its minimum.

Frame scheduling uses the RMB subscription mechanism to define the moment when the processing of the next frame should be started. The first MB of the next frame can be subscribed to start after a specific MB of the current frame. With this simple mechanism it is possible to control the number of frames in flight. Adjusting the number of frames in flight is done by selecting an earlier or later MB with which the first MB of the next frame will be subscribed.

4.4   Frame Priority

Latency is an important characteristic of video decoding systems. The frame scheduling policy described in the previous section reduces the frame latency, since the next frame is scheduled only when a part of the current frame has been decoded. However, when a new frame is scheduled to be decoded, the available cores are distributed equally among the frames in flight. A priority mechanism was added to the TP library in order to reduce the frame latency even further.

The TP library was modified to support two levels of priority. An extra task buffer was implemented to store high priority tasks. When the TP receives a task request, it first checks if there is a task in the high priority buffer. If so this task is selected, otherwise a task in the low priority buffer is selected. With this simple mechanism it is possible to give priority to the tasks belonging to the frame "next in line". Before submitting a new task the process checks if its frame is the frame "next in line". If so the task is submitted with high priority. Otherwise it is submitted with low priority. This mechanism does not lead to starvation because if there is not sufficient parallelism in the frame "next in line" the low priority tasks are selected.

5   Experimental Results

In this section the experimental results are presented. The results include the scalability results of the 3D-Wave (Section 5.1), results of the frame scheduling and priority policies (Section 5.2), impact on the memory and bandwidth requirements (Section 5.3), influence of memory latency (Section 5.4), influence of L1 data cache size on scalability and performance (Section 5.5), the impact of parallelism overhead on scalability (Section 5.6), and the requirements for the CABAC accelerator to leverage a 64-core system (Section 5.7).

To evaluate the 3D-Wave, one second (25 frames) of each sequence was decoded. Longer sequences could not be used due to simulator constraints. The four sequences of the HD-VideoBench using three resolutions were evaluated. Since the result for Rush Hour sequence are close to the average and other sequences vary less than 5% only its results will be presented.

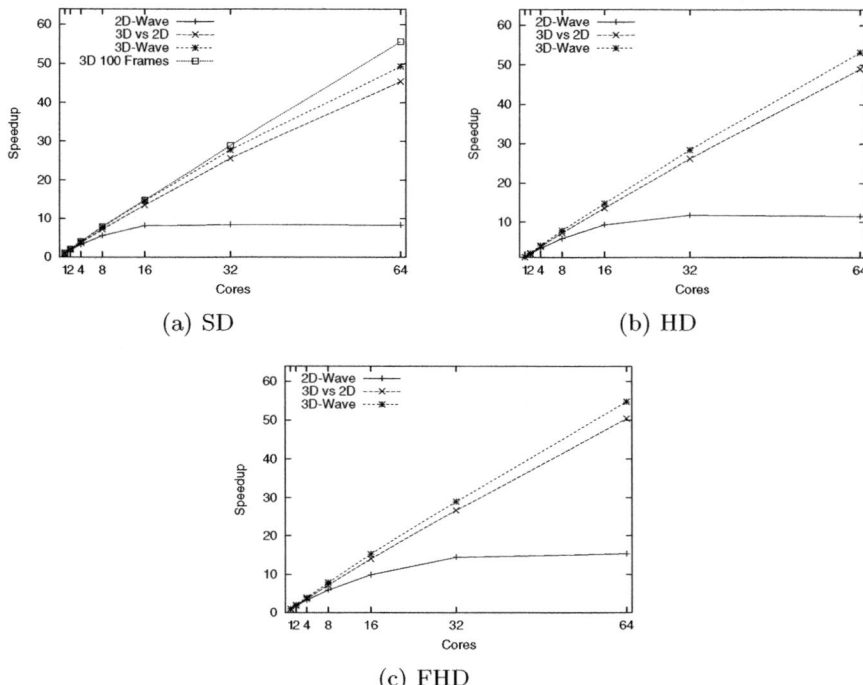

(a) SD (b) HD

(c) FHD

Fig. 7. 2D-Wave and 3D-Wave speedups for the 25-frame sequence Rush Hour for different resolutions

5.1 Scalability

The scalability results are for 1 to 64 cores. More cores could not be simulated due to limitations of the simulator. Figs. 7(a), 7(b), and 7(c) depict the 3D-Wave scalability on p processors $(T_{3D}(1)/T_{3D}(p))$, 2D-Wave scalability $(T_{2D}(1)/T_{2D}(p))$, and 3D-Wave versus 2D-Wave on a single core $(T_{2D}(1)/T_{3D}(p))$, labeled as 3D vs 2D. On a single core, 2D-Wave can decode 39 SD, 18 HD, and 8 FHD frames per second.

On a single core the 3D-Wave implementation takes 8% more time than the 2D-Wave implementation due to administrative overhead for all resolutions. The 3D-Wave scales almost perfectly up to 8 cores, while the 2D-Wave incurs an 11% efficiency drop even for 2 cores due to the following reason. The tail submit optimization assigns MBs to cores per line. At the end of a frame, when a core finishes its line and there is no other line to be decoded, in the 2D-Wave the core remains idle until all cores have finished their line. If the last line happens to be slow the other cores wait for a long time and the core utilization is low. In the 3D-Wave, cores that finish their line, while there is no new line to be decoded, will be assigned a line of the next frame. Therefore, the core utilization as well as the scalability efficiency of the 3D-Wave is higher. Another advantage of the 3D-Wave over the 2D-Wave is that it increases the efficiency of the Tail Submit optimization. In the 2D-Wave the low available parallelism makes the cores stall more due to unsolved intra-frame dependencies. In the 3D-Wave, the available parallelism is much larger which increases the distance between the MBs being decoded, minimizing intra-frame dependency stalls.

For SD sequences, the 2D-Wave technique saturates at 16 cores, with a speedup of only 8. This happens because of the limited amount of MB parallelism inside the frame and the dominant ramp up and ramp down of the availability of parallel MBs. The 3D-Wave technique for the same resolution continuously scales up to 64 cores, with a parallelization efficiency of almost 80%. For the FHD sequence, the saturation of the 2D-Wave occurs at 32 cores while the 3D-Wave continuously scales up to 64 cores with a parallelization efficiency of 85%.

The scalability results of the 3D-Wave increase slightly for higher resolutions. On the other hand, the 2D-Wave implementation achieves higher speedups for higher resolutions since the MB-level parallelism inside a frame increases. However, it would take an extremely large resolution for the 2D-Wave to leverage 64 cores, and the 3D-Wave implementation would still be more efficient.

The drop in scalability efficiency of the 3D-Wave for larger number of cores has two reasons. First, cache trashing occurs for large numbers of cores, leading to many memory stalls, as will be show in the next section. Second, at the start and at the end of a sequence, not all cores can be used because little parallelism is available. The more cores are used, the more cycles are relatively wasted during these two periods. It would be negligible in a real sequence with many frames. To show this Fig. 7(a) also shows the scalability results for 100 frames of the Rush Hour SD sequence. Simulation with HD or FHD sequences with more than 25 frames are not possible because the simulator cannot allocate the required data structures.

For 64 cores the scalability grows from 49.32 to 55.67 when processing 100 instead of 25 frames. The effects of ramp up and ramp down times are minimized when more frames are used. In this case, the scalability results are closer to the results that would be achieved in a real life situation.

5.2   Frame Scheduling and Priority

In this section, experimental results for the frame scheduling and priority policies are presented. The effectiveness of these policies is presented first, then the impact of these policies on the 3D-Wave efficiency.

Fig. 8(a) presents the results of the frame scheduling technique applied to the FHD Rush Hour sequence using a 16-core system. This figure presents the number of MBs processed per ms. It also shows to which frame these MBs belong. In this particular case, the subscribe MB chosen is the last MB on the line that is at 1/3rd of the frame. For this configuration there are at most 3 frames in flight. Currently, the selection of the subscribe MB must be done statically by the programmer. A methodology to dynamically fire new frames based on core utilization needs to be developed.

The priority mechanism presented in Section 4.4 strongly reduces the frame latency. In the original 3D-Wave implementation, the latency of the first frame

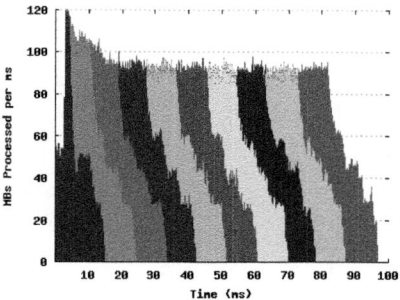
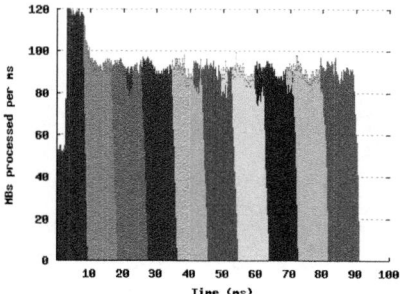

(a) Number of MBs processed per ms using frame scheduling and frames to which these MBs belong

(b) Number of MBs processed per ms using frame scheduling and the priority policy

Fig. 8. Results for frame scheduling and priority policy for FHD Rush Hour on a 16-core processor. Different gray scales represent different frames.

is 58.5 ms, using the FHD Rush Hour sequence with 16 cores. Using the frame scheduling policy, the latency drops to 15.1 ms. This latency is further reduced to 9.2 ms when the priority policy is applied together with frame scheduling. This is 0.1 ms longer than the latency of the 2D-Wave, which decodes frames one-by-one. Fig. 8(b) depicts the number of MBs processed per ms when this feature is used.

Two scenarios were used to analyze the impact of frame scheduling and priority on the scalability. The chosen scenarios use 3 and 6 frames in flight, with and without frame priority. Figs. 9(a) and 9(b) depict the impact of the presented techniques on the scalability. 2D-Wave (2DW) and 3D-Wave (3DW) scalability results are presented as guidelines. In Fig. 9, FS refers to the frame scheduling. The addition of frame priority has no significant impact on the scalability and therefore not shown, as it would decrease legibility. The reported scalability is based on the 2D-Wave execution time on a single core.

Fig. 9(a) shows that 6 frames in flight are not enough to leverage a 64-core system when decoding an SD sequence. The maximum speedup of 23 is the result of the relatively low amount of MB-level parallelism of SD frames. As presented in Fig. 7(a), the 2D-Wave has a maximum speedup of 8. For HD (figure not shown), the performance when 6 frames in flight are allowed is already close to the performance of the original 3D-Wave. The maximum speedups are 24 and 45, for three and six frames in flight, respectively. The latter is 92% of the maximum 3D-Wave speedup. For FHD, depicted in Fig. 9(b), allowing three frames in flight provides a speedup of 46. When 6 frames are used, the difference between the frame scheduler enabled and the original 3D-Wave is only 1%.

5.3   Bandwidth Requirements

In this section, the intra-chip bandwidth requirements for the 3D-Wave and its frame scheduling and priority policies are reported. The amount of data traffic

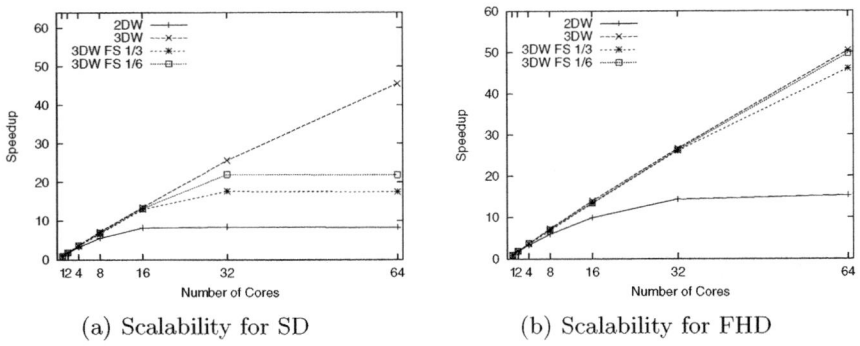

(a) Scalability for SD

(b) Scalability for FHD

Fig. 9. Frame scheduling and priority scalability results of the Rush Hour 25-frame sequence

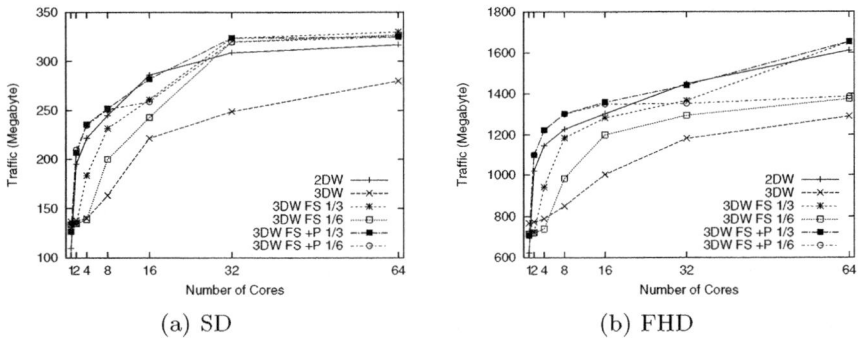

(a) SD

(b) FHD

Fig. 10. Frame scheduling and priority data traffic results for Rush Hour sequence

between L2 and L1 data caches is measured. Accesses to main memory are not reported by the simulator.

The effects of frame scheduling and priority policies on data traffic between L2 and L1 data caches are depicted in Fig. 10(a) and 10(b). The figures depict the required data traffic for SD and FHD resolutions, respectively. In the figures, FS refers to the frame scheduling while P refers to the use of frame priority.

Data locality decreases as the number of cores increases, because the task scheduler does not take into account data locality when assigning a task to a core (except with the tail submit strategy). This decrease in the locality contributes to traffic increase. Due to these effects, the 3D-Wave increases the data traffic by approximately 104%, 82%, and 68% when going from 1 to 64 cores, for SD, HD, and FHD, respectively.

Surprisingly, the original 3D-Wave requires the least communication between L2 and L1 data caches for 8 cores or more. It is approximately 20% to 30% (from SD to FHD) more data traffic efficient than the original 2D-Wave, for 16 cores or more. This is caused by the high data locality of the original 3D-Wave technique.

The 3D-Wave implementation fires new frames as soon as their dependencies are met. This increases the probability of the reference areas of a MB to be present in the system. The probability increases because nearby area of several frames are decoded together, so the reference area is still present in data caches of other cores. This reduces the data traffic because the motion compensation (inter-frame dependency) requires a significant portion of data to be copied from previous frames.

The use of FS and Priority has a negative impact on the L2 to L1 data cache traffic. The use of FS and Priority decreases the data locality, as they increase the time between processing MBs from co-located areas of consecutive frames. However, when the number of frames are enough to sustain a good scalability, the increased data traffic when using FS and Priority is still lower than the data traffic of 2D-Wave implementation. For SD, the data traffic for FS and Priority is higher than the 2D-Wave when the available parallelism is not enough to leverage for 32 and 64 cores. The same happens for the HD using only 3 frames in flight. For FHD, 2D-Wave is the technique that requires most data traffic, together with FS for 3 frames in flight. When the number of frames in flight are enough to leverage to 32 or 64 cores, FS is 4 to 12% more efficient than 2D-Wave. FS and Priority can be 3 to 6% data traffic less efficient than 2D-Wave in the cases when number of frames in flight are insufficient to leverage to the number of cores.

With the data traffic results it is possible to calculate the L2 to L1 bandwidth requirements. The bandwidth is calculated by dividing the total traffic by the time to decode the sequence in seconds. The total amount of intra chip bandwidth required for 64 cores is 21 GB/s for all resolutions of Rush Hour sequence. The bandwidth is independent of the resolution because the number of MBs decoded per time unit per core is the same.

5.4   Impact of the Memory Latency

The type of interconnection used, and the number of cores in the system both influence the memory latency. For increasing number of cores, also the latency of a L2 to L1 data transfer increases. In this section we analyze the impact of this latency on the performance. One second (25 frames) of the Rush Hour sequence, in all three available resolutions, was decoded while with several average memory latencies.

In the previous experiments the average L2 data cache latency was set to 40 cycles. In this experiment the Average Memory Latency (AML) ranges from 40 to 100 cycles in steps of 10 cycles. The latency of the interconnect between L1 and L2 is modelled by adding additional delay cycles to the AML of the L2 cache.

Fig. 11(a) depicts the scalability results for FHD resolution. That is, for each AML, the performance using X cores is compared to the performance using one core. The results show that the memory latency does not significantly affect the scalability. For 64 cores, increasing the AML from 40 to 100 cycles decreases the scalability by 10%. However, the scalability does not equal the absolute

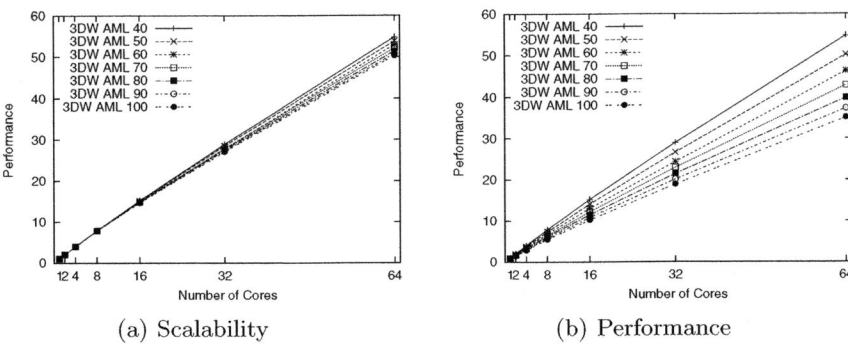

(a) Scalability   (b) Performance

Fig. 11. Scalability and performance for different Average Memory Latency (AML) values, using the 25 frame Rush Hour FHD sequence. In the scalability graph the performance is relative to the execution on a single core, but with the same AML. In the performance graph all performances are relative to the execution on a single core with an AML of 40 cycles.

performance. In Fig. 11(b) the performance is depicted using the execution time one a single core with an AML of 40 cycles as baseline. The performances still scale the same, but the performance for one core is different for every line (in contrast to Fig. 11(a)). The graph shows that in total the system's performance is decreased significantly. That means that large systems might be infeasible if the memory latency increases too much.

5.5   Impact of the L1 Cache Size

We analyzed the influence of the L1 data cache size on the scalability and the amount of L2-L1 traffic. The baseline system has L1 data caches of 64KB, 4-way set-associative, with LRU replacement, and write allocate. By modifying the number of sets in the cache systems with different cache sizes, i.e., 12, 32, 64, 128, and 256KB, were simulated. The results for FHD resolution are depicted in Fig. 12(a). The depicted performance are relative to the decoding time on a single core with the baseline 64KB L1 cache.

The systems with 16KB and 32KB caches have a large performance drop of approximately 45% and 30%, respectively, for any number of cores. The reason for this is depicted in Fig. 12(b), which presents the L1-L2 cache data traffic for FHD resolution. Compared to a system with 64KB caches, the system with 16KB caches has between 3.1 and 4.7 times more traffic while the system with 32KB caches has between 1.8 and 2.5 times more traffic. Those huge increases in data traffic are due to cache misses. For FHD resolution, one MB line occupies 45KB. Preferably, the caches should be able to store more then one MB line, as the data of each line is used in the decoding of the next line and serves as input for the motion compensation in the next frames. For FHD, the 16KB and 32 KB caches suffer greatly from data trashing. As a result there are a lot of write backs to the the L2 cache as well as reads. For smaller resolutions the effects are less.

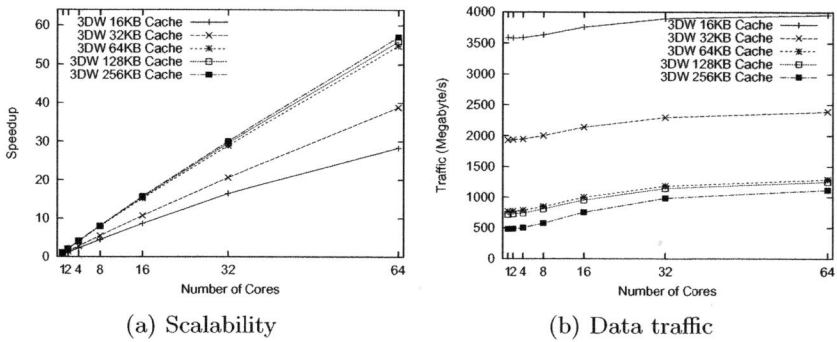

(a) Scalability   (b) Data traffic

Fig. 12. Impact of the L1 cache size on performance and L1-L2 traffic for a 25 frame Rush Hour FHD sequence

For example, for SD resolution using 16KB L1 caches the data traffic increases between 1.19 and 1.66 compared to the baseline with 64KB caches. With 32KB caches, the traffic increases only by approximately 7%.

Using caches larger than 64KB provides small performance gains (up to 4%). The reason for this is again the size of a MB line. Once the dataset fits in the cache, the application behaves like a memory stream application and makes no use of the additional memory space. This is also reflected in the data traffic graph. For FHD, the system with 256KB caches has 13 to 27% less traffic than the 64KB system. For the lower resolutions, the traffic is reduced by at most 10% and the performance gain is at most 4%.

5.6   Impact of the Parallelization Overhead

Alvarez et al. [15] implemented the 2D-Wave approach on an architecture with 64 dual core IA-64 processors. Their results show that the scalability is severely limited by the thread synchronization and management overhead, i.e., the time it takes to submit/retrieve a task to/from the task pool. On their platform it takes up to 9 times as long to submit/retrieve a task as it takes to decode a MB. To analyze the impact of the TLP overhead on the scalability of the 3D-Wave, we replicate this TLP overhead by increasing the Task Pool Library by adding dummy calculation.

The inserted extra overheads are 10%, 20%, 30%, 40%, 50%, and 100% of the average MB decoding time, which is 4900 cycles. Because of the Tail Submit enhancement not every MB requests or submits a task to the Thread Pool. This causes a total performance overhead of only 3% for a single core when comparing the 100% TPL overhead against the baseline 3D-Wave. The effects of this increased overhead is depicted on Figs. 13(a), and 13(b), for SD and FHD resolutions, respectively.

The results for SD resolution show the impact of the increase overhead on the scalability. For 32 cores the scalability is considerably reduced when the overhead is 40% or more. For 64 cores the effects of the extra overhead reduces

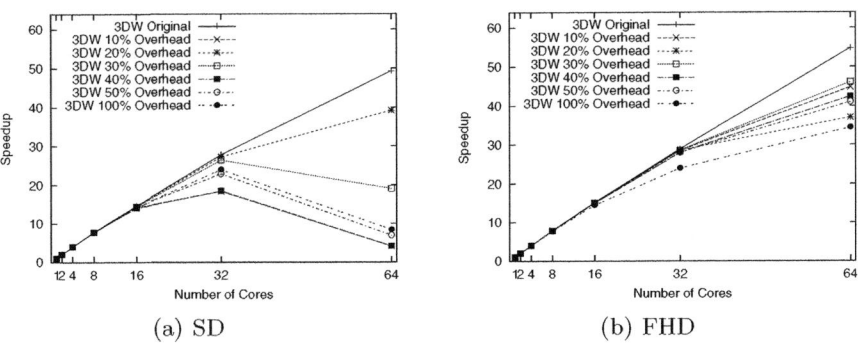

(a) SD   (b) FHD

Fig. 13. TPL overhead effects on scalability for Rush Hour frames

the scalability. The SD resolution is very affected with the increased overhead because the intra frame resolution is comparatively low and the lines are short, which increases task submition per frame. For the HD resolution (figure not shown) the increase in overhead limits the scalability to 32 cores while for FHD it slows down the scalability, but does not limit it. As the resolution increases the requests to TPL per MB ratio decreases and so the impact of the extra overhead. These results show the drastic effects of the overhead on the scalability, even with enhancements that reduces the requests to the parallelization support.

5.7   CABAC Accelerator Requirements

Broadly speaking, H.264 decoding consists of two parts: entropy (CABAC) decoding and MB decoding. CABAC decoding of a single slice/frame is largely sequential while in this paper we have shown that MB decoding is highly parallel. We therefore assumed that CABAC decoding is performed by a specific accelerator. In this section we evaluate the performance required of such an accelerator to allow the 3D-Wave to scale to a large number of cores.

Fig. 14 depicts the speedup as a function of the number of (MB decoding) cores for different speeds of the CABAC accelerator. The baseline accelerator, corresponding to the accelerator labeled "no speedup", is assumed to have the same performance as the TM3270 TriMedia processor. These results were obtained using a trace-driven, abstract-level simulator that schedules the threads given the CABAC and MB dependencies and their processing times. The traces have been obtained using the simulator described in Section 3 and used in the previous sections.

The results show that if CABAC decoding is not accelerated, then the speedup is limited to 7.5, no matter how many cores are employed. Quadrupling the speed of the CABAC accelerator improves the overall performance by a similar factor, achieving a speedup of almost 30 on 64 cores. When CABAC decoding is accelerated by a factor of 8, the speedup of 53.8 on 64 cores is almost the same as the results presented previously which did not consider CABAC. There are several proposals [16] that achieve such a speedup for CABAC decoding. This shows

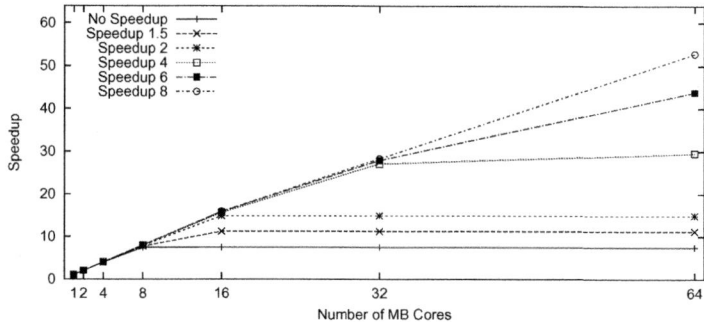

Fig. 14. Maximum scalability per CABAC processor and accelerators

that the CABAC processing does not pose a limitation on the scalability of the
3D-Wave technique. We remark that the 3D-Wave also allows employing multiple CABAC accelerators, since different slices/frames can be CABAC decoded
in parallel, as entropy-decoding dependencies do not cross slice/frame borders.

6   Conclusions

Future CMPs will contain dozens if not hundreds of cores. For such systems,
developing parallel applications that can harness them is the key challenge. In
this paper we have contributed to this challenge by presenting a highly scalable
parallel implementation of H.264 decoding. While a many-core is not necessary
to achieve real-time FHD video decoding, it is likely that future video coding
standards will be computationally more intensive and will be similarly block-
oriented motion-compensation-based. Furthermore, decoding is part of encoding
and real-time encoding is still a challenge. In addition, emerging applications
such as 3D TV are likely to be based on current video coding standards.

   While the idea behind the 3D-Wave was presented in our previous work, in
this paper we have contributed by providing an actual implementation and by
providing exhaustive simulation results. Implementing the 3D-Wave required,
for example, developing a subscription mechanism where MBs are subscribed to
a so-called Kick-off List associated with the MBs in the reference frame(s) they
depend on. Several optimizations have been performed to reduce the overhead
of this mechanism. For example, vector prediction is skipped if it has already
been performed and if two reference MBs are in the same reference frame, only
the one that will be decoded last is added to the list.

   The simulation results show that the 3D-Wave implementation scales almost
perfectly up to 64 cores. More cores could not be simulated due to limitations of
the simulator. Furthermore, one of the main reasons why the speedup is slightly
less than linear is that at the beginning and at the end of decoding a sequence
of 25 frames, not all the cores can be used because little TLP is available. In a
real sequence these periods are negligible. The presented frame scheduling and

priority policies reduce the number of frames in flight and the frame latency. By applying these policies, the frame latency of the 3D-Wave is only 0.1 ms (about 1%) longer than that of the 2D-Wave.

We also measured the amount of data traffic shared L2 and the private L1 data caches. Obviously, increasing the number of cores increases the L2-L1 data traffic, since the cores have to communicate via the L2 cache. 64 cores generate approximately the same amount of L2-L1 traffic as 32 cores, however, and both produce roughly twice as much traffic as a single core. To our initial surprise, the original 3D-Wave generates the least amount of L2-L1 data traffic. This is because the original 3D-Wave exploits the data reuse between a MB and its reference MBs, more so than the 2D-Wave and the 3D-Wave with frame scheduling and priority.

Next we have analyzed the impact of the memory latency and of the L1 cache size. While increasing the average memory latency (AML) hardly affects the scalability (i.e., the speedup of the 3D-Wave running on p cores over the 3D-Wave running on a single core), it of course reduces the performance. Doubling the AML from 40 to 80 cycles reduces the performance on 64 cores by approximately 25%. The results for different L1 data cache sizes show that a 64KB data cache is necessary and sufficient to keep the active working set in cache. Smaller L1 data caches significantly reduce the performance, while larger L1 data caches provide little improvement. The reason is that a single line of MBs is 45KB for FHD and, therefore, caches larger than 45KB can exploit the data reuse between a MB line and the next MB line.

In addition, we have analyzed the impact of the parallelization overhead by artificially increasing the time it takes to submit/retrieve a task to/from the task pool. The 3D-Wave exploits medium-grain TLP (decoding a single MB takes roughly 5000 cycles on the TM3270), so task submission/retrieval should not take too much time. Because of the tail submit optimization, however, not for every MB a task is submitted to the task pool. The results show that even when the parallelization overhead is 50% of the MB decoding time (about 2500 cycles), the speedup on 64 cores is still higher than 41 for FHD. For SD, because it exhibits less TLP and therefore submits more tasks per MB, the effects are more dramatic.

Finally, we have analyzed the performance required of a CABAC accelerator so that CABAC decoding does not become the bottleneck that limits the scalability of the 3D-Wave. The results show that if CABAC decoding is performed by a core with the same speed as the other cores, then the speedup is limited to 7.5, no matter how many cores are employed. If CABAC decoding is accelerated by a factor of 8, however, the speedup for 64 cores is almost the same as when CABAC decoding is not considered but performed beforehand.

Future work includes the development of an automatic frame scheduling technique that only starts to decode a new frame if some cores are idle because of insufficient TLP, the implementation of the 3D-Wave on other platforms such as the Cell and GPGPUs, and the implementation of the 3D-Wave in the encoder. A 3D-Wave implementation of the encoder would provide high definition, low latency encoding on multicores.

Acknowledgment

This work was performed while the first author was visiting NXP Semiconductors and it was partially supported by the European Commission in the context of the SARC integrated project #27648 (FP6), the Ministry of Science of Spain and European Union (FEDER funds) under contract TIC-2004-07739-C02-01, and the European Network of Excellence on High-Performance Embedded Architecture and Compilation (HiPEAC). The authors would like to thank Anirban Lahiri from NXP for his collaboration on the experiments.

References

1. Okano, F., Kanazawa, M., Mitani, K., Hamasaki, K., Sugawara, M., Seino, M., Mochimaru, A., Doi, K.: Ultrahigh-Definition Television System With 4000 Scanning Lines. In: Proc. of NAB Broadcast Engineering Conf., pp. 437–440 (2004)
2. Drose, M., Clemens, C., Sikora, T.: Extending Single-View Scalable Video Coding to Multi-View Based on H. 264/AVC. In: 2006 IEEE Inter. Conf. on Image Processing, pp. 2977–2980 (2006)
3. Meenderinck, C., Azevedo, A., Juurlink, B., Alvarez, M., Ramirez, A.: Parallel Scalability of Video Decoders. Journal of Signal Processing Systems (August 2008)
4. Rodriguez, A., Gonzalez, A., Malumbres, M.P.: Hierarchical Parallelization of an H.264/AVC Video Encoder. In: Proc. Int. Symp. on Parallel Computing in Electrical Engineering, pp. 363–368 (2006)
5. Chen, Y.K., Li, E.Q., Zhou, X., Ge, S.: Implementation of H.264 Encoder and Decoder on Personal Computers. Journal of Visual Communications and Image Representation 17 (2006)
6. van der Tol, E., Jaspers, E., Gelderblom, R.: Mapping of H.264 Decoding on a Multiprocessor Architecture. In: Proc. SPIE Conf. on Image and Video Communications and Processing (2003)
7. International Standard of Joint Video Specification (ITU-T Rec. H. 264— ISO/IEC 14496-10 AVC) (2005)
8. Oelbaum, T., Baroncini, V., Tan, T.K., Fenimore, C.: Subjective Quality Assessment of the Emerging AVC/H.264 Video Coding Standard. In: Int. Broadcast Conf., IBC (2004)
9. Alvarez, M., Salami, E., Ramirez, A., Valero, M.: A Performance Characterization of High Definition Digital Video Decoding using H.264/AVC. In: Proc. IEEE Int. Workload Characterization Symp., pp. 24–33 (2005)
10. Ostermann, J., Bormans, J., List, P., Marpe, D., Narroschke, M., Pereira, F., Stockhammer, T., Wedi, T.: Video Coding with H.264/AVC: Tools, Performance, and Complexity. IEEE Circuits and Systems Magazine 4(1), 7–28 (2004)
11. van de Waerdt, J., Vassiliadis, S., Das, S., Mirolo, S., Yen, C., Zhong, B., Basto, C., van Itegem, J., Amirtharaj, D., Kalra, K., et al.: The TM3270 Media-Processor. In: MICRO 2005: Proc. of the 38th Inter. Symp. on Microarchitecture, pp. 331–342 (November 2005)
12. X264. A Free H.264/AVC Encoder
13. Alvarez, M., Salami, E., Ramirez, A., Valero, M.: HD-VideoBench: A Benchmark for Evaluating High Definition Digital Video Applications. In: Proc. IEEE Int. Symp. on Workload Characterization (2007)

14. Hoogerbrugge, J., Terechko, A.: A Multithreaded Multicore System for Embedded Media Processing. Trans. on High-Performance Embedded Architectures and Compilers 4(2) (2009)
15. Alvarez, M., Ramirez, A., Valero, M., Meenderinck, C., Azevedo, A., Juurlink, B.: Performance Evaluation of Macroblock-level Parallelization of H.264 Decoding on a CC-NUMA Multiprocessor Architecture. In: Proc. of the 4CCC: 4th Colombian Computing Conf. (April 2009)
16. Osorio, R.R., Bruguera, J.D.: An FPGA Architecture for CABAC Decoding in Manycore Systems. In: Proc. of IEEE Application-Specific Systems, Architectures and Processors, pp. 293–298 (July 2008)

Communication Based Proactive Link Power Management*

Sai Prashanth Muralidhara and Mahmut Kandemir

Department of Computer Science and Engineering
Pennsylvania State University, University Park, PA 16802, USA
{smuralid,kandemir}@cse.psu.edu

Abstract. As the number of cores in CMPs increases, NoC is projected to be the dominant communication fabric. Increase in the number of cores brings an important issue to the forefront, the issue of chip power consumption, which is projected to increase rapidly with the increase in number of cores. Since NoC infrastructure contributes significantly to the total chip power consumption, reducing NoC power is crucial. While circuit level techniques are important in reducing NoC power, architectural and software level approaches can be very effective in optimizing power consumption. Any such technique power saving technique should be scalable and have minimal adverse impact on performance. We propose a dynamic, communication link usage based, proactive link power management scheme. This scheme, using a Markov model, proactively manages communication link turn-ons and turn-offs, which results in negligible performance degradation and significant power savings. We show that our prediction scheme is about 98% accurate for the SPEC OMP benchmarks and about 93% over all applications experimented. This accuracy helps us achieve link power savings of up to 44% and an average link power savings of 23.5%. More importantly, it incurs performance penalties as low as 0.3% on average.

1 Introduction

Power inefficiency coupled with limited instruction level parallelism changed the trend from increasing single core frequencies to having multiple relatively simpler cores on a single chip. Driven by this need to have power efficient systems, these chip multiprocessors (CMPs) have become the order of the day [26] [12] [35] [3]. With the projected increase in the number of cores in CMPs [35], limited scalability of bus structures and the need for more on-chip communication bandwidth have become major issues. These issues have given rise to network-on-chip (NoC) [6] [9] [11], which is a more scalable on-chip communication fabric.

The NoC framework addresses the scalability issue effectively. However, in such an NoC based CMP, the issue of power consumption can become a serious limiting factor. This is especially true since the power consumption is projected

---

* This research is supported in part by NSF grants 0811687, 0720645, 0720749, 0702519, 0444345 and a grant from GSRC.

P. Stenström (Ed.): Transactions on HiPEAC IV, LNCS 6760, pp. 135–154, 2011.
© Springer-Verlag Berlin Heidelberg 2011

to increase rapidly as the size of NoCs increase. Therefore, there is a need to develop a wide variety of techniques to reduce chip power consumption.

A major contributor to chip power consumption is the NoC infrastructure. We found that, the NoC framework is responsible for as much as nearly 30% of the total chip power consumption. Communication links form a significant part of an NoC framework and their count increases with the number of cores in a CMP. This calls for power-aware design and power saving schemes which target not only power efficient cores but also power efficient link usage. Since, with the increase in the number of cores and with a similar increase in the number of communication links, possibility of more links being inactive increases dramatically, there is a need for a scalable power saving scheme which can exploit this effectively. Although circuit level and localized techniques are effective to an extent, they are not proactive, and therefore, lose out on important power saving opportunities. In this paper, we propose a completely proactive scheme aimed at link power management.

There have been significant research efforts aimed at characterizing the execution intervals of single-threaded applications into phases [29]. A program phase analysis is a technique of characterizing the program execution intervals into phases based on the similarity in their behavior. In the past, phase characterization has been used in the context of performance [29] [7] and power [15] [13]. We propose that execution of a multi-threaded application on an NoC based CMP can be characterized into phases based on the similarity across inter-core communication patterns. In this context, by communication pattern, we mean the usage of communication links in the system during execution. In case of a shared NUCA cache [17], which we consider, this usage of communication links is due to shared cache accesses and corresponding coherence traffic. The present circuit-level and localized schemes do not use this high level phase characterization information in their link power management. We propose to use the aforementioned phase characterization to implement a Markov based prediction scheme, which predicts the link usage of the next interval. This prediction can be used by a proactive link power management scheme to turn off predicted unused links and also to turn on links that are predicted to be used. The key advantage of this scheme is that, the links that are predicted to be used can be turned on ahead of time such that the turn-on latency is hidden and the performance remains unaltered. We show that this prediction based power management scheme can be very beneficial in reducing link energy consumption. We also note that this power saving scheme is remarkably scalable and can achieve increased power savings with increase in the number of on-chip cores and communication links.

We wish to note three other important points here. Firstly, one of the important goals of our scheme, apart from minimizing energy consumption, is also to minimize the adverse impact on performance. We later show that, our scheme is very accurate in predicting link usage and hence has almost negligible performance impact. Secondly, our scheme can work along with other circuit-level and localized hardware schemes to further maximize the benefits achieved.

Thirdly, as we illustrate later, our scheme is highly scalable and is generic enough to be adaptable across different NoC structures. To summarize, the main contributions of this paper are as follows:

- We classify the execution intervals of a multithreaded application executing on two-dimensional mesh based CMP into phases during runtime based on their similarity in communication link usage.
- We use this classification to implement a Markov prediction based, proactive link power saving scheme. More precisely, we show that a small prediction table can be maintained to make accurate predictions about the future communication link usage during runtime.
- We show that our prediction scheme is highly accurate achieving a prediction accuracy of over 98% in most applications and an average prediction accuracy of about 93% over all the applications we tested. As a result of this high prediction accuracy, the performance penalty incurred by our power management scheme is practically negligible, with an average value of 0.3%. Finally, we present the reduction in energy consumption, which is about 40% for two of the applications. We also present the average energy savings we achieve, which is about 23.5%.

The rest of the paper is organized as follows. Section 2 briefly summarizes the related work pertaining to our area. Section 3 provides a brief description of the NoC based CMP architecture we consider throughout this paper. Section 4 makes a case for a prediction based approach to link power optimization, and Section 5 describes the cache bank access pattern. Section 6 provides a detailed description of phase classification based on link usage. Section 7 talks about the prediction based schemes we employ, and Section 8 provides a detailed description of how our power management scheme is implemented. Section 9 discusses the performance aspect of our scheme. Section 10 talks about the experimental setup, methodology, and results. Finally, we summarize and conclude with Section 11.

2   Related Work

With the growth of CMPs, there have been numerous efforts to optimize power in these systems both in the bus based architectures and the NoC based architectures. Isci et al analyze global dynamic power management policies for CMPs and propose dynamic schemes that perform better than static schemes [14]. Sharkey et al show that global power management outperforms local core-level schemes [28]. Li and Martinez present a scheme to dynamically optimize power consumption of a parallel application executing on a CMP under a given performance constraint [22]. There have been similar efforts to develop power management strategies in the context of NoCs. For example, Benini et al describe an energy-efficient interconnect framework design [4]. By comparison, Simunic et al use closed-loop control concepts to formulate a network-centric power management scheme [31]. There have also been prior research efforts targeting link power savings. Soteriou and Peh propose a dynamic power management scheme to turn off and turn on network links in a distributed fashion depending on network utilization [33]. Shin et al present a static scheme using voltage scalable links to optimize energy consumption [30]. Shang et al apply dynamic voltage scaling to optimize link energy consumption [27]. In comparison, Li et al use profile information to implement a compiler based scheme which increases the link idle periods, thereby enabling the hardware schemes to be more effective in saving power [21]. They also propose a compiler-directed proactive scheme which analyzes the program during compile time and inserts link-activate and turn-off calls [20]. Our scheme differs from these link power management schemes in being a dynamic, runtime scheme which proactively turns off and turns on the interconnection links based on the prediction made by our online prediction module. Also, our dynamic scheme is more general and more widely applicable than compiler-based schemes which can be used only when the source code is available and statically analyzable.

Another related area of work is program phase analysis. Sherwood et al propose the concept of identifying repetitive execution intervals called phases using basic block vector (BBV) similarity [29]. Isci and Martonosi propose a phase analysis scheme for power and demonstrate that performance counter based schemes perform much better than control-flow based schemes such as those based on basic block vector (BBV) analysis when it comes to power [15]. There have been other attempts to use control flow information for program phase classification and consequent performance and power optimizations [13] [7]. Dhodapkar and Smith compare some of these techniques to detect program phases [8]. Perelman et al present a method to utilize phase analysis for parallel applications running on shared memory processors [25].

In this work, we use a flavor of phase characterization in our power management scheme but with important differences. First of all, we use inter-core communication as the basis for our phase characterization of multi-threaded applications. More precisely, intervals of execution which have similar communication patterns are characterized into a single phase. Secondly, we use a more fine grained form of phase analysis in our scheme, wherein, the length of instruction interval used is much shorter than those used in the prior schemes. This is because, we observed that, the inter-core communication, which essentially includes shared cache accesses and coherence traffic, exhibits repetitive behavior but only when looked at in shorter intervals. We further elaborate on this aspect in later sections. In essence, our goal is to identify repetitive behavior of a parallel application execution based on its inter-core communication pattern on the underlying NoC that connects the CMP nodes.

3   Target Architecture

We consider a two-dimensional mesh based NoC that connects the nodes of a CMP, although our approach is equally applicable to other NoC structures. In this architecture, each node (core) has a private level 1 (L1) cache. On the other hand, the level 2 (L2) cache is shared among all the cores and is banked with each core containing an L2 bank. Figure 1 shows a 4×4 mesh structure we use to convey our idea. Most of the time, unless otherwise mentioned, we consider

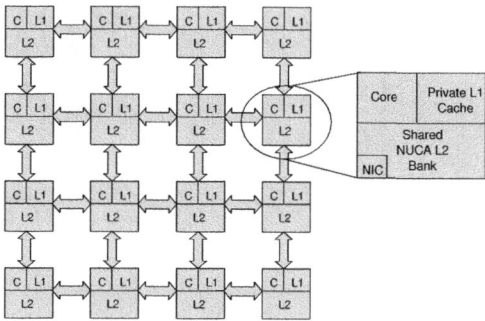

Fig. 1. A 4×4 mesh NoC based CMP. Note that this is a block diagram and not the actual layout, and the routers are not shown for clarity.

this 16 core, 4×4 mesh based CMP with a shared L2 cache which is 16 banked with each of the 16 cores containing an L2 bank. We use a static NUCA [17] scheme in this work although our scheme can be similarly used with dynamic NUCA [17] as well. We would like to emphasize that, in this paper, by "inter-core communication", we always mean an access made by a core to some other core's L2 bank.

4   Empirical Motivation

For any scheme aimed at link power savings to succeed, there should be consider-able periods of execution during which some links are unused. If a multi-threaded application executing on an NoC based CMP uses all of the communication links during the entire period of execution, then any scheme aimed at saving link power will have limited returns. Fortunately, that is not the case in real applications. We profiled several parallel benchmarks from the SPEC OMP [2], NAS [1] and Splash2 [32] benchmark suites running on a 4×4 mesh architecture described in Figure 1. Profiling is done such that the execution is broken down into intervals of 5000 instructions, and links used during these intervals are recorded at the end of each such interval. We computed the percentage of such intervals dur-ing which at least some of the links in the interconnect network are not in use. Figure 2(a) shows our profiling results. As can be observed clearly, during a large percentage of intervals, at least some links are unused. Specifically, on average, in only 10% of intervals, all communication links are used. This is due mainly to the data allocation and the resulting cache bank access pattern exhibited by a program execution as we show in the next section. We also observed that the percentage increases slightly if the instruction interval is shortened. The number of links that are unused in such intervals determine the "window of opportunity", which in other words, means the amount of power savings that can potentially be extracted. The profiling results above serve as the key motivating factor for the scheme we propose in the coming sections.

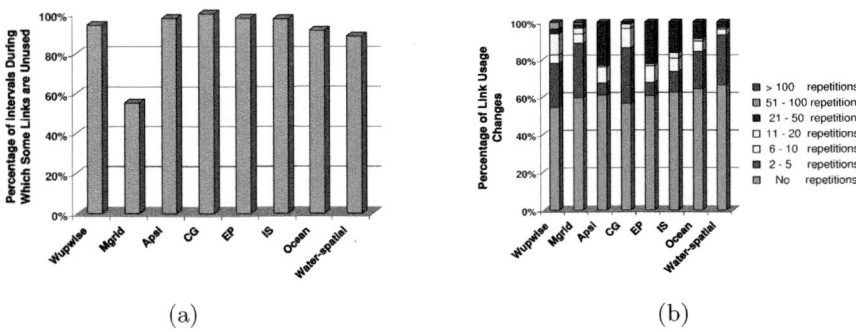

Fig. 2. (a) shows the percentage nof intervals during which at least a few links are unused. We see that, on average, in only about 10% of intervals, all links are used. (b) shows the number of intervals, a new link usage pattern lasts (repeats) before it changes again to a different usage pattern.

Another key factor which needs to be considered is the "repetitive phase behavior" and hence possible "predictability" in parallel application's link usage. During execution, every time a new link usage pattern occurs, an important question is how long does that link usage pattern last before it changes again. Figure 2(b) shows the distribution of the number of times a link usage pattern repeats before there is a change. On average, after 10% of link usage changes, link usage remains the same for 21 to 50 intervals. After 3% of link usage changes, the usage pattern remains the same for 11 to 20 intervals; after 6.6% changes, the same usage remains for 6 to 10 intervals and after 19.1% changes, 2 to 5 times. Overall, on average, whenever a new link usage pattern arises, on nearly 40% of occasions, it remains for more than one interval before it changes again. It is important to note that, we are talking about instruction intervals (intervals of 5000 instructions) here and hence the link usage pattern repeating twice implies that the link usage remains the same for 2×5000, which is for 10,000 instructions. This is an important statistic which hints at repetitiveness and predictability in link usage patterns and possible success of predictive schemes. As we show in the next section, this predictability and repetitiveness results from the data allocation and the cache bank access pattern exhibited by the program execution.

5   Cache Bank Access Pattern

In order to better understand the predictability in link usage patterns and the non-usage of several links during large parts of program execution, we studied how the cores access different L2 cache banks. We executed MGrid application from the SPEC OMP [2] benchmark suite and studied which L2 cache banks are accessed by which cores during each execution interval. Figure 3 shows how different cores access the cache bank present on node 1 during eight consecutive execution intervals. As can be clearly seen, the majority of the accesses to

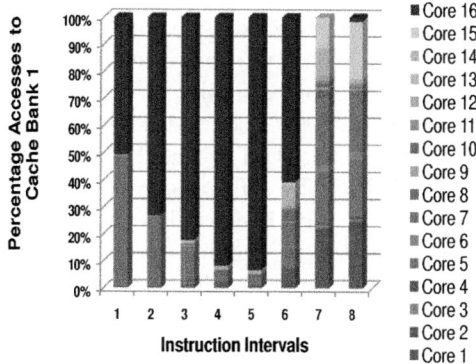

Fig. 3. Access pattern to cache bank 1. Most of the accesses to cache bank 1 are made by core 1.

*cachebank*1 are made by *core*16 followed by *core*5. More importantly, this cache bank access pattern exhibits repetitive behavior across execution intervals as can be seen in Figure 3. This phase behavior in cache bank access manifests into corresponding phase behavior in link usage pattern as shown in Section 4.

6   Link Usage Based Phase Classification

Repetitive behavior is an execution characteristic of most applications. This repetitive behavior can be on the basis of similarity in the basic blocks touched or on the basis of similarity in performance metrics such as cache misses [15]. We use inter-core communication as the basis for characterizing the program execution into phases. Therefore, we classify the execution intervals into phases based on communication link usage. Each execution interval is an interval of 5000 instructions in our classification scheme. Since communication pattern is an application characteristic, instruction interval can be customized for an individual application by using profiling results. Although this interval length can be configured and further tuned as mentioned above, we found that, an interval of 5000 instructions works well for all applications we tested since it captures the repetitive behavior in inter-core communication pattern well. The usage pattern of communication links during execution depends on the data allocations and the data access patterns exhibited by the application, which manifests itself as L2 bank accesses. This means that, as the execution of a parallel application progresses, the L2 cache accesses and hence the communication link usage goes through phases. In this work, we represent the communication link usage in the form of a vector called "Link Vector", and carry out our phase characterization using this novel concept.

6.1   Link Vector

We represent the state of all the links in our NoC in the form of a link vector. Each bit in a link vector represents a link in the NoC and there is bit for every link. Consequently, the number of bits in the link vector is the same as the number in links in the on-chip network. Bit value 1 implies a used state, which means the link is being exercised, and a bit value of 0 implies an unused state, which means the link is idle. For example, in the case of NoC illustrated in Figure 1, the corresponding link vector contains 24 bits with each bit representing the current state of a link in the 4×4 mesh. The link vector of an execution interval is computed by ORing the link usage of all the instructions executed during the instruction interval. This essentially means that, even if a link is used only once during the entire interval, the link vector of the interval denotes that link as being used during the interval. Hence the motivation to have shorter instruction intervals when compared to considerably longer instruction intervals used in other phase characterization works [15] [29]. The effect of aforementioned scenario, where a link which is used only once during the interval and still being considered as used during the entire interval, has been minimized considerably by having shorter instruction intervals.

6.2   Runtime Classification

A simple way to identify phases is by using an identifier called "phase id" and a simple way to store phase information is by maintaining a "phase table", with each row containing the link vector which represents the phase and a uniquely assigned phase identifier. A runtime phase classification scheme would thus involve recording all the phases that have been previously encountered in the phase table and (at the end of every new interval) comparing the interval's link vector with the link vectors of the previously-recorded phases (which essentially involves searching the phase table). If there is a match, then that interval is classified as belonging to that phase. If a match is not found, it is a new phase and is added to the phase table with the link vector of the interval and a newly assigned unique phase id. This process can be performed dynamically making it a runtime classification scheme.

6.3   Classification Example

Figure 4(a) shows a snapshot of the link vectors (of intervals) during a period of execution of the Wupwise benchmark from the SPEC OMP benchmark suite [2]. In this figure, "count", present in each row, indicates the number of contiguous intervals during which the same link vector repeats. The classification (mapping) of intervals to phases which is based on the link vector similarity can be noted.

7   Markov Based Prediction

After classifying the intervals into phases as described in the last section, we use a Markov based prediction mechanism to predict the probable link vector of the next interval just before the end of the current interval. Markov based schemes have been used in the past to implement BBV (basic block vector) based phase prediction [19]. This prediction essentially provides the probable link usage

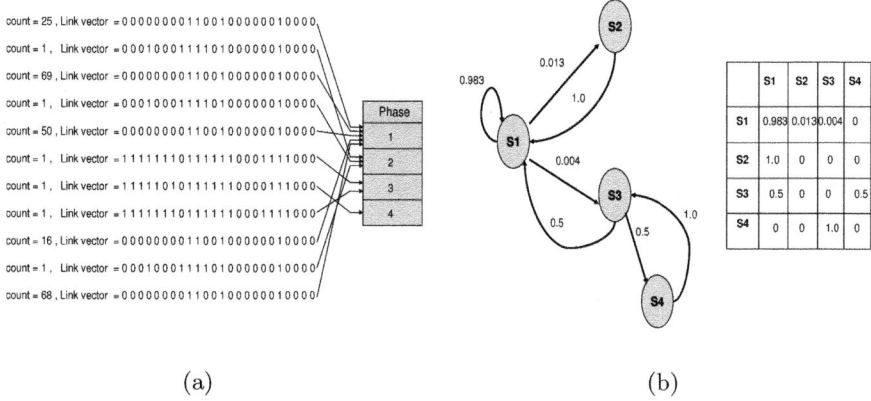

(a)   (b)

Fig. 4. (a) shows a snapshot of link vectors of intervals during a period of execution of the Wupwise multi-threaded benchmark and the phases they map to. Mapping is done based on link vector similarity. (b) depicts a Markov based transition graph and the corresponding prediction table. Prediction is made based on the probabilities contained in the prediction table. The transition graph shows the transition probabilities pictorially.

information of the next interval. This, in turn can be used to proactively turn off the links which are predicted to be not used and pre-activate links that are predicted to be used. This pre-activation is done just ahead of time so that the activation latency is hidden and the link is ready for use when the next interval begins. If the prediction turns out to be correct, we stand to save power. However, if the prediction turns out to be wrong, there is a two-fold penalty. First, there is the performance penalty in waiting for the correct links to power on which had been turned off because of the misprediction. Secondly, there is also the power penalty in turning off and then turning on additional links. Therefore, prediction accuracies are crucial to the effectiveness of this scheme. We describe two prediction schemes based on the Markov model in the next two subsections.

7.1   Basic Markov Prediction

Markov model is a prediction model used frequently in various domains [18] [16] [24]. A specification of the Markov model contains a set of states and a table, containing the transition probabilities from each state to every other state and itself. With this specification, Markov model can make a prediction about the next state, given the present state. This prediction is based on the transition probabilities. The transition probabilities are continuously built and updated as and when state transitions happen, and therefore, these transition probabilities, at any instant, are based on the previous transition history. A basic Markov prediction involves considering the present state and searching the transition probabilities from this present state to every state and choosing the transition which has the maximum probability. In our context, a state is nothing but the link vector of an interval. Figure 4(b) illustrates an example of this scheme. It shows Markov based transition probabilities in the form of a graph and a prediction table at the end of the execution chunk shown in Figure 4(a). Each state in Figure 4(b) corresponds to a phase in the phase table of Figure 4(a). The state S1 corresponds to phase 1, S2 to phase 2 and so on. As an example of Markov based prediction, if the current state is S1, the next state is predicted to be S1 again. As another example, if the current state is S2, then the next predicted state is S1. As a simple illustration of the way transition probabilities are continuously updated, if suppose, S4 now transitions to S2, the new transition probabilities from S4 to S1 and S4 to S4 still remain 0, but the transition probability from S4 to S2 changes from 0 to 0.5 and, the transition probability from S4 to S3 reduces from 1 to 0.5.

7.2   Markov Prediction Using a Threshold

This is similar to the basic Markov prediction scheme explained above with one added quality. Instead of making a prediction based on the maximum probability alone, we base the prediction on another parameter called the "threshold". Specifically, we pick the maximum probability prediction and then, check if its probability is greater than or equal to the pre-specified threshold parameter, and if so, we continue as before by choosing the maximum probability next state as our prediction. However, if the maximum probability is less than the specified threshold value, we do not make any prediction. This scheme is intended to weed out predictions which are based on insufficient previous data or are just too close to call. Note that employing a threshold value, in general, decreases the number of mispredictions, as we show later in the results section. For example, in Figure 4(b), if the present state is S3, the previous scheme would have predicted either state S1 or S4 to be the next state. In contrast, the threshold based scheme with a threshold of 0.67 makes no prediction (for the present state S3) since the maximum probability entry in the row is less than the pre-specified threshold value. The threshold value is a configurable parameter and can be set high if very little performance impact is tolerated and can be set low if some performance impact can be tolerated with a possibility of higher energy savings.

8   Implementation

After having described the important concepts we employ, we now present the implementation details of our scheme. Our proposed predictive link power management can be implemented in two possible ways. One way is to consider a global power manager which manages the power usage of the entire NoC based CMP. Such a global power manager can be implemented as a separate microcontroller to manage chip-wide power usage by controlling the power management of individual cores, as has been previously proposed [14]. It has also been shown that such global power management can be much more efficient and beneficial than local core-level power management schemes [28] [14]. We can extend such a global power manager with a link power management module. Alternately, predictive link management can be implemented using a helper thread which runs parallel to the computation threads and manages the link power. In either case, some hardware support is needed for our scheme to work.

8.1 Required Hardware

Figure 5 shows the hardware details of the link power management module we propose to use. We assume the existence of hardware or software module which can notify us whether a link was used in the previous instruction or not. We now describe the main components and their functionality.

- *Link Vector Register*: This is a 24-bit register that collates the link vector of an instruction interval. This register is reset at the beginning of each interval. After each instruction in the interval, the new link usage information of that previous instruction (in the form of link vector) is ORed into this register. Therefore, at the end of the interval, this register contains the current link vector for the entire interval. Since this is just a single 24-bit register and the operation is relatively simple, its overheads are negligible.

- *Link Vector Table*: This is a 32-entry table that maps each 24-bit link vector entry to a distinct 5-bit phase id. Since this table can contain 32 distinct phases at any given time, phase id is a 5-bit entry. Each row also contains two counters, "correct" and "misprediction", which count the number of correct predictions and the number of mispredictions, respectively. These counters are used to enforce our replacement policy as will be described later. The link vector table is turned on just before the end of each interval to make the prediction. During the rest of the interval, this table is turned to a low-power drowsy mode [10] and hence, the power overhead of maintaining such a table is minimal.

- *Prediction Table*: This is also a 32-row table. This table contains the Markov transition probability information described in Section 7.1. To reiterate, it contains the transition probabilities from each phase (represented by the phase id) contained in the link vector table to all phases contained in the link vector table. This is the table that is used to make the link vector predictions. Like the link vector table, the prediction table is also turned on just before the end of each interval and turned to a drowsy mode [10] otherwise, hence leading to negligible power overhead.

8.2 Functionality

During each instruction interval (which includes 5000 instructions in our experiments), the link usage vector is constructed and stored in the link vector register. Just before the end of an instruction interval, the link vector table is searched to find if there is an entry which matches the value in the link vector register. If a match is found, this means that this particular link usage phase has been seen previously. The corresponding phase id is taken from the link vector table and provided as an input to the prediction table. The prediction table outputs the predicted phase id of the next interval. This predicted phase id is computed using one of the two Markov based prediction schemes described earlier.

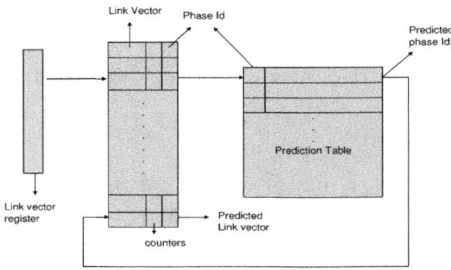

Fig. 5. Hardware needed to implement the Markov based prediction scheme. The main structures needed are the link vector register, the link vector table and the prediction table.

The link vector corresponding to the above predicted phase id is found by searching the link vector table. This link vector represents the predicted link usage during the next interval. Using this, the links which are predicted to be unused are turned off and the links which are predicted to be used but are presently switched off are turned on. We assume hooks to turn-on and turn-off communication links to be present. This whole process is performed just before the beginning of the next interval. How long before the beginning of the next interval a link should be turned on depends on the time needed for the links to turn on. As a result of this, communication links which are predicted to be used are turned on ahead of time considering the link turn-on latency. By doing so, link turn-on latency can be completely hidden and consequently, the potential performance penalty can be avoided. If the prediction is correct, after turning on and turning off appropriate links, the prediction table is updated with the new transition probabilities as described in Section 7.1. On the other hand, if the prediction is wrong, the correct links are turned on, incurring a performance penalty equivalent to the link turn-on latency and also a power penalty. After this, the appropriate counters are updated in the link vector table. If the prediction is correct, the *correct* counter is incremented otherwise the *misprediction* counter is incremented. Therefore, these two counters jointly maintain the information needed to calculate the prediction accuracy of this entry. Later, the transition probabilities are updated as in the case of correct prediction.

8.3   Replacement Policy

The above description is for the case where a match is found in the link vector table. If a match is not found, then this indicates a new phase and needs to be added to the link vector table and the prediction table. There are two possibilities in this case:

• *Tables are not full*: This is the case where the link vector table and the prediction table are not full. As is obvious, the new phase is added to the link vector table as well as the prediction table. Since this is a new phase, no prediction is made.

• *Tables are full*: If the tables are full, we need to find a *victim* to be evicted to make space for this new phase. The victim is selected based on the prediction accuracies. The entry with the lowest prediction accuracy is selected as the victim and evicted. This is where the correct and the misprediction counters come into picture. Using these counters, the phase entry having the lowest prediction accuracy is identified and evicted. The new phase is now added as described before. Using the above prediction accuracy based eviction scheme, the prediction table entries which have not been predicting well are thrown out. This accuracy-oriented replacement mechanism helps us to keep only the phases with good prior predictions in the tables.

8.4   Discussion

An important requisite of any power saving scheme is two-fold. The first requirement is that of minimal performance penalty. Secondly and importantly, power overhead to maintain the hardware needed for the power saving scheme should be minimal and way lower than the power savings achieved. Since our phase classification and prediction is for instruction intervals (of 5000 instructions) and not for individual instructions, the link-usage prediction, link turn-ons and turn-offs are done *only once every 5000 instructions*. Therefore, the overhead to make the prediction, link reactivation latency and link reactivation penalty are incurred at most only once every 5000 instructions. Also, the amount of storage needed by predictive scheme is minimal. The link vector register is a 24-bit register. The link vector table is a 32-entry table and so is the prediction table. Since the link vector table and the prediction table are turned on fully only at the end of each interval, the power penalty they incur is negligible in practice. We factor all the penalties and overheads in our experiments and as can be seen later, the benefits are still considerable. Also, since the prediction is done just before the beginning of the next interval and since the computation is relatively simple, the performance overhead is also expected to be minimal. In addition, as we show in the sensitivity analysis later, by reducing the prediction table size, overhead is dramatically lowered and still the prediction scheme performs really well. We demonstrate later that, reducing the table sizes from 32 entries to 16 or 8 entries still achieves almost the same energy savings. Misprediction penalty is another concern, but as we demonstrate in the next section, since prediction accuracy is very high, this is not a significant factor either. Nevertheless, our results below include *all* the performance and power overheads incurred by the proposed mechanism. Also, since the technique employed by our scheme is very generic and not tied any particular NoC structure, it is very scalable as NoC sizes increase and is also adaptable across various NoC structures.

9   Performance Aspect

In this section, we briefly discuss the performance aspect of our scheme. As noted in Section 5 and seen in Figure 3, there is a repetitive phase behavior in cache bank accesses made by cores. An interesting related aspect is the affinity of the accessing core to the cache bank accessed. In Figure 3, majority of accesses to *cachebank*1 are made by *core*16. Since *core*16 is in the opposite corner from *cachebank*1 in the two-dimensional mesh, there is a considerable access latency involved in making the cache bank access. Therefore, above described phase behavior can be used to move threads closer to cache banks that they access the most, there by reducing the bank access latencies considerably.

10   Evaluation

10.1   Setup

As mentioned previously, we use a 4×4 mesh NoC based 16-core CMP in our experiments. We assume a traditional X-Y routing policy in the NoC. The shared L2 cache is 16 banked SNUCA (static non-uniform cache access) architecture with a bank in every node and each bank is 2MB in size. The link power model we use is taken from [34], and in this model, when a link is turned on, it consumes the same power irrespective of whether it is transmitting data or not due to the link signaling methodology. When a link is turned off, we assume it does not consume any power as in [34]. Table 10.1 presents the default configuration we use in our experimental setup and in the power analysis. The power values in the table are obtained from [5]. We use Simics [23] which is full-system simulator combined with a module we implemented to simulate a 4×4 mesh. This setup is used to compute link usage, support routing, and evaluate link power management.

We tested our scheme with eight parallel (multi-threaded) applications from three different benchmark suites to find the variation in energy savings across different applications. We selected CG, IS and EP applications from the NAS parallel benchmark suite [1] among which IS and EP are known to have a lot of

Link frequency	1GHz
Link reactivation delay	1000cycles
Link reactivation energy	36.2nJ
Power of links for an on-chip switch	0.1446W
Process Technology (Interconnect)	0.07μm
Interconnect type	2D mesh NoC
Processor frequency	1GHz
Number of cores	16

Fig. 6. Default system configuration used

inter-core communications. From the SPEC OMP benchmark suite [2], we selected Mgrid, Wupwise and Apsi applications. Further, we used the Ocean and Water-spatial applications from the Splash2 benchmark suite [32].

10.2   Results

In this section, we present the results for each of the two prediction schemes we presented earlier. For both these schemes, namely, *basic Markov prediction* and *Markov prediction with threshold*, we present the link vector prediction accuracy, the performance penalty incurred and the link energy savings achieved. An important point to be considered for the rest of this paper is that, whenever we present energy savings, we always mean the *effective resulting energy savings*, which is the net energy savings achieved minus the link reactivation energy overhead and the overheads due to additional hardware.

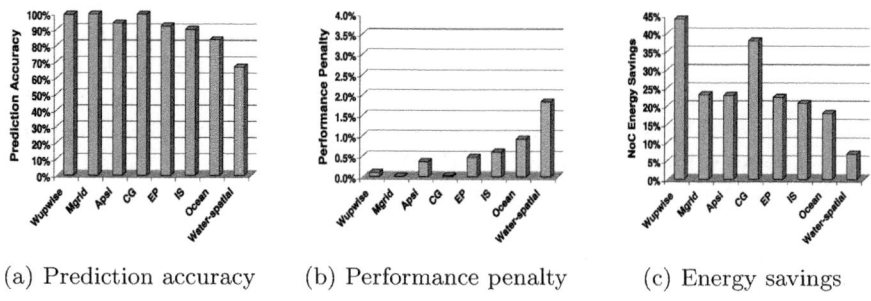

(a) Prediction accuracy   (b) Performance penalty   (c) Energy savings

Fig. 7. Prediction accuracy, performance penalty and the resulting energy savings when the basic Markov prediction scheme is used

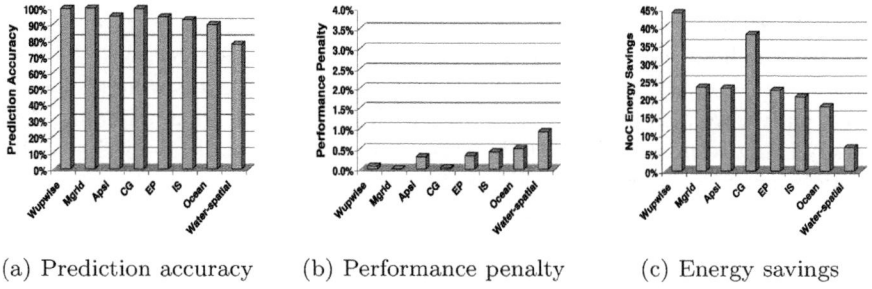

(a) Prediction accuracy   (b) Performance penalty   (c) Energy savings

Fig. 8. Prediction accuracy, performance penalty and the resulting energy savings in the case of Markov prediction using a threshold

Basic Markov Prediction. Figure 7(a) shows the link vector prediction accuracy achieved by this scheme for various applications. The main observation is the variation in the prediction accuracies across applications. As can be clearly seen, most applications have prediction accuracies of well over 95%, with Wupwise, Mgrid and CG having accuracies over 99%. Compared to this, water-spatial has a slightly lower prediction accuracy, probably due to the relatively shorter execution time, which in turn results in smaller learning phases.

Figure 7(b) shows the performance penalties incurred for different applications, over the case where no link power management is employed. This metric is a reflection of the prediction accuracy. The reason for the observed low penalties is two-fold. The main reason is of course the very high link prediction accuracy. Another reason is the fact that the links that are predicted to be used are turned on ahead of time so that the turn-on latency is hidden and the links are up by the time they are going to be used. The main triumph card of our scheme is the extremely low performance penalties which virtually leaves the original performance unaltered. This is in contrast to other hardware schemes which in many cases incur penalties as high as 12%, as mentioned in [20].

In contrast, our scheme results in penalties below 0.5% in most cases except for water-spatial application, which incurs a penalty of 1.5%. As we demonstrate later, the penalties can be further reduced to being almost negligible.

Finally, Figure 7(c) shows the link energy savings achieved by this scheme and as can be seen, Wupwise and CG achieve savings as high as 44% in communication energy. While we present only the NoC energy savings in detail here, our experiments showed that, for the benchmarks we tested, NoC energy consumption constitutes nearly 30% of the total on-chip energy consumption (on-chip energy consumption includes energy consumed by the processing cores, NoC, all cache accesses and other on-chip transactions). This clearly indicates that, NoC energy consumption forms a major component of the total on-chip energy consumption and any significant savings in NoC energy consumption is bound to translate into significant savings in the total on-chip energy consumption.

Markov Prediction Using a Threshold. Figure 8(a), Figure 8(b) and Figure 8(c) show the prediction accuracy, performance penalty and the energy savings, respectively, resulting from this scheme with a pre-specified threshold of 0.5. Later, we also present the results with a different threshold value. Again, the key thing to note is the fact that the performance penalty is further reduced as can be seen in Figure 8(b) and yet the energy savings remain almost the same as in the basic Markov prediction scheme. Hence, incorporating a pre-specified threshold results in further fine tuning of the performance penalties. This happens since the threshold parameter filters out predictions which do not have a good prediction history. Employing this scheme results in performance penalty of less than 1% in all cases and less than 0.5% in all but one application.

10.3 Sensitivity Experiments

In this section, we study the sensitivity of our scheme to various parameters. We alter aspects such as the prediction table size and present the variation in the results. We first reduce the sizes of the link vector table and the prediction table. We reduce the table sizes from 32 entries to 16 entries and 8 entries. Since these tables are the major storage structures used in our prediction scheme, we intend to reduce the sizes in order to further mitigate the power and computation overheads. We use the Markov prediction scheme using a threshold of 0.5 as presented previously. Figure 9 shows the new energy saving and the performance penalty when the table sizes are reduced. As can be clearly seen, the energy gains remain almost the same and surprisingly, there is also a slight reduction in the performance penalty. This reduction is due to our prediction accuracy based replacement policy, which throws out entries with lower prediction accuracies due to the reduced table size, and in the process also reduces the number of mispredictions we experience. These results show clearly that our scheme works beneficially even when the hardware table sizes are as low as just 8 entries.

The two potential factors which can limit the gains achieved by our scheme are the link reactivation energy and the link reactivation latency. In order to find the dependence of the benefits achieved by our scheme on these factors, we

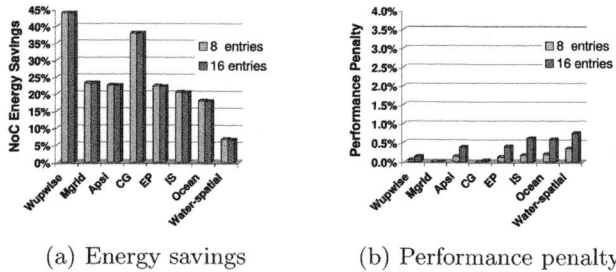

(a) Energy savings   (b) Performance penalty

Fig. 9. Energy saving and the performance penalty values when the table size is reduced to 16 and 8 entries. The prediction scheme used here is the Markov prediction using a threshold of 0.5.

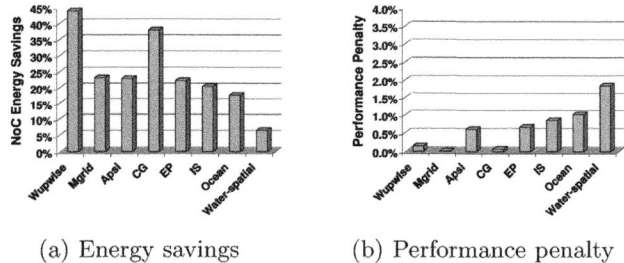

(a) Energy savings   (b) Performance penalty

Fig. 10. Energy savings and the performance penalty when the link reactivation energy and the link reactivation latency values are doubled. The prediction scheme used here is the Markov prediction using a threshold of 0.5.

doubled the link reactivation latency and the link reactivation energy values. We then tested the Markov prediction scheme using a threshold value of 0.5, table size of 32 and with the new, doubled link reactivation latency and link reactivation energy values. The corresponding results can be seen in Figure 10. There is a slight increase in the performance penalty, but even with the increase it is well under 1% for all benchmarks except water-spatial, which has a penalty of just over 1.5%. The reduction in energy savings is negligible as can be seen in Figure 10. This clearly indicates that, even with high reactivation penalties, our scheme performs well and this in turn implies that, the energy saving achieved is not overly sensitive to reactivation penalties.

In the Markov prediction scheme using a threshold, we had earlier used a pre-specified threshold of 0.5. We increased the threshold to 0.8 to check for further reduction in performance penalty. We repeat the experiments with Markov prediction scheme using a threshold value of 0.8 this time around. Figure 11 shows the new results. There is indeed a reduction in performance penalty but the energy savings achieved still remains largely same. This reduction in the performance penalty is due to further fine tuning by the higher threshold value. The higher threshold prevents predictions which do not necessarily have very high probabilities and hence further decreases mispredictions.

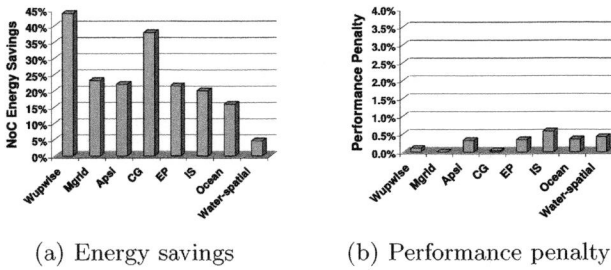

(a) Energy savings   (b) Performance penalty

Fig. 11. Energy savings and the performance penalty achieved in the case of Markov prediction using a threshold when the threshold value is set to 0.8

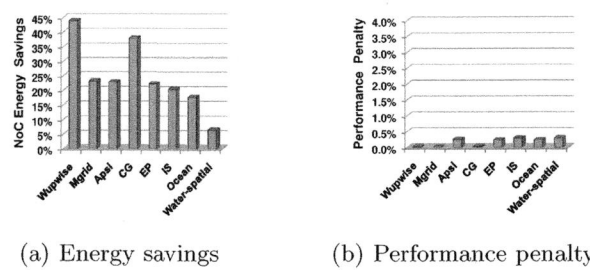

(a) Energy savings   (b) Performance penalty

Fig. 12. Energy savings and the performance penalty achieved in the case of Markov prediction using a threshold of 0.8 when the execution interval is reduced from 5000 instructions to 3000 instructions

Lastly, we reduce the instruction interval from 5000 instructions to 3000 instructions. As can be seen in Figure 12, there is very little change in both power savings and adverse performance impact. Therefore, although performance penalties slightly reduce, instruction interval of 5000 instructions is a better fit, since the overhead of our scheme is incurred only once in 5000 instructions instead of once in 3000 instructions.

11   Concluding Remarks

The goal of this paper is to propose a runtime, proactive scheme for link energy reduction in NoC based CMPs. To that end, we have made the following contributions. First, we have proposed a link usage based dynamic program phase characterization and a technique to use this phase characterization to implement a prediction based pro-active link power management scheme. Second, we have employed this scheme and conducted experiments with various parallel benchmarks and found that our scheme achieves up to 44% in energy savings, and an average saving of about 23.5%. Third, we have found that the most important advantage of our scheme is the remarkably low misprediction rate and hence the low performance penalty which in most cases is below 0.5%.

References

1. http://www.nas.nasa.gov/resources/software/npb.html
2. http://www.spec.org/omp/
3. Cell broadband engine - white paper. IBM (2006)
4. Benini, L., Micheli, G.D.: Powering networks on chips: Energy-efficient and reliable interconnect design for socs. In: Proc. ISSS (2001)
5. Chen, X., Peh, L.-S.: Leakage power modeling and optimization in interconnection networks. In: Proc. ISLPED (2003)
6. Dally, W.J., Towles, B.: Principles and Practices of Interconnection Networks. Morgan Kaufmann, San Francisco (2004)
7. Dhodapkar, A.S., Smith, J.E.: Managing multi-configurable hardware via dynamic working set analysis. In: Proc. ISCA (2002)
8. Dhodapkar, A.S., Smith, J.E.: Comparing program phase detection techniques. In: Proc. MICRO (2003)
9. Duato, J., et al.: Interconnection Networks: An Engineering Approach. IEEE CS Press, Los Alamos (1997)
10. Flautner, K., et al.: Drowsy caches: Simple techniques for reducing leakage power. In: Proc. ISCA (2002)
11. Galles, M.: Spider: A high-speed network interconnect. IEEE Micro 17(1), 34–39 (1997)
12. Hetherington, R.: In The UltraSparc T1 processor. SUN (2005)
13. Huang, M.C., et al.: Positional adaptation of processors: Application to energy reduction. In: Proc. ISCA (2003)
14. Isci, C., et al.: An analysis of efficient multi-core global power managment policies: Maximizing peformance for a given power budget. In: Proc. MICRO (2006)
15. Isci, C., Martonosi, M.: Phase characterization for power: Evaluating control flow based and event counter based techniques. In: Proc. HPCA (2006)
16. Joseph, D., Grunwald, D.: Prefetching using markov predictors. In: Proc. ISCA (1997)
17. Kim, C., et al.: Nonuniform cache architecture for wire-delay dominated network-on-chip caches. In: IEEE Micro: Micro's Top Picks from Computer Architecture Conferences (2003)
18. Latouche, G., Ramaswami, V.: Introduction to matrix analytic methods in stochastic modeling. ASA SIAM, PH Distributions (1999)
19. Lau, J., et al.: Transition phase classification and prediction. In: Proc. HPCA (2005)
20. Li, F., et al.: Compiler-directed proactive power management for networks. In: Proc. CASES (2005)
21. Li, F., et al.: Profile-driven energy reduction in network-on-chips. In: Proc. PLDI (2007)
22. Li, J., Martinez, J.F.: Dynamic power-performance adaptation of parallel computation on chip multiprocessors. In: Proc. HPCA (2006)
23. Magnusson, P.S., et al.: Simics: A full system simulation platform. Computer 35(2), 50–58 (2002)
24. Oly, J., Reed, D.A.: Markov model prediction of i/o requests for scientific applications. In: Proc. ICS (2002)
25. Perelman, E., et al.: Detecting phases in parallel applications on shared memory architectures. In: IPDPS (2006)

26. Ramanathan, R.: Intel multi-core processors: Making the move to quad-core and beyond. Intel White Paper, Intel Corporation (2006)
27. Shang, L., et al.: Dynamic voltage scaling with links for power optimization of interconnection networks. In: Proc. HPCA (2003)
28. Sharkey, J., et al.: Evaluating design tradeoffs in on-chip power management for cmps. In: Proc. ISLPED (2007)
29. Sherwood, T., et al.: Discovering and exploiting program phases. In: IEEE Micro: Micro's Top Picks from Computer Architecture Conferences (December 2003)
30. Shin, D., Kim, J.: Power-aware communication optimization for network-on-chips with voltage scalable links. In: Proc. CODES+ISSS (2004)
31. Simunic, T., Boyd, S.: Managing power consumption in networks on chips. In: Proc. DATE (2002)
32. Singh, J.P., Weber, W.-D., Gupta, A.: Splash: Stanford parallel applications for shared-memory. Computer Architecture News 20(1), 5–44
33. Soteriou, V., Peh, L.-S.: Dynamic power management for power optimization of interconnecttion networks using on/off links. In: Proc. HOT-I (2003)
34. Soteriou, V., Peh, L.-S.: Design space exploration of power-aware on/off interconnection networks. In: Proc. ICCD (2004)
35. Timothy, G.H., Mattson, G.: An overview of the Intel TFLOPS Supercomputer. Intel Technology Journal (1998)

Finding Extreme Behaviors in Microprocessor Workloads*

Frederik Vandeputte and Lieven Eeckhout

ELIS Department, Ghent University (Belgium)
{fgvdeput,leeckhou}@elis.UGent.be

Abstract. Power consumption has emerged as a key design concern across the entire computing range, from low-end embedded systems to high-end supercomputers. Understanding the power characteristics of a microprocessor under design requires a careful study using a variety of workloads. These workloads range from benchmarks that represent typical behavior up to hand-tuned stress benchmarks (so called stressmarks) that stress the microprocessor to its extreme power consumption.

This paper closes the gap between these two extremes by studying techniques for the automated identification of stress patterns (worst-case or extreme application behaviors) in typical workloads. For doing so, we borrow from sampled simulation theory and we provide two key insights. First, although representative sampling is slightly less effective in characterizing average behavior than statistical sampling, it is substantially more effective in finding stress patterns. Second, we find that threshold clustering is a better alternative than k-means clustering, which is typically used in representative sampling, for finding stress patterns. We identify a wide range of extreme behaviors, such as max energy, max power, max CPI, max branch misprediction rate, and max cache miss rate stress patterns. Overall, we can identify extreme behaviors in microprocessor workloads with a three orders of magnitude speedup and an error of a few percent on average.

1 Introduction

Energy, power, power density, thermal hotspots, voltage variation, and related design concerns have emerged as first-class microprocessor design issues over the past few years. And this is the case across the entire computing range, from low-end embedded systems to high-end supercomputers. A detailed understanding of these issues is of primary importance for designing energy-aware, power-aware and thermal-aware microprocessors, their power and thermal management strategies, their power supply unit, and thermal package.

Understanding the power, energy and thermal characteristics of a microprocessor under design requires appropriate benchmarking and simulation methodologies. At the one end of the spectrum, researchers and engineers consider average workload behavior. This is appropriate for studying a microprocessor's average power consumption or

---

* Lieven Eeckhout is a postdoctoral fellow with the Fund for Scientific Research in Flanders (Belgium) (FWO-Vlaanderen). Additional support is provided by the FWO projects G.0232.06 and G.0255.08, and the UGent-BOF project 01J14407.

P. Stenström (Ed.): Transactions on HiPEAC IV, LNCS 6760, pp. 155–174, 2011.
© Springer-Verlag Berlin Heidelberg 2011

thermal map, however, it does not capture more extreme behaviors. At the other end of the spectrum, stressmarks are being used to explore a microprocessor's maximum power consumption [1,2], maximum thermal hotspots [3], and maximum dI/dt behavior [4]. These stressmarks are typically hand-tuned, and push the microprocessor to its extremes in order to understand the microprocessor's worst-case behavior. These stress patterns are not expected to occur during typical operation, however, they can occur and therefore the microprocessor should be able to cope with them.

Microprocessors designed for maximum possible power consumption are not cost-effective though because of the large gap between maximum and typical power consumption. Dynamic thermal management (DTM) techniques [5,6] seek to exploit this gap: the microprocessor cooling apparatus is designed for a wattage less than the maximum power consumption, and a dynamic emergency procedure guarantees that this designed-for wattage level is never exceeded with minimal impact on overall performance. Gunther et al. [7] report that DTM techniques based on clock gating permitted a 20% reduction in the thermal design power for the Intel Pentium 4 processor. Developing and evaluating DTM mechanisms however requires adequate evaluation methodologies for quickly finding the extreme behaviors in typical workloads which are subject to DTM.

Therefore, this paper closes the gap between the two ends of the power benchmarking spectrum by studying ways of identifying *stress patterns* in typical workloads, also called 'worst-case execution behaviors' by Tiwari et al. [8]. More specifically, the goal of this work is to find stress patterns in typical workloads with the least possible simulation time. Identifying stress patterns in typical workloads is important because these stress patterns are expected to occur regularly in practice, much more often than the stress patterns represented by hand-tuned stressmarks. The stress patterns are the execution behaviors that DTM emergency procedures should adequately deal with.

We build on sampled simulation theory for identifying stress patterns in typical workloads. However, in contrast to sampled simulation for which the aim is to estimate *average* performance or power consumption by simulating a representative sample of the entire program execution, the goal in this paper is to leverage sampled simulation theory to find a sample of real program execution that includes stress patterns with *extreme* workload behavior, e.g., max power, max energy, etc. There are two common ways in sampled simulation, statistical sampling (as done in SMARTS [9]) and representative sampling (as done in SimPoint [10]). Our experimental results using the SPEC CPU2000 benchmarks confirm that statistical sampling is generally more accurate than representative sampling for estimating average behavior as shown in prior work [11], however, the new insight provided in this paper is that representative sampling is substantially more effective in identifying stress patterns in typical workloads. The intuitive explanation is that representative sampling uses knowledge about the program structure and execution to find representative sampling units, whereas statistical sampling is largely agnostic to any notion of program structure and execution. Sampling units selected through representative sampling therefore have a higher likelihood of including extreme workload behaviors. In addition, we find that threshold clustering is a better clustering method than k-means clustering (which is commonly used in representative sampling such as SimPoint) for identifying sampling units with extreme workload behavior. The end result is that we can estimate stress patterns in typical workloads with a three orders of magnitude simulation speedup compared to detailed simulation of entire workloads with an error of at most a few percent on average.

In this paper, we make the following contributions[1]:

- We close the gap between sampled simulation focusing on average workload behavior and hand-crafted stressmarks focusing on extreme behavior by identifying stress patterns in typical workloads.
- We make the case that representative sampling is substantially more effective in finding extreme behaviors in microprocessor workloads than statistical sampling, although statistical sampling is (slightly) more effective in capturing average behavior.
- The results in this paper motivate changing current simulation practice. Not only does representative sampling using threshold clustering estimate average performance and power nearly as accurate as statistical sampling, it is substantially more accurate when it comes to estimating stress patterns. And although representative sampling may be more commonly used than statistical sampling in current simulation practice, this paper shows that threshold clustering is substantially more effective than k-means clustering (which is typically being used) for finding stress patterns. In other words, representative sampling with threshold clustering is both effective at estimating average performance as well as stress patterns, whereas prevalent techniques (representative sampling with k-means clustering and statistical sampling) are only effective for estimating average performance.
- We show that the proposed method can be used for finding other flavors of extreme workload behaviors as well, such as high cache miss rate, low IPC, or low branch predictability intervals. These behaviors may be useful for understanding program patterns that lead to these extremities.

We believe this work is timely as power is a primary design concern in today's computer systems, and we are in need for appropriate benchmarking and performance analysis methodologies. In addition, stress patterns will become even more relevant as we enter the multi-core era and the gap between average and peak power widens as the number of cores increases. Benchmarking consortia have also recognized the need for energy- and power-oriented benchmarks and associated benchmarking methodologies. For example, SPEC has developed the SPECpower_ssj2008 benchmark suite [13], that evaluates the performance and power characteristics of volume server class computers. Likewise, EEMBC has released the EnergyBench benchmark suite which reports energy consumption while running performance benchmarks [14].

---

[1] This paper extends 'Finding Stress Patterns in Microprocessor Workloads' [12] by F. Vandeputte and L. Eeckhout, which was published at the International Conference on High Performance and Embedded Architectures and Compilers (HiPEAC) in January 2009. This journal paper provides additional experimental results compared to the conference paper, i.e., it evaluates the method (i) across different microarchitecture configurations, and evaluates the applicability of the proposed method (ii) for identifying stress patterns at very small timescales of a single cycle upto tens or hundreds of cycles, and (iii) for identifying power swing stress patterns.

2 Sampled Simulation

In sampled simulation, only a limited number of *sampling units* from a complete bench-mark execution are simulated in full detail. We refer to the selected sampling units collectively as the *sample*. Sampled simulation only reports performance for the instructions in the sampling units, and discards the instructions in the pre-sampling units. And this is where the dramatic performance improvement comes from: only the sampling units, which account for only a small fraction of the total dynamic instruction count, are simulated in a cycle-by-cycle manner.

There are three major issues with sampling: (i) what sampling units to select, (ii) how to initialize a sampling unit's architecture starting image, and (iii) how to accurately estimate a sampling unit's microarchitecture starting image. This paper only concerns the first issue because the other two issues can be handled easily by leveraging existing technology. For example, the architecture starting image (registers and memory state) can be set through fastforwarding or through checkpointing [15,16]; and the microarchitecture starting image (caches, branch predictors, etc.) can be estimated with microarchitecture state warmup techniques — there is a wealth of literature covering this area, see for example [17,18,19,20,15,16,9].

There are basically two major ways for determining what sampling units to select, namely (i) statistical sampling, and (ii) representative sampling. We now discuss both approaches.

2.1 Statistical Sampling

Statistical sampling takes a number of sampling units across the whole execution of the program. These sampling units are chosen randomly or periodically in an attempt to provide a representative cross-cut of the entire program execution.

Laha et al. [21] propose statistical sampling for evaluating cache performance. They select multiple sampling units by randomly picking intervals of execution.

Conte et al. [17] pioneered the use of statistical sampling in processor simulation. They made a distinction between sampling bias and non-sampling bias. Non-sampling bias results from improperly constructing the microarchitecture starting image prior to each sampling unit. Sampling bias refers to how accurate the sample is with respect to the overall average. Sampling bias is fundamental to the selection of sampling units.

The SMARTS (Sampling Microarchitecture Simulation) approach by Wunderlich et al. [9] proposes *systematic sampling* which selects sampling units periodically across the entire program execution, i.e., the pre-sampling unit size is fixed, as opposed to random sampling. The potential pitfall of systematic or periodic sampling compared to random sampling is that the sampling units may give a skewed view in case the periodicity present in the program execution under measurement equals the sampling periodicity or its higher harmonics. This does not seem to be a concern in practice though as SMARTS achieves highly accurate performance estimates compared to detailed entire-program simulation. The important asset of statistical sampling compared to representative sampling, is that it builds on well-founded statistics theory which enables computing confidence bounds at a given confidence level.

2.2   Representative Sampling

Representative sampling contrasts with statistical sampling in that it first analyzes the program execution to pick a representative sampling unit for each unique behavior. Several approaches have been proposed in representative sampling, and they differ in the way they select the representative sampling units, see for example [22,23,24,25,26], however, the most well known approach is the SimPoint approach proposed by Sherwood et al. [10]. SimPoint picks a small number of sampling units that accurately create a representation of the complete execution of the program. To do so, they break a program's execution into intervals — an *interval* is a contiguous sequence of instructions from the dynamic instruction stream — and for each interval they create a code signature. The code signature is a so called Basic Block Vector (BBV) [27] which counts the number of times each basic block is executed in the interval, weighted with the number of instructions per basic block. After normalizing the BBVs so that the BBV elements sum up to one, they then perform clustering which groups intervals with similar code signatures (BBVs) into so called *phases*. BBV similarity is quantified by computing the Manhattan distance between two BBVs. The intuitive notion is that intervals of execution with similar code signatures have similar architectural behavior, and this has been shown to be the case by Lau et al. [28]. Therefore, only one interval from each phase needs to be simulated in order to recreate an accurate picture of the entire program execution. They then choose a representative sampling unit from each phase and perform detailed simulation on that representative unit. Taken together, these sampling units (along with their respective weights) represent the complete execution of a program. A sampling unit is called a *simulation point* in SimPoint terminology, and each simulation point is an interval on the order of millions, or tens to hundreds of millions of instructions. The simulation points can be used across microarchitectures because the BBVs based on which the simulation points are identified are microarchitecture-independent.

The clustering step in the SimPoint approach is a crucial step as it classifies intervals into phases, with each phase representing distinct program behavior. There exist a number of clustering algorithms; here, we discuss k-means clustering (which is used by SimPoint) and threshold clustering (which we advocate in this paper for identifying stress patterns in typical workloads).

K-means clustering. K-means clustering produces exactly k clusters and works as follows. Initially, k cluster centers are randomly chosen. In each iteration, the distance is calculated for each interval to the center of each cluster, and the interval is assigned to its closest cluster. Subsequently, new cluster centers are computed based on the new cluster memberships. This algorithm is iterated until no more changes are observed in the cluster memberships. It is well known that the result of k-means clustering is dependent on the choice of the initial cluster centers. Therefore, SimPoint considers multiple randomly chosen cluster centers and uses the Bayesian Information Criterion (BIC) [10] to assess the quality of the clustering: the clustering with the highest BIC score is selected.

Threshold clustering. Classifying intervals into phases using threshold clustering can be done in two ways, using an iterative algorithm or using a non-iterative algorithm. The iterative algorithm selects an instruction interval as a cluster center and then computes

Table 1. Processor model assumed in our experimental setup

ROB	128 entries
LSQ	64 entries
processor width	decode, dispatch, issue and commit 4 wide
	fetch 8 wide
latencies	load (2), mul (3), div (20)
L1 I-cache	64KB 2-way set-assoc, 2 cycles
L1 D-cache	64KB 2-way set-assoc, 2 cycles
L2 cache	unified, 2MB 8-way set-assoc, 20 cycles
main memory	150 cycle access time
branch predictor	26Kbit hybrid bimodal/gshare predictor
frontend pipeline	14 stages

the distance with all the other instruction intervals. If the distance measure is smaller than a given threshold θ, the instruction interval is considered to be part of that cluster. Out of all remaining instruction intervals (not part of previously formed clusters), another interval is selected randomly as a cluster center and the above process is repeated. This iterative process continues until all instruction intervals are assigned to a cluster/phase. The θ threshold is expressed as a percentage of the maximum possible Manhattan distance between two intervals; the maximum Manhattan distance between two intervals is 2 assuming normalized BBVs, i.e., the sum across all BBV elements equals one.

The non-iterative algorithm scans all intervals from the beginning until the end of the dynamic instruction stream. If the interval is further away from any previously seen cluster center than a given threshold θ, the interval is considered the center of a new cluster. If not, the interval is assigned to the closest cluster. The non-iterative algorithm is computationally more efficient and performs well for our purpose — we therefore use the non-iterative approach in this paper.

The important advantage of threshold clustering is that, by construction, it builds phases for which its in-phase variability (in terms of BBV behavior) is limited to a threshold θ. This is not the case for k-means clustering: the variability within a phase can vary across phases.

3   Experimental Setup

3.1   Benchmarks and Simulators

We use the SPEC CPU2000 benchmarks and all of their reference inputs in our experimental setup. These benchmarks were compiled and optimized for the Alpha ISA; the binaries were taken from the SimpleScalar website; all benchmarks are run to4 completion.

We use the SimpleScalar/Alpha v3.0 [29] superscalar out-of-order processor simulator. The processor model is configured along the lines of a typical four-wide superscalar microprocessor such as the Alpha EV7 (21364), see Table 1. Power is estimated using Wattch v1.02 [30] and HotLeakage [6] assuming a 70nm technology, 5.6GHz clock frequency and 1V supply voltage. We assume an aggressive clock gating mechanism.

3.2 Sampled Simulation

For statistical sampling, we use periodic sampling, as done in SMARTS [9], i.e., we select a sampling unit every n intervals. We will vary the sampling rate $1/n$ in the results presented in this paper.

For representative sampling, we use SimPoint v3.0 [31] with its default settings. In short, SimPoint computes a BBV per interval, and subsequently performs k-means clustering on randomly projected 15-dimensional BBVs; SimPoint evaluates all values of k between 1 and maxK and picks the best k and random seed per k based on the BIC score of the clustering. We will vary the sampling rate by varying the SimPoint maxK parameter. In the evaluation section of this paper, we will compare k-means clustering versus threshold clustering. When doing so, we replace the k-means clustering algorithm with the threshold clustering algorithm while leaving the rest of the SimPoint software untouched.

In this paper, for both statistical and representative sampling, the interval size is set to 1M (2^{20}) instructions unless mentioned otherwise, i.e., the stress patterns constitute of 1M dynamically executed instructions. This choice does not affect the general conclusions in this paper though — the methodology can be applied to other interval granularities as well, as we will show later in this paper. In fact, we experiment with larger interval sizes — we report 8M-instruction stress patterns as well — and obtain similar results as for the 1M-instruction granularity. However, for smaller interval granularities, there may be practical considerations that prohibit the use of representative sampling, the reason being that the clustering algorithm may become very time-consuming for a large number of intervals. Addressing the computational concerns of clustering large data sets is left for future work.

4 Evaluation

In the evaluation section, we now compare statistical sampling against representative sampling for finding stress patterns in microprocessor workloads. This is done in a number of steps: we present per-benchmark max power stress patterns, as well as processor component power stress patterns; we also evaluate the error versus simulation speedup trade-off; we study the effect of stress pattern granularity; we study max energy stress patterns; and finally, we demonstrate the efficacy of the proposed technique for finding other flavors of extreme behavior, such as max CPI, max cache miss rate and max branch misprediction rate stress patterns.

4.1 Motivation

Before evaluating sampled simulation for identifying stress patterns in typical microprocessor workloads, we first further motivate the problem by showing that the variability over time in power consumption is significant within a single benchmark execution. We therefore compute the power consumption on an interval basis, i.e., we compute the power consumption per interval of 1M instructions in the dynamic instruction stream. This yields a distribution of power consumption numbers. Figure 1 represents this distribution as a boxplot per benchmark. The middle point of the box plot represents the

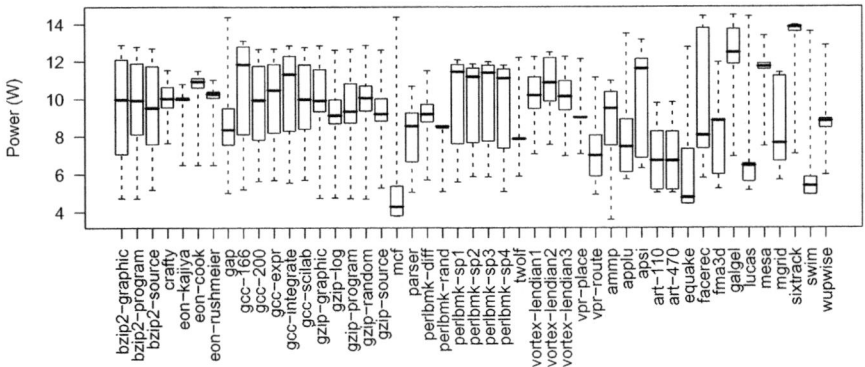

Fig. 1. Boxplots characterizing the distribution of power consumption at the 1M-instruction interval granularity; the boxes represent the 5% and 95% quartiles, and the thick horizontal line in each box represents the median

median power consumption for the entire benchmark execution. The box represents the 5% and 95% quartiles, i.e., 90% of the data lies between these two markers. The outliers are represented by the dashed lines that fall out of the box; the minimum and maximum values are represented by the bottom and top horizontal lines at the ends of the dashed lines, respectively.

The box plots clearly show that there is significant variability over time in power consumption, and, more importantly within the context of this paper, there is a large discrepancy in median versus max power consumption. In fact, for many benchmarks, the max power consumption is substantially higher than its median power consumption, e.g., for mcf the max power consumption is more than three times as high as its median power consumption. And in addition, the bulk of the power consumption numbers falls far below the max power consumption. This illustrates that finding stress patterns for these benchmarks is challenging, i.e., we need to find one of the few intervals that cause max power consumption out of the numerous intervals that constitute the entire benchmark execution — there are typically tens or even hundreds of thousands of 1M-instruction intervals per benchmark.

4.2 Per-benchmark Stress Patterns

We now evaluate the efficacy of sampled simulation in finding stress patterns at the 1M-instruction granularity. For doing so, we assume a $1000\times$ simulation speedup for both statistical and representative sampling compared to the simulation of the entire program execution. Simulation speedup in this paper is defined as the number of instructions in the entire benchmark execution divided by the number of instructions in the sample. This simulation speedup metric does not include the overhead of setting the architecture and microarchitecture starting images, as discussed in Section 2, however, state-of-the-art sampled simulation methods use checkpointing to initialize a sampling unit's starting image, for which the overhead only depends on the number of sampling units (to a first-order approximation). In other words, comparing sampling strategies in terms of simulation speedup can be done by simply comparing the number of sampling units (intervals) in the sample versus the entire program execution.

We simulate all sampling units selected by statistical and representative sampling, respectively, and retain the max power consumption of any of these sampling units. We then compare this sampled maximum against the max power consumption observed across the entire benchmark execution — this is done by simulating the complete benchmark execution while keeping track of the max power consumption at the 1M-instruction interval size. The percentage difference between the max power values is called the *error* which is a smaller-is-better metric: the smaller the error score, the closer the stress pattern identified through sampled simulation reflects the real stress pattern observed across the entire benchmark execution. Figure 2 shows the error in estimating the maximum power consumption. We observe that statistical sampling is less effective in finding stress patterns than representative sampling, i.e., the error can be as high as 60% (and average error of 9.3%) for statistical sampling whereas representative sampling is much more effective. Representative sampling with k-means clustering achieves an average error of 3% (and 14% at most); representative sampling with threshold clustering is even more effective with an average error of 2.3% and a maximum error of at most 11%. The reason for the difference in efficacy between statistical sampling and representative sampling is that representative sampling selects sampling units based on the benchmark execution and structure (through the BBVs that are being collected for finding the distinct phase behaviors), whereas statistical sampling is largely agnostic to any notion of program structure and behavior. In other words, for statistical sampling, the likelihood of hitting upon a stress pattern is inverse proportional to the sampling rate, whereas representative sampling identifies distinct program behavior by looking into the code that is being executed.

The reason why threshold clustering outperforms k-means clustering is that threshold clustering, by construction, bounds the amount of variability within a cluster, whereas k-means clustering does not. In other words, for a given simulation speedup, i.e., for a given number of clusters, threshold clustering will yield more sparsely populated clusters than k-means clustering; i.e., outliers in the data set will end up in separate clusters in contrast to k-means clustering which may group those outliers with its closest, albeit relatively far away, cluster.

The end conclusion is that representative sampling with threshold clustering results in a simulation speedup of three orders of magnitude compared to entire benchmark simulation with an error of at most a few percent on average for finding stress patterns in the SPEC CPU2000 benchmarks. And in addition, respresentative sampling with threshold clustering is more effective than representative sampling with k-means clustering and statistical sampling.

4.3 Processor Component Stress Patterns

In the previous section, the focus was on stress patterns for the entire processor. We now look into stress patterns for individual processor components, such as the instruction window, functional units, caches, branch predictor, etc. This, in conjunction with a microprocessor floorplan, could provide valuable information in terms of power density and thermal hotspots [6]. Figures 3 and 4 quantify the error in estimating average

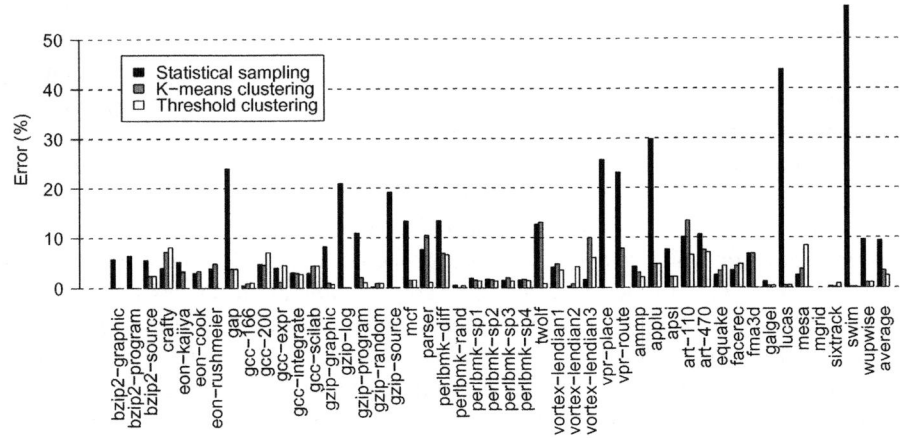

Fig. 2. Error in estimating max power stress patterns

and maximum per-component power consumption, respectively. (We assume a $1000\times$ simulation speedup and present average results computed across all benchmarks.) The interesting observation from these graphs is that both statistical and representative sampling are very accurate in estimating average processor component power consumption (the average error is around 1% on average), however, representative sampling is by far more effective in capturing stress patterns. For representative sampling with threshold clustering, the processor component power error for the stress patterns is less than 5%, whereas representative sampling with k-means clustering and statistical sampling lead to a processor component power error of up to 10% and 20%, respectively.

4.4   Error versus Simulation Speedup

The previously reported results assumed a simulation speedup of three orders of magnitude ($1000\times$). We now explore the trade-off between error and simulation speedup in more detail, see Figure 5 which shows two graphs, one for estimating average power consumption (left graph) and another one for estimating max power consumption (right graph) — these graphs show average results across all benchmarks. The vertical and horizontal axes show percentage error and simulation speedup with respect to simulating the entire benchmark, respectively. For computing these graphs, we simulate all sampling units; for the left graph, we then compute the average power consumption across all sampling units, and compare it against the true average power consumption computed by simulating the entire benchmark; for the right graph, we retain the largest power consumption number of any of the sampling units and compare it against the largest power consumption number observed across the entire program execution. For statistical sampling, one sampling unit is selected every n intervals; this corresponds to a simulation speedup of a factor n. For representative sampling, we set a maxK parameter or θ threshold for the clustering which yields n clusters or sampling units; this corresponds to a n_{total}/n simulation speedup with n_{total} the number of intervals in the entire program execution.

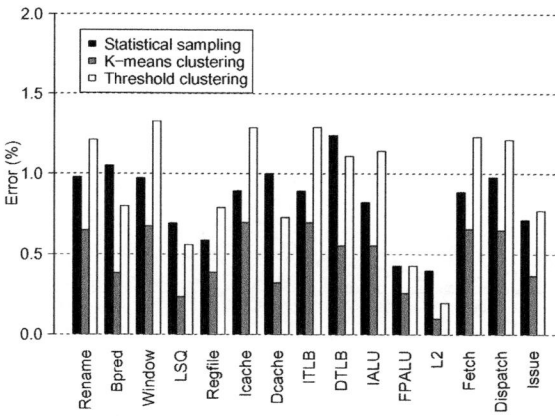

Fig. 3. Error in estimating average power consumption per processor component

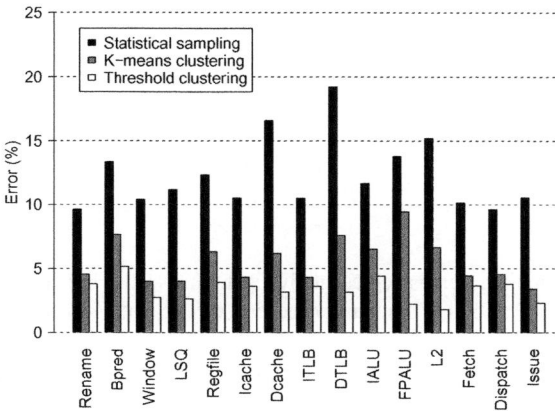

Fig. 4. Error in estimating max power consumption per processor component

We observe that statistical sampling is more accurate than representative sampling for estimating average power consumption, see left graph Figure 5. The results in the left graph confirm the earlier findings by Yi et al. [11] who provide a detailed comparison of statistical and representative sampling for estimating average performance: they found that average performance is more accurately estimated through statistical sampling, however, representative sampling has a better speed versus accuracy tradeoff.

However, when it comes to estimating max power consumption, representative sampling is more effective, and threshold clustering is the most effective approach. In particular, representative sampling with threshold clustering finds an interval with a power consumption number around 2% on average of the max power number found through simulation of the entire benchmark at a simulation speedup of three orders of magnitude. For the same simulation speedup, statistical sampling achieves an error of 10% on average. Or, reversely, for an error of 2%, statistical sampling only achieves a simulation

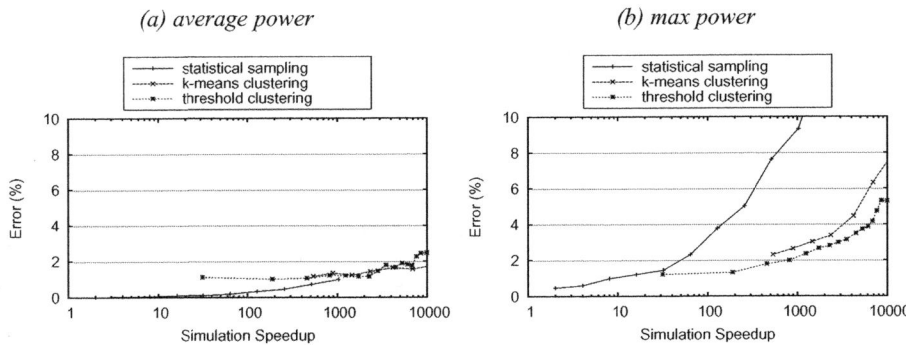

Fig. 5. Statistical sampling versus representative sampling: error as a function of simulation speedup for estimating average power consumption (left graph) and max power (right graph)

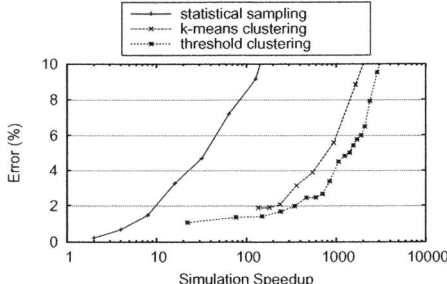

Fig. 6. Statistical sampling versus representative sampling at the 8M-instruction stress pattern granularity: error as a function of simulation speedup for estimating max power

speedup around a factor of 40. In other words, representative sampling with threshold clustering is both faster and more effective in capturing max power stress patterns.

4.5   Stress Pattern Granularity

So far, we considered stress patterns at the 1M-instruction interval granularity. We now consider a larger interval granularity in order to show that representative sampling is equally effective at finding stress patterns at larger granularities. Figure 6 quantifies the efficacy of representative sampling versus statistical sampling at the 8M-instruction granularity. We reach the same conclusion here as before: representative sampling with threshold clustering is most effective.

4.6   Maximum Instantaneous Power Stress Patterns

In the previous sections, we focused on finding stress patterns at the granularity of 1M or 8M instructions. In this section, we focus on finding stress patterns at very small timescale granularities, on the order of a single cycle or tens to hundreds of cycles. In other words, we seek to find stress patterns with maximum power consumption over a

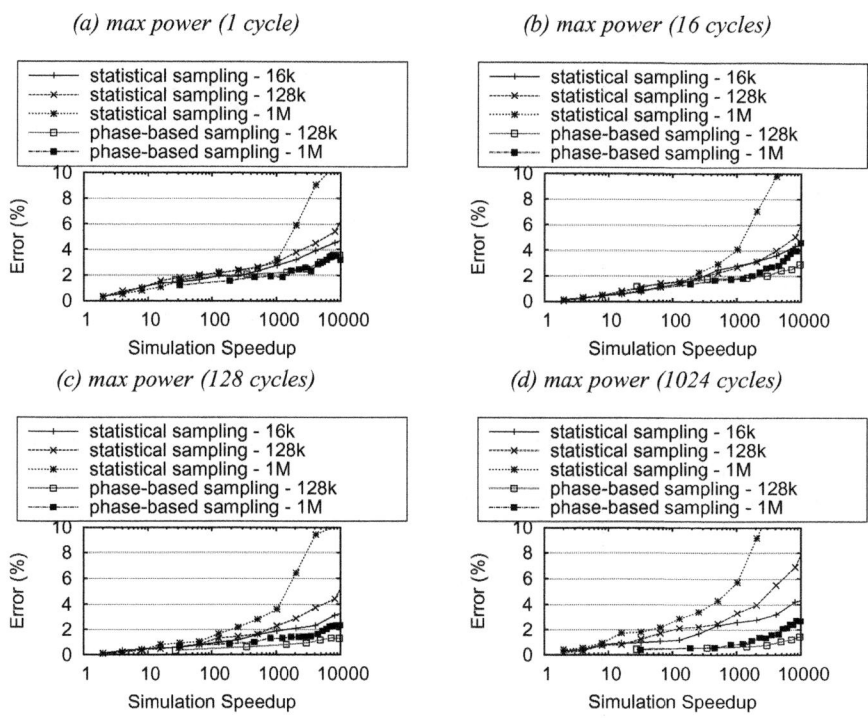

Fig. 7. Statistical sampling versus representative (phase-based) sampling: error as a function of simulation speedup for estimating max power over 1, 16, 128 and 1024 cycles, respectively, using different interval sizes (16K, 128K and 1M instruction intervals for statistical sampling, and 128K and 1M instruction intervals for representative sampling)

very short period of time; this form of stress patterns is important to study for understanding the maximum current that can be drawn from the power supply. In order to do so, we use sampling at a fairly large interval granularity (128K or 1M instructions), and then verify whether the identified intervals contain stress patterns at the smallest timescale. The results for finding maximum power stress patterns over a period of 1, 16, 128 and 1024 cycles are shown in Figure 7. For statistical sampling, we use intervals of 16k, 128k and 1M instructions; for representative (or phase-based) sampling, we use intervals of 128k and 1M instructions, and consider threshold clustering. Although the error tends to be lower for statistical sampling and small-timescale stress patterns compared to stress patterns at larger timescales as discussed previously, we conclude that representative sampling is more accurate than statistical sampling for finding maximum instantaneous power stress patterns.

4.7   Maximum Power Swing Stress Patterns

In Figure 8, the errors for estimating maximum power swings over 32 and 128 cycles are shown. These stress patterns are of great interest for studying the dI/dt problem [4] as the associated current swings may lead to ripples on the voltage supply lines, which may

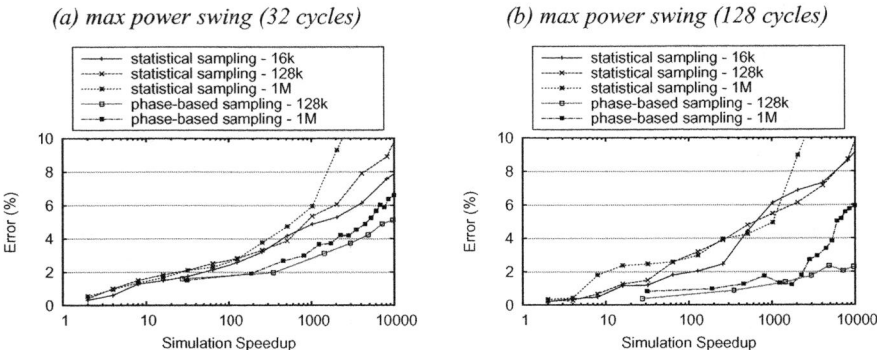

Fig. 8. Statistical sampling versus representative (phase-based) sampling: error as a function of simulation speedup for estimating max power swings of 32 cycles (left graph) and 128 cycles (right graph); different interval sizes are explored: 16K, 128K and 1M instruction intervals for statistical sampling, and 128K and 1M instruction intervals for representative sampling.

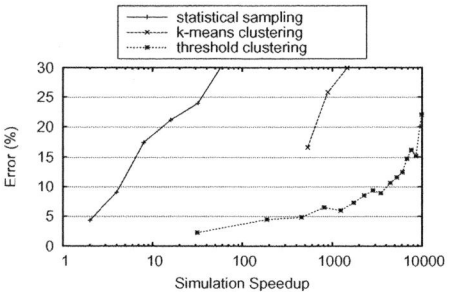

Fig. 9. Statistical sampling versus representative sampling: error as a function of simulation speedup for estimating max energy

introduce timing errors and/or cause circuits to fail. Similar conclusions can be drawn as in the previous section, namely (i) representative sampling outperforms statistical sampling, even when considering small intervals for statistical sampling, and (ii) the difference in accuracy increases for stress patterns at larger granularities.

4.8 Max Energy Stress Patterns

Another flavor of a stress pattern is a max energy stress pattern. Identifying max energy stress patterns is important for battery-operated devices, i.e., a max energy stress pattern represents a poor energy-efficiency code sequence with a high energy-per-instruction (EPI) balance. The results of this evaluation are shown in Figure 9: representative sampling with threshold clustering is by far more effective than statistical sampling for estimating max energy consumption.

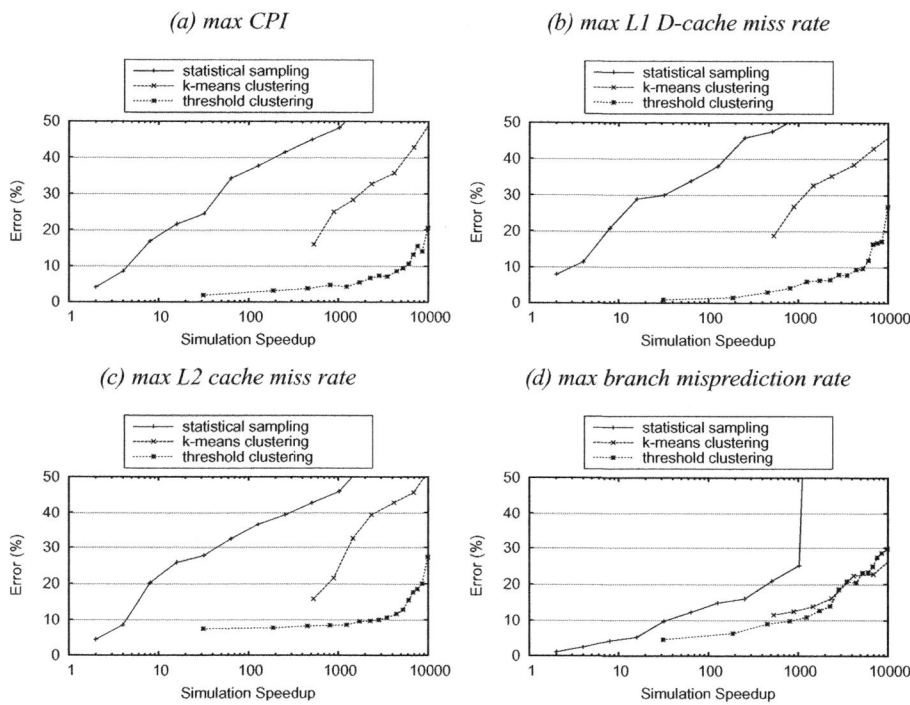

Fig. 10. Finding other flavors of stress patterns: max CPI (top left), max L1 D-cache miss rate (top right), max L2 cache miss rate (bottom left), and max branch misprediction rate (bottom right).

4.9   Other Extreme Behaviors

Representative sampling with threshold clustering is effective at finding other flavors of extreme behaviors as well, beyond energy and power related stress patterns. Figure 10 shows four examples, namely max CPI, max L1 D-cache miss rate, max L2 cache miss rate and max branch misprediction rate stress patterns. In all four examples, representative sampling with threshold clustering is the most effective approach; this is especially the case for the CPI and cache miss rate extreme behaviors. These extreme behaviors can provide valuable insight and understanding about problematic program behaviors and patterns.

4.10   Different Processor Configurations

As a final experiment, we evaluate the effectiveness of finding stress patterns found through representative sampling using threshold clustering across processor configurations. The processor configurations that we consider, are described in Table 2. These three configurations range from a low-end to a high-end aggressive processor configuration. Our fourth configuration is the baseline configuration mentioned earlier in Table 1.

Table 2. Three additional processor configurations

	Config #1	Config #2	Config #3
Decode, issue, commit width	2 wide	4 wide	8 wide
Fetch width	2 wide	8 wide	16 wide
Branch predictor	48Kbit hybrid bimodal/gshare predictor		
ROB entries	48	96	192
LSQ entries	24	48	96
Int ALUs (mult/div units)	2 (1)	4 (1)	8 (2)
FP ALUs (mult/div units)	1 (1)	2 (1)	4 (2)
L1 I-cache size (KB), assoc	8KB,2-way	16KB,4-way	32KB,4-way
L1 D-cache size (KB), assoc	8KB,2-way	16KB,4-way	32KB,4-way
L2 cache size (KB), assoc	512KB,4-way	1MB,4-way	2MB,8-way
Memory latency	150 cycles		

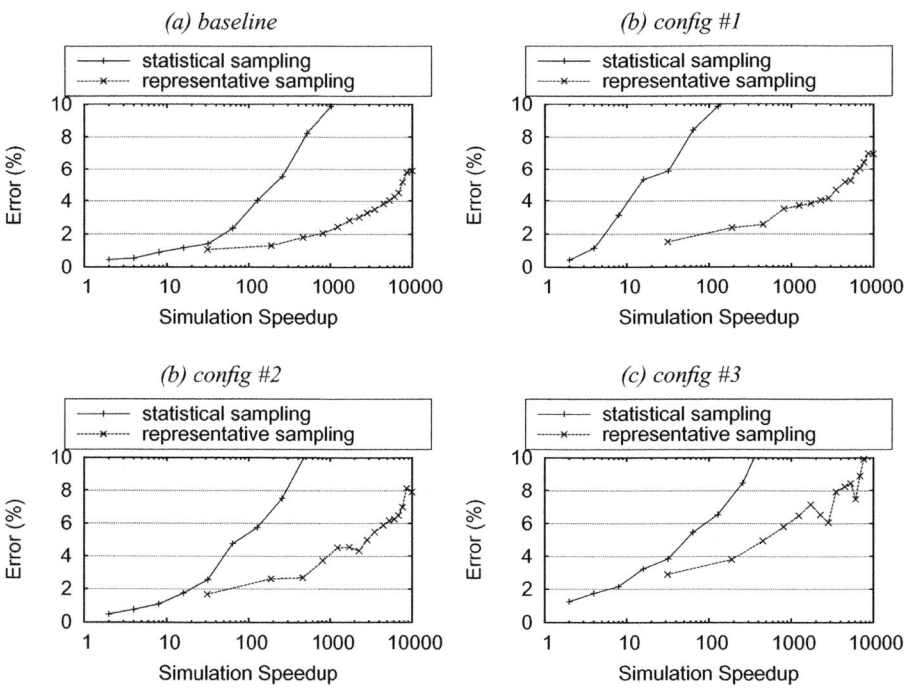

Fig. 11. Statistical sampling versus representative sampling: error as a function of simulation speedup for estimating max power consumption for four different processor configurations

In Figure 11, we compare statistical sampling versus phase-based sampling for finding the max power stress patterns for these four processor configurations. Again, we conclude that phase-based sampling is more effective than statistical sampling.

5   Related Work

Stress testing. In VLSI circuit design, statistically generated test vectors are used to stress a circuit by inducing maximum switching activity [32]. At the microarchitectural level, engineers develop hand-crafted synthetic test cases, so called stressmarks, to estimate maximum power consumption of a microprocessor. This is common practice in industry, see for example [1,33,3]. Recent work by Joshi et al. [34] proposes a framework for automatically developing stressmarks by exploring the space built up by an abstract workload model.

Power phase characterization. A lot of work has been done on characterizing time-varying program behavior, and different authors have been proposing different ways for doing so, such as code working sets [35,36], BBVs [10,37], procedure calls [38], and performance data [39].

Isci and Martonosi [40,41] propose a methodology for tracking dynamic power phase behavior in real-life applications using a real hardware setup. They measure total processor power consumption data using a digital multimeter and simultaneously collect raw performance counter data. They then use the performance counter data to estimate processor component power consumption numbers which they subsequently use to identify power phase behavior at runtime using threshold clustering. Whereas the goal of the work by Isci and Martonosi is on tracking power consumption and power phase behavior at runtime, the focus of our work is on finding stress patterns to guide processor design under extreme workload behavior, which is a related but different problem.

In their follow-on work, Isci and Martonosi [42] compare clustering based on BBVs versus processor component power numbers, and found both approaches to be effective, but processor component power numbers to be more accurate for tracking power phase behavior. The downside of processor component power numbers though is that it requires that the entire benchmark be measured in terms of its power behavior which may be costly in terms of equipment (in case of a real hardware setup) or which may be too time-consuming (in case of a simulation setup). In addition, processor component power numbers are specific to one particular microprocessor implementation. A BBV profile is both inexpensive and fast to measure through software instrumentation, and, in addition, is microarchitecture-independent, i.e., can be used across microarchitectures. Since our goal is to find stress patterns to be used during the design of a processor, we advocate the BBV approach because of its microarchitecture-independence, its low cost and its fast computation.

6   Conclusion

Power consumption has emerged as a key design concern over the entire range of computing devices, from embedded systems up to large-scale data centers and supercomputers. Understanding the power characteristics of workloads and their interaction with the architecture however, is not trivial and requires an appropriate benchmarking methodology. Researchers and engineers currently use a range of workloads for gaining insight into the power characteristics of processor architectures. On the one side, typical workloads such as SPEC CPU and other commercial workloads are used to assess average power consumption. On the other side, hand-crafted stressmarks are being used to understand worst-case behavior in terms of a processor's max power consumption.

This paper closed the gap between these two ends of the power benchmarking spectrum by finding stress patterns in typical microprocessor workloads. An additional requirement was that the simulation time for finding these stress patterns should be as small as possible so that the stress patterns can be used throughput the entire design flow, from early-stage microarchitecture design space exploration down to RTL-level simulation.

In this paper, we advocated and studied sampled simulation as a means of finding these stress patterns. Although sampled simulation is a well studied and mature research area, the objective in this paper is completely different. While the goal of sampled simulation traditionally has been on estimating average performance, the problem addressed in this paper is on estimating worst-case performance rather than average performance, i.e., the goal is to find stress patterns in typical workloads without having to simulate the complete benchmark execution. We found that although statistical sampling is more effective than representative sampling for estimating average behavior, representative sampling is substantially more effective than statistical sampling when it comes to capturing extreme behavior. In addition, we found that threshold clustering is substantially more effective than k-means clustering for finding stress patterns (which is an often used clustering technique for representative sampling). We identify a wide range of extreme behaviors, such as max energy, max average power, max instantaneous power, max dI/dt, max CPI, max branch misprediction rate, and max cache miss rate stress patterns. Our experimental results using the SPEC CPU2000 benchmarks demonstrate that stress patterns can be found with an error of a few percent on average at a simulation speedup of three orders of magnitude.

References

1. Felter, W., Keller, T.: Power measurement on the Apple Power Mac G5. Technical Report RC23276, IBM (2004)
2. Gowan, M.K., Biro, L.L., Jackson, D.B.: Power considerations in the design of the Alpha 21264 microprocessor. In: Proceedings of the 35th Design Automation Conference (DAC), pp. 726–731 (June 1998)
3. Vishmanath, R., Wakharkar, V., Watwe, A., Lebonheur, V.: Thermal performance challenges from silicon to systems. Intel Technology Journal 4(3) (August 2000)
4. Joseph, R., Brooks, D., Martonosi, M.: Control techniques to eliminate voltage emergencies in high performance processors. In: Proceedings of the International Symposium on High-Performance Computer Architecture (HPCA), pp. 79–90 (February 2003)
5. Brooks, D., Martonosi, M.: Dynamic thermal management for high-performance microprocessors. In: Proceedings of the Seventh International Symposium on High-Performance Computer Architecture (HPCA), pp. 171–182 (January 2001)
6. Skadron, K., Stan, M.R., Huang, W., Velusamy, S., Sankaranarayanan, K., Tarjan, D.: Temperature-aware microarchitecture. In: Proceedings of the International Symposium on Computer Architecture (ISCA), pp. 2–13 (June 2003)
7. Gunther, S.H., Binns, F., Carmean, D.M., Hall, J.C.: Managing the impact of increasing microprocessor power consumption. Intel Journal of Technology 5(1) (February 2001)

8. Tiwari, V., Singh, D., Rajgopal, S., Mehta, G., Patel, R., Baez, F.: Reducing power in high-performance microprocessors. In: Proceedings of the Design Automation Conference (DAC), pp. 732–737 (June 1998)
9. Wunderlich, R.E., Wenisch, T.F., Falsafi, B., Hoe, J.C.: SMARTS: Accelerating microarchitecture simulation via rigorous statistical sampling. In: Proceedings of the Annual International Symposium on Computer Architecture (ISCA), pp. 84–95 (June 2003)
10. Sherwood, T., Perelman, E., Hamerly, G., Calder, B.: Automatically characterizing large scale program behavior. In: Proceedings of the International Conference on Architectural Support for Programming Languages and Operating Systems (ASPLOS), pp. 45–57 (October 2002)
11. Yi, J.J., Kodakara, S.V., Sendag, R., Lilja, D.J., Hawkins, D.M.: Characterizing and comparing prevailing simulation techniques. In: Proceedings of the International Symposium on High-Performance Computer Architecture (HPCA), pp. 266–277 (February 2005)
12. Vandeputte, F., Eeckhout, L.: Finding stress patterns in microprocessor workloads. In: Proceedings of the 2009 International Conference on High Performance and Embedded Architectures and Compilers (HiPEAC), pp. 153–167 (January 2009)
13. (SPEC), S.P.E.C.: Specpower_ssj2008, http://www.spec.org/power_ssj2008/
14. Kanter, D.: EEMBC energizes benchmarking. Microprocessor Report (July 2006)
15. Van Biesbrouck, M., Eeckhout, L., Calder, B.: Efficient sampling startup for sampled processor simulation. In: 2005 International Conference on High Performance Embedded Architectures and Compilation (HiPEAC), pp. 47–67 (November 2005)
16. Wenisch, T.F., Wunderlich, R.E., Falsafi, B., Hoe, J.C.: Simulation sampling with live-points. In: Proceedings of the Annual International Symposium on Performance Analysis of Systems and Software (ISPASS), pp. 2–12 (March 2006)
17. Conte, T.M., Hirsch, M.A., Menezes, K.N.: Reducing state loss for effective trace sampling of superscalar processors. In: Proceedings of the International Conference on Computer Design (ICCD), pp. 468–477 (October 1996)
18. Eeckhout, L., Luo, Y., De Bosschere, K., John, L.K.: BLRL: Accurate and efficient warmup for sampled processor simulation. The Computer Journal 48(4), 451–459 (2005)
19. Haskins Jr., J.W., Skadron, K.: Accelerated warmup for sampled microarchitecture simulation. ACM Transactions on Architecture and Code Optimization (TACO) 2(1), 78–108 (2005)
20. Kluyskens, S., Eeckhout, L.: Branch history matching: Branch predictor warmup for sampled simulation. In: Proceedings of the Second International Conference on High Performance Embedded Architectures and Compilation (HiPEAC), pp. 153–167 (January 2007)
21. Laha, S., Patel, J.H., Iyer, R.K.: Accurate low-cost methods for performance evaluation of cache memory systems. IEEE Transactions on Computers 37(11), 1325–1336 (1988)
22. Dubey, P.K., Nair, R.: Profile-driven sampled trace generation. Technical Report RC 20041, IBM Research Division, T. J. Watson Research Center (April 1995)
23. Iyengar, V.S., Trevillyan, L.H., Bose, P.: Representative traces for processor models with infinite cache. In: Proceedings of the Second International Symposium on High-Performance Computer Architecture (HPCA), pp. 62–73 (February 1996)
24. Lafage, T., Seznec, A.: Choosing representative slices of program execution for microarchitecture simulations: A preliminary application to the data stream. In: IEEE 3rd Annual Workshop on Workload Characterization (WWC-2000) Held in Conjunction with the International Conference on Computer Design (ICCD (September 2000)
25. Lauterbach, G.: Accelerating architectural simulation by parallel execution of trace samples. Technical Report SMLI TR-93-22, Sun Microsystems Laboratories Inc. (December 1993)
26. Skadron, K., Ahuja, P.S., Martonosi, M., Clark, D.W.: Branch prediction, instruction-window size, and cache size: Performance tradeoffs and simulation techniques. IEEE Transactions on Computers 48(11), 1260–1281 (1999)

27. Sherwood, T., Perelman, E., Calder, B.: Basic block distribution analysis to find periodic behavior and simulation points in applications. In: Proceedings of the International Conference on Parallel Architectures and Compilation Techniques (PACT), pp. 3–14 (September 2001)
28. Lau, J., Sampson, J., Perelman, E., Hamerly, G., Calder, B.: The strong correlation between code signatures and performance. In: Proceedings of the International Symposium on Performance Analysis of Systems and Software (ISPASS), pp. 236–247 (March 2005)
29. Burger, D.C., Austin, T.M.: The SimpleScalar Tool Set. Computer Architecture News (1997), http://www.simplescalar.com
30. Brooks, D., Tiwari, V., Martonosi, M.: Wattch: A framework for architectural-level power analysis and optimizations. In: Proceedings of the 27th Annual International Symposium on Computer Architecture (ISCA), pp. 83–94 (June 2000)
31. Hamerly, G., Perelman, E., Lau, J., Calder, B.: SimPoint 3.0: Faster and more flexible program analysis. Journal of Instruction-Level Parallelism 7 (September 2005)
32. Chou, T., Roy, K.: Accurate power estimation of CMOS sequential circuits. IEEE Transaction on VLSI Systems 4(3), 369–380 (1996)
33. Srinivasan, V., Brooks, D., Gschwind, M., Bose, P., Zyuban, V., Strenski, P.N., Emma, P.G.: Optimizing pipelines for power and performance. In: Proceedings of the 35th Annual International Symposium on Microarchitecture (MICRO), pp. 333–344 (November 2002)
34. Joshi, A.M., Eeckhout, L., John, L.K., Isen, C.: Automated microprocessor stressmark generation. In: Proceedings of the International Symposium on High-Performance Computer Architecture (HPCA), pp. 229–239 (February 2008)
35. Dhodapkar, A., Smith, J.E.: Managing multi-configuration hardware via dynamic working set analysis. In: Proceedings of the 29th Annual International Symposium on Computer Architecture (ISCA), pp. 233–244 (May 2002)
36. Dhodapkar, A.S., Smith, J.E.: Comparing program phase detection techniques. In: Proceedings of the 36th Annual IEEE/ACM International Symposium on Microarchitecture (MICRO), pp. 217–227 (December 2003)
37. Sherwood, T., Sair, S., Calder, B.: Phase tracking and prediction. In: Proceedings of the 30th Annual International Symposium on Computer Architecture (ISCA), pp. 336–347 (June 2003)
38. Huang, M., Renau, J., Torrellas, J.: Positional adaptation of processors: Application to energy reduction. In: Proceedings of the 30th Annual International Symposium on Computer Architecture (ISCA), pp. 157–168 (June 2003)
39. Duesterwald, E., Cascaval, C., Dwarkadas, S.: Characterizing and predicting program behavior and its variability. In: Proceedings of the International Conference on Parallel Architectures and Compilation Techniques (PACT), pp. 220–231 (October 2003)
40. Isci, C., Martonosi, M.: Identifying program power phase behavior using power vectors. In: Proceedings of the Sixth Annual IEEE International Workshop on Workload Characterization (WWC) (September 2003)
41. Isci, C., Martonosi, M.: Runtime power monitoring in high-end processors: Methodology and empirical data. In: Proceedings of the 36th Annual International Symposium on Microarchitecture (MICRO), pp. 93–104 (December 2003)
42. Isci, C., Martonosi, M.: Phase characterization for power: Evaluating control-flow-based and event-counter-based techniques. In: Proceedings of the International Symposium on High-Performance Computer Architecture (HPCA), pp. 122–133 (February 2006)

Hybrid Super/Subthreshold Design of a Low Power Scalable-Throughput FFT Architecture

Michael B. Henry and Leyla Nazhandali

Virginia Polytechnic Institute and State University,
302 Whittemore , Blacksburg, VA 24061
{mbh,leyla}@vt.edu

Abstract. In this article, we present a parallel implementation of a 1024 point Fast Fourier Transform (FFT) operating with a subthreshold supply voltage, which is below the voltage that turns the transistors on and off. Even though the transistors are not actually switching as usual in this region, they are able to complete the computation by modulating the leakage current that passes through them, resulting in a 20-100x decrease in power consumption. Our hybrid FFT design partitions a sequential butterfly FFT architecture into two regions, namely memory banks and processing elements, such that the former runs in the superthreshold region and the latter in the subthreshold region. For a given throughput, the number of parallel processing units and their supply voltage is determined such that the overall power consumption of the design is minimized. For a 1024 point FFT operation, our parallel design is able to deliver the same throughput as a serial design, while consuming 70% less power. We study the effectiveness of this method for a variable throughput application such as a sensor node switching between a low throughput and high throughput mode, e.g. when sensing an interesting event. We compare our method with other methods used for throughput scaling such as voltage scaling and clock scaling and find that our scaling method will last up to three times longer on battery power. We also analyze the trade-offs involved in our method, including yield and device size issues.

1 Introduction

As Charles Van Loan wrote in his book "The Fast Fourier Transform (FFT) is one of the truly great computational developments of this century. It has changed the face of science and engineering so much that it is not an exaggeration to say that life as we know it would be very difficult without the FFT" [15]. The FFT has had a widespread application in traditional fields such as communication and manufacturing. The advent of wireless sensor networks has created even more applications for the transform. Sensor nodes are often employed to monitor an environment and report interesting data or significant events [1]. The FFT can be used to analyze the raw data in order to identify such events. This is especially important for situations where large amounts of data are collected, but there is

P. Stenström (Ed.): Transactions on HiPEAC IV, LNCS 6760, pp. 175–194, 2011.
© Springer-Verlag Berlin Heidelberg 2011

only an occasional need to report back data. Since the sensor nodes run on either a battery or a limited amount of scavenged energy, and communication costs are still the dominant factor in power consumption, it is usually advantageous to process the data locally and transmit only a message if an interesting event is detected. In an example scenario, a node with an acoustic sensor, which is employed in a field to detect passing vehicles, collects sound samples periodically. It then analyzes the collected data using an FFT to determine if its frequency content includes components representing frequencies found in a moving vehicle such as a humming engine frequency. If so, it records the event and transmits the data to a central station or other nodes depending on how the sensor network is implemented.

It is also highly desirable to be able to scale the throughput of an FFT processor for sensor node applications [8]. Increasing the amount of transformed data yields more resolution in the frequency domain. However, high quality FFTs are computationally intensive and consume high levels of power, which is impractical for wireless sensor nodes. It is therefore suggested that during idle periods, a low throughput FFT is used that consumes less power. When a significant event is suspected, the throughput of the FFT is ramped up so that the data can be analyzed more diligently.

In this article, which is an expansion of [9], we present a low-power parallel implementation of the FFT with scalable throughput. Our novel FFT design partitions a traditional butterfly FFT architecture into two regions, namely memory banks and processing elements, so that the operating voltage of the former region is above the threshold voltage while that of the latter region is below the threshold voltage, which is the voltage that turns the transistors on and off. Above this threshold, transistors operate similar to a switch that let the current flow to either charge or discharge the load. Below the threshold voltage the transistors are not actually switching as usual; instead they are able to complete the computation by modulating the leakage current that passes through them, resulting in a 20-100x decrease in power consumption.

Our proposed design is able to deliver the same throughput as a traditional design while consuming 70 % less power. Furthermore, we study the effectiveness of this method in a variable throughput application. We compare our method with other methods used for scaling the throughput, namely voltage scaling and clock scaling. Our results indicate that in an example scenario, if all these designs are running on 2 alkaline AA batteries and spend 15% of their time in high quality mode and the rest in the low quality mode, our design can last up to 111 days while the other two last only 59 and 40 days respectively. The cost of the decrease in power is a 5x increase in die area. This increase in die area can have some negative side effects, including a decrease in yield and an increase in device size. The parallelization employed allows the use of the fault tolerance technique of redundancy, and two possible redundancy techniques are explored. Also, it is shown that the size of a device using the FFT processor can potentially decrease, because the reduction in power consumption means the size of the energy source can be reduced.

The rest of this article is organized as follows: Section 2 describes the background related to this article, which includes two subsections: one on the fundamentals of FFT operation and the other on the basics of subthreshold operation. In Section 3, we present our novel parallel FFT architecture based on the traditional butterfly design. Section 4 describes our employed methodology to carry out the experiments while Section 5 presents the results of these experiments. Section 6 explores some of the trade-offs of parallelizing to reduce power. 7 presents related work. Finally, in Section 8 we present the conclusions and future directions of this study.

2 Background

2.1 Fast Fourier Transform

The Fast Fourier Transform (FFT), formulated by Cooley and Tukey [6], is an efficient method for calculating the frequency content of a signal. The number of samples in the signal, N, determines the frequency resolution and quality of the FFT. An increase in the number of data points yields more frequency resolution, but takes more computation as the complexity of the transform is equal to $O(N * log_2(N))$. Equation (1) presents the formulas that define the radix-2 FFT.

$$X_k = \sum_{m=0}^{\frac{N}{2}-1} x_{2m} W^{(2m)k} + \sum_{m=0}^{\frac{N}{2}-1} x_{2m+1} W^{(2m+1)k} \tag{1}$$

$$W^n = e^{-\frac{2\pi i}{N} n} \tag{2}$$

Equation (1) breaks up an N point FFT into the sum of two $\frac{N}{2}$ point FFTs. These $\frac{N}{2}$ point FFTs can then be broken up again and again leading to a fast recursive implementation of a DFT. The W coefficients are constants equal to nth roots of unity in the complex plane, traditionally called twiddle factors. Figure 1A shows the signal flow graph of an 8-point FFT. There are 3 levels in

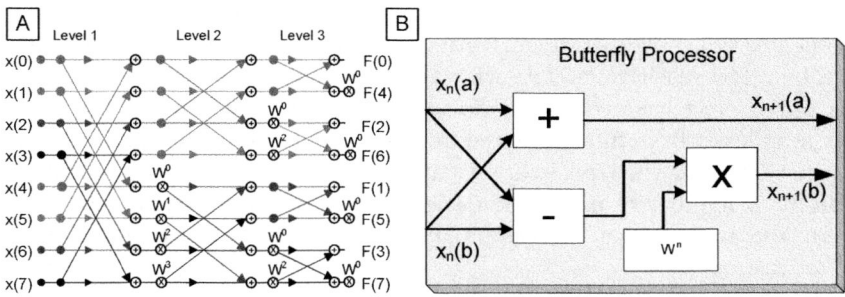

Fig. 1. A. Signal Flow Graph of 8 pt. FFT B. Butterfly processor

an 8-point FFT, corresponding to the $log_2(N)$ term in the complexity. There is a repetitive pattern in the FFT signal flow graph that looks like a butterfly. Each butterfly contains a complex addition, subtraction, and multiplication. It can be seen from the figure that there are 4 butterfly computations in each level, which is half of 8 data points and corresponds to the N term in the complexity. Overall there are $(N * log_2(N))/2$ butterfly operations in this FFT implementation[1]. It is highly impractical to implement this signal flow graph in hardware for a 1024-point FFT due to its large area requirement, so hardware must be reused to perform these calculations. One possibility is to use a single butterfly element and compute all the $(N * log_2(N))/2$ butterfly operations serially. Intermediate values can be stored in and recalled from a memory bank.

2.2 Subthreshold Voltage Operation

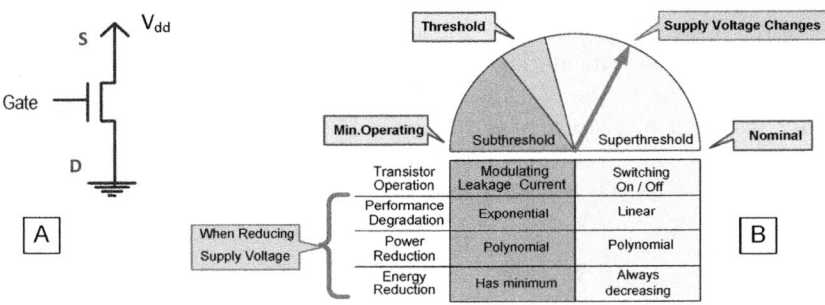

Fig. 2. Overview of sub/superthreshold operation

Figure 2A shows a CMOS transistor identifying its source and gate. When the source voltage is above a certain ***threshold***, the transistor effectively functions like a switch responding to the changes that come from gate voltage. Lowering the voltage source, or voltage scaling, has been a prevalent method for improving the energy efficiency of microprocessors [5,2]. This is due to the fact that reducing the voltage drops the energy consumption of a microprocessor quadratically, while decreasing its performance linearly. The lower limit for voltage-scaling has typically been restricted to half the nominal voltage - the voltage that hardware is designed to typically operate at. Until recently, this limit has only been imposed upon by a few sensitive circuits with analog-like operation such as sense amplifiers. However, it has been known for some time that standard CMOS gates operate seamlessly from full-voltage source to well below the threshold voltage - the voltage that turns the transistor on - at times reaching as low as 100mV [11,16]. Recently, a number of prototype designs have demonstrated that with careful design and replacement of these analog-like devices with standard switching

---

[1] There are other ways to implement FFT. However, the Cooley-Tukey algorithm discussed in this article is by far the most common implementation of FFT due to its efficiency.

counterparts, it is possible to extend the traditional voltage-scaling limit to below the threshold voltage, i.e., **subthreshold-voltage**[2] region [23,21,12].

Figure 2B provides an overview of subthreshold and superthreshold operation differences. First, the transistors are not switching as normal in the subthreshold region; instead they modulate the leakage current that passes through to charge or discharge their load and eventually perform computation. This, in turn, results in exponential degradation of performance in the subthreshold region as opposed to linear degradation when voltage is reduced in superthreshold[3]. Moreover, because the system operates at much lower voltages, it becomes more susceptible to some manufacturing and operational problems such as process variation and soft errors. These issues, as well as accurate modeling of subthreshold leakage are currently under investigation by several research groups in the VLSI and digital electronics area who have shown promising results [20,13,10,23]. The focus of this article is not providing a solution to some of these known problems for subthreshold operation. Instead, we present an example of the new opportunities this technology provides to designers by showcasing an architecture for FFT with scalable throughput and ultra low power consumption.

3   Implementation

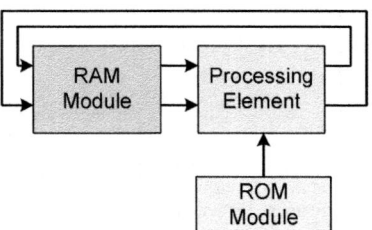

Fig. 3. FFT Architecture

The 1024 point FFT architecture used in this article is based on [18] and is implemented in a 90 nm technology. It consists of three major modules: RAM, processing element, and ROM. The processing element (PE) performs the FFT calculations and contains at least one butterfly processor shown in Figure 1B. The butterfly processor implements a complex addition, subtraction, and multiplication. The multiplication is implemented using a Booth multiplier and the addition is implemented using efficient carry select adders. The architecture processes 32 bit complex numbers, where 16 bits represent the real portion and 16 bits represent the complex portion, all in the Q15 fixed point format.

---

[2] In this document, we may use super/subthreshold words in place of super/subthreshold-voltage for brevity.

[3] In order to obtain power and frequency trends for the butterfly processor in the subthreshold region, a post layout simulation was performed using extracted parasitics and a Fast-SPICE program.

The ROM module stores the constant twiddle coefficients while the RAM module is responsible for storing inputs, outputs and intermediate values. The PE takes in three inputs: the first two inputs are either the input signals, or the intermediate values that are the result of a previous butterfly operation. The third operand is a constant W^n coefficient, taken from the ROM. The W^n coefficients are arranged around the unit circle in the complex plane, but the FFT only uses coefficients with positive imaginary parts. There is also symmetry of the coefficients on the left half and right half of the unit circle, so overall 256 32-bit coefficients are needed in the ROM for a 1024 point transform. The architecture implements the FFT using decimation in frequency, which means initially, the RAM holds the 1024 32-bit input values, and they get replaced with intermediate and eventually output values as the FFT progresses.

3.1   Parallelization and Throughput Scalability

It is well-known that the parallelism present in applications such as the FFT can be utilized to improve the energy efficiency of the system without sacrificing performance [4]. In our design, we exploit the unique characteristics of subthreshold operation in this context. Traditional parallel designs focus on increasing the throughput of a system. Our design exploits parallelism in a different way, by adding parallel units and slowing them down to match the original throughput. To slow down the parallel units, the supply voltage is reduced which greatly reduces the power consumption. We will show that the optimal supply voltage for the parallel FFT architecture is in the subthreshold region.

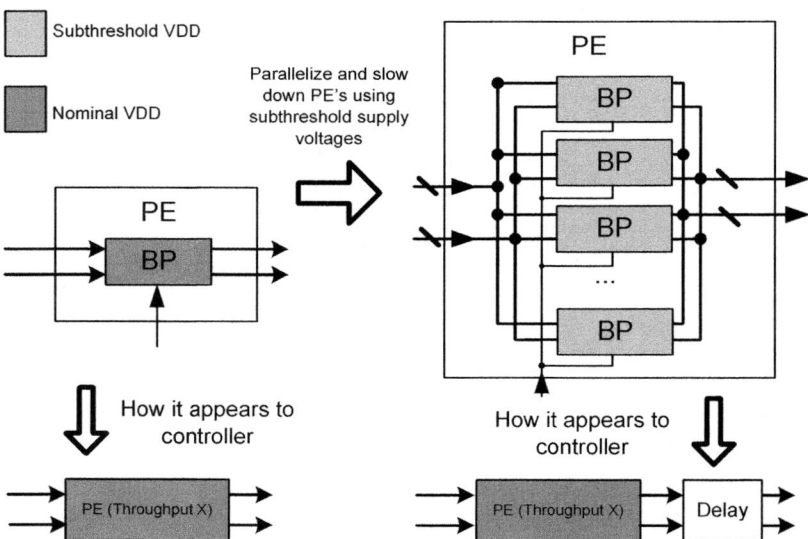

Fig. 4. Parallelization of the PEs: Butterfly processors are added to the processing element and their supply voltage is reduced so the throughput remains the same. To the controller, this only appears as a delay from the input to the output.

Our goal is to design an FFT architecture to operate with minimum energy given a desired level of performance. In order to achieve this, the number of butterfly processors (BPs) within the processing element (PE) is increased and the supply voltage to the processors is decreased such that the throughput remains constant, as shown in Figure 4. Even though a processing element may contain a number of butterfly processors, it must still only have three inputs and two outputs. The processing element, therefore, needs a data distribution bus that distributes the serial data from the RAM to each butterfly processor, and a collection bus that forms the processed data back into a serial stream. The PE uses a common bus and a multiplexer to accomplish the data distribution and collection respectively. Data is distributed in a staggered fashion to the BPs, and is collected on the other end in a staggered fashion. The supply voltage of the BPs is scaled such that the existing data in a BP is processed before new data is sent to it. The PE, therefore, exhibits the same throughput no matter how many BPs it contains. The only difference is that there is increased latency of the PE, which grows linearly with respect to the number of BPs.

The parallelization lends itself well to a scalable throughput design. At maximum throughput, all of the BPs in the PE are activated and are processing data. To reduce the throughput, only some of the BPs are active and the rest are powered off. Ideally, the operating voltage of these remaining BP's should be adjusted to achieve maximum energy efficiency. However, as we will show in Section 5, the benefits of this ideal method does not justify the extra burden of adding voltage scaling capability to the circuitry. Instead, we simply power off a certain number of BP's while leaving the rest to run at the same speed. We call this method *active unit scaling.*

With more than one BP running in parallel, one can envision a design where the RAM bank is split into multiple banks, each running at a lower speed than the original RAM and feeding the slow-running BP units. As an example, the 1024-word RAM bank can be split into two separate 512-word banks. Both of these RAM modules, i.e. the single bank or dual bank, are capable of supplying data at the same rate, but each 512-word RAM banks is now required to run at half the speed of the original one. Because of the relaxed speed requirement, the supply voltage of the two 512-word banks can be reduced, resulting in reduction of the RAM power. The penalty is the area taken up by the additional controller logic in the second bank, as well as the additional routing. We study the practicality of this method and present our findings in the results section.

4   Methodology

Table 1 shows the tool chain used for the synthesis and simulation of our design. In the rest of this section, we present the detailed methodology for the two major experiments done to study our proposed design.

Table 1. Tool Chain

HDL Language	Verilog
HDL Simulator	Synopsys VCS
Technology	Industry level 90 nm
Synthesis	Synopsys Design Compiler
RAM/ROM memory compiler	Industry level memory compiler
Voltage Scaling Characterization	Synopsys HSPICE, NanoSim
Power Simulation	Synopsys Primetime PX

4.1   Minimum Energy Architecture

The purpose of this experiment is to compute the optimum number of parallel butterfly processors as well as their operating voltage in order to achieve minimum energy consumption for a given throughput. Since the throughput is kept constant, the energy consumption is directly related to the power and we use these two terms interchangeably. To carry out this experiment, we use the trends presented in Section 2.2, which give the power consumption and the frequency (or throughput) of a BP for a given supply voltage. The inverse of this is used to determine the supply voltage - and then, power consumption - of a BP running at a given throughput. The throughput of the processing element with a single butterfly processor at nominal voltage is referred to as $TP_{Nominal}$, and is the target throughput for the minimum energy architecture. It is possible to increase the number of BPs in the PE and maintain $TP_{Nominal}$ by reducing the supply voltage of the BPs. Herein, n will refer to the number of parallel BPs in the PE. In order to achieve $TP_{Nominal}$ in a processing element, the throughput of each individual butterfly processor must be $\frac{TP_{Nominal}}{n}$. Using the characterization curves, the supply voltage that yields a BP throughput of $\frac{TP_{Nominal}}{n}$ will be determined and the power consumption at that speed will be noted. The total power consumption of the PE is the power consumption of a BP at $\frac{TP_{Nominal}}{n}$ throughput times n. The power consumption of the bus needed to distribute and collect data from n BPs will also be determined and added to the BPs' power consumption. The *minimum energy architecture* will be defined as the FFT architecture with n BPs that consumes the least amount of power, while maintaining a throughput of $TP_{Nominal}$.

4.2   Throughput Scaling

As stated in the introduction, there is a desire to dynamically scale the throughput of the FFT architecture. During idle times, fewer data points can be used in the FFT, and the throughput of the FFT processor can be reduced. Figure 5 shows an example scenario in a wireless sensor network. From $t0$ to $t1$, the hardware is performing a 256 point FFT and the hardware has reduced the throughput of the FFT processor. At $t1$, an event is detected and the hardware shifts to a 1024 point FFT. At this point, the hardware is running at its

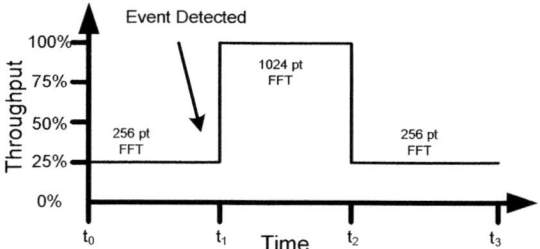

Fig. 5. Example sensing scenario

maximum throughput. From $t2$ to $t3$, the hardware goes back to a 256 point FFT. The duty cycle of the FFT hardware will be defined by Equation (3), or the time the hardware spends at max throughput divided by total time.

$$DutyCycle = \frac{t_2 - t_1}{t_3 - t_0} \qquad (3)$$

Four different methods will be examined that can be used to reduce the throughput of the FFT hardware and save power. The first method is clock scaling, where the clock speed to the PE is reduced. The supply voltage remains at nominal 1V. This will be done to the $n = 1$ FFT architecture (one BP per PE). The second method is dynamic voltage scaling, where the clock speed *and* supply voltage are the PE is reduced. This will also be done to the $n = 1$ FFT architecture. The third method will be the active unit scaling mentioned in Section 3.1. The minimum energy architecture will be used for this method. The fourth method is the ideal method for throughput scaling. The methodology presented in 4.1 presents a methodology that, for a target throughput, finds the number of parallel units and the supply voltage that minimizes energy. The ideal method of throughput scaling would use this methodology for each reduced target throughput. Thus, whenever the throughput needs to be lowered, a predetermined number of parallel units would be shut off, and the supply voltage would be adjusted such that the resulting architecture is the minimum energy architecture for the lowered throughput. The four methods of voltage scaling will be tested over various throughputs and the power consumption will be determined. It will also be determined, for a given duty cycle defined by Equation (3), how long each of the throughput scaling methods can last on two alkaline AA batteries (at 1500 mAh each) while executing the sensing scenario in Figure 5.

5   Results

5.1   Synthesis Results

Table 2 shows the results of the memory compiler and the synthesized verilog code at nominal voltage (1.0 V) and maximum speed.

Table 2. Synthesis Results of the FFT Architecture

Butterfly critical path	4.43 ns
Butterfly throughput	222 MHz
Butterfly power consumption	19.6 mW @ 222 MHz
Butterfly area	0.0498 mm^2
RAM access time	0.89 ns
RAM power	6.22 mW @ 444 MHz
RAM area	0.126 mm^2
ROM access time	0.74 ns
ROM power	1.13 mW @ 111 MHz
ROM area	0.024 mm^2

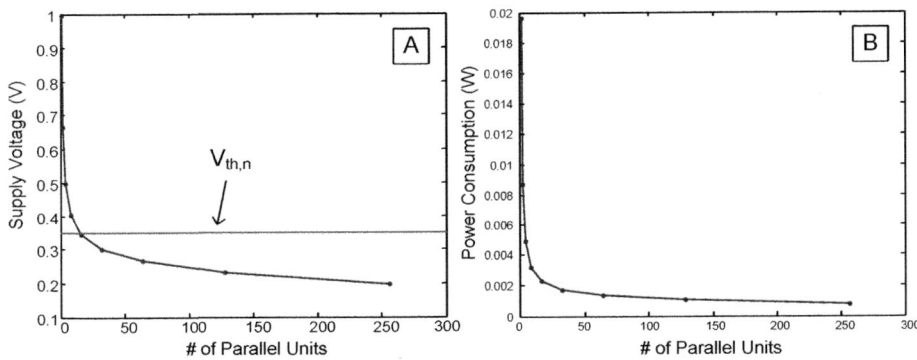

Fig. 6. A. Supply voltage for a given number of BPs. B. Power consumption of the PE for a given number of BPs, not including bus overhead for a constant throughput of 222 MHz.

5.2 Minimum Energy Architecture Experiment Results

Figure 6B shows the power consumption (not including bus overhead) of the processing element (PE) for a given number of butterfly processors (BP) inside the PE. The throughput is kept constant at 222 MHz while decreasing the supply voltage. The power decreases dramatically at first, but as the supply voltage reaches the subthreshold region, there are diminishing returns for adding more elements. As the number of BPs increases, the power consumption of the bus increases due to the increased load capacitance and increased number of flip flops required for distribution and collection of data. Figure 7A shows the data distribution and collection overhead for a given number of butterfly processors. The power consumption of the PE decreases with additional BPs while the power consumption of the bus increases with additional BPs, so there is a point where the PE reaches its maximum power efficiency for the targeted throughput. Since the throughput is kept constant, all the power savings translate to energy savings. Figure 7B shows the total power consumption of the entire FFT architecture.

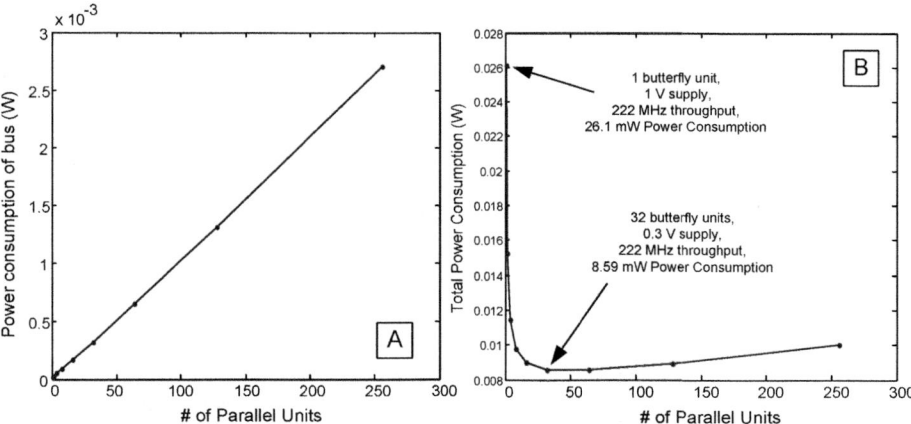

Fig. 7. A. Power consumption of the data distribution and collection bus within the PE. B. Total power consumption of the entire architecture for a given number of BPs including RAM, ROM, bus, and controller.

This includes the RAM, ROM, and controller power. According to the figure, the minimum energy is achieved at $n = 32$.

5.3   Throughput Scaling Experiment Results

Figure 8A shows the results of the throughput scaling in terms of power consumption. The clock scaling and the supply voltage scaling methods are identical at 100 % duty cycle operating at nominal voltage of 1.0 V and running at maximum speed of 222 MHz. However, at lower duty cycles, the dynamic voltage scaling outperforms the clock scaling because it reduces the power quadratically. Meanwhile, our proposed active unit scaling method outperforms both traditional methods in all cases. Figure 8B shows the results of the experiment mentioned in Section 4.2, where the throughput is varied between a 256 point FFT and a 1024 point FFT at various duty cycles. Figure 8B presents the number of days our throughput method, as well as the two traditional methods, can survive while running off two heavy duty alkaline AA batteries. The proposed active unit scaling architecture lasts longer than the other two architectures for all possible duty cycle scenarios. As shown in Figure 8B, at around 30 % duty cycle, our proposed architecture using active unit scaling can last up to 3 months while the other two methods can barely survive beyond a month.

As mentioned in Section 3.1, the ideal method of throughput scaling is to adjust both the supply voltage and the number of active BPs. In other words, to achieve maximum energy efficiency while scaling the throughput, one has to identify the optimum number of BPs and their operating voltage for the desired reduced throughput using the method shown in Section 4.1. Instead, we proposed a simple method to simply turn off a pre-calculated number of BP's to achieve the same result. Figure 9A shows the proposed active unit scaling method versus the ideal method with respect to the target throughput. This

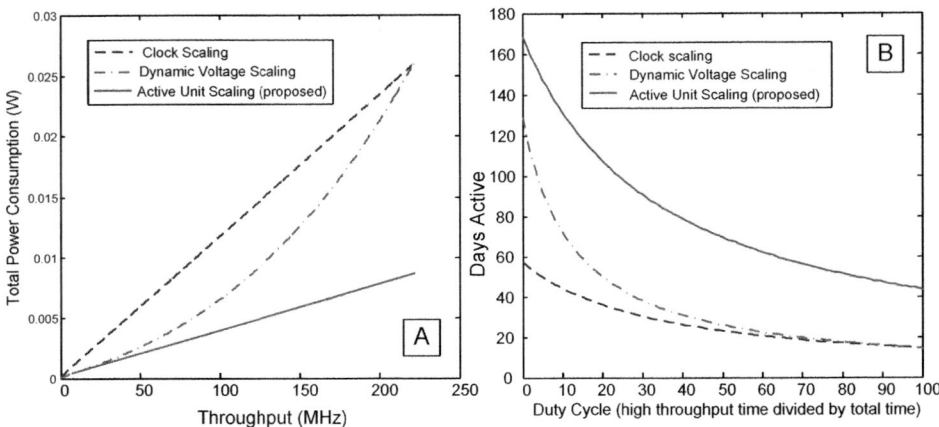

Fig. 8. A. Total power consumption of proposed active unit scaling compared to clock scaling and voltage scaling. B. Number of days the above designs can remain active on 2 AA batteries with respect to duty cycle.

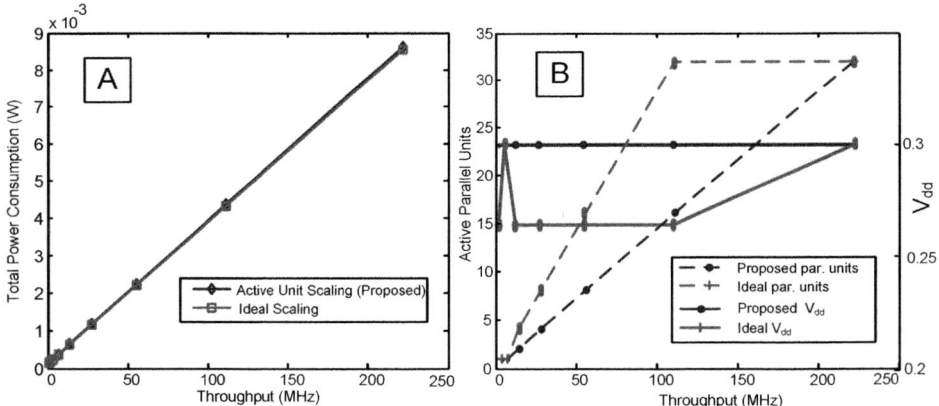

Fig. 9. A. Power consumption of Proposed Active Unit Scaling and Ideal throughput scaling w.r.t. throughput. B. Number of active parallel units and supply voltage of Proposed Active Unit Scaling and ideal throughput scaling w.r.t. throughput.

figure shows that the proposed active unit scaling achieves a power consumption that is very close to the ideal method. In addition, the ideal throughput scaling method involves more control logic and a fine tune control of the supply voltage. Figure 9B shows the number of active parallel units and the supply voltage of the two methods. The number of active parallel units with the ideal method does not follow a predictable pattern and thus would be hard to implement. The proposed method, on the other hand, shuts down a linear number of parallel units. For example, to achieve a throughput that is one half of the maximum, half of the parallel units would be shut off. Also, the ideal method requires a finely tunable variable voltage source, which can be difficult to implement. The proposed method, on the other hand, uses a constant supply voltage. Overall, the proposed active unit throughput scaling method only consumes slightly more power than the ideal throughput scaling method, but is significantly simpler to implement.

5.4 Comparisons

Table 3 compares the non parallelized FFT architecture with two parallelized FFT architectures. While $n = 32$ constitutes the minimum energy architecture, the $n = 16$ design provides a sweet spot with only a slight increase in power and half of the area overhead. The total power consumption includes that for processing, RAM, ROM, and the bus.

Table 3. Comparison of different number of BPs

	$n = 1$	$n = 16$	$n = 32$
Total Power @ 222MHz	26.11 mW	9.00 mW	8.54 mW
Total Area	0.200 mm^2	0.947 mm^2	1.74 mm^2
PE Supply Voltage	1.0 V	0.344 V	0.30 V
Days on 2 AA bat. @ Max Duty Cyc.	14	42	44
Days on 2 AA bat. @ 15 % Duty Cyc.	40 (CS), 59 (DVS)	111	118

5.5 Splitting the RAM Bank

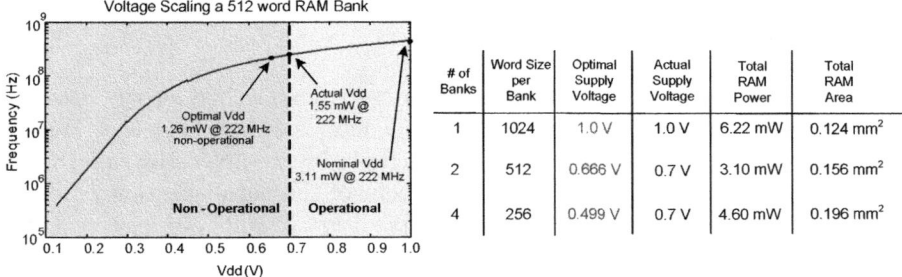

Fig. 10. Splitting the RAM bank and reducing the supply voltage

Figure 10 shows how the frequency of a 512-word 32-bit RAM bank scales with the supply voltage, which results in significant power savings. However, in practice, it is known that regular 6T SRAM cells are not able to function below 0.7 V in 90 nm technology [24][4]. Therefore, even though splitting the RAM bank ideally calls for lowering the voltage, we cannot go beyond 0.7 V. The table in

---

[4] Currently, there are designs of SRAM cells that are functional near or below threshold voltage. However, they require additional transistors.[3]

Figure 10 shows the result of our analysis. It can be seen that given the restriction on lowering the supply voltage, splitting the RAM into two banks provides the most power efficient design by reducing the memory power consumption by more than half while incurring little area overhead.

6   Trade-offs

The obvious penalty for reducing the power consumption through parallelization is the increase in area. With the recent advances in packaging and the steady decrease in feature size, area is becoming less of a design factor when compared to performance and power consumption. The increase in area, however, can still have some negative side effects that must be addressed. First, adding more transistors means that there is an increased probability of faults in the FFT processor. These faults can be mitigated using fault tolerance techniques, and two techniques will be examined in this section. Second, the increase in die area can also increase the total device size, which may be unacceptable in some applications. The effect of the parallelization on the total area of a packaged chip is difficult to determine because the total area is also dependent on the pin count and packaging method. Lowering the power consumption of the processor, however, means that the size of the energy source of the device can potentially be reduced. Two applications that use the FFT processor will be examined: one powered by a solar cell and one powered by a lithium ion battery. It will be shown that in some cases, the size of the device is dominated by the energy source, and the increase in die area from parallelization is well worth the large decrease in the size of the energy source.

6.1   Yield

The increased area from the proposed power reduction method also increases the probability that the FFT system as a whole contains a fault or defect. Without fault tolerance techniques, a defect in a single butterfly processor could render the whole FFT processor inoperable. A benefit of the parallelization procedure is that it inherently allows the use of the traditional fault tolerance technique of redundancy. Two redundancy techniques with the parallelized FFT architecture are examined. The first technique can retain the optimal number of parallel units in the presence of a fault by inserting one or more backup cores. The second technique does not add backup cores and simply shuts down faulty cores, which leads to non-optimal power consumption.

Backup Cores: The backup core technique inserts extra backup cores that can be activated to replace an existing faulty core. This technique is well suited for the proposed architecture because the butterfly processors (BP) are homogenous and connected to a common bus. Figure 11 shows an example architecture that uses backup BPs. Each non-backup BP is assigned a unique ID. A global counter that increments through the unique IDs is sent alongside the data bus. When

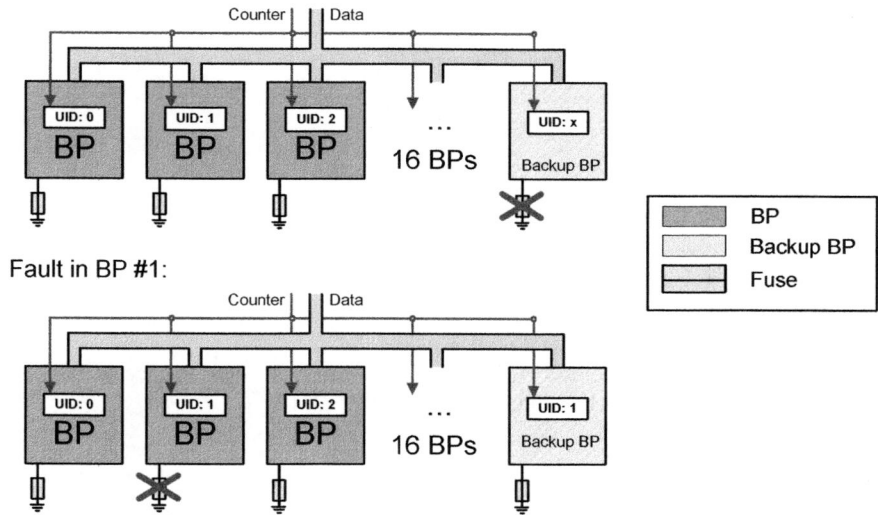

Fig. 11. Backup core method for fault tolerance, which retains optimal number of parallel units, but increases area

the counter matches a BP's unique ID, the BP latches the data from the bus. To implement the backup core method, the backup cores would need to contain a programmable ID. If a fault is detected in a non-backup BP, it is shut down (through fusible links, supply voltage gating, etc.) and a backup BP adopts the faulty core's unique ID. Estimating the optimum number of backup BPs to obtain a satisfactory yield is out of the scope of the article, but has been addressed thoroughly in other papers [14]. This method has three advantages: First, even in the presence of faulty BPs, it is possible to maintain the optimal operating point. Second, the controller that distributes and receives data from the parallel units does not have to be modified. Since the backup BP adopts the faulty BP's unique ID, to the controller it appears as if nothing has changed. Finally, the supply voltage to the system remains unchanged. A disadvantage of the backup core method is the extra area occupied by the backup BPs.

Core Shutdown: Section 4.1 gives a procedure for finding the optimal supply voltage for a given number of parallel units and a target throughput. This indicates that if one or more butterfly processors are faulty, it is possible to shut them down, raise the supply voltage of the remaining units, and still meet the throughput requirements. This method is considered non-optimal because, in the presence of faults, it uses less than the optimal number of parallel units in terms of power consumption. Figure 12 gives the supply voltage and power consumption for a given number of parallel units from 12 to 16, and a target throughput of 222 MHz. It can be seen that reducing the number of usable parallel units and increasing the supply voltage to meet the target throughput only slightly

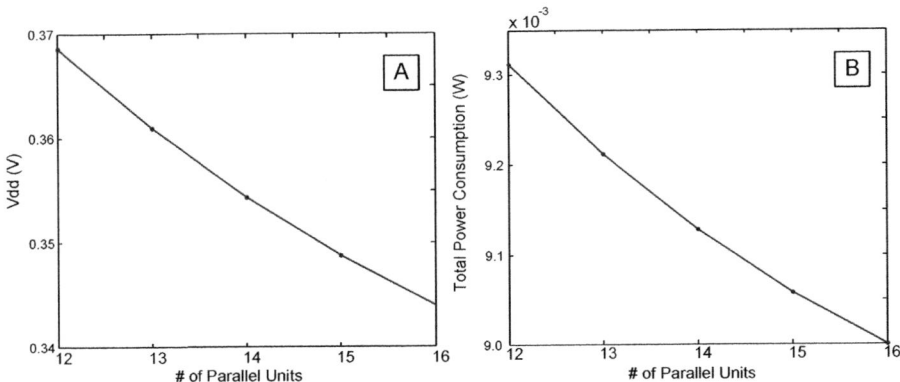

Fig. 12. A. Supply voltage and B. Power consumption in the presence of faulty cores, for the core shutdown method. Throughput = 222 MHz.

raises the power consumption. Combining the data in Figure 12 with redundancy yield analysis, such as that in [14], could yield a histogram with different bins for varying levels of power consumption. Non-optimal core shutdown appears to be an effective fault tolerance method, however there are some drawbacks. First, the controller that distributes and collects the data would have to be flexible enough to handle a variable number of parallel units. Controller design also becomes more difficult because the number of parallel units is now no longer restricted to powers of two. The remaining operational BPs would have to work faster in order to meet the throughput constraint, so the clock speed would need to be adjusted. Finally, the supply voltage to the parallel units must be raised. Depending on how the power networks are distributed, this may mean that the supply voltage to other portions of the chip must be raised, leading to a greater increase in power consumption.

6.2   Power Source Size Reduction

Table 3 shows that with the parallelization method outlined, a power reduction of around 70 % is possible for an FFT application. Depending on the energy source, a reduction in power consumption means the size of the energy source can be reduced. This is especially true for mobile applications that must run off of a battery or scavenged energy. To show this, the area of the $n = 1$ single single core architecture in Table 3 will be compared to the parallelized $n = 16$ architecture in Table 3 for an application using solar power and an application powered by a lithium-ion battery, all running at 222 MHz.

Solar Power: The first device in question is a solar powered mobile FFT device. The device must run indefinitely, so the power output of the solar cell must match the power consumption of the FFT processor. For the sake of simplicity, it will be assumed that the solar cell receives constant direct sunlight, so a power output of 15 mW/cm^2 will be used, which is typical of modern mass produced solar cells

[19]. Also, integrated circuit packaging and other peripheral electronics will be ignored. Table 4 shows the die area and solar cell area of the single core device and the parallelized $n = 16$ device.

Table 4. Area reduction of solar cell powered application

FFT Architecture	Power Cons.	Area	
		Die	Solar Cell
Single core $n = 1$	26.11 mW	0.200 mm^2	1.741 cm^2
Parallelized $n = 16$	9.00 mW	0.947 mm^2	0.600 cm^2

Battery Powered: The second device in question is a battery powered mobile FFT device. It is be assumed that the device is scattered in an environment, the battery cannot be replaced or recharged, and the device must last for 10 days. The battery in question is a 4.2 V lithium-ion battery with an energy capacity of 11.6 mW-days/cm^3 [22]. It will be assumed that the battery is 5mm thick, for an energy capacity of 5.8 mW-days/cm^2. For this device, non-linear battery effects, integrated circuit packaging and other peripheral electronics will be ignored. Table 5 shows the die area and battery area of the single core device and the parallelized $n = 16$ device.

Table 5. Area reduction of battery powered application

FFT Architecture	Power Cons.	Area	
		Die	Battery
Single core $n = 1$	26.11 mW	0.200 mm^2	45.02 cm^2
Parallelized $n = 16$	9.00 mW	0.947 mm^2	15.52 cm^2

It is clear from both Table 4 and Table 5 that the size of the power sources can potentially dominate the area of the device. As was said previously, it is hard to determine if an increase in the area of a subsystem leads to an overall increase in area of the packaged chip. What is clear, however, is that reducing the power consumption can lead to a reduction in size of the energy source of the system. In most cases, even if the size of the packaged chip has to be increased due to parallelization, this would be outweighed by large decrease in the size of the energy source.

7 Related Work

[23] presented a 180 mV FFT architecture that runs in the subthreshold region. The entire architecture runs at subthreshold voltage and the resulting through-put is very low due to a 164 Hz clock cycle at 180 mV and 10 kHz at 350 mV.

Our design, on the other hand, only runs the processing elements at subthreshold voltage, and parallelizes the processing to achieve a throughput typical of nominal voltage FFT processors. In addition, the architecture in [23] would have to use dynamic voltage scaling to achieve a higher throughput, and it was shown that our active unit scaling architecture outperforms dynamic voltage scaling. [17] presented a general purpose processor for the purposes of wireless sensor networks that runs in the subthreshold region. The processor is only capable of executing simple commands and a program to execute an FFT operation would be very slow due to the low clock frequency and the lack of FFT specific hardware. [7] presented a design methodology for parallel cores running at near threshold voltage. The cores were general purpose processors with caches, and they executed parallel software routines. Our work is different in that we present minimum energy hardware for a specific application.

8   Conclusion

In this article, we presented a novel FFT architecture based on the traditional butterfly-based FFT architecture, and greatly reduced its power consumption by exploiting parallelism. Additional butterfly processors were added, and their supply voltage was reduced while keeping the overall throughput constant. We showed that the optimum operating voltage of butterfly processors is well below the threshold voltage at around 0.3 V. The transistors still operate at this voltage, not by turning on and off, but by modulating the leakage current passing through them. The RAM module of the design however, was kept to operate in superthreshold at 0.7 V maximizing power efficiency while keeping the SRAM cells functional, resulting in a hybrid super/subthreshold design. By exploiting the parallelism in the processing element of the architecture, we were able to achieve 68 % reduction in total power consumption of the FFT architecture. A 10 % reduction is obtained by splitting the SRAM bank into two banks and scaling their voltage from nominal 1 V to 0.7 V. This total reduction of 78 % is obtained at the expense of increasing the area of the design by about a factor of 5. Even though the area increase may seem significant, the reduced cost of silicon and the increased need for ultra low power applications such as wireless sensor networks promotes such design directions. Also, the decrease in power consumption in some applications means that the required size of the energy source decreases, which can counteract the increase in chip area.

In addition, we proposed an efficient method to enable scaling the throughput of our design by turning off some of the active subthreshold parallel units without changing their supply voltage. We compared our method to traditional methods of clock scaling and dynamic voltage scaling by simulating the designs running on two AA batteries. Over the entire range of possible duty cycles of high throughput to low throughput, the active unit scaling outlasted the other two methods by a wide margin. At 15 % duty cycle, the active unit scaled design lasted 111 days, compared to 59 and 40 days for dynamic voltage scaling and clock scaling respectively. Future work would include fabricating a complete

ASIC design of our proposed FFT architecture, which would allow exploration of yield and process variation. Moreover, we intend to develop a general model for estimating how various architectures will benefit from the minimum energy architecture and active unit scaling methods detailed in this article.

References

1. Akyildiz, I.F., Su, W., Sankarasubramaniam, Y., Cayirci, E.: Wireless sensor networks: a survey. Computer Networks (Amsterdam, Netherlands: 1999) 38(4), 393–422 (2002)
2. Burd, T.D., Brodersen, R.W.: Energy efficient cmos microprocessor design. In: HICSS 1995: Proceedings of the 28th Hawaii International Conference on System Sciences (HICSS 1995), p. 288. IEEE Computer Society, Washington, DC (1995)
3. Calhoun, B.H., Chandrakasan, A.: A 256kb sub-threshold SRAM in 65nm CMOS. In: IEEE International Solid-State Circuits Conference, ISSCC 2006. Digest of Technical Papers, pp. 2592–2601 (Febraury 2006)
4. Chandrakasan, A.P., Brodersen, R.W.: Low Power Digital CMOS Design. Kluwer Academic Publishers, Norwell (1995)
5. Chandrakasan, A.P., Sheng, S., Brodersen, R.W.: Low-power CMOS digital design. IEEE Journal of Solid-State Circuits 27(4), 473–484 (1992)
6. Cooley, J.W., Tukey, J.W.: An algorithm for the machine calculation of complex fourier series. Mathematics of Computation 19(90), 297–301 (1965)
7. Dreslinski, R.G., Zhai, B., Mudge, T., Blaauw, D., Sylvester, D.: An energy efficient parallel architecture using near threshold operation. In: 16th International Conference on Parallel Architecture and Compilation Techniques, PACT 2007, pp. 175–188 (September 2007)
8. Heinzelman, W.R., Sinha, A., Wang, A., Chandrakasan, A.P.: Energy-scalable algorithms and protocols for wireless microsensornetworks. In: Proceedings of the IEEE International Conference on Acoustics, Speech, and Signal Processing, ICASSP 2000, Istanbul, Turkey, vol. 6, pp. 3722–3725 (2000)
9. Henry, M.B., Nazhandali, L.: Hybrid super/Subthreshold design of a low power scalable-throughput FFT architecture. In: Seznec, A., Emer, J., O'Boyle, M., Martonosi, M., Ungerer, T. (eds.) HIPEAC 2009. LNCS, vol. 5409, pp. 278–292. Springer, Heidelberg (2009)
10. Jayakumar, N., Khatri, S.P.: A variation tolerant subthreshold design approach. In: DAC 2005: Proceedings of the 42nd Annual Conference on Design Automation, pp. 716–719. ACM Press, New York (2005)
11. Kao, J., Narendra, S., Chandrakasan, A.: Subthreshold leakage modeling and reduction techniques. In: Proc. International Conference on Computer-Aided Design (November 2002)
12. Kim, C.H.I., Soeleman, H., Roy, K.: Ultra-low-power DLMS adaptive filter for hearing aid applications. IEEE Transactions on Very Large Scale Integration (VLSI) Systems 11(6), 1058–1067 (2003)
13. Kim, T.-H., Eom, H., Keane, J., Kim, C.: Utilizing reverse short channel effect for optimal subthreshold circuit design. In: ISLPED 2006: Proceedings of the 2006 International Symposium on Low Power Electronics and Design, pp. 127–130. ACM Press, New York (2006)
14. Koren, I., Koren, Z.: Defect tolerance in VLSI circuits: techniques and yield analysis. Proceedings of the IEEE 86(9), 1819–1838 (1998)

15. Loan, C.V.: Computational frameworks for the fast Fourier transform. Society for Industrial and Applied Mathematics, Philadelphia (1992)
16. Meindl, J.D., Davis, J.A.: The fundamental limit on binary switching energy for terascale integration (TSI). IEEE JSSCC 35 (February 2002)
17. Nazhandali, L., Zhai, B., Olson, J., Reeves, A., Minuth, M., Helfand, R., Pant, S., Austin, T., Blaauw, D.: Energy optimization of subthreshold-voltage sensor network processors. SIGARCH Comput. Archit. News 33(2), 197–207 (2005)
18. Pirsch, P.: Architectures for Digital Signal Processing. Wiley, West Sussex
19. Raghunathan, V., Kansal, A., Hsu, J., Friedman, J., Srivastava, M.: Design considerations for solar energy harvesting wireless embedded systems. In: IPSN 2005: Proceedings of the 4th International Symposium on Information Processing in Sensor Networks, p. 64. IEEE Press, Piscataway (2005)
20. Raychowdhury, A., Paul, B., Bhunia, S., Roy, K.: Computing with subthreshold leakage: device/circuit/architecture co-design for ultralow-power subthreshold operation. IEEE Transactions on Very Large Scale Integration (VLSI) Systems 13(11), 1213–1224 (2005)
21. Sze, V., Blazquez, R., Bhardwaj, M., Chandrakasan, A.: An energy efficient subthreshold baseband processor architecture for pulsed ultra-wideband communications. In: Proceedings of the IEEE International Conference on Acoustics, Speech and Signal Processing, ICASSP 2006, Toulouse, vol. 3 (2006)
22. Tarascon, J.M., Gozdz, A.S., Schmutz, C.: Performance of bellcore's plastic rechargeable liion batteries. Solid State Ionics
23. Wang, A., Chandrakasan, A.: A 180-mv subthreshold FFT processor using a minimum energy design methodology. IEEE Journal of Solid-State Circuits 40(1), 310–319 (2005)
24. Yamaoka, M., Maeda, N., Shinozaki, Y., Shimazaki, Y., Nii, K., Shimada, S., Yanagisawa, K., Kawahara, T.: Low-power embedded SRAM modules with expanded margins for writing. In: IEEE International Solid-State Circuits Conference, ISSCC 2005. Digest of Technical Papers, pp. 480–611 (February 2005)

Transaction Reordering to Reduce Aborts in Software Transactional Memory

Mohammad Ansari, Mikel Luján, Christos Kotselidis, Kim Jarvis,
Chris Kirkham, and Ian Watson

The University of Manchester
{ansari,mikel,kotselidis,jarvis,chris,watson}@cs.manchester.ac.uk

Abstract. In transactional memory, conflicts between two concurrently executing transactions reduce performance, reduce scalability, and may lead to aborts, which waste computing resources. Ideally, concurrent execution of transactions would be ordered to minimise conflicts, but such an ordering is often complex, or unfeasible, to obtain. This paper identifies a pattern, called *repeat conflicts*, that can be a source of conflicts, and presents a novel technique, called *steal-on-abort*, to reduce the number of conflicts caused by repeat conflicts. Steal-on-abort operates at runtime, and requires no application-specific information or offline preprocessing. Evaluation using a sorted linked list, and STAMP-vacation with different contention managers show steal-on-abort to be highly effective at reducing repeat conflicts, which leads to a range of performance improvements.

1 Introduction

Recent progress in multi-core processor architectures, coupled with challenges in advancing uniprocessor designs, has led to mainstream processor manufacturers adopting multi-core designs. Modest projections suggest hundred-core processors to be common within a decade. Although multi-core has re-invigorated the processor manufacturing industry, it has raised a difficult challenge for software development.

The execution time of software has improved on successive generations of uniprocessors thanks to the increasing clock frequency, and complex strategies designed to take advantage of instruction-level parallelism. However, on future multi-core processors this 'free' improvement will not materialise unless the software is multi-threaded, i.e., parallelised, and thus able to take advantage of the increasing number of cores. Furthermore, the number of cores predicted in future processors suggests software will need to scale to non-trivial levels.

Parallel (or concurrent) programming using *explicit locking* to ensure safe access to shared data has been the domain of experts, and is well-known for being challenging to build robust and correct software. Typical problems include data races, deadlock, livelock, priority inversion, and convoying. Parallel applications also usually take longer to build, and correcting defects is complicated by the

P. Stenström (Ed.): Transactions on HiPEAC IV, LNCS 6760, pp. 195–214, 2011.
© Springer-Verlag Berlin Heidelberg 2011

difficulty in reproducing errors. However, the move to multi-cores requires adoption of parallel programming by the majority of programmers, not just experts, and thus simplifying it has become an important challenge.

Transactional Memory (TM) is a new parallel programming model that seeks to reduce programming effort, while maintaining or improving execution performance, compared to explicit locking. The need to simplify parallel programming, as indicated earlier, has led to a surge in TM research. In TM, programmers are required to mark those blocks of code that access shared data as *transactions*, and safe access to shared data by concurrently executing transactions is ensured implicitly (i.e., invisibly to the programmer) by a TM system. The TM system searches for conflicts by comparing each executing transaction's data accesses against that of all other concurrently executing transactions, also known as *conflict detection* or *validation*. If conflicting data accesses are detected between any two transactions, one of them is *aborted*, and usually restarted immediately. Selecting the transaction to abort, or *conflict resolution*, is based upon a policy, typically referred to as a *contention management policy*. If a transaction completes execution without aborting, then it *commits*, which makes its changes to shared data visible to the whole program.

In order to achieve high scalability on multi-core architectures, it is important that the number of conflicts is kept to a minimum, as conflicts require the execution of conflict resolution code, which reduces effective parallelism by deviating execution from application code. Effective parallelism is further reduced by the grace period offered by some contention management policies to the victim transaction of a conflict, during which the non-victim transaction must wait. Finally, if the conflict leads to an abort, then not only is effective parallelism reduced by restarting the aborted transaction and repeating work performed previously, but computing resources used in executing the aborted transaction are also wasted. This is made worse in certain (update-in-place) TM implementations, which use further computing resources in rolling back any updates made by the aborted transaction.

The order in which transactions are executed concurrently can affect the number of conflicts that occur, and given complete information a priori it may be possible to determine an optimal order (or schedule) that minimises the number of conflicts. However, in practice this is difficult to achieve because complete information is not available for many programs, e.g., due to dynamic transaction creation, or because it is impractical to obtain. Additionally, even if complete information is available, the search space for computing the optimal order of transactions is likely to be unfeasibly large.

This paper presents a novel technique called *steal-on-abort*, which aims to improve transaction ordering at runtime. As mentioned earlier, when a transaction is aborted it is typically restarted immediately. However, due to close temporal locality, the immediately restarted transaction may *repeat its conflict* with the original transaction, which may lead to another aborted transaction. Steal-on-abort targets such a scenario: a transaction that is aborted is not restarted immediately, but instead 'stolen' by the non-aborted transaction, and queued behind it, thus preventing the two transactions from conflicting again. Two key advantages of steal-on-abort are that it requires no application-specific information or offline pre-processing, and it is only executed when an abort occurs, thus adding no overhead when transactions are largely committing. Even when aborts do occur in large numbers, the evaluation suggests that the overhead of steal-on-abort is low.

Steal-on-abort is evaluated using DSTM2 [1], a Software TM (STM) implementation, that has been modified to employ random *work stealing* [2] to execute transactions. Steal-on-abort is evaluated with different contention managers using two widely used benchmarks in TM: a sorted linked list [3], and STAMP-vacation [4]. The evaluation reveals hundred-fold performance improvements for some contention managers, while negligible performance difference for others.

The remainder of this paper is organised as follows: Section 2 introduces steal-on-abort, and Section 4 its implementation in DSTM2, along with strategies for tuning it to particular workload characteristics. Section 6 evaluates steal-on-abort's performance in the benchmarks mentioned earlier. Section 7 discusses recent related work. Finally, Section 8 completes the paper with a summary.

2 Steal-on-abort

In all TM implementations, conflict resolution is invoked when a data access conflict between two concurrently executing transactions is detected. Conflict resolution may give the victim transaction a grace period before aborting it, but once a transaction is aborted then typically it is restarted immediately. However, we observed that the restarted transaction may conflict with the same opponent transaction again, which we refer to as a *repeat conflict*, and lead to another abort.

In general it is difficult to predict the first conflict between any two transactions, but once a conflict between two transactions is observed, it is logical not to execute them concurrently again (or, at least, not to execute them concurrently unless the repeat conflict is avoided). Steal-on-abort takes advantage of this idea, and consists of three parts. First, it does not restart the aborted transaction immediately; the opponent transaction 'steals' the aborted transaction, and hides it. This dynamic reordering avoids repeat conflicts from occurring, since the two transactions are prevented from executing concurrently. Secondly, the thread whose transaction has been stolen acquires a new transaction to execute. The new transaction has an unknown likelihood of conflict, whereas the stolen transaction has a higher likelihood of conflicting due to the chance of a repeat conflict. If the new transaction commits, then throughput may improve. Thirdly, when a transaction commits it releases all the transactions it has stolen.

Since steal-on-abort relies on removing repeat conflicts to improve performance, the more repeat conflicts that occur in an application, the more effective steal-on-abort is likely to be. In applications that have a high number of unique aborts, i.e., few of them are repeat conflicts, steal-on-abort may be less effective at improving results. It is worth noting that steal-on-abort, like most contention management policies, reorders transactions with the aim of improving performance, which has implications for fairness. The effect on fairness is dependent on application characteristics, and it is beyond the scope of this paper to provide a complete analysis of steal-on-abort's impact.

Steal-on-abort's design complements the current function of conflict resolution. As the name suggests, steal-on-abort will only reorder transactions when the call to abort a transaction is made, not when a conflict is detected. Existing and future contention management policies can be used to respond to conflicts as usual, and steal-on-abort will only come into play when a transaction is aborted. This maintains the flexibility of using different contention management policies, while still attempting to reduce repeat conflicts.

3   Effectiveness and Applicability

However, the contention management policy can influence the performance of steal-on-abort. For example, steal-on-abort's benefit could be reduced when using the Greedy contention management policy [5], which in some cases causes the victim transaction to wait indefinitely for a resumption notification from its opponent. Since the victim is not aborted, steal-on-abort is never invoked. Conversely, steal-on-abort could have a greater impact when contention management policies such as Aggressive, which immediately aborts the opponent transaction, are used.

The benefit of steal-on-abort also changes with the method of updating shared data employed. Update-in-place requires an aborted transaction to roll back original values to shared objects as part of its abort operation. Steal-on-abort is likely to provide better throughput with update-in-place, than deferred-update, since steal-on-abort may reduce the number of aborts that occur, and thus the number of times roll back is performed. Deferred-update typically has a much faster abort operation, and consequently may see a lesser benefit from steal-on-abort.

Visibility of accesses also affect the benefit of steal-on-abort. The detection of repeat conflicts requires one transaction be active while another concurrently executing (active) transaction conflicts with it, and aborts, multiple times. Such a scenario can only occur when visible accesses are used: either read, write, or both, with both giving greater likelihood of detecting repeat conflicts. Steal-on-abort is not applicable if both reads and writes are invisible, as conflicts cannot be detected between active transactions, which prevents repeat conflicts from occurring. Furthermore, the quicker the accesses are detected, the higher the chance of repeat conflicts. As a result, steal-on-abort is likely to be most effective when visible reads and visible writes are used in conjunction with eager validation (i.e., checking for conflicts upon each data access, as opposed to lazy validation, which checks for conflicts after executing the transaction, not as each access is performed). This should not come as a surprise; steal-on-abort attempts to reduce conflicts, and a configuration with visible accesses and eager validation is most suited to the quick detection of conflicts.

4   Implementation in DSTM2

This section details the concrete implementation of steal-on-abort in DSTM2, and then goes on to explain the two design variants of steal-on-abort evaluated in this paper. DSTM2, like most other STM implementations [6–8], creates a number of threads that concurrently execute transactions, and is extended to support the three key parts of steal-on-abort. First, each thread needs to store transactions stolen by its currently executing transaction. Second, each thread needs to acquire a new transaction if its current transaction is stolen. Finally, a safe mechanism for stealing active transactions is required. We implemented a thread pool framework to support the first two parts, and a lightweight synchronisation mechanism to implement the third part.

4.1   Thread Pool Framework

DSTM2, like other STMs [6–8], creates a number of threads that concurrently execute transactions. This is extended into a thread pool model where application threads submit transactional jobs to a thread pool that executes transactions. The thread pool model simplifies the task of stealing and releasing transactions, and for acquiring new transactions when a thread's transaction is stolen.

The thread pool comprises of worker threads, and Figure 1 illustrates that each worker thread has its own work queue holding transactional jobs, in the form of a deque (double-ended queue) named `mainDeque`. A transactional job is simply an object that holds parameters needed to execute a transaction. In remainder of this paper we use the terms transaction and job, and the terms deque and queue, interchangeably. Per-thread deques are used as a single global deque may result in high synchronisation overhead. Worker threads acquire jobs from the head of their own queue, and place it in the thread-local variable `currentJob`, to execute. Worker threads acquire a job when their current job commits, or is stolen through steal-on-abort. The benchmarks used in this paper were modified to load jobs onto each thread's `mainDeque` in a round-robin manner during benchmark initialisation, which is excluded from the execution times reported.

In order to keep threads busy, randomised work stealing [2] is used for load balancing. Figure 2 illustrates work stealing in action. If a thread's deque is empty, then work stealing attempts to steal a job from the tail of another randomly selected thread's deque. If a job is not available in the other thread's deque, then yet another thread is randomly selected. In any one attempt to steal jobs from other threads, the threads from which theft has already been attempted are recorded so that random selection is performed only over the remaining threads. If a job is obtained through work stealing, then it is stored in the thread variable `currentJob`, and not in any deque. Since each thread's deque can be accessed by multiple threads concurrently, it needs to be thread-safe. As DSTM2 is Java-based, the deque used is a `java.util.concurrent.LinkedBlockingDeque`.

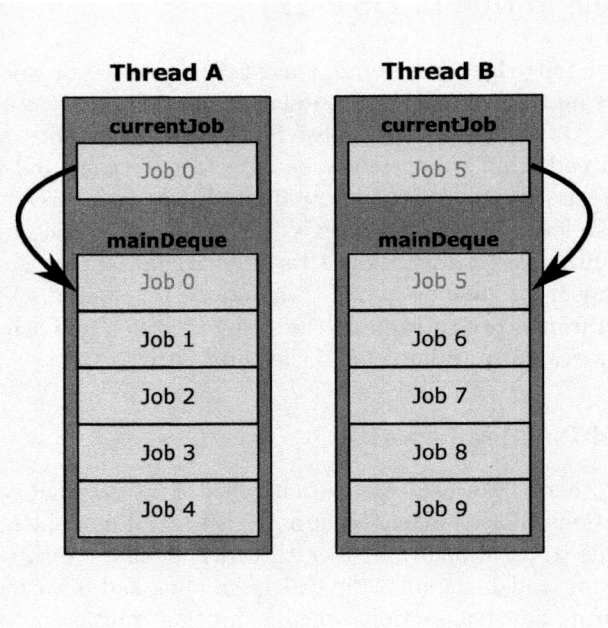

Fig. 1. DSTM2 is modified to implement per-thread deques that store transactional jobs. Threads take jobs from the head of their own deque

4.2   Steal Operation

To implement the steal operation, a second private deque, named `stolenDeque`, is added to each worker thread to hold jobs stolen by an executing transaction. Once a transaction commits, the jobs in the `stolenDeque` are moved to the `mainDeque`. The second deque is necessary to hide stolen jobs otherwise they may be taken through randomised work stealing, and executed concurrently by other threads while the current transaction is still active, which re-introduces the possibility of a repeat conflict.

Figure 3 illustrates steal-on-abort in action. Steal-on-abort is explained from the perspectives of the victim thread (the one from which the aborted transaction is stolen) and the stealing thread. Each thread has an additional flag, called `stolen`. If a victim thread detects its transaction has been aborted, it waits for its `stolen` flag to be set, following which it first attempts to acquire a new job, and then clears the `stolen` flag. The victim thread must wait on the `stolen` flag, otherwise access to the variable `currentJob` may be unsafe.

The stealing thread operates as follows. In DSTM2, a transaction is aborted by using Compare-And-Swap (CAS) to change its status flag from `ACTIVE` to `ABORTED`. If the stealing thread's call to abort the victim thread's transaction in this manner is successful, it proceeds to steal the victim thread's job that is stored in its `currentJob` variable, and places the job in the stealing thread's `stolenDeque`. After the job is taken, the victim thread's `stolen` flag is set.

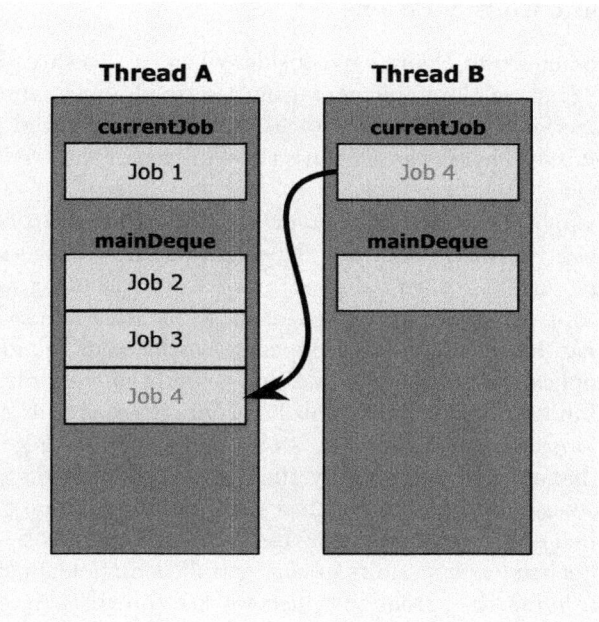

Fig. 2. If a thread's deque is empty, it steals work from the tail of another, randomly selected, thread's deque

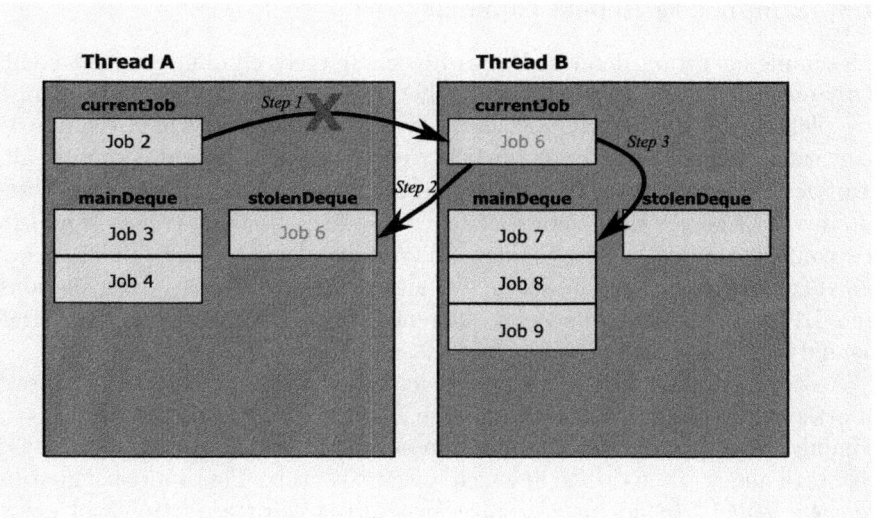

Fig. 3. Steal-on-abort in action. Thread A is executing a transaction based on Job 2, and Thread B is executing a transaction based on Job 6. In step 1, thread A's transaction conflicts with, and aborts, Thread B's transaction. In step 2, thread A steals thread B's job, and places it in its own stolenDeque. In step 3, after thread A finishes stealing, thread B gets a new job, and starts executing it immediately.

4.3   Semantic Considerations

There are two important changes to consider when using a thread pool to execute transactions. First, in the implementation described above, application threads submit transactional jobs to the thread pool to be executed asynchronously, rather than executing transactions directly. This requires a trivial change to the application code.

Secondly, application threads that previously executed a transactional code block, and then executed code that depended on the transactional code block (e.g. code that uses a return value obtained from executing the transactional code block), are not easily supported using asynchronous job execution. This dependency can be accommodated by using synchronous job execution; for example, the application thread could wait on a condition variable, and be notified when the submitted transactional job has committed. Additionally, the transactional job object could be used to store a return value from the committed transaction that may be required by the application thread's dependent code. Such synchronous job execution requires a simple modification to the implementation described already. However, the use of asynchronous job execution, where possible, is preferred as it permits greater parallelism. Solely using synchronous job execution limits the extent to which worker threads may execute simultaneously, as the maximum number of jobs would be limited to the number of application threads.

4.4   Eliminating Repeat Conflicts

The implementation described does not completely eliminate repeat conflicts. As transactions are abort-stolen by the currently executing transaction, they are placed in a steal queue associated with the thread in which the aborter is executing. When the transaction being executed by a thread commits, all the transactions in the thread's steal queue are moved to the thread's work queue. However, there is still a chance of repeat conflict. Imagine transaction T1 and T2 conflict, and T2 is abort-stolen by (and serialised behind) T1. Transaction T3 then conflicts with transaction T1, and abort-steals it. Now transactions T1 and T2 are in the steal queues of different threads (so T2 is no longer serialised behind T1), and could possibly conflict again.

A second approach is for *per-transaction steal queues*. When a transaction abort-steals another, it adds it to its own internal steal queue. Once a transaction commits, it releases its abort-stolen transactions from its internal steal queue into the work queue of the thread in which it was executing. This approach guarantees repeat conflicts do not occur, since an abort-stolen transaction will never be made visible until its stealer commits. This approach has been investigated, but is not presented in this paper, as the former approach is sufficiently efficient at reducing repeat conflicts for the evaluation performed.

5   Steal-on-Abort Strategies

Two steal-on-abort strategies that differ in when they choose to re-execute a stolen job are described and evaluated. When an aborted job is stolen, and subsequently moved from the `stolenDeque` to the `mainDeque`, it can either be placed at the head of the `mainDeque`, or the tail.

Steal-Tail. If jobs are placed at the tail, the thread will execute the stolen jobs last, although the job may be executed earlier by another thread due to work stealing. As an example of where Steal-Tail may benefit, the round-robin allocation of jobs means jobs that were created close in time will likely be executed close in time. For benchmarks with a close relationship between a job's creation time and its data accesses, executing a stolen job right after the current job may lead to conflicts with other transactions, therefore placing stolen jobs at the tail of the deque may reduce conflicts.

Steal-Head. If jobs are placed at the head, the thread will execute the stolen jobs first. For benchmarks that do not show the temporal locality described above, placing jobs at the head of the deque may take advantage of cache locality to improve performance. For example, data accessed by transaction A, which aborts and steals transaction B's job, is likely to have at least one data element (the data element that caused a conflict between the two transactions), in the processor's local cache.

6   Evaluation

This section presents highlights the potential performance benefit of using steal-on-abort, and analyses how such benefits are achieved, and the overhead of using steal-on-abort. As mentioned already, this paper only evaluates the per-thread steal queues implementation. In this section, 'Normal' refers to execution without steal-on-abort, Steal-Head refers to steal-on-abort execution where stolen jobs are moved to the head of the `mainDeque`, and Steal-Tail refers to execution where stolen jobs are moved to the tail. All execution schemes utilise the thread pool framework described earlier.

6.1   Platform

The platform used to execute benchmarks is a 4 x dual-core (8-core) Opteron 880 2.4GHz system with 16GB RAM, running openSUSE 10.1, and using Sun Hotspot Java VM 1.6 64-bit with the flags `-Xms4096m -Xmx14000m`. Benchmarks are executed using DSTM2 set to using the shadow factory, eager validation, and visible accesses. Benchmarks are executed with 1, 2, 4, and 8 threads, each run is repeated 6 times. Mean results are reported with ± 1 standard deviation error bars.

6.2   Benchmarks

The benchmarks used to evaluate steal-on-abort[1] are linked list [3], and STAMP-vacation [4]. Hereafter, they are referred to as List, and Vacation, respectively. List is a microbenchmark that transactionally inserts and removes random numbers from a sorted linked list. Vacation is a non-trivial transactional benchmark from the STAMP suite (version 0.9.5) ported to DSTM2 that simulates a travel booking database with three tables to hold bookings for flights, hotels, and cars. Each transaction simulates a customer making several bookings, and thus several modifications to the database. The number of threads used represents the number of concurrent customers.

Evaluating steal-on-abort requires the benchmarks to generate large amounts of transactional conflicts, and the method of achieving high contention for each benchmark is described. List is configured to perform 20,000 randomly selected insert and delete transactions with equal probability. Additionally, after executing its code block, each transaction waits for a short delay, which is randomly selected using a Gaussian distribution with a standard deviation of 1.0, and a mean duration of 3.2ms. The execution time of the average committed transaction in List is 6ms before the delays were added. The delays are used to simulate transactions that perform extra computation while accessing the data structures. This also increases the number of repeat conflicts. To induce high contention in Vacation, it is configured to build a database of 128 relations per table, and execute 1,024,768 transactions, each of which performs 50 modifications to the database. The small size of the table, and the large number of modifications per transaction, results in high contention.

6.3   Contention Managers

A contention manager (CM) is invoked by a transaction that detects a conflict with another (opponent) transaction. In this evaluation, three CMs are used to provide coverage of the published CM policies: Aggressive [3], Polka [9], and Priority. Aggressive immediately aborts the opponent transaction. Polka, the published best CM, gives the opponent transaction time to commit, before aborting it. Polka waits exponentially increasing amounts of time for a dynamic number of iterations (equal to the difference in the number of read accesses performed by the two transactions). The parameters for Polka are based on the defaults [9]. Priority immediately aborts the younger of the two transactions based on their timestamps.

Steal-on-abort should be most effective with Aggressive and Priority, as they immediately make a call to abort the victim transaction. Conversely, steal-on-abort should be less effective with Polka, as it chooses to give the victim transaction a grace period before aborting it. In scenarios with high contention, Aggressive and Polka are more likely to cause transactions to temporarily

---

[1] Reviewer's note: The SHCMP paper also used a red-black tree benchmark. This has been omitted to make space for further analysis of steal-on-abort's results with linked list and STAMP-vacation.

livelock as they always choose to abort the opponent transaction. Priority will not livelock transactions since it is always selects the same transaction to abort (the one with the younger timestamp). Aggressive and Polka abort the opponent to provide non-blocking progress guarantees by preventing a transaction becoming indefinitely blocked behind a zombie opponent transaction. Priority does not provide such a guarantee.

6.4 Throughput

Figure 4 shows the transaction throughput results for List and Vacation. Looking at the Normal results (i.e., without steal-on-abort), the Aggressive CM gives the worst performance in both benchmarks, as the high contention scenarios cause the transactions to livelock due to Aggressive's policy to abort the opponent. The Polka CM fares better due to its grace period allowing opponents to commit, but the policy to abort the opponent still causes transactions to livelock. Priority gives the best performance in both benchmarks, as it does not necessarily always abort the opponent, and thus avoids transactions livelocking.

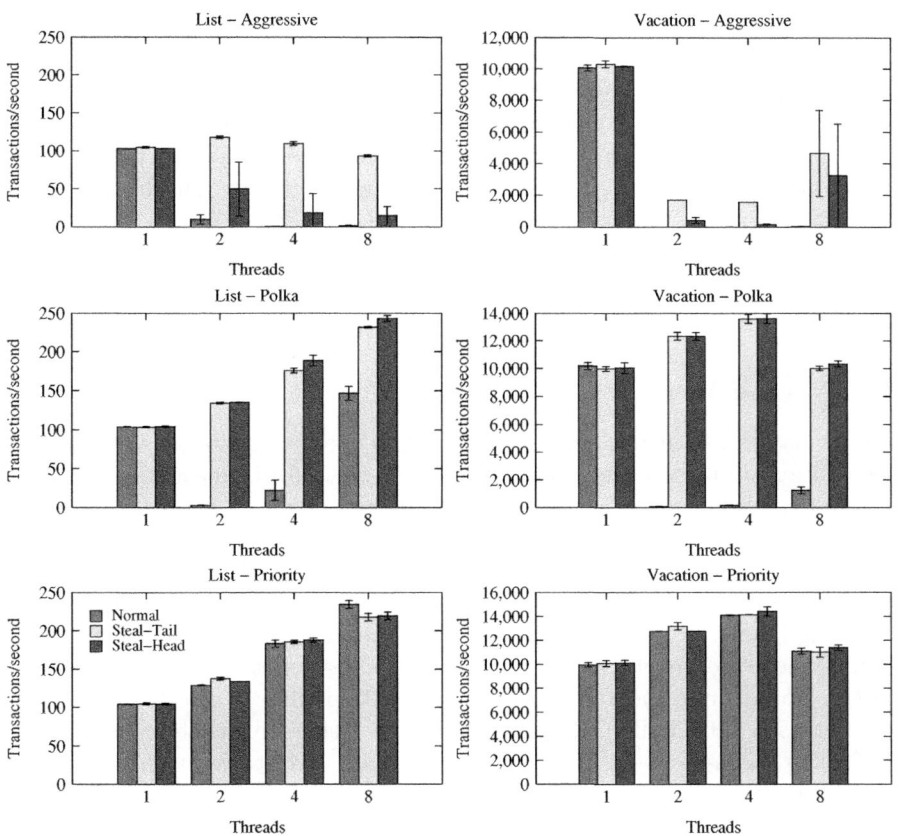

Fig. 4. Throughput results. Higher is better.

Looking at the steal-on-abort results (i.e., both Steal-Tail and Steal-Head), Aggressive and Polka benefit significantly, while Priority sees no benefit of using steal-on-abort, with performance degrading slightly at eight threads in List. As explained earlier, Aggressive and Polka may livelock conflicting transactions through repeated conflict and abort. This raises the number of repeat conflicts that occur, which results in better throughput with steal-on-abort. Since Priority does not suffer from such livelock, it has fewer repeat conflicts, and thus benefits less from steal-on-abort. However, as mentioned earlier, there is a trade off in using Priority: it provides weaker non-blocking progress guarantee compared to Aggressive and Polka.

Drilling down further, Aggressive sees Steal-Tail give higher performance than Steal-Head in both List and Vacation. Steal-Head's large standard deviations in List with Aggressive, and both Steal-Head's and Steal-Tail's in Vacation at eight threads, are due to (data not shown here) execution either completing in a short duration, or approximately 5 times greater duration than the short duration. Comparing profiling data from the high and low throughput runs reveals that the low throughput runs are caused by the throughput falling almost instantaneously early in the execution, and then failing to recover. Although the reason for the drop in throughput is not known, it indicates an opportunity to improve steal-on-abort to avoid, or resolve, the condition that caused the drop in throughput, and achieve high throughput with greater consistency.

Polka sees Steal-Head give marginally higher performance than Steal-Tail in List, and at eight threads in Vacation, in contrast to the results with Aggressive. This contrast suggests that the steal-on-abort strategies are not only more suited for certain application traits, but also the CM used. It is also worth noting that Steal-Head improves Polka's performance such that it is within 3% of Priority's performance. Thus, it is possible to have both the performance of Priority, and the non-blocking progress guarantee of Polka.

6.5   Wasted Work

The transactional metric wasted work [10] is the proportion of execution time spent in executing aborted transactions, and is useful in measuring the cost of aborted transactions in terms of computing resources. It is used here to see if steal-on-abort reduces this cost.

Figure 5 shows wasted work results. No transactional aborts occur in single thread execution since there are no other concurrent transactions to cause conflicts, and thus all single thread execution results have no wasted work. The results show the benchmarks' high contention parameters result in Aggressive and Polka spending nearly all of their execution time in aborted transactions (except List with Polka). This supports the suggestion that transactions are livelocked. There is negligible impact on wasted work of using steal-on-abort with Priority, which suggests a lack of repeat conflicts.

With Aggressive, Steal-Tail reduces wasted work by larger margins than Steal-Head in both benchmarks. Steal-Tail reduces wasted work by 30% to 70% in List, and 15% to 80% in Vacation. With Polka, Steal-Head reduces wasted by a

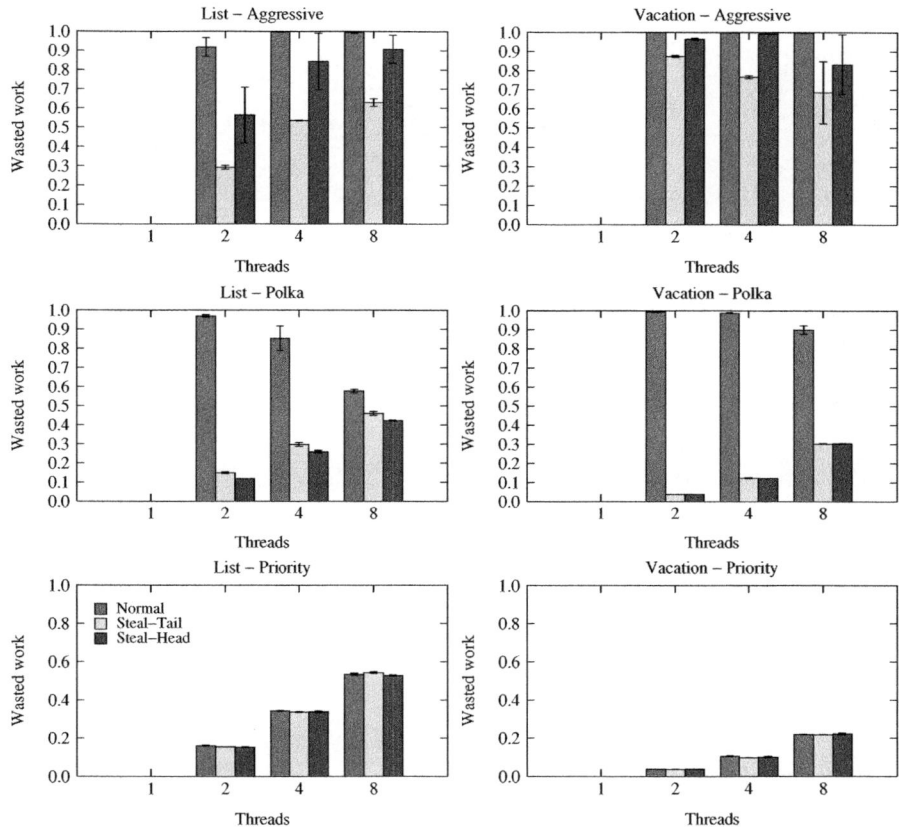

Fig. 5. Proportion of total execution time spent in aborted transactions (wasted work). Lower is better.

slightly larger margin than Steal-Tail in both benchmarks. Steal-Head reduces wasted work by 57% to 87% in List, although the reduction decreases with the number of threads, and 95% to 99% in Vacation. These results reflect the trends seen in the throughput results seen earlier. Also, we mentioned earlier that steal-on-abort improves Polka's performance to within 3% of Priority's, and this is reflected in the similarity in wasted work between Polka with steal-on-abort, and Priority.

6.6   Aborts Per Commit (APC)

The aborts per commit ratio (APC) is the number of aborts divided by the number of commits. It is another indicator of the efficiency with which computing resources are utilised, but it is not as useful as wasted work because it ignores the durations of the aborted and committed transactions. We investigate it here because steal-on-abort should reduce APC in benchmarks that exhibit repeat conflicts.

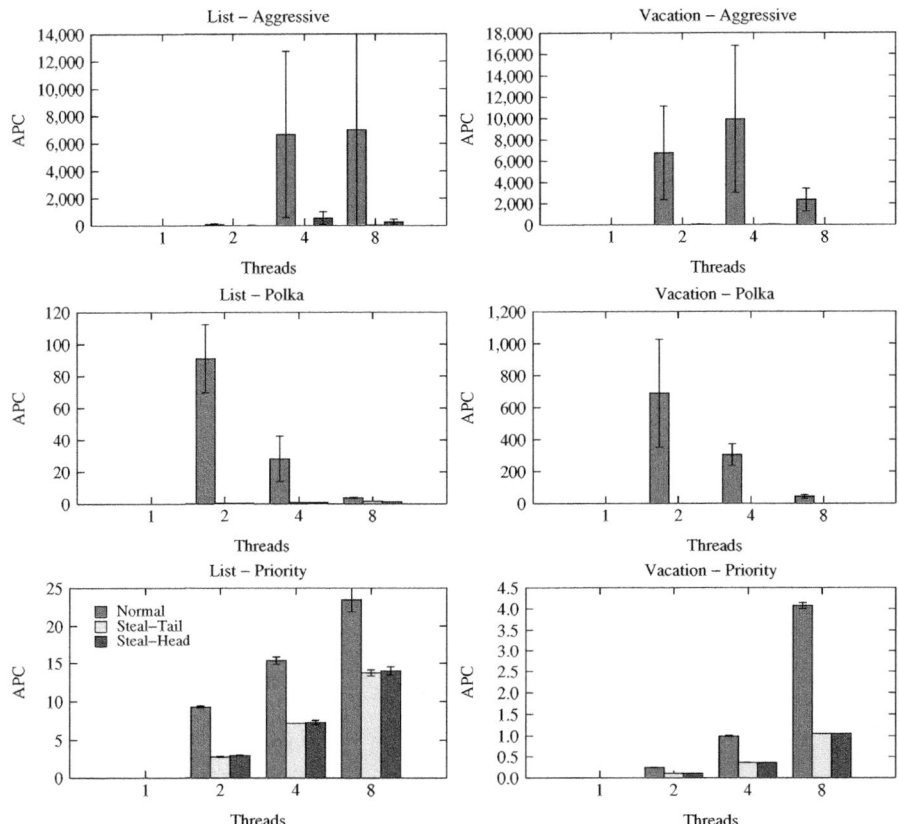

Fig. 6. APC results. Lower is better.

Figure 6-presents APC results. Using Aggressive, on average steal-on-abort has a low APC compared to Normal, but Normal exhibits significant variance in APC between runs of the same benchmark configuration. Polka's results paint a similar picture, except that the APC is significantly lower, and consistently falls as the number of threads increases. Polka's lower APC is due to the grace time that Polka offers an opponent transaction, which delays the call to perform an abort, and thus reduces the total number of aborts. Given the performance improvements of steal-on-abort for Aggressive and Polka, it is plausible that the high APC value with Normal is due to a large number of repeat conflicts.

Priority has a very low APC compared to Aggressive and Polka, attributable to the lack of livelock. Steal-on-abort reduces APC compared to Normal, but this does not correlate with the wasted work or throughput results shown in earlier sections. This implies that, on average, transactions make greater progress with steal-on-abort than Normal, but still get aborted eventually.

6.7   Repeat Conflicts

This section examines the amount of time spent in repeat conflicts. Figure 7 shows histograms of the distribution of time spent in aborted transactions (wasted work) for a given number of conflicts with a particular transaction. As an example, consider transaction T1 aborts seven times before committing, thus it has seven lots of wasted work. Four aborts occur through conflict with transaction T2, two with T3, and one with T4. The time wasted in the executions of T1 that conflicted with, and were aborted by, T2 are added to column '4', the two lots associated with T3 are added to column '2', and the one lot associated with T4 is added to column '1'. For brevity, only the eight thread results are discussed, although better performance improvements were observed with fewer threads. Furthermore, results with Aggressive are not presented as there is significant variance in the repeat conflict results from one run to another.

Since steal-on-abort should target repeat conflicts it should reduce the amount of time in all but the first column. For Polka, this is confirmed by the results: Steal-Tail reduces time in the remaining columns (repeat conflicts) by 99% in List, and 99% in Vacation. Furthermore, the results show that repeat conflicts represent a significant proportion of the total wasted work: 65% in List, and 96% in Vacation. Thus, steal-on-abort is highly effective at reducing the number of repeat conflicts, even they occur in large proportions. In contrast, for Priority the number of repeat conflicts is quite low, which confirms previous suspicions, and explains why steal-on-abort did not improve performance with Priority as significantly as with Aggressive and Polka. Also, although there are differences

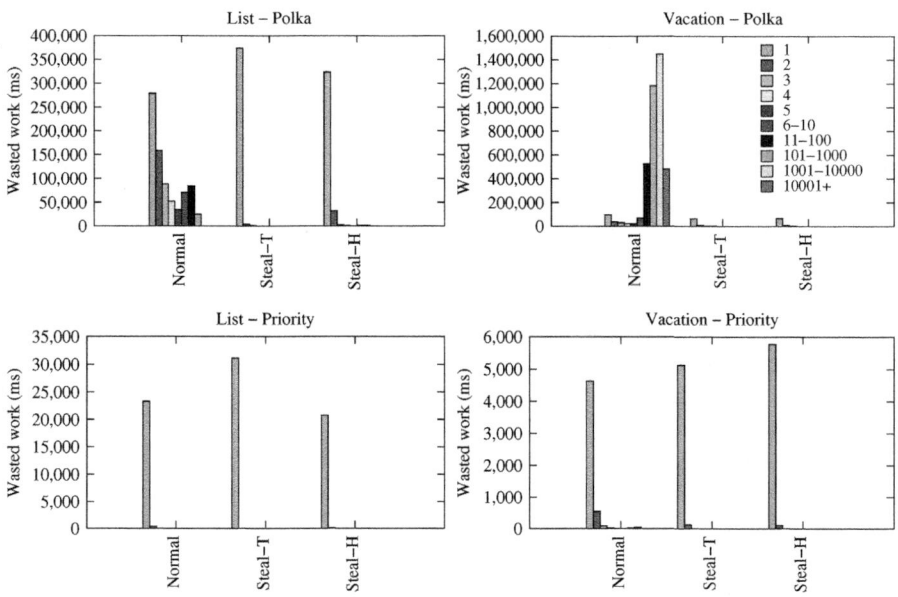

Fig. 7. Repeat conflict distribution. Lower is better.

in repeat conflict distribution results between Normal and steal-on-abort for Priority, recall that the difference in wasted work between them was minimal.

This raises the obvious question of whether steal-on-abort could benefit applications that use Priority since, so far, repeat conflicts have arisen due to the policies of Aggressive and Polka livelocking conflicting transactions. The answer is yes, steal-on-abort could benefit applications that use Priority. Recall Priority aborts transactions that are younger. Thus, a younger transaction can repeatedly conflict and abort against an older transaction. The longer the older transaction remains active, the more repeat conflicts and aborts possible. In such a case, steal-on-abort may improve performance with Priority when the aborted transaction is stolen, and then replaced with a new transaction from the work queue, which may or may not commit, and thus improve performance. This strategy was not useful in these benchmarks as they were configured to have generally high contention, and thus all transactions, including the new transaction from the work queue, had a high likelihood of conflicting with some other transaction, and the lower likelihood of a repeat conflict became insignificant.

It is worth noting that steal-on-abort increases single conflict (non-repeat) wasted work in most cases. In Polka this is because repeat conflicts are being reduced to single conflicts so their wasted work is allocated to the single conflict column. However, the increase in single conflict wasted work is less than the decrease in repeat conflict wasted work because steal-on-abort prevents repeat conflicts from occurring, which leads to the reduction in wasted work shown earlier. In Priority the increase in single conflict wasted work is also due to steal-on-abort attempting a new transaction on abort, whereas Priority may attempt the same transaction repeatedly (if it is younger than its opponent).

6.8   Steal-on-Abort Overhead

Steal-on-abort consists of two short operations, and we have not tried to measure the overhead of these directly as the overhead of the measurement code is likely to distort the results. Thus, we attempt to measure the overhead of steal-on-abort indirectly. The first source of overhead is performing the steal operation. Figure 8 shows average committed transaction durations for each benchmark, which includes the overhead of the steal operation. Only results for Polka are shown, as its high number aborts suggests steal-on-abort is invoked a large number of times. Taking the standard deviations into account, generally the overhead of stealing transactions seems negligible. Furthermore, the transactions in Vacation are significantly shorter than those in List, yet stealing transactions does not add noticeable overhead.

The reductions in average committed transaction durations with steal-on-abort are due to Polka's policy. Polka causes transactions to wait for their opponents, which increases the average time it takes to execute a transaction that eventually commits if it encounters conflicts. Since steal-on-abort reduced the amount of time spent in repeat conflicts, it should also have reduced the total number of conflicts, which in turn should have reduced the average committed transaction's duration.

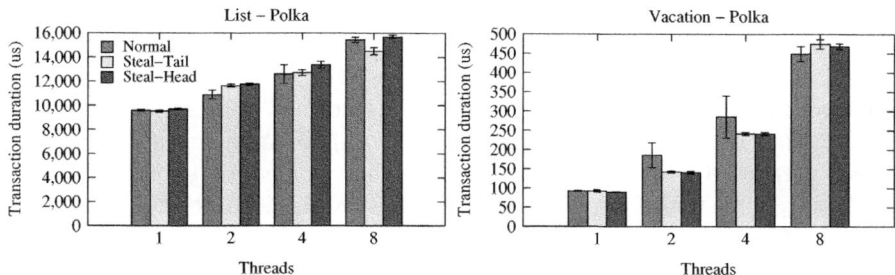

Fig. 8. Average Committed Transaction Duration (microseconds). Lower is better.

The other major source of steal-on-abort overhead is due to moving transactions in the `stolenDeque` to the `mainDeque` after the local transaction commits. The in-transaction metric (InTx), which is the proportion of execution time spent in executing transactions, is used to measure this overhead. For the benchmarks used in this evaluation there are two major sources of out-of-transaction execution: work stealing, and moving transactions between deques after a transaction commits. Since Normal execution also utilises work stealing, the difference between Normal and steal-on-abort execution should approximately represent the cost of moving jobs between the deques.

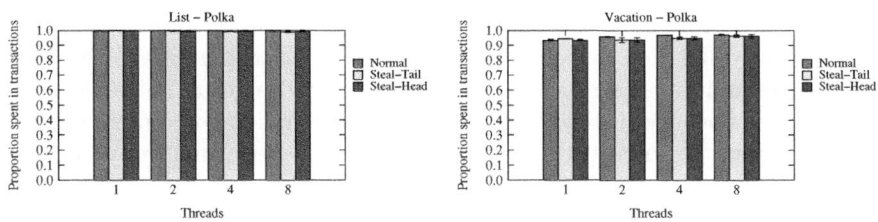

Fig. 9. Proportion of total execution time spent within transactions. Higher is better.

Figure 9 shows the InTx results, again only with Polka. It identifies that there is negligible overhead in moving jobs between deques and work stealing in List. However, in Vacation the overhead becomes visible, with most strategies observing an overhead of 3%. This equates to an average overhead of moving jobs of 2.8 microseconds per transaction. However, this cost is related to the number of jobs moved between deques, and with Steal-Tail this averages to 2.2 jobs per transaction.

7   Related Work

Limited research has been carried out in transaction re-ordering for improving TM performance. Bai *et al.* [11] introduced a key-based approach that colocates transactions based on their calculated keys. Although their approach improves performance, it requires an application-specific formula to calculate keys for transactions. Furthermore, performance is based on the effectiveness of the formula, and it may be difficult to generate such formulae for some applications. In contrast, our approach does not require any application-specific information.

Dolev *et al.* recently published work similar to steal-on-abort called CAR-STM [12], which also attempts to reorder transactions to minimise repeat conflicts. CAR-STM uses a thread pool with multiple work queues to execute transactions. Application threads submit transactional jobs to the thread pool, and then suspend until the transaction is committed by one of the thread pool's worker threads (i.e., use synchronous job execution). CAR-STM consists of two parts: collision avoidance, and collision resolution.

Collision avoidance is an interface to support (optional) application-supplied conflict prediction routines. If supplied, these routines are used to queue transactions that are likely to conflict into the same work queue, rather than using round robin distribution. This concept is a simpler version of the adaptive key-based scheduler of Bai *et al.* [11] described above.

Collision resolution is similar to steal-on-abort; transactions that conflict are queued behind one another. CAR-STM also describes the per-thread and per-transaction steal queues. However they do not explore the design space as thoroughly; they do not attempt to support existing contention management policies, and they do not investigate stealing strategies such as releasing stolen transactional jobs to the head or tail of a work queue. Furthermore, CAR-STM supports only synchronous job execution, and does not support work stealing, thus threads can be left idle, which reduces its performance potential. The thread pool implementation described in this paper recognises that not all scenarios require the application thread to wait for the transaction to complete, and allows asynchronous job execution, which can improve performance by increasing the number of jobs available for execution through work stealing, and by reducing the synchronisation overhead between application threads and thread pool worker threads.

8   Summary

This paper has presented an evaluation of a new runtime approach, called steal-on-abort, that dynamically re-orders transactions with the aim of reducing the number of aborted transactions caused by repeat conflicts. Steal-on-abort requires no application specific information or offline pre-processing. Two different steal-on-abort strategies were introduced that differed in either executing stolen transactions immediately, or executing them last.

Steal-on-abort was evaluated against two widely used benchmarks in TM: a sorted linked list microbenchmark, and STAMP-vacation, a non-trivial TM benchmark. Performance improvements were observed when using the Aggressive and Polka CM policies, and Polka is the published best CM. Further analysis showed steal-on-abort improved their performance by eliminating repeat conflicts, and also showed that steal-on-abort is highly effective at removing repeat conflicts, even when they occur in significant proportions.

However, no benefit was observed with the Priority CM policy, and Priority provided the best non-steal-on-abort performance in the benchmarks used. Priority's policy provides weaker non-blocking progress guarantees than Aggressive and Polka, which allowed it to avoid livelocks they encountered. This reduced the number of repeat conflicts with Priority, and thus also the benefit of steal-on-abort. This introduces a trade off when selecting CM policies: high performance and weaker progress guarantees, or vice versa. However, steal-on-abort eliminated this trade off as it improved Polka's performance to within 3% of Priority's performance, and combined high performance, and superior progress guarantees.

References

1. Herlihy, M., Luchangco, V., Moir, M.: A flexible framework for implementing software transactional memory. In: OOPSLA 2006: Proceedings of the 21st Annual Conference on Object-Oriented Programming Systems, Languages, and Applications, pp. 253–262. ACM Press, New York (2006)
2. Blumofe, R.D., Joerg, C.F., Kuszmaul, B.C., Leiserson, C.E., Randall, K.H., Zhou, Y.: Cilk: An efficient multithreaded runtime system. Journal of Parallel and Distributed Computing 37(1), 55–69 (1996)
3. Herlihy, M., Luchangco, V., Moir, M., Scherer III, W.N.: Software transactional memory for dynamic-sized data structures. In: PODC 2003: Proceedings of the 22nd Annual Symposium on Principles of Distributed Computing, pp. 92–101. ACM Press, New York (2003)
4. Minh, C.C., Trautmann, M., Chung, J., McDonald, A., Bronson, N., Casper, J., Kozyrakis, C., Olukotun, K.: An effective hybrid transactional memory system with strong isolation guarantees. In: ISCA 2007: Proceedings of the 34th Annual International Symposium on Computer Architecture, pp. 69–80. ACM Press, New York (2007)
5. Guerraoui, R., Herlihy, M., Pochon, B.: Toward a theory of transactional contention managers. In: PODC 2005: Proceedings of the 24th Annual Symposium on Principles of Distributed Computing, pp. 258–264. ACM Press, New York (2005)
6. Marathe, V., Spear, M., Herio, C., Acharya, A., Eisenstat, D., Scherer III, W., Scott, M.L.: Lowering the overhead of software transactional memory. In: TRANSACT 2006: First ACM SIGPLAN Workshop on Transactional Computing (June 2006)
7. Dice, D., Shalev, O., Shavit, N.: Transactional locking II. In: Dolev, S. (ed.) DISC 2006. LNCS, vol. 4167, pp. 194–208. Springer, Heidelberg (2006)
8. Felber, P., Fetzer, C., Riegel, T.: Dynamic performance tuning of word-based software transactional memory. In: PPoPP 2008: Proceedings of the 13th ACM SIGPLAN Symposium on Principles and Practice of Parallel Programming, pp. 237–246. ACM Press, New York (2008)

9. Scherer III, W., Scott, M.L.: Advanced contention management for dynamic software transactional memory. In: PODC 2005: Proceedings of the 24th Annual Symposium on Principles of Distributed Computing, pp. 240–248. ACM Press, New York (2005)

10. Perfumo, C., Sonmez, N., Cristal, A., Unsal, O., Valero, M., Harris, T.: Dissecting transactional executions in Haskell. In: TRANSACT 2007: Second ACM SIGPLAN Workshop on Transactional Computing (August 2007)

11. Bai, T., Shen, X., Zhang, C., Scherer, W.N., Ding, C., Scott, M.L.: A key-based adaptive transactional memory executor. In: IPDPS 2007: Proceedings of the 21st International Parallel and Distributed Processing Symposium, pp. 1–8. IEEE Computer Society Press, Los Alamitos (2007)

12. Dolev, S., Hendler, D., Suissa, A.: Car-stm: Scheduling-based collision avoidance and resolution for software transactional memory. In: PODC 2007: Proceedings of the 26th Annual ACM Symposium on Principles of Distributed Computing, pp. 125–134. ACM Press, New York (2008)

A Parallelizing Compiler Cooperative Heterogeneous Multicore Processor Architecture

Yasutaka Wada, Akihiro Hayashi, Takeshi Masuura, Jun Shirako,
Hirofumi Nakano, Hiroaki Shikano, Keiji Kimura, and Hironori Kasahara

Department of Computer Science and Engineering, Waseda University
3-4-1 Ohkubo, Shinjuku-ku, Tokyo 169-8555, Japan
{yasutaka,ahayashi,masuura,shirako,hnakano,
shikano,kimura,kasahara}@kasahara.cs.waseda.ac.jp

Abstract. Heterogeneous multicore architectures, integrating several
kinds of accelerator cores in addition to general purpose processor cores,
have been attracting much attention to realize high performance with low
power consumption. To attain effective high performance, high application software productivity, and low power consumption on heterogeneous
multicores, cooperation between an architecture and a parallelizing compiler is important. This paper proposes a compiler cooperative heterogeneous multicore architecture and parallelizing compilation scheme for
it. Performance of the proposed scheme is evaluated on the heterogeneous multicore integrating Hitachi and Renesas' SH4A processor cores
and Hitachi's FE-GA accelerator cores, using an MP3 encoder. The heterogeneous multicore gives us 14.34 times speedup with two SH4As and
two FE-GAs, and 26.05 times speedup with four SH4As and four FE-
GAs against sequential execution with a single SH4A. The cooperation
between the heterogeneous multicore architecture and the parallelizing
compiler enables to achieve high performance in a short development
period.

1 Introduction

The demands for high performance, low power consumption, cost effectiveness
and short software development period have been increasing in the area of consumer electronics such as mobile phones, games, digital TVs, and car naviga-
tion systems. To satisfy these demands, multicore processors[1–8] have been
attracting much attention. Especially in consumer electronics, heterogeneous
multicores[9–15], that integrate general purpose processor cores and various accelerator cores such as dynamically reconfigurable processors (DRPs), digital signal processors (DSPs), graphic processors and/or matrix processors (MTXs)[16]
on a chip, have been researched to achieve both high performance with low cost
and low power consumption.

Many types of heterogeneous multicores are being developed such as Larrabee
[9], CELL[10], Stream processor[11], MP211[12], SH4A heterogeneous multicore
[13], and Single-ISA heterogeneous multicore[14]. In addition, development environments or language extensions like CUDA[17] come to be used to make it easy

P. Stenström (Ed.): Transactions on HiPEAC IV, LNCS 6760, pp. 215–233, 2011.
© Springer-Verlag Berlin Heidelberg 2011

to use accelerator cores. However, parallelizing application programs for various configurations of heterogeneous multicore processors is human-intensive and rather difficult. Therefore, a parallelizing compiler, which automatically extracts parallelism from a sequential program and schedules tasks to heterogeneous cores considering data transfer overhead, is required to minimize development periods of application softwares.

A parallelizing compiler for heterogeneous multicore systems has to schedule tasks to various types of hardware resources. Some task scheduling algorithms have been proposed for heterogeneous systems with availability constraints of resources[18, 19]. Though some heuristic scheduling algorithms assume to be used at compile-time[20, 21], a parallelizing compiler employing such task scheduling algorithms has not been developed before.

This paper proposes a parallel compilation scheme with a static scheduling scheme[22] for coarse grain task parallel processing[23] and a heterogeneous multicore architecture to support the compiler parallelization. The developed compiler is based on the OSCAR multigrain parallelizing compiler[24]. In the proposed compilation scheme, the compiler groups general purpose processor cores on a chip hierarchically to utilize hierarchical parallelism of a program effectively. In this processor grouping, accelerator cores are not included in the hierarchical grouping of general purpose processor cores so that the compiler can improve the availability of accelerator cores even if the number of them is less than the number of general purpose processor cores. Then, the compiler applies a static scheduling scheme extended for a heterogeneous multicore processor and optimizes data transfer timings considering overlapping with task executions. The proposed heterogeneous multicore architecture is developed for cooperating with the OSCAR heterogeneous compiler. Each accelerator core on this architecture is equipped with simple processor core to control the accelerator core. This controller makes it possible that the compiler adjusts the granularity of tasks can be executed on accelerators to apply the static scheduling. In addition, each core on a chip has the same memory architecture. This memory homogeneity supports the static scheduling scheme with memory and data transfer optimization by the compiler.

The remainder of this paper is organized as follows: Overviews of a heterogeneous multicore architecture cooperative with the parallelizing compiler are discussed in Section 2. Overviews of a compilation flow for heterogeneous multicore processors are described in Section 3. A coarse grain task parallel processing method for the heterogeneous multicore architecture is explained in Section 4. A coarse grain task scheduling scheme on the heterogeneous multicore architecture considering data transfers is proposed in Section 5. An experimental performance evaluation using an MP3 encoder program is described in Section 6.

2   A Heterogeneous Multicore with OSCAR-Type Memory Architecture

The proposed heterogeneous multicore architecture (Fig. 1) is based on homogeneous OSCAR-type memory architecture[22, 25, 26]. The architecture has

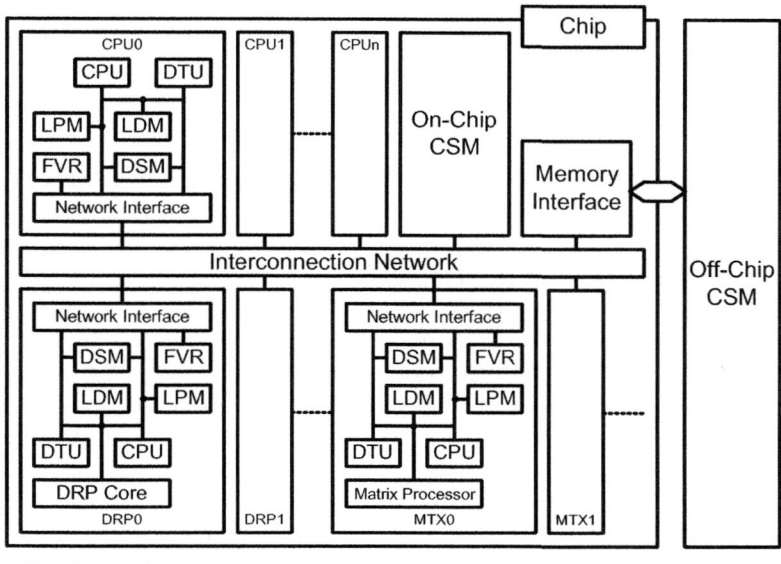

- DTU : Data Transfer Unit
- FVR : Frequency/Voltage Control Register
- LPM : Local Program Memory
- LDM : Local Data Memory
- DSM : Distributed Shared Memory
- CSM : Centralized Shared Memory

Fig. 1. OSCAR Heterogeneous Multicore Architecture

multiple processor elements (PEs) and centralized shared memories (CSM) connected by an interconnection network like multiple buses or crossbar network. A general purpose PE has a general purpose processor core (CPU). An accelerator PE has an accelerator core such as a dynamically reconfigurable processor (DRP) and a matrix processor (MTX) with a small controller processor core. This controller helps to make synchronizations among PEs, data transfers, and some simple calculations, so that OSCAR compiler can apply static scheduling scheme as explained in Section 5 even if the input program has complex control flow structure. For example, control flow structures such as conditional branches can be processed by the controller. This paper focuses on the applications that the compiler can apply the static scheduling scheme in the cooperation with this architecture.

Each general purpose and accelerator PE has a local data memory (LDM), a distributed shared memory (DSM), a data transfer unit (DTU) and frequency voltage control registers (FVR). The Local data memory stores PE private data in a program. The distributed shared memory is a dual port memory used for data transfers between PEs and low-latency synchronizations. Different from cache memory, the local data memory and the distributed shared memory are managed by software to handle real-time applications. The data transfer unit is an advanced DMA Controller which enables overlapping task execution and data transfer. OSCAR compiler controls and optimizes data transfer timings and data allocation for the PEs using these memories and DTUs with the support of this homogeneous memory architecture. To make the task cost estimation by the compiler easy and precise, this architecture expects to use simple CPU cores as the general purpose cores.

3   A Compilation Flow for Heterogeneous Multicore Processors

For a heterogeneous multicore, the parallelizing compiler needs to know which tasks in the program can be executed and accelerated by which accelerator cores and their execution costs. However, it is difficult to develop a compiler that can deal with every type of accelerator core. In the proposed scheme, special purpose compilers for the accelerators developed by their vendors is used to find the tasks which can be accelerated, to calculate the execution costs, and to generate object code for the accelerator cores.

Fig. 2 shows a compilation flow for heterogeneous multicore processors. First, special purpose compilers for accelerator cores are used to generate source code with directives indicating task execution costs on the accelerator. This source file is input to OSCAR heterogeneous parallelizing compiler. OSCAR compiler parallelizes and optimizes the program, then generates parallel execution code for the heterogeneous multicore processor. To generate the execution code, OSCAR compiler uses the object codes generated by the special purpose compilers for accelerator cores. This paper focuses on OSCAR parallelizing compiler and the compiler cooperative heterogeneous multicore architecture assuming that the special purpose compilers are supplied by the vendors and can be used.

4   Coarse Grain Task Parallel Processing on a Heterogeneous Multicore Processor

This section presents coarse grain task parallel processing on a heterogeneous multicore processor. In this scheme, OSCAR compiler generates coarse grain tasks (Macro-Tasks, MTs) hierarchically and decides the hierarchical processor grouping to utilize parallelism among them.

4.1   Coarse Grain Task Parallel Processing

For coarse grain task parallel processing, the compiler decomposes the target program into three kinds of coarse grain tasks (Macro-Tasks, MTs), such as a block of pseudo assignment statements (BPA), a repetition block (RB), a subroutine block (SB). After generation of Macro-Tasks from the source program, the data dependencies and control flow among Macro-Tasks are analyzed, and Macro-Flow Graphs (MFGs) are generated. A Macro-Flow Graph (Fig. 3a) represents control flow and data dependencies among Macro-Tasks. Nodes represent Macro-Tasks, solid edges represent data dependencies among Macro-Tasks, and dotted edges represent control flow. A small circle inside a node represents a

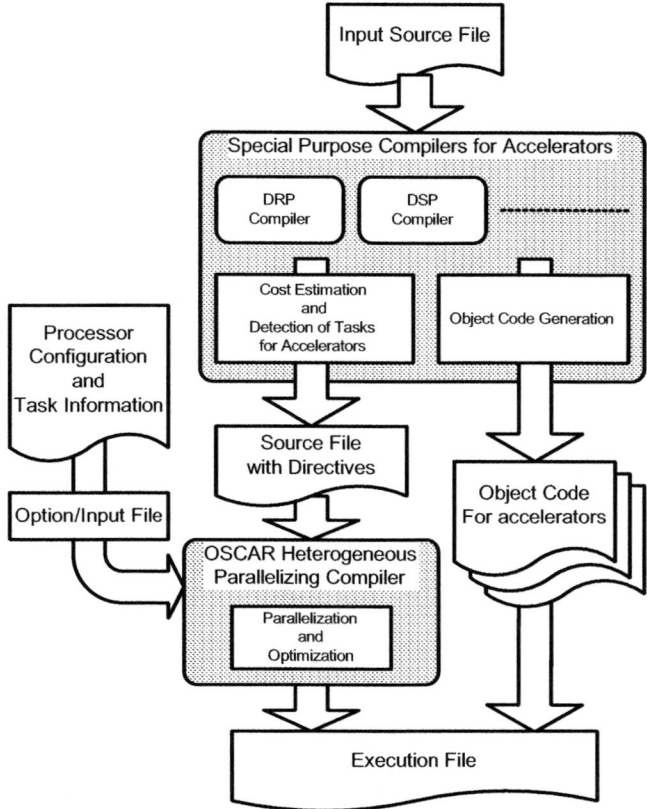

Fig. 2. A Compilation Flow for Heterogeneous Multicores

conditional branch inside the Macro-Task. Though arrows of edges are omitted in the Macro-Flow Graph, it is assumed that the directions are downward.

Then, to extract coarse grain task parallelism among Macro-Tasks from the Macro-Flow Graph, Earliest Executable Condition Analysis[27] is applied to the Macro-Flow Graph and a Macro-Task Graph (MTG) is generated (Fig. 3b). Macro-Task Graphs represent coarse grain task parallelism among Macro-Tasks. Nodes represent Macro-Tasks. A small circle inside a node represents conditional branches. Solid edges represent data dependencies. Dotted edges represent extended control dependencies. Extended control dependency means ordinary normal control dependency and the condition on which a data dependence predecessor of a Macro-Task is not executed. Solid and dotted arcs connecting solid and dotted edges have two different meanings. A solid arc represents that edges connected by the arc are in AND relationship. A dotted arc represents that edges connected by the arc are in OR relationship. Though arrows of edges are omitted assuming downward direction, edges having arrow represents original control flow edges, or branch direction in Macro-Flow Graph. If SB or RB has nested inner layer, Macro-Tasks and Macro-Task Graphs are generated hierarchically.

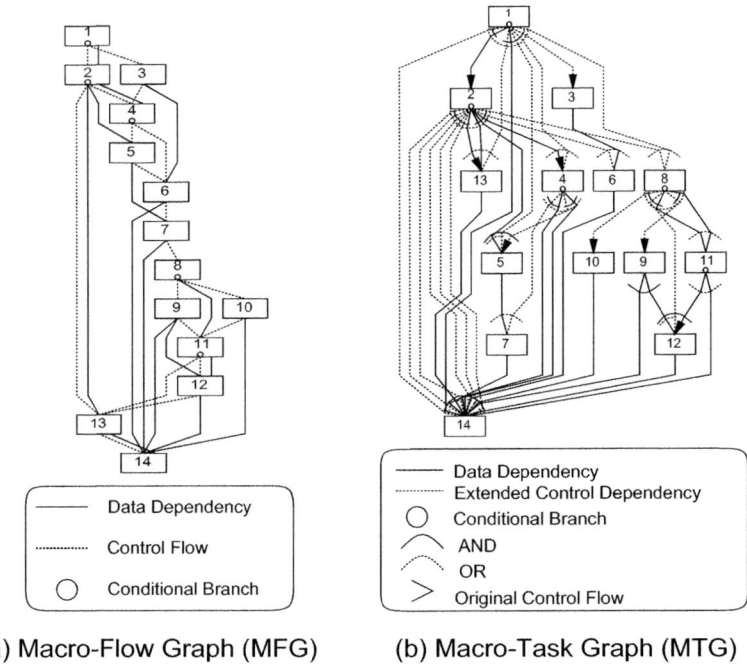

(a) Macro-Flow Graph (MFG)   (b) Macro-Task Graph (MTG)

Fig. 3. Examples of Macro-Flow Graph (MFG) and Macro-Task Graph (MTG)

After generation of Macro-Tasks and Macro-Task Graphs, Macro-Tasks are assigned to Processor-Groups (PGs). A Processor-Group is a group of processor elements (PEs), and its grouping is performed logically. If the Macro-Task Graph has only data dependencies,the compiler schedules Macro-Tasks to Processor-Groups at compile time (static scheduling). The static scheduling scheme can minimize data transfer, task assignment and synchronization overhead. If the Macro-Task Graph has conditional branches among Macro-Tasks, the dynamic scheduling is applied. In this case, the compiler generates scheduling codes to assign Macro-Tasks to Processor-Groups at run-time[24, 26] though only the static scheduling scheme is used in this paper.

In addition, if SB or RB has coarse grain task parallelism inside them, PEs are grouped hierarchically and hierarchical parallelism is utilized. OSCAR compiler applies the automatic processor grouping scheme[28, 29] to decide the layers to be applied coarse grain task parallel processing and its processor grouping.

4.2   Hierarchical Processor Grouping Considering OSCAR Heterogeneous Multicore Architecture

To apply coarse grain task parallel processing with static scheduling effectively, processor elements (PEs) are grouped into Processor-Groups (PGs) hierarchically

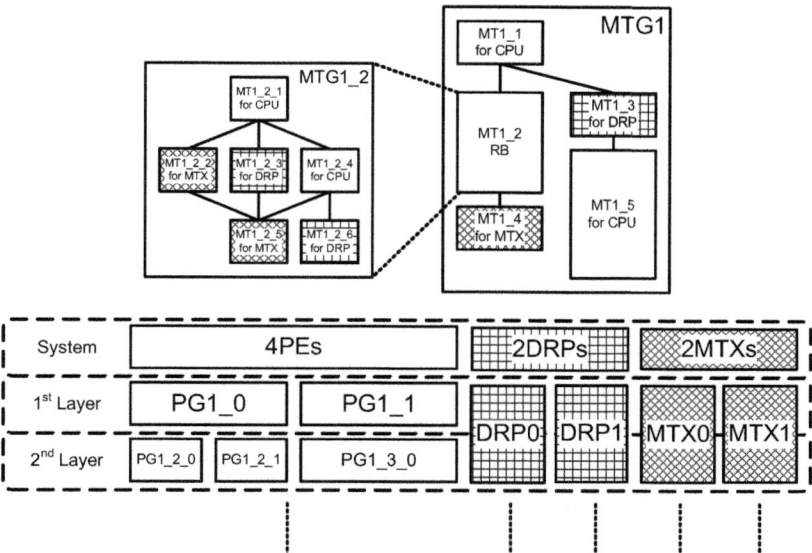

Fig. 4. An Example of Processor Grouping considering OSCAR Heterogeneous Multicore Architecture

while considering coarse grain task parallelism. General purpose PEs on a heterogeneous multicore processor are hierarchically grouped, while considering nested parallelism of the source program or nested structure of Macro-Task Graphs. Different from general purpose PEs, accelerator PEs are not grouped hierarchically, since the number of accelerator PEs is usually less than the number of the general purpose PEs and not enough to be assigned to deeply nested Macro-Task Graphs. In the proposed scheme, accelerator PEs are free from hierarchical grouping of general purpose PEs, and can be used by any nested layers of Macro-Task Graphs efficiently. After the processor grouping, OSCAR compiler schedules Macro-Tasks (MTs) to Processor-Groups or to accelerator PEs at compile time.

Fig. 4 shows an example of hierarchical processor grouping for a heterogeneous multicore processor. In this example, the multicore system has four general purpose PEs and two kinds of accelerator PEs such as two DRP cores and two matrix processor cores (MTXs)[16]. In the 1st layer Macro-Task Graph (MTG1), general purpose PEs are grouped into two Processor-Groups (PG1_0 and PG1_1) and Macro-Tasks (MTs) in this layer is assigned to these Processor-Groups. While the MT1_2 having coarse grain task parallelism internally is executed on PG1_0, PG1_0 is grouped into two Processor-Groups (PG1_2_0 and PG1_2_1) hierarchically. DRPs and MTXs are grouped according to their types or functionality, and can accept requests to execute Macro-Tasks from any Macro-Task Graph.

5   A Static Scheduling Algorithm for OSCAR Heterogeneous Multicore Architecture

This section presents a static scheduling scheme for coarse grain tasks on OS-CAR heterogeneous multicore architecture. In this scheme, the compiler schedules Macro-Tasks to Processor-Groups composed of general purpose PEs and accelerator PEs to minimize execution time while considering load balancing and data transfer timing.

5.1   A Task Scheduling Scheme for Heterogeneous Multicores

To schedule Macro-Tasks in the input program to heterogeneous cores, the characteristics of Macro-Tasks and PEs must be considered. For example, some Macro-Tasks are assignable to accelerator PEs (PEs having accelerator cores), however, the other Macro-Tasks cannot be executed on accelerator PEs. In most cases, the assignable Macro-Tasks result in highly effective execution if they are assigned to accelerators. Different from accelerator PEs, general purpose PEs (PEs having only general purpose processor cores) can execute all Macro-Tasks.

The task scheduling algorithm for heterogeneous multicore implemented in OSCAR compiler consists of eight steps:

Step 1. Preparation.

Step 1-1. Calculate each Macro-Task cost on a general purpose PE and each assignable accelerator PE.

Step 1-2. Calculate scheduling priority of each Macro-Task (see Section 5.2 for more details).

Step 2. Initialization.

Step 2-1. Set the scheduling time to zero.

Step 2-2. Add the 1st layer Macro-Task Graph to the list of Macro-Task Graphs under the scheduling process.

Step 3. Extracting ready tasks.

Extract ready Macro-Tasks from the Macro-Task Graphs in the list of Macro-Task Graphs under the scheduling process. Ready Macro-Tasks are Macro-Tasks that satisfy the following requirements at current scheduling time :

– satisfying Earliest Executable Condition[27]
– having a Processor-Group or an assignable accelerator PE which is free at current scheduling time

If there is no ready Macro-Task, then go to Step 8.

Step 4. Task selection.

Select a Macro-Task to be scheduled (target Macro-Task) from the ready Macro-Tasks according to the priorities.

Step 5. Completion time estimation.

Estimate execution completion time of the target Macro-Task on

– each Processor-Group which is free at current scheduling time
– each accelerator PE which can execute the target Macro-Task

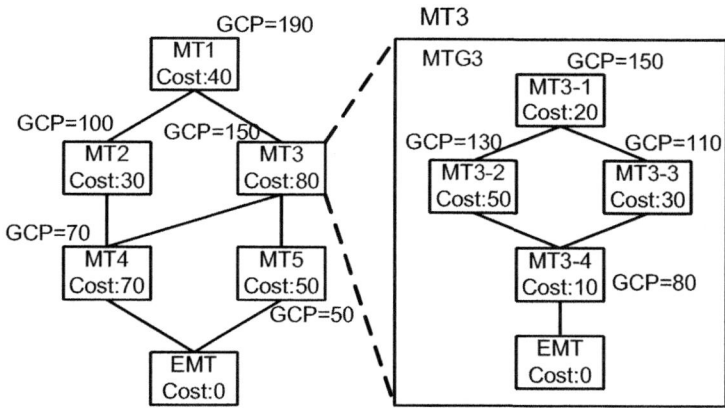

Fig. 5. Global CP Length

(To estimate the completion time, data transfer timings are calculated as mentioned in Section 5.3 and 5.4.)

Step 6. Macro-Task assignment.

Assign the target Macro-Task to the Processor-Group or the accelerator PE gives the earliest completion time.

Step 7. Examination of inside of the Macro-Task.

If the assigned Macro-Task has Macro-Task Graphs to be applied coarse grain parallel processing inside, add it to the list of Macro-Task Graphs in the scheduling process.

Step 8. Updating the scheduling time.

   Step 8-1. Update the scheduling time until the time when a Macro-Task is completed next.

   Step 8-2. If there is a Macro-Task Graph that all of the Macro-Tasks inside have been completed at the updated scheduling time, remove it from the list of Macro-Task Graphs under the scheduling process.

   Step 8-3. If all of the Macro-Tasks are completed, then exit. If not, then go to Step 3.

5.2   A Scheduling Priority

In this paper, global critical path length (global CP length, GCP) is used as the scheduling priority. Global CP length is the longest path length from the exit node of main program to each Macro-Task calculated considering hierarchical Macro-Task Graph structure. Fig. 5 is an example of hierarchical Macro-Task Graphs and global critical path length (GCP) of each Macro-Task (MT). For example, the longest path length from the exit node (EMT) of MTG3 to MT3-3 is 40, and the longest path length from the exit node of the main program to the end of MT3 is 70. Therefore, the longest path length, or global critical path length of MT3-3 is 110, or 40 + 70.

5.3   Estimating Completion Time of a Macro-Task

In the proposed task scheduling scheme, OSCAR compiler estimates completion time of a Macro-Task considering characteristics of the Macro-Task (MT) and processor elements (PEs), and overlapping data transfers with task executions. OSCAR compiler estimates a Macro-Task cost by adding up the costs of instructions inside the task. In the case of loops, the number of iterations is estimated using initial and final value of the loop index, or the size of array accessed in the task. If more precise costs are required, profiling results may be used. In both cases, OSCAR compiler can schedule Macro-Tasks effectively if relative costs among Macro-Tasks are correct.

Before estimating the completion time of a Macro-Task, the completion time of data transfers needed by the target Macro-Task DT_{end} is estimated as:

$$DT_{end} = \max[DT_{load}, \max_{MT_p \in PRED}\{DT_{send}(p)\}],$$

where $PRED$ is the set of predecessors of the target Macro-Task, $DT_{send}(p)$ is the completion time of data transfers from a predecessor MT_p, and DT_{load} is the completion time of data loadings from CSM. These data transfers are scheduled while considering overlapping with task executions (section 5.4). Then, completion time of the target Macro-Task (MT_{fin}) is estimated as:

$$MT_{fin} = \max(T_{free}, DT_{end}) + COST_{MT} + DT_{store},$$

where T_{free} is the time that the Processor-Group or the accelerator PE comes to be free, DT_{end} is the completion time of the data transfers, $COST_{MT}$ is the execution cost of the target Macro-Task on the Processor-Group or the accelerator PE, and DT_{store} is the cost of the data storing to CSM. If the target Macro-Task has Macro-Task Graphs inside it, its completion time is estimated by applying this scheduling scheme to the Macro-Task Graphs inside recursively.

5.4   Overlapping Data Transfers and Task Executions

On a heterogeneous multicore architecture proposed in Section 2, data can be transferred by the data transfer unit (DTU)[13] effectively. In current implementation, the data transfer unit is driven at the beginning or the end of a Macro-Task execution. Once a data transfer is driven, the data transfer is performed asynchronously with task executions on CPU cores or accelerator cores. OSCAR compiler searches data transfer timing while considering the statuses of interconnection network and memory ports. Data loadings from centralized shared memory and data sending among processor elements are scheduled as earlier as possible while considering overlapping with task executions, and data storings to centralized shared memory are scheduled to be overlapped with task executions if possible.

Fig. 6 shows an example of the scheduling result with data transfers. This figure shows the case that one general purpose PE (CPU0) and one accelerator

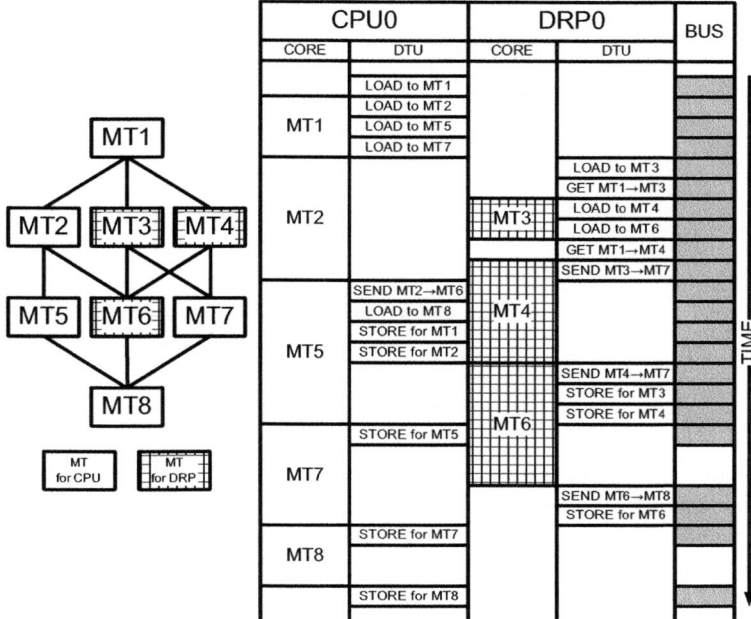

Fig. 6. An Example of Task Scheduling Result considering Overlapping Data Transfers and Task Executions

PE with DRP (DRP0) are connected with single bus. In this example, "LOAD" means data loading from centralized shared memory (CSM), "STORE" means data storing to CSM, "SEND" means data storing/sending to remote distributed shared memory (DSM) and "GET" means data loading/getting from remote DSM. For example, data loading from CSM to the PE that executes Macro-Task named MT4 ("LOAD to MT4") is overlapped with the execution of MT3.

6   Performance Evaluation

This section evaluates the performance of the proposed heterogeneous multicore architecture and task scheduling algorithm.

6.1   The Evaluated Multicore Architecture

In this evaluation, the heterogeneous multicore processor having up to eight PEs on a chip is used. SH4A[30] processor cores are used as the general purpose processor cores and controllers of accelerator PEs, and FE-GAs[13, 31] are used as DRP cores of accelerator PEs. Triple buses are used as the interconnection network, and centralized shared memory has four memory banks. Table 1 shows the minimum access costs of distributed shared memory (DSM), local data memory(LDM), and centralized shared memory (CSM). Local DSM access needs 1

Table 1. Minimum Access Costs for LDM, DSM, and CSM

DSM	1 Clock Cycle
DSM (Remote)	4 Clock Cycles
LDM	1 Clock Cycle
CSM	16 Clock Cycles (off-chip) 4 Clock Cycles (on-chip)

Table 2. MP3 Encode Parameters

# of frames evaluated	16 frames of Stereo PCM
Sample Rate	44.1 [kHz]
Bit Rate	128 [kbps]

clock cycle, remote DSM access needs 4 clock cycles, LDM access needs 1 clock cycle, on-chip CSM access needs 4 clock cycles and off-chip CSM access needs 16 clock cycles at 300MHz. A clock accurate simulator of the heterogeneous multicore architecture is used for this evaluation.

6.2 The Evaluated Application

In this evaluation, an MP3 encoder program written in FORTRAN77 is used. This program is implemented based on the "UZURA MPEG1/LayerIII encoder in FORTRAN90"[32]. Tasks can be executed by accelerator PEs are specified by compiler directives. OSCAR compiler[24] extracts parallelism from the sequential program and schedules its coarse grain tasks to the general purpose processor PEs, namely SH4A cores, and accelerator PEs with FE-GA cores. The encode parameters are shown in Table 2. The input PCM data is allocated on the centralized shared memory initially. Profiling results are used for the task scheduling. Only the main encoding loop is measured to reduce the influence of I/O and calculation of the initial values.

The Structure and Parallelism of an MP3 Encoder. Fig. 7a shows the program structure of MP3 encoder. The MP3 encoder program consists of Sub-Band Analysis, MDCT, Psycho-Acoustic Analysis, Quantization, and Huffman Coding. In the MDCT, the result from the sub-band analysis of the previous frame is used. In psycho-acoustic analysis, the result from the psycho-acoustic analysis of the previous frame is used. Except these stages that need to deliver data among frames, multiple frames can be encoded at the same time. In the program used for this evaluation, 16 frames of PCM data are encoded in the same iteration of main-loop of encoding (Fig. 7b). In this evaluation, it is assumed that local memory (local data memory and distributed shared memory) size is large enough to store the data to encode the 16 frames.

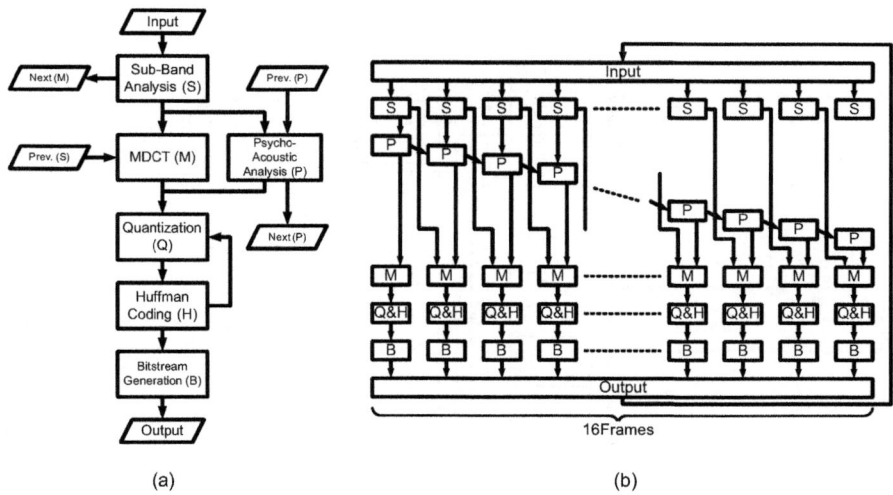

Fig. 7. The Program Structure and the Task Graph of the Evaluated MP3 Encoder

Code Mapping for the ALU Array of FE-GA. In this evaluation, "P", "M", "Q&H" and a part of "S" (Fig. 7b) can be executed and accelerated by accelerator PEs having FE-GAs. Their execution costs on accelerator PEs are precisely estimated in clock level using the amount of input data and the code mapping for the ALU array on FE-GA.

FE-GA core has 24 ALU cells and 8 MULT cells, and these cells are connected to the memory via a crossbar switch. Fig. 8 shows a part of code mapping of MP3 sub-band analysis to FE-GA. The k's loop can be accelerated with the FE-GA's ALU array (Fig. 8a). In the code mapping of this part (Fig. 8b), the k's loop is divided into two parts for the effective use of ALU/MULT cells.

Estimated speedup on accelerator PEs is shown in Fig. 9. The estimated speedup is the average of the sixteen frames used in this evaluation. A part of sub-band analysis and psycho-acoustic analysis are comparatively simple processions, which give us 67.06 times speedup and 61.76 times speedup against a single general purpose PE, respectively. Because the task of Quantization and Huffman Coding ("Q&H" in Fig. 7b) is complex, it gives us 4.36 times speedup. On the average, 6.73 times speedup is given by an accelerator PE with FE-GA core against a general purpose PE.

6.3 Performance on OSCAR Heterogeneous Multicore by OSCAR Compiler

The parallel processing performance of an MP3 encoder on the OSCAR heterogeneous multicore by OSCAR heterogeneous parallelizing compiler is shown in Fig. 10. The horizontal axis shows the configurations of the processor cores and centralized shared memory (namely, on-chip CSM or off-chip CSM). The vertical axis shows the speedup against the sequential execution using one general

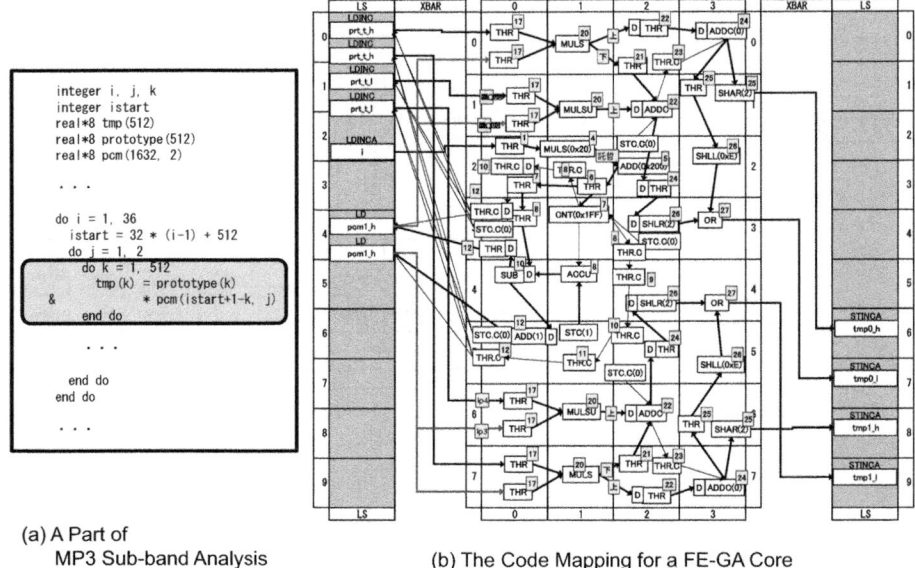

(a) A Part of
MP3 Sub-band Analysis

(b) The Code Mapping for a FE-GA Core

Fig. 8. A Sample Code to be Accelerated by FE-GA and its Mapping for ALU Array of FE-GA

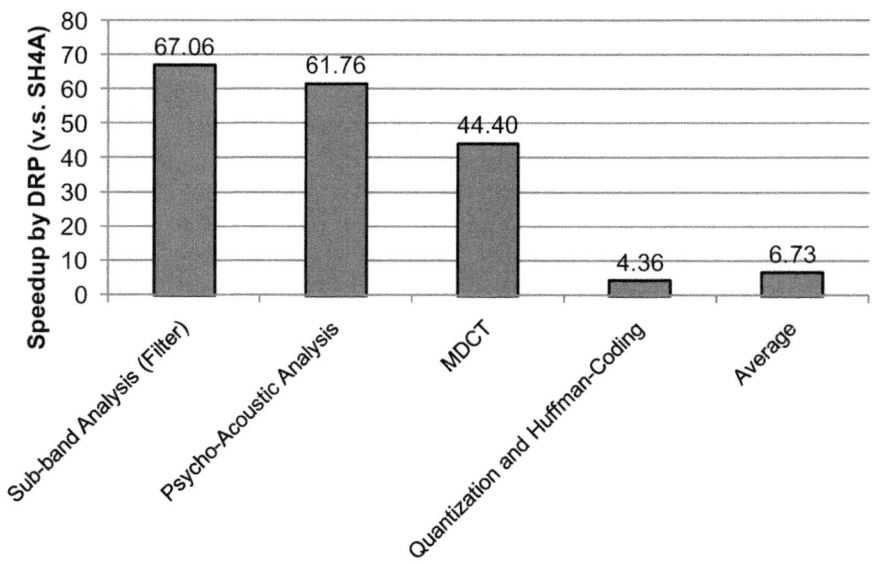

Fig. 9. Speedup of the MP3 Encoder by an Accelerator PE (DRP)

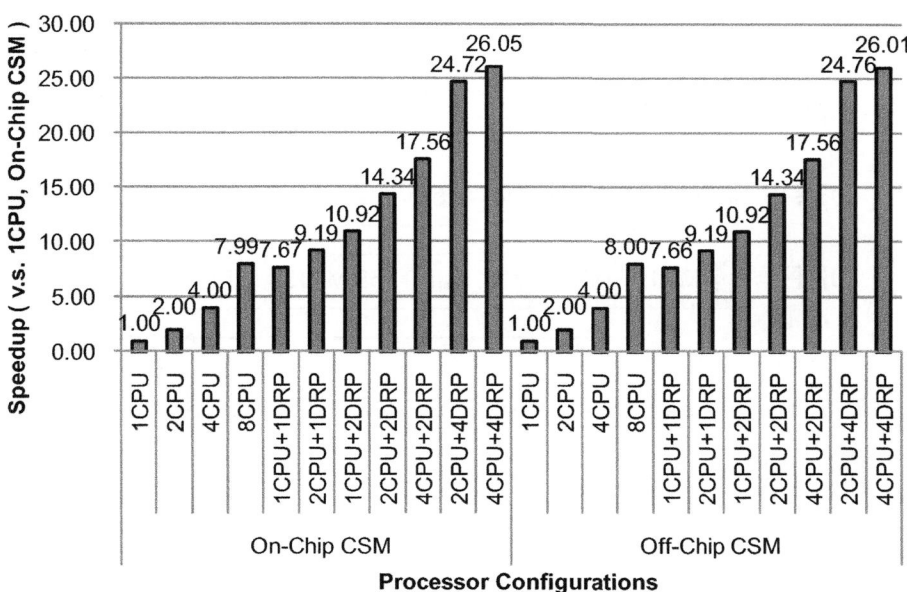

Fig. 10. The Performance of the MP3 Encoder on the OSCAR Heterogeneous Multi-core using OSCAR Compiler

purpose PE and on-chip CSM. "nCPU+mDRP" are the numbers of general purpose PEs (CPUs in the figure) and accelerator PEs with FE-GAs (DRPs). "On-Chip" means on-chip CSM and "Off-Chip" means off-chip CSM.

The configurations of 2CPU, 4CPU and 8CPU with on-chip CSM give us 2.00, 4.00 and 7.99 times speedup against 1CPU, respectively. The proposed heterogeneous parallelizing compilation scheme with architecture supports is effective even on a homogeneous multicore environment. With heterogeneous configurations, the configurations of 1CPU+1DRP, 2CPU+1DRP, 1CPU+2DRP, 2CPU+2DRP, 4CPU+2DRP, 2CPU+4DRP and 4CPU+4DRP give 7.67, 9.19, 10.92, 14.34, 17.56, 24.72 and 26.05 times speedup against 1CPU, respectively. Effective use of accelerator PEs gives a much higher performance compared with the number of PEs.

Even if the CSM is out of the chip, the homogeneous configurations of 2CPU, 4CPU and 8CPU give us 2.00, 4.00, 8.00 times speedup against 1CPU, respectively, and the heterogeneous configurations of 1CPU+1DRP, 2CPU+1DRP, 1CPU+2DRP, 2CPU+2DRP, 4CPU+2DRP, 2CPU+4DRP and 4CPU+4DRP give us 7.66, 9.19, 10.92, 14.34, 17.56, 24.76 and 26.01 times speedup. This is because the data are effectively assigned to local memories (local data memories and distributed shared memories) and data transfers are overlapped with task execution with the use of data transfer units (DTUs), or DMA controllers.

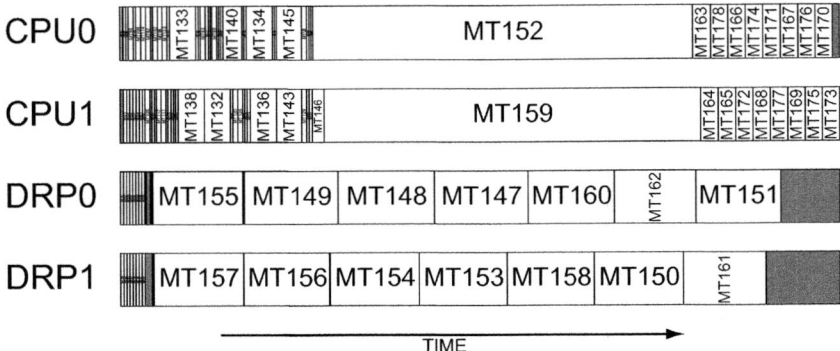

Fig. 11. The Execution Trace of the Configuration of 2CPU+2DRP with off-chip CSM

Fig. 11 shows the execution trace of 2CPU+2DRP with off-chip CSM. MT152 and MT159 are the Macro-Tasks of Quantization and Huffman Coding ("Q&H" in Fig 7b) and executed by the general purpose PEs, though they can be assigned to accelerator PEs. If they are assigned to accelerator PEs, the total processing time of the program becomes larger than the schedule. In the proposed compilation scheme, a Macro-Task, which might require more processing time if it is assigned to an accelerator PE, is automatically assigned to a general purpose PE to utilize CPUs and accelerators effectively.

7   Conclusions

This paper has proposed OSCAR heterogeneous multicore architecture and an automatic parallelizing compilation scheme using static coarse grain task scheduling. The performance is evaluated on the heterogeneous multicore processor with low power SH4A processor cores as general purpose PEs (CPUs), and FE-GA dynamically reconfigurable processor (DRP) cores as accelerator PEs using an MP3 encoder implemented based on "UZURA MPEG1/LayerIII encoder in FORTRAN90". In this evaluation, the heterogeneous configurations give us 14.34 times speedup with two CPUs and two DRPs and 26.05 times speedup with four CPUs and four DRPs against sequential execution on one CPU with the on-chip centralized shared memory (CSM). Also, with the off-chip CSM, the heterogeneous multicore give us 14.34 times speedup with two CPUs and two DRPs and 26.01 times speedup with four CPUs and four DRPs by data localization to local data memories and distributed shared memories and data transfer overlapping using intelligent DMA controllers.

References

1. Hammond, L., Hubbert, B.A., Siu, M., Prabhu, M.K., Chen, M., Olukotun, K.: The stanford hydra CMP. IEEE Micro 20, 71–84 (2000)
2. ARM Limited: ARM11 MPCore Processor Technical Reference Manual (2005)

3. Friedrich, J., McCredie, B., James, N., Huott, B., Curran, B., Fluhr, E., Mittal, G., Chan, E., Chan, Y., Plass, D., Chu, S., Le, H., Clark, L., Ripley, J., Taylor, S., Dilullo, J., Lanzerotti, M.: Design of the Power6 microprocessor. In: Digest of Technical Papers of the 2007 IEEE International Solid-State Circuits Conference, pp. 96–97 (February 2007)

4. Taylor, M.B., Kim, J., Miller, J., Wentzlaff, D., Ghodrat, F., Greenwald, B., Hoffman, H., Johnson, P., Lee, J.W., Lee, W., Ma, A., Saraf, A., Seneski, M., Shnidman, N., Strumpen, V., Frank, M., Amarasinghe, S., Agarwal, A.: The raw microprocessor: A computational fabric for software circuits and general purpose programs. IEEE Micro 22, 25–35 (2002)

5. Sankaralingam, K., Nagarajan, R., Liu, H., Kim, C., Huh, J., Burger, D., Keckler, S.W., Moore, C.R.: Exploiting ILP, TLP, and DLP with the polymorphous TRIPS architecture. In: Proceedings of the 30th Annual International Symposium on Computer Architecture, pp. 422–433 (June 2003)

6. Shiota, T., Kawasaki, K., Kawabe, Y., Shibamoto, W., Sato, A., Hashimoto, T., Hayakawa, F., Tago, S., Okano, H., Nakamura, Y., Miyake, H., Suga, A., Takahashi, H.: A 51.2GOPS 1.0GB/s-DMA single-chip multi-processor integrating quadruple 8-Way VLIW processors. In: Digest of Technical Papers of the 2005 IEEE International Solid-State Circuits Conference, pp. 194–593 (February 2005)

7. Sohi, G.S., Breach, S.E., Vijaykumar, T.N.: Multiscalar processors. In: Proceedings of 22nd Annual International Symposium on Computer Architecture, pp. 414–425 (June 1995)

8. Vangal, S., Howard, J., Ruhl, G., Dighe, S., Wilson, H., Tschanz, J., Finan, D., Iyer, P., Singh, A., Jacob, T., Jain, S., Venkataraman, S., Hoskote, Y., Borkar, N.: An 80-Tile 1.28TFLOPS network-on-chip in 65nm CMOS. In: Digest of Technical Papers of the 2007 IEEE International Solid-State Circuits Conference, pp. 98–589 (February 2007)

9. Seiler, L., Carmean, D., Sprangle, E., Forsyth, T., Abrash, M., Dubey, P., Junkins, S., Lake, A., Sugerman, J., Cavin, R., Espasa, R., Grochowski, E., Juan, T., Hanrahan, P.: Larrabee: A many-core x86 architecture for visual computing. ACM Transactions on Graphics 27(3) (2008)

10. Pham, D., Asano, S., Bolliger, M., Day, M.N., Hofstee, H.P., Johns, C., Kahle, J., Kameyama, A., Keaty, J., Masubuchi, Y., Riley, M., Shippy, D., Stasiak, D., Suzuoki, M., Wang, M., Warnock, J., Weitzel, S., Wendel, D., Yamazaki, T., Yazawa, K.: The design and implementation of a first-generation CELL processor. In: Digest of Technical Papers of the 2005 IEEE International Solid-State Circuits Conference, pp. 184–592 (February 2005)

11. Khailany, B., Williams, T., Lin, J., Long, E., Rygh, M., Tovey, D., Dally, W.J.: A programmable 512 GOPS stream processor for signal, image, and video processing. In: Digest of Technical Papers of the 2007 IEEE International Solid-State Circuits Conference, pp. 272–602 (February 2007)

12. Torii, S., Suzuki, S., Tomonaga, H., Tokue, T., Sakai, J., Suzuki, N., Murakami, K., Hiraga, T., Shigemoto, K., Tatebe, Y., Ohbuchi, E., Kayama, N., Edahiro, M., Kusano, T., Nishi, N.: A 600MIPS 120mW 70μA leakage triple-CPU mobile application processor chip. In: Digest of Technical Papers of the 2005 IEEE International Solid-State Circuits Conference, pp. 136–589 (February 2005)

13. Ito, M., Todaka, T., Tsunoda, T., Tanaka, H., Kodama, T., Shikano, H., Onouchi, M., Uchiyama, K., Odaka, T., Kamei, T., Nagahama, E., Kusaoke, M., Nitta, Y., Wada, Y., Kimura, K., Kasahara, H.: Heterogeneous multiprocessor on a chip which enables 54x AAC-LC stereo encoding. In: Proceedings of the 2007 IEEE Symposium on VLSI Circuits, pp. 18–19 (June 2007)
14. Kumar, R., Tullsen, D.M., Ranganathan, P., Jouppi, N.P., Farkas, K.I.: Single-ISA heterogeneous multi-core architectures for multithreaded workload performance. In: Proceedings of the 31st Annual International Symposium on Computer Architecture, pp. 64–75 (June 2004)
15. Shikano, H., Suzuki, Y., Wada, Y., Shirako, J., Kimura, K., Kasahara, H.: Performance evaluation of heterogeneous chip multi-processor with MP3 audio encoder. In: Proceedings of the IEEE Symposium on Low-Power and High Speed Chips, pp. 349–363 (April 2006)
16. Noda, H., Tanizaki, T., Gyohten, T., Dosaka, K., Nakajima, M., Mizumoto, K., Yoshida, K., Iwao, T., Nishijima, T., Okuno, Y., Arimoto, K.: The circuits and robust design methodology of the massively parallel processor based on the matrix architecture. In: Digest of Technical Papers of the 2006 Symposium on VLSI Circuits, pp. 210–211 (2006)
17. NVIDIA Corporation: NVIDIA CUDA Compute Unified Device Architecture Programming Guide (2008)
18. Xie, T., Qin, X.: Stochastic scheduling with availability constraints in heterogeneous clusters. In: Proceedings of the 2006 IEEE International Conference on Cluster Computing, pp. 1–10 (September 2006)
19. Sih, G.C., Lee, E.A.: A compile-time scheduling heuristic for interconnection-constrained heterogeneous processor architectures. IEEE Transactions on Parallel and Distributed Systems 4, 175–187 (1993)
20. Chan, W.Y., Li, C.K.: Scheduling tasks in DAG to heterogeneous processor system. In: Proceedings of the 6th Euromicro Workshop on Parallel and Distributed Processing, pp. 27–31 (January 1998)
21. Topcuoglu, H., Hariri, S., Wu, M.Y.: Performance-effective and low-complexity task scheduling for heterogeneous computing. IEEE Transactions on Parallel and Distributed Systems 13, 260–274 (2002)
22. Kasahara, H., Honda, H., Narita, S.: Parallel processing of near fine grain tasks using static scheduling on OSCAR (Optimally SCheduled Advanced multiprocessoR). In: Proceedings of Supercomputing '90, pp. 856–864 (November 1990)
23. Kimura, K., Kodaka, T., Obata, M., Kasahara, H.: Multigrain parallel processing on OSCAR CMP. In: Proceedings of the 2003 International Workshop on Innovative Architecture for Future Generation High-Performance Processors and Systems (January 2003)
24. Ishizaka, K., Miyamoto, T., Shirako, J., Obata, M., Kimura, K., Kasahara, H.: Performance of OSCAR multigrain parallelizing compiler on SMP servers. In: Proceedings of the 17th International Workshop on Languages and Compilers for Parallel Computing (September 2004)
25. Kimura, K., Wada, Y., Nakano, H., Kodaka, T., Shirako, J., Ishizaka, K., Kasahara, H.: Multigrain parallel processing on compiler cooperative chip multiprocessor. In: Proceedings of the 9th Annual Workshop on Interaction between Compilers and Computer Architectures, pp. 11–20 (February 2005)
26. Kasahara, H., Ogata, W., Kimura, K., Matsui, G., Matsuzaki, H., Okamoto, M., Yoshida, A., Honda, H.: OSCAR multi-grain architecture and its evaluation. In: Proceedings of the 1997 International Workshop on Innovative Architecture for Future Generation High-Performance Processors and Systems, pp. 106–115 (October 1997)

27. Kasahara, H., Honda, H., Mogi, A., Ogura, A., Fujiwara, K., Narita, S.: A multi-grain parallelizing compilation scheme for OSCAR (Optimally scheduled advanced multiprocessor). In: Proceedings of the Fourth International Workshop on Languages and Compilers for Parallel Computing, pp. 283–297 (August 1991)

28. Obata, M., Shirako, J., Kaminaga, H., Ishizaka, K., Kasahara, H.: Hierarchical parallelism control for multigrain parallel processing. In: Pugh, B., Tseng, C.-W. (eds.) LCPC 2002. LNCS, vol. 2481, pp. 31–44. Springer, Heidelberg (2005)

29. Shirako, J., Nagasawa, K., Ishizaka, K., Obata, M., Kasahara, H.: Selective inline expansion for improvement of multi grain parallelism. In: The IASTED International Conference on Parallel and Distributed Computing and Networks, pp. 128–134 (February 2004)

30. Yoshida, Y., Kamei, T., Hayase, K., Shibahara, S., Nishii, O., Hattori, T., Hasegawa, A., Takada, M., Irie, N., Uchiyama, K., Odaka, T., Takada, K., Kimura, K., Kasahara, H.: A 4320MIPS four-processor core SMP/AMP with individually managed clock frequency for low power consumption. In: Digest of Technical Papers of the 2007 IEEE International Solid-State Circuits Conference, pp. 100–590 (February 2007)

31. Kodama, T., Tsunoda, T., Takada, M., Tanaka, H., Akita, Y., Sato, M., Ito, M.: Flexible engine: A dynamic reconfigurable accelerator with high performance and low power consumption. In: Proceedings of the IEEE Symposium on Low-Power and High Speed Chips, pp. 393–408 (April 2006)

32. UZURA3: MPEG1/LayerIII encoder in FORTRAN90, http://members.at.infoseek.co.jp/kitaurawa/index_e.html

A Modular Simulator Framework for Network-on-Chip Based Manycore Chips Using UNISIM

Xiongfei Liao, Wu Jigang, and Thambipillai Srikanthan

Centre for High Performance Embedded Systems, School of Computer Engineering
Nanyang Technological University, Singapore 639798
{liao0016,asjgwu,astsrikan}@ntu.edu.sg

Abstract. NoC-based manycore chips are considered as emerging platforms of significant importance but so far there is no public accessible architectural simulator which allows coupled simulation of NoC and cores for relevant research. This paper presents a modular cycle-level simulator framework developed using UNISIM and its applicability is exemplified by building a simulator which models a message-passing distributed memory architecture with an NoC and supports coupled simulation. Simulation of a MPI-based parallel program on this simulator shows that performance metrics, such as throughput, delay and overhead, can be accurately evaluated with the captured data of flits and messages. Simulators for different functionalities and architectures can be constructed by using this framework.

1 Introduction

We are heading for a "manycore era" following the Moore's Law [1]. A typical manycore chip may have hundreds, even thousands of relatively small compute cores on a single die. On such chips, one or more cores and other resources are encapsulated into a tile. These tiles commonly are connected by Network-on-Chip (NoC). Tile-based architecture overcomes the limits by wire delay, reduces design complexity and power consumption, and hence enables scalability of designs [2]. Examples of NoC-based chips include Intel's 80-tile chip [3] and Tilera's 64-core TILE64 [4]. NoC-based manycore chips are considered as emerging platforms of significant importance. Accordingly, there are numerous research activities aimed at these platforms.

Simulators have been widely used for evaluating different hardware designs without building costly physical hardware systems and for obtaining detailed performance metrics. Therefore, suitable architectural simulators for NoC-based manycore chips are indispensable. However, to the best of our knowledge, there is no public accessible simulator which integrates industry-level cores into NoC infrastructure and runs real parallel applications on these cores.

This paper reports our work of developing a modular cycle-level architectural simulator framework using UNISIM [5,6] and it can be used to construct simulators supporting coupled simulation of NoC and cores for NoC-based manycore chips. Major features of the framework are as follows:

- This framework has an on-chip network built upon pipelined routers which have a modular architecture and support wormhole switching and virtual-channel flow

P. Stenström (Ed.): Transactions on HiPEAC IV, LNCS 6760, pp. 234–253, 2011.
© Springer-Verlag Berlin Heidelberg 2011

control. Various parameters of on-chip network, such as dimension, sizes of flit and packet, routing algorithms, etc., are configurable and performance metrics such as throughput, delay and overhead can be captured. This framework can be applied in studies of on-chip networks as described in section 5.

- This framework is designed as a foundation (section 2) for building simulators for manycore chips with different architectures. Using suitable core interfacing strategy, various cores can be connected to NoC via network interfaces and network access operations are explicitly exposed to cores. Communicating with each other, different parts of parallel applications can be distributed and run on cores. The process of building a such simulator using the framework is elaborated in section 4.
- This framework can be used to construct simulators which support typical parallel programming models such as message-passing and shared-memory. We demonstrate this by constructing a sample simulator which supports message-passing in section 4 and by suggesting an extension for shared-memory in section 5.
- This framework is developed using UNISIM environment. Many independent modules composing the simulator framework are connected through signals and these modules can be easily changed or replaced by others, enabling component re-use, fast customization and easy upgrading. Details of them are described in section 3.
- This framework is developed as a cycle-level model of UNISIM which is characterized by a high accuracy on performance evaluation comparing to the real hardware and it helps the exploration of fine-grained parallelism. In section 4, we manifest this by running a parallel application on the aforementioned simulator and elaborate the captured data of high accuracy.

The rest of this paper is organized as follows. Section 2 introduces a baseline architecture of NoC-based manycore chips for which the framework is built. Section 3 elaborates the design and implementation of the framework. Section 4 describes the process of building a simulator using the framework and the experimental results of simulating a parallel program on it. Section 5 suggests several applications of this framework. Section 6 discusses related work and section 7 concludes the paper.

2   A Baseline Architecture for NoC Based Manycore Chips

In this section, a preliminary and extensible architecture for NoC based manycore chips is described. The chosen topology of its on-chip network is mesh because mesh is regular, simple and predictably scalable with regard to power and area [7]. This architecture serves as a foundation for building NoC based manycore chips with different and sophisticated architectures.

2.1   A Network-on-Chip and Its General Structure of Tiles

Figure 1(a) shows an NoC with its tiles arranged as 4×4 2D mesh. Each tile has its coordinates and a unique identity (id). The coordinates of the tiles at the left-top corner and the right-bottom corner are $(0, 0)$ and $(3, 3)$ respectively. A tile's id is calculated with its coordinates (x, y) following the formula $id = y * width\_of\_mesh + x$.

Above NoC implements techniques such as wormhole switching and virtual-channel flow control. Here, credit-based flow control mechanism [23] is adopted. Each tile contains a router and routers are connected to ones in neighboring tiles with physical links.

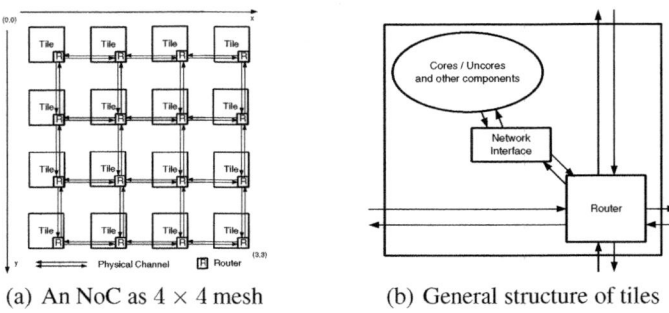

(a) An NoC as 4×4 mesh   (b) General structure of tiles

Fig. 1. Structures of a NoC and its tiles

In an NoC supporting switching technique, the granularity of data transfer is usually defined as follows. The unit of data transferred in a single cycle on a link is called a *phit* (physical unit). The unit of data for synchronization at link-level flow control is called a *flit* (flow control unit) and a flit is at least as large as a phit. Multiple flits constitute a *packet*. Specially, a short packet which has only one flit is called HDT flit. Further, several packets make up *messages* that modules connected to NoC send to each other.

Different NoCs use different phit, flit, packet and message sizes. Æthereal [9] uses phits of 32 bits, flits of 3 phits, and packets and messages of unbounded length. SPIN [10] uses phits and flits of 36 bits, and packets can be unbounded in length. For simplicity, a flit has the same size of a phit in the NoC of our framework and the size of a flit is configurable for users.

The first flit of a packet, i.e., header flit, contains routing information which is used by routers to decide header flit's route. Other flits of the same packet, i.e., body and tail flits, follow header flit's route. A flit may traverse several intermediate routers until it arrives at the destination tile.

The general structure of tiles in above architecture is shown in Figure 1(b). A tile contains one or more cores/uncores, other hardware components, a network interface (NI) and a router. A router is regarded as a part of a tile because a router is commonly put inside a tile on the physical floorplans on many NoC-based chips. An NI acts as a bridge between a router and resources in the same tile.

2.2   Virtual Channel Router

A virtual channel router of above NoC is shown in Figure 2. Its structure is similar to routers in [24][25][27]. Its major components are: several pairs of physical input/output channels, virtual channels (including buffers) for physical input channels, a routing logic, a virtual channel allocator, a switch allocator, and a crossbar switch. Credit input/output lines exist between routers which pass information of availability and buffer status of virtual channels.

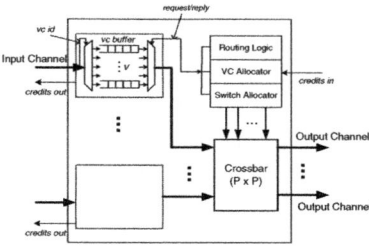

Fig. 2. A virtual channel router

The numbers of pairs of physical channels are variable for routers at different locations of mesh. For the routers located at corners, the number of pairs is 3. One pair of input/output channels are connected from/to NI in the same tile. Other two pairs of input/output channels are connected from/to routers of neighboring tiles. For routers on the borders of and internal to the mesh, the numbers of pairs are 4 and 5 respectively.

3   Design and Implementation of the Framework

This section first describes the layers of design of the framework. Then, design and implementation of the most important module, virtual channel router, and its inner modules are elaborated. Further, the considerations in NI's design are discussed. Finally, the configurable parameters and the performance metrics of the framework are introduced.

The framework is developed on Ubuntu 7.10 and compiled with GCC 4.2.3. UNISIM environment is kept at the version of May 17, 2008. The tool valgrind is used to prevent potential memory errors.

3.1   Layers of Software Design

Following the practices of UNISIM, the framework is designed and implemented in layers. At innermost layer, each tile manages its inner modules such as router, network interface, compute core and other components. The number of ports in a router is dynamically managed according to its tile's location in the mesh.

The middle layer of the simulator manages all tiles and connections between them. The clock of all tiles are set at this layer. The connections between input and output ports of tiles are established here. Users could change the topology of network-on-chip of simulators by modifying connections between tiles.

The outermost layer implements functionalities such as instantiation of a simulator and its control of execution. During the instantiation of the simulator, various modules of it are created and connected. Additionally, services provided by UNISIM are used to setup executable images of cores and to complete initialization of memory. We also adopt a good practice that all signals of the simulator are checked at every cycle. The command line is parsed to get input parameters from users and these parameters are used to configure the simulator and to control its behaviors.

3.2   Virtual Channel Router and Its Inner Modules

The virtual channel router in Figure 2 is designed as a UNISIM hardware module which contains other components. Some of these components are designed as hardware modules: input channel, output channel, virtual channel allocator and switch allocator. Remaining components, routing logic and crossbar switch, are common C++ classes.

The variable numbers of ports/connections of routers are calculated according to the coordinates of tiles. Subsequently, pairs of input and output channel modules are created when a router is instantiated.

Routing Logic (RL) and Crossbar Switch (CS)

Routing logic is implemented in a common C++ class named *RoutingAlgorithms*, instead of a hardware module. Resource request conflicts are handled at modules virtual channel allocator and switch allocator. Routing algorithms are designed as static methods of this class. Each method accepts a routing request and returns a routing result. A routing request contains information such as id of the current tile, ids of source tile and destination tile. A routing result indicates the direction of the physical output channel.

Currently implemented routing algorithms include X-Y routing (a simple deterministic routing [12]), Odd-Even adaptive routing [13] and Fully Adaptive routing [14] and table-based routing. The table-based routing is implemented by adding to each router a routing table whose entries define routing information between source and destination nodes. Data of tables are loaded from configuration files when routers are instantiated. Other routing algorithms, such as source routing, DyAD adaptive routing [15] and NoP adaptive routing [16], can be added by introducing relevant data structures and methods.

Crossbar switch is modeled by connecting each output port of input channels to each input port of output channels. The connections are setup when the router is instantiated. Control of this switch is placed in switch allocator module. When an input channel is granted with permission of passage, it can send out flits. Otherwise, it has to wait.

Input Channel (IC)

Input channel module manages multiple virtual channels (VCs) and flit buffer slots for them. The numbers of VCs and buffer slots of each VC are configurable. Buffer of a VC are organized as a FIFO queue. Each VC stores the routing result of handling a header flit which is applied to body and tail flits of the same packet.

A pipelined router processes flits in steps. In our design, an input channel module contains five inner modules to process flits: *stage buffer*, *stage route compute*, *stage VC allocation*, *stage port allocation* and *stage switch traversal*. A pipeline with six stages formed by these modules is discussed later.

Virtual Channel Allocator (VCA)

When a header flit is processed in an IC, *stage VC allocation* module sends a request to VCA to acquire a virtual channel id ($vcid$) in next router or local NI. More than one such requests in the same cycle lead to conflicts and VCA arbitrates these requests following service policies.

In addition, VCA keeps values of credits of neighboring routers and local NI. These values are updated based on inputs from credit input lines from neighboring routers and local NI. They are used together with service policies in making allocation decisions.

Switch Port Allocator (SPA)

After flits obtaining the route information including $vcid$ and output physical channel, they come to *stage port allocation* modules of ICs. These modules send requests to SPA for acquiring permissions for flits to pass the crossbar switch. Similar to VCA, in a same clock cycle, there could be conflicts due to multiple requests. Relevant service policies have to be applied to solve these conflicts.

Output Channel (OC)

Major functionalities of OC modules include receiving flits passed from output ports of ICs and sending these flits to ICs of next routers or local NI. Accordingly, each OC module has two categories of registers to store flits for buffering. One category is for storing the flits passed from ICs and there is one register for each IC. These registers are named as *input registers*. The other category is for storing the flits which will be sent to VCs of IC in next router or local NI. The number of registers of this category equals to the number of VCs of IC in next router or local NI. These registers are named *output registers*. OC also moves flits from the input registers to appropriate output registers.

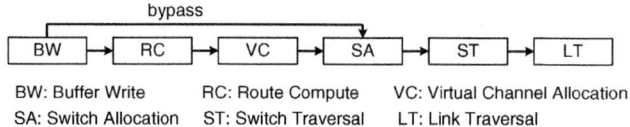

BW: Buffer Write   RC: Route Compute   VC: Virtual Channel Allocation
SA: Switch Allocation   ST: Switch Traversal   LT: Link Traversal

Fig. 3. Pipeline of the virtual channel router

Pipeline of Router

The traversal of flits of a packet through the above router can be divided into several steps which form a pipeline with six stages shown in Figure 3. These stages are described as follows:

1) *(Buffer writing)* When a header flit h of a packet p arrives at a router r from one of its ICs, $vcid$ contained in h is read and flit h is stored into a buffer slot of the virtual channel VC_{vcid} if VC_{vcid} is not occupied. After h is saved, VC_{vcid} is marked as "occupied" and the number of available buffer slots of VC_{vcid} is reduced by 1. VC_{vcid} is occupied by packet p until all p's flits are transferred. Credit values of this IC which reflect status of resources are passed to the neighboring routers via "credits out" lines. This stage is called "buffer writing" and implemented in the *stage buffer* module.

2) *(Route compute)* Then, flit h is passed from *stage buffer* module to *stage route compute* module. Here, a request for routing for h is sent to routing logic. A reply contains routing result, i.e., the OC to be used by h, is received and saved in related data structure of VC_{vcid}. This stage is called "route compute". After this stage, h is sent to *stage VC allocation* module for virtual channel allocation.

3) *(Virtual channel allocation)* A request for allocating a VC in next router or local NI is sent to VCA for flit h. VCA makes decision based on the targeted OC, current service policy (such as round-robin) and the availability of VCs in next router or local NI (passed from "credits in" lines). Reply containing the allocated virtual channel id, denoted as $nextvcid$, is sent back from VCA if $VC_{nextvcid}$ is available. If no VC is available, the reply contains a specified value, i.e., $VCID\_NULL$, and requests for

allocation keep being sent in following clock cycles until a VC is allocated to h. The *nextvcid* is also saved at VC_{vcid} and $vcid$ in the header flit h is updated to *nextvcid*. The routing information for h saved at VC_{vcid} will be used by the body and tail flits of the same packet p for their transfers. This stage is named "virtual channel allocation".

4) (*Switch port allocation*) After stage "virtual channel allocation", flit h is passed to *stage port allocation* module. For each flit, including header, body and tail, a request for switch passage permission is sent to SPA. SPA makes port allocation decision based on related service policies. SPA controls the crossbar switch by granting permissions to corresponding ICs. This stage is named "switch port allocation".

5) (*Switch traversal*) Flits granted passage permission for the crossbar are passed to input ports of the appropriate OCs. When the tail flit of packet p passes the crossbar switch, the VC of the current IC which has been allocated to p can be freed for transfers of other packets. This stage is named "switch traversal" and implemented in the *stage switch traversal* module.

6) (*Link traversal*) The flits at the OCs are transferred to next routers or local NI. This stage can be regarded as implemented in output channel module. After this, flits are transferred to a neighboring router or local NI.

In Figure 3, there is a bypass path between stage *buffer writing* and stage *switch allocation*. It is used by the body and tail flits which don't need to go through the stages such as "route compute" and "virtual channel allocation".

3.3   Network Interface (NI)

NIs are usually considered as the glue logic necessary to adapt compute cores to the NoC. A typical NI in physical implementation contains front-end and back-end sub-modules [23] [8]. Functionalities of an NI could include core interfacing, packetization, flow control, clock adaptation, reliability, security, etc. Since we are implementing NI for architectural simulators, the functionalities of NI in our framework are simplified to only include core interfacing, packetization and flow control. Moreover, the cores, NIs and NoC share a common clock.

Core interfacing and packetization are closely related. The communication between cores, i.e., message passing between cores, comprises of three stages: the packet assembly, packet transmission and the packet disassembly and delivery. The commonly used packetization strategies are software library based, on-core module based and wrapper based [11]. In our framework, the on-core module based strategy is chosen since it has low latency and high flexibility at modest cost of hardware complexity including additional registers and logic and an increase in instruction set [11]. In addition, this strategy makes network access operations directly exposed to the ISA which paves the way for a tighter coupling of computation and communication [23].

The flow control of NI involves interactions with both router and compute core connected to it [23]. When the NoC cannot accept new packets any more because of congestion, NI can still accept new transactions from connected core if it has enough decoupling buffering resources. To a certain extent, this mechanism can decouple core computation with its requests for non-blocking communication services. However, when NI runs out of buffers, the congestion in NoC has impact on the core's behavior in that the core has to be stalled if it requires additional communication services.

3.4 Configurable Parameters of the Framework

Several parameters of the framework are designed as configurable. Some can be set when simulators are compiled and others can be changed when simulators run. These parameters and their brief descriptions are as follows.

- *NoC size* is specified with number of rows and number of columns of NoC.
- *Flit size* is the maximum number of bytes one flit can accommodate.
- *Packet size* is the maximum number of flits a packet could accommodate.
- *Routing algorithm* is used by routing logic in routers. Currently supported routing algorithms in the framework are: XY, Odd-Even, Fully Adaptive, Table-based.
- *Routing table file* is a text file containing information for routing tables of routers.
- *VC number* is the number of virtual channels each physical channel supports.
- *Buffer depth of virtual channel* is the number of buffers for flits at each virtual channel. A buffer slot accommodates a flit.
- *Buffer depth of NI* is the size of buffer (in packets) for messages at each NI.
- *Service policy* is the policy used to arbitrate conflicts at virtual channel allocator or switch port allocator. The default policy is first-come-first-service (FCFS).

There are several configurable parameters related to traffic and message/packet injection used by Noxim [37] and NIRGAM [38]. These parameters are not included in our framework since traffic and message/packet injection are determined by parallel workloads running on cores. When constructing simulators for NoC infrastructure research, relevant parameters can be added.

3.5 Metrics for Performance Evaluation

Similar to [12][16], two metrics, *throughput* and *average delay*, are chosen in our framework to evaluate performance of NoC.

For message-passing, metric *throughput (TP)* is defined as follows:

$$TP = \frac{Total\ received\ flits}{Number\ of\ nodes \times Total\ cycles}$$

where *Total received flits* refers to the number of whole flits that arrive at their destination nodes, *Number of nodes* is the number of network nodes, and *Total cycles* is the number of clock cycles elapsed between the occurrence of the first message generation and the last message reception. Thus, message throughput is measured in flits/cycle/node. It is the fraction of the maximum load ($TP = 1$) that the network is capable of physically handling, assuming that each node receives a flit in each cycle.

Delay of a message m is defined as time in clock cycles that elapses between the occurrence of m's header flit injection into the network at the source node and the occurrence of m's tail flit reception at the destination node. Metric *average delay (D)* is defined as follows:

$$D = \frac{1}{N} \sum_{i=1}^{N} D_i$$

where N is the total number of messages reaching their destination nodes and D_i is the delay of message i.

This framework is different from other simulators in that it integrates compute cores to run parallel applications. Therefore, performance evaluation of NI is mandatory and *average overhead* is proposed for this. During the transfer of a message from source to destination, there are overheads in the source and destination NIs. These overheads are resulted from the activities in NIs such as data movement, packetization and flow control etc. Concept of *lifetime* is introduced. Lifetime of a message m is defined as time in clock cycles that elapses between the beginning of m's transferal at the source node and the occurrence of m's consumption at the destination node. Thus, overhead of m equals to difference of its lifetime and its delay. Metric *average overhead (H)* is defined as:

$$H = \tfrac{1}{K} \sum_{i=1}^{K} H_i = \tfrac{1}{K} \sum_{i=1}^{K} (L_i - D_i)$$

where K is the total number of messages consumed by their destination nodes, D_i is the delay of message i and L_i is the lifetime of message i.

To calculate values of these performance metrics for simulations, detailed information is recorded in data structures of relevant components such as routers and NIs.

4   Constructing a Simulator for NoC Based Manycore Chips

In this section, we show the extensibility of the framework by constructing a simulator that models NoC-based manycore chips with a message-oriented distributed memory architecture which is commonly used in embedded domain.

As discussed in section 3.3, on-core module based interfacing strategy is used. Thereby, the architectural extension to computer core and added instructions are introduced first. Then the details of NI implementation are described. Following that, programming interfaces are designed to enable the simulator to run parallel applications. Finally, a simple MPI application is executed on this simulator and the various captured data for performance evaluation are elaborated. These highly accurate data manifest the capabilities of the simulators based on our framework.

This paper focuses on presenting the framework itself. Therefore, sophisticated simulators supporting more communication primitives and their applications to evaluate message-passing benchmarks such as NAS Parallel Benchmarks [21] will be reported in our future work.

In this simulator, a PowerPC 405 core is incorporated into each tile and connected to NoC through NI, shown in Figure 4(a). PowerPC 405 is a single-issue, scalar core with a 5-stage pipeline. It has many features desired for future manycore chips [1].

4.1   Interfacing PowerPC 405 Core with NoC

1) Architectural Extensions to PowerPC 405 Core
PowerPC 405 core is extended in the way that an NI is regarded as an accelerator to it. In detail, a pair of input/output ports are added to PowerPC 405 core. The signals of these ports are of type *nireq*, a class wrapping the data passed via these ports. The core sends commands to and gets data from the connected NI through these ports.

A *nireq* signal contains the following: *1)* a command passed to NI from PowerPC 405 core indicating to send/receive a message; *2) id* of message specified by application; *3)* tile id of destination (source) for sending (receiving) message; *4)* the effective address of memory where the data of message to fetch (store) for sending (receiving); *5)* length of message in bytes. Here, a simple message format is used. The first word (32 bits) of a message is the length of the message in bytes excluding the first word.

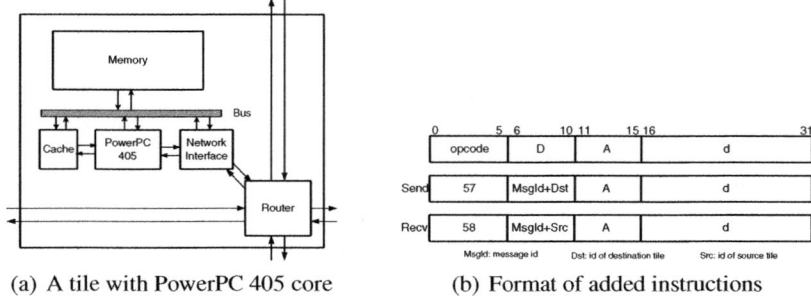

(a) A tile with PowerPC 405 core   (b) Format of added instructions

Fig. 4. Extensions to Structure of Tile and ISA of PowerPC 405

2) Extensions to Instruction Set of PowerPC 405

To expose network access operations to PowerPC 405 core, two instructions are added to PowerPC ISA. The mnemonics of them are "send" and "recv" respectively. They are designed in the same format with integer load/store instructions such as **lwz** and **stw**, shown in Figure 4(b). Opcode fields of "send" and "recv" are 57 and 58 respectively. Filed D indicates a register and its content is denoted as (D). The higher 16 bits of (D) indicates id of the message to be sent or to be received. The lower 16 bits of (D) indicates id of destination tile for "send" and id of source tile for "recv". Field A is a register and field d is an immediate. $(A)+d$ indicates the message's address in memory.

To support these instructions, it is necessary to modify the assembler to produce object codes. The back-end of the GNU assembler which is part of the binutils collection of tools is modified as follows. Two entries are added to the array of structure "powerpc_opcode", i.e., powerpc_opcodes[], in file *opcodes/ppc-opc.c*. They are as follows:

> { *"send"*, *OP(57)*, *OP_MASK*, *PPC405*,{*RS, D, RA0*}},
> { *"recv"*, *OP(58)*, *OP_MASK*, *PPC405*,{*RS, D, RA0*}},

After the binutils tools are built, a new cross-compiler is generated using crosstool 0.43 [18] for gcc 4.1.0 and glibc 2.3.6 which can generate object codes for these instructions.

3) Functionalities of Added Instructions

During their execution, these two instructions "block" the pipeline of PowerPC 405 until they finish. When such an instruction finishes, the length of message sent or received is passed to PowerPC 405 core by NI and this value is kept in the register D.

Instruction "send" is handled by PowerPC 405 core like store instructions. First, the core passes to NI a nireq signal containing message id, destination id and starting address of the message in memory. Then, NI fetches data of the message from memory hierarchy and NI sends them to NoC. After the whole message is sent, NI returns the number of bytes sent to the core and instruction "send" finishes.

Instruction "recv" is handled like load instructions. Similarly, the core first passes to NI a nireq signal containing message id, source tile id and starting address to store received message. Then, NI checks the arrival of expected message and moves its data to specified memory address. After whole message is sent to memory, NI returns the number of bytes received to the core and the "recv" instruction finishes.

4) Finite State Machines in Network Interface

An NI contains two finite state machines (FSMs) for "send" and "recv" instructions respectively. When an NI starts to send a message to NoC, the "send" FSM works as follows. *1)* NI first sends one memory request to memory hierarchy to get message's head containing the length of the whole message. *2)* After the length is obtained, successive memory requests are prepared and then sent to memory hierarchy to get the whole message. *3)* When replies to above memory requests come, NI stores them in buffer. *4)* Each cycle, even before the whole message arrives, NI tries to organize packets from its buffer and put them into an outgoing queue. NI also tries to send to NoC a flit of the packet at the head of the queue. *5)* After the whole message is sent, NI returns the number of bytes sent to the core and the "send" FSM transfers to the idle state.

The "recv" FSM works in a similar manner. The difference lies in the reverse direction of data flow, i.e., from NoC to memory hierarchy. When packets come before the "recv" instruction which accepts them, they are kept in the buffer of NI if empty slots are available. When the buffer of NI is fully occupied, flits of packets are kept in buffers in routers and flow control mechanism eventually takes in action.

In NoC designs, data that a packet accommodates may not be of same size of a memory request, the alignments of data are unavoidable. Additionally, in order that NI works properly as above described, some modifications have been made to the cache module and bus module provided by UNISIM for the purpose of cache coherence.

4.2   Programming Interfaces

Several level of programming interfaces have been designed to make programming easier. They are described as follows.

1) Low-level C Wrapper Functions

The "send" and "recv" instructions are wrapped in two C functions "_send" and "_recv" as below. Assembly intrinsics of "send" and "recv" are embedded in C codes and thereby only modifications to GNU assembler are needed.

```
int _send(int msg_tile_ids, char* message) { asm ("send 3, 0(4)"); }
int _receive(int msg_tile_ids, char* message) { asm ("recv 3, 0(4)"); }
```

For these functions, it is necessary to understand procedure interfaces and register conventions for PowerPC processors. In assembly of PowerPC, general purpose register GPR_n is represented by number n. According to [19], GPR_1 is used as stack pointer register (*SP*). GPR_3, GPR_4, ..., are used to store the first, second, ..., parameter passed from caller of a function. GPR_3 is also used to store the first word of the return value if the function has return value.

Table 1. High-level wrapper functions

int Send(int msgId, int tileId, char* msg, int len)	int Receive(int msgId, int tileId, char* msg, int len)

{
  char *temp, *t;
  int iLen = len;
  int msg_tile_ids = msgId << 16 + tileId;
  temp = (char*)malloc((iLen + 5)*sizeof(char));
  if(temp == NULL) { return 0; }
  memset(temp, 0, iLen + 5);
  temp[0] = ((iLen & 0xff000000) >> 24);
  temp[1] = ((iLen & 0x00ff0000) >> 16);
  temp[2] = ((iLen & 0x0000ff00) >> 8);
  temp[3] = ((iLen & 0x000000ff));
  t = &temp[4];   memcpy(t, msg, len);
  iLen = _send(msg_tile_ids, temp);
  free(temp);   return iLen;
}
	{
	  char *temp, *t;
	  int iLen = len + 32;
	  int msg_tile_ids = msgId << 16 + tileId;
	  temp = (char*)malloc(iLen * sizeof(char));
	  if(temp == NULL){ return 0; }
	  memset(temp, 0, iLen);
	  iLen = _receive(msg_tile_ids, temp);
	  memcpy(msg, temp, iLen);
	  msg[iLen] = 0;
	  free(temp);
	  return iLen;
	}

In "_send", msg_tile_ids contains mixture of message id and destination tile id and *message* is the address of the message to be sent. These parameters are passed to GPR_3 and GPR_4 respectively. The instruction "send" can get desired values. Similarly, in "_receive", msg_tile_ids contains mixture of message id and source tile id and *message* is the address to save the message.

No *return* statement appears in above functions. Thus, a value set by "send" or "recv", i.e., length of message, is intact and returned to caller via GPR_3.

2) High-level C Wrapper Functions

Two high-level C wrapper functions , "Send" and "Receive", are added to release the burdens of using low-level functions such as calculating msg_tile_ids, preparing message in correct format and allocating buffer, etc.

Shown in Table 1, calculations of msg_tile_ids are included. Buffers for temporary store are managed as well. In addition, in "Send", codes are added to calculate length of a message and put it at the beginning bytes of the message. In "Receive", extra 32 bytes are allocated to save an extra memory request in NIs for non-aligned data.

3) Massage-Passing Interface (MPI)

MPI is a standard interface for message-passing [17] that supports point-to-point communications and collective operations. Programs using MPI typically employ single program, multiple data (SPMD) parallelism. MPI APIs are usually organized in layers and a layered implementation is adopted in this simulator. Point-to-point operations, *MPI_Send* and *MPI_Recv*, are implemented based on above "Send" and "Receive". Similar to [20], MPI collective operations such as *MPI_Bcast*, *MPI_Reduce*, *MPI_Barrier* and *MPI_Gather* are implemented on top of point-to-point operations using linear algorithm. The details of *MPI_Send* and *MPI_Recv*, are as follows:

```
void MPI_Send (void *value, int len, MPI_Datatype type, int dest, int tag, MPI_Comm comm)
{
    int size, destTileId, iUnitSize, iLen, iMsgId = 0, iReturn = 0;
    MPI_Comm_size(comm, &size);    assert(dest < size);
    destTileId = grp_array[comm].member[dest]; //grp_array manages groups of processes.
    if( type == MPI_INT ) {    iUnitSize = sizeof(int);    }
    else if( type == MPI_FLOAT ) {    iUnitSize = sizeof(float);    }
    else if ( type == MPI_DOUBLE ) {    iUnitSize = sizeof(double);    }
    else {    printf("MPI_Send: datatype is unknown");    return;    }
    iLen = len * iUnitSize;   iMsgId = tag;   iReturn = Send(iMsgId, destTileId, value, iLen);
}
void MPI_Recv (void *value, int len, MPI_Datatype type, int src, int tag,MPI_Comm comm,
                            MPI_Status *status) {
    int size, srcTileId, iMsgId = 0, iReturn = 0;
    MPI_Comm_size(comm, &size);    assert(src < size);
    srcTileId = grp_array[comm].member[src];
    iMsgId = tag;      iReturn = Receive(iMsgId, srcTileId, value, len);
    status→tag = tag;   status→source = src;   status→length = iReturn;
}
```

MPI environment is setup in API *MPI_Init*. In it, each MPI process reads a configuration file whose name is passed from command line. This file contains the information of one-to-one mapping between tile ids and ranks of processes related to a communicator. Currently, only communicator *MPI_COMM_WORLD* is used. APIs *MPI_Comm_rank* and *MPI_Comm_size* are based on above information as well.

4.3   Evaluation of a Parallel Program Using MPI

A Linux OS plugin provided by UNISIM, *PowerPCLinux*, is attached to PowerPC 405 core in each tile. These plugins can load ELF32 files compiled and statically linked to UNISIM libraries by the aforementioned cross-compiler. A configuration file is used to pass command line parameters to each core. Parameters for an application include local tile id, MPI configuration file and log file for debugging. The cores which run a same parallel workload are synchronized for termination of simulation. Upon termination of simulation, the detailed data of flits and messages are saved into files on hard disc.

To elaborate the captured data of high accuracy, a parallel program using MPI to calculate the value of PI (π) is evaluated on the simulator. In it, root process ($rank = 0$) accepts number of steps of calculation (n) from console and broadcasts it using *MPI_Bcast* to all non-root processes associated with the same communicator. Then, partial results from non-root processes are collected using *MPI_Reduce* and added at root process to get the final result for above n. The program finishes when root process gets the zero value of n ($n = 0$) and non-root processes get this value from root process. Link to its code is: *http://www-unix.mcs.anl.gov/mpi/usingmpi/examples/simplempi/cpi_c.htm*.

A simulator with 9 tiles arranged as 3×3 mesh is generated. Several relevant parameters of it are as follows. Sizes of level-1 instruction and data caches are 8K respectively. Bus buffer depth is 16. Routing algorithm is X-Y routing. NI buffer depth is 16. The number of virtual channel is 2. Virtual channel buffer depth is 8 and flit size is 64 bits.

In simulation, all 9 cores participate in the calculation and each core runs a process. Root process runs on a tile at corner, shown in Fig. 5. The mapping of processes to tiles is saved in configuration file which is used by *MPI_Init*. The time in cycle when simulations start is set as 0. Two consecutive inputs to number of steps n are 50 and 0.

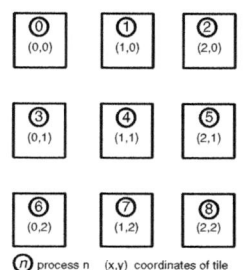

Fig. 5. Root process runs on a tile at corner

The execution of the program takes 948921 cycles. The estimated value of PI (π) is 3.1416258780877069 and its error related to a predefined value is 0.0000332244979138. Part of experimental data of flits and messages are presented in Table 2 and 3 respectively. Since each message is contained in a packet, information of packets is omitted.

Information of Flits

The simulator records the important events in the whole life of any flit. The first column of Table 2 contains partial identity information of flits. Each flit is labeled with its source tile id, destination tile id, tag of the message to which it belongs and the serial number of it in the message. "Generated Cycle" contains the time in cycle when the flit is created by its source NI and "Consumed Cycle" contains the time in cycle when the data of it is handled by destination NI. The combination of "Flit" and "Generated Cycle" can be used to uniquely identify a flit. The "NoC Entry Cycle" indicates the time in cycle when a flit leaves the source NI for the local router. The "NoC Exit Cycle" indicates the time in cycle when a flit leaves a router and enters the input channel of destination NI. Table 2 lists information of six flits. The first / last three flits are for the communications between root process and process 1 ($rank = 1$) / process 8 ($rank = 8$).

Information of Messages

Messages in the simulation are displayed in Table 3. Meanings of columns of the table are as follows. The first column gives the partial identity information of a message which includes the message's source tile id, destination tile id and tag. "Send Start" indicates the time in cycle when the PowerPC 405 core executes a "send" instruction and sends a command to source NI to initialize a sending session. "Send End" is the time in cycle when the NI finishes sending the message and returns value to the core.

Table 2. Relevant Details of Some Flits in the Simulation

Flit (s,d,t,f)	Generated Cycle	NoC Entry Cycle	NoC Exit Cycle	Consumed Cycle
(0,1,0,0)	167744	167745	167761	167762
(1,0,0,0)	259214	259215	259231	480429
(0,1,0,0)	698098	698099	698115	698116
(0,8,0,136)	406135	406136	406177	406178
(8,0,0,0)	493480	493481	493521	611577
(8,0,0,0)	935986	935987	936027	936028

Note: s: source tile id; d: destination tile id; t: message tag; f: flit id.

Table 3. Relevant Details of All Messages in the Simulation

Msg	Send (cycle)		Recv (cycle)		Length		Delay	Overhead (cycles)			SynCost
(s, d, t)	Start	End	Start	End	bytes	flits	cycles	Total	Send	Recv	cycles
(0,1,0)	167739	167746	141578	167764	4	1	16	9	6	3	26183
(0,2,0)	201778	201785	141279	201812	4	1	25	9	6	3	60530
(0,3,0)	235755	235762	141313	235780	4	1	16	9	6	3	94464
(0,4,0)	269954	269961	141546	269988	4	1	25	9	6	3	128439
(0,5,0)	303978	303985	141403	304020	4	1	33	9	6	3	162614
(0,6,0)	337996	338003	141555	338030	4	1	25	9	6	3	196472
(0,7,0)	372055	372062	141285	372096	4	1	32	9	6	3	230808
(0,8,0)	406130	406137	141739	406180	4	1	41	9	6	3	264438
(1,0,0)	259209	259216	480423	480431	8	1	16	221206	6	221200	221192
(2,0,0)	293089	293096	499276	499284	8	1	24	206171	6	206165	206157
(3,0,0)	327055	327062	518013	518021	8	1	16	190950	6	190944	190936
(4,0,0)	361385	361392	536752	536760	8	1	24	175351	6	175345	175337
(5,0,0)	391083	391090	555368	555376	8	1	32	164261	6	164255	164247
(6,0,0)	425227	425234	574111	574119	8	1	24	148868	6	148862	148854
(7,0,0)	459150	459157	592908	592916	8	1	33	133733	6	133727	133719
(8,0,0)	493475	493482	611571	611579	8	1	40	118064	6	118058	118050
(0,1,0)	698093	698100	292207	698118	4	1	16	9	6	3	405908
(0,2,0)	732258	732265	326144	732291	4	1	24	9	6	3	406144
(0,3,0)	766428	766435	360124	766453	4	1	16	9	6	3	406326
(0,4,0)	800515	800522	394383	800548	4	1	24	9	6	3	406162
(0,5,0)	834477	834484	424122	834518	4	1	32	9	6	3	410393
(0,6,0)	868314	868321	458135	868347	4	1	24	9	6	3	410209
(0,7,0)	902106	902113	492019	902148	4	1	33	9	6	3	410126
(0,8,0)	935981	935988	526439	936030	4	1	40	9	6	3	409588

Note: Msg: message; s: source tile id; d: destination tile id; t: message tag; SynCost: synchronization cost.

"Recv Start" and "Recv End" have the similar meanings but for a "recv" instruction. Length of a message is represented by bytes and flits, as shown in column "Length". Delay of a message is the difference of the "NoC Exit Cycle" of its tail flit and the "NoC Entry Cycle" of its header flit, i.e., the period of time that a message stays in NoC. According to definition in section 3.5, "total overhead" can be calculated as ("Recv End" - "Send Start" - "Delay"). "Total overhead" can be further divided into "Send Overhead" and "Recv Overhead" where "Send overhead" is calculated as ("NoC Entry Cycle" of header flit - "Send Start") and "Recv Overhead" is calculated as ("Recv End" - "NoC Exit Cycle" of tail flit).

During the simulation, there are 24 messages transferred in the NoC. Eight messages containing value of n (50, 4-byte integer) are sent from root process to non-root processes, listed in the first 8 rows of Table 3. Eight messages containing the partial results (8-byte double) are sent from non-root processes to root process, shown in the second 8 rows of Table 3. Eight messages from root process to non-root processes containing $n = 0$ are displayed in the last 8 rows.

Discussions

Two important issues should be pointed out. First, captured data are cycle accurate and performance metrics can calculated easily with these data of high accuracy. Metric Throughput (TP) can be obtained based on information of flits. Metrics delay and overhead can be calculated using information of messages.

Second, analysis on these data indicates a new metric is helpful to performance evaluation of coupled simulation. A study at "Overhead" in Table 3 reveals that the middle 8 rows have much higher values of "Total Overhead" than other 16 rows. These values come largely from "Recv Overhead" which is caused by the fact that "Recv" instruction to accept the message comes later than the "Send" instruction sending this message. After such a message is sent, it waits for the corresponding "Recv" instruction in buffers of NI in the destination tile or buffers of some routers. By contrast, those small values of "Total Overhead" are resulted from the fact that the "Recv" instruction to accept a message comes earlier than the corresponding "Send" instruction. The cores executing "Recv" instruction wait for the desired messages to arrive.

Disadvantages exist for both above situations. For situation where messages wait for acceptance in NI or buffers in routers, these idle messages hold and waste the limited and precious resources for long periods. For situation where cores executing "Recv" instructions wait for desired messages, the compute cycles are wasted without doing any useful work. A new metric, namely *synchronization cost*, is proposed to quantify these disadvantages. The collected synchronization costs of messages are displayed in the last column, i.e., "SynCost", in Table 3. When synchronization costs are reduced, the performance can be improved, or the resources can be better used, or both can be achieved. Therefore, synchronization cost can be used as an indicator for performance and resource-utilization efficiency.

5   Applications of the Framework

Several examples of applying the framework are described in this section.

1. **Constructing Simulators with Various Functionalities and Architectures**
   This is realized by incorporating various IP Cores ranging from general CPU to special processing logics into tiles.By incorporating IP cores of same type or different types, simulators for homogeneous or heterogeneous architectures can be created. This is feasible because UNISIM supports modeling in both sequential logic and combinational logic.

2. **Constructing Simulators Supporting Shared-Memory Programming Model**
   Cache coherence on shared-memory platforms is widely discussed [28][29]. An extended structure of a tile for supporting shared-memory programming model is shown in Figure 6(a) where a tile has private Level-1 cache and shared Level-2 cache. It can be extended from Figure 1(b) by integrating one compute core, Level-1 cache, Level-2 cache, directory and other modules.

3. **Constructing Simulators for NoC Infrastructure Research**
   This framework can be applied in research which emphasizes on NoC infrastructure. Some research doesn't consider particularities of applications. For them,

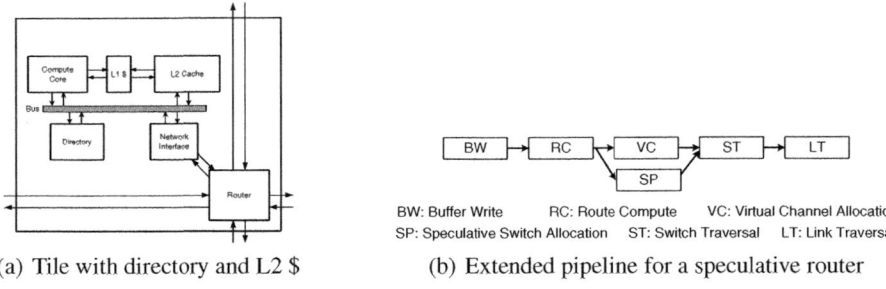

(a) Tile with directory and L2 $ (b) Extended pipeline for a speculative router

Fig. 6. Examples of Applications

simple cores can be used in tiles. Some cores generate and inject packets into NoC while the others accept packets from NoC. Foci can be put on the performance metrics, routing algorithms, router, etc. Topology of NoC can be changed as described in section 3.1. These simulators are similar to Noxim [37] and NIRGAM [38]. In addition, based on the basic pipeline in Figure 3, sophisticated router models can be constructed and evaluated. The speculative router discussed in [24] is shown in Figure 6(b) and it can be modeled by changing the basic pipeline. Similarly, the fast router in [26] can be simulated after appropriate adaptations.

6   Related Work

6.1   NoC Research and Related Simulators

There have been many research activities aimed at Network-on-Chip. Networking techniques are re-examined in on-chip scenario [22][23]. New devices are studied and developed [24,25,26,27]. Techniques for integration are studied [28,29,30]. Experiences are summarized [31] and roadmap for future research is discussed [32].

Unfortunately, there is no public accessible simulator for NoC based manycore chips which connects industrial level cores and runs real applications on them. We surveyed several good simulators in related areas. FAST [33] is a functionally accurate simulation toolset for manycore chips but it is limited to IBM's proprietary Cyclops-64 architecture. Orion [34] and LUNA [35] are especially developed for power simulation of on-chip interconnection networks and they don't consider compute cores. NoC simulators such as NNSE [36], Noxim [37] and NIRGAM [38] have flexibilities in configuring parameters of on-chip network and capabilities to obtain performance metrics. But they don't integrate compute cores and can not run real applications to simulate behaviors of whole chips. When we started this work in Dec. 2007, the only topology supported by UNISIM environment was bus.

6.2   UNISIM Environment

Overview of UNISIM   UNISIM is a structural simulator environment built on top of SystemC for hardware modeling. Its core consists of a compilation engine and a library.

The library defines modules, ports, signals, etc. The compilation engine produces C++ source files of a simulator from the set of leaf and hierarchical modules defining it. The produced files are compiled and linked to the library to create the simulator executable.

UNISIM environment currently supports two types of modeling: transaction-level modeling (TLM) and cycle-level modeling (CLM). TLM-level simulators are fast and able to simulate full systems. Cycle-level simulators have high accuracy on performance evaluation. Our framework is developed as a cycle-level model.

There is an online repository of UNISIM environment [6]. It has many cycle-level modules for reusable hardware blocks and several cycle-level simulators for case study. UNISIM has been successfully used to develop complex cycle-level simulators including CellSim [39] which models IBM's Cell, a modern heterogeneous multiprocessor.

Cycle-level Modeling in UNISIM. UNISIM provides a set of rules for modular hardware modeling. A hardware module is a derived class of UNISIM class *module* and can have states. A module only exposes interfaces and its implementation is hidden.

A hardware module can be reused in different designs as a plug-in. Modules can be connected through ports. A connection is established when an output port is linked to an input port of the same type through signals. A connection has three different signals: *data*, *accept* and *enable*. The signal *data* is typed signal to pass data of various types. The signals *accept* and *enable* are simple boolean signals. By establishing connections, a set of modules could define a hierarchical hardware architecture.

UNISIM also provides a well defined communication protocol to implement the interactions between pairs of modules. Passing values between two modules is as follows: a sender module writes data to its output ports and a receiver module reads data from corresponding input ports. Processes are designed in modules to define their behaviors in response to changes in signals of ports. A communication transaction is initialized at a sender module by sending data via *data* signal of output ports; the receiver module can accept them or not by setting *accept* signal of the corresponding input port as **true** or **false**; the sender can enable or disable the transaction by setting *enable* signal of the output port as **true** or **false**. In this way, centralized controls are distributed among modules with connection signals in UNISIM-based simulators.

UNISIM designs service/client relations via interfaces to enable interactions without using hardware ports. A interface is a set of standardized calls which acts as a contract between service and client. Any module importing a service automatically benefits from it. UNISIM utilizes services to implement many simulator-independent functionalities which are technology- and software- related. Services are easy to be modified or replaced due to their independency. Several examples of services are: loader, thread, memory, debugger, OS and syscall etc. All registered services are managed by a Service Manager which helps interaction and debugging. Developers can give names to modules and ports for debugging purpose. Moreover, APIs are provided to check signals during simulation to avoid the "unknown" status.

7 Conclusions

We have discussed a baseline architecture for NoC based manycore chips. Based on it, we have designed and implemented a framework for building simulators modeling the above mentioned chips. Further, we have demonstrated its extensibility by constructing a simulator for a message-passing architecture and by capturing relevant data of high accuracy with simulating a parallel program on it. Analysis of above data shows the framework's capabilities for coupled simulation of NoC and cores. Several proposed applications of the framework show that it can readily be applied to various NoC-based research. The simulation framework will be available for download at http://www.chipes.ntu.edu.sg/contents/resources/Resources.htm in near future.

Acknowledgements

We thank anonymous referees for their constructive comments. Our thanks also go to Dr. Sylvain Girbal at ALCHEMY Group of INRIA Saclay for his help in explaining details of UNISIM in correspondences.

References

1. Asanovic, K., et al.: The Landscape of Parallel Computing Research: A View from Berkeley. TR UCB/EECS-2006-183, UC Berkeley (2006)
2. Benini, L., De Micheli, G.: Networks on Chips: A New SoC Paradigm. IEEE Computer 35, 70–78 (2002)
3. Vangal, S., et al.: An 80-tile 1.28TFlops Network-on-Chip in 65nm CMOS. In: Proceedings of ISSCC 2007 (2007)
4. Tilera (2008), http://www.tilera.com
5. August, D., et al.: UNISIM: An Open Simulation Environment and Library for Complex Architecture Design and Collaborative Development. IEEE Comp. Arch. Letters (August 2007)
6. UNISIM (2008), https://unisim.org/site
7. Balfour, J., Dally, W.J.: Design Tradeoffs for Tiled CMP On-Chip Networks. In: International Conference on Supercomputing (2006)
8. Radulescu, A., et al.: An efficient on-chip NI offering guaranteed services, shared-memory abstraction, and flexible network configuration. IEEE Trans. on CAD of Integrated Circuits and Systems 24(1), 4–17 (2005)
9. Goossens, K., et al.: A Ethereal network on chip: concepts, architectures, and implementations. IEEE Design & Test of Computers 22(5), 414–421 (2005)
10. Guerrier, P., Greiner, A.: A generic architecture for on-chip packet-switched interconnections. In: Proceedings of DATE 2000 (2000)
11. Bhojwani, P., Mahapatra, R.: Interfacing Cores with On-chip Packet-Switched Networks. In: Proceedings of VLSI 2003 (2003)
12. Pande, P.P., et al.: Performance Evaluation and Design Trade-offs for Network on Chip Interconnect Architectures. IEEE Transactions on Computers 54(8) (2005)
13. Chiu, G.-M.: The odd-even turn model for adaptive routing. IEEE Transactions on Parallel and Distributed Systems 11(7) (2000)
14. Zhou, J., et al.: Adaptive fault-tolerant wormhole routing in 2D meshes. In: International Parallel and Distributed Processing Symposium (2001)
15. Hu, J., Marculescu, R.: DyAD - smart routing for networks-on-chip. In: Proceedings of ACM/IEEE DAC (2004)
16. Asica, G., et al.: Implementation and analysis of a New Selection Strategy for Adaptive Routing in Networks-on-Chip. IEEE Transactions on Computers 57(6) (2008)

17. Message Passing Interface Forum, http://www.mpi-forum.org/
18. GCC/glibc cross toolchains (2008), http://www.kegel.com/crosstool
19. Hoxey, S., et al.: The PowerPC Compiler Writer's Guide. IBM (1996)
20. Saldana, M., Chow, P.: TMD-MPI: An MPI Implementation for Multiple Processors Across Multiple FPGAs. In: Proceedings of FPL (2006)
21. NAS Parallel Benchmarks (2008),
    http://www.nas.nasa.gov/Resources/Software/npb.html
22. Dally, W.J., Towles, B.P.: Principles and Practices of Interconnection Networks. Morgan Kaufmann Publishers, San Francisco (2003)
23. Benini, L., De Micheli, G.: Networks on Chips: Technology and Tools. Morgan Kaufmann Publishers, San Francisco (2006)
24. Peh, L.-S., Dally, W.J.: A Delay Model and Speculative Architecture for Pipelined Routers. In: Proceedings of ISCA 2001 (2001)
25. Mullins, R., et al.: Low-Latency Virtual-Channel Routers for On-Chip Networks. In: Proceedings of ISCA 2004 (2004)
26. Kumar, A., et al.: A 4.6Tbits/s 3.6GHz Single-cycle NoC Router with a Novel Switch Allocator in 65nm CMOS. In: Proceedings of 25th ICCD (2007)
27. Hoskote, Y., et al.: A 5-GHz Mesh Interconnect for a Teraflops Processor. IEEE Micro 27(5), 51–61 (2007)
28. Zhang, M., Asanovic, K.: Victim Replication: Maximizing Capacity while Hiding Wire Delay in Tiled Chip Multiprocessors. In: Proceedings of ISCA 2005 (2005)
29. Brown, J.A., et al.: Proximity-aware directory-based coherence for multi-core processor architectures. In: Proceedings of SPAA 2007 (2007)
30. Azimi, M., et al.: Integration Challenges and Tradeoffs for Tera-scale Architectures. Intel Technology Journal (2007)
31. Agarwal, A.: Tiled Multicore Processors: The Four Stages of Reality. Keynote talk, Micro 40 (2007)
32. Owens, J.D., et al.: Research Challenges for On-Chip Interconnection Networks. IEEE Micro 27(5), 96–108 (2007)
33. del Cuvillo, J., et al.: FAST: A Functionally Accurate Simulation Toolset for the Cyclops-64 Cellular Architecture. In: MoBS 2005 Workshop in Conjunction with ISCA 2005 (2005)
34. Wang, H., et al.: Orion: A Power-Performance Simulator for Interconnection Networks. In: Proceedings of MICRO, vol. 35 (2002)
35. Eisley, N., Peh, L.-S.: High-Level Power Analysis for on-Chip Networks. In: Proceedings of CASES, vol. 7 (2004)
36. Lu, Z., Thid, R., et al.: NNSE: Nostrum network-on-chip simulation environment. In: Design, Automation and Test in Europe Conference (2005)
37. Noxim (2008), http://sourceforge.net/projects/noxim
38. Jain, L., et al.: NIRGAM: A Simulator for NoC Interconnect Routing and Application Modeling. In: Design, Automation and Test in Europe Conference (2007)
39. CellSim (2007), http://pcsostres.ac.upc.edu/cellsim/doku.php

Software Transactional Memory Validation – Time and Space Considerations

Adam Welc and Bratin Saha

Programming Systems Lab
Intel Corporation
Santa Clara, CA 95054
{adam.welc,bratin.saha}@intel.com

Abstract. With single thread performance hitting the power wall, hardware architects have turned to chip-level multiprocessing to increase processor performance. As a result, issues related to the construction of scalable and reliable multi-threaded applications have become increasingly important. One of the most pressing problems in concurrent programming has been synchronizing accesses to shared data among multiple concurrent threads.

Traditionally, accesses to shared memory have been synchronized using lock-based techniques resulting in scalability, composability and safety problems. Recently, transactional memory has been shown to eliminate many problems associated with lock-based synchronization, and transactional constructs have been added to languages to facilitate programming with transactions. Hardware transactional memory (HTM) is at this point readily available only in the simulated environments. Furthermore, some of the TM systems relying on the hardware support are hybrid solutions that require TM operations to be supported in software as well. Therefore, providing an efficient software transactional memory (STM) implementation has been an important area of research. One of the largest overheads in an STM implementation is incurred in the validation procedure (that is, in ensuring correctness of transactional read operations).

This paper presents novel solutions to reduce the validation overhead in an STM. We first present a validation algorithm that is linear in the number of read operations executed by a transaction, and yet does not add any overhead to transactional reads and writes. We then present an algorithm that uses bitmaps to encode information about transactional operations and further reduces both the time and space overheads related to validation. We evaluate the effectiveness of both algorithms in the context of a state-of-the-art STM implementation.

1 Introduction

With single thread performance hitting the power wall, hardware architects have turned to chip-level multiprocessing (CMP) to increase processor performance. All major processor vendors are aggressively promoting CMPs in the mainstream computing market. In a CMP environment, applications have to be concurrent to exploit the computing power of the hardware platform. As a result, issues related to the construction of scalable and reliable multi-threaded applications have become increasingly important. One

P. Stenström (Ed.): Transactions on HiPEAC IV, LNCS 6760, pp. 254–273, 2011.
© Springer-Verlag Berlin Heidelberg 2011

of the most pressing problems in concurrent programming has been the mediation of accesses to shared memory by multiple concurrent threads of execution.

Today, programmers use lock-based synchronization to manage concurrent accesses to shared memory. However, lock-based synchronization leads to a number of software engineering problems as well as scalability bottlenecks resulting from oversynchronization, which is often a result of programmers attempting to ensure correctness. Transactional memory [5–8, 13] avoids many problems associated with lock-based synchronization by eliminating deadlocks, providing safe composition, and enabling application scalability through optimistic concurrency. Accordingly, there has been a lot of recent interest in adding transactional constructs to programming languages, and in providing high performance implementations of transactional memory.

Transactional memory (TM) can be implemented both as a hardware (HTM) [9–11], or as a software (STM) [6, 7, 13, 15] system. For use as a programming construct, a TM system must support transactions of unbounded size and duration, and allow transactions to be integrated with a language environment. While these requirements can be satisfied by the HTM systems [2, 12], hardware support necessary to implement such systems is complicated and, additionally, the HTM systems require a specific transactional semantics to be "baked" into hardware. As a result, the time frame for deployment of such systems is highly unpredictable. Some of these problems are alleviated by the hybrid TM systems [3, 14], but these systems, while implementing some transactional functionality in hardware, still rely on the software transactional memory support to a smaller or a larger extent. Thus, a high performance STM is likely to be crucial for deploying transactional memory as a programming mechanism.

Some of the best performing STMs constructed so far use optimistic read concurrency [7, 13], wherein the run-time system optimistically executes a transaction and then validates all the read operations before committing its results. However, the validation procedure constitutes one of the major costs of such STM systems [13]. In this paper, we present a number of novel mechanisms to reduce the STM validation cost, and thereby to make the STM implementation more efficient. We also evaluate the effectiveness of the solutions we developed on a number of transactional workloads.

This paper makes two novel contributions:

- We present and evaluate a validation algorithm that is linear in the number of read operations executed by a transaction, does not add overhead to STM read and write operations, and does not suffer from false conflicts. Other solutions we are aware of are either of higher complexity [13], impose additional overhead on transactional memory access operations to reduce validation overhead [7], or are imprecise and may lead to an unspecified number of false conflicts [16].
- We present and evaluate an algorithm that further reduces validation overhead by using bitmaps to represent information about transactional operations in a compressed form. Using bitmaps reduces both space and time overheads of validation. This enhancement is important since even a linear validation scheme can incur a substantial overhead for a long running transaction. Other STMs using bitmaps for validation [16] use them as the sole validation scheme. Therefore, to reduce the number of spurious aborts, the algorithm must use very large maps which negates any space savings, and can still lead to unpredictable performance degradation.

The rest of the paper is organized as follows. Section 2 gives a brief overview of the existing validation algorithms in STMs with optimistic read concurrency and motivates the need for more efficient solutions. Section 3 describes a novel optimized validation algorithm linear in the number of reads executed by a transaction that is both precise and imposes no additional overhead on transactional data access operations. Section 4 presents a validation algorithm that compresses information about shared memory operations executed by a transaction into bitmaps. In Section 5 we evaluate performance of the presented algorithms. Finally, Section 6 contains the related work. and Section 7 contains the final conclusions.

2   Overview

Our work is set in the context of an STM that implements optimistic read concurrency using version numbers, and pessimistic write concurrency using exclusive write locks [13]. This type of STM has been independently proven to achieve high run-time performance [7]. In this type of STM every access to a shared data item is mediated using a *transaction record* (also called *STM Word* [7]). A transaction record may contain either a version number or a *lock pointer*. A lock pointer points to a data structure representing an exclusive lock and containing information about the lock owner.

If a transaction record associated with a given data item contains a version number, then other transactions are allowed to read this data item. Otherwise, only the lock owner is allowed to access this data item. Lock acquisition and release is controlled by the 2PL [4] protocol – locks are acquired when the transaction is active and released only upon transaction termination. Version numbers get incremented by the writers to indicate modifications of data items.

Every reader records a version number associated with a data item it is about to read in its local *read set*. A read set entry consists of a pointer to the transaction record associated with the data item being read and the recorded version number. A committing transaction validates its read operations by comparing the version numbers in its local read set with the current version numbers stored in the corresponding transaction records in the main memory. If all the version numbers match, all reads are considered valid and the transaction can commit.

Every writer records a version number associated with a data item it is about to write in its local *write set*. An entry in the write set, similarly to a read set entry, consists of a pointer to the transaction record associated with the data item being written and the recorded version number. Version numbers recorded in the write set are used by the terminating transactions during the lock release procedure to restore transaction records to their "unlocked" state.

We have described the STM data structures at an abstract level to ease the presentation. We will dive into the details in the later sections when we describe the algorithms.

2.1   Motivation

Processing of the read set during validation is a potential source of significant overhead. Ideally this overhead should be reduced as much as possible while, at the same time,

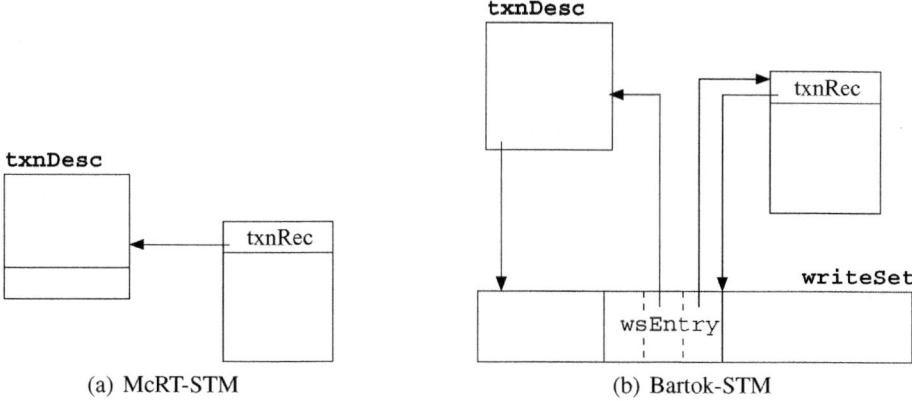

Fig. 1. Data item locked by a transaction

keeping the cost of transactional data access operations low. Unfortunately, these two requirements are somewhat contradictory, as we will demonstrate through the analysis of solutions used by two highly efficient and well documented STMs, one by Harris *et al.* implemented in Bartok optimizing compiler [7] (from now on we will call it Bartok-STM to emphasize a distinction from Harris's previous STM implementation [5]) and the other, by Saha *et al.*, called McRT-STM [13]. Both STMs use version numbers to validate correctness of read operations and exclusive locks for ensuring correctness of write operations, as described previously.

In both STMs a transaction can read or write a data item that has already been locked only if it already owns the lock. This *ownership test* must be implemented efficiently since it is executed for every transactional memory operation. The approach used in McRT-STM is illustrated in Figure 1(a). The transaction record (txnRec) associated with the locked data item points directly to the lock owner's *transaction descriptor* (txnDesc), which allows for direct identification of the lock owner. In Bartok-STM, for reasons described later in this section, the lock pointer points to an entry in the lock owner's write set. In order to facilitate the ownership test, in Bartok-STM an entry in the write set contains (in addition to a transaction record pointer and a version number) a pointer to the lock owner's transaction descriptor. As a result, in the case of Bartok-STM, identification of the lock owner involves two levels of indirection instead of just one. The essence of the scheme used in Bartok-STM is illustrated in Figure 1(b). The transaction record points to an entry (wsEntry) in the lock owner's write set (writeSet)[1], the middle slot of which contains a pointer to the lock owner's transaction descriptor. The remaining slots of the write set entry contain a back-pointer to the transaction record (right-most slot) and a version number (left-most slot) as described in Section 2. Additionally, in both STMs both the read set and the write set of a given transaction are accessible via the transaction descriptor (this information has been omitted from the figures for clarity).

---

[1] Only one entry in the write set is distinguished to improve clarity of the figure.

The choice of the solution for the ownership test affects not only the efficiency of the data access operations but also the efficiency of the validation procedure. Consider a scenario where a transaction reads a data item (recording the version number), then locks the same data item and writes to it. The validation procedure must then verify that no other transaction modified this item between the read and the subsequent write operation. This is achieved by comparing a version number recorded (upon read) in the read set with a version number recorded by the same transaction (upon the following write) in the write set.

In Bartok-STM the time to perform this comparison is constant. The entry in the read set representing a locked data item points to the transaction record associated with this item while, as illustrated in Figure 1(b), the transaction record points to the lock owner's write set. Hence the version number recorded in the write set can be quickly recovered. The validation algorithm is then linear in the size of the read set. In McRT-STM the entry in the read set representing a locked data item also points to the transaction record associated with this item but the transaction record, as illustrated in Figure 1(a), points to the transaction descriptor representing the owner of the lock. In this case the verification procedure needs to scan the lock owner's write set (accessible through the lock owner's transaction descriptor) to locate the version number for the appropriate data item. This results in an algorithm whose complexity is $O(M \times N)$ where M is the size of the read set and N is the size of the write set.

In summary, Bartok-STM features a fast validation procedure at a cost of an additional level of indirection during the ownership tests and an additional value that needs to be stored in every write set entry, whereas McRT-STM implements a much slower validation procedure but avoids a second level of indirection when testing lock ownership as well as additional write set space overhead. The first major contribution of our current work is a novel algorithm that combines the benefits of both algorithms described earlier in this section – its complexity is linear in the size of the read set, a single write set entry consists of only two slots and the additional level of indirection during ownership tests is avoided as well. However, even such an algorithm can incur a significant overhead for long running transactions, both in terms of validation time as well as the space overhead of maintaining the read set. Therefore we also present an algorithm that limits (and can potentially eliminate) the need for maintaining and processing a transaction's read set.

3   Optimized Linear Validation

We implemented the optimized validation algorithm in McRT-STM and compared it with the original validation algorithm described in Section 2. In order to maintain the low cost of the lock ownership test, the new algorithm guarantees that it is sufficient for a transaction accessing a data item to only inspect the contents of the transaction record to determine lock ownership (no additional levels of indirection are involved). At the same time, it avoids multiple searches of the write set during validation [2]. The new

---

[2] These searches were necessary in the original validation algorithm present in McRT-STM to determine the validity of accesses to data items that have been first read and then written by the same transaction.

algorithm works by temporarily modifying the contents of transaction records during the validation procedure to allow easy access to the version numbers recorded (upon write) in the write set.

3.1 Algorithm Overview

In the original validation algorithm, a transaction record could only contain either a version number or a lock pointer (pointing to a transaction descriptor) at any given time. These two cases were distinguished by checking a designated low-order *version bit* of the value stored in a transaction record. A transaction record contained a version number if the bit was set, and contained a lock pointer (indicating that the data item is locked) if the bit was cleared. We took advantage of this property when developing the new optimized validation algorithm.

In the new algorithm, when a data item is unlocked the transaction record associated with this data item contains the version number and the version bit is set. When a data item is locked, however, its transaction record can either contain a pointer to the lock owner's transaction descriptor (when the corresponding transaction is active) or a pointer to an entry in the lock owner's write set (when the lock owner's transaction is being validated). In both these cases the version bit is unset. Since the meaning of the version bit remains the same when a transaction is active, the access operations on the shared data do not have to change and, as a result, remain as efficient as in the original algorithm. Any data access operation of a given transaction can proceed if the bit is set since the item is unlocked. If the bit is unset, the operation of a given transaction can proceed only if the contents of the transaction record points to its own transaction descriptor. Otherwise, the transaction record points to either another transaction's descriptor, or to an entry in another transaction's write set. We would like to emphasize that, unlike in the approach adopted by Bartok-STM, a transaction record is only made to point to an entry in the write set for the duration of the validation procedure, and then only if the transaction writes a location after reading it. This is important since an optimizing compiler can statically detect many or even all situations when a location is read and then subsequently written. Exclusive locks for such locations can then be acquired at the point of a read without loss of efficiency and validation for such locations can be skipped altogether. If all write-after-read situations are eliminated, our algorithm neither incurs an overhead during transactional access operations, nor during the validation procedure.

3.2 Validation Procedure

During a transaction's validation procedure we need to be able to distinguish transaction records associated with data items that have been read and then subsequently written, and are currently locked by the validating transaction. While the validation procedure is in progress, these transaction records can only point either to the validating transaction's descriptor or to an entry in the validating transaction's write set. Since pointers are aligned we designate another low-order bit (called *validation bit*) for this purpose.

The validation procedure consists of the following phases. Phases 2 and 3 are optional and depend on the result of executing phase 1.

```
bool VALIDATE(TxnDescriptor *txnDesc) {

  // ************ PHASE 1 ************
  bool writeAfterReadPresent = FALSE;

  FOREACH rsEntry IN txnDesc->readSet {
   IF (*(rsEntry->txnRec) != rsEntry->version) {
    // version numbers do not match
    IF ((*(rsEntry->txnRec) & ~VALIDATE_MASK) == txnDesc) {
     // written by the validating transaction
     // but not yet marked as such - mark it
     *(rsEntry->txnRec) = txnDesc | VALIDATE_MASK;
     writeAfterReadPresent = TRUE;
    }
    ELSE RETURN FALSE; // validation failure
   }
  }

  // other phases may be unnecessary
  IF (!writeAfterReadPresent) RETURN TRUE;

  // ************ PHASE 2 ************
  FOREACH wsEntry IN txnDesc->writeSet {
   IF (*(wsEntry->txnRec) & VALIDATE_MASK)
    *(wsEntry->txnRec) = wsEntry | VALIDATE_MASK;
  }

  // ************ PHASE 3 ************
  FOREACH rsEntry IN txnDesc->readSet {
   IF ((*(rsEntry->txnRec) & ~VALIDATE_MASK) == txnDesc &&
       POINTS_TO_WRITE_SET(*(rsEntry->txnRec), txnDesc)) {
    // transaction record  points to txnDesc's write set;
    // compare version numbers in both sets
    IF ((*(rsEntry->txnRec))->version != rsEntry->version)
     RETURN FALSE;
   }
  }
  RETURN TRUE;
}
```

Fig. 2. Optimized linear validation procedure

1. **Validate and Mark**: For every entry in the read set of the validating transaction inspect the contents of the transaction record to which it points. If the transaction record contains the same version number as the one recorded in the read set, proceed to the next read set entry (the read is valid). If the transaction record contains the validating transaction's descriptor (with the validation bit set or unset) then the validating transaction both read and wrote the same data item. Set the validation bit

(if not yet set) and proceed to the next read set entry. In all other cases the validation procedure fails. We do not execute the subsequent phases if the transaction did not have a write-after-read situation, or the validation failed.

2. **Redirect**: For every entry in the write set of the validating transaction inspect the contents of the transaction record to which it points. If the validation bit of the value stored in the transaction record is set, redirect the transaction record to point to the currently inspected entry in the write set (keeping the validation bit set).

3. **Verify**: For every entry in the read set of the validating transaction inspect the contents of the transaction record to which it points. If the validation bit of the value stored in the transaction record is set and the transaction record contains a pointer to an entry in the validating transaction's write set, compare the version number stored in the read set with the version number stored in the write set. If the values are equal, proceed to the next read set entry; otherwise the validation procedure fails. Please note that the write set entry in McRT-STM, unlike the write set entry in Bartok-STM, consists of only two slots. Therefore, in case a transaction record points to a write set entry of some lock owner (not necessarily the one being validated), we need an alternative solution for lock owner identification. [3] We take advantage of the fact that in McRT-STM write set is composed of memory chunks aligned on a fixed-size boundary. This allows us to store a pointer to the lock owner's transaction descriptor at a fixed offset from the base of each chunk and access it using simple pointer-arithmetic operations.

The pseudo-code describing the new linear validation algorithm is presented in Figure 2 with all three phases explicitly distinguished. The VALIDATE_MASK constant represents a mask used to mask out the validation bit. The POINTS_TO_WRITE_SET procedure summarizes actions (bit operations and the lock owner identification test) required to determine if the value stored in the transaction record points to an entry in the write set of the transaction executing the validation procedure.

Please note that if the validation procedure is executed upon transaction termination, the clean-up of transaction records can be piggy-backed on the lock release procedure which has to be executed regardless of the validation procedure's result. Only if validation is performed while the transaction is in progress (*e.g.* for periodic validation) the explicit cleanup (involving an additional pass over the write set) is required. Please note that even though the complexity of the algorithm is $O((M \times 2) + N)$ in the worst case (M is the size of the read set and N is the size of the write set), the additional passes through the read set and the write set are only necessary if the validating transaction read and then subsequently wrote to some data items it has accessed. If it is possible to detect these kinds of situations it is beneficial to eagerly acquire a write lock at the point of read to guarantee that the data item will not be modified by a different transaction between the read and the write. If all such cases are detected, then the complexity of the new validation algorithm is reduced to $O(M)$. Prior work describes a compiler analysis that performs this task [1, 7].

---

[3] In Bartok-STM a pointer to the lock owner's descriptor is stored directly in the third slot of the write set.

4   Bitmap-Based Validation

Similarly to the optimized linear validation procedure, the bitmap-based algorithm has been implemented in the context of McRT-STM. The original validation procedure used in McRT-STM requires processing of the entire read set (of the size equal to the number of reads performed by the validating transaction) to detect conflicts with respect to updates performed by other transactions. A general idea behind the bitmap-based validation algorithm is to coarsen the granularity of conflict detection by compressing information recorded in the read set into a form of a bitmap, optimizing the validation procedure towards mostly-read-only transactions. Bitmaps are used to detect conflicts only on the first attempt to commit a transaction and, upon validation failure and transaction abort, the original validation procedure is used on the following commit attempts of the re-executed transaction. Unlike the optimized linear validation algorithm described in Section 3, the bitmap-based algorithm requires modification of the code fragments implementing transactional read and write operations, called *read and write barriers*.

The bitmap-based algorithm assumes that every eligible transaction (as described below, bitmaps should not be used to detect conflicts under certain circumstances) initially uses bitmaps to detect conflicts and only upon failed validation and a resulting abort uses the original validation procedure during the subsequent re-execution. The write barriers execute both the code required to support the original validation procedure and the code implementing the algorithm using bitmaps. This is required because enough information must be maintained at all times to facilitate conflict detection with respect to other transactions that may be using different versions of the validation procedure at the same time. The read barriers use a conditional to decide which version of the validation procedure is currently used and to choose the appropriate sequence of code to execute. The expected benefit is the reduction of overheads related to both the time required to execute the read barriers and the validation procedure itself (no need to either maintain or process a read set) at a cost of potentially increasing both the number of aborts and the cost of the write barrier. A detailed description of the bitmap-based algorithm is presented below.

4.1   Overview

We use two transaction-local bitmaps (*local read map* and *local write map*) to record reads and writes performed by the transaction to all shared data items. We currently use maps of the 64-bit size to achieve high efficiency of operations used to manipulate bitmaps. Every slot (bit) in the bitmap represents access to a single shared data item. A slot in the map corresponding to the data item being accessed is computed using the address of the data item. In case the address of a data item accessed inside of a transaction using the bitmap-based algorithm changes while this transaction is still active (*e.g.* as a result of a copying garbage collector moving objects around), all currently active transactions using the same scheme must be aborted.

A *global write map* is maintained to record updates performed by all transactions executing concurrently. Information about all updates performed by a successfully committed transaction (stored in its local write map) is merged with the information

```
void BEGIN(TxnDescriptor *txnDesc, int64 globalMap) {
 IF (txnDesc->useBitmaps) {
  WHILE(TRUE) {
   int tCount = globalMap & COUNT_MASK;

   IF (tCount == 0) {
    // reset map
    IF (UPDATE_MAP_CAS(0, tCount+1)) BREAK;
   }
   ELSE IF (tCount < COUNT_MAX && (globalMap & MAP_MASK) == 0) {
    // increment count
    IF (UPDATE_MAP_CAS(globalMap, tCount+1)) BREAK;
   }
   ELSE {
    // disable bitmap-based validation
    txnDesc->useBitmaps = false;
    ORIGINAL_BEGIN(txnDesc);
    BREAK;
   }
  }
 }
 ELSE ORIGINAL_BEGIN(txnDesc);
}
```

Fig. 3. Transaction begin

currently represented in the global write map (initially empty). Additionally, a transactions counter is maintained to represent the number of concurrently executing transactions. Merging of local and global maps needs to happen only if the counter is greater than one. Transactional reads are validated by computing an intersection of the local read map that belongs to the committing transaction and the global write map. If the intersection is empty, validation is successful, otherwise it fails and the transaction is aborted. As mentioned previously, in some situations all transactions using the bitmap-based scheme may have to be aborted. This can be easily handled by setting all the bits in the global map to one.

Bitmaps should be used to detect conflicts only if the number of concurrently executing transactions is relatively low (otherwise there is a high chance of quickly filling up the global write map which would lead to conflicts being detected often). This allows us to set the maximum value of the transactions counter to a low value (currently 32), and to implement it using the (5) lowest bits of the global write map. Updates to the counter and the global write map can then be performed atomically using a single 64-bit CAS (atomic compare-and-swap) operation.

4.2 Transaction Begin

If at the start of a transaction the transactions counter is equal to zero then the transaction clears the global write map, increments the counter and proceeds. If the transactions counter is greater than zero (another transaction is already executing) and either the

```
void COMMIT(TxnDescriptor *txnDesc, int64 globalMap) {
 IF (txnDesc->useBitmaps) {
  int tCount = globalMap & COUNT_MASK;
  int64 mapIntersect = txnDesc->readMap & globalMap;

  // update map both on commit and on abort
  UPDATE_MAP_CAS(globalMap | txnDesc->writeMap, tCount  1);
  IF (mapIntersect != 0) {
   // use original algorithm on re-execution
   txnDesc->useBitmaps = false;
   ABORT();
  }
 }
 ELSE {
  // use bitmap-based validation next time
  txnDesc->useBitmaps = true;
  ORIGINAL_COMMIT(txnDesc);
 }
}
```

Fig. 4. Transaction commit

global write map is non-empty or the maximum value of the counter has been reached, then the starting transaction uses the original validation procedure (a separate flag is used to maintain this information – in such case only the original validation procedure is attempted at commit time). In all other cases, no action is required and the transaction is free to proceed.

Falling back to the precise validation procedure in case of non-empty global write map is required to avoid a problem of never clearing the map in case the number of concurrently executing transactions is high (in particular, if a new transaction is often started before all the previously executed ones are committed). In other words, we use bitmaps to detect conflicts only for transactions that are started before the first update of the global write map.

The pseudo-code representing the transaction begin operation is presented in Figure 3. The useBitmaps flag is used to determine if bitmaps should be used at all for validation purposes. Procedure UPDATE_MAP_CAS() is an abbreviation for an operation using a single CAS to update both the contents of the map (passed as the first parameter) and the counter (passed as the second parameter) – it returns TRUE upon successful update and FALSE upon failure. The COUNT_MASK and MAP_MASK constants are used to mask the appropriate bits of the word representing the global map to extract the transactions counter and the contents of the map, respectively. The COUNT_MAX constant represents the maximum counter value.

4.3   Transaction Commit

In case bitmaps are used to detect conflicts (as indicated by the appropriate flag), the committing transaction computes the intersection of its local read map and the global write map to validate correctness of its read operations.

```
int64 TAG_MAP(int64 localMap, int *addr) {
 int slot = (addr >> BITS_IGNORED) % MAP_SIZE;
 int64 slotMask = FIRST_MAP_SLOT << slot;
 RETURN localMap | slotMask;
}

int READ_BARRIER(TxnDescriptor *txnDesc,int *addr) {
 IF (txnDesc->useBitmaps)
  txnDesc->readMap = TAG_MAP(readMap, addr);
 ELSE ORIGINAL_READ_BARRIER(txnDesc, addr);
 RETURN *addr;
}

void WRITE_BARRIER(TxnDescriptor *txnDesc,
                   int *addr, int newValue) {
 txnDesc->writeMap = TAG_MAP(writeMap, addr);
 ORIGINAL_WRITE_BARRIER(txnDesc, addr);
 *addr = newValue;
}
```

Fig. 5. Read and write barriers

If the intersection is empty then the validation succeeds, otherwise the committing transaction is aborted and re-executed. In both cases, the committing transaction merges contents of its local write map with the contents of the global write map and decrements the transactions counter. The merging of write maps is required in both cases since the updates performed by the committing transaction have already been reflected in the main memory and other transactions need to be notified about the possibility of a conflict. The pseudo-code representing the transaction commit operation is presented in Figure 4. Note that upon failure of the procedure using bitmaps the flag to disable optimized procedure is set and the transaction is aborted to be re-executed using the original algorithm. In case the optimized procedure has been disabled, it is re-enabled for a given transaction descriptor upon execution of the original commit procedure.

4.4   Barriers

The read and write barriers, presented in Figure 5, have been modified to implement tagging of the local maps. The TAG_MAP() procedure is shared between all the barriers. We found out experimentally that in order to achieve the best distribution of values in the map we should ignore a certain number of bits in the address (represented by the BITS_IGNORED constant) when computing the map slot number. The FIRST_MAP_SLOT constant represents the first available slot number (determined by how many low order bits are used to store the transactions count). Note that in the case of the read barrier, we execute either the code fragment that supports the original procedure or the code fragment that supports the algorithm using bitmaps. In the case of the write barrier the code supporting both styles of validation must be executed.

% reads	hash-table		b-tree	
	1 CPU	16 CPUs	1 CPU	16 CPUs
10	0.9991	0.9907	1.0229	0.9545
30	0.9920	0.9745	1.0238	0.9048
50	1.0006	0.9577	1.0178	1.2029
70	0.9975	0.9758	1.0102	0.9501
90	0.9943	0.9667	0.9856	0.9624

Fig. 6. Execution times

5   Performance Evaluation

In this section we will present results of the performance evaluation of both the new optimized linear validation algorithm and the bitmap-based validation algorithm. Both solutions are implemented in the context of McRT-STM and evaluated on the Intel Xeon^{TM} 2.2 GHz machine with 16 CPUs and 16 GB of RAM running Red Hat Enterprise Linux Release 3 (with 2.4.21-28.ELsmp kernel). Both new algorithms are being compared with the original validation algorithm present in McRT-STM.

The evaluation is based on measuring execution times and other execution metrics (such as aborts) of two transactions-enabled benchmarks implementing accesses to common data structures: hash-table and b-tree. The first benchmark uses an implementation of a hash-table where hashing conflicts between a fixed number of buckets are resolved through chaining, and the second benchmark uses a standard implementation of a b-tree. In both cases, all data structure operations are enclosed in atomic blocks and the benchmarks execute a varying mixture of read and update operations on a given data structure, where an update is either an addition of an element to a given data structure or a removal of an element from a given data structure (in all configurations the number of additions was equal to the number of removals). Additionally, because transactions in the hash-table benchmark are longer than those in the b-tree benchmark, and are therefore more prone to conflicts, they perform periodic validations of their read sets to "catch" situations when their read sets become invalid earlier than at transaction commit. The total number of operations performed by all threads was 2^{17}, unless noted otherwise.

5.1   Optimized Linear Validation

The first set of numbers verifies that in the common case the performance of the new linear validation algorithm does not negatively affect the overall performance of the system. We first executed both benchmarks using one thread running on a single CPU to model workloads that do not exhibit any contention. We also executed both benchmarks using 16 threads running on 16 CPUs, even though we did not expect the contention to have any effect on the performance of the algorithm. In both uncontended and contended cases we varied the percentage of reads (vs. the percentage of updates) from 10% of reads to 90% of reads. We summarize the results obtained for both the hash-table benchmark and the b-tree benchmarks in Table 6. The table reports execution times for the new linear algorithm normalized with respect to the execution times of the original algorithm.

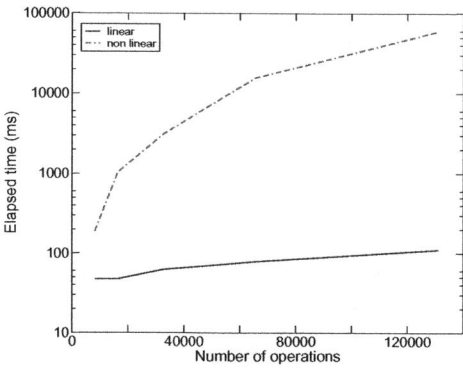

Fig. 7. Execution times – linear algorithm vs. non-linear algorithm

The analysis of the numbers presented in Table 6 confirms that in the common case the performance of both algorithms is comparable. In the case of single-threaded execution the difference in performance rarely exceeds 1%. The larger differences observed during multi-threaded runs are due to jitter in the results we obtained, which we were unable to eliminate fully despite averaging over 25 runs.

Despite both algorithms performing similarly in the common case, the performance of the original validation algorithm is expected to degrade quite dramatically, dropping exponentially as the number of write-after-read occurrences grows. At the same time, the execution time of the new validation algorithm is expected to only grow linearly in the number of operations. In order to confirm this hypothesis, we measured execution times of a microbenchmark that pulls every entry from a given pre-initialized data structure (hash-table) and then both reads and writes a value stored in that entry. We vary the number of entries (and thus operations performed) from 2^{13} to 2^{17} and plot the execution times (total execution time of the micro-benchmark in microseconds using a logarithmic scale) in Figure 7. As we can observe, our hypothesis indeed holds – performance of the new algorithm remains linear while the performance of the original algorithm rapidly degrades as the number of write-after-read operations increases.

5.2   Bitmap-Based Validation

The first set of numbers represents an "ideal" case for the bitmap-based validation procedure, used to gauge a potential benefit of using the optimized procedure – both benchmarks were executed within a single thread on a single physical CPU. As a result no aborts could ever occur. Additionally we measured impact of different implementation components on the overall performance. Figure 8 describes execution times for both benchmarks, differentiating between separate components (represented by different bars). All execution times are normalized with respect to the "baseline" case, that is execution times for a version of the system that uses the original validation procedure only.

The first bar is an exception – it represents execution time for the configuration using the original validation procedure where the *verification step* (part of the validation

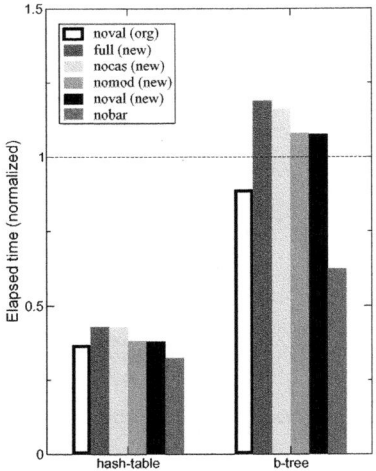

Fig. 8. Overhead split – 1 thread, 1 CPU

procedure performed either at commit time or during periodic validation) has been omitted. In other words, it constitutes our ideal target in terms of expected performance – our major goal is to reduce overheads related to performing the verification step. The verification step represents one of two major components contributing to the overheads related to supporting any STM algorithm using optimistic readers – the other one is related to work performed during data accesses (in the barriers). The last bar represents execution time where in addition to omitting the verification step, both read and write barriers have also been removed (and all the data access operations turned into "regular" loads and stores). The difference between these two bars represents the cost of the barriers. Please note, that the execution time described by the last bar represents both algorithms (original and bitmap-based) – by omitting the verification step as well as the barriers these versions of the system have been effectively unified.

The second bar represents a fully functional system supporting the bitmap-based validation procedure (the remaining bars, even though correctly executing their respective workloads in the single-threaded case could behave incorrectly in the presence of multiple concurrent threads). The third bar represents a version of the algorithm where the CAS operations used to update the global map and the transactions counter have been replaced by regular writes. The fourth bar represents a version of the algorithm where the modulo division operation used to compute the appropriate slot in the map has been replaced (in addition to removing CAS operations) with a bit-wise AND operation extracting the n lowest bits of the address. Using the n lowest bits for slot computation is unlikely to provide a good distribution of slots in the map – in the case of real-life workloads it might be difficult to accept. The fifth bar represents a version of the algorithm where the configuration represented by the previous (fourth) bar has been further modified to completely omit the verification step of the bitmap-based procedure (similarly to the verification step for the original procedure being removed in case of the first bar).

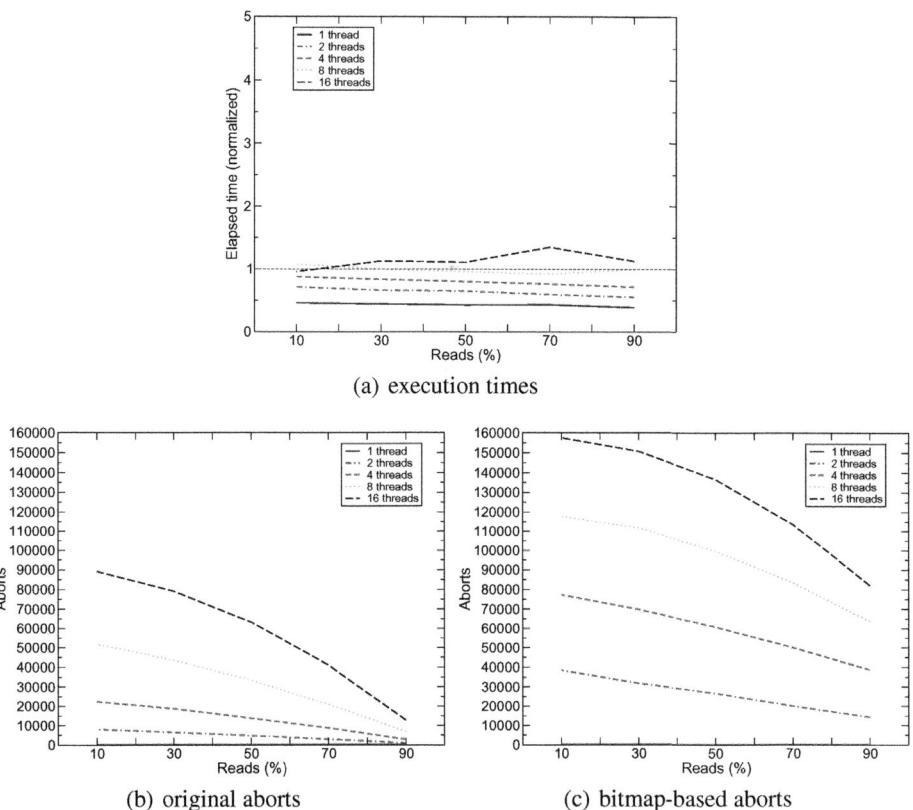

(a) execution times

(b) original aborts   (c) bitmap-based aborts

Fig. 9. Hash-table benchmark

The first conclusion that can be drawn from the analysis of Figure 8 is that we can expect high performance gains from optimizing the verification step only in the case of the hash-table benchmark, as indicated by the size of the first bar. It is a direct result of both a large number of locations read by every transaction executed in this benchmark (orders of magnitude more than for the b-tree benchmark) and periodic validations performed by transactions for the locations they have read.

The first bar, as mentioned before, represents optimization potential. The difference between the height of the first bar and the height of the fifth bar represents the difference in the barrier cost between the original scheme and the optimized scheme and, as we can see, the cost of the barriers in the bitmap-based validation procedure is larger than for the original.

As a result, if the optimization potential is small, and the difference in the barrier cost between the original (the first bar) and the optimized (the fifth bar) [4] versions of the validation procedure is high (as is the case of the b-tree benchmark), no performance improvement is observed.

---

[4] Despite applying (unsafe) simplifications to the barrier code, as described previously, and represented by the third bar and the fourth bar.

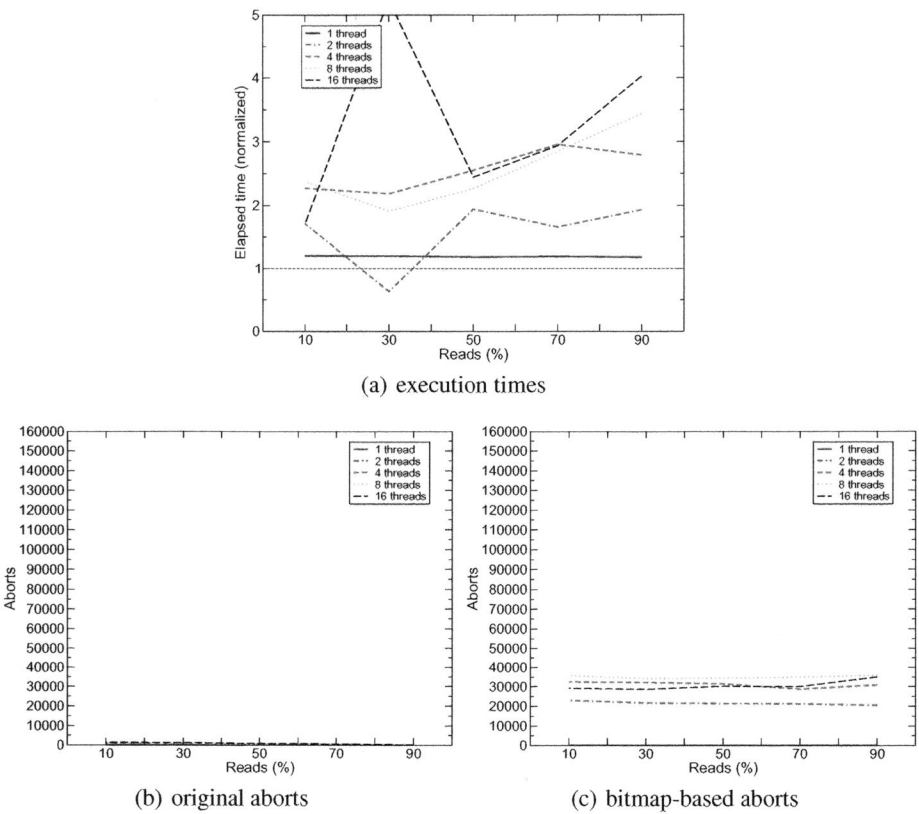

(a) execution times

(b) original aborts   (c) bitmap-based aborts

Fig. 10. B-tree benchmark

The second set of numbers attempts to answer the question of how both the bitmap-based validation procedure behaves under contention. Figure 9(a) and Figure 10(a) plot execution times for the hash-table benchmark and the b-tree benchmark, respectively. The graphs reflect execution times for the bitmap-based scheme normalized with respect to execution times using the original validation procedure under varying levels of contention: 1–16 threads running on 1–16 CPUs respectively, and percentage of reads (vs. the percentage of updates) varying from 10% of reads to 90% of reads. Let us first analyze performance of the hash-table benchmark (Figure 9(a)). The bitmap-based procedure outperforms the original algorithm for configurations running up to 8 threads on 8 CPUs, but starts performing worse than the original algorithm at the highest level of contention (when 16 threads on 16 CPUs are being run). As we can observe, the increase in the number of aborts for the configurations using the bitmap-based validation procedure (plotted in Figure 9(c) seems to have relatively small impact on the overall performance. The performance of the bitmap-based algorithm is better than that of the original one for all but the most contended configuration despite the number of aborts being quite dramatically increased with respect to the numbers for the original validation procedure (plotted in Figure 9(b)). We believe that the explanation for this behavior lies in periodic validations of all the data read by transactions executed in this benchmark. The cost of periodic validation is very low when using the bitmap-based version of the procedure (a transaction intersects the maps and either proceeds or aborts) whereas in the case of the original algorithm traversal of the entire read set is required. As a result, the cost of a (failed) transactional execution is potentially much higher in the case of the original algorithm.

The analysis of the execution times for the b-tree benchmark is much simpler. The bitmap-based procedure is unable to outperform the original algorithm (with the exception of execution anomalies – explanation is presented below) as indicated on Figure 10(a). Also, the increase in the number of aborts has the expected impact on performance. Aborts for both types of algorithms are plotted on Figure 10(b) (original validation procedure) and Figure 10(c) (bitmap-based validation procedure) with the number of aborts for the original algorithm being extremely small.

When running the benchmarks, similarly to the experiments we performed for the new optimized linear algorithm, we observed a degree of variability between different runs of the same benchmark (observed over 25 runs of every configuration) and a significant amount of jitter. This effect is much more visible in the case of the b-tree benchmark whose running time is short – we believe that benchmark runs where the bitmap-based scheme performed better than the original one are a direct result of this behavior. Therefore, we repeated our measurement for the b-tree benchmark with the number of iterations increased by the factor of four to increase the execution times. Unfortunately the variability has not been eliminated but the overall conclusion remains the same – no performance benefit can be expected from running any of the b-tree benchmark configurations when using the bitmap-based validation procedure.

One of the conclusions that can be drawn from the analysis of these results is that adding any additional overheads to the read and write barriers should be avoided when implementing similar solutions. The increased barrier cost dwarfed any potential performance improvement of the verification step for the b-tree benchmark. A more general conclusion is that while the bitmap-based validation procedure has potential to improve the performance over the original algorithm, it is not suitable for a general purpose system in its current form as it performs well only under selected workloads (large number of reads, potentially in conjunction with frequent periodic validations) and may degrade performance when used as the primary validation procedure. At the same time, the approach presented could prove itself useful in case the validation procedure must be invoked much more frequently (*e.g.* at every data access operation, in the extreme case). In such cases, the additional overheads described above could appear to be more tolerable.

6   Related Work

A linear validation algorithm has been proposed by Harris *et al.* [7] and implemented in the context of their STM system. However, in their solution transaction records associated with locked data items always (throughout the entire lifetime of the lock owner) point to the appropriate entry in the lock owner's write set. As a result, and unlike in our own linear algorithm, the ownership tests performed during transactional memory access operations require an additional level of indirection.

Bitmaps have been previously used to support the validation algorithm by Welc *et al.* [16]. In their system, however, the validation procedure using bitmaps is the primary one. As a result, in order to achieve a reasonable precision of the validation procedure, they must use large bitmaps (16,000 slots) which may have negative impact on both the memory footprint as well as on the time it takes to execute the validation procedure. Additionally, imprecision resulting from the (exclusive) use of bitmaps for validation may result in repeated transaction aborts, whereas in our system a transaction can be aborted only once as a result of using information about reads in a compressed form (subsequent re-executions use the original validation algorithm).

7   Conclusions

In this paper we presented two novel STM validation algorithms and evaluated their performance in a context of an efficient STM implementation. While the linear validation algorithm is a clear improvement over the original algorithm used in McRT-STM, the bitmap-based algorithm, though able to improve performance in case of some benchmarks, is in its current form unfit for deployment as the primary STM validation algorithm.

References

1. Adl-Tabatabai, A.-R., Lewis, B.T., Menon, V., Murphy, B.R., Saha, B., Shpeisman, T.: Compiler and runtime support for efficient software transactional memory. In: PLDI 2006 (2006)
2. Ananian, C.S., Asanovic, K., Kuszmaul, B.C., Leiserson, C.E., Lie, S.: Unbounded transactional memory. In: HPCA 2005 (2005)
3. Damron, P., Fedorova, A., Lev, Y., Luchangco, V., Moir, M., Nussbaum, D.: Hybrid transactional memory. In: ASPLOS 2006 (2006)
4. Gray, J., Reuter, A.: Transaction Processing: Concepts and Techniques. In: Data Management Systems. Morgan Kaufmann, San Francisco (1993)
5. Harris, T., Fraser, K.: Language support for lightweight transactions. In: OOPSLA 2003 (2003)
6. Harris, T., Marlow, S., Peyton-Jones, S., Herlihy, M.: Composable memory transactions. In: PPoPP 2005 (2005)
7. Harris, T., Plesko, M., Shinnar, A., Tarditi, D.: Optimizing memory transactions. In: PLDI 2006 (2006)
8. Herlihy, M., Luchangco, V., Moir, M., Scherer III, W.N.: Software transactional memory for dynamic-sized data structures. In: PODC 2003 (2003)
9. Herlihy, M., Moss, J.E.B.: Transactional memory: Architectural support for lock-free data structures. In: ISCA 1993 (1993)
10. Martínez, J.F., Torrellas, J.: Speculative synchronization: Applying thread-level speculation to explicitly parallel applications. In: ASPLOS 2003 (2003)
11. Rajwar, R., Goodman, J.R.: Transactional lock-free execution of lock-based programs. In: ASPLOS 2002 (2002)
12. Rajwar, R., Herlihy, M., Lai, K.: Virtualizing transactional memory. In: ISCA 2005 (2005)

13. Saha, B., Adl-Tabatabai, A.-R., Hudson, R.L., Minh, C.C., Hertzberg, B.: A high performance software transactional memory system for a multi-core runtime. In: PPoPP 2006 (2006)
14. Saha, B., Adl-Tabatabai, A.-R., Jacobson, Q.: Architectural support for software transactional memory. In: MICRO 2006 (2006)
15. Shavit, N., Touitou, D.: Software transactional memory. In: PODC 1995 (1995)
16. Welc, A., Hosking, A.L., Jagannathan, S.: Transparently reconciling transactions with locking for Java synchronization. In: Bateni, M. (ed.) ECOOP 2007. LNCS, vol. 4609. Springer, Heidelberg (2007)

Tiled Multi-Core Stream Architecture

Nan Wu, Qianming Yang, Mei Wen, Yi He, Ju Ren,
Maolin Guan, and Chunyuan Zhang

Computer School, National University of Defense Technology
Chang Sha, Hu Nan, P.R. of China, 410073
nanwu@nudt.edu.cn

Abstract. Conventional stream architectures focus on exploiting ILP and DLP in the applications, although stream model also exposes abundant TLP at kernel granularity. On the other side, with the development of model VLSI technology, increasing application demands and scalability challenges conventional stream architectures. In this paper, we present a novel Tiled Multi-Core Stream Architecture called TiSA. TiSA introduces the tile that consists of multiple stream cores as a new category of architectural resources, and designed an on-chip network to support stream transfer among tiles. In TiSA, multiple levels parallelisms are exploited on different granularity of processing elements. Besides hardware modules, this paper also discusses some other key issues of TiSA architecture, including programming model, various execution patterns and resource allocations. We then evaluate the hardware scalability of TiSA by scaling to 10s~1000s ALUs and estimating its area and delay cost. We also evaluate the software scalability of TiSA by simulating 6 stream applications and comparing sustained performance with other stream processors and general purpose processors, and different configuration of TiSA. A 256-ALU TiSA with 4 tile and 4 stream cores per tile is shown to be feasible with 45 nanometer technology, sustaining 100~350 GFLOP/s on most stream benchmarks and providing ~10x of speedup over a 16-ALU TiSA with a 5% degradation in area per ALU. The result shows that TiSA is a VLSI- and performance-efficient architecture for the billions-transistors era.

1   Introduction

With VLSI technology scaling, increasing numbers of transistors can fit onto one chip. In 2010, more than 1 billion transistors may be integrated on chip. In a 45-nanometer technology, a 32-bit ALU with multiplier requires only 0.044mm^2 of chip area. In this technology, over two thousand of these multipliers could fit on a single 1 cm^2 chip and could be easily pipelined to operate at over 1 GHz. At this speed, these multipliers could provide 2 Teraops per second of arithmetic bandwidth [1]. The challenge is translating these physical potential to efficient computation resource. In general-purpose processor, most of chip area is used to exploit Instruction Level Parallelism (ILP) and implement cache memory hierarchy to reduce average memory access latency.

For some important application domains, such as multi-media, graphic, cryptography and scientific modeling, special architecture with stream model may break through the

P. Stenström (Ed.): Transactions on HiPEAC IV, LNCS 6760, pp. 274–293, 2011.
© Springer-Verlag Berlin Heidelberg 2011

challenge. Stream model is a novel stream programming model originated from vector parallel model. In such stream programming model, an application is usually composed of a collection of data streams passing through a series of computation kernels. Each stream is a sequence of homogeneous data records. Each kernel is a loop body that is applied to each record of the input stream [2]. In stream program level, the producer-consumer relation between kernel and stream exposes explicitly TLP between kernels, and between loading streams and running kernels, while in kernel program level, data streams and intensive computation intra-kernel expose abundant DLP and ILP. High predictability and abundant parallelism of stream model provide significant advantages. In stream architecture, more software and compiler management technology can be used to avoid dynamic instruction parallelism extraction such as super scalar and instruction speculation technology. Moreover, latency tolerance and processing a batch of data at one time in stream architecture make long latency of memory reference and communication can be tolerated, and the achieved throughput is addressed. Thus, application-specific architectures which are based on or compatible with stream model have achieved cost--efficient high performance, such as Imagine[6], Merrimac[12], FT64[13], CELL[9].

Along with the increasing demand for performance of processor and the broadening application domain of stream model, stream application and algorithm is more complexity. For SBR and UAV, the demand for performance has already achieved 1TFLOPS in 2004 [3]. To achieve the performance, there are at least 1000 1GHz ALUs requested on a chip. These require stream architecture has good scalability of performance and resource. Therefore, for epoch of more than one billion transistors in one chip, architecture innovation is necessary to keep performance and cost efficiency of stream architecture.

This paper presents Tiled Multi-core Stream Architecture (TiSA). We describe TiSA's hardware architecture, programming model and resource allocation. Then we analysis hardware overhead based on scaling cost model, and evaluate TiSA's performance for several applications. The result shows that TiSA is a VLSI- and performance-efficient architecture for the billions-transistors era.

2   Motivation

The scaling of conventional stream processor has reached the limit. Typical stream architecture, Imagine supporting ILP and DLP is consists of 8 clusters (4 ALU/cluster) while both the number of clusters and ALUs intra-cluster can be increased (two scaling dimensions: inter-cluster and intra-cluster). However prior research has shown that stream architecture like Imagine with 16 clusters (4 ALU/cluster) would achieve the best performance efficiency. The scaling of more than 64 ALUs will cause the decrease of the performance efficiency, and the downside will be more obvious as the number of ALUs increases [1].

On the other hand, the application domains of conventional stream processor is very limited in terms of the follows: 1. Orignal two level scaling methods may results in increasing demand for DLP of application, but stream application may not provide more DLP or longer stream length, that results in inefficient computation or short stream effect[2]; 2. Intensive computation is necessary to make full use of stream architecture. For stream processor with 48 ALUs, the threshold is about 33 Ops/w

(33 arithmetic operations/ memory reference), which is growing annually for future stream processors as off-chip bandwidth grows more slowly than arithmetic bandwidth. That means the requirement for application's computation intensity is increasing. 3. As stream application domains are broader, only supporting ILP and DLP is not enough for stream architecture. 4. The single SIMD execution mode makes some restrictions because there are irregular streams in stream application that may not be suitable for SIMD mode [4].

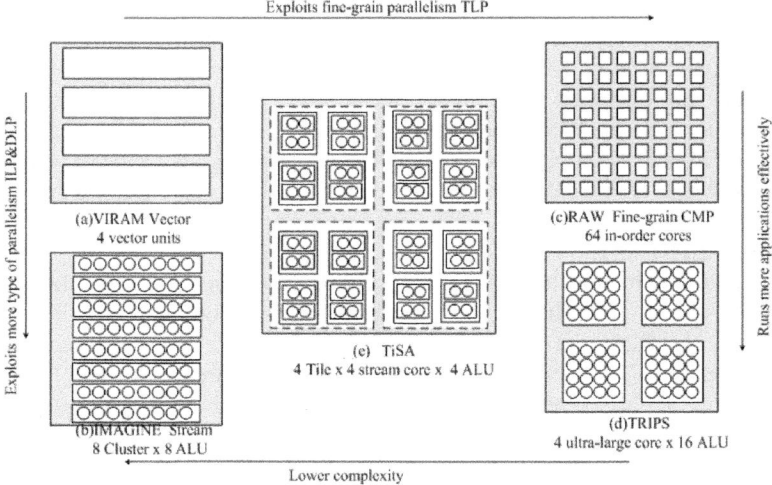

Fig. 1. Granularity of parallel processing elements on a chip

In fact, stream applications usually exhibit mix features with ILP, DLP, TLP in terms of several types of control and memory reference behaviors. Supporting multiple parallel execution modes simultaneously is more suitable for these. There are several approaches. Figure 1 shows several typical stream architectures. The important difference in them is the parallel processing granularity. The left two processors in figure 1, VIRAM [5] and Imagine [6], work in SIMD mode whereas their DLP granularity are word and record respectively. Both of them provide high performance for stream applications while not suitable for irregular stream and exploiting TLP. The right two processors in figure 1, RAW [7] and TRIPS [8], support multiple parallel execution modes simultaneously and are general for several types of workloads including stream application. RAW uses a set of uniform hardware to support all parallel execution modes, while TRIPS uses different sets of hardware to support different parallel execution modes respectively. Both of them are tile architecture, also are CMP, which is suitable for TLP rather than kernel level parallelism, DLP and TLP inside kernel. From figure 1 we can see that from left to right parallel processing elements is decomposed into tiles gradually to exploit fine-grain parallelism TLP, while from right to left parallelism execution modes supported by processors become less and the complexity of processor becomes lower. There are also be seen that from top to bottom, the granularity of process unit become larger which enable run more applications efficiently.

Thus, novel stream architecture targets on running more stream applications by increasing the granularity of process unit and supporting several parallelism execution modes. Tiled Multi-Core Stream Architecture (TiSA) is shown in middle of figure 1, which supports several types of parallelism execution modes including TLP exploited by tiles, kernel level parallelism exploited by stream cores, ILP and DLP exploited by ALUs intra-cores. Compared to conventional stream architecture, TiSA provides following advantages: 1. The number of tiles can be scaled without more DLP of stream application demanded. It can improve the stream processor's scalability as described in section 6. 2. Several parallel execution patterns supported enable more applications with different parallelism requirements run on TiSA. 3. It can reduce the threshold of intensive computation. Since each core may perform a kernel, several cores share the computation executed in a core before. 4. Fault tolerance can be implemented through the same task is executed in different tiles. 5. It inherits the advantages of processor with multiple cores. In multi-core, the communication latency on die is about 20 cycles and the on-die interconnect bandwidth between cores will be >100 Tera bytes/second [10].

3   The TiSA Architecture

The TiSA architecture uses large, coarse-grained tile to achieve high performance for stream applications with high computing intensity, and augments them with multiple execution pattern features that enable the tile to be subdivided for explicitly concurrent applications at different granularities. Contrary to conventional large-core designs with centralized components that are difficult to scale, the TiSA architecture is heavily partitioned to avoid large centralized structures and long wire runs. These partitioned computation and memory elements are connected by 2D on-chip networks with multiple virtual point-to-point communication channels that are exposed to software schedulers referred in section 5 for optimization. Figure 2 shows a diagram of the TiSA architecture, which consists of following major critical components.

Tile is a partition of computation elements. It consists of multiple *stream cores* and a *network bridge*. As shown in Figure 2, four stream cores compose a tile. The organization is tightly coupled between stream cores in a tile while loosely coupled between tiles.

Stream Core adopting simplified classical stream processor architecture [2] is the basic computation module of TiSA. It is optimized for executing kernels of stream applications. Each stream core has its own instruction controllers—*Stream Controller* and *Micro-controller*, and data storage—*Stream Register File* (SRF), and multiple arithmetic *clusters*. Clusters are controlled by the micro-controller in SIMD+VLIW pattern. A cluster is composed of a set of full-pipelined ALUs performing one multiply-add operation per cycle, and some non-ALU function units including 1 iterative unit to support operations like divide and square-root, 1 juke-box unit to support conditional streams [1], 1 COMM unit connected to an inter-cluster switch for data communication between clusters, and a group of local register files. Taking a 4 clusters x 4 ALUs configured stream core for example, the peak arithmetic performance of 32 floating-point operations per cycle can be achieved in a single core. In order to exploit DLP and ILP efficiently, the components of the stream core

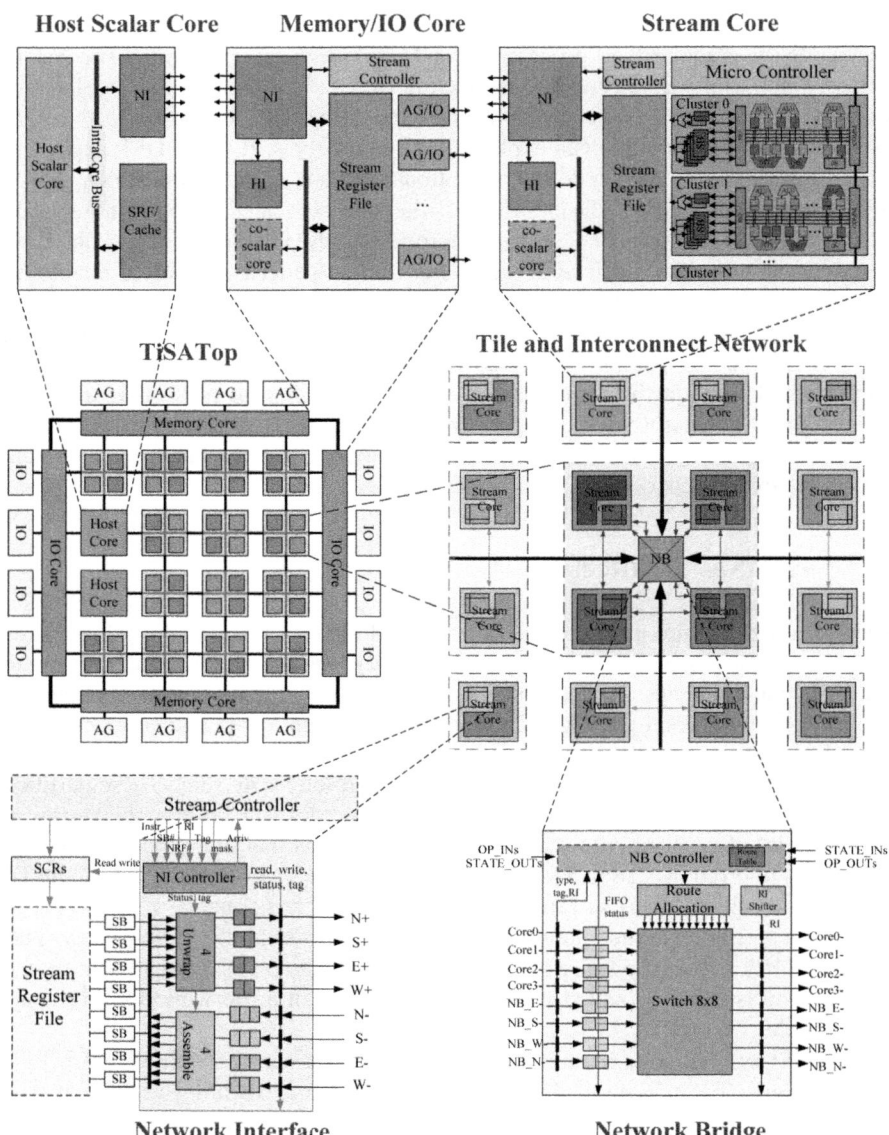

Fig. 2. TiSA architecture overview

mentioned before are scaleable leading to varied configurations and at tradeoffs design time. Furthermore, in our plan the stream core could be heterogeneous, even some special function unit or re-configurable circuit could be used. Besides this, there are some standard components in all types of cores including *Network Interface* (NI), *Host Interface* (HI) and *co-scalar core* (optional, run-time system software [11] and few scalar code can be chosen to execute in it), which are necessary to guarantee uniform interface.

Memory/IO **Core** has multiple *Address Generators* (AG) or IO interfaces as shown in Figure 2, which are able to provide multiple DRAM or IO access channels in DMA mode without processor control. It is optimized for stream access by hardware memory scheduling design [26].

Host Scalar Core is a high performance scalar processor. There could be one or more hose cores in TiSA. It is responsible for sending stream operations to stream/memory/IO core and synchronizes kernel execution and stream transfer. Meanwhile, host scalar core also processes some serial scalar codes that are not suitable for streamization. Host scalar core could be on-chip or off-chip (depend on complexity of implementation but not the architecture demands). A MIPS like embedded processors [14] are used as host scalar core and co-scalar in our simulation and prototype.

Interconnect Networks are constructed by *Network Interface* (NI), *Network Bridge* (NB) and data wires. The topology of the networks is divided into two levels: intra-tile and inter-tile, as shown in Figure 2. Figure 2 also shows the structure of NI and NB. The stream cores are directly connected to their nearest neighbors in the same tile by NI, and deliver streams to any remote cores in other tile through NB. Different commutation protocols are designed for data and op transfer in networks respectively. As figure 3 shows, data stream can only be transferred in batch pattern. A batch is consists of a long sequence stream elements between a header and a tailer. Header is used to construct a point-to-point exclusive visual channel between NI and NB before transfer, while a tailer is used to destruct the channel after transfer. This method results in the large startup overhead (~100s cycle) but high throughput (about 1 word per cycle) and payload. Thus, it can be done efficiently for large blocks of data stream that allows the overheads to be amortized over many data elements. On the contrary, stream operations and scalar data are translated in package pattern that has much lower startup overhead but fewer payloads that a stream op may be decomposed to multiple packages.

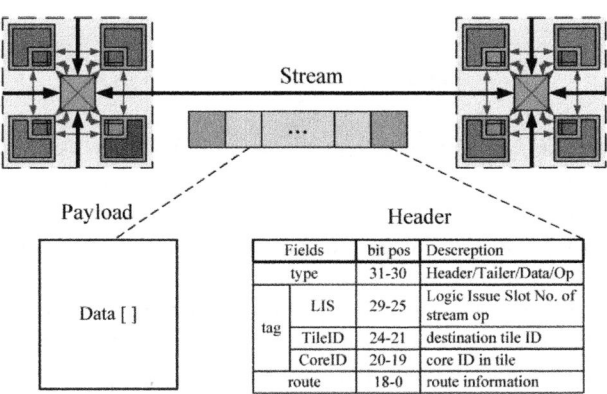

Fig. 3. Transferring stream data

Running mechanism of TiSA is a software/hardware cooperative mechanism shown in Figure 5. When main program is running on host scalar core, software dispatcher [11] sends stream operations such as load kernel, load input data stream, invoke kernel,

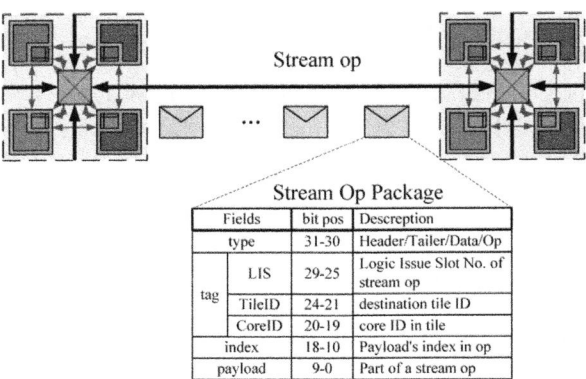

Fields		bit pos	Descreption
type		31-30	Header/Tailer/Data/Op
tag	LIS	29-25	Logic Issue Slot No. of stream op
	TileID	24-21	destination tile ID
	CoreID	20-19	core ID in tile
index		18-10	Payload's index in op
payload		9-0	Part of a stream op

Fig. 4. Transferring stream operation

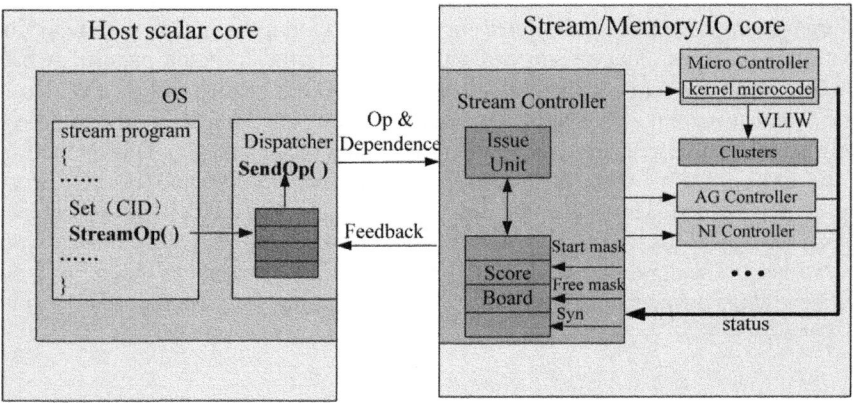

Fig. 5. Running mechanism of TiSA

store output data stream, and communicate stream to Stream Controller of each core through HI. Stream controller dynamically issues each stream operation to corresponding module to execute. This mechanism guarantees the flexibility, and decrease the load of host scalar core as central control unit by puts most dynamical control into each stream core.

Kernel's microcode is preloaded by *load kernel* operation as a stream. Then, when a stream operation to invoke a kernel is received from the stream controller, the micro-controller starts fetching and issuing VLIW instructions from the local microcode instruction storage to each functional unit in the arithmetic clusters. During kernel execution, each cluster executes an identical series of VLIW instructions on stream elements, and the multiple clusters then write output elements in parallel back to one or more output streams in the SRF.

4   Programming Model

Corresponding to the TiSA's hardware structure, this paper extends conventional stream programming model. TiSA's stream programming model exposes the inherent parallelism of stream applications including TLP, ILP, DLP, and kernel level parallelism.

A stream application in TiSA is divided into three levels: stream thread level, stream scheduling level and kernel execution level. The instance of the model is shown in Figure 6.

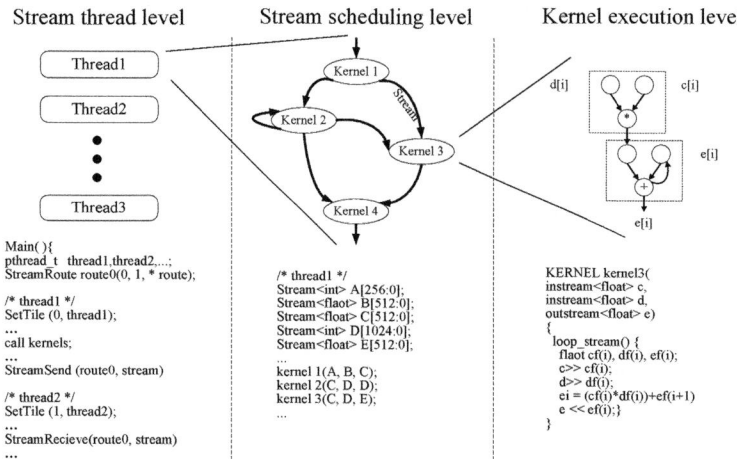

Fig. 6. TiSA's stream programming model

At the top, the stream thread level using a derivative of StreamC that has specific library functions to facilitate the multithreading programming on multi-tile system. It provides C++ like syntax for the programmer to code stream thread. Threads are explicitly declared and assigned to a tile using the *SetTile(index of tile, thread)* function. Thread communication and synchronization is also explicit and exposed to the programmer. Threads transfer data between processors using the *StreamSend (StreamRoute, stream)* and *StreamRecieve(StreamRoute, stream)*. A *StreamRoute* variable, which is declared as a global variable in the stream program, defines a route between two tiles in the networks. The code of a stream program shown in Figure 7 gives an example of two threads running on different tiles. Kernels in a thread are scheduled over stream cores by software scheduler described in section 5.

At the stream scheduling level, a stream thread is decomposed to a series of computation kernels. This done using primary StreamC language [11]. StreamC includes stream operations for transferring streams of data to and from the tile, for defining control and data flow between kernels and for invoke kernels. Note that the storage of stream and the communication operation are also encapsulated as stream operations and distributed to memory core or IO core. At last, StreamC will be translated into C++ library functions by the stream compiler [11].

The kernel level specifies computation. The details of arithmetic operation and data executing mode are defined at this level. It describes execution of single kernel in KernelC language [11]. At last, kernel will be translated into kernel's microcode by the kernel complier.

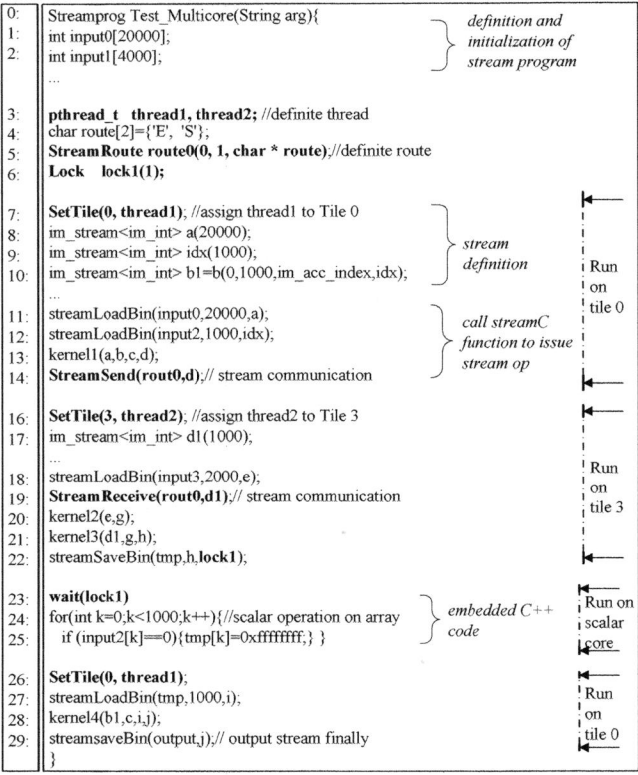

Fig. 7. An instance of stream program

The TiSA's stream programming model exposes kernel level TLP. Beside of the traditional instruction level SIMD and MIMD execution pattern, we extend three new kernel level MIMD execution patterns on TiSA: *MKMS(*Multi Kernel Multi Stream*)*: each stream core executes different kernels and processes different stream, the parallelism between kernels can be either time-multiplexed or space-multiplexed; *SKMS* (Single kernel Multi Stream): all cores execute the same kernel but processing different streams; *MKSS* (Multi Kernel Single Stream): multiple cores are combined to deal with the same stream. Different with the traditional execution patterns, the new execution patterns have the computation granularity of kernel rather than instruction, the data granularity of stream but not word. Multi parallel granularity with different execution patterns is more conformable for programmer to map the stream model to TiSA. In addition, the efficiency of control, computation and bandwidth may be improved by coarser granularity. For example, software managed SRF provide greater

```
......                                              12 SteamReceive ( IN: OUT: 'd1' )
3 streamLoadBin ( IN: OUT: 'a' )                       OUT: d1 ( 0, 1000, , stride, 1, 1 )
   OUT: a ( 0, 20000, , stride, 1, 1 )                 RI:  0 1 'route'
   tile: 0                                             tile: 3
!! WARNING: Double-buffered output stream 'a'. !!   13 kernelLoad ( IN: 'kernel2 ucode' )
4 streamLoadBin ( IN: OUT: 'b' )                       IN: kernel2 ucode ( 0, 3960, , stride, 1, 1 )
   OUT: b ( 0, 4000, , stride, 1, 1 )                  tile: 3
   tile: 0                                          14 kernel2 ( IN: 'e' OUT: 'g' )
5 streamLoadBin ( IN: OUT: 'idx' )                     IN: e ( 0, 2000, , stride, 1, 1 )
   OUT: idx ( 0, 1000, , stride, 1, 1 )               OUT: g ( 0, 2000, , stride, 1, 1 )
   tile: 0                                             tile: 3
6 kernelLoad ( IN: 'kernel1 ucode' )               15 kernelLoad ( IN: 'kernel3 ucode' )
   IN: kernel1 ucode ( 0, 4000, , stride, 1, 1 )       IN: kernel3 ucode ( 0, 2432, , stride, 1, 1 )
   tile: 0                                             tile: 3
7 kernel1 ( IN: 'a' 'b' OUT: 'c' 'd' )              ......
   IN: a ( 0, 20000, , stride, 1, 1 )              19 streamLoadBin ( IN: OUT: 'i' )
   IN: b ( 0, 4000, , stride, 1, 1 )                   OUT: i ( 0, 2000, , stride, 1, 1 )
   OUT: c ( 0, 2000, , stride, 1, 1 )                  tile: 0
   OUT: d ( 0, 1000, , stride, 1, 1 )              20 kernelLoad ( IN: 'kernel4 ucode' )
   tile: 0                                             IN: kernel4 ucode ( 0, 5584, , stride, 1, 1 )
!! WARNING: Double-buffered input stream 'a'. !!       tile: 0
8 StreamSend ( IN: 'd' )                           21 kernel4 ( IN: 'b*' 'c' 'i' OUT: 'j' IDX: 'idx' )
   IN: d ( 0, 1000, , stride, 1, 1 )                   IN: b* ( 0, 1000, , index,  index: idx ( 0,
   RI:  0 1 'route'                                        1000, , stride, 1, 1 ), 1 )
   tile: 0                                             IN: c ( 0, 2000, , stride, 1, 1 )
9 streamLoadBin ( IN: OUT: 'kernel2 ucode' )           IN: i ( 0, 2000, , stride, 1, 1 )
   OUT: kernel2 ucode ( 0, 3960, , stride, 1, 1 )      OUT: j ( 0, 2000, , stride, 1, 1 )
   tile: 3                                             IN: idx ( 0, 1000, , stride, 1, 1 )
......                                                  tile: 0
                                                    ......
```

Fig. 8. A segment of stream program's profile

placement freedom and application-aware replacement, these are performed at a coarse granularity to amortize the associated overheads [17] as show in figure 9.

5   Resource Allocation

There are two types of key resources in TiSA, one is computation resource, and another is network resource. As referred in section 4, on top level of TiSA, programmer explicitly assigns both tile and route. And fortunately, in a stream core, resources allocation including allocation of SRF, kernel microcode storage and function units in cluster have been solved by current stream processor's complier [11]. Therefore, in this section we mainly discuss the resource allocation method for stream cores in a tile. There are two major aims of allocation. The first is distributing kernels over stream cores rather balance. The second is reducing the path conflict of stream communication on the network. We just introduce a basic method of resource allocation in tile here due to limited paper length.

Because the stream model is a highly structured model, which has few branches of data dependence and most of its data flow and the kernel invoke in a thread are predictable, the stream compiler can get considerable accurate Kernel-Stream data flow directed acyclic graph (DAG) by a *profile*. Figure 8 shows the complier-produced profile of the stream program shown in figure 7. Based on the DAG, we can introduce *kernel scheduling* algorithm, which is shown in figure 9(a), into stream complier to allocate the recourse in the tile. Inside the kernel scheduling, an extracted communication scheduling algorithm [16] called *stream route scheduling* are used to produce the route on the network for streams as figure 9(b) shows.

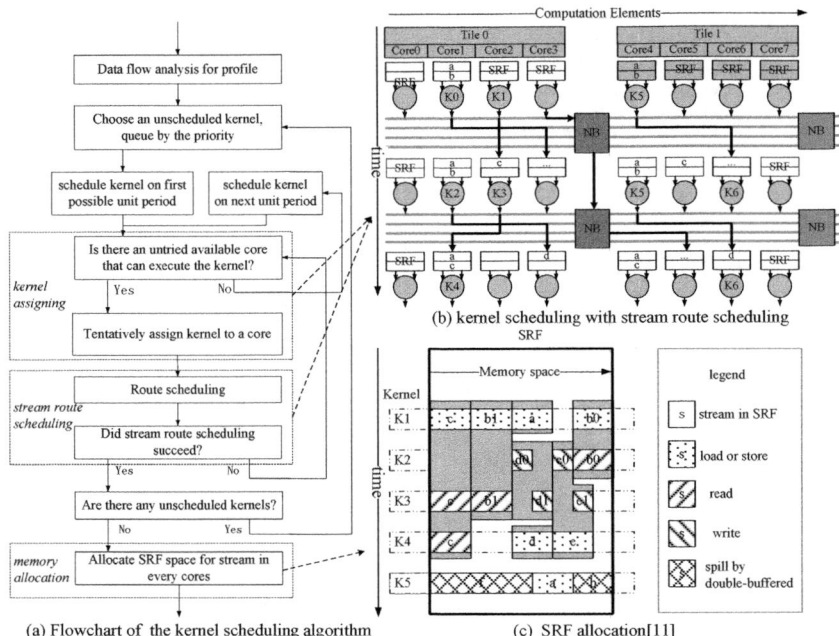

(a) Flowchart of the kernel scheduling algorithm   (c) SRF allocation[11]

Fig. 9. Compiler managed resource allocation in tile

6   Hardware Scalability: VLSI Costs

This section discusses the hardware scalability of TiSA with three scaling dimensions: intra-cluster scaling, inter-cluster scaling and tile-core scaling. The VLSI cost model follows the methodology developed in [18] (0.40 square microns in the 0.18 micron technology) adapted to the design of the TiSA [13] with the additional tile mechanism introduced in this paper. We focus on area and delay in this paper, while the energy of a stream processor is highly correlated to area as shown in [1].

According to the cost model, the area of a stream processor can be modeled by constructing a processor from a set of basic modules: the clusters (including ALUs, local register files, non-ALU FUs and intra-cluster switch), the SRF, the microcontroller, the inter-cluster switch and the networks (including NI, NB and wires). Some key parameters of these components that will be used in estimate are presented in Table 1. Other components such as the host scalar core and memory system contribute nearly a constant factor to total area that roughly equal to the area of a single stream core with 4cluster x 4ALUs [1] [25]. In addition, these components are not or lightly scaled with the number of ALUs, so they are not considered in this study.

Figure 10, 11 and 12 show the area per ALU for intra-cluster, inter-cluster and tile-core scaling of TiSA. All charts are normalized to the value for a stream core with 4 clusters x 4 ALUs. Figure 10 indicates that the area dependence on the intra-cluster dimension is much stronger than on cluster and core scaling. Configurations with an ALU of 16–32 (4~8 per cluster) are roughly equivalent in terms of hardware cost, but

Table 1. Major scaling coefficients

Parameter	Description	Value
A_{LRF}	Configuration of local register file	32 entries with 1 read port and 1 write port
A_{ALU}	Configuration of ALU	32 bits add, logic and multiplication operation
A_{SP}	Configuration of Scratchpad unit	2048 entries with 32 words each
b	Data width of the stream architecture	32
b_1	Additional VLIW instruction width per function unit	40 bit
b_2	Numbers of VLIW instruction can be stored in microcontroller	2048
Co	Numbers of co-scalar core per tile	0
H	Numbers of host scalar core	1
G	AG required per T	1
N_{SP}	Scratchpad units required per N_{ALU}	0.25
N_{COMM}	COMM units required per N_{ALU}	0.25
N_{SR}	Square-Root units required per N_{ALU}	0.25
N_{JB}	Juke-Box units required per N_{ALU}	0.25
N_{IO}	Numbers of I/O units in cluster	8
N_{CORE}	Numbers of stream cores in a micro-tile	4
I_{CLSB}	Initial number of cluster SBs	8
I_{r}	Required number of non-cluster SBs	8
m	Average numbers of LRF per function unit need	3
VC_{NI}	Number of channels per Network Interface	4
VC_{NB}	Number of channels per Network Bridge	12
N_{ALU}	Numbers of ALU in cluster	scalable
C	Numbers of clusters per stream core	scalable
T	Numbers of macro-tile	scalable

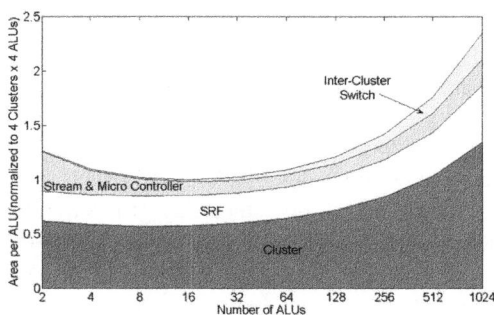

Fig. 10. Area of intra-cluster scaling

further scaling along the intra-cluster axis is not competitive because of the N^2 term of the intra-cluster switch and the increased instruction store capacity required to support wider VLIW instructions. As shown in figure 11, increasing the number of ALUs utilizing cluster dimension leads to better scaling. When scaling cluster dimension beyond 256 ALUs, the inter-cluster switch area significantly increases the area per ALU. As the figure 12 shown, tile-core scaling have much softer increment of area/ALU. With 4 clusters x 4 ALUs stream core, configurations up to 1000s ALUs are within about 5% of the optimal area.

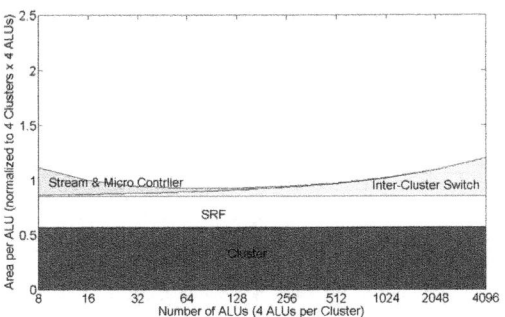

Fig. 11. Area of inter-cluster scaling

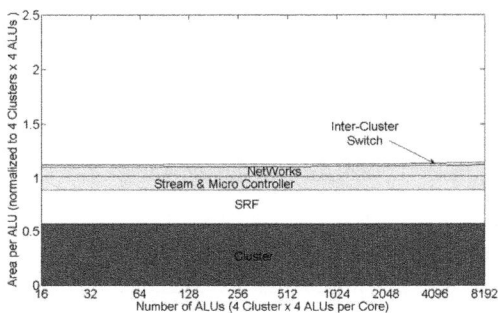

Fig. 12. Area of tile-core scaling

Comparing to the area, delay may be more critical in the modern VLSI technology on some extent. For intra-cluster scaling, the worst-case switch delays of intra-cluster and inter-cluster communications are shown in Figure 13. As ALU increases, inter-cluster wire delay grows considerably. This delay is dominated by the wire delay between the large clusters. The intra-cluster delay grows at a lower rate, and includes significant components of both logic and wire delay. Worst-case switch delays with inter-cluster scaling are shown in Figure 14. Intra-cluster delay stays constant because the size of each cluster does not change. Increased inter-cluster delay is incurred mostly from wire delay and not logic delay. Worst-case switch delays of tile-core scaling are shown in figure 15, Both Intra-cluster and inter-cluster delay stay constant because the size of each stream core does not change. Intra-core networks delay can be divided in to two parts: intra-tile delay and inter-tile delay. The former also stay constant for the fixed size of each tile, while the latter grows considerably that is incurred mostly from wire delay.

Although all scaling techniques lead to greater switch delays, the grid layout of the inter-core networks switches can be fully pipelined by NI and NB, meaning that scaling incurs additional switch traversal latency, but does not affect overall processor clock rates. This is worthwhile for the inter-core commutation at stream granularity that is not sensitive to latency but throughput. The delays of pipelined networks are shown in figure 16.

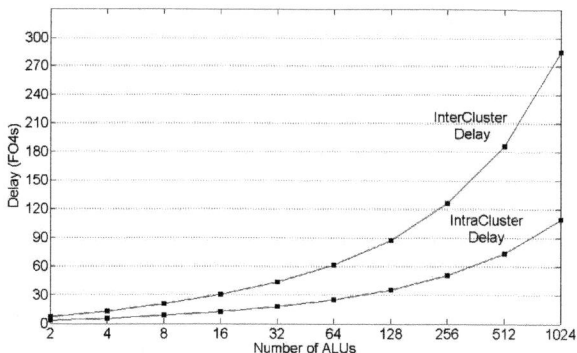

Fig. 13. Delay of intra-cluster scaling

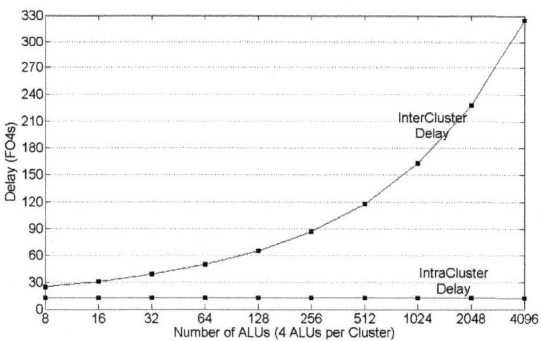

Fig. 14. Delay of inter-cluster scaling

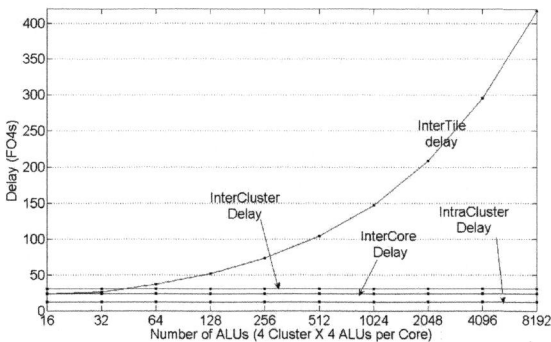

Fig. 15. Delay of tile-core scaling (non pipelined)

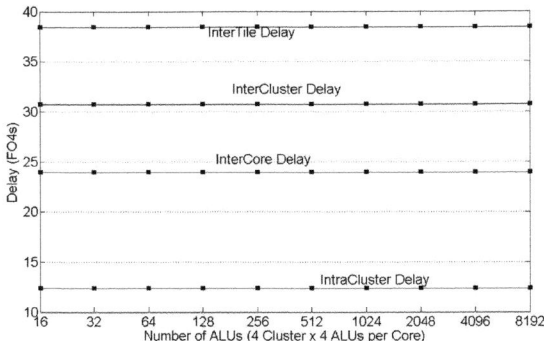

Fig. 16. Delay of tile-core scaling (pipelined by NI, NB)

In summary, the scaling estimation on area and delay show that TiSA architecture can be area- and delay- efficiently scaled to thousands of ALUs by combining multiple dimension scaling.

7   Hardware Scalability: VLSI Costs

In this section, we evaluate the TiSA architecture for a suit of stream application benchmark [19], and compare with Merrimac and FT64 stream processors and some general-purpose processors. We perform the analysis using a cycle-accurate simulator----modified ISIM[20] for stream architecture and memory system, including DRAM timing. Except for our additive module for inter-core control, communication and memory access, TiSA use the same configuration to simulate single stream core as well as FT64 and Merrimac. All benchmarks are streamized by algorithm described in [19] and full optimized for multiple stream cores, and written in the streaming style with TLP extended StreamC/KernelC described in section 4. The simulations use the parameters of TiSA as described in table 2. When a fair comparison is possible, we directly compare TiSA's sustained performance with that of other stream processors as FT64 and Merrimac. On some extent, FT64 can be seen as a single stream core of TiSA, while Merrimac is rather equal to an enhanced single stream core.

Results for benchmarks are summarized in table 1. Both CONV2D and MATMUL are ILP and DLP abundant that achieve a high arithmetic performance by SKMS pattern, at 275.1 and 358.9 GFLOPS respectively. FFT3D is characterized by lot of available DLP and ILP but places higher demands on the memory system. After each FFT stage, stream should scatted by bit reverse pattern and change the computing dimension of the data [17], stream reorganization on some stream cores and long strides DRAM access reduce the overall application performance, SKMS and MKMS pattern are hybrid in implementation of FFT3D. Table 3 compares the performance of FFT3D on mainstream commerce general-purpose processors. It shows that stream architecture have obvious advantages as opposed to general architecture for stream application, no matter on peak arithmetic performance or sustained performance. StreamFEM has regular SIMD pattern within a kernel but includes MKMS constructs in the stream level

Table 2. Performance evaluation summary of TiSA architecture

Application	Dataset	FT64 (16 ALU) 1 stream core x 4 cluster			Merrimac (64 ALU) [19] 1 stream core x 16 cluster			TiSA (256 ALU) 4 tile x 4 stream core		
		GFLOP/s	%Busy	%Peak	GFLOP/s	%Busy	%Peak	GFLOP/s	%Busy	%Peak
CONV2D	2052^2	9.8	99%	61%	78.6	99%	61%	275.1	91%	54%
MATMUL	512^2	13.4	94%	84%	117.3	98%	92%	358.9	78%	71%
FFT3D	128^3	4.9	90%	28%	37.3	89%	29%	100.7	64%	20%
StreamFEM	Euler	9.0	94%	56%	60.4	85%	47%	132.8	51%	26%
StreamMD	11475	6.1	92%	38%	46.5	86%	36%	190.6	82%	37%
StreamCDP	AE	1.1	42%	7%	7.4	30%	6%	17.8	19%	3%
StreamSPAS	1594	0.4	21%	3%	3.1	14%	2%	18.6	21%	4%

Table 3. Performance comparison of FFT3D on TiSA, FT64, Merrimac and general purpose processors. General purpose processor's results are referred from [19].

Processor	Frequency	Peak GFLOP/s	Sustained GFLOP/s	% of Peak
General Purpose Processor				
Intel Pentium 4　(Prescott)	3.6GHz	7.2	2	28%
IBM Power5	1.65GHz	6.6	1.5	23%
AMD dual-core Opteron	2.2GHz	8.8	.1.5	17%
Stream Processor				
FT64	500MHz	16	4.5	31%
Merrimac	1GHz	128	37.3	29%
TiSA	1GHz	512	100.7	20%

program to exploit irregular TLP. This irregularity causes some imbalance and control overheads, but the application has high arithmetic intensity and achieves quit high arithmetic performance at 132.8GFOP/S. StreamMD can be divided into many strips to exploit TLP, where each particle only interacts with a small number of neighboring particles. In addition, it is preferred to implement in MKMS pattern because different neighbor degree among particle cause redundant computing and access in SIMD pattern. By MKMS control and data access as well as a numerically complex kernel with many divide and square root operations, it achieves a significant performance at 190.6 GFLOPS. StreamSPAS has similar characteristic with StreamMD, but the performance potential on TiSA is hindered by the small number of operations within the inner loop of the computation. StreamCDP have very low arithmetic intensity because of the simple computations involved, so it performs worse no matter which stream architectures of three is. In a word, on the Multi-tile TiSA system, most of these benchmarks achieve much higher absolute arithmetic performance over traditional stream processors and general-purpose processors.

On the other hand, we are more concerned about performance-efficient of TiSA's scalability. Firstly, as shown in table 3, 16-core TiSA achieves 20% peak performance on FFT3D that is even higher than a dual-core general-purpose processor AMD

Opteron. This implies that for compute-intensive application, the stream model is more scaling efficient than the general model.

Secondly, table 2 illustrates that TiSA has its computing clusters busy over 50% of the execution cycles on many of the tested applications except StreamCDP and StreamSPAS, this implies that TiSA has quit high data accessing and transferring efficient to feed so many ALUs.

Finally, we coarsely simulate applications performance on cases TiSA scaling to more cores, figure 17 illustrate the four applications' normalized speedup and efficiency on different configurations with 1~64 stream cores (each core includes 4 cluster x 4 ALU). As the number of cores increases, the number of AG and the size of application datasets are reasonably enlarged (stencil matrix of Conv2D are enlarged as well). It can be analyzed from the result that for typical stream application full of pure DLP and ILP such as CONV2D and FFT3D, TiSA achieves considerable speedup with increment of ALUs. When comparing a 64-core to a single core TiSA, speedups of up to 24x and 19x are achieved. Although performance efficiency is descending on some extent, the increment of dataset and compute density partly compensate for the loss of efficiency. For stream application hybrid with DLP and TLP such as StreamMD, TiSA maintained efficiency on scaling (decrement of %peak < 5%) and achieves well speedup (up to 22x) by various parallel execution patterns at kernel level. For application with very low arithmetic intensity such as StreamCDP, the result benefit from scaling is low. Overall, simulation result show that TiSA's performance efficiency decreased on scaling, which is unavoidable for multi-core and parallel architecture, however, at least in the domain of stream application, TiSA still maintains relatively high efficient from single-core (16 ALUs) to 64-core (1024 ALUs), and therefore obtain much higher absolute performance.

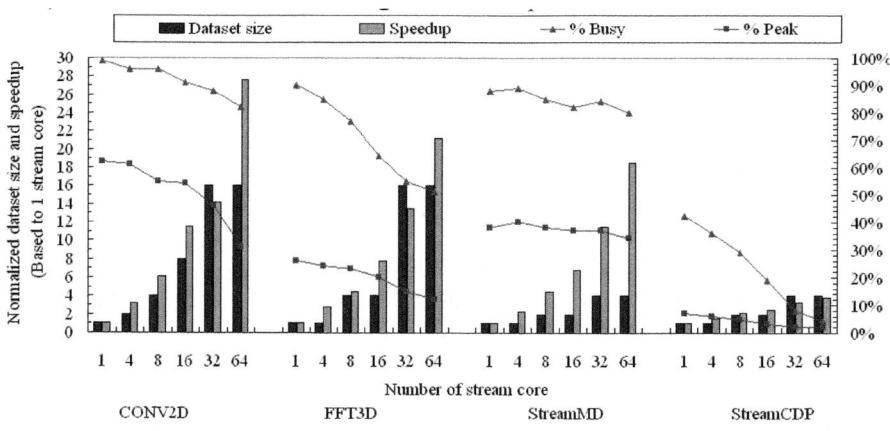

Fig. 17. Performance scalability of TiSA

Beside core dimension, stream architecture like TiSA can also be scaled along intra-cluster and inter-cluster dimension, whose performance efficiency has been detailed discussed in [1].

8   Related Work

Multi-core scaling is necessary as technology enables more ALUs to fit on a single chip. Many corporations and universities have made lots of significant researches on the multi-core data-parallel architectures, such as Cell [9] processor developed by IBM/Sony/Toshiba, RAW [7] designed by MIT, TRIPS [5] designed by Texas University, Smart Memory [21] designed by Stanford, Niagara [22] developed by SUN, and Tile64 [23] and Cellular Automata [24] developed by TILERA.

Different with them, TiSA focuses on the stream model [2]. TiSA introduces the tile as a new category of architectural resources to processing kernel level TLP, and presents an on-chip network to support stream transfer between tiles. In TiSA, multiple level parallelisms are exploited on different granularity of processing elements.

In another work, classical stream processor such as Imagine [6], Merrimac[12] and FT64[13] only support exploiting ILP and DLP in stream model. TiSA supports multithreaded stream programming and the multi-core scaling leading to more efficient scalability for thousands of ALUs.

9   Conclusions

TiSA is a multi-tile stream processor for applications including media, signal processing, and parts of scientific computing, which is facing future Microarchitecture with billions of transistors. It consists of multiple tiles that are connected by on-chip networks, and each tile includes multiple stream cores. The programming model of TiSA is different from that of traditional stream programming because of the addition of tile. We extend conventional stream programming model to three levels as to two levels (stream level and kernel level) by adding a stream thread level, and software scheduler could be used to allocate multi-kernels that belong to threads to running on stream cores in tile. TiSA's stream programming model exposes the inherent parallelism of stream applications including four levels: TLP of threads among tiles; Kernel level parallelism among stream cores, DLP inside each stream core, and ILP inside ALU cluster. According to TiSA's stream programming model, there are MKMS, SKMS, MKSS execution patterns besides SIMD could be supported. It is more convenient for programmer to develop real stream applications.

According to the VLSI cost model, this paper estimates the area and delay of TiSA stream processor with intra-cluster, inter-cluster and inter-tile scaling. Our analysis shows that scaling to 4 tiles with 4 stream cores (16 ALUs per stream core) incurs only modest penalties for area. Moreover, this paper evaluates performance for a set of benchmarks as the number of tiles increases. Our results show that TiSA can scale effectively.

In summary, TiSA accords with the trend of billions of transistors VLSI technology in future.

Acknowledgements. We would like to thank Professor Xuejun Yang and all colleagues of 610 department. When we developed FT64 stream processor together, some good ideas had been generated. Our research was supported by the National Nature Science Foundation of China under NSFC No. 60673148 and 60703073, 863 Project of China under contract 2007AA01Z286, and Research Fund for the Doctoral Program of Higher Education of China under SRFDP No. 20069998025. Several of the authors received support from the National University of Defense Technology and/or Computer School graduate fellowships.

References

1. Khailany, B.: The VLSI Implementation and Evaluation of Area-and Energy-Efficient Streaming Media Processors. PhD thesis, Stanford,University (2003)
2. Rixner, S.: Stream Processor Architecture. Kluwer Academic Publishers, Boston (2001)
3. Bond, R.: High Performance DoD DSP Applications. In: 2003 Workshop on Streaming Systems (2003), http://catfish.csail.mit.edu/wss03/
4. Wen, M., Wu, N., Li, H., Zhang, C.: Multiple-Morphs Adaptive Stream Architecture. Journal of Computer Science and Technology 20(5) (September 2005)
5. Kozyrakis, C.E., et al.: Scalable Processors in the Billion-Transistors Era: IRAM. IEEE Computer 30(9) (September 1997)
6. Khailany, B., Dally, W.J., Kapasi, U.J., Mattson, P., et al.: Imagine: media processing with streams. IEEE Micro (March/April 2001)
7. Taylor, M.B., et al.: Evaluation of the Raw Microprocessor: An Exposed-Wire-Delay Architecture for ILP and Streams. In: ISCA 2004 (2004)
8. Sankaralingam, K., et al.: Exploiting ILP, TLP, and DLP with the Polymorphous TRIPS architecture. In: 30th Annual International Symposium on Computer Architecture (May 2003)
9. Hofstee, H.P.: Power Efficient Processor Architecture and the Cell Processor. In: Proc. of the 11th International Symposium on High Performance Computer Architecture (February 2005)
10. Fang, J.: Challenges and Opportunities on Multi-core Microprocessor. In: Srikanthan, T., Xue, J., Chang, C.-H. (eds.) ACSAC 2005. LNCS, vol. 3740, pp. 389–390. Springer, Heidelberg (2005)
11. Mattson, P.R.: A Programming System for the Imagine Media Processor. PhD thesis, Stanford University (2002)
12. Dally, W.J., et al.: Merrimac: Supercomputing with Streams. In: Proc. of Supercomputing 2003 (November 2003)
13. Wen, M., Wu, N., Zhang, C., Wu, W., Yang, Q., Xun, C.: FT64: Scientific Computing with Stream. In: Aluru, S., Parashar, M., Badrinath, R., Prasanna, V.K. (eds.) HiPC 2007. LNCS, vol. 4873, pp. 209–220. Springer, Heidelberg (2007)
14. Larus, J.: SPIM: A MIPS Simulator, http://pages.cs.wisc.edu/~larus/spim.html
15. Das, A., Mattson, P., Kapasi, U., Owens, J., Rixner, S., Jayasena, N.: Imagine Programming System User's Guide 2.0 (June 2004), http://cva.stanford.edu/Imagine/project/
16. Mattson, P.: Communication scheduling. In: Proceedings of the Ninth International Conference on Architectural Support for Programming Languages and Operating Systems, Cambridge, MA (November 2000)
17. Nuwan, S.: Jayasena, Memory Hierarchy Design for Stream Computing. Stanford Ph.D. Thesis (2005)
18. Khailany, B., Dally, W.J., Rixner, S., Kapasi, U.J., Owens, J.D., Towles, B.: Exploring the VLSI Scalability of Stream Processors. In: Proceedings of the 9th Symposium on High Performance Computer Architecture, Anaheim, California (February 2003)

19. Erez, M.: Merrimac - High-Performance and High-Efficient Scientific Computing with Streams. PhD thesis, Stanford University (2006)
20. Das, A., Mattson, P., Kapasi, U., Owens, J., Rixner, S., Jayasena, N.: Imagine Programming System Developer's Guide (2002), http://cva.stanford.edu/Imagine/project/
21. Mai, K., Paaske, T., Jayasena, N., Ho, R., Dally, W.J., Horowitz, M.: Smart memories: A modular reconfigurable architecture. In: International Symposium on Computer Architecture (June 2000)
22. Kongetira, P., Aingaran, K., Olukotun, K.: Niagara: A 32-way multithreaded Sparc processor. IEEE Micro, 25(2) (March/April 2005)
23. (2007), http://www.tilera.com/products/processors.php
24. Zhirnov, V., Cavin, R.: Greg Leeming, Kosmas Galatsis, An Assessment of Integrated Digital Cellular Automata Architectures. IEEE Computer (January 2008)
25. Wu, W., Wen, M., Wu, N., He, Y., et al.: Research and Evaluating of a Multiple-dimension Scalable Stream Architecture. Acta Electronic Sinica (May 2008)
26. Ahn, J.H.: Memory and Control Organizaions of Stream Processors, Ph.D. Thesis, Stanford University (2007)

An Efficient and Flexible Task Management
for Many Cores

Yuan Nan[1,2], Yu Lei[1,2], and Fan Dong-rui[1]

[1] Key Laboratory of Computer System and Architecture, Institute of Computing Technology,
Chinese Academy of Sciences, Beijing 100190
[2] Graduate University of Chinese Academy of Sciences, Beijing 100039
{yuannan,yulei,fandr}@ict.ac.cn

Abstract. This paper presents the design and implementation of a runtime system (named "GodRunner") on Godson-T many-core processor to support task-level parallelism efficiently and flexibly. GodRunner abstracts underlying hardware resource, providing ease-of-use programming interface. A two-grade task management mechanism is proposed to support both coarse-grained and fine-grained multithreading efficiently. Two load-balanced scheduling policies are combined flexibly in GodRunner. The software-controlled task management makes GodRunner more configurable and extensible than hard-wired ones. The experiment shows that the tasking overhead in GodRunner is as small as hundreds of cycles, which is about the hundreds of times faster than the conventional Pthread based multithreading on a SMP machine. Furthermore, our approach scales well and supports fine-grained tasks as small as 20k cycles optimally.

Keywords: many-core architecture, runtime system, task management.

1 Introduction

Previous techniques of increasing single-thread performance through faster clock rate have finally run up against power limits and diminishing returns. Computer industry has widely consensus that future performance increases must largely come from increasing the number of processing cores on a die. This has led to swift changes in computer architectures in recent years: multi-core processors become everywhere, and many-core processors have entered the lexicon. Furthermore, *Moore's Law* suggests that the number of on-chip processing cores will increase exponentially. It is anticipated that future microprocessors will accommodate tens, hundreds or even thousands of processing cores, implicating that *thread-level parallelism* (TLP) will become increasingly important.

Godson-T is a processor prototype of many-core architecture designed with 65nm CMOS technology, shown in Figure 1(a). Godson-T has 64 homogeneous, dual-issue and in-order processing cores running at 1GHz. The 8-pipeline processing core supports MIPS-4 ISA with synchronization instruction extensions. Each processing core has a 16KB 2-way set-associative private instruction cache and a 32KB local memory. The local memory functions as a 32KB 4-way set-associative private data

P. Stenström (Ed.): Transactions on HiPEAC IV, LNCS 6760, pp. 294–310, 2011.
© Springer-Verlag Berlin Heidelberg 2011

cache in default. It can also be configured as an explicitly-controlled and globally-addressed Scratched-Pad Memory (SPM), or a hybrid of cache and SPM. To utilize tremendous on-chip bandwidth, horizontal data communication between SPMs is enabled on Godson-T. A DMA-like coprocessor Data Transfer Agent (DTA) is built in each processing core for fast data communication. There are 16 address-interleaved L2 cache banks (256KB each) distributed along the perimeter of the chip. The L2 cache is shared by all processing cores and can serve up to 64 outstanding cache accessing requests in total. Four L2 cache banks in the same side of the chip share a memory controller. The memory hierarchy of Godson-T is shown in Figure 1(b).

A low-complexity synchronization-based cache coherence protocol on Godson-T [1] provides the efficient support of traditional multithreading with cache organization. This makes Godson-T Scope-Consistent [2].

A dedicated synchronization manager provides architectural support for fast mutual exclusion, barrier and single/wait synchronization. The 8×8 and 128-bit-width packet-switching mesh network connects all on-chip units. The network employs deterministic X-Y routing policy and provides total 2TB/s on-chip bandwidth among 64 processing cores.

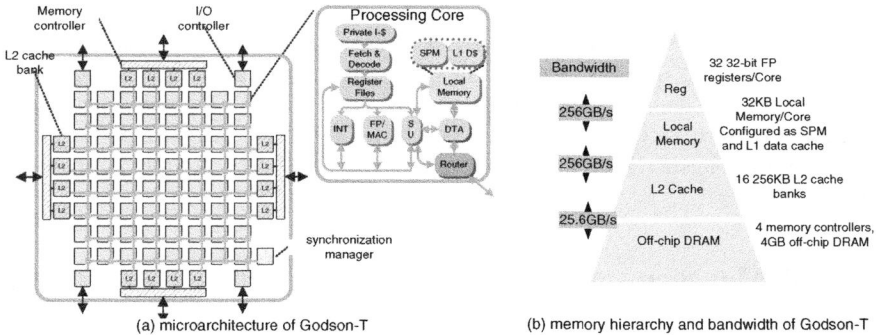

(a) microarchitecture of Godson-T   (b) memory hierarchy and bandwidth of Godson-T

Fig. 1. The Godson-T processor architecture

Given a many-core processor like Godson-T, or more processing cores, the challenge is that how to efficiently utilize large computation capability on the chip. It is notoriously difficult for parallel programmers to orchestrate threads with much underlying architecture details, so that simple and reasonable programming abstraction is necessary. This challenge is more likely to be overcome by promising programming models, compiler technology and runtime systems. On the motivation of this, we design and implement a novel task management for Godson-T many-core architecture in our runtime system named "GodRunner", focusing on efficiently abstracting a large number of underlying hardware threading units and providing familiar programming APIs.

Fine-grained multithreading has gained more and more attention in recent years. As core population increases, fined-grained multithreading programs achieve dynamic load-balancing without rewritten of programs. Besides, on-chip parallel architecture provides unique opportunities for fast communication and synchronization, which makes fine-grained multithreading more viable. However, tasking overhead (i.e.

creation, termination and scheduling of tasks) impacts much on performance, especially for fine-grained tasks. On conventional parallel system, software is usually responsible for the task management. Creating or terminating a thread typically takes tens of thousands cycles penalty on such systems [3], which makes these system only suitable for very coarse-grained thread-level parallelism to amortize the threading overhead. Some dedicated architecture supports for tasks [4][5][6] claim that they obtain near-optimum performance for sets of benchmarks composed of fine-grained tasks. However, we argue that the hardware approaches are not flexible enough to implement more sophisticated scheduling algorithms for different purposes (e.g. power-efficiency, off-chip bandwidth consumption, and etc), which is very important for runtime system running broad kinds of applications with different characteristics and requirements.

In this paper, we propose a two-grade mechanism that makes task management ultra efficient for both coarse-grained and fine-grained multithreading on many-core processor. The first grade mechanism is used for traditional coarse-grained thread level parallelism, while the second one is particularly designed for much finer grained thread level parallelism by latency tolerance. We also combine two well-known task scheduling algorithms together for flexible load balancing management. The theoretical and experimental studies show that our task management is efficient for both coarse-grained and fine-grained tasks. The rest of the paper is organized as follows. Section 2 demonstrates the design and implementation of two-grade task management mechanism in GodRunner, and makes insightful theoretical analysis based on performance models. Section 3 evaluates and analyzes performance of proposed mechanism. Section 4 introduces related work. And section 5 concludes the paper.

2   Task Management Mechanism

The factors affecting performance on parallel architecture are quite complex and unpredictable with static analysis. Runtime system is more and more regarded as an accessible method to improve performance since it is capable of supervising the dynamic execution states and optimizing the execution on-the-fly. Task management is a cornerstone of runtime systems for many-core processors. From programmer's view, a successful task management design should have the following **3 objectives:**

(1) Encapsulates subtle hardware details and provides a simple abstraction without unreasonable programming constraints. For example, programming should not be restricted by the number of threading units and the spatial distribution of them.

(2) Efficient for either coarse-grained or fine-grained thread level parallelism. In more detail, there are two key factors to obtain the efficiency: (a) the overhead of the task management itself should be minimized; (b) all threading units should be kept busy by dynamic load balancing.

(3) Flexible to configure or extend. Performance is deteriorated by complex reasons besides load imbalacing problem. For example, contended accesses to shared resource (e.g. off-chip memory bandwidth). Moreover, performance is not the only objective sometimes, like power consumption constraint in embedding computing.

The objective 3 implies the software approach, which is bad for the objective 2. In this section, we present detailed design and implementation of task management in GodRunner to pursuit all the three objectives listed above.

2.1 Overview of GodRunner Task

GodRunner task model adopts *create-join* task model inspired by Pthread [7] which is familiar to the programmers. Therefore, a large amount of parallel program sources written in Pthread programming model can be ported on Godson-T conveniently. An execution of a program can be partitioned into many tasks (in our terminology, *task* is high-level programming abstraction which is not necessarily bind to hardware threading unit). A GodRunner task is created when a triple *<entry program counter, input parameters, execution context>* is set up by another task. The task is said "ready" and placed in some task ready queue. When the task is chosen by the scheduler and executing on the threading unit, the task is "running". After the task retired, the task is said "zombie" and placed in the queue of completed tasks. Finally, the task is "retired" after it is joined by the other task. GodRunner tasks feature non-preemptive execution, because context-switch incurs save-restore overhead and cache thrashing, especially inappropriate for fine-grained tasking environment. Therefore, a task will keep executing on a threading unit until it terminates. Non-preemptive execution can make *execution context* initialization simple and fast, for example, stack could be statically allocated to each threading unit, so that the time-consuming dynamic allocation is avoided.

GodRunner permits program to create more tasks than hardware threading units, and transparently allocates them to the threading units at runtime. GodRunner is responsible for swapping the completed task out from thread, and scheduling a new one in, see Figure 2.

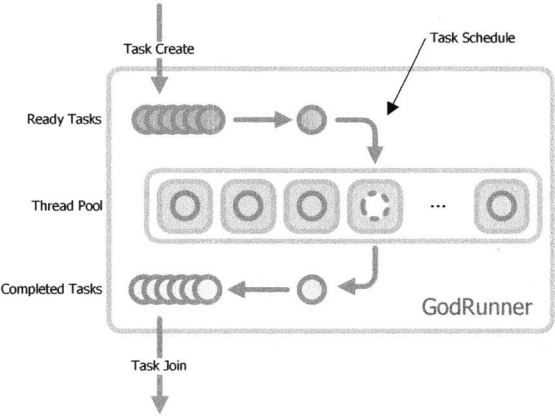

Fig. 2. Responsibility and role of GodRunner

There is potentially a deadlock problem when the non-preemptive "running" tasks are dependent on the "ready" tasks that can never be scheduled to run since the "running" tasks occupy all the threading units. For example, considering a program recursively *create* a child task and then *join* it, finally all tasks on threading units want to join their child tasks but there are not enough threading units to execute the created child tasks. We provide a task scheduling algorithms flexibly to address the problem and leave the detailed description in section 2.3.

2.2 Task Management API

The software is responsible for creating, terminating and synchronizing tasks by inserting appropriate Pthread-like API invocations to GodRunner C library. We make some improvement for performance issues, such as batched thread operation and flexible joining operation. A brief description of major APIs for task management is given below.

int gtask_create(void *func, mask_t mask, unsigned argc, void *argv)

Create a task. *func* specifies the program counter of created task embodied in function; and *mask* indicates some control information like scheduling policy and join policy; *argc* and *argv* specify input parameters of created task; the function returns *task_id* of created task if successful.

void gtask_create_batch(int *task_id, void *func, mask_t mask, unsigned iteration, unsigned argc, void *argv)

Create a set of identical tasks with different input parameters. *iteration* specifies the count of tasks should be create; *argc* and *argv* specify all input parameters of created tasks. This API is particularly useful in SPMD or paralleling loops. Creation penalty can be significantly reduced by scheduling identical operations in batches.

void gtask_exit(void *ret)

Task terminates and returns. *ret* specifies returned data to parent or ancestor task. It should be mentioned that GodRunner permits task to return to arbitrary task, not only its direct parent. For example, a task can directly return to some ancestors for performance benefits.

void gtask_join(unsigned task_id, void *ret)

Join a retuned task specified by *task_id*, returned data is copied to space specified by *ret*. Note that some tasks need not to be joined dependent of *mask* parameter in creation. Furthermore, a task is not necessarily to be joined by its direct parent. These changes enable the program to violate the join dependence between tasks and make the computation not fully-strict, but they bring the performance sometimes.

Task synchronization primitives (i.e. lock/unlock, barrier, signal/wait) are also provided as function calls (e.g. **godsont_lock**, **godsont_barrier_wait**, …). These APIs typically execute several special synchronization instructions on Godson-T.

2.3 Task Scheduling Algorithm

Different types of task scheduling algorithms can be incorporated into GodRunner flexibly. Two well-known task scheduling algorithms for dynamic load balancing, *work-stealing* [11] and *conditional-spawning* [5], are supported in our task management mechanism. A brief description of these two scheduling algorithms is shown below.

Work-Stealing (WS). Every Threading Unit (TU) has a Local Task Stack (LTS) logically to maintain unexecuted tasks created locally. When a task is created by a TU, the task frame is pushed onto the top of the local LTS; when a task terminates, the TU pops a "ready" task from the top of the LTS when the LTS is not empty and continues to execute the new task; otherwise the TU will randomly select another TU as the victim and steal a "ready" task from the bottom of victim's LTS. Work-stealing is proved a simple and efficient scheduling algorithm for dynamic load balancing and good cache locality.

Conditional-Spawning (CS). Task creation does not actually spawn a new task as if there are not enough threading units. Instead, the creation of the child task changes to a local function call to the computation of the child task. Logically, it seems that parent task could "context-switch" into child task through function call, and return after its completion. Conditional-spawning scheduling algorithm is introduced in GodRunner to address the deadlock problem described in 2.1, because the program could never have a chance to spawn new tasks when threading units are insufficient. It breaks the premise of the deadlock. Therefore, the scheduling algorithm could eliminate the programming restriction posed on non-preemptive task model.

GodRunner combines both scheduling algorithms flexibly: different tasks in a same program can be scheduled by different algorithms. In section 3, we study the performance issue of the two scheduling algorithms, and will see that the performance of work-stealing slightly outperforms conditional spawning in our implementation.

2.4   Two-Grade Task Management Mechanism

Since the communication and the synchronization latency are dominated, coarse-grained multithreading is encouraged on conventional SMP or CC-NUMA machines. Hence, large input data set is usually advocated to achieve good scalability. In this case, task management overhead is not very critical to performance, since it can be amortized by long life-cycle execution of tasks. As many-core architecture emerges in recent years, it is viable to execute much finer grained of tasks, since the communication and the synchronization overhead are significantly reduced by fabricating large amount of threading units in same package. However, task management becomes very critical as the tasks getting smaller, so that minimizing task management overhead is of major concern.

GodRunner provides two-grade task management mechanism. The first grade is used for conventional coarse-grained multithreading, while the second one is specially designed for fine-grained multithreading. The same programming interfaces are exhibited in both of the grades. The two task scheduling algorithms, work-stealing and conditional-spawning are also implemented in both cases.

Before running a program, a proper grade of task management mechanism need to be chosen according to the number of available threading units and the grain size of tasks. The differences between the two mechanisms originate from the different requirements of the coarse-grained and the fine-grained multithreading.

2.4.1   The 1st Grade of Task Management Mechanism (TMM1)

The assumption of the TMM1 implementation is that tasks will execute for a long period, so that the tasking overhead itself is less important. To maximize the delivered throughput, the design principles of TMM1 should focus on minimizing its usage of on-chip resource, reducing the chance contending with applications. As a result, we implement TMM1 based on cache configuration on Godson-T. The task management process is only triggered when task APIs are invoked.

There are two major shared data structures in TMM1: *the state table of threading units*, and *the state table of tasks*. Accessing these shared data should be mutual exclusively protected by either critical section or atomic synchronization instruction. To enhance the performance, we take advantage of light-weight mutual exclusion operations (i.e. test-and-set, fetch-and-add on Godson-T) to reduce the penalty of locks as far as we can.

Two major task management processes of TMM1 are depicted in Figure 3.

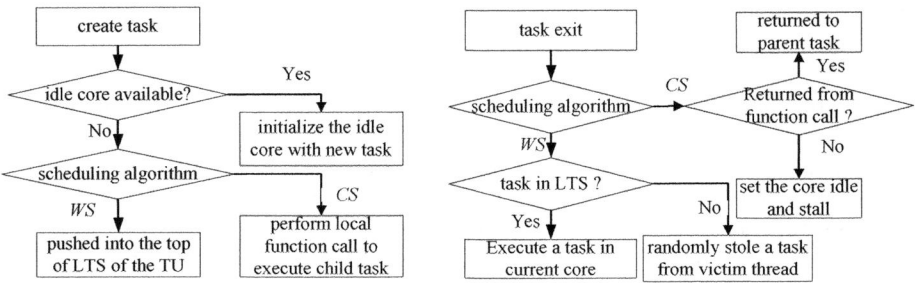

Fig. 3. Task management process in TMM1

2.4.2   The 2nd Grade of Task Management Mechanism (TMM2)

TMM1 is customized to efficient support for coarse-grained multithreading. There are several inefficiencies making TMM1 unsuitable for fine-grained multithreading:

(1) It is not very efficient due to frequently accessing shared data (i.e. *the state table of threading units, and the state table of tasks*) exclusively, incurring much cache coherence penalty (i.e. flush and invalidation of cache blocks). As a result, creating a task typically consumes more than one thousand cycles without network contention. Moreover, mutual exclusion with critical sections dose not scale well on large-scale system;

(2) From Figure 3, it is shown that creation and termination of a task typically accompanies the scheduling process, e.g. initialize an idle threading unit, or steal a task from the others. This time-consuming scheduling process degrades single task performance. However, it is not necessarily bind to task creation or termination;

(3) The TMM1 itself a parallel program with plenty of locks and lock-free data operations– notoriously messy to orchestrate, debug and tune.

These problems come from accessing shared data mutual exclusively. When more than one threads intend to upgrade same shared data, accesses should be dealt with serially. Meanwhile, the shared data should be purged from the former host cache before being owned by the next cache. It seems that the shared data just "walks" among caches. Unfortunately, the penalty of the "walk" contributes to the critical path of application's performance. In fine-grained multithreading paradigm with frequent task management, the penalty seems much more delinquent. To mitigate the problem, we propose a novel approach to manage tasks in TMM2. The basic principle of TMM2 is that the control of the shared accesses moves instead of the movement of the shared data. As a result, the operations on shared data are grouped together, and executed by a dedicated thread (called the helper thread). Review the case that more than one user threads intend to upgrade same shared data. If all the shared accesses from different user threads are performed by one helper thread so that the shared data can be treated as private data, which never "walks". The isolation semantic of shared data accesses can be naturally guaranteed by single-thread program order. Moreover, since the shared data is not needed by user threads after the update, user threads can immediately do its following work after passing the control on shared data accessing to the helper thread. Therefore, no more threads wait for each other in this case. The serialization overhead of the critical sections can be hided in computations. To realize the principle on Godson-T, a runtime helper thread dedicated to the task management is used. Besides this, intensive optimizations directly featuring Godson-T architecture are done for performance issues. In TMM2:

(1) When the processor starts, a runtime thread is assigned to maintain shared data structure mentioned in 2.4.1 and manage the creation, termination and join of tasks. The processes of creation, termination and join of tasks are split into two stages. The first stage without any shared data access is done by user threads themselves. After that, user threads generate the one-sided requests to notify the runtime thread through horizontal communication enabled on Godson-T. After that, the user threads need not wait for the returned response and continue to execute its following operations. The helper thread handles the second stage of these requests. For instance, creation of a task only initializes a task frame on side of user thread, scheduling of the new created task is done in runtime thread. Therefore, tasking overhead are decoupled — part of work handled by user threads and the other part handled by runtime threads. User task latency could be tolerated by overlapping the execution of the two parts. Work containing accesses of shared data is done serially in the helper thread, so that all locks are eliminated in TMM2 anymore. It is foreseen that many other performance-critical parallel functions can benefit from this approach, which is beyond the scope of the paper.

(2) Putting data in SPM as much as possible for fast and deterministic access. In our implementation, 31KB memory of the runtime thread is configured as SPM and the spare 1KB as a small data cache to accommodate data stacks of the runtime thread. On the contrary, only 1KB memory is configured as SPM unit of user threads by default, so that 31KB memory is left for user programs. Runtime thread maintains almost all shared data on local SPM, while user threads also maintain some necessary task and synchronization information on their SPMs. The limited on-chip storage restricts the size of task structures stored in SPM. If active task structures (with *ready*, *running* and *zombie* state) exceed the number that can accommodated on SPM, the spilled task structures are maintained in less-efficient cache memory. 512 reusable task structures are maintained in our implementation, which is sufficient for most cases.

(3) Task prefetch scheme is used to further tolerate interconnection latency, thus thread reuse latency can be minimized. When a task terminates, the thread unit chooses a prefetched task from its local prefetch buffer maintained on local SPM. The helper thread is responsible for choosing prefetch tasks for threading units and pushing them to the local prefetch buffers of the threading units;

(4) Runtime thread communicates with user threads by writing information to SPM of each other. For example, if user threads want to notify the runtime thread, they just write information to corresponding memory locations of runtime thread's SPM memory remotely. Although supported in Godson-T, remote SPM memory read is not encouraged since it lengthens critical path. Therefore, communications between runtime thread and user thread are almost asynchronous, which helps further hiding interconnection latency.

Two major task management processes of TMM2 are depicted in Figure 4.

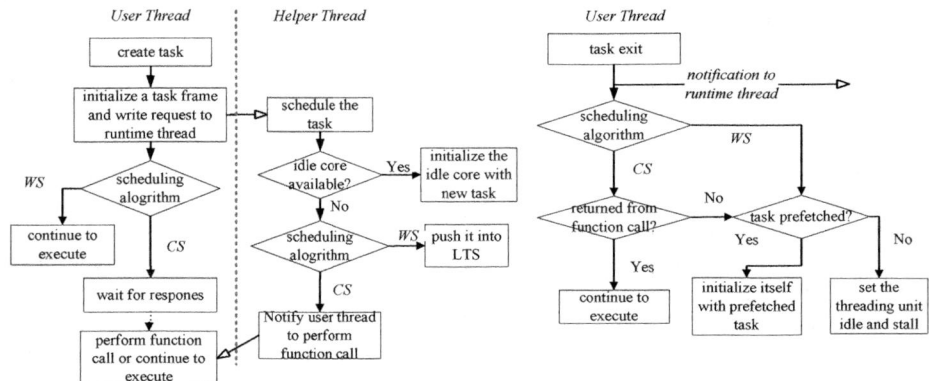

Fig. 4. Task management process in TMM2

2.5   Performance Model

This section is expected to answer the question that how to choose the grade of task management mechanisms to maximize the delivered performance by understanding the application and the processor issues. We build a simple performance model to make insightful understanding of the two-grade task management mechanism.

Intuitively, performance is tightly related to the grain size of tasks and the number of threading units. Let P denote the number of threading units, G denote the average grain size of tasks, N denote the number of tasks. Assume that N is large enough.

Tasking overhead T_O for a task is defined as overall time of task creation, join and termination for **one** task measured in the execution cycles.

In TMM1, the tasking overhead can be divided into two parts: the serialized-execution part T_S (due to mutual exclusively accesses of shared data) and the paralleled-executed part T_P. The total execution time of the program is:

$$T_{TMM1} = \frac{(G + T_P) \times N}{P} + T_S \times N \qquad \text{(Equation 2.5.1)}$$

In TMM2, the tasking overhead for a single task can also be divided into two parts: the overhead T_U on the user thread side and overhead T_R on the runtime helper thread. Ideal execution time of program should be:

$$T_{TMM\,2-U} = \frac{(G + T_U) \times N}{P - 1}$$ (Equation 2.5.2)

(T_R is not considered since its overhead can be hided)

For choosing TMM1, let $T_{TMM1} < T_{TMM2}$. According to the measured overhead in TMM1 and TMM2, we set $T_S=160$, $T_P=2300$, and $T_U=400$. And we get another equation:

$$P < \sqrt{43.94 + G/160} - 5.44$$ (Equation 2.5.3)

If we foreknow the amount of threading units and the average size of the tasks, then we can calculate equation 2.5.3 to see if the relationship stands. If it is validated, we should choose TMM1, otherwise choose TMM2. For example, for $P=64$, TMM1 will be chosen as if G is larger than 77383 cycles. For $P=2$, TMM1 will be chosen as if G is larger than only 1826 cycles.

Another observation revealed from the performance model is that TMM2 also has its bottleneck if user threads create and terminate tasks (namely, generate task management requests) too fast, which makes the helper thread overfed.

The saturated work time of runtime thread is:

$$T_{TMM\,2-R} = T_R \times N$$ (Equation 2.5.4)

Then real execution time of program should be fixed to:

$$T_{TMM\,2} = \max\{T_{TMM\,2-R}, T_{TMM\,2-U}\}$$ (Equation 2.5.5)

Therefore, if $T_{TMM2-R} > T_{TMM2-U}$, the performance will not scalable due to our task management mechanism. The measured T_R in TMM2 is approximately 400 cycles. The overhead will deteriorate delivered performance if $G < 300 \times P - 700$ (Equation 2.5.6). In theoretical analysis, TMM2 can optimally support the task grain size as small as 20K cycles on 64 threading units. For G is smaller than 20000 cycles, the clustered task management mechanism is proposed: on-chip user threads are partitioned into several clusters. Each cluster is managed by a dedicated runtime helper thread. Performance and scalability is guaranteed since threading units within same cluster could never saturate corresponding runtime helper thread by applying equation 2.5.6 within the cluster. However, it is a bit more complex than TMM2 that communications among runtime threads must be carefully handled. This new grade of task management mechanism TMM3 is working-on-progress.

3   Experimental Study and Result

3.1   Experimental Methodology and Benchmark

Experiments are conducted on the cycle-accurate Godson-T architecture simulator (GAS). Major architecture configurations we used in experiments are listed in Table 1.

Table 1. Experimental architecture parameters

Processing Core	
Processing Core	64 cores, in-order, dual-issue, each running at 1GHz
Load-to-Use Latency	3 cycles
FMAC Unit Latency	4 cycles
Memory Subsystem	
L1 I-Cache	16KB, 2-way set associative, 32B/cacheline.
Local Memory	Configured to 32KB SPM, 16 64-bit-width SRAM sub-banks with 2 memory ports each (1 for read, 1 for write).
L2 Cache	16 banks, total 4MB, 8-way set-associative, 64B/cacheline.
Memory Controller & Off-chip DRAM	4 memory controllers, running at same clock rate as the processing core. 64-bit FSB. Each memory controller controls a 1GB DDR2-800 DRAM. DRAM clock is 400MHz, $t_{CAS}=5$, $t_{RCD}=5$, $t_{RP}=5$, $t_{RAS}=15$, $t_{RC}=24$ measured in memory clock.
Contentionless Latency	
L1 I-Cache hit	1 cycle
SPM load/store hit	1 cycle
Mesh network	2 cycles per hop
L2 hit	12~40 cycles according to routing distance
Off-chip memory	62~120 cycles according to routing distance and DRAM access pattern (e.g. whether the access is on the same row as previous ones)

Microbenmarks are composed on Godson-T to evaluate the raw performance of task management mechanism without any interference. The first microbenchmark is for measuring the tasking API overhead and the runtime overhead, we compare the overhead of TMM1, TMM2 on Godson-T with Pthread overhead on a SMP machine with 8 dual-core AMD Opteron processor. (See Section 3.2)

We developed a Radom Program Generator (RPG) to generate sets of different microbenchmarks randomly spawning tasks with randomized computation workload (the workload is simulated by empty loops). These generated microbenchmarks should conform to the given generation restrictions (i.e. the total workload of a program, the average workload/grain of each task, the grain variation of tasks, and the max count of tasks that a task can spawn). Therefore, we can generate program benchmarks with given behavior to test how capable our implementation is and the how accurate the theoretical performance model is. For these generated benchmarks, performance and scalability of TMM1 and TMM2 are evaluated and compared with an optimal (zero-latency) task management mechanism. (See Section 3.3)

Four kernels of SPLASH-2 benchmark [13] with default input data set are used to evaluate the efficiency of TMM1. Speedup of these kernels and the proportion of corresponding threading overhead are shown. (See Section 3.4)

3.2   Evaluating API and Runtime Overhead

Table 2 lists the API and Runtime overheads of TMM1, TMM2 on Godson-T and Pthread on a SMP machine with an 8 dual-core AMD Opteron processors running at 2.6GHz. Note that only task creation overhead is measured with Pthread, since the remaining Pthread APIs cannot be precisely or directly measured. Detailed reasons are listed in columns. In TMM2, the overhead of task scheduling handled by the helper thread consumes another 120 cycles, which is not listed in the table. It is shown that both TMM1 and TMM2 significantly outperform Pthread in task creation. Furthermore, task creation can greatly benefit from batch operation. In batch mode, task creation of TMM1 is **84x** faster than that of Pthread normalized to same processor clock rate, while TMM2 is **143x** faster. The impressive speedup allows programs with much finer grained of tasks. We believe that other tasking overheads of Pthread not shown in the table also could not compete with GodRunner.

Table 2. Task API and Runtime Overhead

	TMM1's API	TMM2's API	TMM2's Helper	Pthread
Create	1038 cycles	154 cycles	107 cycles	~50000 cycles
Create 60 tasks in batches	13705 cycles	8038 cycles	6754 cycles	(no such API call)
Join	646 cycles	237 cycles	55 cycles	(difference among the collected data is too large)
Exit	~900 cycles	~100 cycles, zero-latency thread reuse with task prefetch	29 cycels	(cannot be measured)

3.3 Evaluating Microbenchmarks

Three sets of benchmarks are generated by RPG. Programs in the same set are of the same average grain size of tasks (grain size of 20k cycles, 40k cycles, 60k cycles, and 80k cycles). Grain size variation is set up to 50% to simulate different grains of tasks exist in same program. It means that workload of a task is randomly generated ranging from 50% to 150% of the average workload per task. In our experiments, a task can spawn up to 64 child tasks, and the total amount of tasks is set to 1024.

The normalized speedups of TMM1, TMM2 and optimal task management are shown in Figure 5. The optimal task management uses work-stealing scheduling algorithm, and task creation and termination cost zero penalty to performance. The result shows that TMM2's performance can be nearly optimal when the average grain size of tasks is as small as 20k cycles on 64 threading units, as illustrated in theoretical analysis. For the average task grain size as coarse as 60k cycles, TMM1 gets almost optimal performance and scalability as well as TMM2 on 64 threading units. For the 80k-cycles task grain size, we observe that the performance of TMM1 slightly outperform TMM2, which validates the prediction of our performance model in section 2.5.

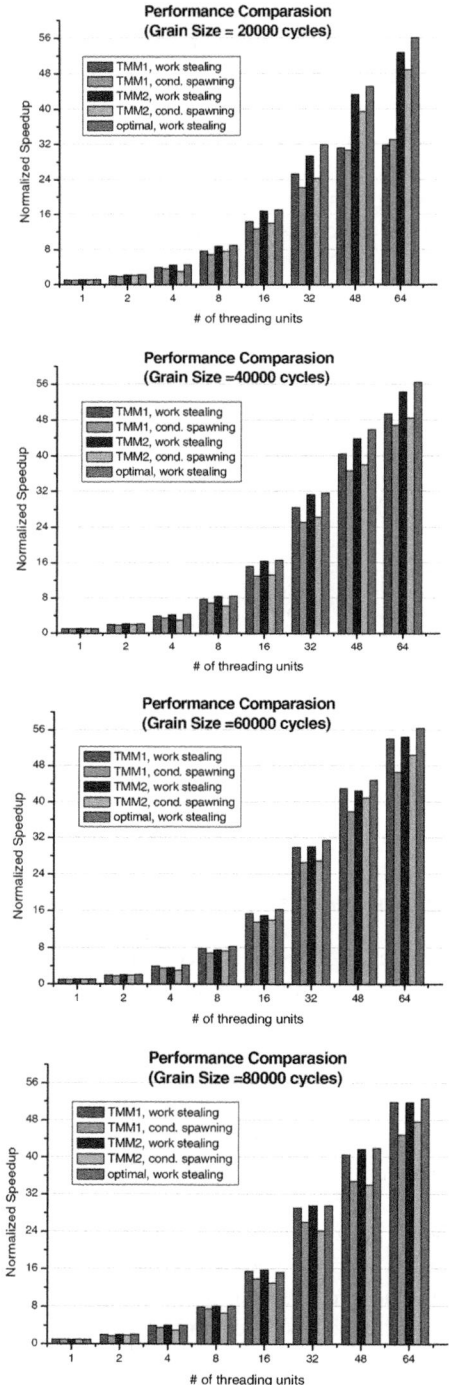

Fig. 5. Performance comparisons with microbenchmarks generated by RPG

It is also observed that in our implementation, the performance of work-stealing scheduling outperforms conditional-spawning scheduling, especially when the grain size of tasks gets larger or the number of participated threading units increases. The first reason is that conditional spawning algorithm creates new tasks lingeringly, so it is more probably that idle threading units shall wait for a new spawned task for a period of time. The second reason is that in TMM2, task creation in conditional spawning scheduling cannot extract the benefit from decoupled mechanism as much as work-stealing algorithm, since the creating task always needs to wait for runtime's response and determine whether to perform the task creation as a function call or not.

3.4   Evaluating SPLASH-2 Kernels

The four SPLASH-2 kernels FFT, RADIX, LU and CHOLESKY are evaluated with default input set. , even though the default input data set is too small for SMP or CC-NUMA machines TMM1 is used in the experiments since SPLASH-2 represents traditional coarse-grained multithreaded programs. All the kernels are programmed with SPMD paradigm that would easily benefit from our batched task operations. The result shows that the speedup of these kernels is comparable to that on ideal memory described in original SPLASH-2 paper, see Figure 6. The proportion of the task management overhead is usually smaller than 1‰ of the overall execution time even though 64 threads are running, which means TMM1 is efficient enough for these benchmarks.

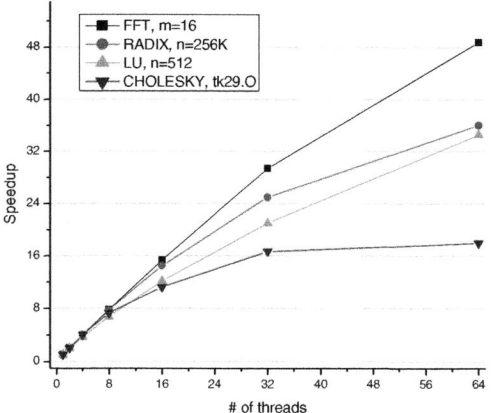

Fig. 6. The speedup of SPLASH-2 kernels

4   Related Work

Portability on off-the-shelf multithreaded platforms is emphasized of many related work such as LWP [8], Nano-Thread [9], TAM [10], Pthread [7], Cilk [11] and EARTH [12]. To achieve this goal, these runtime systems or threading libraries need to be written in common software interface provided by another threading libraries or

OS, e.g. Cilk can construct over Pthread library. Therefore, tasking overhead could be large, so that they only fit for coarse-grained task parallelism.

CAPSULE [5] is a runtime software taking advantage of proposed architecture support on SMT processor. Conditional spawning scheduling algorithm is adopted to change the grains of tasks dynamically. GodRunner shows that conditional spawning scheduling could resolve some synchronization problem with non-preemptive task model, but it can not deliver performance as well as work-stealing algorithm on many-core architecture as evaluated from experiments.

Carbon [4] introduces hard-wired task manager controlled by dedicated task management instructions. It obtains nearly optimal performance on a set of RMS benchmarks composed of fine-grained tasks on ring-based multi-core architecture. The decoupled design of TMM2 in GodRunner is similar to Carbon, but software-approach TMM2 more focuses on reducing shared data overhead. By minimizing data movement overhead, TMM2 also provides optimal performance for the fine-grained task management. Besides hardware complexity, Carbon is not flexible enough to extend task scheduling algorithms for different purpose. Even though Carbon is very fast, theoretical performance analysis in Section 2.5 shows that decoupled design suffers from scalability problem when the grain size of tasks is small or the number of threading units is large. The pure hardware approach also could not address the problem as flexible as the software one.

TiNy Threads (TNT) [3] is thread virtual machine for Cyclops-64 architecture. As in GodRunner, TNT uses on-chip memory for deterministic data access, so tasking overhead in TNT is comparable small to that in GodRunner. However, programming with TNT is much more restrictive which limits the usage of TNT. For example, programmer cannot create tasks more than hardware threading units.

5   Conclusion

The tradeoff between high performance and ease of programming makes a grand challenge for parallel computing. GodRunner is an attempt to address the challenge by providing an efficient and flexible task management on many-core processor.

GodRunner abstracts underlying threading units, providing a flat, non-restrictive programming vision. The Pthread-like task management APIs is quite familiar to parallel programming community.

Two-grade task management mechanism is proposed to address the efficiency problem of task management. The first grade of task management mechanism (TMM1) is used for coarse-grained multithreading, while the second grade mechanism (TMM2) is especially designed for fine-grained multithreading. By identifying the bottleneck of traditional task management, TMM2 adopts a novel decoupled framework by introducing a runtime helper thread. Thus, a part of tasking overhead could be hidden. The mechanism also eliminates shared data movements and mutual exclusive data accesses. The choice of the two grades is determined through a simple performance model considering application and architecture issues. Intensive optimizations make our task management extremely efficient. Cycle-accurate simulations show that the measured API overheads in GodRunner is very efficient, for example, task creation can be 89~143x faster than the Pthread's on the

SMP machine. The experimental results validate our performance model and show that TMM2's performance can be optimal even the grain size of tasks is as small as 20k cycles. Evaluation of SPLASH2 kernels with small input data set shows that the task management of TMM1 only causes <1‰ overhead.

Besides distributed work-stealing scheduling algorithm, conditional-spawning is adopted to address the deadlock problem on non-preemptive task model. GodRunner is also a flexible platform to extend new scheduling algorithms.

Acknowledgement

This work is supported by the National Natural Science Foundation of China under Grant No.60736012; the National Grand Fundamental Research 973 Program of China under Grant No. 2005CB321600.

References

[1] Huang, H., Yuan, N., Lin, W., et al.: Architecture Supported Synchronization-Based Cache Coherence Protocol For Many-Core Processors. In: 2nd Workshop on Chip Multiprocessor Memory Systems and Interconnects, In Conjunction with the 35th International Symposium on Computer Architecture, Beijing, China (June 2008)

[2] Iftode, L., Singh, J.P., Li, K.: Scope Consistency: A Bridge between Release Consistency and Entry Consistency. In: Proc. of the 8th Annual ACM Symposium on Parallel Algorithms and Architectures (1996)

[3] Cuvillo, J.D., Zhu, W.R., Hu, Z., Gao, G.R.: TiNy threads: a thread virtual machine for the cyclops64 cellular architecture. In: Proceedings of 19th IEEE International Parallel and Distributed Processing Symposium, The Colorado, The USA (April 2005)

[4] Kumar, S., Hughes, C.J., Nguyen, A.: Carbon: Architectural Support for Fine-Grained Parallelism on Chip Multiprocessors. In: Proceedings of 34th International Symposium on Computer Architecture, San Diego, California, USA (June 2007)

[5] Palatin, P., Lhuillier, Y., Temam, O.: CAPSULE: hardware-assisted parallel execution of component-based Programs. In: Proceedings of 39th Annual IEEE/ACM International Symposium on Microarchitecture, Florida, USA (December 2006)

[6] Chen, J., Juang, P., Ko, K., Contreras, G., Penry, D., Rangan, R., Stoler, A., Peh, L., Martonosi, M.: Hardware-Modulated Parallelism in Chip Multiprocessors. In: Proceedings of Workshop on Design, Architecture and Simulation of Chip Multi-Processors Conference (dasCMP), Spain, pp. 54–63 (November 2005)

[7] Mueller, F.: Pthreads library interface. Technical report, Department of Computer Science, Florida State University (July 1993)

[8] Rosenberg, J.: LWP user manual. Technical Report CMUITC- CMUITC-85-037, Information Technology Center, Carnegie- Mellon University (June 1985)

[9] Nikolopoulos, D.S., Polychronopoulos, E.D., Papatheodorou, T.S.: Efficient runtime thread management for the Nano-Threads programming model. In: Proceedings of the 2nd IPPS/SPDP Workshop on Runtime Systems for Parallel Programming, Orlando, Florida, March 30, pp. 183–194 (1998)

[10] Culler, D.E., Goldstein, S.C., Schauser, K.E., Eicken, T.V.: TAM – a compiler controlled threaded abstract machine. Journal of Parallel and Distributed Computing (July 1993)

[11] Frigo, M., Leiserson, C.E., Randall, K.H.: The implementation of the Cilk-5 multithreaded language. In: Proceedings of the ACM SIGPLAN 1998 Conference on Programming Language Design and Implementation (June 1998)

[12] Theobald, K.B.: EARTH: An Efficient Architecture for Running Threads. PhD dissertation, McGill University (May 1999)

[13] Woo, S.C., Ohara, M., Torrie, E., Pal Singh, J., Gupta, A.: The SPLASH-2 Programs: Characterization and Methodological Considerations. In: Proceedings of the 22nd International Symposium on Computer Architecture, Santa Margherita Ligure, Italy, pp. 24–36 (June 1995)

On Two-Layer Brain-Inspired Hierarchical Topologies – A Rent's Rule Approach –

Valeriu Beiu[1,2], Basheer A.M. Madappuram[1,2],
Peter M. Kelly[2], and Liam J. McDaid[2]

[1] Faculty of Information Technology, United Arab Emirates University, Al Ain, UAE
Center for Neural Inspired Nano Architectures (CNINA)
[2] School of Intelligent Systems, University of Ulster, Magee, UK
{vbeiu,basheera}@uaeu.ac.ae, {pm.kelly,lj.mcdaid}@ulster.ac.uk

Abstract. This research compares the brain's connectivity (based on different analyses of neurological data) with well-known network topologies (originally used in super-computers) using Rent's rule. The comparison reveals that brain connectivity is in good agreement with Rent's rule. However, the known network topologies fall short of being strong contenders for mimicking brain's connectivity. That is why we perform a detailed Rent-based (top-down) connectivity analysis of generic two-layer hierarchical network topologies. This analysis aims to identify generic two-layer hierarchical network topologies which could closely mimic brain's connectivity. The range of granularities (*i.e.*, number of gates/cores/neurons) where such mimicking is possible are identified and discussed. These results should have implications for the design of future networks-on-chip in general, and for the burgeoning field of multi/many-core processors in particular (in the medium term), as well as for forward-looking investigations on emerging brain-inspired nano-architectures (in the long run).

Keywords: Connectivity, network topology, network-on-chip, communication, nano-architecture, Rent's rule, neural networks, brain.

1 Introduction

Interconnection (both at the low technological level as well as the highest architectural level) is certainly the most challenging problem facing the development of tera-scale and multi-/many-core systems of the future [1]. The potentially huge processing power offered by these parallel architectures will only be realized if the interconnection problem is addressed satisfactorily. Finding a solution to this problem is therefore a subject of intense research interest to the academic and manufacturing community [2].

The computing performance of future applications will need real-time processing of terabytes of information. Applications in areas where data is generated by billions of people for information sharing, businesses and entertainments, global real-time monitoring of movements, full body scan and health assessment, as well as management and visualization in such fields as genetics, geophysics, finance, and computational neuroscience, are some examples where huge processing power will be required [3].

P. Stenström (Ed.): Transactions on HiPEAC IV, LNCS 6760, pp. 311–333, 2011.
© Springer-Verlag Berlin Heidelberg 2011

Architectural innovation will be the major means by which the increased computational performance demanded by such applications will be achieved [4], [5]. Industry has clearly recognized this game change [6], and consequently hardware is witnessing multi- to many- to 1000s-core platform development. This will also impact on software [7] and will create the need for a paradigm shift in software languages to cope with the massive parallelism which will result from the new innovative architectures.

To date interconnect in multi-/many-cores have employed buses or crossbar switches between the cores and cache banks. Chip implementations such as the Cell (IBM, Sony and Toshiba) employ multiple ring networks to interconnect the nine processors (cores) on the chip and use software-managed memory to communicate between the cores, rather than conventional cache-coherency protocols. In the recent past we have also witnessed an explosion of multi-core processors: Niagra with 8 cores (Sun), the 80-core Teraflop chip (Intel), as well as more specialized chips like the network processors from Cisco (Silicon Packet Processor having 188 RISC processors, while the Quantum Flow Processors hosts 40 Tensilica cores), or the graphic processors from Nvidia (*e.g.*, Tesla with 128 cores and Fermi with 512 cores), and many more in the pipeline. The future tera-scale (*i.e.*, having 10^{12} devices) processors will need to connect, not only the large number of cores, but also to other hardware units with specific purposes. As more elements are packed onto a tera-scale chip, there is a correspondingly greater challenge to enable the rising on-chip communication. Studies have shown that the interconnect design and micro architecture will play a significant role in determining the overall performance of tera-scale chips [8], [9]. The problem is that crossbar and even more specialized network topologies do not scale well to 1000s of cores. As the number of cores increases interconnection dimensions decrease and create problems imposed by their physical size. Besides the obvious *performance problems*—increased delays and rising power—associated with interconnect scaling, several other *interconnect-related issues* are very troublesome: resistivity degradation, material integration issues, high-aspect ratio, wire coverage, planarity control, leading to a plethora of *reliability-related concerns* (due to electrical, thermal, and mechanical stresses in a multilevel wire stack, as well as cross-coupling and heating). Interconnects must also be robust in the face of failures, and have a lifetime that can span several generations of processor designs. Interconnects must also have efficient power management that scales down power consumption to match the more efficient utilization of the cores. That is why the industry needs on-chip topologies that scale well to future 1000s-core systems.

On one side, structures in the brain are characterized by massive interconnections, but contrary to common thought most of these are local with a quite sparse global interconnect network [10]. On the other side, cortical neurons possess an average of 8,000 (up to a maximum of 100,000) synaptic connections, which differentiate them significantly from present day CMOS gates having an average of four inputs only. Still, future cores might approach neurons' *fan-ins* (*i.e.*, on the order of a few 100s of inputs). With on the order of 10^{10} neurons in the human cortex, and about 10^{14} synaptic connections [11], the brain certainly exhibits a highly optimized interconnection scheme. Nature has always been inspirational in various engineering developments, and it is easy to envisage that it might serve as inspiration for future interconnection networks supporting massively parallel multi-/many-cores due to its reduced power consumption and high reliability [12] (see also [13]).

It is almost two decades ago that Miller [14] clearly stated that semiconductor chips suffer from an impedance matching (or voltage-transforming) crisis which will only be aggravated by scaling: *"Small devices carry small currents and are therefore essentially high-impedance (and low-capacitance) devices, both for outputs and inputs, but electrical transmission is unavoidably low impedance (or high capacitance per unit length)"*—a fact recently re-emphasized by Yablonovitch [15]. In 2000, Sakurai [16] also drew the (now obvious) conclusion that the interconnects—rather than transistors—will be the major factor determining the cost, delay, power, reliability and turn-around time of the future semiconductor industry. Unfortunately, *"the miniaturization of interconnects, unlike transistors, does not enhance their performance"* [17]—as once interconnect scaling challenges are overcome, wires will still degrade delay and increase power consumption (see also [2]).

Interconnect delays and power are crucially important factors, and if we consider an older 1.0µm technology (using Al and SiO_2 dielectric) the transistor delay was 20ps, and the RC delay of a 1mm line was 1ps, while in a projected 32nm technology (using Cu and low-k dielectric) the transistor delay will be 1ps, and the RC delay of a 1mm line will be 250ps [18]. In addition, in the next five years up to 80% of microprocessor power will be consumed by interconnect [19], [20]. This *communication challenge* [21] has received significantly less attention than power/heat [16]–[18], [22], and more recently reliability [23]–[28]. This in spite of the fact that *communication is clearly bridging the power and reliability challenges* [2], as on-chip communications are getting more-and-more power hungry and less-and-less reliable (or equivalently, more-and-more sensitive to noise and variations [29], [30]).

Key important issues for coping with the efficient realization of future tera-scale architectures will be:

- *interconnect topologies*;
- *communication protocols*; and
- *encoding*.

These will require intense and extensive investigation. In this paper only the first of these aspects, namely *interconnect topologies*, will be dealt with. Rent's rule is first discussed followed by a brief description of known computer interconnect (network) topologies which are then compared to the connectivity of the brain. In this research much use is made of Rent's rule [31], [32] and also of a fresh interpretation of Rent's rule reported in [33], [34]. The aim of this research is to identify generic interconnect (network) topologies which could be a better fit for future brain-inspired nano-architectures, looking for hybrid (hierarchical) combination of two network topologies which would allow us to optimally approach (mimic) the brain's connectivity.

2   Rent's Rule

Rent's empirical rule is a power law that describes the interconnectivity of computer hardware components. It was first presented to the technical community in the work of Landman and Russo in 1971 [31]. This work was based on *an interpretation* of Rent's two internal memoranda from 1960 [32] that introduced his methods (and graphical techniques) to illustrate the relationship between attributes of computer hardware components (for details see [33] and [34]).

For over four decades, Rent's rule—a power law used for estimating the average *number of I/O terminals* (N_{IO}) required to connect a (sub-region of a) circuit as a function of the *number of gates* N_{GATES} (or sub-blocks) in that region:

$$N_{IO} = k \cdot N_{GATES}^p \qquad (1)$$

went through stages of neglect and popularity. The inputs to this model are two empirical parameters that are referred to as Rent parameters:

- Rent exponent p ($0 < p < 1$); and
- Rent coefficient k.

Smaller values of the Rent exponent p represent placement optimization of the gates and/or sub-blocks, while $p = 1$ implies that there is no placement optimization whatsoever.

The 1971 paper of Landman and Russo [31] has been referenced extensively in the literature of several scientific fields, including semiconductor circuitry, computer systems, applied mathematics, applied sciences, and semiconductor manufacturing technology. The interested reader should consult [34] for a very detailed list of applications. One of the most important applications of the 1971 work has been the derivation of models which provide *estimates for the wire-length distributions, average wire length, and total interconnection length required to wire chip circuitry correctly* [35]–[42]. Still, Rent's rule has hardly been used in the quickly growing nano-architecture community, except for a handful of contributions. These include a joint discussion of Moore's and Rent's laws [43], followed by detailed analyses of switching requirements and programmable interconnects [44], [45], and more recently [46], [47] by nanoelectronics testability analyses, leading to most intriguing results.

Rent's rule has been recently revisited in [33] and [34], and a new interpretation of Rent's memos was formulated. When referring back to the original memoranda written by Rent [32], Lanzerotti, Fiorenza, and Rand described in detail the contents of Rent's two memoranda as well as his approach. They derived a *historically-equivalent interpretation* of Rent's memos and proved that this is very well suited for today's computer components. In fact, the new interpretation was shown to provide improved wire-length distribution models with better quantitative agreement with the actual measurements and more accurate estimates of wire-length distribution and wire-length requirements for real VLSI designs (when compared to the prior interpretations) [42]. The new historically-equivalent interpretation describes a power law that relates N_{GATES} to the *total number of connections* (N_{CONN}) used in a design:

$$N_{CONN} = k_R \times N_{GATES}^{p_R}. \qquad (2)$$

Using data from six units in the IBM POWER4 core designs, Lanzerotti, Fiorenza, and Rand have plotted on a log-log graph N_{GATES} in each design versus N_{IO}, as well as versus N_{CONN}. A version based on the data reported in Table 1 from [48] (which provides information on the 18 control logic designs used inside the IBM POWER4 IFU), can be seen in Fig. 1. All of these have shown that the new interpretation of Rent's rule might be more accurate than the one presented by Landman and Russo [31], the dispersion being significantly smaller. Average values of k_R and p_R have been determined from the range of parameter pair $\{k_R, p_R\}$ reported in [33]: $k_R = 2.835$ ($1.02 \leq k_R \leq 4.65$) and $p_R = 1.085$ ($0.92 \leq p_R \leq 1.25$).

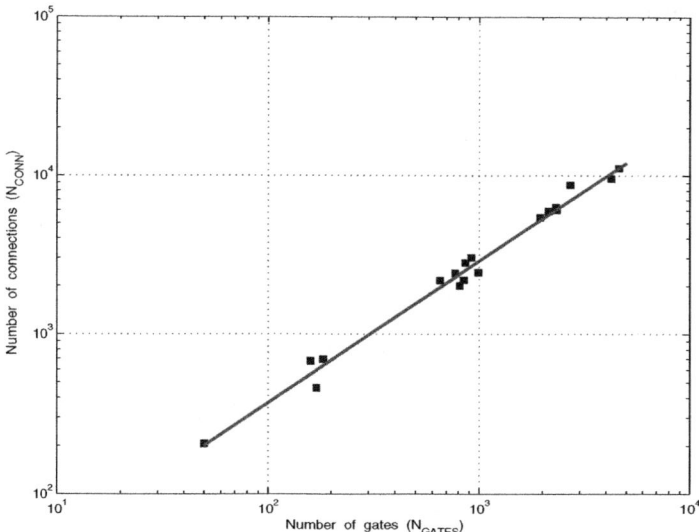

Fig. 1. Number of connections N_{CONN} as a function of the number of gates N_{GATES} for eighteen POWER4 IFU designs (adapted from [48])

If $F_{IN}(i)$ is the fan-in of gate i and F_{IN_avg} is the *average fan-in* (of one gate), the new interpretation of Rent's rule implies that:

$$
\begin{aligned}
N_{CONN} &= \sum_{i=1}^{N_{GATES}} [F_{IN}(i)+1] \\
&= N_{GATES}(F_{IN\_avg}+1)
\end{aligned}
\tag{3}
$$

$$
N_{GATES}(F_{IN\_avg}+1) = k_R \times N_{GATES}^{p_R}
\tag{4}
$$

$$
F_{IN\_avg}+1 = k_R \times N_{GATES}^{p_R-1}.
\tag{5}
$$

These equations suggest that:

- as F_{IN} is (bounded by) a (small) constant, p_R should be (slightly) higher than (but quite close to) 1; while
- as N_{GATES} is increased (towards tera-scale levels), p_R should be (slowly) decreasing towards 1.

In fact things are even simpler (or should we say quite trivial) with this interpretation as $N_{CONN} = (1+F_{IN\_avg}) \times N_{GATES}$, which implies that $p_R = 1$ and $k_R = (1+ F_{IN\_avg})$. Obviously, the *fan-in* is the one and only (very important) parameter in this new interpretation.

Before going further, we should mention that extensions of Rent's rule for accommodating heterogeneous systems [49] as well as to 3D integration [50] have been suggested and investigated.

3   Interconnection Topologies

Many topological characteristics of computer (interconnect) networks have been explored over the years [51]. Their development was effectively stimulated by the evolution of supercomputers. Characteristics such as *degree, diameter, number of links*, and many other cost functions have been computed and reported for network topologies such as: crossbar, binary hypercube, torus, generalized hypercube, spanning bus hypercube, hierarchical cubic network, cube connected cycle, hyper-deBruijn, folded Peterson, hyper-mesh, fat tree, to name but a few. These have long been advocated (and some even used) for (massively) parallel computing and supercomputers. A revived interest has became apparent due to the current evolution of multi-/many-cores processors. The relationships between the *number of processing elements* (also known as network *size*, or equivalently N_{PROC} or N_{GATES} or simply N) and N_{CONN} (also known as connections or links) for various computer network topologies are presented synthetically in Table 1. N_{CONN} are given as a function of N, and a reference to the literature is included also. Normally w is 2 which corresponds to a binary tree type of branching, while larger integers are possible (*e.g.*, $w = 3$ for a ternary tree type of branching, and so on).

Table 1. Connectivity of known computer networks of size N

Network (of size N)	Connections N_{CONN}	Reference
Cube Connected Cycles	$3N/2$	[52]
Spanning Bus Hypercube	$N\log_w N /w$	[53]
Fat tree	$N\log_w N$	[54]
Torus	$N\log_w N$	[51]
Hyper-Mesh	$N\log_w N$	[55]
Generalized Hypercube	$N\log_w N \times (w-1)/2$	[56]
Hierarchical Cubic Network	$N\log_2 N /4 + N/2$	[57]
Hyper-deBruijn	$N\log_2(N - c + 4)/2$	[58]
Binary Hypercube	$N\log_2 N /2$	[59]
Mesh Hypercube	$N(\log_2 N + 3)/2$	[60]
Folded Peterson	$3N\log_{10} N /2$	[61]
Crossbar	$N(N - 1)/2$	[51]

As can be seen, almost all of these have N_{CONN} of the order $O(N\log N)$ with a few exceptions. On one end, the cube connected cycles (CCC) have a connectivity which grows only linearly $O(N)$ with the number of nodes. On the other end, the crossbar (XB), which is one of the "highly cited" in the small but growing nanoarchitecture community, has $(N^2 - N)/2$ connections being $O(N^2)$. A plot of all these networks, including Rent's rule (average as black dotted line, and range as yellow area) can be seen in Fig. 2. It shows that most of the computer networks follow reasonably close the average of Rent's rule, with XB is the only significant exception.

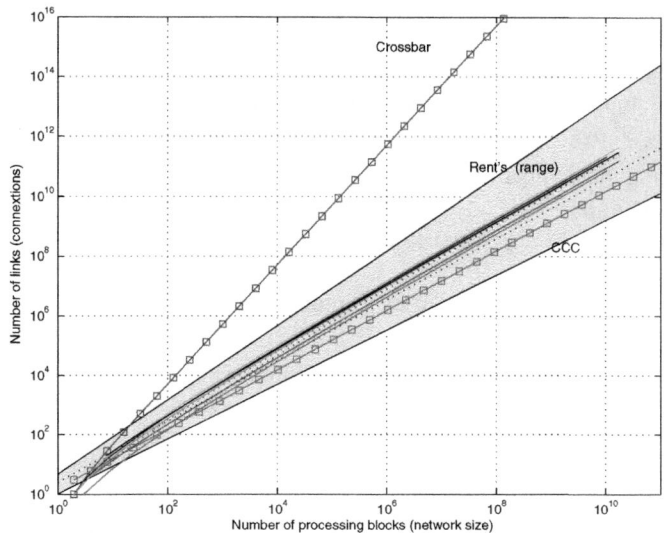

Fig. 2. N_{CONN} versus size for Rent's rule (black dotted line) and its range (yellow) and the network topologies presented in Table 1 (crossbar and cube connected cycles are the two extremes)

Obviously, all these network topologies have to satisfy Rent's rule. Based on the old interpretation (eq. (1) and Fig. 1) Rent exponent should be $p < 1$, while the new interpretation (eq. (2)) implies $p_R = 1$. Apparently there is a contradiction, as the computer networks presented in Table 1 are having between N and N^2 "connections." The explanation is that "connections" here represent in fact *the number of possible connections* the networks could be configured to make, and not *the number of wires*, which is in all cases linear with the number of gates/devices. As an example here, XB has N vertical and N horizontal wires, which give $2N$ (long) wires. On the other hand, XB could have N^2 two-terminal devices, hence the number of "short" wires could be $2N^2$. Still, these networks exhibit *programmability* which should allow them to emulate larger *fan-ins*.

From a VLSI point of view, the occupied *area* would be a much more interesting parameter (than *size* and N_{CONN}), and there are many results presenting detailed layout/area analyses of various network topologies (a fresh reference on these lines being [62]). When going into implementation details one should also keep in mind that in VLSI long wires are normally buffered and maybe multiplexed. Such approaches would depart from a straightforward Rent-based (*number of connections = f(size)*) analysis, and that is why they will not discussed here.

4   On the Brain's Connectivity

By looking at nature, one finds that the mammalian brain is one of (if not) the most efficient network of processing elements currently known to mankind: on the order of 10^{10} processing elements (*i.e.*, neurons) and 10^{14} connections (*i.e.*, synapses) [11], let alone that each synapse has an associated (low-precision) weight. There is no doubt that mammals' brains have evolved to operate efficiently—the unknown(s) being the particular optimization cost(s). A smaller brain will certainly require fewer materials and less energy for 'construction,' 'maintenance,' and 'operation' (*i.e.*, lighter skeletal elements and muscles, and less energy). Obviously, the size of a nervous system could be reduced by:

- reducing the number of neurons (a certain minimum is still required for adequate functioning);
- reducing the average size of neurons (*e.g.*, by reducing their *fan-in* and/or *fan-out*);
- laying out the neurons such as to reduce (optimize) the (total wiring) lengths of their (inter)connections.

At the highest level, the brain is segregated into white (of volume W) and gray (of volume G) matter. White matter contains long axons implementing long-range connections (*i.e.*, global communications) between cortical areas. In human brain, these long axons occupy about 44% of the white matter volume, hence $N_{CONN} \sim 0.44W$ (the element count could be linearly related to volume through density). On the other hand, the gray matter contains cell bodies, dendrites, and axons for information processing and local communication [9]. Axons and dendrites constitute about 60% of the gray matter, which suggest that $N_{CONN} \sim 0.6G$, and also that $N_{NEU} \sim 0.4G$. This indicates a quite *high degree of local communication* (*i.e.*, analogous to the implementation of local area networks). This 60% wiring fraction is probably optimizing the (local) delays by balancing transmission speeds (and also energy) as well as component densities [63]. In the case of neurons, reducing the diameter of axons reduces the speed at which signals travel, hence, increasing their delays. But, this also reduces axon volume, allowing for packing neurons closer together, hence tending to shorten delays. Although such a view of the brain is simplistic, it still captures the fact that the brain could be modeled as a hierarchical communication network consisting of (at least) two (different) sub-networks: a global and a local one.

For various mammalian species, as brain size increases, the volume W of the white matter beneath the cortex tends to increase faster than the volume G of the cortical gray matter according to a power law [64]:

$$\log_{10} W = (1.23 \pm 0.01)\log_{10} G - (1.47 \pm 0.04) . \tag{6}$$

This power scaling law is very strongly supported by experimental data (see Fig. 3):

$$W = 10^{-1.47} \times G^{1.23} . \tag{7}$$

As a first approximation this would imply that $N_{CONN} = k_B \times N^{p_B}$, being *a cortical (equivalent of) Rent's rule* [65], [66], with $k_B = 10^{-1.47}$ and $p_B = 1.23$ (as it relates N_{CONN}, *i.e.*, the number of axons in W, to N_{NEU}, *i.e.*, the number of neurons in G).

Just like the wires connecting components in semiconductor chips, the connections between neurons occupy a substantial fraction of the total volume, and the 'wires' (axons and dendrites) are expensive to operate as dissipating energy during signaling. In fact, *although the human brain represents only 2% of the total body weight, it consumes 20% (going up to 40% for kids) of its resting energy—which is obviously quite expensive!* However, nature has an important advantage over electronic circuits.

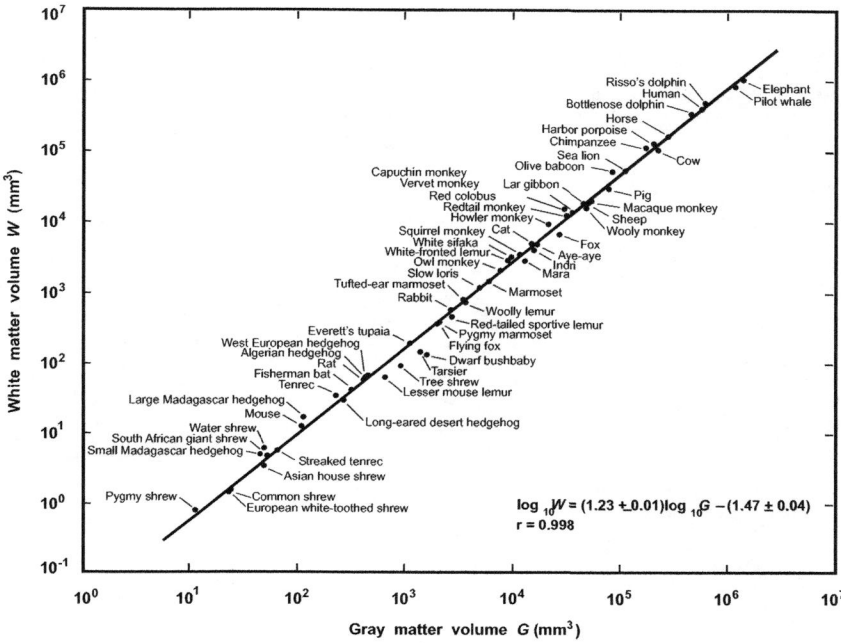

Fig. 3. The volume of white versus the volume of gray matter for 59 mammalian species (see [64])

In mammals' brains components are connected in 3D space, whereas even the most advanced microprocessor use only a small number of layers of planar (2D) wiring. This could be (one of) the reason(s) why wiring occupies 40% to 60% of the whole brain's volume—which is still considerably less than the 90% of today's VLSI chips.

Impressive advances in brain scanning have evolved from positron emission tomography PET (developed about twenty years ago), to magnetic resonance imaging MRI (developed about ten years ago). Variations include *functional* MRI (fMRI), *blood oxygen level-dependent* (BOLD) MRI, and recently *diffusion* MRI. For a fresh review the interested reader should consult [67]. All of these have led to quite precise mapping of brain's connectivity [68] (see also [69]–[71]). Diffusion imaging is an MRI technique introduced in the mid 80's which provides a very sensitive probe of biological tissues architecture [72]. The rapidly developing *diffusion tensor* MRI (DT-MRI) offers means of probing the structural arrangement of tissue at the cellular level, and has been used extensively to estimate the brain connectivity. This technique can also be used to map the path of (white matter) tracts in the brain in vivo non-invasively, using so-called *tractography methods*.

In [73] two new approaches (*flow based connectivity*, and *distance based connectivity*) have been investigated to measure the white matter connectivity in human brains. Both approaches use DT-MRI and can provide numerical measures of brain connectivity. Sebastiani, Pasquale, and Barone [74] presented an alternate approach for quantifying the degree of connectivity between human brain regions from DT-MRI data. In their approach, the connectivity between pairs of white matter points is quantified by *minimizing the weighted length of the curves within white matter connecting the points to each other*. Techniques like the ones just mentioned,

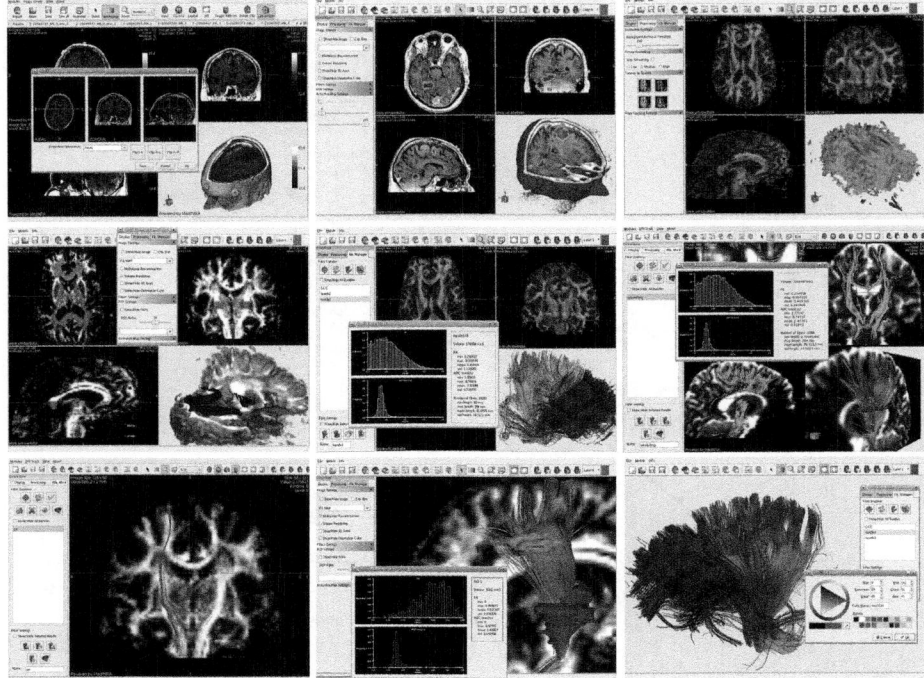

Fig. 4. From left-to-right and top-to-bottom: classical visualization; fMRI activation map; DT-MRI analysis; selection of region of interest (ROI); output statistics; output statistics and DT-MRI track projections; DT-MRI track projections; bundle extraction with ROI; and fiber tracking (generated with MedINRIA, see: http://www-sop.inria.fr/ asclepios/software/MedINRIA/)

or like those detailed in [75], open up the possibility of studying the connectivity of the brain in very great details. To get a feeling of the tremendous advances in this burgeoning field we present some results generated with MedINRIA in Fig. 4 and several fiber tracking views in Fig. 5.

All of these are supporting the somehow unexpected scarcity of the long interconnects in the brain. The detailed map of the full set of neurons and synapses within the nervous system of an organism is known as a connectome (see http://en.wikipedia.org/wiki/Connectome), and the National Institutes of Health has just launched a US\$ 30 million project (http://www.humanconnectomeproject.org/) to map the circuitry of the healthy adult human brain. In fact, another comprehensive attempt to reverse-engineer the mammalian brain (in order to understand brain function and dysfunction through detailed simulations) has already started in 2005. It is known as the Blue Brain Project [76], and impressive simulation results of neocortical column (10,000 biologically accurate individual neurons) have already been presented/published.

From the work of Lanzerotti, Fiorenza, and Rand [33] (based on POWER4 units), we have taken the average values for $k_R = 2.835$ and $p_R = 1.023$. Besides this new interpretation of Rent's rule, we have also included the brain by using $k_B \approx 10^{-1.47}$ and $p_B \approx 1.23$ (as a straightforward interpretation of eq. (7)). A log-log plot is presented in

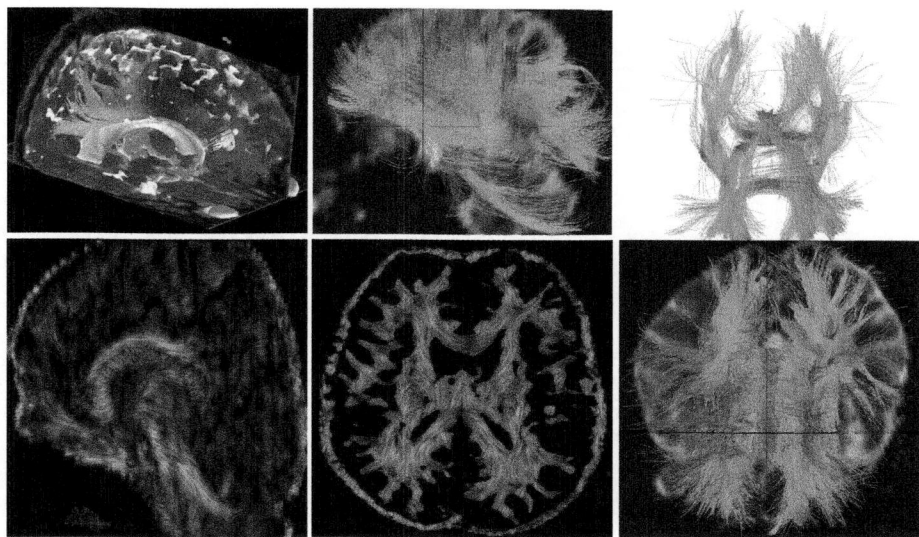

Fig. 5. Several different fiber tracking views

Fig. 6, which shows Rent's average (as a dotted line), Rent's range of values (as a yellow area), together with the brain. This plot shows that:

- *the brain seems to slightly outperform Rent's rule* as falling below Rent's rule average (even below the lowest range of values for small size networks);
- almost all the network topologies follow quite closely Rent's rule average;
- CCC seems to be the strongest contender, with XB apparently the weakest (exhibiting the steepest slope).

Still, the approach we have taken is far from accurate as N_{CONN} would need to include not only the global connections $0.44W$, but also the local ones (in the gray matter), which are about $0.6G$. On top of these, the new interpretation of Rent's rule counts each connection twice (once as input and also as output), hence $N_{\text{CONN}} \sim 2(0.44W + 0.6G)$. This interpretation leads to a more accurate estimate:

$$\log_{10}\left(\frac{N_{\text{CONN}} - 3N_{\text{NEU}}}{0.88}\right) = 1.23\log_{10}\left(\frac{N_{\text{NEU}}}{0.4}\right) - 1.47 \tag{8}$$

$$\log_{10}(N_{\text{CONN}} - 3N_{\text{NEU}}) = 1.23\log_{10}N_{\text{NEU}} - 1.036 \tag{9}$$

$$N_{\text{CONN}} = 0.092N_{\text{NEU}}^{1.23} + 3N_{\text{NEU}}. \tag{10}$$

This hardly changes anything if at all, as the growth of N_{CONN} is still governed by $p_{\text{B}} \approx 1.23$ (eqs. (7) and (10)).

Finally, we have plotted in Fig. 7:

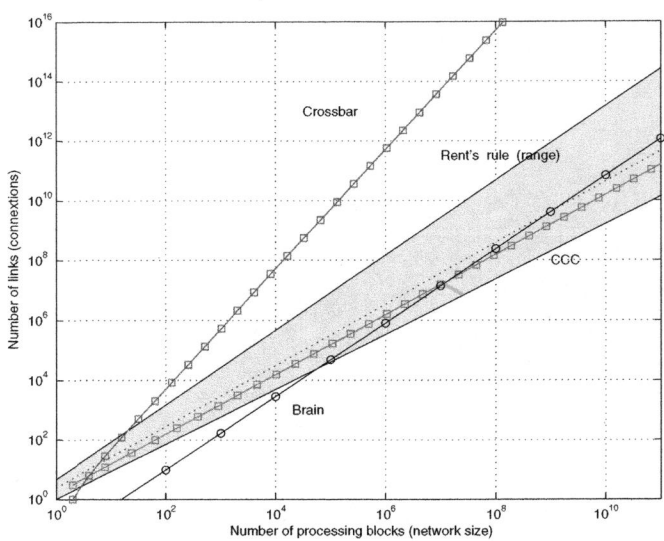

Fig. 6. N_{CONN} versus size (gates or neurons) for Rent's rule average (dotted line), Rent's rule range (yellow), and Brain's connectivity (using eq. (7))

- data for several IBM POWER4 units (also presented in Fig. 2); as well as
- the brain using neurological data for human ($N_{NEU} = 2...3 \times 10^{10}$, $N_{CONN} = 1.5...2.5 \times 10^{14}$), macaque ($N_{NEU} = 2 \times 10^9$, $N_{CONN} = 2.2 \times 10^{13}$), cat ($N_{NEU} = 1.08 \times 10^9$, $N_{CONN} = 9.05 \times 10^{12}$), rat ($N_{NEU} = 6.5 \times 10^7$, $N_{CONN} = 5.45 \times 10^{11}$), and mouse ($N_{NEU} = 1.6...2.6 \times 10^7$, $N_{CONN} = 1...2.2 \times 10^{11}$).

These results show that the brain has a (much) higher connectivity than suggested by eq. (7) or (10). This is due to the fact that eq. (7) considers only the connections in the white matter (*i.e.*, it ignores local connections in the gray matter). Fig. 7 also shows that the brain's average based on neurological data (red dotted line in Fig. 7) is parallel to Rent's average (black dotted line), which is inline with the new interpretation of Rent's rule: the average (black dotted line) corresponds to *fan-in* = 3 (as $k_R = 2.835$), while neurological data (red dotted line) corresponds to *fan-in* = 8000.

Last but not least, we also want to mention here that neural communication and computations are closely entangled with reliability [77]–[84], hence ideally these aspects should be dealt with jointly.

5   Hierarchical Solutions

Inspired by the previous analysis of the brain, we have already investigated the behavior of two-layer hierarchical networks combining two known network topologies: a local and a global one (see [85], [86]). Those studies were not able to identify an optimal solution, but only to rank nine different two-layer hierarchical combinations. In this paper we will expand on those in several ways:

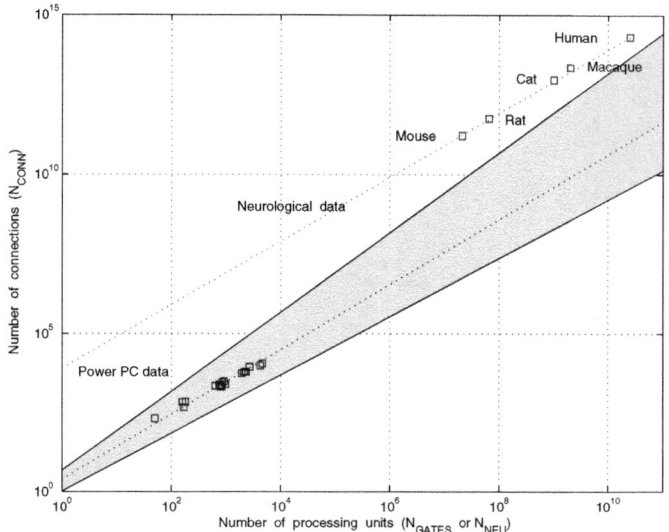

Fig. 7. N_{CONN} versus size for Rent's rule and its range, together with: POWER PC data (blue squares on Rent's average), as well as neurological data (for human, macaque, cat, rat, and mouse)

- We will try to identify an optimal solution.
- We will extend our search to generic networks based on a Rent type of connectivity (instead of a few particular known network topologies, as we have done before).
- We will consider both multiple-wire (bus) connections as well as single-wire connections for the global network.

Hierarchical solutions when applied to emerging many-to-1000s core scenario can be understood as follows. Inside each core the connections form a local network, while among the cores connections form a global network. For example, if the inside-core network (local) is the XB, and if the inter-core network (global) is the CCC, this will represent a CCC-of-XBs two-layer hierarchical network [86]. For any two-layer hierarchical network the total number of connections can be exactly calculated as:

$$N_{CONN} = N_{PROC} \times N_{CONN}(\text{per core}) +$$
$$N_{CONN}(\text{amongst cores}) \times [1 \ldots N_{GATES}(\text{per core})]. \tag{11}$$

Here N_{CONN} is the total number of connections, N_{PROC} is the number of processors (cores) inside a chip, and $N_{CONN}(\text{per core})$ is the number of connections inside a core. This equation has two parts:

- the first part is the sum of all connections representing the local (inside a core) networks; and
- the second part is the sum of all connections forming the global (among the many-/multi-cores) network.

The multiplication factor $[1 \ldots N_{GATES}(\text{per core})]$ represents the number of wires which are used by each of the connections forming the global (inter-core) network.

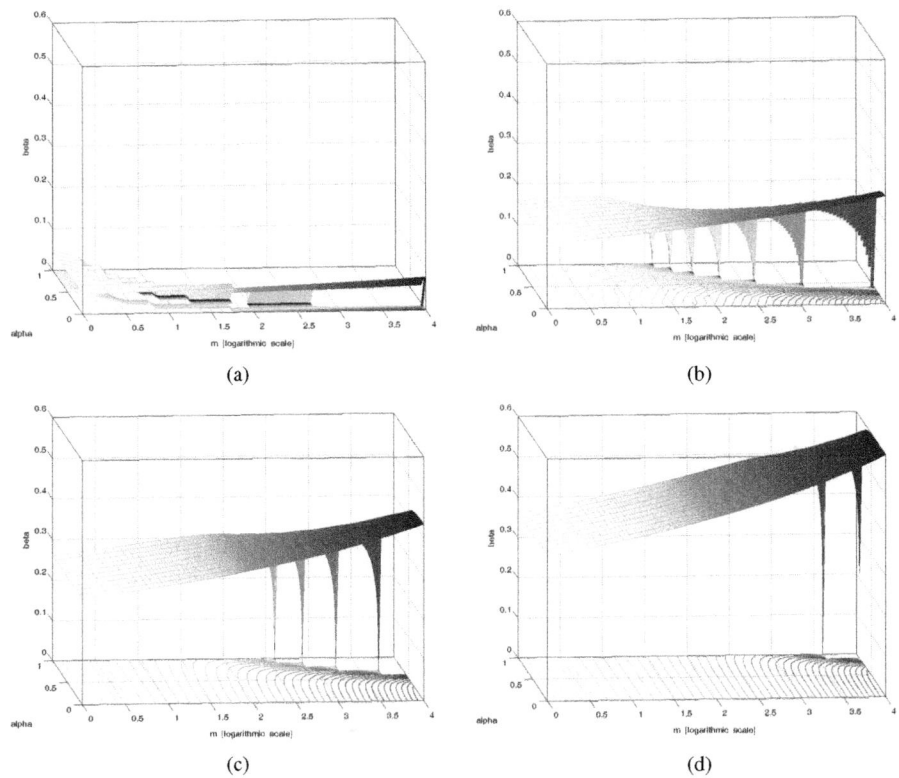

(a) (b) (c) (d)

Fig. 8. β as a function of m and α when m-wide busses are used for the global connections (10^{10} connections), and for average *fan-ins* of: (a) 4 (current VLSI circuits); (b) 40; (c) 400; (d) 4000 (half of the neurons' average *fan-in*)

Hence, if this factor is 1 the global network will use only single-wire connections, while otherwise the global network will be made of multiple-wire (bus) connections.

Let us suppose that N is the total number of gates the chip has, and that m is the number of gates inside each core. This implies that the number of cores is $N_{\text{PROC}} = N/m$ (this number has to be an integer). Additionally, we shall consider that a generic network has a connectivity of the form $X^{1+\alpha}$ (power law similar to Rent's rule), where X is the number of gates and α is between 0 and 1 (with 0 corresponding to a CCC-type of network and 1 corresponding to a XB-type of network). Similarly, the second (global) network will have a connectivity of the form $Y^{1+\beta}$ ($0 \leq \beta \leq 1$). For example, if $\alpha = \beta = 1$ this would mean that the two-layer hierarchical network is a XB-of-XBs, while if $\alpha = \beta = 0$ the two-layer hierarchical network could be a CCC-of-CCCs; a combination like *e.g.* $\alpha = 1$ and $\beta = 0$ would represent a CCC-of-XBs. What would fractional values of α and β represent? Obviously, two networks satisfying $X^{1+\alpha}$ and $Y^{1+\beta}$. And which networks would these be? Here the answer is more nuanced, but one possible implementation is to use random dynamical networks [87] satisfying the above mentioned growth rates.

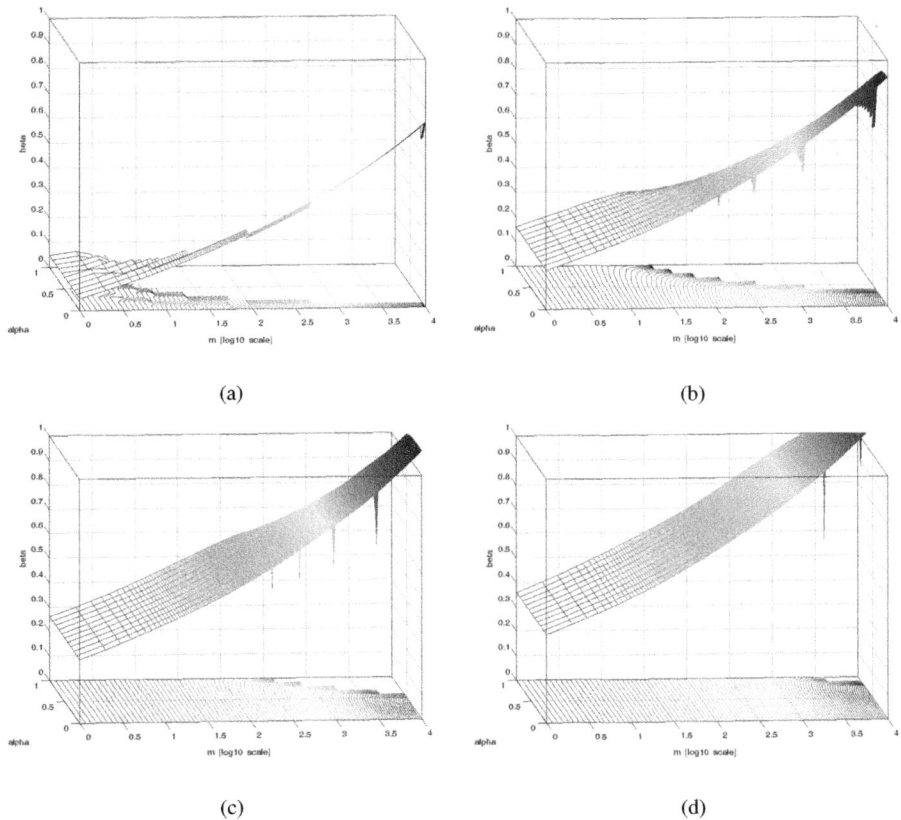

(a)   (b)

(c)   (d)

Fig. 9. β as a function of m and α when single wires are used for the global connections (10^{10} connections), and for average *fan-ins* of: (a) 4 (current VLSI circuits); (b) 40; (c) 400; (d) 4000 (half of the neurons' average *fan-in*)

Using two generic networks, a local one as $m^{1+\alpha}$ and a global one as $(N/m)^{1+\beta}$ in eq. (11), and considering the extreme case when the multiplication factor is N_{GATES}(per core) = m, we obtain:

$$N_{CONN} = (N/m) \times m^{1+\alpha} + (N/m)^{1+\beta} \times m$$
$$= N \times m^{\alpha} + N \times (N/m)^{\beta}. \qquad (12)$$

To explore the implications for α and β, we solve eq. (12) as follows (keep in mind that N_{CONN}/N represents the average *fan-in* F_{IN_avg}):

$$F_{IN\_avg} = N_{CONN}/N = m^{\alpha} + (N/m)^{\beta} \qquad (13)$$

$$\beta = \log(F_{IN\_avg} - m^{\alpha}) / (\log N - \log m). \qquad (14)$$

Eq. (14) is plotted in Fig. 8 for different values of *fan-in* viz. 4, 40, 400 and 4000 (*i.e.*, from CMOS gates going towards neurons) while varying α in steps of 0.1 and m in between 1 and 10,000, with $N = 10^{10}$. Our interest is to identify minimum values for

β for all possible α and m combinations. The most obvious combination is $\alpha = 1$ and $m = fan\text{-}in$, which makes $\beta = 0$, but any $m^\alpha = fan\text{-}in$ will do. $Fan\text{-}in = 4$ is the current standard in VLSI design. Further, *fan-ins* of 40, 400 and 4000 have been simulated for analysis purpose only, and do not represent the CMOS gates available today, but:

- multi-/many-cores (the trend being to move towards 1000s of cores, these would correspond to higher *fan-ins*, say 32, 64, 128, etc.);
- neurons (these are estimated to process about 8000 inputs on average, hence analysis with *fan-in* = 8000 are of interest when trying to understand the brain).

These figures show that for $m^\alpha = fan\text{-}in$ significant improvements are possible as β drops towards zero.

When considering a single-wire (multiplication factor of 1) instead of an m-bit bus, eq. (12) is modified and the solution is:

$$\beta \qquad = [\log(F_{IN\_avg} - m^\alpha) + \log m] / (\log N - \log m). \qquad (15)$$

This equation has been used to plot Fig. 9, for the same conditions as Fig. 8 (*i.e.*, $N = 10^{10}$, $\alpha = 0\ldots1$, $m = 1\ldots10,000$, and *fan-in* = 4, 40, 400, and 4000). These plots show a slightly different picture, with β growing with increasing m. Still, the same α and m combinations ($m^\alpha = fan\text{-}in$) minimize β to $\log(fan\text{-}in^{1/\alpha})/\log(N/fan\text{-}in^{1/\alpha})$.

These results strongly support an organization of the brain in neocortical columns, also known as hypercolums (see http://en.wikipedia.org/wiki/Neocortical_column). If a neuron has a *fan-in* of 8000, it follows that for $\alpha = 1$ (locally fully connected) and $m = 8000$ we have $\beta = 0$. Hence, 100 minicolumns of about 80 neurons each would be a possible solution as $m = 100\times80 = 8000$ (a neocortical column). These numbers are consistent with published data [88]–[90] as well as simulations [76], [91]. Even if each neuron would use 7999 synapses for local (inside the column) connections and only 1 synapse for the global (outside the column) connections, the aggregate bandwidth of a neocortical column would be that of a 8000-wide bus.

6 Conclusions

The new interpretation of Rent's rule allows for a very simple interpretation of connectivity $N_{CONN} = (1+fan\text{-}in)\times N_{GATES}$. Obviously, this translates into $3N_{transistors}$ for classical circuits, or $2N_{devices}$ for any 2-terminal devices, and $8000N_{NEU}$ for the human brain. The major difference is that neurons have a significantly larger (average) *fan-in*, hence a neuron should not be assimilated to a gate, and should be weighted up against a core. In fact, like any cell, a neuron has several *internal networks for information processing*, and classical logic methods—including Rent's rule—have recently been used to analyze their behavior [92].

The results presented in this paper show that two-layer hierarchical networks would be able to mimic brain's connectivity, while particular (*fan-in*, m, α) combinations can significantly reduce the complexity of the global network (β). The tradeoff between the two networks is a highly nonlinear one (see Figs. 8 and 9) allowing for a quite simpler (sparser) global network. One possible solution for m close to *fan-in* is to rely on a highly connected (α close to 1) local network (*e.g.*, XB of size $fan\text{-}in^{1/2}\times fan\text{-}in^{1/2}$), followed by a sparsely connected (β below $\log(\textit{fan-in}^{1/\alpha})/\log(N/\textit{fan-in}^{1/\alpha})$) global network (second layer). Additionally, although apparently wasting on wires, it seems to be much better to use parallel instead of serial connections for the global (inter-core) network. As a very practical example, a 1024-core chip with a *fan-in* of 64 per core, should use 8×8 XBs in the first layer, followed by a serial/ring/CCC network of 64-bit buses in the second layer (between the 1024/64 = 16 crossbars).

Future work should concentrate on detailed estimates of the length of the wires (connections). Results like [93]–[98], should be revisited, and should be followed by thorough re-evaluations of the tradeoffs between *performance-area-power-energy* [99]–[101] versus *reliability* [23]–[29], [102], as well as by investigating these in the context of alternate communication (encoding) techniques, like those discusses in [103]–[105], or by photonic ones [106]–[108].

Acknowledgments. This research was partly supported by the Research Affairs of the UAE University (under contracts no. 03-01-9-11/07 and no. 01-02-9-11/07), partly by an EPSRC project *Biologically Inspired Architecture for Spiking Neural Networks in Hardware*, and partly by a British Council PMI2 Connect grant *Brain-inspired Interconnects for Nanoelecronics*.

This document is an output from the PMI2 Project funded by the UK Department for Innovations, Universities and Skills (DIUS) for the benefit of the United Arab Emirates Higher Education Sector and the UK Higher Education Sector. The views expressed are not necessarily those of DIUS, nor British Council.

Many thanks to D. Hammerstrom for inviting one of us (V. Beiu) to the *NSF Architectures for Silicon Nanoelectronics and Beyond: A Workshop to Chart Research Directions* (Portland State University, Portland OR, USA, Sep. 13-14, 2005, http://web.cecs.pdx.edu/~strom/nsf_workshop/). This has made us aware of paper [64], which represents the starting point of the results presented here.

References

1. International Technology Roadmap for Semiconductors (ITRS), 2007 Edition and 2008 Upadate, SEMATECH, Austin, TX, USA (2009), http://public.itrs.net/
2. Cavin, R.K., Zhirnov, V.V., Herr, D.C., Avila, A., Hutchby, J.: Research directions and challenges in nanoelectronics. J. Nanoparticle Res. 8, 841–858 (2006)
3. Santo, B., Adee, S.: Multicore made simple. IEEE Spectrum 46, 32–36 (2009)
4. Ye, T.T., De Micheli, G.: Physical planning for on-chip multiprocessor networks and switching fabrics. In: Proc. Intl. Conf. Appl.-Specific Syst. Arch. & Proc. (ASAP 2003), Hague, The Netherlands, June 24-26, pp. 97–107 (2003)
5. Beiu, V., Rückert, U., Roy, S., Nyathi, J.: On nanoelectronic architectural challenges and solutions. In: Proc. Intl. Conf. Nanotech. (IEEE-NANO 2004), Munich, Germany, August 17-19, pp. 628–631 (2004)
6. Reed, D.: Multicore: Let's not focus on the present. Proc. Intl. Super Comp. Conf. (SC 2007), Reno, NV, USA, November 10-16 (2007),
http://gamma.cs.unc.edu/SC2007/DanReedSlides.pdf
7. Asanovic, K., Bodik, R., Demmel, J., Keaveny, T., Keutzer, K., Kubiatowicz, J., Morgan, N., Patterson, D., Sen, K., Wawrzynek, J., Wessel, D., Yelick, K.: A view of the parallel computing landscape. Comm. ACM 52, 56–67 (2009)

8. Kolodny, A.: Networks on Chip – Keeping up with Rent's rule and Moore's law. In: Proc. Intl. Workshop Syst.-Level Intercon. Predict. (SLIP 2007), Austin, TX, USA, March 17-18, p. 55 (2007),
http://www.sliponline.org/SLIP07/presentations/4A_Kolodny.pdf

9. Lee, H.G., Chang, N., Ogras, U.Y., Marculescu, R.: On-chip communication architecture exploration: A quantitative evaluation of point-to-point, bus, and network-on-chip approaches. ACM Trans. Design Autom. Electr. Syst. 12, art. 23, 1–20 (2007)

10. Wen, Q., Chklovskii, D.B.: Segregation of the brain into gray and white matter: A design minimizing conduction delays. PLoS Comp. Biol. 1, 617–630 (2005)

11. Azevedo, F.A.C., Carvalho, L.R.B., Grinberg, L.T., Farfel, J.M., Ferretti, R.E.L., Leite, R.E.P., Jacob Filho, W., Lent, R., Herculano-Houzel, S.: Equal numbers of neuronal and nonneuronal cells make the human brain an isometrically scaled-up primate brain. J. Comp. Neurol. 513, 532–541 (2009)

12. Jóźwiak, L.: Life-inspired systems and their quality-driven design (keynote paper). In: Grass, W., Sick, B., Waldschmidt, K. (eds.) ARCS 2006. LNCS, vol. 3894, pp. 1–16. Springer, Heidelberg (2006)

13. Wyss Institute for Biologically Inspired Engineering,
http://wyss.harvard.edu/

14. Miller, D.A.B.: Optical for low-energy communication inside digital processors: Quantum detectors, sources, and modulators as efficient impedance converters. Optics Lett. 14, 146–148 (1989)

15. Yablonovitch, E.: The impedance-matching predicament: A hurdle in the race toward nano-electronics. In: Center for NanoScience (CeNS) Workshop: Emerging Nanosystems – From Quantum Manipulations to Nanobiomachines, Venice, Italy, p. 20 (September 2006), http://www.cens.de/uploads/media/CeNS_proceedings06.pdf

16. Sakurai, T.: Design challenges for 0.1μm and beyond. In: Proc. Asia & South Pacific Design Autom. Conf (ASP-DAC 2000), Tokyo, Japan, pp. 553–558 (January 2000)

17. Davis, J.A., Venkatesan, R., Kaloyeros, A., Beylansky, M., Souri, S.J., Banerjee, K., Saraswat, K.C., Rahman, A., Reif, R., Meindl, J.D.: Interconnect limits on gigascale integration (GSI) in the 21st century. Proc. IEEE 89, 305–324 (2001)

18. Davis, J.A., Meindl, J.: Interconnect Technology and Design for Gigascale Integration. Kluwer, Dordrecht (2003)

19. Magen, N., Kolodny, A., Weiser, U., Shamir, N.: Interconnect-power dissipation in a microprocessor. In: Proc. Intl. Workshop Syst.-Level Intercon. Predict (SLIP 2004), Paris, France, pp. 7–13 (February 2004)

20. Intel, Intel demonstrates industry's first 32nm chip and next-generation Nehalem microprocessor architecture, September 18 (2007),
http://www.intel.com/pressroom/archive/releases/2007/20070918corp_a.htm

21. Meindl, J.D.: Beyond Moore's law: The interconnect era. Comp. in Sci. & Eng. 5, 20–24 (2003)

22. Dally, W.J.: The end of denial architecture and the rise of throughput computing. In: Intl. Symp. Asynch. Circ. & Syst. (ASYNC 2009), Chapel Hill, NC, USA, May 17-20 (2009),
http://asyncsymposium.org/async2009/slides/dally-async2009.pdf, Also presented at HiPC 2009 and DAC 2009,
http://videos.dac.com/46th/wedkey/dally.html

23. Kuo, W.: Challenges related to reliability in nano electronics. IEEE Trans. Reliab. 55, 569–570 (2006)

24. Beiu, V., Ibrahim, W.: On computing nano-architectures using unreliable nano-devices. In: Lyshevski, S.E. (ed.) Handbook of Nano and Molecular Electronics, ch. 12, pp. 12.1–49. Taylor & Francis, London (2007)

25. Heins, M.: In the eye of the DFM/DFY storm. EE Times, May 25 (2007), http://www.eetimes.com/showArticle.jhtml?articleID=199702741

26. McKee, S.A. (ed.): Special Issue on Reliable Computing. ACM J. Emerg. Tech. Comp. Syst. 3 (July 2007)

27. Jeng, S.-L., Lu, J.-C., Wang, K.: A review of reliability research on nanotechnology. IEEE Trans. Reliab. 56, 401–410 (2007)

28. Lau, C., Orailoglu, A., Roy, K. (eds.): Special Issue on Nano-electronic Circuits and Nano-architectures. IEEE Trans. Circ. & Syst. I 54 (November 2007)

29. Beiu, V., Ibrahim, W., Makki, R.Z.: On wires driven by a few electrons. In: Proc. Intl. Northeast Workshop Circ. & Syst. (NEWCAS 2009), Toulouse, France, June 28-July 1, pp. 1–4 (2009); art. 5290448

30. Beiu, V., Ibrahim, W.: On CMOS circuit reliability from the MOSFETs and the input vectors. In: Proc. Intl. Conf. Dependable Syst. & Nets. (DSN 2009), Estoril, Lisbon, Portugal, June 29-July 2 (2009) (in press), http://spiderman-2.laas.fr/WDSN09/WDSN09_files/Texts/WDSN09-2-2-Beiu.pdf

31. Landman, B.S., Russo, R.L.: On a pin versus block relationship for partitions of logic graphs. IEEE Trans. Comp. C-20, 1469–1479 (1971)

32. Rent, E.F.: Microminiature packaging—Logic block to pin ratio. IBM Memoranda, November 28-December 12 (1960) (see also [34])

33. Lanzerotti, M.Y., Fiorenza, G., Rand, R.A.: Interpretation of Rent's rule for ultralarge-scale integrated circuit designs, with an application to wirelength distribution models. IEEE Trans. VLSI Syst. 12, 1330–1347 (2004)

34. Lanzerotti, M.Y., Fiorenza, G., Rand, R.A.: Microminiature packaging and integrated circuitry: The work of E. F. Rent, with an application to on-chip interconnection. IBM J. R&D 49, 777–803 (2005)

35. Donath, W.E.: Placement and average interconnection lengths of computer logic. IEEE Trans. Circ. & Syst. 26, 272–277 (1979)

36. Bakoglu, H.B.: Circuits, Interconnections, and Packaging for VLSI. Addison-Wesley, Reading (1990)

37. Davis, J.A., De, V.H., Meindl, J.D.: A stochastic wire-length distribution for gigascale integration (GSI)—Part I: Derivation and validation. IEEE Trans. Electr. Dev. 45, 580–589 (1998)

38. Davis, J.A., De, V.H., Meindl, J.D.: A stochastic wire-length distribution for gigascale integration (GSI)—Part II: Applications to clock frequency, power dissipation, and chip size estimation. IEEE Trans. Electr. Dev. 45, 590–597 (1998)

39. Christie, P., Stroobandt, D.: The interpretation and application of Rent's rule. IEEE Trans. VLSI Syst. 8, 639–648 (2000)

40. Dambre, J., Stroobandt, D., Campenhout, J.V.: Toward the accurate prediction of placement wire length distributions in VLSI circuits. IEEE Trans. VLSI Syst. 12, 339–348 (2004)

41. Das, S., Chandrakasan, A.P., Reif, R.: Calibration of Rent's rule models for three-dimensional integrated circuits. IEEE Trans. VLSI Syst. 12, 359–366 (2004)

42. Lanzerotti, M.Y., Fiorenza, G., Rand, R.A.: Predicting interconnect requirements in ultra-large-scale integrated control logic circuitry. In: Proc. Intl. Workshop Syst. Level Interconn. Predict. (SLIP 2005), San Francisco, CA, USA, pp. 43–50 (April 2005)

43. Otten, R.H.J.M., Stravers, P.: Challenges in physical chip design. In: Proc. Intl. Conf. Comp. Aided Design (ICCAD 2000), San Jose, CA, USA, pp. 84–91 (November 2000)

44. DeHon, A.: Rent's rule based switching requirements. In: Proc. Syst.-Level Intercon. Predict. Workshop (SLIP 2001), Sonoma, CA, USA, pp. 197–204 (March 2001)

45. DeHon, A.: Unifying mesh- and tree-based programmable interconnect. IEEE Trans. VLSI Syst. 12, 1051–1065 (2004)

46. Kumar, A., Tiwari, S.: Testing and defect tolerance: A Rent's rule based analysis and implications on nanoelectronics. In: Proc. Intl. Symp. Defect & Fault Tolerance VLSI Syst. (DFT 2004), Ithaca, NY, USA, pp. 280–288 (October 2004)

47. Tiwari, S., Kumar, A., Liu, C.C., Lin, H., Kim, S.K., Silva, H.: Electronics at nanoscale: Fundamental and practical challenges, and emerging directions. In: Proc. Conf. Emerg. Tech. – Nanoelectr. (NanoSingapore 2006), Singapore, pp. 481–486 (January 2006)

48. Lanzerotti, M.Y., Fiorenza, G., Rand, R.A.: Impact of interconnect length changes on effective materials properties (dielectric constant). In: Austin, T.X. (ed.) Proc. Intl. Workshop Syst. Level Interconn. Predict. (SLIP 2007), Austin, TX, USA, pp. 73–80 (March 2007)

49. Zarkesh-Ha, P., Davis, J.A., Loh, W., Meindl, J.D.: On a pin versus gate relationship for heterogeneous systems: Heterogeneous Rent's rule. In: Proc. Intl. Custom Integr. Circ. Conf (CICC 1998), Santa Clara, CA, USA, May 11-14, pp. 93–96 (1998)

50. Joyner, J.W., Zarkesh-Ha, P., Meindl, J.D.: Global interconnect design in a three-dimensional system-on-a-chip. IEEE Trans. VLSI Syst. 4, 367–372 (2004)

51. Dally, W.J., Towels, B.: Principles and Practices of Interconnection Networks. Elsevier/Morgan Kaufmann, San Mateo, CA, USA (2004)

52. Preparata, F.P., Vuillemin, J.: The cube-connected cycles: A versatile network for parallel computation. Comm. ACM 24, 300–309 (1981)

53. Wittie, L.D.: Communication structures for large networks of microcomputers. IEEE Trans. Comp. 30, 264–273 (1981)

54. Leiserson, C.E.: Fat-trees: Universal networks for hardware-efficient supercomputing. IEEE Trans. Comp. 34, 892–901 (1985)

55. Szymanski, T.: Hypermeshes optical interconnection networks for parallel computing. J. Par. & Distrib. Comp. 26, 1–23 (1995)

56. Bhuyan, L.N., Agrawal, D.P.: Generalized hypercube and hyperbus structures for a computer network. IEEE Trans. Comp. 33, 323–333 (1984)

57. Ghose, K., Desai, K.R.: Hierarchical cubic networks. IEEE Trans. Comp. 6, 427–435 (1995)

58. Ganesan, E., Pradhan, D.K.: The hyper-deBruijn networks: Scalable versatile architecture. IEEE Trans. Par. & Distrib. Syst. 4, 962–978 (1993)

59. Saad, Y., Schultz, M.H.: Topological properties of hypercubes. IEEE Trans. Comp. 37, 867–872 (1988)

60. Louri, A., Sung, H.: A scalable optical hypercube-based interconnection network for massively parallel computing. Appl. Optics 33, 7588–7598 (1994)

61. Ohring, S., Das, S.K.: Folded Petersen cube networks: New competitors for the hypercubes. IEEE Trans. Par. & Distrib. Syst. 7, 151–168 (1996)

62. Balkan, A.O., Qu, G., Vishkin, U.: Mesh-of-trees and alternative interconnection networks for single-chip parallelism. IEEE Trans. VLSI Syst. 17, 1419–1432 (2009)

63. Laughlin, S.B., Sejnowski, T.J.: Communication in neural networks. Science 301, 1870–1874 (2003)

64. Zhang, K., Sejnowski, T.J.: A universal scaling law between gray matter and white matter of cerebral cortex. Proc. Natl. Acad. Sci. USA 97, 5621–5626 (2000)

65. Beiu, V., Amer, H., McGinnity, M.: On global communications for nano-architectures –
    Brain versus Rent's rule. In: Proc. Conf. Design Circ. & ICs (DCIS 2007), Seville, Spain,
    pp. 305–310 (November 2007)
66. Hammerstrom, D.: Biologically inspired nanoarchitectures. In: Computer-Aided Network
    Design Workshop (CAND 2007), Long Beach, CA, USA (September 2007)
67. Le Bihan, D.: The 'wet mind': Water and functional neuroimaging (introductory review).
    Phys. Med. and Biol. 52(7), R57–R90 (2007)
68. Jirsa, V.K., McIntosh, A.R. (eds.): Handbook of Brain Connectivity. Springer:
    Complexity (Understanding Complex Systems), Berlin (2007)
69. Le Bihan, D., Urayama, S., Aso, T., Hanakawa, T., Fukuyama, H.: Direct and fast
    detection of neuronal activation in the human brain with diffusion MRI. Proc. Natl. Acad.
    Sci. USA 103, 8263–8268 (2006)
70. Achard, S., Salvador, R., Whitcher, B., Suckling, J., Bullmore, E.: A resilient, low-
    frequency, small-world human brain functional network with highly connected
    association cortical hubs. J. Neurosci. 26, 63–72 (2006)
71. Achard, S., Bullmore, E.: Efficiency and cost of economical brain functional networks.
    PLoS Comput. Biol. 3, 174–183 (2007)
72. Merboldt, K.D., Hanckie, W., Frahm, J.: Self-diffusion NMR imaging using stimulated
    echoes. J. Magnetic Resonance 64, 479–486 (1985)
73. O'Donnell, L., Haker, S., Westin, C.-F.: New approaches to estimation of white matter
    connectivity in diffusion tensor MRI: Elliptic PDEs and geodesics in a tensor-warped
    space. In: Dohi, T., Kikinis, R. (eds.) MICCAI 2002. LNCS, vol. 2488, pp. 459–466.
    Springer, Heidelberg (2002)
74. Sebastiani, G., Pasquale, F., Barone, P.: Quantifying human brain connectivity from
    diffusion tensor MRI. J. Math. Imag. & Vision 25, 227–244 (2006)
75. Prados, E., Soatto, S., Lenglet, C., Pons, J.-P., Wotawa, N., Deriche, R., Faugeras, O.:
    Control theory and fast marching techniques for brain connectivity mapping. In: Proc.
    Intl. Conf. Comp. Vis. & Pattern Recog. (CVPR 2006), New York, NY, USA, vol. 1, pp.
    1076–1083 (June 2006)
76. The Blue Brain Project, http://bluebrain.epfl.ch/
77. Bialek, W., Rieke, F.: Reliability and information transmission in spiking neurons.
    Trends Neurosci. 15, 428–434 (1992)
78. Stevens, C.F.: Neuronal communication. Cooperativity of unreliable neurons. Current
    Biol. 4, 268–269 (1994)
79. Smetters, D.K., Zador, A.: Synaptic transmission: Noisy synapses and noisy neurons.
    Current Biol. 6, 1217–1218 (1996)
80. Lisman, J.E.: Bursts as a unit of neural information: Making unreliable synapses reliable.
    Trends Neurosci. 20, 38–43 (1997)
81. Zador, A.: Impact of synaptic unreliability on the information transmitted by spiking
    neurons. J. Neurophysiol. 79, 1219–1229 (1998)
82. Manwani, A., Koh, C.: Detecting and estimating signals over noisy and unreliable
    synapses: Information-theoretic analysis. Neural Comp. 13, 1–33 (2001)
83. Levy, W.B., Baxter, R.A.: Energy-efficient neuronal computation via quantal synaptic
    failures. J. Neurosci. 22, 4746–4755 (2002)
84. Chklovskii, D.B.: Exact solution for the optimal neuronal layout problem. Neural
    Comp. 16, 2067–2078 (2004)
85. Madappuram, B.A.M., Beiu, V., Kelly, P.M., McDaid, L.J.: On Brain-inspired
    Connectivity and Hybrid Network Topologies. In: Proc. Intl. Symp. Nanoscale Archs.
    (NanoArch 2008), Anaheim, CA, USA, pp. 54–61 (June 2008)

86. Beiu, V., Madappuram, B.A.M., McGinnity, M.: On Brain-inspired Hybrid Topologies for Nano-architectures — A Rent's Rule Approach. In: Proc. Intl. Conf. Embedded Comp. Syst. (IC-SAMOS 2008), Samos, Greece, pp. 33–40 (July 2008)

87. Teuscher, C., Gulbahce, N., Rohlf, T.: Assessing random dynamical network architectures for nanoelectronics. In: Proc. Intl. Symp. Nanoscale Archs. (NanoArch 2008), Anaheim, CA, USA, pp. 16–23 (June 2008)

88. Karbowski, J.: Optimal wiring principle and plateaus in the degree of separation for cortical neurons. Phys. Rev. Lett. 86, 3674–3677 (2001)

89. Johansson, C.: Towards cortex isomorphic attractor neural networks. Lic. Thesis, School Comp. Sci. & Comm., Royal Inst. Tech. (KTH), Stockholm, Sweden (June 2004), http://www.nada.kth.se/~cjo/publications/lic.pdf

90. Silver, R., Boahen, K., Grillner, S., Kopell, N., Olsen, K.L.: Neurotech for neuroscience: Unifying concepts, organizing principles, and emerging tools. J. Neurosci. 27, 11807–11819 (2007)

91. Djurfeldt, M., Lundqvist, M., Johansson, C., Rehn, M., Ekeberg, Ö., Lansner, A.: Brain-scale simulation of the neocortex on the IBM Blue Gene/L supercomputer. IBM J. R& D (Sp. Issue Appls. of Massively Par. Syst.) 52, 31–41 (2008)

92. Reda, S.: Using circuit structural analysis techniques for network in system biology. In: Proc. Intl. Workshop Syst.-Level Intercon. Predict. (SLIP 2009), San Francisco, CA, USA, July 26-27, pp. 37–44 (2009)

93. von Neumann, J.: The Computer and the Brain. Yale Univ. Press, New Haven (1958)

94. Hammerstrom, D.: The connectivity analysis of simple associations –or– How many connections do we need? In: Anderson, D.Z. (ed.) Neural Info. Proc. Syst. (NIPS 1987), pp. 338–347. Amer. Inst. of Physics (IoP), Denver (1988)

95. Vitányi, P.M.B.: Locality, communication, and interconnect length in multicomputers. SIAM J. Comput. 17, 659–672 (1988)

96. Fernández, A., Efe, K.: Bounds on the VLSI layout complexity of homogeneous product networks. In: Proc. Intl. Symp. Parallel Archs., Algs. & Networks (ISPAN 1994), Kanazawa, Japan, pp. 41–48 (December 1994)

97. Legenstein, R.A.: The wire-length complexity of neural networks. PhD dissertation, Inst. Theor. Comp. Sci., Graz Univ. Tech., Graz, Austria (November 2001), http://www.igi.tugraz.at/legi/psfiles/legi_diss.pdf

98. Kyogoku, T., Inoue, J., Nakashima, H., Uezono, T., Okada, K., Masu, K.: Wire length distribution model considering core utilization for system on chip. In: Proc. Intl. Symp. VLSI (ISVLSI 2005), Tampa, FL, USA, pp. 276–277 (May 2005)

99. Ho, R.: On-chip wires: Scaling and efficiency. PhD dissertation, EE Dept., Stanford Univ., Stanford, CA, USA (August 2003), http://www-vlsi.stanford.edu/papers/rh_thesis.pdf

100. Ho, R.: Interconnection technologies. In: Workshop on On- and Off-Chip Interconn. Nets for Multicore Syst. (OCIN 2006), Stanford, CA, USA (December 2006), http://www.ece.ucdavis.edu/~ocin06/talks/ho.pdf

101. Burleson, W., Maheshwari, A.: VLSI Interconnects: A Design Perspective. Elsevier/Morgan Kaufman, San Francisco, CA, USA (in progress); Burleson, W.: Statistical design issues and tradeoffs in on-chip interconnects. In: Intl. Forum Appl.-specific Multi-Proc. SoC (MPSoC 2006), Estes Park, CO, USA (August 2006), http://www.mpsoc-forum.org/2006/slides/Burleson.pdf

102. Joachim, C., Ratner, M.A.: Molecular electronics: Some views on transport junctions and beyond. Proc. Natl. Acad. Sci. USA 102, 8801–8808 (2005)

103. Heimburg, T., Jackson, A.D.: On soliton propagation in biomembranes and nerves. Proc. Natl. Acad. Sci. USA 102, 9790–9795 (2005)
104. Ricketts, D.S., Li, X., Sun, N., Woo, K., Ham, D.: On the self-generation of electrical soliton pulses. IEEE J. Solid-State Circ. 42, 1657–1668 (2007)
105. Tuffy, F., McDaid, L.J., Kwan, V.W., Alderman, J., McGinnity, T.M., Santos, J.A., Kelly, P.M., Sayers, H.: Inter-neuron communication strategies for spiking neural networks. Neurocomp. 71, 30–44 (2007)
106. Beausoleil, R.G., Kuekes, P.J., Snider, G.S., Wang, S.-Y., Williams, R.S.: Nanoelectronic and nanophotonic interconnect. Proc. IEEE 96, 230–247 (2008)
107. Johnson, R.C.: HP targets silicon phonics. EE Times, May 14 (2008), http://www.eetimes.com/showArticle.jhtml?articleID=207800143
108. Merritt, R.: Potholes seen on road to silicon photonics. EE Times, January 28 (2009), http://www.eetimes.com/showArticle.jhtml?articleID=212903357

Advanced Packet Segmentation and Buffering Algorithms in Network Processors

Daniel Llorente, Kimon Karras, Thomas Wild, and Andreas Herkersdorf

Lehrstuhl für Integrierte Systeme
Technische Universität München
Munich, Germany
{daniel.llorente,kkarras,thomas.wild,herkersdorf}@tum.de

Abstract. Memory subsystem performance is rapidly becoming an important bottleneck in network processing, partially because packets must be segmented to prevent memory fragmentation. Depending on segment length, accesses to memory are short and thus inefficient or long and hence storing efficiency drops. Besides, segments have one-to-one associated descriptors which require a large control buffer and high management effort to update them. Our contribution consists in allowing multiple segment lengths for packet segmentation even for a single packet. We propose two new segmentation algorithms that ensure a minimum number of segments, so as to achieve maximum packet throughput, while maintaining a high level of memory efficiency together with reducing the amount of control resources needed. Both algorithms are evaluated using a variety of packet traces and realistic system configurations in order to determine how different choices impact the performance and the storage efficiency. The findings were then used to realize the SmartMem Buffer Manager in VHDL, which was tested in a Virtex-4 FPGA and its performance measured to verify the simulation results and validate the higher performance of the proposed algorithms.

Keywords: Network Processing, Memory Management, Segmentation.

1 Introduction

So far Network Processors (NPs) have been used mostly in applications where only the packet header was retrieved/written-back from/to the packet memory, like IP forwarding. However, the advent of more complex Deep Packet Inspection (DPI) applications, like virus scanning and packet encryption, raises the bar regarding memory system performance since now the entire packet must be read from and written to the memory for processing. To provide enough memory bandwidth, NP vendors include multiple DRAM and SRAM channels in commercial NPs, a solution which significantly raises system complexity and thus cost. Moreover, the current approach will prove insufficient in the future since memory speedup is not at par with network throughput advances.

The extended processing increases the buffer storage requirements since data stays in the NP for a longer period of time. When taking into account additional phenomena

P. Stenström (Ed.): Transactions on HiPEAC IV, LNCS 6760, pp. 334–353, 2011.
© Springer-Verlag Berlin Heidelberg 2011

such as port contention and queuing delays we end up with a very large buffer which can only be implemented economically using dynamic memory, typically commodity DDR2-SDRAM or more efficient but costlier Reduced Latency DRAM. While this solves the size issue, the limited throughput and higher access latency of such memories reduces the system's performance. Hence, additional methods to enhance memory performance are needed.

Multithreading support and ad hoc caches partially hide DRAM latency by allowing parallel task execution, as do multiple level memory subsystems which combine SRAM and DRAM. Mudigonda et al. [1] reviewed several of these methods and concluded that the minimal set of mechanisms should include at least multithreading and one level of caching. However, in contrast to general purpose processors, the specifics of NP's application generate a low cache-hit percentage due to low spatial and temporal row locality. Thus the beneficial impact of caches is mitigated.

The different sorts of traffic have different processing and Quality-of-Service requirements, which makes packets to leave in a different order than they arrived. Hence the buffer cannot be managed using simple structures like FIFO queues and stacks that only output data in a specific order. Traffic cannot be either stored on the fly because variable-length packets may leave small free spaces behind after packet transmission. This problem is known as external fragmentation and occurs whenever incoming large packets cannot be accommodated in the memory because free space is fragmented. In order to prevent fragmentation loss, NPs organize the buffer in fixed-size segments, which successfully prevents fragmentation but cannot simultaneously achieve high storing efficiency and allow for long and efficient data burst to the memory. Besides, having a large number of segments implies provisioning the corresponding control buffer size and straining the memory interface constantly updating control. Moreover, as control size requirements grow, the use of DRAM for control data buffering becomes necessary, which further reduces the system performance.

We propose two new segmentation algorithms using multiple segment sizes for packet segmentation in NPs. These algorithms bring a considerable improvement in system performance without loss in storing efficiency. This is because the algorithms enable the use of long segments where possible thus allowing for more efficient bus and memory accessing while still using short segments for small data fragments. The multiple segment pools are resized dynamically allocating memory blocks upon demand so no external fragmentation occurs. What is more, the lower number of segments per packet leads to strong reductions in the size of control data as well as additional performance increases due to less control management effort. We have tested these algorithms using multiple levels of abstraction, each further refining the selection of segment sizes to explore the ones that better adapt to the packet length pattern found in nowadays networks.

This paper is based on the work presented in the SAMOS IC VIII Conference [2], where our algorithms were first introduced. It has been extended to include the SmartMem Buffer Manager, a hardware prototype that implements the most efficient segmentation algorithms found in terms of performance and storing efficiency. Memory is administrated using an advanced memory management mechanism based on Bitmaps, which further reduces control memory requirements while accelerating control operations. We discuss the accelerator architecture, its implementation as well as its performance results running on an FPGA device, which demonstrate that multiple-size packet segmentation clearly increases packet throughput.

The paper is structured as follows presenting an overview of the state-of-the-art. In section 3, we describe the two segmentation algorithms proposed and in section 4, we show the methodology followed during our investigations and the models utilized therein. In section 5 we use a two level simulation approach to provide a comprehensive investigation of several configuration parameters that affect algorithm performance. Section 6 describes the implementation of a module which utilizes the described concepts and its achieved performance. Finally section 7 summarizes our findings and provides pointers for future research.

2 Previous Work

The preferred segment size in the first generation of commercial NPUs like Intel's IXP12xx series [3], Hifn's PowerNP NP4GS3 [4], Freescale's C-Port C-5 [5] or in the PRO3 prototype [6] was 64 bytes. Two main factors led to this decision: (1) small segments offer a fair storing efficiency [7] and (2) ATM cells are 53-Bytes long, which makes it convenient to use segments rounded-up to the next power of two.

Newer devices utilize more complicated schemes. The Intel IXP24xx and IXP28xx families [8] allow for dividing the receive (Rx) and transmit (Tx) buffers in up to three partitions. The partitions coexist, each with a different segment size, though each packet must be segmented using only the appropriate segment size and stored into the corresponding partition. This approach is similar to an IBM patent [9], where the packet buffer is divided into two partitions, each of which corresponds to a segment size. Each packet is segmented according to its length and then stored to the appropriate partition.

Segmenting packets into 64-byte segments leads to reduced performance due to the fact that it necessitates multiple bus and memory transactions per packet [10]. In contrast, larger segment sizes can benefit from reduced bus arbitration and higher DRAM performance since they can take advantage of higher spatial row locality [11].

Moreover, the number of segments is directly coupled with the amount of control resources needed, as each segment has a descriptor one-to-one associated. Descriptors contain pointers to other segments so in that way, multitude of segments can be chained together [6]. Linked Lists deliver simplicity of use yet with the drawback of requiring several accesses to the control buffer, hence generating high load on the memory interface and longer packet fetching latencies [22].

Activating different rows in the same bank incurs a significant performance penalty in dynamic memories. Thus several optimization techniques pursue to maximize accessing consecutive columns within the same row (burst mode), therefore avoiding activation and pre-charge latencies [12]. Additionally such conflicts can be partially avoided by reordering requests to avoid consecutive accesses to the same bank [10][12].

In NPs, a numerous set of hardware accelerators assist the processing cluster in common tasks like packet classification, table lookup, pattern matching or Cyclic

Redundancy Check calculation. Data transfers between various devices are commonly handled by such hardware devices, the simplest of which is a Direct Memory Access (DMA). The CPU may instruct the device to perform a single transfer (for example the IXP1200 follows this approach) or assign to it a list of tasks to be performed (scatter & gather DMAs). Other NPs incorporate more complex accelerators that segment/reassemble packets and queue/dequeue them without CPU intervention [3][5]. The most complex of such devices, called Buffer Managers or Memory Manager Units (MMU), even manage the packet buffer as well as its associated control structures [13][14] autonomously.

In our system we employ a Buffer Manager that implements the new segmentation schemes together with an advanced control mechanism based on Bitmaps instead on linked list [22]. This is done to upgrade the inflexible solutions found in current devices that neither deliver the desired performance without incurring in low storing efficiency, nor reduce the requirement in control buffer size.

3   Algorithm Description

As stated above, Fixed Size Segmentation (FSS) schemes are limited to either optimizing memory efficiency or minimizing the number of segments per packet, which can lead to an excessive amount of control information or memory waste. In this section, two algorithms are proposed which both utilize a finite number of segment sizes to divide a packet into multiple segments each of which might be of a different segment size. The segment sizes are defined during the systems configuration. The goal is to bridge the gap between the number of segments per packet and memory efficiency with an algorithm that achieves high performance in both parameters concurrently.

3.1   Memory Efficiency Optimized Algorithm (MEO)

The first of the two algorithms proposed here aims at optimizing the memory efficiency achieved by selecting segments that are the optimal fit for each packet. Using this algorithm a packet is segmented into several segments of different size from a selection of possible segment sizes, in contrast to the approaches by Intel [8] and IBM [9], which divide each packet into segment of one size, selected from a pool of several possible alternatives.

The algorithm processes each packet, testing all the available segment sizes from biggest to smallest until one, which is smaller than the current data amount (which initially is the packet length, but is reduced as the packet is segmented), is found. This

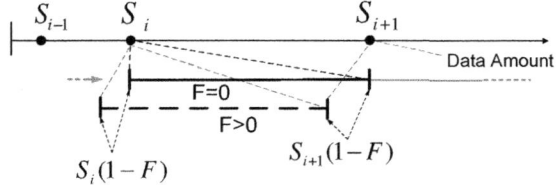

Fig. 1. Iterative selection of segment sizes for packet allocation

will be the largest segment which can be completely filled with data from this packet. Then a segment of that size is created, its size is subtracted from the packet length and the process is repeated for the remaining packet length until the entire packet has been stored. Figure 1 illustrates the criteria for segmenting a packet. S_i denotes the segment size tested at any time while S_{i-1} and S_{i+1} are the previous and next segment sizes respectively. The dashed boundary indicates the area in which the data amount must be located for the segment S_i to be selected.

The parameter F, called the ranging factor, can be used to shift the segmentation selection boundaries, thus allowing for the dynamic manipulation of the trade-off between memory efficiency and segment number by loosely regulating the number of segments the algorithm commits for each packet. The greater the ranging factor, the more the lower bound expands. The upper bound of S_i is defined by the lower bound of S_{i+1}. Here, the increase of the range factor means that instead of allocating three 128 byte segments we allocate one 512 byte segment. This is because the remainder length range with F=0 is from 512 to 1024 bytes while with F=0.3 it is from 358 to 716 bytes. The increase of F thus results in reduced number of segments per packet but also in reduced memory efficiency.

3.2   Segment Number Limited Algorithm (SLA)

The algorithm described in section A attempts to optimize memory efficiency without however providing a hard bound on the number of segments in which it can divide a packet. Such a limitation can be useful in order to enable a more deterministic approach, which can allow us to better optimize control data structures (e.g. to avoid linked lists to store packet segment descriptors). In the SLA algorithm a packet is still divided into segments selected from a predefined pool of segment sizes, however the implementation of the selection process is different.

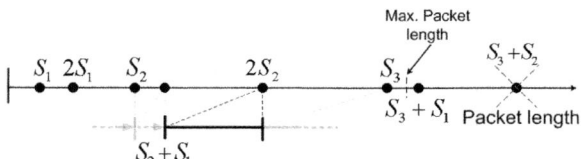

Fig. 2. Criteria for selecting sizes by limiting the number of segments per packet (SLA)

Table 1. Example of two different packet segmentation results for a 1392 Byte Packet and 128-512-1024 Byte segment sizes using the MEO algorithm

Ranging factor	F=0	F=0.3
1st segment	1024	1024
2nd segment	128	512
3rd segment	128	-
4th segment	128	-
Memory Efficiency	98.8 %	92 %

Assume that N is the number of segments sizes available to the segmentation algorithm, while M is the maximum number of segments per packet the algorithm is allowed to allocate. Here we calculate all the possible combinations between all of the available segment sizes for the specific values of N and M. Figure 2 illustrates this for 3 segment sizes and a maximum of 2 segments per packet allowed.

In this case the following combinations are available: { S_1, 0, 0}, {0, S_2, 0}, {0, 0, S_3 }, { S_1, S_2, 0}, { S_1, 0, S_3 }, {0, S_2, S_3 }, { $2S_1$, 0}, {0, $2S_2$, 0}, {0, 0, $2S_3$ }.

Some results which are larger than the maximum packet length are discarded. Only the one which is immediately larger than the maximum packet length needs to be considered. After calculating all possible combinations within the limitations we define, we then compare the packet length to all of the calculated results in order to determine the combination that is immediately larger than the packet size. This ensures optimal efficiency while limiting the maximum number of segments to the defined number.

4 Design Flow

A three stage approach was used in the investigation into the proposed segmentation algorithms, modeling or implementing the system at different levels of abstraction, as Figure 3 illustrates. Each lower level provides higher simulation accuracy but also requires increased effort to model, as well as longer simulation times to execute. The goal was thus to explore a large number of options using a fast high level model (written in C++) and a large variety of stimuli (e.g. PCAP files), then move into a much more detailed system level model (in SystemC) and finally when the selection of the various algorithm parameters had been sufficiently narrowed down, to implement the Buffer Manager in synthesizable VHDL.

The significant number of parameters (number of segment sizes N, segment size values, F, M) that may be tuned in any of the two algorithms creates a huge number of different variations (a few hundred) that need to be considered. To counter this, a high level model which behaviorally captures the memory subsystem was developed. Its purpose is to provide high speed evaluation of each algorithm without significant compromises in result accuracy.

The first stage in the investigation should provide a preliminary estimation of algorithm performance and a selection of the fittest solutions. The results from this initial sorting were used as input for further simulation with the more detailed system level model, which provides a much more detailed rendition of the system, including different instances of a system bus, processing units and memory subsystem, which can be interconnected in various configurations. This second stage in the investigation aims at implementing the most promising algorithm variations, but this time extracting performance data regarding the entire system and not only the algorithms itself. With this system level model, we expect to observe a close correlation between average segments per packet and throughput, which validates the approach followed in the early stage of the study.

The SmartMem System C System-level model captures an entire NP system while focusing on its memory subsystem performance and MMU functionality. It combines transaction-level accuracy for internal engine behaviour with a cycle-accurate modelling for critical performance bottlenecks like the bus and the memory controller. Several degrees of freedom allow a comprehensive exploration of factors that affect performance like memory devices, buffer mapping, number of memory interfaces, transfer length and destination address, memory controller policy or internal interconnect architecture. Moreover, the Buffer Manager (BM) architecture's [13] functionality is accurately modelled, including packet segmentation algorithm, control structures, free-address lookup, packet reassembly or internal transactions.

The model utilizes a CPU cluster for packet processing. Each CPU contains its own local cache and is connected to the rest of the system via a common bus. To emulate the CPU load on the bus and memory, a basic processing delay together with different request patterns depending on the application type were considered. Queue system delays match are random one, which match common queuing latency distributions, based on measurements taken from real routers found in [15, 16] as well as [17], showing that packet delays across a router can be approximated with a Weibull distribution.

The final stage is the coding of a buffer manager module in VHDL, which incorporates the findings of the previous steps of this investigation together with advanced control structures to manage the packet buffer. The implementation is configurable and thus can be used to test several variations (of the segment sizes) and is used to verify the results of both models on a prototype hardware implementation. What limits us to testing only a small subset of these variations is the significant time it takes to re-synthesize the system, reprogram the FPGA and execute the measurements each time.

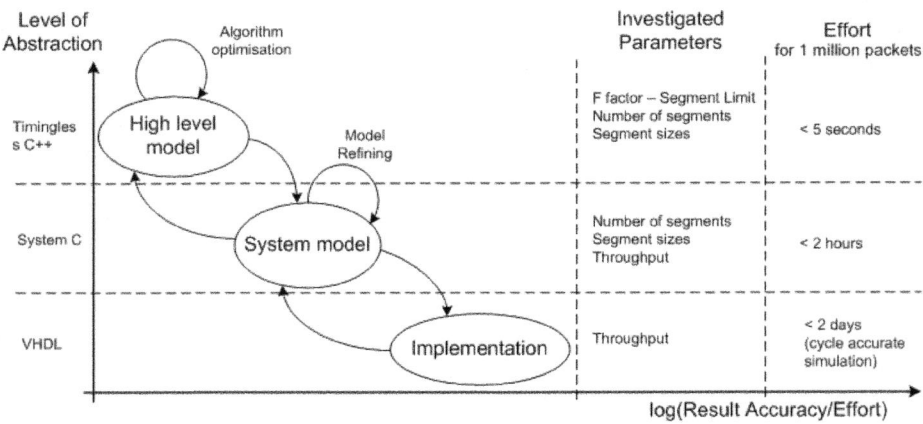

Fig. 3. Strategy for the investigation of packet segmentation

5   Packet Segmentation Analysis

The number of segment sizes available to the segmentation algorithm has a direct effect on the efficiency and control overhead it achieves. A thorough look into typical packet size distributions found in various sources (the Advanced IMIX [18], various PCAP files from both edge and core network sources [19][20]) is used for a preliminary selection of segment size combinations.

From such a study, we conclude that most packets can be broadly categorized into a small (less than 100 bytes), a medium (around 500 bytes) and a large (more than 640 bytes) packet size. This means that to provide acceptable coverage for theses packet size ranges, we need at least three packet segment sizes, for one of these areas. Thus solutions with less than 3 segment sizes should not provide comparable performance, while the ones with more than 4 segment sizes should not provide any significant improvement since the packet size spectrum must already be adequately covered by solutions with a smaller number of appropriate segment sizes.

To verify this we simulated seven PCAP files from both core network OC-48/192 links [19][20], as well as slower access network ones [20] as stimuli. The files contained in total more than 2 million packets of varying packet sizes and traffic patterns. Table 2 provides the origin, number of packets and packet size distribution for these files. From these data we can also extract a sensible distribution for the memory size allocated to each segment size pool during the simulations. 16 MB of memory are used in total which are divided into 3 or 4 pools depending on how many segment sizes are used. When 3 segment sizes are used the distribution is 12-33-55% per segment size and when 4 segment sizes are used the distribution is 8-16-28-48%, from the smallest to the largest segment size used respectively.

As stated previously, the most important parameters to evaluate the performance of a segmentation algorithm are the number of segments per packet and the memory efficiency. To achieve this we graph the memory efficiency achieved versus the average number of segments for each algorithm variation.

Table 2. Stimuli Information

Type of traffic	No. of packets	Packet size distribution		
		40-319	320-639	640-
OC-192 Backbone	1017247	85.54	2.62	11.84
OC-48 Backbone	226255	70.56	8.86	20.58
OC-48 Backbone	274544	65.19	9.46	25.35
OC-48 Backbone	675191	55.07	11.05	33.88
LAN–P2P	76702	54.41	5.1	40.49
LAN Online gaming	24806	68.78	1.17	30.05
LAN–HTTP/video streaming	88498	37.47	0.41	62.12

Table 3. Best Performing Algorithms

Algo-rithm	Segment Size Combination	M	F	Mem. Efficiency	Avg. no. of Segments
MEO	256-512-1024	-	0,3	77.59	1.37
	64-256-1024	-	0,3	93.08	2.05
	64-128-512-1024	-	0,3	93.08	1.83
	32-64-256-1024	-	0	96.63	3.71
SLA	32-64-256-1024	4	-	95.54	2.09
	64-128-512-1024	2	-	92.05	1.38
	64-128-512-1024	5	-	94.33	1.58
	256-512-1024	2	-	77.70	1.35

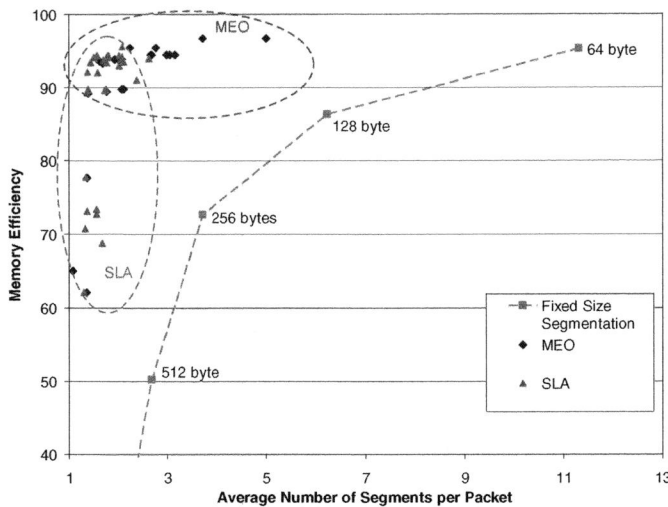

Fig. 4. Overview of segmentation algorithm performance (SLA, MEO and FSS)

Thus in figure 4 the optimal solution would be in the upper left corner of the graph. For clarity reasons this figure does not include all possible combinations but only the best performing ones for each algorithm (marked MEO and SLA respectively), as well present an average of the results obtained for the seven PCAP files, in which each result from each PCAP files contributes equally to the total. Additionally we include the performance of the fixed size segmentation algorithm as a reference.

Both the MEO and SLA achieve hugely improved results in comparison with the fixed segmentation scheme for all shown combinations. Table 3 provides a list of the best performing solutions from both algorithms. The table verifies the design goals for the two algorithms. For both three and four segment sizes the MEO reaches higher memory efficiency than the SLA. The difference increases to more than 20% as the segment number limit in the latter becomes stricter (e.g. when 2). It is important to note that for a loose limit the SLA algorithm performance tends to converge with that of the MEO. Thus the most interesting parameters here are a relatively low segment number limit, which offer somewhat decreased memory efficiency but with a lower average segment number and a hard limit on the maximum number of segments in which a packet may be split.

Regarding the selection of segment sizes, our original assumptions are confirmed. We see that when using three segment sizes both algorithms perform better with a small- medium-large segment size combination, where the large segment size is almost always 1024 bytes (2048 ones result in a significant drop in memory efficiency).

The medium size is in most cases 256 bytes, which enables us to cover medium sized packets with 2 or 3 segments, while providing enough granularity to efficiently cover other packet sizes as well. As small segment size, 64 bytes represents the most reasonable choice as the 32-byte segment brings only marginal improvement in memory efficiency but with a significant increase in the number of segments generated and the 128 byte one result in somewhat overall reduced memory efficiency.

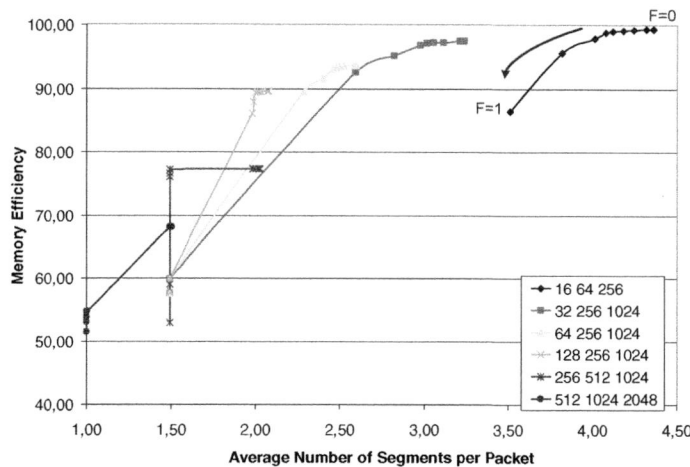

Fig. 5. Variation of memory efficiency and average segment size with the F factor (MEO)

Modifying the range factor in the memory efficiency optimized algorithm provides an easy way to alter the balance of the memory efficiency vs. number of segments per packet trade-off so as to cover a wide area of system requirements. To verify this we have simulated the algorithm with an F value varying from 0 to 1 in 0.1 increments, using the segment size combinations that achieved the most promising results in the previous analysis. Figure 5 illustrates the results from these simulations.

An increase of both the memory efficiency and the average number of segments per packet as the F factor decreases is always noticeable, while a value of 0.3 seems to provide the best tradeoff. When using combinations with large segment sizes this trend is distorted due to the fact that the expanded segmentation range borders begin overlapping and in worst cases even completely cover one another.

Based on these results we can select some variations of the two algorithms to test greater detail with our system level model. More specifically the MEO algorithm is used with both three (64-256-1024 bytes) and four (64-128-256-1024 bytes) segment sizes and an F of 0.3 as these proved to be the best all-around performers in the previous investigation. From the SLA algorithm we select a four (64-128-512-1024 bytes) segment size variant with a maximum segment number of two. Since the performance of both algorithms tends to converge as the segment number limit increases we chose a variant with a maximum of only two segment sizes as this provides both excellent memory efficiency and minimization of control overhead.

6   System Level Simulation

This section utilizes the system model to further refine the evaluation of the systems performance and gain insight into the influence of additional functional and architectural parameters, such as memory type, memory access pattern and system topology. For these simulations the model has been configured to use four processing cores. A cycle-accurate model of IBM's 64-bit Processor Local Bus (PLB) bus [20] is used for

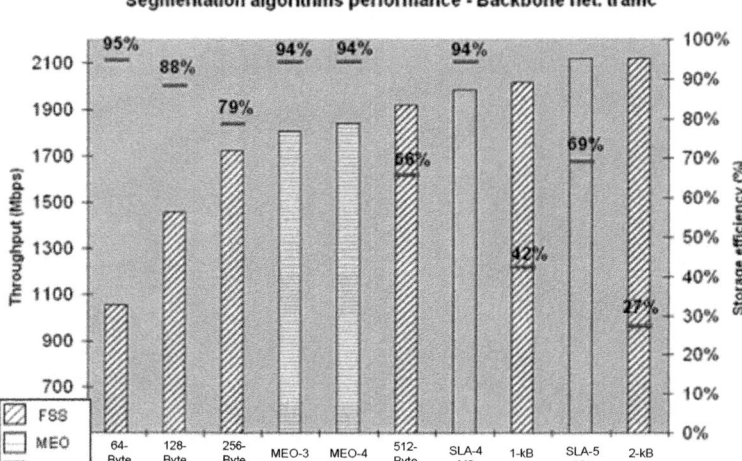

Fig. 6. Tradeoff between storage efficiency and throughput obtained for various segmentation algorithms with backbone traffic

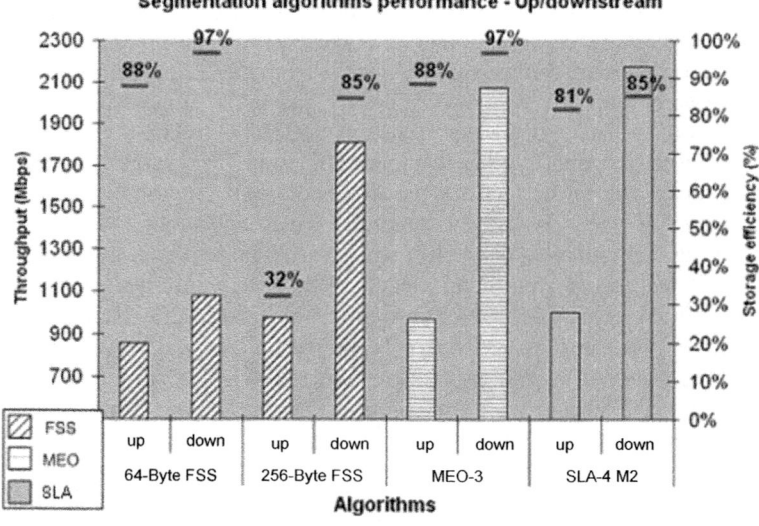

Fig. 7. Throughput and memory efficiency results for up- and downstream traffic

module communication. The bus works at 100 MHz with an arbitration time of 3 cycles. Initially the system is configured with one DDR-200 SDRAM memory which acts as a packet buffer and is connected to the PLB bus via an advanced memory controller which supports arbitrary length without command access reordering and a bus attached SRAM memory which is used as control buffer.

6.1 Segmentation Algorithm Performance

The most important parameter that the system level model allows us to evaluate is the system throughput. As Figure 6 demonstrates, the fixed size segmentation provides a linear tradeoff with 64-byte achieving excellent memory efficiency but low throughput, 2048-byte the exact opposite and everything else falling somewhere in between, with 256-byte representing a reasonable compromise. Still better, the MEO algorithm with three segment sizes (1024, 256 and 64 Bytes) achieves approximately 100 Mb/s of throughput more in comparison to the 256-Byte FSS, while achieving 15% more storage efficiency. The SLA algorithm performances are 15%-23% higher (approx. 300 Mb/s more) while efficiency improves by 10%-15% in comparison to the FSS. It is possible that transitory traffic patterns with concentration of packets of a specific size may cause a storage efficiency drop if the segment sizes used are not appropriately selected. We demonstrate this by replacing the backbone stimuli by user's upstream traffic which contains a high concentration of small packets. Figure 7 illustrates such a scenario for a subset of the most promising segmentation algorithms since the multiple simulation needed for up- and downstream traffic are time consuming. If only 256-Byte segments are available, storage efficiency drops down to 32%, while for example SLA-4 M2 hits a satisfactory 81%. On the other hand throughput is predictably lower when smaller packets have to be processed. Even in this case our algorithms achieve better performance by about 100 Mb/s. Our segmentation algorithms prove again superior when the traffic pattern contains an unusual amount of large packets, which is typical of downstream in last mile traffic. Results show again better performance because large packets are more effectively transferred to the memory in long bursts rather than split in several requests.

From the results of the previous section we conclude that the SLA algorithm with 4 available segment sizes (64-128-512-1024 bytes) and a maximum segment number of 2 is the best choice since it combines very high throughput, low segment number per packet and a bound on the maximum number of segments per packet. This segment number constrain also allows using the control structures presented in [22].

6.2 CPU Access Impact on Performance

The processing cluster accesses the packet buffer, and so places additional strain on the interconnection infrastructure and the memory interface. Packet processing requires in many cases simple IP forwarding, which means that the packet header should be fetched from memory and the updated header written back once processing is done. However more complex packet processing applications require the entire packet data, which has to fetched from and written back to the memory.

Figure 8 shows the throughput obtained for incoming in packets requiring either IP forwarding or payload processing in different percentages. Additionally the decay of performance with respect to values obtained without CPU accesses to the memory (as in Figure 6) is illustrated. This is repeated for four segmentation algorithms with backbone network traffic. The number of CPUs does not affect results provided they do not become the bottleneck of the system. First of all we confirm the general trend observed in previous simulations: longer segments lead to better performance, even when the CPU generates short accesses per packet (right most case).

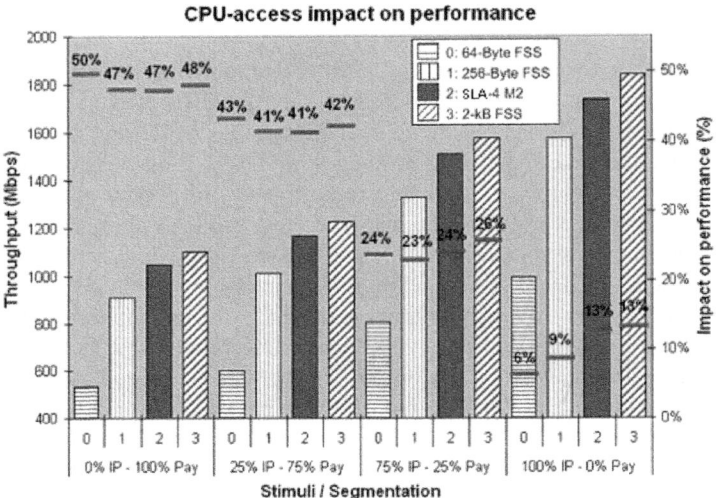

Fig. 8. Throughput obtained for different CPU cluster access schemes

In general, the impact on performance decreases whenever a higher proportion of packets require payload processing. Obviously, this is due to the extra data traffic which increases the load to up to four times the line rate (100% payload processing). Most importantly, our algorithm suffers no additional impact since a 50%-performance decrease is visible for all included segmentation schemes, demonstrating that regardless of the processing requirements our segmentation scheme provides significantly improved performance.

6.3 Impact of Memory Subsystems

A further step in our investigation is to determine the impact of various memory technologies and system topologies on the algorithm's performance. Since the packet buffer in NPs is usually implemented using commodity DDR SDRAM chips, it is interesting to evaluate how the performance of various DDR technologies and speed grades affects the overall system throughput in conjunction with the newly proposed algorithms. Figure 9 summarizes the results of this investigation which demonstrate that faster memory types only marginally increase the overall system performance regardless of the segmentation scheme used.

This can be attributed to the fact that the latency of a memory access depends only partially on the actual memory technology, so faster memories bring only marginal improvements to the total transfer completion time. Moving the packet buffer to on-chip SRAM is more effective, since SRAM latency is significantly lower than any DRAM device (10 ns in the model). However, current fabrication technologies do not allow for the integration of the necessary amount of SRAM either on chip or on a PCB board. Additionally we confirm that using longer segments proportionally increases performance independently of the memory type.

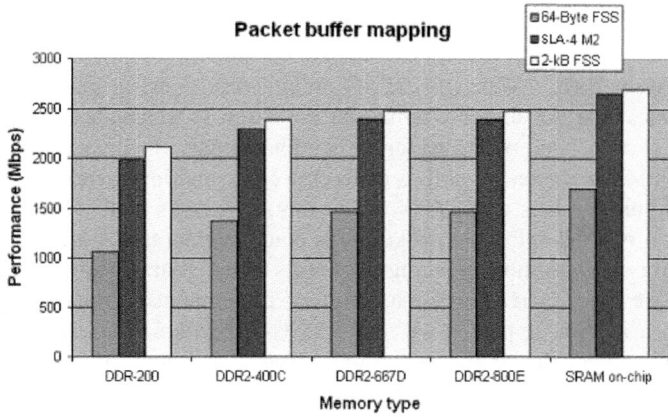

Fig. 9. Throughput for different packet buffer mappings

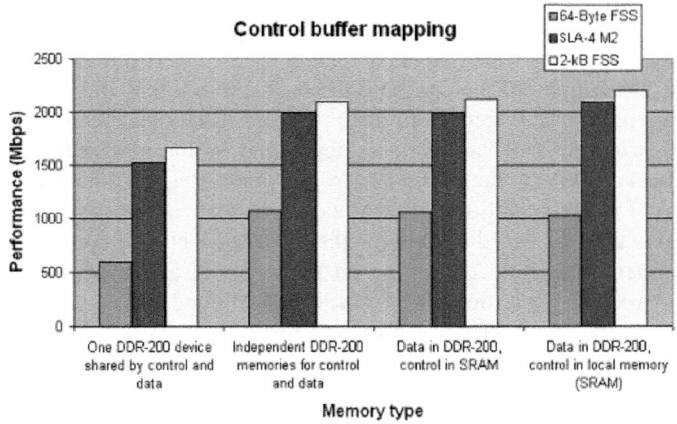

Fig. 10. Throughput obtained for different control buffer mappings

Also of interest is the impact of various system topologies which is illustrated in Figure 10. In contrast to the reference scenario where packet SDRAM memory and control SRAM memory were attached to the same bus, we try utilizing one common SDRAM buffer for both packet and control data, which brings a significant performance reduction regardless of the segmentation algorithm used. Moving the control buffer to a separate DRAM memory has no effect on system throughput. In comparison it is much beneficial to keep control data in a local memory in the BM.

A final parameter investigated was the bus burst length. Some buses limit this to avoid master starvation due to long data transfers. When we introduced this limitation in our model, we observed for example a performance degradation of 16.33% (256-Byte FSS) and 27.63% (2048-Byte) in comparison to an unlimited burst length. These results discourage constraining the maximum bus transfer. This is only possible when CPUs and BM do not share the bus, as long bursts increase CPU bus access latency.

7 SmartMem Buffer Manager Implementation

The SmartMem Buffer Manager (SBM) architecture consists mainly of three functional modules, the RX and TX units and the Address Manager (AM). It supports a full-duplex flow of data while managing simultaneously the packet buffer and its associated control structures as well as different segmentation schemes (SLA and FSS).

The RX unit receives and stores the incoming packets in local SRAM. Then the segmentation module splits the packet in as many segments as required, according to the algorithm configuration. The segment sizes allowed are those powers of two between 64 Bytes and 2 KB up to a maximum of 24 segments per packet, the maximum required for a 1536-Byte packet with the FSS-64 algorithm. Once the packet structure has been calculated, the segmentation unit requests memory space accordingly from the Address Manager. The segment addresses are already available in an internal cache to accelerate the transfer of data as no waiting for control operations is necessary. Next, the storing unit transfers the segment data to the external Packet Buffer through the Peripheral Local Bus (PLB). We use an optimized bus interface that allows burst transfers of up to 2 KB, so as to increase the bus usage by reducing the arbitration and transfer times. As the PLB Bus supports simultaneous read and write transfers, two master interfaces have been included so as to optimize bus utilization.

A Packet Descriptor (PD) containing the segment pointers and context data (input port, packet length, etc) is generated once the packet data has been completely transferred. This structure is of variable size depending on the maximum number of segments per packet (M) of the configured segmentation algorithm being its minimum size 128 bits for segmentations with M equal to one or two segments per packet. Every additional 64-bit word allows for three extra 16-bit pointers with their corresponding segment type field. Keeping all the segment addresses in the PD has the advantage of reducing data fetching latency as no linked list needs to be parsed. Inconveniently as the M parameter grows, additional memory space has to be reserved for the implementation of the queue system, typically built up out of linked PDs. However this overhead does not play a role when using the algorithm proposed (SLA-N4-M2) as only two segment addresses are stored. This is the same size that would be needed when using pointers to keep track of head and tail of linked lists.

An interrupt to the CPU Core signals that a new packet has been stored and is available for processing. A CPU running a typical packet forwarding application would quickly become the system's bottleneck, thus preventing the correct grasp of segmentation's influence on performance. For the assessment of maximum throughput we use four engines that emulate the CPU behavior. These engines fetch the PD from the BM to immediately loop it back and trigger packet transmission. As soon as the TX unit receives a new PD, it starts to retrieve the corresponding data segments from the packet buffer into its local memory. Data is stored there continuously hence accomplishing packet reassembly. Afterwards segment addresses are returned to the AM, where they are discarded in parallel and made available for reuse. The transmission concludes once the packet has been completely sent to the corresponding output port.

The SBM requires control structures to manage a packet buffer typically with a size in the order of hundreds of MB or even more. In our case, the Address Manager [22] uses an advanced method that allocates memory dynamically using a combination of bitmaps and double linked lists that track big memory blocks completely avoiding external fragmentation. This novel organization strongly reduces the control buffer requirements, which enables mapping the control buffer in a resizable local buffer built out of multiple BlockRAMs (on-chip SRAM). Its advantages include accelerating control data updating, reducing memory bandwidth and avoiding the need to dedicate off-chip memory for the control buffer thus cutting on chip packaging costs.

Finally, the implementation of the SBM on a Xilinx's Virtex-IV FX60 FPGA requires 2.556 Slices out of a total of 25.280 (~10%) running at 100 MHz. At that speed, four 32-bit ports allow a maximum traffic of 3.2 Gbps (full-duplex). The memory subsystem becomes the system's bottleneck before reaching that speed, which allows us to observe the maximum throughput with different segmentations.

7.1   Measurements and Concept Verification

Our central thesis in this paper is to demonstrate that by using multiple segment sizes for packet segmentation it is possible to achieve a performance close to that using only one large segment per packet and simultaneously getting high storing efficiency. Figure 12 shows the throughput measured at the system's output with four different segmentation strategies: FSS with segment sizes 64, 256 and 2 KB, and our SLA algorithm with four segment sizes (64, 128, 512 and 1 KB) constrained to a maximum of two segment sizes per packet (SLA-N4-M2).

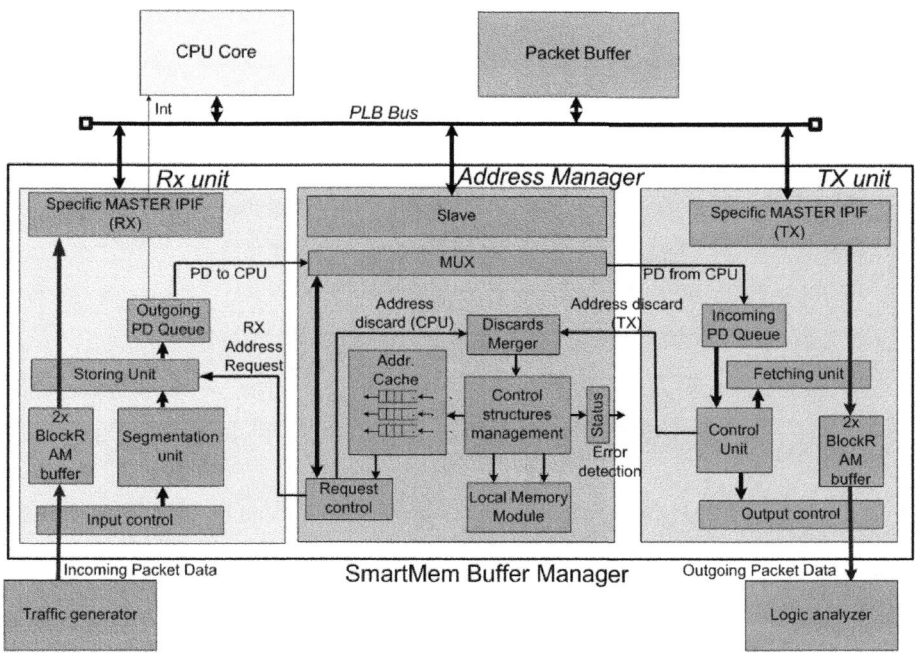

Fig. 11. Buffer Manager Implementation Schematic

First we proceed by stimulating the system with a continuous stream of fix-sized packets, which helps to better distinguish the effect of different packet sizes on performance. For that experiment, the packet buffer is mapped on a 64-bit DDR-SDRAM-200 interfaced through the Xilinx's IP Core library controller. The SLA algorithm achieves better results than state-of-the-art FSS 64 independently of the packet size chosen. Performance is between 9 and 109% higher, increasing this percentage as packet sizes get larger. A similar observation can be made when comparing SLA and FSS-256 figures, though SLA's performance is only better when using the 512 and 1024-Byte segments. Again, the number of segments per packet is the decisive factor that drives performance, so the best throughput is invariably obtained when the complete packet fits into one segment.

The previous experiment demonstrates that segmentation and performance are tightly coupled. In order to evaluate the contributions in this context, we switch the mapping of the data buffer from the previous DDR-SDRAM 200 to a 32-bit SRAM running at 100 MHz. Next we proceed by stimulating again with fix-sized packets and keeping SLA-N4-M2 as segmentation algorithm (Figure 13).

At a first glance, it can be observed that SRAM performs in several cases faster than dynamic memory, which was expected. But remarkably, that difference is bigger for those packet sizes that require two segments than for those contained in just one segment. This indicates that those memory subsystems based on dynamic memory (the usual case in commercial NPs) are much more sensitive to packet segmentation than those mapped on SRAM. To put it in other words, it is particularly beneficial to use large segments with dynamic memory.

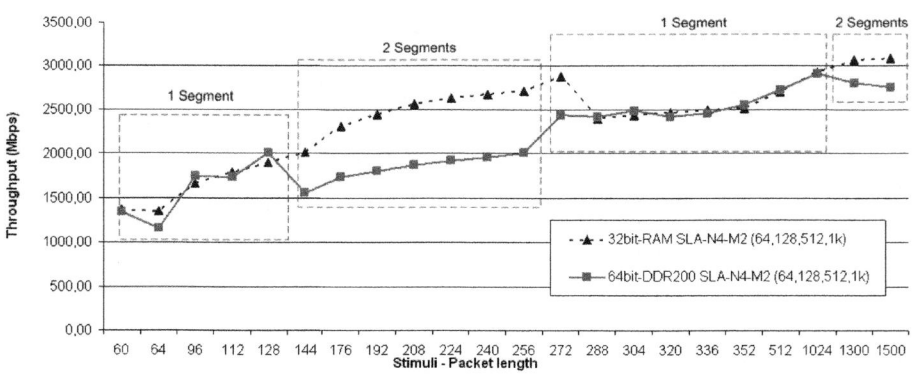

Fig. 12. SBM with the packet buffer mapped on SRAM and DDR-SDRAM

The reason for this effect is the activation/pre-charge latencies when accessing DDR-SDRAM. Every segment requires one memory access, which in turn requires activating the corresponding memory bank as well as writing back data to refresh the transistor value (access is destructive in one-transistor memories). Requesting large chunks of data reduces latency and by extension optimizes the system's performance.

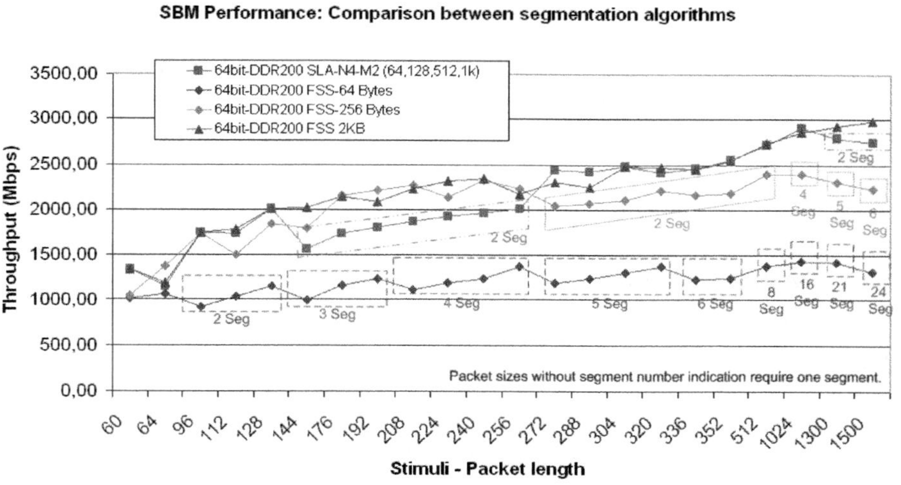

Fig. 13. Performance comparison of four different segmentation algorithms

Moreover a small amount of large accesses improve data transmission over the bus due to the reduction of associated arbitration, handshake and acknowledge latencies, though it must be taken into consideration that large bursts increase the chance of collisions (and thus of higher latency) when requesting bus access. Finally, algorithms with low average number of segments per packet need smaller Packet Descriptors, which reduces the load on the bus. FSS-64/256 algorithms require enlarged PDs to keep up to 24/8 segment addresses while in comparison SLA-N4-M2 generates a maximum of two segments per packet.

8   Conclusions and Future Work

This paper presents two novel, advanced segmentation algorithms for network processors that aim to decisively increase system throughput in comparison with current state-of-the-art segmentation schemes. This is achieved by finding a sweet spot between the number of segments per packet and memory efficiency. Algorithm configurations with 3 or 4 segment sizes like 64–256–1024 and 64–128–512–1024 provide excellent all around performance with both proposed algorithms. They achieve significantly increased throughput in comparison to the traditionally used fixed size segmentation scheme, while maintaining very high memory efficiency. Additionally the impact of increased CPU load on the memory was demonstrated without affecting the superior performance offered by the proposed algorithms.

Additionally we studied the impact of several memory types and system topologies on our algorithms and validated their superiority in a variety of conditions using an abstract system model. We observed that faster memory types bring relatively small improvements in system performance and that decoupling the control from the data buffer leads to significantly higher throughput. Finally we coded the selected algorithms on a Virtex 4 FGPA as part of a Buffer Manager module and measured its performance. The results verify the throughput benefits of the proposed algorithms.

Our future work consists in upgrading the buffer manager to include automatic header forwarding to the processing cluster according to packet classification preprocessing, which should lead to an acceleration of the cluster operation while offloading the packet buffer interface of inefficient CPU accessing.

Acknowledgement. This work has been funded by the Bavarian Ministry of Economic Affairs, Infrastructures, Transport and Technology under grant reference IUK 178/001 (SmartFlow).

References

1. Mudigonda, J., Vin, H.M., Yavatkar, R.: Overcoming the memory wall in packet processing: hammers or ladders? In: Proceedings of the 2005 ACM Symposium on Architecture for Networking and Communications Systems (2005)
2. Karras, K., Llorente, D., Wild, T., Herkersdorf, A.: Improving Memory Subsystem Performance in Network Processors with Smart Packet Segmentation. In: SAMOS IC VIII, Samos, Greece, July 21-24 (2008)
3. Intel IXP12xx Network Processor, http://www.intel.com/design/network/products/npfamily/ixp1200.htm
4. Allen, J.R., Bass, B.M., Basso, C., Boivie, R.H., Calvignac, J.L., Davis, G.T., Frelechoux, L., Hed-des, M., Herkersdorf, A., Kind, A., Logan, J.F., Peyravian, M., Rinaldi, M.A., Sabhikhi, R.K., Siegel, M.S., Waldvogel, M.: IBM PowerNP network preocessor: Hardware, software and applications. IBM Journal of Research and Development 47(2/3), 177–193 (2003)
5. Freescale C-5e Network Processor, http://www.freescale.com/webapp/sps/site/prod_summary.jsp?code=C-5E&nodeId=01M994862703126
6. Vlachos, K., Orphanoudakis, T., Papaeftathiou, Y., Nikolaou, N., Pnevmatikatos, D., Konstantoulakis, G., Sanchez-P, J.A.: Design and performance evaluation of a Programmable Packet Processing Engine (PPE) suitable for high-speed network processors units. Microprocessors and Microsystems 31(3), 188–199 (2007)
7. O'Kane, S., Sezer, S., Lit, L.: A Study of Shared Buffer Memory Segmentation for Packet Switched Networks. In: Proceedings of the Advanced int'L Conference on Telecommunications and Int'l Conference on Internet and Web Applications and Services, Washington, DC, vol. 55 (February 2006)
8. Intel IXP2400 Network Processor, http://download.intel.com/design/network/ProdBrf/27905302.pdf
9. Georgiou, C.J., Salapura, V.: Dynamic reallocation of data stored in buffers based on packet size. US Patent 7003597 (February 2006)
10. Jahangir, H., Satish, C., Vijaykumar, T.N.: Efficient use of memory bandwidth to improve network processor throughput. In: Proceedings of the 30th Annual International Symposium on Computer Architecture, vol. 31(2), pp. 300–313 (May 2003)
11. Ykman-Couvreur, C., Lambrecht, J., Verkest, D., Catthoor, F., Nikologiannis, A., Konstantou-lakis, G.: System-level performance optimization of the data queueing memory management in high-speed network processors. In: Proceedings of the Design Automation Conference, pp. 518–523 (2002)

12. Papaefstathiou, I., Orphanoudakis, T., Kornaros, G., Kachris, C., Mavroidis, I., Nikolo-giannis, A.: Queue Management in Network Processors. In: Design, Automation and Test in Europe 2005, vol. 3, pp. 112–117 (2005)
13. Llorente, D., Karras, K., Meitinger, M., Rauchfuss, H., Wild, T., Herkersdorf, A.: Accele-rating Packet Buffering and Administration in Network Processors. In: International Sym-posium on Integrated Circuits (September 2007)
14. Kornaros, G., Papaefstathiou, I., Nikologiannis, A., Zervos, N.: A Fully-Programmable Memory Man-agement System Optimizing Queue Handling at Multi Gigabit Rates. In: Proceedings of the 40th Conference on Design Automation (2003)
15. Papagiannaki, K., Veitch, D., Hohn, N.: Origins of Microcongestion in an Access Router. In: Barakat, C., Pratt, I. (eds.) PAM 2004. LNCS, vol. 3015, pp. 126–136. Springer, Hei-delberg (2004)
16. Papagiannaki, K., Moon, S., Fraleigh, C., Thiran, P., Diot, C.: Measurement and Analysis of Single-Hop Delay on an IP Backbone Network. IEEE Journal on Selected Areas in Communications, Special Issue on Internet and WWW Measurement, Mapping, and Mod-eling, 3rd quarter (2003)
17. Fu, J., Hagsand, O., Karlsson, G.: Queueing behavior and packet delays in network proces-sor systems. In: Proceddings of the IEEE Workshop on High Performance Switching and Routing (2006)
18. Spirent Communication Test Methodology Journal, IMIX (Internet MIX) Journal (March 2006)
19. NLANR PMA: Special Traces Archive,
    http://pma.nlanr.net/Special/chronIndex.html
20. CAIDA OC-48 Trace Archive,
    http://www.caida.org/data/passive/index.xml#oc48
21. CoreConnect bus architecture,
    http://www-306.ibm.com/chips/products/coreconnect/
22. Llorente, D., Karras, K., Wild, T., Herkersdorf, A.: Buffer Allocation for Advanced Packet Segmentation in Network Processors. In: Application-specific Systems, Architectures and Processors 2008, Leuven, Belgium, July 2-4 (2008)

Energy Reduction by Systematic Run-Time Reconfigurable Hardware Deactivation

W.G. Osborne, W. Luk, J.G.F. Coutinho, and O. Mencer

Department of Computing,
Imperial College London, UK
{wgo,wl,jgfc,o.mencer}@imperial.ac.uk

Abstract. This paper describes a method of developing energy-efficient run-time reconfigurable hardware designs. The key idea is to systematically deactivate part of the hardware using word-length optimisation techniques, and then select the most optimal reconfiguration strategy: multiple bitstream reconfiguration or component multiplexing. When multiplexing between different parts of the circuit, it may not always be possible to gate the clock to the unwanted components in FPGAs. Different methods of achieving the same effect while minimising the area used for the control logic are investigated. A model is used to determine the conditions under which reconfiguring the bitstream is more energy-efficient than multiplexing part of the design, based on power measurements taken on 130nm and 90nm devices. Various case studies, such as ray tracing, B–Splines, vector multiplication and inner product are used to illustrate this approach.

1 Introduction

The increasing cost of circuit fabrication has led to the adoption of reconfigurable technology, which enables a circuit to be altered more quickly. Although these devices are flexible, they may not always be as efficient as application-specific integrated circuits (ASICs) — dynamic power is up to 12 times higher on average for a variety of circuits (9 times when embedded blocks are used) [1]. Reconfiguration can, however, be exploited to reduce power consumption because the circuit can be adapted to suit the current scenario. Two methods have been proposed to achieve this. The first is bitstream reconfiguration which involves reconfiguring the circuit [2], possibly deactivating part of it. The second is multiplexer-based reconfiguration, in which parts of the circuit are selected based on input stimuli [3], [4], [5]. Multiplexing has the advantage that it can be applied when the circuit cannot be modified.

Designing power-efficient circuits is a challenging task [6]. One method is to reduce the dynamic power. Clock gating [7], [8] — deactivating the inactive parts of a circuit — has been shown to reduce dynamic power [9] although this is not always the case [10]. Clock gating is not always possible in FPGAs, so alternative approaches are investigated. A method of multiplexing the input to arithmetic

P. Stenström (Ed.): Transactions on HiPEAC IV, LNCS 6760, pp. 354–369, 2011.
© Springer-Verlag Berlin Heidelberg 2011

operators, which involves feeding constant zero into parts of the circuit, is combined with word-length optimisation to reduce energy. Bitstream reconfiguration may be applied to give a similar result, although it has disadvantages. The long reconfiguration time and high power consumption incurred while reconfiguring the chip can lead to inefficient hardware devices given that a high reconfiguration frequency may be required. In order to determine the most efficient approach, the size of the reconfiguration interval must be known.

To summarise, multiplexer-based reconfiguration provides fast, power-efficient reconfiguration, but results in designs with a large area and high power consumption. Bitstream reconfiguration has a long reconfiguration time, with a high power consumption, but provides small, power-efficient designs. The aim of this paper is to show how these two methods can be combined with recent work on word-length optimisation to produce energy-efficient designs. The innovative elements of the proposed approach are:

1. Two methods, multiplexer-based reconfiguration and bitstream reconfiguration, are combined with word-length optimisation to develop run-time reconfigurable designs (section 3).
2. Derivation of the conditions under which multiplexer-based reconfiguration should be chosen in preference to multiple bitstream reconfiguration (section 4).
3. Comparison of the two different reconfiguration methods (section 5).
4. An implementation of the approach for various case studies: ray tracing, B–Splines, vector multiplication and inner product (section 6).

This paper is an extension of our previous work [11] and includes a reconfiguration model covering designs running at different clock frequencies (section 4). Additional results have been obtained on a chip using a different process technology (section 6), along with a more in-depth analysis.

2 Related Work

Word-length optimisation is a common method of reducing power consumption of hardware circuits by minimising the width of arithmetic operators. Brooks and Martonosi [12] show that often, the full width of an arithmetic operator is not required. The authors propose the use of clock gating to reduce the power consumption when part of an operator is not in use, resulting in power savings of between 45%-60% for the SPECint95 and MediaBench benchmark suites. Packing operators into single units is also proposed to increase speed. A similar method [13] has been proposed to reduce the width of subtraction operators.

Zhang et al. [9] analyse the effect of clock gating on power efficiency showing that FPGAs, although not as efficient as ASICs, can achieve significant power reductions. Clock gating may not always be the most energy-efficient solution even though it is the most power-efficient solution in some cases. Cadenas et al. [10] implement a clock gating technique in a pipelined Cordic core with the goal of reducing bit-switching, however, they do not obtain power improvements.

Since program executions often change their behaviour based on input data, the circuit needs to evolve at run time in order to keep the error to a minimum. Bitstream reconfiguration involves reconfiguring part or all of the FPGA to contain a small, power-efficient circuit. Another approach is based on using multiplexers and demultiplexers for time multiplexing designs [3], [4], [5]. This method supports fast reconfiguration but requires a large area. One further disadvantage is that configurations must be known at compile time because they need to be installed on the chip at start-up. Multiple bitstream reconfiguration can be adopted when downloading new configurations.

Control-flow analysis can be used to detect when to reconfigure the design. Styles and Luk [14] use information about branch frequencies to reduce the hardware required for branches that are infrequently taken. Bondalapati and Prasanna [15] reconfigure the circuit at run time to reduce the execution time by up to 37%. Word-length optimisation can benefit from this approach since the error accumulated during the execution of a program depends on its control-flow.

3 Approach

Our proposed approach has three elements:

- Word-length optimisation is used to determine where to save power (section 3.1). This involves locating parts of the design that are not required at a given instant so that they can be deactivated. The components are either separated into different bitstreams (bitstream reconfiguration) or multiplexed (section 3.2), and deactivated when not required (sections 3.3).
- An energy model to determine when to use the different strategies (section 4).
- A reconfiguration strategy to determine how to save power (section 5).

3.1 Word-Length Optimisation

Word-length optimisation involves reducing the precision of variables such that power consumption can be minimised. This, combined with a reconfiguration strategy can result in an energy reduction [11]. Here, a method of guaranteeing accuracy constraints [16] while adapting to different error requirements is shown to reduce energy.

Every variable involved in arithmetic operations has an associated range and precision. The range and precision optimisation is accuracy-guaranteed, which means that any operations performed by the compile-time analysis are guaranteed to produce a specified accuracy irrespective of the input data. Since these results will be conservative, run-time analysis can be employed so that the results are guaranteed for a specific set of input data. Arithmetic is performed on errors instead of numeric values to calculate the worst-case error on the output, given errors on the inputs. ROSE [17] is adopted to analyse a C++ application and create a hardware circuit. Due to the large number of cores, they are generated automatically along with hardware interfaces, and then connected together.

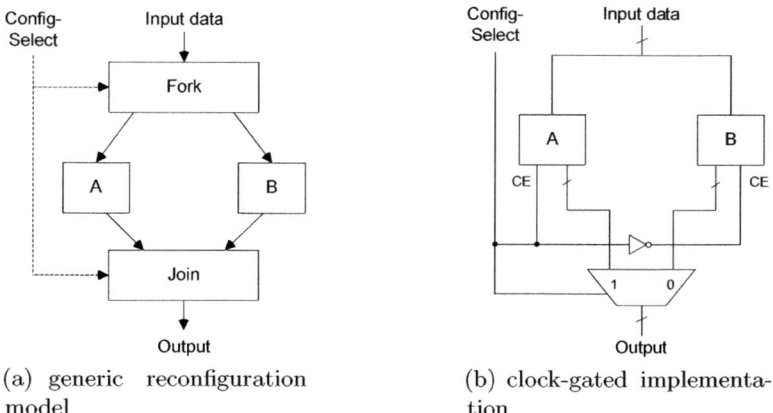

(a) generic reconfiguration model

(b) clock-gated implementation

Fig. 1. A model of a reconfigurable design, configured with *Config-Select*. The clock-gated implementation is also shown.

3.2   Reconfiguration with Multiplexers

Modelling reconfigurable circuits [3], [4] requires specialist development tools [18] to make efficient use of the resources available. In the general case, these models describe a circuit as a set of interchangeable blocks, A and B in figure 1(a). Multiplexers provide a way of rapidly (cycles as opposed to milliseconds) reconfiguring the circuit, allowing data to be routed to the active part via control blocks (*Fork* and *Join*). This methodology assumes that every block can reside on the chip at a given time. An abstract model has also been proposed [19], in which the control blocks are virtual. It may be the case that the multiplexed components do not reside on the same chip but are separate systems.

Here, an extension to this approach is proposed in the case that the control blocks are mapped to real multiplexers and demultiplexers, controlling data flow to the reconfigurable regions. Since only one of the regions will be active at any one time, the clock to the inactive regions can be stopped, as shown in figure 1(b). A reconfiguration controller activates and deactivates different configurations. When it is not possible to stop the clock to these regions (as explained in section 3.3), the input is set to constant zero to reduce signal transitions.

When blocks A and B in figure 1 are identical apart from different constant coefficients there are two options. The first option is to optimise the blocks independently by making use of constant propagation techniques. Although a high performance may be achievable, a large area is often required. The other option is to time-multiplex constants with a block that supports both A and B. Some examples will be presented in section 6.1, comparing the time-multiplexed constant coefficient approach with multiple bitstream reconfiguration.

3.3 Reducing Power Consumption in FPGAs

One option to reduce power consumption is clock gating which provides a means of reducing switching activity, and hence dynamic power consumption, by disabling registers from reading external data. Clock gating is supported by current FPGA devices through the use of dedicated on-chip resources. The Xilinx Virtex series of devices contain a clock gating block, BUFGCE, which provides a way to turn on or turn off a global clock net [7], resulting in power savings, both from the clock net, and the registers attached to it. However, the number of such clock gating blocks may be limited — there are only 16 BUFGCE elements on a Xilinx XC2VP30 FPGA and fewer on smaller devices, such as the Xilinx XC3S500E. When more are required, the clock-enable input may be used to gate the register in each configurable logic element. This method can be used to support reconfigurable word-length optimisation, however, to simplify the designs and reduce the area, the inputs are multiplexed.

It is possible that several components can be grouped together so that they share a single clock gating control, such that the number of clock gating elements matches the number of specialised clock gating blocks from a given device. Due to the number of functional blocks that are used, this approach is not adopted. A coarse-grain approach using clock-enable inputs on cores could also be employed.

3.4 Combining Reconfiguration Approaches

Several steps must be completed in order to combine different methods of reconfiguration — bitstream reconfiguration and multiplexer-based reconfiguration. The methodology can be summarised in the following steps.

1. The circuit is divided into blocks, one for each phase. Word-length analysis is one method of partitioning the design; different configurations are created based on the accuracy required.
2. The different configurations are managed by a controller. There may be a single controller for a small system or many distributed controllers for larger systems. When there are many configurations, multiplexers may be replaced with dedicated decoders to reduce the area of the controller.
3. Identical regions in different configurations are extracted to minimise area and the reconfiguration overhead. An efficient algorithm based on weighted bipartite graphs [19] has been proposed to automate this step. When bitstream reconfiguration is adopted, each configuration can be optimised independently, making use of techniques such as constant propagation. When multiplexing is adopted it may be more efficient to optimise a group of configurations, for example, several constant multipliers may be replaced by a single multiplier to reduce area.
4. For reconfigurable designs with partial bitstreams, support for heterogeneous architectures [20] (in which the placement of different configurations is not restricted to identical regions of the FPGA) and online routing [21] (different types of communication primitive have different power and delay characteristics) can be included.

In the general case, power-efficient designs can be produced by clock gating the deactivated parts, or by having multiple bitstreams in which the deactivated parts have been eliminated. In the next section the conditions under which each reconfiguration strategy should be employed are discussed. The implementation constraints are outlined in section 5 with an analysis showing when each strategy should be selected for a given device.

4   Deriving Reconfiguration Conditions

In many applications such as ray tracing and feature extraction, the algorithm's control-flow is dependent on input data. This means that the functionality of the system will change as input data changes, so static word-length optimisation will have a reduced effect because when the system functionality changes, the word-lengths will need to change. Based on stimuli, which may come from outside the system or be generated by the system, the word-lengths will adapt in such a way as to reduce the power consumption of the system, while keeping the error to a minimum.

When the multiplexer-based approach is used, there is an increase in power consumption because the entire design resides on the chip, regardless of whether it is active at a particular time. Multiple bitstream reconfiguration does not have this overhead, but has a long reconfiguration time coupled with an increase in power consumption; for this reason a model to determine the most efficient reconfiguration strategy is used.

4.1   Speed Considerations

First, the following terms are defined:

- t_{eb}: time spent on execution between successive bitstream configurations.
- t_{eg}: time spent on execution between successive multiplexer configurations.
- t_b: time spent on reconfiguring resources between successive executions.
- t_g: time spent on reconfiguring multiplexer elements between successive executions.

The total run-time with reconfigurable multiplexing and multiple bitstream reconfiguration is obtained by summing the respective elements.

In general, $t_g < t_b$ since reconfiguring the multiplexers may only take a few cycles, but $t_{eg} > t_{eb}$ since a multiplexed design is larger and usually slower than the corresponding bitstream configuration. Hence, the total run time depends on which term dominates. For instance, when execution time is short compared with reconfiguration time, designs employing multiplexers are likely to be faster than the corresponding designs with multiple bitstream reconfiguration.

In general, a design using multiple bitstream reconfiguration is likely to have a higher clock frequency because it has a smaller area. Place and route tools are therefore more likely to be able to pack elements closer together. It is possible

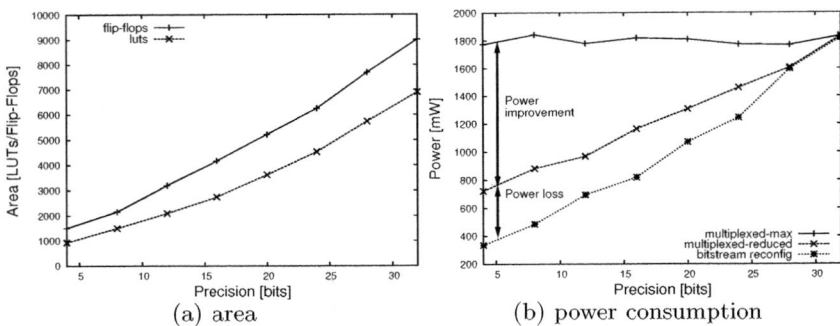

Fig. 2. Area and power consumption of the B-Splines benchmark on the Xilinx XC2VP30

to increase the clock frequency of a design with multiplexers by using a different clock frequency for each block (figure 1), by having multiple clock domains in the design; this will, however, only be applicable when a coarse-grain approach is adopted.

4.2   Energy Considerations

Figure 2(b) shows the power saving of a B–Splines benchmark with simulated inputs; 8-bit counters providing a uniform toggling input over the length of the variable. The inputs are shifted to avoid the tools optimising operations, for example, a multiplier being reduced to a squared operator or an addition being converted to a 1 bit shift. The graph compares two designs. The first, *bitstream reconfig*, is one which has been optimised by reducing the width of operators, for example multipliers, in such a way that it satisfies the error requirement given on the x-axis. Figure 2(a) shows the corresponding area.

This is compared with the second design, capable of running at two precisions: the precision given on the x-axis, *multiplexed-reduced*, and 32 bits of accuracy, *multiplexed-max*. The first design is one which would be employed if the bitstream were reconfigured to the optimal configuration, the second is one in which the design remains on chip and part of it is deactivated to achieve a reduced precision. Since the entire design, including the inactive part, remains on-chip, the design is larger than one using the minimum logic resulting from multiple bitstream reconfiguration; hence, the multiplexer-based design consumes more power during execution for a given precision. This difference is shown in figure 2 as *Power loss*. When the accuracy required is increased, the fluctuation caused by the place and route tools and chip temperature [22] becomes so great that the difference in power consumption between the two designs is not very pronounced. In general, when only a single precision is required, less power is consumed. This is because the active logic is performing the same task, and the inactive logic in the larger design is consuming power, largely due to the clock tree still toggling.

All designs operate with the same number of pipeline stages. In some cases it may be preferable to reduce the number of pipeline stages for designs employing bitstream reconfiguration to reduce the power consumption further, thus increasing the power loss caused by keeping the entire design on-chip. Overheads such as power dissipation of the controller, required to select a precision, are not included. Any Block RAM used in the design will not have its precision reduced because all values must be stored at their maximum precision. There may therefore be a small power improvement when a large RAM is required.

Multiple bitstream reconfiguration may consume more power during the reconfiguration process than the multiplexer-based design, so the conditions are derived under which one method is more efficient than the other. The analysis is based on energy consumption, which takes into account execution time and reconfiguration time, as well as the associated power consumption.

First, the following terms are defined:

- p_{eb}: power spent on execution between successive configurations using multiple bitstreams.
- p_{eg}: power spent on execution between successive configurations using multiplexers.
- p_b: power spent reconfiguring bitstreams between successive executions.
- p_g: power spent reconfiguring multiplexers between successive executions.

From figure 2, the total energy used by the multiplexer approach is:

$$\sum(t_{eg} \times p_{eg}) + \sum(t_g \times p_g)$$

A summation is used to show that there may be multiple reconfigurations. The total energy of a reconfigurable design with multiple bitstreams is calculated as follows:

$$\sum(t_{eb} \times p_{eb}) + \sum(t_b \times p_b)$$

$\sum(t_g \times p_g)$ is usually small, so it is ignored. Given:

$$\delta p = p_{eg} - p_{eb}$$
$$t_{gb} = t_{eg} - t_{eb}$$

(δp can be obtained from figure 2, *Power loss*) the multiplexer-based approach will require less energy the corresponding designs with multiple bitstream reconfiguration when:

$$\sum(t_{eg} \times \delta p) + \sum(t_{gb} \times p_{eb}) < \sum(t_b \times p_b)$$

When $\sum(t_{gb} \times p_{eb})$ is small compared with other terms, it can be neglected. In this case, both circuits operate at the same clock frequency. Assuming that there are n reconfigurations (which are assumed to be uniformly distributed and use a similar amount of energy per iteration), then:

$$\sum(t_b \times p_b) = n \times t_b \times p_b$$

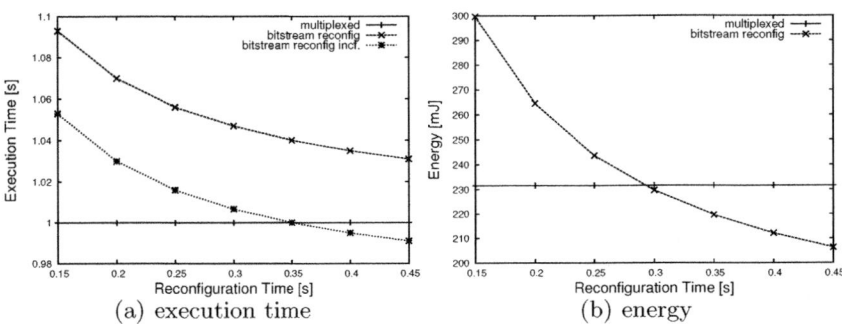

Fig. 3. Variation in run-time and energy for designs exhibiting different reconfiguration intervals for an inner-product design with a word-length of 20 bits

and t_{ae}, the average time spent on execution between reconfigurations, can be defined by:

$$n \times t_{ae} = \sum t_{eg}$$

Hence, a simple estimate for the average reconfiguration time is:

$$t_{ae} < (t_b \times p_b)/\delta p \tag{1}$$

for designs employing multiplexers to be more efficient, provided that the power loss does not vary significantly between reconfigurations. From figure 2, given t_{ae}, which depends on the application, the average precision required can be calculated. In addition to determining the condition that favours multiplexing in achieving a low energy design, the above model can be used in various ways. For instance, it enables us to study quantitatively how energy consumption varies with the frequency of reconfiguration: more frequent reconfiguration favours multiplexer-based reconfiguration, while less frequent reconfiguration favours multiple bitstream reconfiguration.

4.3   Reconfiguration Interval

The reconfiguration interval, that is, the length of time between reconfigurations occurring, affects power consumption and execution time. In practice, the interval width may have a certain distribution associated with it, but for simplicity a fixed width is looked at. Since multiple bitstream reconfigurable designs do not contain as much logic on-chip, they can sometimes run faster. When the circuits can run at different speeds (xMHz and yMHz, where $x < y$), the energy consumed for multiple bitstream reconfiguration to be more efficient is:

$$(p_b \times t_b) + (\delta rp \times t'_{eb}) < (\delta p \times t_{eg}) + (t_b \times p_{eb})$$

where δrp is the difference in power consumption at the different speeds and t'_{eb} is the time between reconfigurations at the faster speed. When both designs must complete at the same time:

$$t'_{eb} = t_{eg} - t_b$$
$$y = \frac{x \times t_{eg}}{t'_{eb}}$$

Figure 3 shows how the reconfiguration interval affects the run-time and energy requirements. The graphs show that a reconfiguration interval of 0.35 seconds or more means that a design employing bitstream reconfiguration will be more efficient than using multiplexers to reconfigure the device. To estimate power consumption at an arbitrary clock frequency, power consumption readings are taken at different frequencies and interpolation used by separating the active and inactive components. When this method is used alone, the energy will not increase significantly by increasing the clock frequency; the power will increase but the execution time will decrease. In practice, it may increase because additional hardware may be required.

5 Reconfiguration Strategy

In order to save power and allow a circuit to adapt to different input conditions, two methods of reconfiguration are used. This means that the circuit can adapt to changing conditions, enabling it to have a different accuracy depending on the output accuracy requirement. When a lower accuracy is required the circuit can be reconfigured to save power by either reconfiguring the bitstream or multiplexing components. Using a lower accuracy can have the same effect as reducing the bandwidth, accelerating the application.

5.1 Multiplexing and Bitstream Reconfiguration

The ability to multiplex components can be realised in several different ways. As explained in section 3.3, clock gating is not always possible with FPGAs. For example, word-length optimisation requires more dedicated clock gating elements than are available, so methods of producing a similar effect are investigated. One approach is to connect several smaller cores together, for example multipliers, creating a larger core. Components are then disabled using the clock enable port to reduce power when the accuracy of the full core is not required. This method can be inefficient because one large core can be optimised more fully than several independent cores connected together. Since only the clock enable port on flip-flops are used to save power, the clock is still toggling and therefore consumes more power than an ASIC design in, which the clock can be completely gated. Another option is to use a more global clock gating technique whereby entire arithmetic operators are selected, for example multipliers with different precisions, instead of gating individual bits; this is not done here because it requires a large area.

To reduce the area overhead of multiplexing components, the lower-order bits of the input are set to zero to minimise signal transitions in the circuit, which produces a similar effect to clock gating the unwanted bits. In both cases, signal

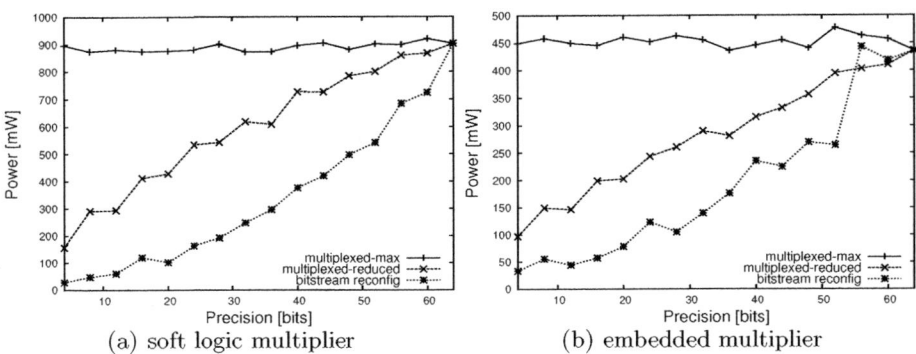

(a) soft logic multiplier   (b) embedded multiplier

Fig. 4. Power saving for a 64-bit multiplier by reducing the precision

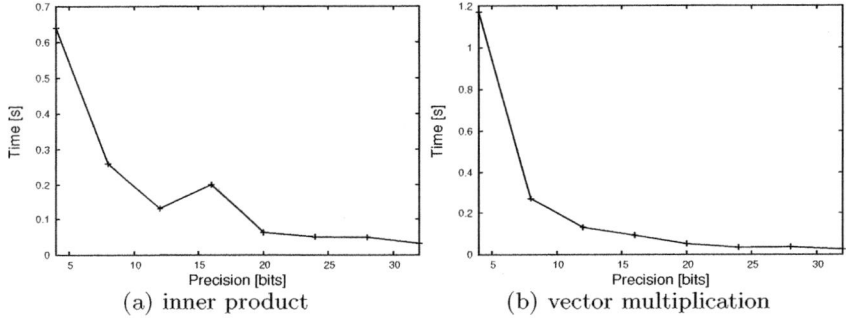

(a) inner product   (b) vector multiplication

Fig. 5. Average execution time, above which multiple bitstream reconfiguration becomes more efficient than multiplexing

transitions have been reduced to zero on the inactive part of the circuit, however, in this case the clock is still toggling. Figure 4 shows the power consumption of a 64-bit multiplier with different precisions, changed by setting the unwanted bits to zero. This method has a 1% area overhead because the inputs must be multiplexed. This overhead can increase in larger designs as routing becomes more complex. Figure 4(a) shows how a soft multiplier built from LUTs is affected by signal transition rates; figure 4(b) shows how an embedded multiplier is affected.

Bitstream reconfiguration is the most flexible technique enabling all or part of the bitstream to be reconfigured. With a smaller design on the chip, the power consumed will be lower. The disadvantage is that there are speed and power overheads associated with the reconfiguration process.

5.2   Comparing Reconfiguration Strategies

Figure 5 shows how the average execution time given by equation (1) varies with output precision. It indicates how long it takes before the overhead of reconfiguring the design by multiplexing components becomes more costly than reconfiguring the bitstream. When applying the model, 14ms [23] is used for the average reconfiguration time and 1500mW [24] for the average reconfiguration power. The overheads of using multiplexers are taken from the designs in section 6. Although this may be an under-estimate of reconfiguration time when the entire chip is to be reconfigured, the graphs still show that leaving the entire design on-chip can be more efficient. The same estimate is used for two chips: the Xilinx XC2VP30 and XC3S500E. Fore more accurate estimates, the reconfiguration power consumption overhead should be measured for each specific device.

The time before bitstream reconfiguration becomes more efficient than multiplexing components is almost constant when designs are configured using the word-length optimisation approach (section 3.1). Figure 5 shows what happens when time-multiplexed constants are adopted (section 3.2). In this case, either a set of constant multipliers are used in the multiple bitstream approach, or standard multipliers with multiplexed constants are used. As the accuracy requirement increases, the constant multipliers become more efficient, favouring the multiple bitstream approach, despite its reconfiguration overhead.

6   Results

All designs are synthesised with Handel–C 5 and Xilinx ISE 10.1. The power consumption is measured by attaching an ammeter to the 1.5V VCCINT jumpers (on the XC2VP30) and the 1.2V VCCINT jumpers (on the XC3S500E) which supply power to the FPGA. As well as automatically generating the required arithmetic cores and hardware interfaces, FPGA and board information is used to generate the clock interface. Digital clock managers (DCMs) are automatically inserted to ensure that all designs operate at the same clock frequency — 100MHz, although the circuits can run significantly faster in most cases.

6.1   Inner Product and Vector Multiplication

Figures 6 and 7 show how area and power vary with target precision for designs using time-multiplexed constant coefficients (see section 3.2) and designs using multiple bitstreams, optimised by constant propagation. The gap between the design dedicated to a single set of constants and the one capable of using multiple sets of constants grows as the word-length increases. The larger this gap, the more favourable bitstream reconfiguration is because the power loss caused by a larger than required design is so high that the reconfiguration overhead becomes less significant. Figure 5 shows how long it takes for the energy loss to become greater than the energy required to reconfigure the chip.

6.2   Uniform Cubic B-Splines

B-Splines equations are used in image deformation applications [25] and can be accelerated with dedicated hardware, such as FPGAs. Figure 2 shows the

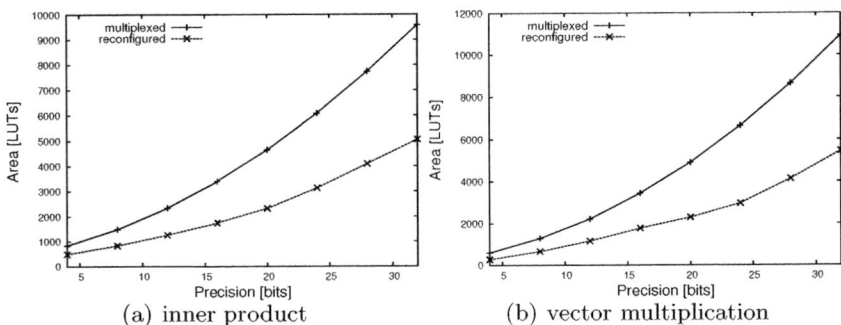

Fig. 6. Variation in area with word-length for a constant inner product and constant vector multiplier using multiplexed constant inputs against those using a single constant input, on the Xilinx XC2VP30

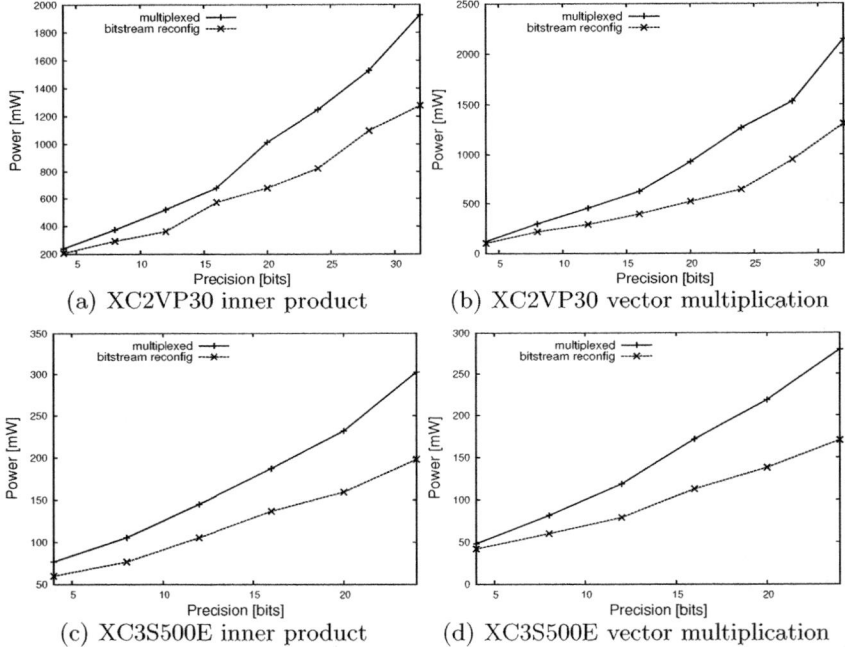

Fig. 7. Variation in power consumption with word-length for a constant inner product and constant vector multiplier using multiplexed constant inputs against those using a single constant input

power consumption and area of the B–Splines circuit. Section 4.2 describes the associated power overheads that come with fast on-chip reconfiguration and the implications of selecting each reconfiguration strategy. Although there is a large power loss caused by keeping the entire design on-chip, there is a large saving when combining word-length optimisation with the approach of modelling reconfiguration.

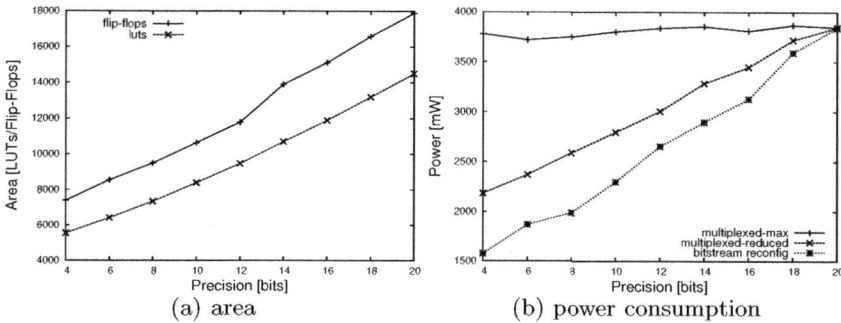

Fig. 8. Area and power consumption of the ray tracer at different output precisions on the Xilinx XC2VP30

6.3   Ray Tracing

The bottleneck in most ray-tracers is the ray-object intersection. For every ray, it must be determined whether it will intersect with an object or be unaffected. The more imprecise the arithmetic operators, the lower the image quality produced. If the hardware design were implemented to cater for less accurate image creation, the precision could be greatly reduced to conserve power. Since the ray tracer should be able to deal with any scene, the word-lengths are reduced at run time to minimise power consumption. Figure 8 shows the area and dynamic power saving of the ray tracer at different output precisions for the multiplexer-based approach and multiple bitstream reconfiguration.

Although the power loss is large, when the reconfiguration time is less than 0.1 seconds, keeping every component of the design on-chip will reduce energy. Since this is a large design, the estimate for reconfiguration time may be too small. The longer the reconfiguration time, the more beneficial multiplexing becomes.

7   Conclusion

In this paper, an approach for developing reconfigurable designs with either multiplexer-based reconfiguration or multiple bitstream reconfiguration has been shown. A model has been developed to determine which approach produces the most energy-efficient designs given the reconfiguration interval. Word-length optimisation should be used to reduce the power consumed by circuits, but also combined with the reconfiguration strategy determined by the model, to reduce the energy used by the system.

Current and future work includes automating the method outlined in section 3, extending the proposed approach to cover reconfigurable designs that make use of partial bitstream reconfiguration, and quantifying the trade-offs of these methods for a wide variety of devices. We are investigating the types of controller and the associated reconfiguration strategies, and their impact on power and energy consumption; phase information [26] is being analysed to accomplish this study. The effect of pipelining on energy reduction per operation [27] is also being explored.

Acknowledgements

The support of the UK EPSRC, FP6 hArtes (Holistic Approach to Reconfigurable Real Time Embedded Systems) project, Celoxica, Agility and Xilinx is gratefully acknowledged.

References

1. Kuon, I., Rose, J.: Measuring the gap between FPGAs and ASICs. IEEE Transactions on Computer-Aided Design of Integrated Circuits and Systems 26(2), 203–215 (2007)
2. Becker, J., Hübner, M., Hettich, G., Constapel, R., Eisenmann, J., Luka, J.: Dynamic and partial FPGA exploitation. Proceedings of the IEEE 95(2), 438–452 (2007)
3. Courtney, T., Turner, R., Woods, R.: Mapping multi-mode circuits to LUT-based FPGA using embedded MUXes. In: Proceedings of the IEEE Symposium on Field-Programmable Custom Computing Machines, pp. 318–327. IEEE Computer Society Press, Los Alamitos (2002)
4. Luk, W., Shirazi, N., Cheung, P.Y.K.: Modelling and optimising run-time reconfigurable systems. In: Proceedings of the IEEE Symposium on Field-Programmable Custom Computing Machines, pp. 167–176. IEEE Computer Society Press, Los Alamitos (1996)
5. Turner, R.H., Woods, R.F.: Design flow for efficient FPGA reconfiguration. In: Cheung, P.Y.K., Constantinides, G.A. (eds.) FPL 2003. LNCS, vol. 2778, pp. 972–975. Springer, Heidelberg (2003)
6. Farrahi, A.H., Sarrafzadeh, M.: FPGA technology mapping for power minimization. In: Hartenstein, R.W., Servit, M.Z. (eds.) FPL 1994. LNCS, vol. 849, pp. 66–77. Springer, Heidelberg (1994)
7. Klein, M.: Power considerations in 90nm FPGA designs. Xcell Journal (Fourth Quarter), 56–59 (2005)
8. Stephenson, J.: Design guidelines for optimal results in FPGAs. Altera (2005), http://www.altera.com/literature/cp/fpgas-optimal-results-396.pdf
9. Zhang, Y., Roivainen, J., Mämmelä, A.: Clock-gating in FPGAs: A novel and comparative evaluation. In: Proceedings of the 9th EUROMICRO Conference on Digital System Design: Architectures, Methods and Tools, pp. 584–590 (August 2006)
10. Cadenas, O., Megson, G.: Power performance with gated clocks of a pipelined Cordic core. In: Proceedings of the 5th International Conference on ASIC, vol. 2, pp. 1226–1230. IEEE, Los Alamitos (2003)
11. Osborne, W.G., Luk, W., Coutinho, J.G.F., Mencer, O.: Reconfigurable design with clock gating. In: Proceedings of the International Conference on Embedded Computer Systems: Architectures, Modeling and Simulation, pp. 187–194. IEEE, Los Alamitos (2008)
12. Brooks, D., Martonosi, M.: Value-based clock gating and operation packing: Dynamic strategies for improving processor power and performance. ACM Transactions on Computer Systems 18(2), 89–126 (2000)
13. Moshnyaga, V.G.: Reducing switching activity of subtraction via variable truncation of the most-significant bits. Journal of VLSI Signal Processing Systems 33(1), 75–82 (2003)

14. Styles, H., Luk, W.: Exploiting program branch probabilities in hardware compilation. IEEE Transactions on Computers 53(11), 1408–1419 (2004)
15. Bondalapati, K., Prasanna, V.K.: Dynamic precision management for loop computations on reconfigurable architectures. In: Proceedings of the IEEE Symposium on Field-Programmable Custom Computing Machines, pp. 249–258. IEEE Computer Society Press, Los Alamitos (1999)
16. Lee, D., Abdul Gaffar, A., Cheung, R.C.C., Mencer, O., Luk, W., Constantinides, G.A.: Accuracy-guaranteed bit-width optimization. IEEE Transactions on Computer-Aided Design of Integrated Circuits and Systems 25(10), 1990–2000 (2006)
17. Quinlan, D.J., Schordan, M., Yi, Q., Saebjornsen, A.: Classification and utilization of abstractions for optimization. In: Margaria, T., Steffen, B. (eds.) ISoLA 2004. LNCS, vol. 4313, pp. 57–73. Springer, Heidelberg (2006)
18. Luk, W., Shirazi, N., Cheung, P.Y.K.: Compilation tools for run-time reconfigurable designs. In: Proceedings IEEE Symposium on Field-Programmable Custom Computing Machines, pp. 56–65. IEEE Computer Society Press, Los Alamitos (1997)
19. Shirazi, N., Luk, W., Cheung, P.Y.K.: Automating production of run-time reconfigurable designs. In: Proceedings of the IEEE Symposium on Field-Programmable Custom Computing Machines, pp. 147–156. IEEE Computer Society Press, Los Alamitos (1998)
20. Becker, T., Luk, W., Cheung, P.Y.K.: Enhancing relocatability of partial bitstreams for run-time reconfiguration. In: Proceedings of the IEEE Symposium on Field-Programmable Custom Computing Machines, pp. 35–44. IEEE Computer Society Press, Los Alamitos (2007)
21. Paulsson, K., Hübner, M., Becker, J.: On-line optimization of FPGA power-dissipation by exploiting run-time adaption of communication primitives. In: Proceedings of the 19th Annual Symposium on Integrated Circuits and Systems Design, pp. 173–178. ACM, New York (2006)
22. Becker, T., Jamieson, P., Luk, W., Cheung, P.Y.K., Rissa, T.: Power characterisation for the fabric in fine-grain reconfigurable architectures. In: Proceedings of the 5th Southern Conference on Programmable Logic, pp. 77–82. IEEE, Los Alamitos (2009)
23. Griese, B., Vonnahme, E., Porrmann, M., Rückert, U.: Hardware support for dynamic reconfiguration in reconfigurable SoC architectures. In: Becker, J., Platzner, M., Vernalde, S. (eds.) FPL 2004. LNCS, vol. 3203, pp. 842–846. Springer, Heidelberg (2004)
24. Becker, J., Hübner, M., Ullmann, M.: Power estimation and power measurement of Xilinx Virtex FPGAs: Trade-offs and limitations. In: Proceedings of the 16th Symposium on Integrated Circuits and Systems Design, pp. 283–288. IEEE Computer Society, Los Alamitos (2003)
25. Jiang, J., Luk, W., Rueckert, D.: FPGA-based computation of free-form deformations. In: Cheung, P.Y.K., Constantinides, G.A. (eds.) FPL 2003. LNCS, vol. 2778, pp. 1057–1061. Springer, Heidelberg (2003)
26. Styles, H., Luk, W.: Compilation and management of phase-optimized reconfigurable systems. In: Proceedings of the International Conference on Field Programmable Logic and Applications, pp. 311–316. IEEE, Los Alamitos (2005)
27. Wilton, S.J., Ang, S.S., Luk, W.: The impact of pipelining on energy per operation in Field-Programmable Gate Arrays. In: Becker, J., Platzner, M., Vernalde, S. (eds.) FPL 2004. LNCS, vol. 3203, pp. 719–728. Springer, Heidelberg (2004)

A Cost Model for Partial Dynamic Reconfiguration

Markus Rullmann and Renate Merker

Technische Universität Dresden, Dresden, Germany
markus.rullmann@gmx.de, renate.merker@tu-dresden.de

Abstract. In this paper we present a new approach to minimize costs for partial dynamic reconfiguration of FPGAs. First, we develop a general Module Transition Model (MTM). In the MTM the reconfiguration is modeled at the granularity of reconfigurable resources, hence the model can take advantage of the partially identical configurations. The MTM targets both, minimum reconfiguration time and data. After it, the MTM is used at two diffent levels: (1) We apply the MTM to minimize binary configuration data, i.e. to generate cost efficient bitstreams for reconfigurable systems. It is shown how our model relates to previously established reconfiguration techniques. The improvements in reconfiguration time and bitstream size are demonstrated on an example. (2) We apply the MTM for high level designs, as the model also provides a measure for the similarity of reconfigurable circuits. The model describes in detail, which circuit elements are static and which need to be reconfigured. We use the model to derive a cost function in a high level synthesis tool to derive an allocation with minimal reconfiguration costs.

1 Introduction

Partial dynamic reconfiguration is used to adapt the FPGA configuration at *run-time* to the needs of the application that runs on the FPGA. While this technique allows a more efficient use of logic resources, the reconfiguration leads to a time overhead and overhead to store configuration data. Hence, the objective for an efficient dynamic reconfiguration should be to minimize these reconfiguration costs.

There exist a range of methods that can improve reconfiguration costs. The known methods can be divided into one of the following categories: improved device architectures, reconfiguration management at runtime, bitstream compression, and 'minimal' reconfiguration.

Coarse grain architectures take a fundamentally different approach to implement digital systems: These architectures consist of word level arithmetic functions or even primitive processors and word level interconnect. The programming models differ from the circuit centric approach of FPGAs. In this work FPGA architectures are considered.

In a reconfigurable system, the reconfiguration control organizes the reconfiguration of modules. The freedom available to schedule and place modules in the

P. Stenström (Ed.): Transactions on HiPEAC IV, LNCS 6760, pp. 370–390, 2011.
© Springer-Verlag Berlin Heidelberg 2011

reconfigurable area can be exploited to reduce the runtime overhead with configuration prefetching[1], caching[2], or smart reconfiguration scheduling [3][4][5]. Both configuration prefetching and caching require unused device resources in FPGAs to be effective. All presented methods assume reconfiguration costs that depend on the module area only.

There exist several schemes for bitstream compression [6][7][8][9]. They can reduce the space needed to store the bitstreams, but currently the configuration logic does not accept compressed bitstreams directly. However bitstream compression requires additional configuration decompression that must be implemented on the FPGA. In addition, bitstream compression does not reduce the often critical reconfiguration time.

Both techniques, reconfiguration management and bitstream compression complement our proposed method to minimize the bitstreams itself, because they can be used in combination with our method.

There are several approaches that exploit circuit similarities in order to achieve low reconfiguration cost. Most approaches target gate-level netlists, cf. [10][11]. Boden et.al. [12] incorporate runtime reconfiguration into high level synthesis as well. In their approach an application is not split into tasks for reconfiguration. Instead frequent reconfiguration of small parts of the circuit is assumed which is not effective for current FPGAs. In [13], Moreano et.al. describe a method to merge different dataflow graphs into one reconfigurable datapath. In his work, the additional data multiplexers are considered as reconfiguration cost. They do not provide a global cost model for the reconfiguration between multiple dataflow graphs.

Generally, an application is divided into *reconfigurable modules* that perform the data processing. Existing reconfiguration techniques consider the reconfigurable modules as inseparable entities. Moreover, reconfiguration is treated independently of the actual configuration of the FPGA.

In this paper we develop a general reconfiguration model, the *module transition model* (MTM). It is predicated on the fact, that not all resources allocated by a module need to be reconfigured, if the new module uses partially the same configuration of some resources of the FPGA. So it describes reconfiguration inherently as partial reconfiguration.

A similar state based model has been presented by Heron et al. [14]. They use the model in a virtual hardware handler to manage the device reconfiguration. In addition to their approach, we use the MTM to establish a measure for the reconfiguration overhead. While Heron et al. propose a generic approach to design circuits for more efficient partial reconfiguration, we show how the MTM can be used generate optimized datapaths from high-level specifications automatically.

We use this MTM to model the re-use potential of reconfigurable resources with the objective to get minimum reconfiguration costs. Due to the general approach of the MTM we can use it at two different levels: (1) at binary level: The model is used in a tool that creates a set of configuration bitstreams, minimal in terms of reconfiguration time or bitstream size. Obviously, this optimization approach complements previous techniques mentioned above. Further, we demonstrate that a substantial reduction in reconfiguration costs can be achieved, when compared to existing methods such as the Xilinx modular design flow [15] and the CombitGen tool [16]. (2) at structural level: The MTM provides a measure of similarity between reconfigurable modules at structural level. We implemented a tool that optimizes the mapping of dataflow graphs to device resources such that minimal reconfiguration costs are achieved.

In the next section an elaborate motivation for our approach is given.

This article extends the work presented in [17] as follows: We provide a concise formulation of the optimization problems that achieve minimal reconfiguration costs. We further present the virtual architecture (VA) model as a generic approach to evaluate the reconfiguration cost at structural level. We highlight the differences when applying the VA model between digital circuits and in the synthesis of circuits from dataflow graphs. This article includes benchmark results for a number of applications.

2   Motivation

Partial dynamic reconfiguration in FPGAs is usually associated with a module based design approach, see Figure 1. At first, the designer defines a *reconfigurable area* on the device. Second, he implements the reconfigurable tasks as modules on the reconfigurable area. At runtime the resources in the reconfigurable area are reconfigured to run the different tasks.

Using standard methodology, the reconfiguration cost of the implementation depends on the layout of the reconfigurable area. Each reconfiguration is performed by loading a partial *bitstream* into the device. The configuration bitstream itself is composed of *configuration frames* that contain any data needed to configure the entire reconfigurable area. A configuration frame is the smallest reconfigurable unit in a device; the size of a frame and configurable logic that is associated with each frame depends on the FPGA device. Because the standard bitstreams contain all data for a reconfigurable area, the size of these bitstreams is large, typically hundreds of kilobyte. The *configuration port* of the device has only a limited bandwidth. Together, this leads to configuration times in the order of some hundred microseconds. As a conclusion, configuration data becomes often to large for on-chip storage and frequent reconfiguration leads to considerable runtime overhead.

If the properties of reconfiguration data is analyzed in detail, it can be observed that the data does not differ completely between reconfigurable modules: (1) some of the reconfiguration frames are equal in two designs and (2) the data in two frames that configure the same part of the device frequently exhibit only a few different bytes (see frame/data differences in Figure 1). This has implications on the device reconfiguration at runtime. After the initial device configuration, the reconfigurable area is always in a known configuration state. When a new configuration must be established on this area, a new bitstream is used to program the associated device resources. In the ideal case, the reconfiguration programs only the device resources that need a different configuration. Currently the granularity of the reconfiguration is limited by the configuration frame size. For an efficient partial reconfiguration, only configuration frames that contain new configuration data are used to program the reconfigurable area. This is only possible if the current configuration and the frame-based differences are known at runtime.

The configuration data themselves are the result of the circuit design and the place and route tools. The configuration data of two modules can become very similar if the initial design exhibits a similar circuit structure and the tools place and route the circuits similarly.

In this paper we investigate how the above mentioned observations can be exploited to decrease the runtime overhead of dynamic reconfiguration. Our contributions are as follows. We introduce a state-based model to describe the runtime reconfiguration. The model is used to compute a reconfiguration cost metric at two layers: (1) for the configuration data the number of necessary configuration frames is computed for the reconfiguration between modules, and (2) for the digital circuit we compute the similarity in terms of circuit elements and the interconnect in the circuit. The cost metric is used to generate bitstreams that lead to more efficient reconfiguration at runtime and to generate digital datapaths within a high level synthesis tool that exhibit superior similarity between the circuits in reconfigurable modules.

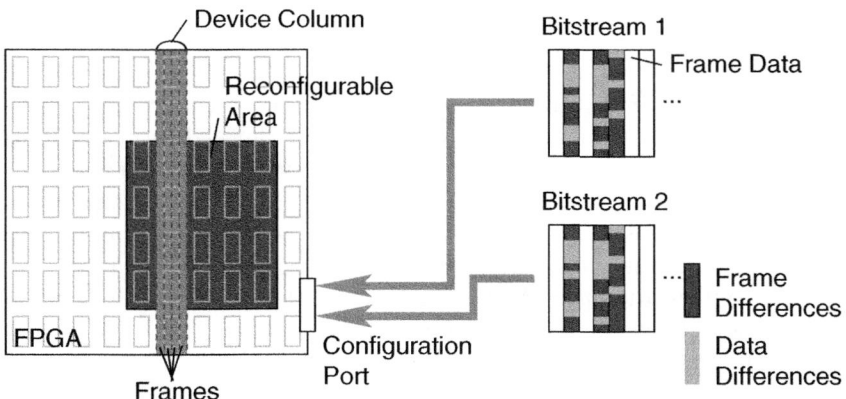

Fig. 1. Illustration of module-based partial reconfiguration

3   Module Transition Model (MTM)

In this section we introduce a general model, so called Module Transition Model (MTM), for partial reconfiguration as the basis of our approach. It allows us to evaluate reconfiguration costs and to perform optimizations on the configurations in order to reduce these costs.

The MTM describes the states (configurations $n_1, \ldots n_4$) of a device and the transitions (i.e. the reconfiguration from n_1 to n_2 etc.) between states. The device configuration that realizes a reconfigurable module puts the device in a certain state. A transition from one state to another is realized by partial reconfiguration of some of the device resources. The MTM can be described using a configuration transition graph $G(\mathcal{N}, \mathcal{E})$: Each state is represented by a node $n_i \in \mathcal{N}$. A transition from state n_i to state n_j is possible if the graph $G(\mathcal{N}, \mathcal{E})$ contains the directed edge $e = (n_i, n_j) \in \mathcal{E}$ with $n_i, n_j \in \mathcal{N}$. In Figure 2a an example of a configuration transition graph is given.

We assume that a reconfigurable area consists of m individually configurable elements, e.g. configuration frames. The configuration vector $\mathbf{d}(n_i) = [d(n_i)_1, d(n_i)_2, \ldots, d(n_i)_m]$ describes the configurations $d(n_i)_k$ of the configurable elements k, $k = 1 \ldots m$, for realizing state (configuration) n_i. We further define a reconfiguration bitmap $\mathbf{r} : \mathcal{E} \mapsto \{0, 1\}^m$, where $\mathbf{r}(e = (n_i, n_j)) = [r(e)_1, r(e)_2, \ldots, r(e)_m]$ describes which of the configurable elements k have to be reconfigured ($r(e)_k = 1$) or not ($r(e)_k = 0$) during reconfiguration from state n_i to state n_j.

The main purpose of the MTM is the quantification of the costs that originate from the partial dynamic reconfiguration of the device. Two fundamental measures can be defined on the basis of the MTM. The number of configurable elements that must be reconfigured on a transition $e = (n_i, n_j)$ determines the time required for the reconfiguration. Therefore we define the total reconfiguration time t of an instance of G as follows:

$$t = \sum_{e \in \mathcal{E}} ||\mathbf{r}(e)||_1 = \sum_{e \in \mathcal{E}} \sum_{k=1}^{m} r(e)_m. \tag{1}$$

The total reconfiguration time t describes the number of configurable elements that must be reconfigured if all transitions in G are performed once. The measure represents the time overhead at runtime associated with partial reconfiguration. If necessary, the terms in Equation 1 can be scaled by factors that describe the reconfiguration cost of a configurable element and the transition probability between configurations. However, in this paper we neglect these factors.

For each configuration $n_j \in \mathcal{N}$ it is important to know how much data for the reconfigurable elements must be available at runtime. From the MTM it appears that all configuration data that is needed for any transition to a specified state n_j. If computed for any configuration $n_j \in \mathcal{N}$ it yields the total configuration size s:

$$s = \sum_{n_j \in \mathcal{N}} || \bigvee_{n_i \in \mathcal{N}} \mathbf{r}((n_i, n_j))||_1. \tag{2}$$

As before we neglect any element and configuration specific weighting in Equation 2.

The reconfiguration costs are normalized to represent the average size per configuration $\bar{s}$ and the average reconfiguration time $\bar{t}$:

$$\bar{s} = \frac{s}{N} \text{ and } \bar{t} = \frac{t}{E} \quad \text{with} \quad N = |\mathcal{N}| \text{ and } E = |\mathcal{E}|.$$

Both quantities count the number of reconfigurable elements that must be stored for a configuration or that must be loaded on reconfiguration. The quantities can be interpreted for binary configuration data as follows: each reconfigurable element corresponds to one configuration frame. The size of a configuration frame (frame_size) is used as an architecture dependent scaling factor. The average storage size for raw configuration data evaluates to:

$$\bar{s}_{\text{data}}/KB = \bar{s} \times \text{frame\_size}/KB.$$

Similarly, the average reconfiguration time can be computed by using the configuration frame size and the speed of the configuration interface (data_rate) of the device as scaling factors:

$$\bar{t}_{\text{data}}/s = \bar{t} \times \frac{\text{frame\_size}/KB}{\text{data\_rate}/\frac{KB}{s}}.$$

4   Reconfiguration Costs for Binary Configuration Data

In this section, we apply the MTM to binary configuration data of Xilinx Virtex FPGAs. Therefore the model is refined such that the special properties of reconfiguration in these devices are handled correctly. We develop two new techniques to create bitstreams that are minimal in configuration size and reconfiguration time. We also discuss existing models for dynamic reconfiguration in the context of the MTM.

Dynamic reconfiguration is restricted by the configuration architecture in the FPGA. E.g. in Xilinx Virtex FPGAs, the smallest unit of configuration data is a configuration frame which corresponds to a configurable element. The size of such a frame depends on the FPGA device. We assume there are m configuration frames required to configure a fixed reconfigurable area. Each configuration frame is written to a specific frame address in the device. Within the MTM, each frame is associated with an element of the configuration vector $d(n_i)_k$ with $1 \leq k \leq m$, i.e. $d(n_i)_k$ yields the data for a configuration frame k. Similarly, a configurable element must be reconfigured by a configuration frame if $r((n_j, n_i))_k = 1$. In partially reconfigurable devices, only frames k with different configuration data $d(n_i)_k \neq d(n_j)_k$ need to be reconfigured.

The following example demonstrates the application of the MTM to frame based, partial reconfiguration.

Example 1. In Figure 2a the configuration transition graph for four modules is shown. If the device is in state n_1 and must be reconfigured to establish state n_2, the frames 3 and 5 must be reconfigured, $\mathbf{r}((n_1, n_2)) = [00101]$.

In Virtex FPGAs the configuration data is assembled to so-called bitstreams that are sent to a configuration port of the device. A bitstream contains control information for the configuration port, the frame address and data as well as checksum data. They can be created from raw frame data only with extra processing overhead. Most FPGA-based reconfigurable systems rely on these offline-assembled bitstreams, because they can be directly transferred to the

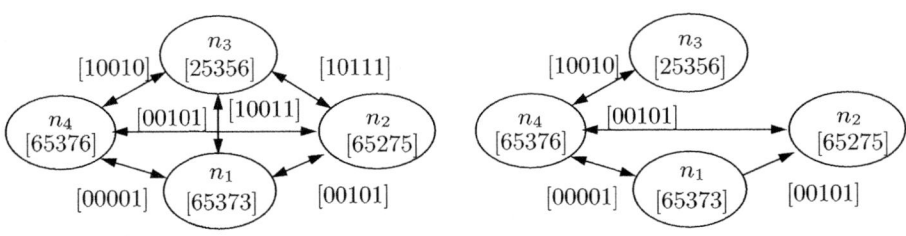

(a) Configuration Transition Graph for Example 1

(b) Configuration Transition Graph for Example 5

Fig. 2. Configuration transition graphs for (a) Example 1 and (b) Example 5: the nodes $n_1, \ldots, n_4$ are labeled with the frame configuration $[d(n_i)_1 \ldots d(n_i)_5]$. The edges are labeled with the reconfiguration bitmap $[r(n_i)_1 \ldots r(n_i)_5]$.

configuration interface of the device from the memory. Bitstreams can be created from raw frame data only with extra processing overhead. However, there are also approaches that modify bitstreams at runtime (e.g. [18]). We assume that a finite set of bitstreams must be created at design time for the reconfigurable system. The choice of available bitstreams is crucial to achieve low configuration size and reconfiguration time. With the MTM we can create minimal bitstreams for reconfigurable systems with respect to configuration size and reconfiguration time.

In the following the MTM is augmented such that the transitions in between configurations are performed by bitstreams. The number of configuration frames in the bitstreams are not necessarily identical to the number of configuration frames required by a transition, but a transition can be realized by a bitstream if it contains at least the necessary configuration frames. We model the execution of the state transitions in $G(\mathcal{N}, \mathcal{E})$ using bitstreams as follows: We define a finite set $\mathcal{B}$ of bitstreams. The elements $b_{l,i} \in \mathcal{B}$, $l < |\mathcal{N}|$, represent the specific bitstreams that perform the partial reconfiguration to establish state n_i. The function $\mathbf{f} : \mathcal{B} \mapsto \{0, 1\}^m$ assigns a configuration bitmap to each bitstream. The bitstream $b_{l,i}$ contains the configuration frame $d(n_i)_k$ if $f(b_{l,i})_k = 1$. The bitstream $b_{l,i}$ can only be used to realize transition $(n_j, n_i) \in \mathcal{E}$ if all configuration frames required by $\mathbf{r}(n_j, n_i)$ are associated with the bitstream, i.e.:

$$\forall k \in \{1, \ldots m\} \; : \; f(b_{l,i})_k \geq r((n_j, n_i))_k. \tag{3}$$

When a set of bitstreams is computed for a configurable system, the associated problem has three variables: the bitstreams $b_{l,i} \in \mathcal{B}$, the configuration bitmap $\mathbf{f}$, and the mapping $c : \mathcal{E} \mapsto \mathcal{B}$ of the MTM transitions $e \in \mathcal{E}$ to the bitstreams $b_{l,i} \in \mathcal{B}$.

The original equations to compute the total bitstream size and the total reconfiguration time (Equations 1 and 2) are replaced by their bitstream related equivalents. Now the configuration size s is a function of the deployed bitstreams and the reconfiguration time t is a function of the bitstream size each transition has been mapped to:

$$s = \sum_{b \in \mathcal{B}} ||\mathbf{f}(b)||_1 \quad \text{and} \quad t = \sum_{e \in \mathcal{E}} ||\mathbf{f}(c(e))||_1. \tag{4}$$

4.1 Existing Methods

With the MTM we are able to model two already existing reconfiguration models: Xilinx Modular Design Flow [15] and CombitGen [16]. Both models define exactly one bitstream per module, hence $\forall n_j \in \mathcal{N} : c((\cdot, n_j)) = b_{0,n_j}$. The models also assume full reconfigurability, e.g. G is complete. Thus $N = |\mathcal{B}|$ and $E = N(N-1)$.

Xilinx Modular Design Flow. The standard method to implement reconfigurable modules is based on the Xilinx modular design flow [15]. In a floorplanning step, the designer selects the areas for the reconfigurable modules on the device and defines busmacros, through which the reconfigurable modules connect to the static part of the design and other modules. The configuration data size and reconfiguration time for a reconfigurable module is defined by the selected area, regardless of the module contents.

The modular design flow includes all configuration frames in the bitstream for a module, e.g. $||\mathbf{f}(b)||_1 = m$. The equations in (4) reduce to:

$$s = mN \quad \text{and} \quad t = mN(N-1) \tag{5}$$

Example 2. For the MTM in Figure 2a, the Xilinx modular design flow yields $\mathbf{f}(c((n_2, n_1))) = \mathbf{f}(c((n_3, n_1))) = \mathbf{f}(c((n_4, n_1))) = [11111]$, cf. Figure 3a.

CombitGen. The CombitGen tool [16] exploits the fact that the modules that are placed at the same area do not necessarily differ in all configuration frames. Some configuration frames might be equal in all modules, if the associated resources are configured equally, or if the resources are not used by the modules. CombitGen processes all modules for the same area and excludes configuration frames that are equal in *all modules* from the reconfiguration data. If the modules are very densely populated or if resource configuration differs substantially, no reconfiguration frames will be saved and the reconfiguration cost are equal to that of the Xilinx modular design flow.

The CombitGen tool includes all frames in a bitstream that need to be reconfigured for any transition to that module configuration. Equation 6 computes the k-th element of the configuration bitmap:

$$f(b_{0,n_j})_k = \bigvee_{n_i \in \mathcal{N}} r((n_i, n_j))_k \quad \text{with } 1 \leq k \leq m. \tag{6}$$

In case G is complete and the function $\mathbf{r}$ is commutative, i.e. $\mathbf{r}((n_i, n_j)) = \mathbf{r}((n_j, n_i))$, then the configuration bitmap becomes a constant vector $\mathbf{f}(b_{l,i}) = \mathbf{f}_0$ for all bitstreams. Since at most all frames need to be reconfigured, the following unequation holds:

$$||\mathbf{f}_0||_1 \leq m. \tag{7}$$

For the CombitGen method, the equations in (4) reduce to:

$$s = ||\mathbf{f}_0||_1 N \quad \text{and} \quad t = ||\mathbf{f}_0||_1 N(N-1) \tag{8}$$

Example 3. For the MTM in Figure 2a, CombitGen yields $\mathbf{f}(c((n_2, n_1))) = \mathbf{f}(c((n_3, n_1))) = \mathbf{f}(c((n_4, n_1))) = [10111]$. Figure 3b illustrates the mapping of all transitions reaching configuration n_1 to a single bitstream $b_{0,1}$.

Both equations for s, t in (5) and (8) differ only by factor $N - 1$. Hence, the total bitstream size and total reconfiguration time are minimized both at the same time, if only one bitstream per module is used.

4.2   Novel Methods for Bitstream Generation

In this section we show how to use our model for the minimization of reconfiguration costs at binary level. We describe two novel methods to obtain a set of configuration bitstreams that lead to optimal solutions in terms of total configuration size and total reconfiguration time within our model. The first method yields a set of bitstreams such that each transition in the MTM can be realized directly by an associated bitstream, the second method yields a reduced set of bitstreams, for which some direct transitions are replaced by a sequence of transitions.

Reconfiguration by Direct Transition. In this model we assume, that each transition in $\mathcal{E}$ is mapped to a bitstream in $\mathcal{B}$. The function c and the configuration bitmap $\mathbf{f}$ can be chosen to minimize either the total bitstream size or the total reconfiguration time for a configuration transition graph $G(\mathcal{N}, \mathcal{E})$.

With the bitstream-based definition of the configuration size and the reconfiguration time – see Equation 4 – it is possible to compute bitstream assignments that are optimal in either way. In our tool we use an Integer Linear Program (ILP) to solve associated optimization problems. The problem formulation is given in Program 1. In the problem there are as many bitstreams possible as there are transitions in G, hence $|\mathcal{B}| = |\mathcal{E}|$. However not all bitstreams must be used in the derived solution. We introduce a binary variable $\beta_{l,j,i}$ that is set to 1 if the transition (n_j, n_i) is realized by bitstream $b_{l,i}$. Thus the solution of $\beta_{l,j,i}$ defines the function c. Equation 10 ensures that each transition is mapped to exactly one bitstream. In order to compute a valid configuration bitmap $\mathbf{f}$ for the selected mapping we ensure with Equation 11 that each necessary frame is contained in the bitstream and thus Condition 3 is fullfilled. The OR operation ($\bigvee$) is converted into a linear constraint by our ILP class library.

Program 1.   Minimal Bitstream Size or Minimal Reconfiguration Time

Minimize:

$$s = \sum_{b_{l,i} \in \mathcal{B}} \sum_{k=1}^{m} f(b_{l,i})_k \quad \text{or} \quad t = \sum_{(n_j, n_i) \in \mathcal{E}} \sum_{b_{l,i} \in \mathcal{B}} \beta_{l,j,i} \sum_{k=1}^{m} f(b_{l,i})_k \tag{9}$$

Subject to:

$$\forall (n_j, n_i) \in \mathcal{E} : 1 = \sum_{\substack{l,i \text{ with} \\ b_{l,i} \in \mathcal{B}}} \beta_{l,j,i} \tag{10}$$

$$\forall 0 \leq k < m : f(b_{l,i})_k = \bigvee_{(n_j, n_i) \in \mathcal{E}} r((n_j, n_i))_k \beta_{l,j,i} \tag{11}$$

Example 4. For the MTM in Figure 2a, reconfiguration to state n_1 with minimal time can be achieved with $\mathbf{f}(c((n_2, n_1))) = [00101]$, $\mathbf{f}(c((n_3, n_1))) = [10011]$, and $\mathbf{f}(c((n_4, n_1))) = [00001]$ In Figure 3c, it is shown that every possible transition to configuration n_1 is realized by a different bitstream. Clearly, each bitstream is smaller than the bitstream created by CombitGen in Figure 3b, which yields to faster reconfiguration.

Reconfiguration with a Transition Sequence. In contrast to previous methods, it is also possible to replace the direct transition between states as a sequence of alternative transitions. This method allows us to define a reduced graph $G'(\mathcal{N}, \mathcal{E}' \subset \mathcal{E})$ with fewer transitions. However we make sure that each transition in the original graph G can be realized by a sequence of transitions in the reduced graph G'. A sequence of transitions is defined as a path $\mathcal{P}_e$. The substitution of a single transition e by a sequence $\mathcal{P}_e$ of transitions can be exploited to reduce the total bitstream size further, but at the extend of increased reconfiguration time.

For the reduced graph G', we seek to find a subset of transitions $\mathcal{E}' \subset \mathcal{E}$ such that for each $e = (n_j, n_i) \in \mathcal{E}$ there exists a path $\mathcal{P}_e = \{(n_j, \cdot), \ldots, (\cdot, n_i)\}$. The path $\mathcal{P}_e$ is an ordered set of edges with $\mathcal{P}_e \subset \mathcal{E}'$. We require the path $\mathcal{P}_e$ to cause minimal reconfiguration time $\sum_{e' \in \mathcal{P}_e} \|\mathbf{f}(c(e'))\|_1$ along this path. The total bitstream size s and the total reconfiguration time t when using the transition sequences becomes:

$$s = \sum_{b \in \mathcal{B}} \|\mathbf{f}(b)\|_1 \quad \text{and} \quad t = \sum_{e \in \mathcal{E}} \sum_{e' \in \mathcal{P}_e} \|\mathbf{f}(c(e'))\|_1. \tag{12}$$

Example 5. The configuration transition graph shown in Figure 2b contains only the minimal subset of transitions necessary to realize all transitions from Example 1. A reconfiguration (n_2, n_1) is given by $\mathcal{P}_{(n_2, n_1)} = \{(n_2, n_4)(n_4, n_1)\}$. With a function $\mathbf{f}(c((n_2, n_4))) = [00101]$ and $\mathbf{f}(c((n_4, n_1))) = [00001]$ the reconfiguration time is proportional to 3 configuration frames.

While the original problem, i.e. reconfiguration by direct transition, consisted of finding a set of bitstreams and the function c, here we have to determine the reduced set of transitions $\mathcal{E}'$ as well as the minimum path for each transition of the original set $\mathcal{E}$. In the ILP model we assume that any edge from the set $\mathcal{E}$ can be contained in the solution. We use the binary variable γ_e to determine if edge $e \in \mathcal{E}$ is present in $\mathcal{E}'$ ($\gamma_e = 1$) and hence, if e is mapped to a bitstream as well, cf. (Equation 14). The model is built using a set $\mathcal{P}_e$ of pre-computed paths with $\{\mathcal{P}_e, \ldots\} \in \mathcal{P}'_e$ that are available for the solution. For small problem instances it is possible to include any path $\mathcal{P}_e$ that can realize transition e in the ILP model, for larger graphs G it is useful to limit the length of the path in order to reduce the complexity of the ILP model. The complete ILP is given in Program 2. A path $\mathcal{P}_e$ is available if all edges are included in the solution (Equation 15), hence the binary variable $\delta_e = 1$. In the cost function, we include only the path with the lowest sum of transition costs t_e. The term T defines an upper bound for t_e.

Program 2. Transition Sequence: Minimal Bitstream Size or Minimal Reconfiguration Time

Minimize:
$$s = \sum_{b_{l,i} \in \mathcal{B}} ||\mathbf{f}(b_{l,i})||_1 \quad \text{or} \quad t = \sum_{e \in \mathcal{E}} t_e \tag{13}$$

Subject to:

$$\forall (n_j, n_i) \in \mathcal{E} : \gamma_e = \sum_{\substack{l,i \text{ with} \\ b_{l,i} \in \mathcal{B}}} \beta_{l,j,i} \tag{14}$$

$$\forall \mathcal{P}_e : \delta_e = \bigwedge_{e \in \mathcal{P}_e} \gamma_e \tag{15}$$

$$\forall e : 1 \leq \sum_{e' \in \mathcal{P}_e} \delta'_e \tag{16}$$

$$\forall e : t_e = \min_{\mathcal{P}_e \in \mathcal{P}'_e} \sum_{e' \in \mathcal{P}_e} ||\mathbf{f}(c(e'))||_1 \delta_e + T(1 - \delta_e) \tag{17}$$

$$\forall 1 \leq k \leq m : f(b_{l,i})_k = \bigvee_{(n_j, n_i) \in \mathcal{E}} r((n_j, n_i))_k \beta_{l,j,i} \tag{18}$$

So far we have shown how the bitstream-based partial reconfiguration fits in our reconfiguration model. The original tool flow from Xilinx uses a simple scheme of full reconfiguration of all resources associated with the reconfigurable area. The CombitGen approach extends this model as follows: the bitstreams for each configuration contain only frames that are different to any other configuration. Our transition model shows that both Xilinx and CombitGen are not always optimal solutions in terms of total configuration size and total reconfiguration time. In order to derive optimal solutions with respect to our model, we have developed two ILP models that can be used to generate optimal sets of bitstreams. Figure 3 illustrates the mapping of transitions in the MTM to bitstreams using the proposed methods.

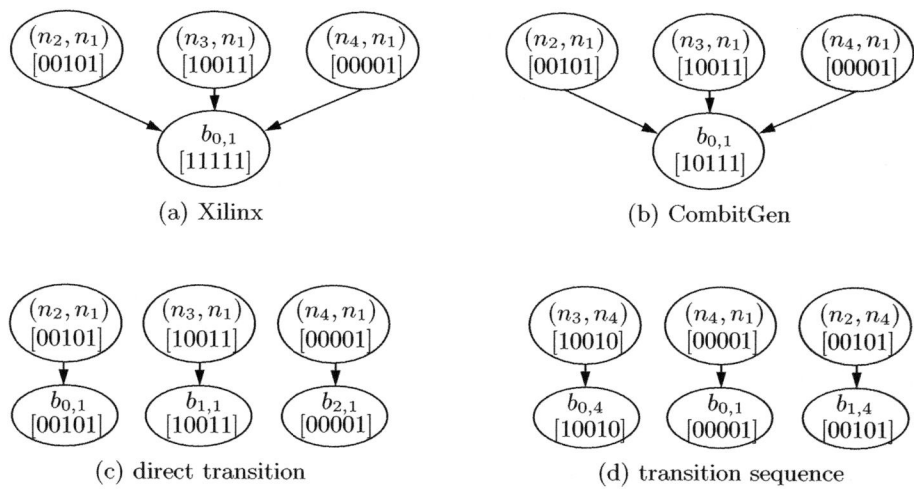

Fig. 3. Mapping of MTM transitions to bitstreams for configuration n_1: all transitions are realized by one bitstream that contains all frames (a), or only by the necessary frames (b). In (c) each transition is mapped to an individual bitstream to ensure minimum reconfiguration time. In (d) the mapping of all transitions required to realize the original transitions $(\cdot, n_1)$: $\mathcal{P}_{(n_2,n_1)} = \{(n_2, n_4), (n_4, n_1)\}$, $\mathcal{P}_{(n_3,n_1)} = \{(n_3, n_4), (n_4, n_1)\}$, $\mathcal{P}_{(n_4,n_1)} = \{(n_4, n_1)\}$ is shown. The reduced reconfiguration transition graph G' for (d) is shown in Figure 2b.

4.3   Examples

For demonstrating our approach we investigated the reconfiguration costs computed with the MTM for the module configurations of Example 1 and for a real world example, a set of four reconfigurable video filters implemented on the ESM platform [19]. We developed a tool that generates bitstreams that are minimal in terms of size or reconfiguration time. The functionality of the bitstreams was successfully verified on the ESM platform. The results are given in Table 1. As expected, the average reconfiguration time and bitstream sizes are equal if the reconfiguration method of Xilinx or CombitGen are used. However, our method allows us to reduce average reconfiguration times by almost 50 % when compared to the original Xilinx method. The penalty is an overhead of 23 % in bitstream size. Vice versa, the bitstream size could be reduced by more that 50 % if the transition sequence method is used. The reconfiguration time in this case is comparable to the CombitGen approach.

5   Reconfiguration Cost Estimation at Structural Level

In this section we demonstrate how the MTM can be used to generate reconfigurable designs with reduced reconfiguration costs at structural level. Therefore we aim to find implementations for the specified tasks which are as similar as

Table 1. Comparison of the different reconfiguration models for Example 1 and the ESM video filter application. The table lists the resulting average reconfiguration times $\bar{t}$ and bitstream sizes $\bar{s}$ for each method. The numbers are given in configuration frames. For the reconfiguration by direct transition the bitstreams have been optimized to achieve minimal bitstream size or minimal reconfiguration time.

	Example 1		ESM Video Filter	
	$\bar{t}$	$\bar{s}$	$\bar{t}$	$\bar{s}$
Xilinx	5.00	5.00	88.00	88.00
CombitGen	4.00	4.00	61.00	61.00
Direct Transition, Min. Size	3.50	4.00	61.00	61.00
Direct Transition, Min. Time	2.33	6.50	44.83	108.50
Transition Sequence, Min. Size	2.58	2.25	63.66	41.25

possible to each other. The improved similarity of any two circuits is represented in the MTM as a reconfiguration bitmap **r** that indicates fewer reconfigurable resources.

5.1   Reconfiguration Cost Reduction for Digital Circuits

In contrast to binary configuration data, the implementation of a task is often described as a so-called netlist. A netlist describes used circuit elements, the configuration of the circuit elements (e.g. the LUT contents), and the interconnect between the elements. We are using an equivalent graph representation of the netlists for our purpose. The netlist graph $G_i(\mathcal{R}_i, \mathcal{W}_i)$ of task i consists of a set $\mathcal{R}_i$ of resource instances r_i and the set $\mathcal{W}_i$ of interconnect wires w_i between those resources. The graph representation describes the configuration for a task at a structural level as opposed to the bit level of the binary configuration data.

The amount of reconfigurable resources for each transition $e \in \mathcal{E}$ depends on the placement of circuit elements and the routing of the circuit interconnect. For our reconfiguration cost estimation we do not use device specific place and route information, instead we use the following two assumptions: (1) two circuit elements with equal configuration that are placed at the same device resource cause no reconfiguration cost and (2) two connections that describe the interconnect between two such circuit elements cause no reconfiguration cost, too. Thus in order to improve reconfiguration cost we need to define which circuit elements must be placed in the same device resources in order to take advantage of the circuit similarity.

At structural level, there exists no fixed architecture for which reconfiguration costs can be measured in configuration frames. Instead, we define a *virtual architecture* (VA) that is used as a basis for the cost functions s, t. The VA defines a super-netlist that includes the resources required for all tasks. Formally, the VA is a graph $G^{\cup}(\mathcal{R}^{\cup}, \mathcal{W}^{\cup})$ that describes a set $\mathcal{R}^{\cup}$ of resources r_k and a set $\mathcal{W}^{\cup}$ of wires w_q used by any task $G_i(\mathcal{R}_i, \mathcal{W}_i)$.

The allocation $a : \bigcup_i \mathcal{R}_i \mapsto \mathcal{R}^\cup$ of the resource $r_i \in \mathcal{R}_i$ of graph G_i to resource $r \in \mathcal{R}^\cup$ in the VA is the key to obtain the circuit similarity: two resources $r_i \in \mathcal{R}_i$ and $r_j \in \mathcal{R}_j$ with $i \neq j$ are placed on the same device resource if they are mapped to the same resource in the VA, i.e. $a(r_i) = a(r_j) \in \mathcal{R}^\cup$. The set $\mathcal{W}^\cup$ of wires in the VA follows implicitly from the allocation a as well:

$$\mathcal{W}^\cup = \{w = (a(r_1), a(r_2))|\ (r_1, r_2) \in \bigcup_i \mathcal{W}_i\}. \tag{19}$$

Two interconnects $(r_{1i}, r_{2i}) \in \mathcal{W}_i$ and $(r_{1j}, r_{2j}) \in \mathcal{W}_j$ with $i \neq j$ can be realized using the same routing in the device if the source and drain nodes are allocated each to the same resources in the VA. It follows that in this case both wires are mapped to the same wire in the VA, i.e. $(a(r_{1i}), a(r_{2i})) = (a(r_{1j}), a(r_{2j}))$.

The allocation function a allows us to describe the implementation of a netlist G_i on the VA, represented by $G^\cup(\mathcal{R}^\cup, \mathcal{W}^\cup)$. For each netlist G_i, the allocation a translates the netlist into a configuration vector $\mathbf{d}(n_i) = (\dots, d(n_i)_k, \dots, d(n_i)_q, \dots)$ with $1 \leq k \leq |\mathcal{R}^\cup|, |\mathcal{R}^\cup| + 1 \leq q \leq |\mathcal{W}^\cup|$ as follows:

- $d(n_i)_k$ denotes the configuration of a resource $r \in \mathcal{R}_i$, if $a(r) = r_k \in \mathcal{R}^\cup$, otherwise it is 0.
- $d(n_i)_q$ is 1 if $(r_1, r_2) \in \mathcal{W}_i$ and $(a(r_1), a(r_2)) = w_q \in \mathcal{W}^\cup$, otherwise it is 0.

Hence, the configuration vector $\mathbf{d}(n_i)$ defines the resource *and* connection configuration of $G^\cup$ to realize task G_i.

The reconfiguration function $\mathbf{r}$ can be defined in accordance with the MTM on the basis of the configuration vector:

$$r(n_i, n_j)_k = \begin{cases} 1 & \text{if } d(n_i)_k \neq d(n_j)_k \wedge d(n_j)_k \neq 0 \\ 0 & \text{otherwise} \end{cases} . \tag{20}$$

The equation yields $r(n_i, n_j)_k = 1$ if the resource in the target configuration is configured and the configuration of that element deviates from the previous configuration.

The following example illustrates how the netlists of the tasks are mapped to a VA and how the reconfiguration costs that result from this mapping are computed.

Example 6. Figure 4a shows an example set of three netlists G_1, G_2, G_3 which correspond to the states n_1, n_2, n_3 in the configuration transition graph. Given the set $\mathcal{R}^\cup = \{b, c, d, e\}$ of VA resources, a possible allocation a is described in Table 2. E.g. the resources 1, 5 and 10 of the netlists are allocated to the same resource b of the VA. The node mapping defines also the connections in the VA: e.g. the three edges $(1, 2), (5, 6)$, and $(10, 8)$ are mapped to the same connection (b, c) of the VA. Note that there are many other node allocations possible for the three netlists; Table 2 describes only one allocation.

We have shown how the reconfiguration costs can be measured with our cost model at structural level. It appears that the actual cost depends on the mapping

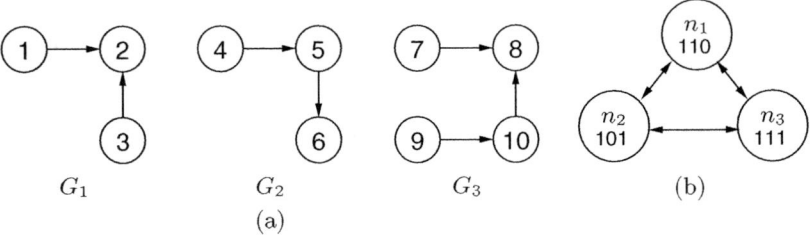

Fig. 4. (a) The three netlists G_1, G_2, G_3 for Example 6. In (b) the configuration transition graph that results from the allocation given in Table 2 is shown. The nodes are labeled with the state name n_1, n_2, n_3 and the part of the configuration vector that describes the use of connections in the VA.

Table 2. Allocation of nodes and edges for Example 6

	n_1	n_2	n_3	$a(r)$	$(a(r_1), a(r_2))$	$u_{\mathcal{R}\cup}$	$u_{\mathcal{W}\cup}$
Nodes r	1	5	10	b		3	
	2	6	8	c		3	
	3		7	d		2	
		4	9	e		2	
Edges (r_1, r_2)	$(1,2)$	$(5,6)$	$(10,8)$		(b,c)	3	
	$(3,2)$		$(7,8)$		(d,c)	2	
		$(4,5)$	$(9,10)$		(e,b)	2	
$\mathbf{d}(n_i)$	$[1110\,110]$	$[1101\,101]$	$[1111\,111]$				

function a of the netlists to the VA. In our work we aim to find a mapping function a such that low reconfiguration costs are achieved. There exists a variety of approaches to find an optimal mapping with respect to the cost functions s, t, e.g. exact solutions with ILP and approximations using heuristics.

A typical netlist for a single task may contain hundreds or thousands of resources. It appears that it is often infeasible to find optimal or even good mappings to a VA. The netlists consist of resources that describe FPGA logic directly. The fine grained representation often obscures the logical structure of a circuit that consists of ALU operations, register files and word level multiplexers. In order to reduce the problem complexity, we treat the reconfiguration not at netlist level but we investigate the mapping of dataflow graphs to a VA.

5.2   Reconfiguration Cost Reduction in High Level Synthesis

In this section we assume that the tasks are specified as dataflow graphs (DFGs). The nodes in a DFG represent operations and the edges describe data dependencies between operations. We want to reduce the reconfiguration cost when these tasks are implemented on an FPGA. Obviously it is possible to synthesize the

DFGs into fine grained netlists independent from each other and subsequently one can find a mapping that reduces reconfiguration costs.

Instead we use the VA model directly during the synthesis of DFGs into reconfigurable datapaths. At first we create a VA that provides enough resources to map all DFG operations to it. During synthesis the allocation of the DFG operations to these resources is optimized such that low reconfiguration costs are achieved. As for the netlist mapping, the data dependencies are implicitly mapped to connections in the VA. The result is a VA that consists of word level operations and interconnect – and a configuration vector for each configuration that describes the utilization of the VA for each task.

This method has several advantages compared to a netlist based approach: The mapping of operations to resources provides additional freedom in the optimization. The treatment of word level operations and interconnect reduces the problem complexity. Finally, several trade-offs between resource use and reconfiguration costs are feasible during optimization.

The modifications necessary to the model presented in Sect. 5.1 are only of minor nature. In fact, a task $G_i(\mathcal{R}_i, \mathcal{W}_i)$ describes a DFG instead of a netlist. If resource sharing is allowed then the mapping function a may map several DFG nodes to the same resource in the VA. Thus it is possible that several different data dependencies use different resources as data source but the same resource as target of a data transfer. The resulting conflict is resolved by inserting steering logic to control the dataflow. The VA nodes consist of complex word level operations, e.g. ALUs or complex functions, with a fixed configuration. Hence the configuration vector describes whether such a resource is used or not.

Although it is possible to use the cost functions in Equations 1 and 2 directly, it is possible to derive a simplified cost functions by using the following assumptions: (a) the MTM describes full reconfigurability, i.e. $G(\mathcal{N}, \mathcal{E})$ is complete, (b) all elements of the VA can be configured individually, and (c) the configuration vector describes only the use of an element in the VA but not the configuration. The reuse function $u_{\mathcal{R}^\cup} : \mathcal{R}^\cup \mapsto \mathbb{N}$ describes how often a DFG node is mapped to a resource $r \in \mathcal{R}^\cup$ of the VA for all tasks. The reuse function $u_{\mathcal{W}^\cup} : \mathcal{W}^\cup \mapsto \mathbb{N}$ describes how often a data dependency in a DFG is mapped to a connection $w \in \mathcal{W}^\cup$ of the VA for all tasks. Now, the total configuration size s can be computed from the sum of all VA elements that are in use by any configuration. With the reuse functions $u_{\mathcal{R}^\cup}, u_{\mathcal{W}^\cup}$ the total configuration size is now:

$$s = \sum_{r \in \mathcal{R}^\cup} u_{\mathcal{R}^\cup}(r) + \sum_{w \in \mathcal{W}^\cup} u_{\mathcal{W}^\cup}(w). \tag{21}$$

The total reconfiguration time t can also be rewritten by using the reuse function:

$$t = \sum_{r \in \mathcal{R}^\cup} [N - \mathcal{R}^\cup(r)] u_{\mathcal{R}^\cup}(r) + \sum_{w \in \mathcal{W}^\cup} [N - u_{\mathcal{W}^\cup}(w)] u_{\mathcal{W}^\cup}(w). \tag{22}$$

Example 7. In Table 2, the reuse functions $u_{\mathcal{R}^\cup}$ and $u_{\mathcal{W}^\cup}$ are given for resources and connections. The connection (d, c) is used in two configurations, hence $u_{\mathcal{W}^\cup}((d, c)) = 2$. The cost metrics yield $s = 17$ and $t = 8$.

The Equations 21 and 22 relate the reconfiguration cost to the reuse of elements in the VA. If more elements are reused then the size of the configuration is reduced as well as the total reconfiguration time. However it is not guaranteed that an allocation function a yields optimal results in terms of configuration size and reconfiguration time at the same time.

5.3   Benchmark Data

The use of the MTM to structural design descriptions is twofold: the MTM provides a measure for reconfiguration cost at structural level and the measure can be used to find a mapping that achieves low reconfiguration cost. We have implemented a high-level synthesis tool that maps DFGs to reconfigurable datapaths with a high reuse of logic and interconnect. The control is implemented separately by our tool, cf. [20]. The DFGs extracted from ANSI-C sources with a modified C-Compiler. The tool employs the VA model described in this paper to map all tasks within one step and to improve resulting reconfiguration cost. In this section we present data for several sets of reconfigurable tasks. The benchmarks are characterized in Table 3.

Table 3. Benchmark characteristics

Benchmark	Task	Control Blocks	Operations	Variables	Data Dependencies
ADPCM	adpcm_encode	35	126	24	199
	adpcm_decode	29	105	24	161
EDGE	sobel_hv	9	113	36	204
	sobel_h	9	100	33	177
	sobel_v	9	100	33	175
JPEG_DCT	jpeg_dct	6	178	43	378
	jpeg_idct	9	267	59	563
RGB_YUV	ycrcb2rgb	3	26	16	32
	rgb2ycrcb	3	24	13	28

In our tool, we select resource types for the DFG operations from a macro library and perform scheduling in a preprocessing step. For the reconfiguration optimization step we first generate a VA that provides one resource for each operation. In the main processing we use a simulated annealing approach to find a high-quality mapping of operations to VA elements with respect to the cost function. The cost function can be set up for different optimization targets: minimize the mean resource requirements or minimize the mean resource reconfiguration.

Here we present results for three different setups: In setup a, the mapping of each task is performed such that each datapath is of minimal size in both resource and interconnect. We assume that no information on the reuse of datapath elements is available and that all resources must be reconfigured. Similarly in setup b the mapping objective is the minimal size of each task. In this setup

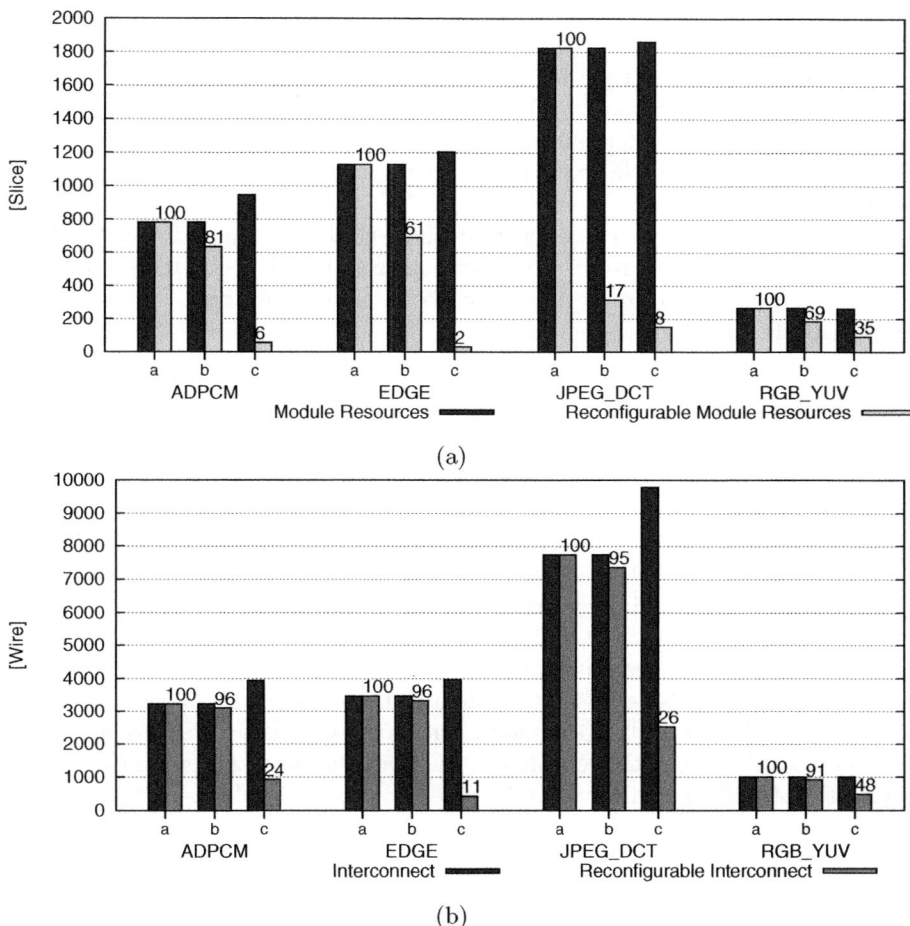

Fig. 5. Comparison of HLS results for different cost function settings. Figure (a) shows the average use of resources and the average reconfigurable resources that implement the datapath operations (without steering logic). Figure (b) shows the average use of interconnect and the average reconfigurable interconnect of the datapaths. The relative amount in % is printed on top of the reconfigurable elements. The setups used in a,b,c are explained in the text.

we compute the configuration cost on the basis of our VA model. Finally in setup c we optimize the mapping such that minimal reconfiguration cost for resources and interconnect are achieved, the size of the datapath is not considered.

The results are summarized in Figure 5. The charts show how many resources/interconnect is required on average for each benchmark task set and how many resources/interconnect must be reconfigured on average between the tasks. It can be seen that, if the DFG mapping is only optimized for datapath size, only few resources and interconnect can be reused and that most of the datapath must be reconfigured (typ. >60 % of resources and >95 % of the inter-connect, setup b). In contrast, if mapping is optimized for low reconfiguration cost (setup c), we observe that the datapath reconfiguration is much reduced, according to our cost model. For the benchmarks we achieve typically <10 % resource and <26 % interconnect reconfiguration for the larger examples. The datapaths consume little more resources because this is not the target of the optimization.

From our results we conclude that the MTM in conjunction with the VA model allows us to measure the inherent similarity of tasks. It can further be used as a cost metric in high-level synthesis to optimize task implementations especially for partial reconfiguration.

6   Summary

We have described the MTM model to analyse reconfiguration costs at different levels of abstraction. The model provides measures to evaluate the total bit-stream size and the total reconfiguration time, which are not necessarily equiv-alent. When the model is applied to binary configuration data, absolute costs can be measured. For this case we provided an extension that covers the use of a finite set of bitstreams. The configuration bitstreams which realize all transitions can be minimal in reconfiguration time or in terms of configuration costs.

The model can also be used to estimate the reconfiguration costs at a higher design level. The benefits are twofold: The model provides a measure for the sim-ilarity of modules, e.g. the reconfiguration costs that are inherent in the modules. Also, the identified similarity can be passed on to the implementation tools. The tools can use the similarity information to generate cost optimal implementa-tions that decrease the reconfiguration costs at the binary level [21]. The analysis at a higher level has considerable advantages: the resource configuration can be optimized with much better granularity, and the operations have no fixed allo-cation. The MTM can be used to determine the allocation that minimizes the reconfiguration costs. Another application is reconfigurable architecture design: The VA for a given allocation describes a reconfigurable architecture that can implement the modules set with minimum reconfiguration costs.

References

1. Hauck, S.: Configuration prefetch for single context reconfigurable coprocessors. In: Proceedings of the 1998 ACM/SIGDA Sixth International Symposium on Field Programmable Gate Arrays, pp. 65–74 (1998)
2. Li, Z., Compton, K., Hauck, S.: Configuration caching management techniques for reconfigurable computing. In: FCCM, pp. 22–38 (2000)
3. Walder, H., Platzner, M.: Online scheduling for block-partitioned reconfigurable devices. In: Design, Automation and Test in Europe Conference and Exhibition, pp. 290–295 (2003)

4. Ahmadinia, A., Bobda, C., Teich, J.: A dynamic scheduling and placement algorithm for reconfigurable hardware. In: Müller-Schloer, C., Ungerer, T., Bauer, B. (eds.) ARCS 2004. LNCS, vol. 2981, pp. 125–139. Springer, Heidelberg (2004)
5. Angermeier, J., Teich, J.: Heuristics for scheduling reconfigurable devices with consideration of reconfiguration overheads. In: IEEE International Symposium on Parallel and Distributed Processing, IPDPS 2008, pp. 1–8 (April 2008)
6. Stepien, P., Vasilko, M.: On feasibility of FPGA bitstream compression during placement and routing. In: International Conference on Field Programmable Logic and Applications, FPL 2006, pp. 1–4 (August 2006)
7. Huebner, M., Ullmann, M., Weissel, F., Becker, J.: Real-time configuration code decompression for dynamic FPGA self-reconfiguration. In: Proceedings of the 18th International Parallel and Distributed Processing Symposium (April 2004)
8. Pan, J.H., Mitra, T., Wong, W.F.: Configuration bitstream compression for dynamically reconfigurable FPGAs. In: IEEE/ACM International Conference on Computer Aided Design, ICCAD 2004, pp. 766–773 (November 2004)
9. Li, Z., Hauck, S.: Configuration compression for virtex FPGAs. In: The 9th Annual IEEE Symposium on Field-Programmable Custom Computing Machines, FCCM 2001, pp. 147–159 (2001)
10. Shirazi, N., Luk, W., Cheung, P.: Automating production of run-time reconfigurable designs. In: Proc. IEEE Symposium on FPGAs for Custom Computing Machines, pp. 147–156 (April 1998)
11. Rakhmatov, D., Vrudhula, S.B.K.: Minimizing routing configuration cost in dynamically reconfigurable FPGAs. In: Proceedings 15th International Parallel and Distributed Processing Symposium, pp. 1481–1488 (April 2001)
12. Boden, M., Fiebig, T., Meissner, T., Rulke, S., Becker, J.: High-level synthesis of HW tasks targeting run-time reconfigurable FPGAs. In: IEEE International Parallel and Distributed Processing Symposium, IPDPS 2007, pp. 1–8 (March 2007)
13. Moreano, N., Borin, E., de Souza, C., Araujo, G.: Efficient datapath merging for partially reconfigurable architectures. IEEE Transactions on Computer-Aided Design of Integrated Circuits and Systems 24(7), 969–980 (2005)
14. Heron, J., Woods, R., Sezer, S., Turner, R.: Development of a run-time reconfiguration system with low reconfiguration overhead. The Journal of VLSI Signal Processing 28(1-2), 97–113 (2001)
15. Xilinx Inc.: Xapp290 – Two Flows for Partial Reconfiguration: Module Based or Difference Based (September 2004)
16. Claus, C., Müller, F.H., Zeppenfeld, J., Stechele, W.: A new framework to accelerate Virtex-II pro dynamic partial self-reconfiguration. In: IEEE International Parallel and Distributed Processing Symposium, IPDPS 2007 (March 2007)
17. Rullmann, M., Merker, R.: A cost model for partial dynamic reconfiguration. In: Najjar, W., Blume, H. (eds.) International Conference on Embedded Computer Systems: Architectures, Modeling and Simulation (IC-SAMOS), Samos, Greece, pp. 182–186 (July 2008)
18. Kalte, H., Lee, G., Porrmann, M., Ruckert, U.: Replica: A bitstream manipulation filter for module relocation in partial reconfigurable systems. In: Proceedings of the 19th IEEE International on Parallel and Distributed Processing Symposium (April 2005)
19. Göhringer, D., Majer, M., Teich, J.: Bridging the gap between relocatability and available technology: The Erlangen Slot Machine. In: Athanas, P.M., Becker, J., Brebner, G., Teich, J. (eds.) Dynamically Reconfigurable Architectures. Dagstuhl Seminar Proceedings, Internationales Begegnungs- und Forschungszentrum für Informatik (IBFI), Schloss Dagstuhl, Germany (2006)

20. Rullmann, M., Merker, R., Hinkelmann, H., Zipf, P., Glesner, M.: An integrated tool flow to realize runtime-reconfigurable applications on a new class of partial multi-context FPGAs. In: 19th International Conference on Field Programmable Logic and Applications (FPL 2009), pp. 92–98. IEEE Press, Prague (2009)
21. Rullmann, M., Merker, R.: A reconfiguration aware circuit mapper for FPGAs. In: 14th Reconfigurable Architectures Workshop of the IEEE International Parallel & Distributed Processing Symposium - IPDPS 2007 (2007)

Heterogeneous Design in Functional DIF

William Plishker, Nimish Sane, Mary Kiemb, and Shuvra S. Bhattacharyya

Department of Electrical and Computer Engineering, and Institute for Advanced
Computer Studies,
University of Maryland at College Park, USA
{plishker,nsane,kiemb,ssb}@umd.edu
http://www.ece.umd.edu/DSPCAD

Abstract. Dataflow formalisms have provided designers of digital signal processing (DSP) systems with analysis and optimizations for many
years. As system complexity increases, designers are relying on more
types of dataflow models to describe applications while retaining these
implementation benefits. The semantic range of DSP-oriented dataflow
models has expanded to cover heterogeneous models and dynamic applications, but efficient design, simulation, and scheduling of such applications has not. To facilitate implementing heterogeneous applications,
we utilize a new dataflow model of computation and show how actors
designed in other dataflow models are directly supported by this framework, allowing system designers to immediately compose and simulate
actors from different models. Using examples, we show how this approach
can be applied to quickly describe and functionally simulate a heterogeneous dataflow-based application such that a designer may analyze and
tune trade-offs among different models and schedules for simulation time,
memory consumption, and schedule size.

Keywords: Dataflow, Heterogeneous, Signal Processing.

1   Introduction

For a number of years, dataflow models have proven invaluable for application
areas such as digital signal processing. Their graph-based formalisms allow designers to describe applications in a natural yet semantically rigorous way. Such
a semantic foundation has permitted the development of a variety of analysis
tools, including determining buffer bounds and efficient scheduling [1]. As a result, dataflow languages are increasingly popular. Their diversity, portability,
and intuitive appeal have extended them to many application areas with a variety of targets (e.g., [2][3][4])

   As system complexity and the diversity of components in digital signal processing platforms increases, designers are expressing more types of behavior in
dataflow languages to retain these implementation benefits. While the semantic
range of dataflow has expanded to cover quasi-static and dynamic interactions,
efficient functional simulation and the ability to experiment with more flexible

P. Stenström (Ed.): Transactions on HiPEAC IV, LNCS 6760, pp. 391–408, 2011.
© Springer-Verlag Berlin Heidelberg 2011

scheduling techniques has not. Complexity in scheduling and modeling has impeded efforts of a functional simulation that matches the final implementation. Instead, designers are often forced to go all the way to implementation to verify that dynamic behavior and complex interaction with various domains are correct. Correcting functional behavior in the application creates a developmental bottleneck, slowing the time to implementation on a heterogeneous platform.

To understand complex interactions properly, designers should be able to describe their applications in a single environment. In the context of dataflow programming, this involves describing not only the top level connectivity and hierarchy of the application graph, but also the functionality of the graph actors (the functional modules that correspond to non-hierarchical graph vertices), preferably in a natural way that integrates with the semantics of the dataflow model they are embedded in. Once the application is captured, designers need to be able to evaluate static schedules (for high performance) alongside dynamic behavior without loosing semantic ground. With such a feature set, designers should arrive at heterogeneous implementations faster.

To address these designer needs, we present a new dataflow model called *enable-invoke dataflow* (EIDF), a preliminary version of which was published in [5]. EIDF permits the natural description of actors for a variety of dynamic (and static) dataflow models. Even if the actors adhere to different models of dataflow, being described in EIDF ensures that they may be composed and functionally simulated together. Leveraging our existing *dataflow interchange format* (DIF) package [6], we implement an extension to DIF based on a restricted form of EIDF, called *core functional dataflow* (CFDF), that facilitates the simulation of heterogeneous applications. This extension to DIF, called *functional DIF*, allows designers to verify the functionality of their application immediately as we showed in preliminary work in [7]. From this working application, designers may focus on efficient schedules and buffer sizing, and thus are able to arrive at quality implementations of heterogeneous systems quickly.

This article is organized in the following fashion: relevant background is covered in Section 2 and related research is discussed in Section 3. The semantics for our dataflow formalisms are presented in Section 4 while their relationship to other dataflow models is covered in Section 5. The implementation of functional DIF is covered in Section 6. Two design examples are discussed in Section 7 and Section 8 summarizes and concludes the work.

2   Background

2.1   Dataflow Modeling

Modeling DSP applications through coarse-grain dataflow graphs is widespread in the DSP design community, and a variety of dataflow models has been developed for dataflow-based design. A growing set of DSP design tools support such dataflow semantics [8][9]. Ideally, designers are able to find a match between their application and one of the well studied models, including cyclo-static dataflow (CSDF) [10] , synchronous dataflow (SDF) [1], single-rate dataflow, homogeneous synchronous dataflow (HSDF), or a more complicated model such as boolean dataflow (BDF) [11].

Common to each of these modeling paradigms is the representation of computational behavior as a dataflow graph. A dataflow graph G is an ordered pair (V, E), where V is a set of vertices (or nodes), and E is a set of directed edges. A directed edge $e = (v_1, v_2) \in E$ is an ordered pair of a source vertex $v_1 \in V$ and a sink vertex $v_2 \in V$. A *source function, src* : $E \rightarrow V$, maps edges to their source vertex, and a *sink function, snk* : $E \rightarrow V$ gives the sink vertex for an edge. Given a directed graph G and a vertex $v \in V$, the set of incoming edges of v is denoted as $in(v) = \{e \in E | snk(e) = v\}$, and similarly, the set of outgoing edges of v is denoted as $out(v) = \{e \in E | src(e) = v\}$.

2.2 Dataflow Interchange Format

To describe the dataflow applications for this wide range of dataflow models, application developers can use the *dataflow interchange format* (DIF) [6], an approach founded in dataflow semantics and tailored for DSP system design. *The DIF language* (TDL) provides an integrated set of syntactic and semantic features that can fully capture essential modeling information of DSP applications without over-specification. From a dataflow point of view, TDL is designed to describe mixed-grain graph topologies and hierarchies as well as to specify dataflow-related and actor-specific information. The dataflow semantic specification is based on dataflow modeling theory and independent of any design tool.

To utilize the DIF language, *the DIF package* (TDP) has been built. Along with the ability to transform DIF descriptions into a manipulable internal representation, TDP contains graph utilities, optimization engines, algorithms that

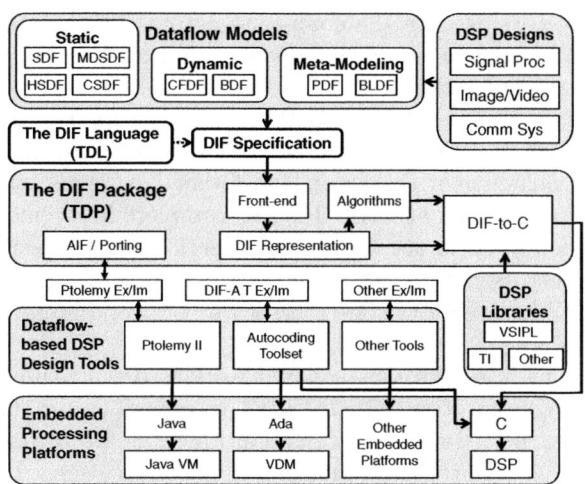

Fig. 1. DIF based design flow

may prove useful properties of the application, and a C synthesis framework [12]. These facilities make the DIF package an effective environment for modeling dataflow applications, providing interoperability with other design environments, and developing new tools. An overview of the DIF design flow using TDP is shown in Figure 1.

Beyond these features, TDP is also suitable as a design environment for implementing dataflow-based application representations. Describing an application graph is done by listing nodes and edges, and then annotating dataflow specific information. TDP also has an infrastructure for porting applications from other dataflow tools to DIF [13]. What is lacking in TDP is the ability to simulate functional designs in the design environment. Such a feature would streamline the design process, allowing applications to be verified without having to go to implementation.

3   Related Work

A number of development environments utilize dataflow models to aid in the capture and optimization of functional application descriptions. Ptolemy II encompasses a diversity of dataflow-oriented and other kinds of models of computation [14]. To describe an application subsystem, developers employ a director that controls the communication and execution schedule of an associated application graph. If an application developer is able to write the functionality of an actor in a prescribed manner, it will be polymorphic with respect to other models of computation. To describe an application with multiple models of computation, developers can insert a "composite actor" that represents a subgraph operating with a different model of computation (and therefore its own director). In such hierarchical representations, directors manage the actors only at their associated levels, and directors of composite actors only invoke their actors when higher level directors execute the composite actors. This paradigm works well for developers who know a priori the modeling techniques with which they plan to represent their applications.

Other techniques employ SystemC to capture actors as composed of input ports, output ports, functionality, and an execution FSM, which determines the communication behavior of the actor [15]. Other languages specifically targeting actor descriptions such as CAL [16]. For complete functionality in Simulink [9], actors are described in the form of "S-functions." By describing them in a specific format, actors can be used in continuous, discrete-time, and hybrid systems. LABVIEW [8] even gives designers a way of programmatically describing graphical blocks for dataflow systems.

Semantically, perhaps the most related work is the Stream Based Function (SBF) model of computation [17]. In SBF, an actor is represented by a set of functions, a controller, state, and transition function. Each function is sequentially enabled by the controller, and uses on each invocation a blocking read for each input to consume a single token. Once a function is done executing, the transition function defines the next function in the set to be enabled.

Functional DIF differs from these related efforts in dataflow-based design in its integrated emphasis on a minimally-restricted specification of actor functionality, and support for efficient static, quasi-static, and dynamic scheduling techniques. Each may be critical to prototyping overall dataflow graph functionality. Compared to models such as SBF, functional DIF allows a designer to describe actor functionality in an arbitrary set of fixed modes, instead of parceling out actor behavior as side-effect free functions, a controller, and a transition function. Functional DIF is also more general than SBF as it permits multi-token reads and can enable actors based on application state. As designers experiment with different dataflow representations with different levels of actor dynamics, they need corresponding capabilities to experiment with compatible scheduling techniques. This is a key motivation for the integrated actor- and scheduler-level prototyping considerations in functional DIF.

4   Semantic Foundation

4.1   Enable-Invoke Dataflow

We propose a new dataflow model in which an actor specification is divided into enable and invoke. We call this model *enable-invoke dataflow* (EIDF). Any application based on EIDF also adheres to the dataflow formalism described in Section 2.1, where each of the vertices are actors that implement separate enable and invoke capabilities. These capabilities correspond, respectively, to testing for sufficient input data, and executing a single quantum (invocation) of execution for a given actor.

Each actor also has a set of *modes* in which it can execute. This set of modes can depend upon the type of dataflow model being employed or it may be user-defined. Each mode, when executed, consumes and produces a fixed number of tokens. This set of modes can depend upon the type of dataflow model being employed or it may be user-defined. Given an actor $a \in V$ in a dataflow graph, The *invoking function* for an actor a is defined as:

$$\kappa_a : (I_a \times M_a) \rightarrow (O_a \times Pow(M_a)), \tag{1}$$

where $I_a = X_1 \times X_2 \times \ldots \times X_{|in(a)|}$ is the set of all possible inputs to a, where X_i is the set of possible tokens on the edge on input port i of actor a. After a executes, it produces outputs $O_a = Y_1 \times Y_2 \times \ldots \times Y_{|out(a)|}$, where Y_i is the set of possible tokens on the edge connected to port i of actor a, where $|out(a)|$ is the number of output ports. In general, invoking an actor can change the mode of execution of the actor, so the invoking function also produces the set of modes that are valid next. If no mode is returned (i.e., an empty mode set is returned), the actor is forever disabled.

To ensure that an invoking mode has the necessary inputs to run to completion, we utilize the *enabling function* which for a is defined as:

$$\varepsilon_a : (T_a \times M_a) \rightarrow \mathbb{B}, \tag{2}$$

where $T_a = \aleph^{|in(a)|}$ is a tuple of the number of tokens on each of the input edges to actor a (here, $|in(a)|$ is the number of input edges to actor a); M_a is the set of modes associated with actor a; and the output is *true* when an actor $a \in V$ has an appropriate number of tokens for mode $m \in M_a$ available on each input edge, and *false* otherwise. An actor can be executed in a given mode at a given point in time if and only if the enabling function is true-valued.

The separation of enable and invoke capabilities helps in prototyping efficient scheduling techniques. Scheduling is key to executing dataflow models, since minimal emphasis is placed on execution ordering in the paradigm of dataflow-based application specification. Scheduling is therefore a necessary part of dataflow graph execution, and furthermore, scheduling has major impact on key implementation metrics, including memory requirements, performance, and power consumption (e.g., see [18]).

Dynamic dataflow behaviors require special attention to schedule to retain efficiency and minimize the loss of predictability. The enable function is designed so that if desired, one can use it as a "hook" for dynamic or quasi-static scheduling techniques to rapidly query actors at runtime to see if they are executable. For this purpose, it is especially useful to separate the enable functionality from the remaining parts of actor execution.

These remaining parts are left for the invoke function, which is carefully defined to avoid computation that is redundant with the enable function. The restriction that the enable method operates only on token counts within buffers and not on token values further promotes the separation of enable and invoke functionality while minimizing redundant computation between them. At the same time, this restriction does not limit the overall expressive power of EIDF, which is Turing complete, as enabling and invoking functions can be formulated to describe BDF actors. Since BDF is known to be Turing complete, and EIDF is at least as expressible as BDF, EIDF can express any computable function and important dynamic dataflow models.

The restrictions in EIDF can therefore be viewed as design principles imposed in the architecting of dataflow actors rather than restrictions in functionality. Thus, flexible and efficient support for prototyping with dynamic and quasi-static scheduling techniques is an important motivation for EIDF. Such techniques are generally needed when dynamic dataflow behavior is present, and may be convenient for early-stage prototyping of static dataflow behaviors by simplifying the construction of schedulers.

In summary, the EIDF model is tailored to natural actor design and also facilitates dataflow modeling for rapid prototyping. EIDF is a generic model with its semantics independent of the underlying dataflow model used to describe a particular application. Thus, one can efficiently experiment with different specialized dataflow formats in the context of a given application. It is also possible to integrate dynamic parameterization (i.e., parameters whose values can be set and changed dynamically) into EIDF for example, through the meta-modeling framework of parametrized dataflow [19], to yield parameterized EIDF (PEIDF). Such rigorous integration of dynamic parameterization into EIDF is a useful topic for future work.

4.2   Core Function Dataflow

For a formalism customized to functional DIF, we derive a special case of the EIDF model that we refer to as *core functional dataflow* (CFDF). In the case of the EIDF model, the invoking function returns a set of valid modes of execution for an actor. This allows for non-determinism as an actor can be invoked in any of these valid modes. In the deterministic CFDF model, actors must proceed deterministically to one particular mode of execution whenever they are enabled. Hence, the invoking function should return only a single valid mode of execution instead of a set. The generic definition of the invoking function can be modified as

$$\kappa_a^* : (I_a \times M_a) \to (O_a \times M_a), \tag{3}$$

With this restricted form of invoking function, only one mode can meaningfully be interrogated by the enabling function. As long as the modes of an actor are themselves deterministic, requiring a single, unique next mode ensures that the resulting application is deterministic.

4.3   Functional DIF Semantic Hierarchy

Functional DIF is the realization of the CFDF semantics in our DIF package. Figure 2 shows the new hierarchical structure of functional DIF semantics with respect to the DIF package. DIF Graph is at the highest hierarchical level in the DIF semantics. EIDF represents our generalized, enable-invoke dataflow abstraction for applications specified by non-deterministic dataflow models. It provides a mechanism to handle generic methods that form a basis for many common dataflow models.

As described earlier, CFDF is a restricted form of EIDF for modeling deterministic dataflow applications. CFDF is the most general form of dataflow that we consider in our development of dataflow representations in DIF that have functional capabilities (as opposed to abstract dataflow graphs for application analysis). We are actively expanding the sub-tree rooted at CFDF to enable an increasing set of specialized dataflow modeling techniques available.

5   Translation to CFDF/EIDF

Many common dataflow models may be directly translated to CFDF in an efficient and intuitive manner. In this section we show such constructions, demonstrating the expressibility of CFDF and how the burden of design is eased when starting from an existing dataflow model.

5.1   Static Dataflow

SDF, CSDF, and other static dataflow-actor behaviors can be translated into finite sequences of CFDF modes for equivalent operation. Consider, for example, CSDF, in which the production and consumption behavior of each actor a is

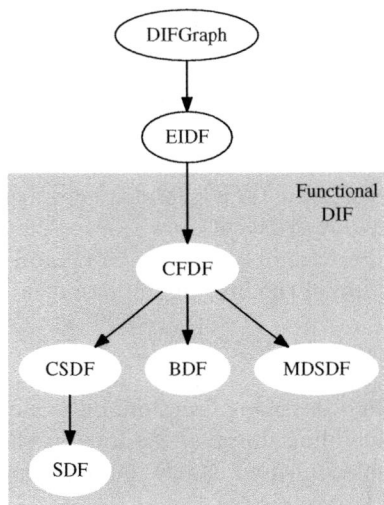

Fig. 2. Functional DIF semantic hierarchy

divided into a finite sequence of periodic phases $P = (1, 2, ..., n_a)$. Each phase has a particular production and consumption behavior. The pattern of production and consumption across phases can captured by a function ϕ_a whose domain is P_a. Given a phase $i \in P_a$, $\phi_a(i) = (G_i, H_i)$, where G_i and H_i are vectors indexed by the input and output ports of a, respectively, that give the numbers of tokens produced and consumed on these edges for each port during the ith phase in the execution of actor a.

To construct a CFDF actor from such a model, a mode is created for each phase, and we denote the set of all modes created in this way by M_a. Given a mode $m \in M_a$ corresponding to phase $p \in P_a$, the enable method for this mode checks the input edges of the actor for sufficient numbers of tokens based on what the phase requires in terms of the associated CSDF semantics. Thus, for each input port z of a, mode m checks for the availability of at least $G_p(z)$ tokens on that port, where $\phi(p) = (G_p, H_p)$. For the complementary invoke method, the consumption of input ports is fixed to G_p, the production of output ports is fixed to H_p. The next mode returned by the invoke method must be the mode corresponding to the next phase in the CSDF phase sequence. Since any SDF actor can be viewed as a single-phase CSDF actor, the CFDF construction process for SDF is a specialization of the CSDF-to-CFDF construction process described above in which there is only one mode created.

5.2 Boolean Dataflow

Boolean dataflow (BDF) adds dynamic behavior to dataflow. The two fundamental elements of BDF are Switch and Select. Switch routes a token from its input to one of two outputs based on the Boolean value of a token on its control input. The concept of a control input is also utilized for Select, in which the value of the control token determines which input port will have a token read and forwarded to its one output.

To construct a CFDF actor that implements BDF semantics, we create a mode that is dedicated to reading that input value, which we call the control mode. The result of this examination sends the actor into either a true mode or a false mode that corresponds to that control port. In the case of Switch, this implies three modes with behavior described in Table 1. Note that a single invocation of a Switch in BDF corresponds to two modes being invoked in the CFDF framework. For a strict construction of BDF, only the Switch and Select actors are needed for implementation, but CFDF does permit more flexibility, allowing designers to specify arbitrary behavior of true and false modes as long as each mode has a fixed production and consumption behavior.

Table 1. The behavior of modes in a Switch actor

mode	consumes		produces	
	Control	Data	True	False
Control	1	0	0	0
True	0	1	1	0
False	0	1	0	1

5.3 Gustav Function

While EIDF is designed to handle non-deterministic applications, it is also useful for certain cases of deterministic behavior in which CFDF is not expressible enough. The EIDF generalization of multiple next modes provides the expressibility necessary for some of these cases. Consider the Gustav function [20] the behavior of which is described in Table 2. Like the Switch actor in BDF, certain behaviors are tied to the value of tokens. The behavior is deterministic, but conditioned on the values presented at the inputs. To determine which two tokens should be processed, the values on the inputs must be known. This presents a problem for blocking read semantics like that of CFDF. Switch is implementable by splitting the token production and consumption into separate phases such that the dataflow behavior can be conditioned on the value of tokens. In the case of the Gustav function, it cannot be known *a priori* which token to read to indicate which token to read next. For example, the actor cannot simply wait for the value of input I_1 because the next mode to be processed might be m_3 implying a token might not appear on I_1 leaving the actor forever waiting while valid data is ready to be processed on the other two inputs.

Fortunately, EIDF is capable of processing these inputs by leveraging multiple possible next modes. Consider the subset of Gustav traces presented in Figure 3. Initially, the actor attempts to read a single token off any port, which is represented by the set of initial valid modes: $ReadI_1$, $ReadI_2$, and $ReadI_3$. By allowing any one of those modes to become enabled (and then successfully invoked), we avoid blocking on any one port. Once a token is read in (in our

Table 2. The behavior of the Gustav Function

modes	consumes		
	I_1	I_2	I_3
m_1	T	F	
m_2	F		T
m_3		T	F

example, a token from I_1), the actor waits for a token from one of the other two ports. Once two tokens are received, the data may be ready for processing, or may need to wait for a final token on the last remaining port. Once an action mode has been successfully invoked, it returns an appropriate set of read modes to continue processing.

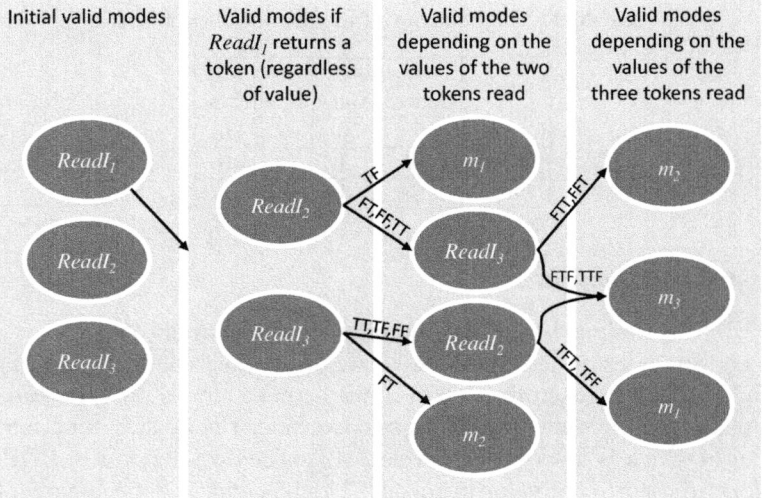

Fig. 3. Example traces through the EIDF implementation of the Gustav Function

The key to this implementation is using non-deterministic mechanisms present in EIDF to capture the unique deterministic behavior of this function. The Gustav function is another benchmark for expressibility that shows the power of EIDF. With only 6 modes (one for each input read, and one for each action), we are able to describe and implement the Gustav function in a natural way amenable for implementation.

6 Design and Implementation

To construct an efficient realization of CFDF, extensions to the DIF package have been made carefully. The following section discusses these changes, along with the functionality needed to simulate CFDF applications.

6.1   Software Architecture

The DIF package has been restructured to extend it to functional DIF. We have introduced an library of actors described in the Java programming language for use in functional DIF applications. Actors are objects derived from a base class that provides each actor with mode and edge interfaces along with base methods for the enabling and invoking functions, called the enable method and the invoke method respectively. Modes can be created either by a user through an API or automatically, based on other information about the application (e.g., the sequence of phases in a cyclo-static dataflow representation). While a designer will redefine an actor's class methods to define the proper functionality, the enable method is always restricted to only checking the number of tokens on each input (as per the enabling function definition). The invoke method may read values from inputs, but it must consume them as tokens. In other words, when a mode is invoked on an actor, the actor consumes a fixed number of tokens that is associated with that mode, and no more values are read. In either case, we expect designers to effectively construct a case statement of all of the possible modes for a given actor, and fill in the functionality of each mode in a case.

6.2   Scheduler and Simulator

We have used the *generalized schedule tree* (GST) [21] representation to represent schedules generated by schedulers in functional DIF. The GST representation is a generalization of the (binary) schedule tree representation developed for R-schedules [22]. The GST representation can be used to represent dataflow graph schedules irrespective of the underlying dataflow model or scheduling strategy being used. GSTs are ordered trees with leaf nodes representing the actors of an associated dataflow graph. An internal node of the GST represents the loop count of a schedule loop (an iteration construct to be applied when executing the schedule) that is rooted at that internal node. The GST representation allows us to exploit topological information and algorithms for ordered trees in order to access and manipulate schedule elements. To functionally simulate an application, we need only generate a schedule for the application, and then traverse the associated GST to iteratively enable (and then execute, if appropriate) actors that correspond to the schedule tree leaf nodes. Note that if actors are not enabled, the GST traversal simply skips their invocation. Subsequent schedule rounds (and thus subsequent traversals of the schedule tree) will generally revisit actors that were unable to execute in the current round.

We can always construct a *canonical schedule* for an application graph. This is the most trivial schedule that can be constructed from the application graph. The canonical schedule is a single appearance schedule (a schedule in which actors of the application graph appear once) which includes all actors in some order. In terms of the GST representation, a canonical schedule has a root node specifying the loop count of 1 with its child nodes forming leaves of the schedule tree. Each leaf node points to a unique actor in the application graph. The ordering of leaf nodes determines the order in which actors of the application graph are traversed. When the simulator traverses GST, each actor in the graph is fired, if it is enabled.

7   Design Example - Polynomial Evaluation

Polynomial evaluation is a commonly used primitive in various domains of signal processing, such as wireless communications and cryptography. Polynomial functions may change whenever senders transmit data to receivers. The kernel is the evaluation of a polynomial $P_i(x) = \sum_{k=0}^{n_i} c_k \times x^k$, where $c_1, c_2, \ldots, c_n$ are coefficients, x is the polynomial argument, and n_i is the degree of the polynomial. Since the coefficients may change at runtime, a programmable *polynomial evaluation accelerator* (PEA) is useful for accelerating the computation of multiple P_i's.

7.1   Programmable PEA

Since the degree and the coefficients may change at runtime (e.g., for different communications standards or different subsystem functions), a programmable polynomial evaluation accelerator (PEA) is useful for accelerating the computation of multiple P_i 's in a flexible way. To this end, we design a PEA with the following instructions: *reset, store polynomial*(STP), *evaluate polynomial*, and *evaluate block*. *Evaluate polynomial* is for a single evaluation, and *evaluate block* is for bulk evaluation of the same polynomial.

Since data consumption and production behavior for the PEA depends on the specific instruction, a PEA actor cannot follow the semantics of conventional dataflow models, such as SDF. However, if we define multiple modes of operation, we can capture the required dynamic behavior as a collection of CFDF modes. Following this principle, we have implemented the PEA as a single CFDF actor. In our functional description of the actor, we defined different modes according to the four PEA instructions. These modes are summarized in Table 3.

Table 3. The behavior of the PEA modes

mode	consumes		produces	
	Control	Data	Result	Status
Normal	1	0	0	0
Reset	0	0	0	0
Store Poly	0	1	0	1
Evaluate Poly	0	1	1	1
Evaluate Block	0	1	1	1

The normal mode (like the "decode" stage in a typical processor) reads an instruction and determines the next operating mode of the datapath. Of particular note here is the behavior of STP, in which a variable number of coefficients is read. Each individual mode is restricted to one particular consumption rate, so when the STP mode is invoked, it reads a single coefficient, stores it, and updates an internal counter. If the counter is less than the total number of coefficients to be stored, invoke returns STP as the next mode, so it will continue reading until done. Note that persistent internal variables ("actor state variables"), such as a counter, can be represented in dataflow as self-loop edges (edges whose source and sink actors are identical), and thus, the use of internal variables does not violate the pure dataflow semantics of the enclosing DIF environment. In future versions, we plan to incorporate parameterized dataflow [1] semantics to implement STP as a single PEA mode with a dynamically parameterized mode consumption rate.

Using an implementation based on the same behavior implemented by the functional DIF actor, we were able to compactly specify the behavior of the PEA in functional DIF. Through simulation of our functional DIF implementation, we verified its correctness and confirmed it produced the same output of a Verilog implementation we wrote of the same actor and test bench. A comparison of simulation time for the PEA between functional DIF and Verilog is shown in Table 4. We simulated this Verilog description using Modelsim version 6.3 SE. We used two different test bench input files and measured the time spent in simulation. Functional DIF improved the simulation time by over a factor of four in this example. Because the simulation of the Functional DIF description occurs at a higher level than Modelsim, we expect the speedups could be even higher. However, it is worth noting that we have not spent any time performance tuning the DIF simulator. We believe that with more performance tuning these speedup number should improve dramatically.

Table 4. Simulation times of Verilog and Functional DIF for the PEA test bench with two different sets of instructions

Instruction set	Verilog Simulation Time (ms)	Functional Simulation Time (ms)	DIF Speedup
Case 1	250	55	4.6x
Case 2	170	33	5.1x
Average	210	44	4.9x

7.2   Multi-PEA Design

To illustrate the problem of heterogeneous complexity, we suppose that a DSP application designer might use two PEA actors customized for different length polynomials. For this application, we restrict the PEA's functionality to be a CSDF actor with two phases: reading the polynomial coefficients and then processing a block of x's to be evaluated, as shown in Table 5. The overall PEA system is shown in Figure 4. Two PEA actors are in the same application and made them selectable by bracketing them with a Switch and a Select block. To

Table 5. The behavior of the CSDF implementation of the restricted PEA used in the dual PEA application

Actor	mode	consumes Data	produces Result
PEA1	Store Poly	4	0
	Evaluate Block	15	15
PEA2	Store Poly	7	0
	Evaluate Block	15	15

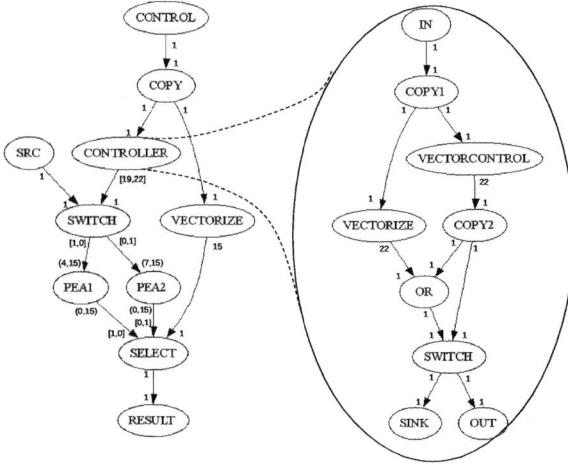

Fig. 4. A pictorial representation of the dual PEA application

manage the two PEA actors properly, this design requires control to select the *PEA1* or *PEA2* branch. In this system, the CSDF PEA actors consume a different number of polynomial coefficient tokens, so the control tokens driving the switch and select on the datapath must be able to create batches of 19 and 22 tokens, respectively for each path. If the designer is restricted to only Switch and Select for BDF functionality, the balloon with *CONTROLLER* shows how this can be done.

This design can certainly be captured with model oriented approach, pulling the proper actors into super-nodes with different models. But like many designs, this application has a natural functional hierarchy in it with the refinement of *CONTROLLER* and with *PEA1* and *PEA2*. We believe that competing design concerns of functional and model hierarchy will ultimately be distracting for a designer. With this work, we focus designers on efficient application representation and not model related issues.

Immediate simulation of the dual PEA application is possible to verify correctness by using the canonical schedule. We simulated the application with a random control source and a stream of integer data. A nontrivial schedule tree

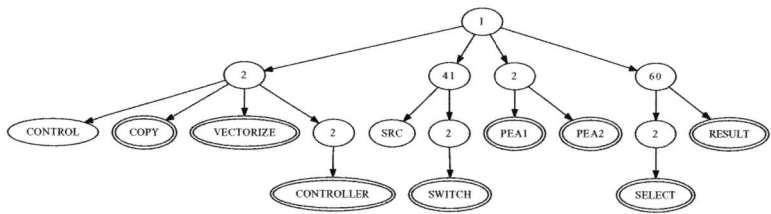

Fig. 5. Single appearance schedule for the dual PEA system

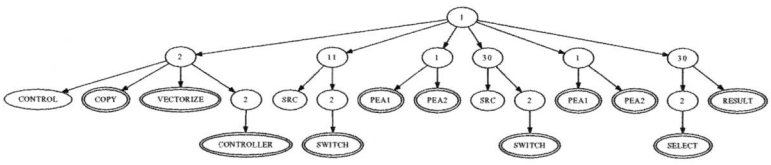

Fig. 6. Multiple appearance schedule for the dual PEA system

can significantly improve upon the canonical performance. Given that the probability of a given PEA branch being selected is uniform, we can derive a single appearance schedule shown in Figure 5, where each leaf node is annotated with an actor and each interior node is annotated with a loop count. Leaf nodes are double ovals to indicate they are guarded by the enabling function, while a single oval is unguarded. Figure 6 shows a manually designed multiple appearance schedule (a schedule in which actors may appear more than once) that attempts to process polynomial coefficients first, before queuing up data to be evaluated, to reduce buffering. Note that the *SRC* and *CONTROL* actor are unguarded as they require no input tokens to successfully fire.

We also implemented an M channel uniform discrete Fourier transform (DFT) filter bank and a sample rate conversion application. We constructed the decimated uniform DFT filter bank using a mixed-model consisting of CSDF and SDF actors. The sample rate conversion application is based on concepts found in [23] and [12]. Results for these different implementations with different schedules are summarized by Table 6. We simulated 10,000 evaluations running on a 1.7GHz Pentium with 1GB of physical memory. We measured the time it took to complete enough iterations to complete all of the evaluations and maximum total queue size. The manually designed schedules performed notably better than the canonical schedule. Such insight can be invaluable when considering the final implementation of the controller logic.

8   Conclusions and Future Work

In this work, we have presented a new dataflow approach to enable the description of heterogeneous applications that utilize multiple forms of dataflow. This

Table 6. Simulation times and max buffer sizes of the dual PEA design

Application	Schedule	Simulation Time (s)	Max observed buffer size (tokens)
Dual PEA - BDF Strict	Canonical	6.88	2,327,733
	Single appearance	1.72	1,729
	Multiple appearance	1.59	1,722
Dual PEA - CFDF	Canonical	3.57	1,018,047
	Single appearance	0.95	1,791
	Multiple appearance	0.99	1,800
DFT Filter	Canonical	0.91	17
	Single appearance	1.02	24
Sample Rate Conv	Canonical	9.15	9,394
	Single appearance	1.43	2,408

is based on a new dataflow formalism, a construction scheme to translate from existing dataflow models to it, and a simulation framework that allows designers to model and verify interactions between those models. With this approach integrated into TDP, we demonstrated it on the heterogeneous design of a dual polynomial evaluation accelerator. Such an approach allowed us to functionally simulate the design immediately and then to focus on experimenting on schedules and dataflow styles to improve performance.

This new dataflow model and modeling technique have many aspects for further work. One of the ongoing efforts focuses on developing generalized scheduling technique for CFDF graphs, in particular those representing dynamic applications. Such a technique would explore the fact that production and consumption rates of an actor are fixed for any given mode. This fact can be exploited to decompose a given dynamic CFDF graph into a set of static graphs that interact dynamically. Although the number of such static dataflow graphs can grow exponentially, application specific reachability analysis can be performed to include only a subset of all possible static graphs. The existing scheduling techniques for static dataflow models can then be leveraged for scheduling such static graphs. These schedules interact with each other dynamically. The GST framework discussed earlier provides an elegant way of representing such generalized schedules and simulating heterogeneous applications inside functional DIF. We believe the profiling results supplied by functional DIF could also provide valuable information for improving complex schedules automatically. We also plan to support parameterized dataflow modeling, which will permit more natural description of certain kinds of dynamic behavior, without departing from strong dataflow formalisms.

Acknowledgments

This research was sponsored in part by the U.S. National Science Foundation (Grant number 0720596), and the US Army Research Office (Contract number TCN07108, administered through Battelle-Scientific Services Program).

References

1. Lee, E.A., Messerschmitt, D.G.: Synchronous dataflow. Proceedings of the IEEE 75(9), 1235–1245 (1987)
2. Shen, C., Plishker, W., Bhattacharyya, S.S., Goldsman, N.: An energy-driven design methodology for distributing DSP applications across wireless sensor networks. In: Proceedings of the IEEE Real-Time Systems Symposium, Tucson, Arizona, pp. 214–223 (December 2007)
3. Hemaraj, Y., Sen, M., Shekhar, R., Bhattacharyya, S.S.: Model-based mapping of image registration applications onto configurable hardware. In: Proceedings of the IEEE Asilomar Conference on Signals, Systems, and Computers, Pacific Grove, California, pp. 1453–1457 (October 2006) (invited paper)
4. Plishker, W.: Automated Mapping of Domain Specific Languages to Application Specific Multiprocessors. PhD thesis, University of California, Berkeley (January 2006)
5. Plishker, W., Sane, N., Kiemb, M., Anand, K., Bhattacharyya, S.S.: Functional DIF for rapid prototyping. In: Proceedings of the International Symposium on Rapid System Prototyping, Monterey, California, pp. 17–23 (June 2008)
6. Hsu, C., Corretjer, I., Ko., M., Plishker, W., Bhattacharyya, S.S.: Dataflow interchange format: Language reference for DIF language version 1.0, user's guide for DIF package version 1.0. Technical Report UMIACS-TR-2007-32, Institute for Advanced Computer Studies, University of Maryland at College Park (June 2007); Also Computer Science Technical Report CS-TR-4871
7. Plishker, W., Sane, N., Kiemb, M., Bhattacharyya, S.S.: Heterogeneous design in functional DIF. In: Proceedings of the International Workshop on Systems, Architectures, Modeling, and Simulation, Samos, Greece, pp. 157–166 (July 2008)
8. Johnson, G.: LabVIEW Graphical Programming: Practical Applications in Instrumentation and Control. McGraw-Hill School Education Group, New York (1997)
9. The MathWorks Inc.: Using Simulink. Version 3 edn. (January 1999)
10. Bilsen, G., Engels, M., Lauwereins, R., Peperstraete, J.A.: Cyclo-static dataflow. IEEE Transactions on Signal Processing 44(2), 397–408 (1996)
11. Buck, J.T., Lee, E.A.: Scheduling dynamic dataflow graphs using the token flow model. In: In Proceedings of the International Conference on Acoustics, Speech, and Signal Processing (April 1993)
12. Hsu, C., Ko, M., Bhattacharyya, S.S.: Software synthesis from the dataflow interchange format. In: Proceedings of the International Workshop on Software and Compilers for Embedded Systems, Dallas, Texas, pp. 37–49 (September 2005)
13. Hsu, C., Bhattacharyya, S.S.: Porting DSP applications across design tools using the dataflow interchange format. In: Proceedings of the International Workshop on Rapid System Prototyping, Montreal, Canada, pp. 40–46 (June 2005)
14. Eker, J., Janneck, J., Lee, E.A., Liu, J., Liu, X., Ludvig, J., Neuendorffer, S., Sachs, S.R., Xiong, Y.: Taming heterogeneity - the Ptolemy approach. Proceedings of the IEEE, Special Issue on Modeling and Design of Embedded Software 91(1), 127–144 (2003)
15. Haubelt, C., Falk, J., Keinert, J., Schlichter, T., Streubühr, M., Deyhle, A., Hadert, A., Teich, J.: A systemc-based design methodology for digital signal processing systems. EURASIP J. Embedded Syst. (1), 15–15 (2007)
16. Eker, J., Janneck, J.: Caltrop—language report (draft). Technical memorandum, Electronics Research Lab, Department of Electrical Engineering and Computer Sciences, University of California at Berkeley California, Berkeley, CA (2002)

17. Kienhuis, B., Deprettere, E.F.: Modeling stream-based applications using the SBF model of computation. In: Proceedings of the IEEE Workshop on Signal Processing Systems, pp. 385–394 (September 2001)
18. Sriram, S., Bhattacharyya, S.S.: Embedded Multiprocessors: Scheduling and Synchronization. Marcel Dekker, Inc., New York (2000)
19. Bhattacharya, B., Bhattacharyya, S.S.: Parameterized dataflow modeling for DSP systems. IEEE Transactions on Signal Processing 49(10), 2408–2421 (2001)
20. Berry, G.: Bottom-up computation of recursive programs. ITA 10(1), 47–82 (1976)
21. Ko, M., Zissulescu, C., Puthenpurayil, S., Bhattacharyya, S.S., Kienhuis, B., Deprettere, E.: Parameterized looped schedules for compact representation of execution sequences. In: Proceedings of the International Conference on Application Specific Systems, Architectures, and Processors, Steamboat Springs, Colorado, pp. 223–230 (September 2006)
22. Murthy, P.K., Bhattacharyya, S.S.: Shared buffer implementations of signal processing systems using lifetime analysis techniques. IEEE Transactions on Computer-Aided Design of Integrated Circuits and Systems 20(2), 177–198 (2001)
23. Dalcolmo, J., Lauwereins, R., Ade, M.: Code generation of data dominated DSP applications for FPGA targets. In: Proceedings of the International Workshop on Rapid System Prototyping, pp. 162–167 (June 1998)

Signature-Based Calibration of Analytical Performance Models for System-Level Design Space Exploration

Stanley Jaddoe, Mark Thompson, and Andy D. Pimentel

Computer Systems Architecture group
Informatics Institute, University of Amsterdam, The Netherlands
{m.thompson,a.d.pimentel}@uva.nl

Abstract. The Sesame system-level simulation framework targets efficient design space exploration of embedded multimedia systems. Even despite Sesame's high efficiency, it would still fail to explore large parts of the design space simply because system-level simulation is too slow for this. Therefore, Sesame uses analytical performance models to provide steering to the system-level simulation, guiding it toward promising system architectures and thus pruning the design space. In this paper, we present a mechanism based on execution profiles, referred to as *signatures*, to calibrate these analytical models with the aim to deliver trustworthy estimates. Moreover, we also present a number of experiments in which we evaluate the accuracy of our signature-based performance models using a case study with a Motion-JPEG encoder and the Mediabench benchmark suite for performing off-line calibration of the models.

1 Introduction

The increasing complexity of modern embedded systems, which are more and more based on (heterogeneous) MultiProcessor-SoC (MP-SoC) architectures, has led to the emergence of system-level design. A key ingredient of system-level design is the notion of high-level modeling and simulation in which the models allow for capturing the behavior of system components and their interactions at a high level of abstraction. As these high-level models minimize the modeling effort and are optimized for execution speed, they can be applied at the early stages of design to perform, for example, Design Space Exploration (DSE). Such early DSE is of eminent importance as early design choices heavily influence the success or failure of the final product.

With our Sesame modeling and simulation framework [1,2], we target efficient system-level design space exploration of embedded multimedia systems, allowing rapid performance evaluation of different architecture designs, application to architecture mappings, and hardware/software partitionings. Key to this flexibility is the separation of application and architecture models, together with an explicit mapping step to map an application model onto an architecture model.

Although Sesame's system-level simulations allow for evaluating different application/architecture combinations in a highly efficient fashion, it would typically fail to explore large parts – let alone the entire span – of the design space. This is because system-level simulation is still too slow for comprehensively exploring the design space,

P. Stenström (Ed.): Transactions on HiPEAC IV, LNCS 6760, pp. 409–425, 2011.
© Springer-Verlag Berlin Heidelberg 2011

which is at its largest during the early stages of design. For this reason, Sesame uses analytical models [3,4] to provide steering to the system-level simulation, guiding it toward promising system architectures and therefore allowing for *pruning* the design space. These analytical models, which include models for performance, power and cost estimation, are used for quickly searching the design space by means of multi-objective optimization using evolutionary algorithms. So far, this analytical modeling stage lacked a systematic method for deriving the model parameters that specify application requirements and architecture capabilities. Clearly, the accuracy of these analytical models is highly dependent on the correct determination of these parameters.

In this paper, which extends [5], we focus on the performance estimation part of our analytical models (i.e. the power and cost models are not addressed) and present a technique based on execution profiles, referred to as *signatures*, that allows for deriving the application and architecture specific parameters in these analytical performance models. Using an experiment with a Motion-JPEG encoder application and an ARM-based target MP-SoC architecture, we validate the accuracy of our approach by comparing the estimations of our signature-based analytical model with those from simulation. Moreover, we also present an experiment in which we perform so-called *off-line training* of our signature-based performance model using the Mediabench benchmark suite [6], after which this externally calibrated model is again applied to the Motion-JPEG case study.

The remainder of the paper is organized as follows. In the next section, we introduce the basic analytical system model [3,4] for which we want to derive the model parameters. Section 3 describes how we determine application specific model parameters via a profiling mechanism based on signatures. Section 4 describes how architecture specific parameters are derived using a comparable mechanism. In Section 5, we put together the pieces of the puzzle presented in Sections 3 and 4 to actually construct signature-based analytical performance models. Section 6 presents initial validation results of our approach using an experiment with a Motion-JPEG encoder application. Moreover, it also presents results from an experiment in which we study off-line training of our signature-based performance models using the Mediabench benchmark suite. Section 7 describes related work, and Section 8 concludes the paper.

2   Basic Analytical System Model

In the Sesame framework, applications are modeled using the Kahn Process Network (KPN) [7] model of computation. The use of KPNs is motivated by the fact that this model of computation nicely fits the targeted multimedia-processing application domain and is deterministic. The latter implies that the same application input always results in the same application output, irrespective of the scheduling of the KPN processes. This provides complete scheduling freedom when, as will be discussed later on, mapping KPN processes onto MP-SoC architecture models for quantitative performance analysis and design space exploration. In a KPN, parallel processes communicate with each other via unbounded FIFO channels. By executing the application model, each Kahn process records its actions in order to generate its own *trace of application*

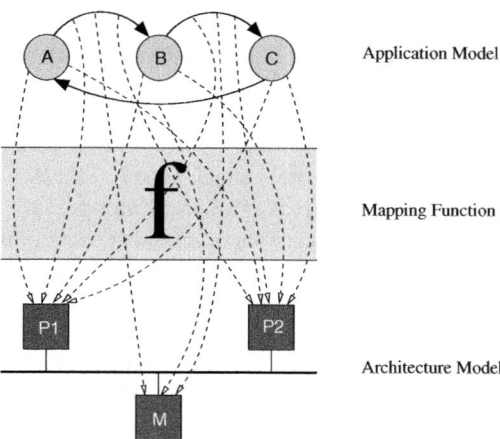

Fig. 1. An example mapping problem

events which is necessary for driving an architecture model. There are three types of application events, divided in two groups: *execute* events for computational behavior and *read* and *write* events for communication behavior.

The architecture models in Sesame are cycle-approximate TLM models and simulate the performance consequences of the computation and communication events generated by an application model. Architecture models are constructed from building blocks provided by a library containing template models for processing cores, and various types of memories and interconnects.

Since Sesame makes a distinction between application and architecture models, it needs an explicit mapping step to relate these models for co-simulation. In this step, the designer decides for each application process and FIFO channel a destination architecture model component to simulate its workload. Here, Sesame provides support for modeling a variety of scheduling policies in case multiple application processes are mapped onto a single architectural processing element. Mapping applications onto the underlying architectural resources is an important step in the design process, since the final success of the design can be highly dependent on these mapping choices. In Figure 1, we illustrate this mapping step on a very simple example. In this example, the application model consists of three Kahn processes and FIFO channels. The architecture model contains two processors and one shared memory. To decide on an optimum mapping, many instances need to be considered (and thus simulated). In realistic cases, in which the underlying architecture can also be varied during the process of design space exploration, simulation of all points in the design space is infeasible. Therefore, analytical models are needed to prune the design space, steering the designer towards a small set of promising design points which then can be simulated. The remainder of this section provides an outline of the basic analytical performance model [3,4] we use in Sesame for design space pruning, after which the subsequent sections present our signature-based mechanism to calibrate this analytical model.

The application models in Sesame are represented by a graph $KPN = (V_K, E_K)$ where the sets V_K and E_K refer to the Kahn processes and the directed FIFO channels between these processes, respectively. For each process $a \in V_K$, we define $B_a \subseteq E_K$ to be the set of FIFO channels connected to process a, $B_a = \{b_{a1}, \ldots, b_{an}\}$. For each Kahn process, we define a computation requirement, shown with α_a, representing the computational workload imposed by that Kahn process onto a particular component in the architecture model. The communication requirement of a Kahn process is not defined explicitly, rather it is derived from the channels attached to it (i.e., B_a). We have chosen this type of definition for the following reason: if the Kahn process and one of its channels are mapped onto the same (processor) component, the communication overhead experienced by the Kahn process due to that specific channel is simply neglected. For the communication workload imposed by the Kahn process, only those channels that are mapped onto a memory component are taken into account. So, our model neglects internal communications and only considers external communications. Formally, we denote the communication requirement of the channel b with β_b. To include memory latencies into our model, we require that mapping a channel onto a specific memory asks computation tasks from the memory. To express this, we define the computational requirement of the channel b from the memory as α_b. Here, it is ensured that the parameters β_b and α_b are only taken into account when the channel b is mapped onto an external memory. The actual determination of the above application model parameters will be addressed in the next section.

Similarly to the application model, the architecture model is also represented by a graph $ARC = (V_A, E_A)$ where the sets V_A and E_A denote the architecture components and the connections between the architecture components, respectively. In our model, the set of architecture components consists of two disjoint subsets: the set of processors (P) and the set of memories (M), $V_A = P \cup M$ and $P \cap M = \emptyset$. For each processor $p \in P$, the set $M_p = \{m_{p1}, \ldots, m_{pj}\}$ represents the memories which are reachable from the processor p. We define processing capabilities for both the processors and the memories as c_p and c_m, respectively. These parameters need to be set such that they reflect processing capabilities for processors, and memory access latencies for memories. The determination of these parameters will be addressed in Section 4.

The above model needs to adhere to a number of constraints, such as that each Kahn process has to be mapped to a processor, each channel has to be mapped to a processor (in case of local communication) or memory, and so on. For a formal description of these constraints, we refer to [3,4].

3   Application Requirements

As indicated in the previous section, we need to determine the model parameters for application requirements (α_a, α_b and β_b) and architecture capabilities (c_p and c_m). To this end, we present an approach based on execution profiles of application events, referred to as *signatures*, to determine these model parameters. In the remainder of this section, we focus on the derivation of the model parameters – via these signatures – for application requirements. The next section will address the derivation of the model parameters for architecture capabilities, which is done using the signature mechanism as well. As will become clear, our approach strictly adheres to the concept of 'separation of concerns' [8], separating application (requirements) from architecture (capabilities) signatures.

Table 1. Table (a) shows the currently defined AIS instructions with their index in the vector-based process signatures. Table (b) lists the event trace of process k_1, and Table (c) shows an execution trace of op_1 as obtained by an ARM ISS (left column) and the corresponding AIS instructions (right column).

Signature index	AIS opcode	Description
1	AIS_BMEM	Block memory transfers
2	AIS_MEM	Memory transfers
3	AIS_BRANCH	Branches
4	AIS_COPROC	Co-proc. instructions
5	AIS_IMUL	Int. multiplications
6	AIS_ISIMPLE	Simple Int. arithmetic
7	AIS_OS	Software interrupts
8	AIS_UNKNOWN	Non-mappable instruction

(a)

read	f_2
execute	op_1
write	f_1
read	f_2
execute	op_2
write	f_1
execute	op_1
write	f_1
write	f_1

(b)

ARM instruction	AIS opcode	ARM instruction	AIS opcode
bl 0x81c4;	AIS_BRANCH	str r3, [fp, #−16];	AIS_MEM
mov ip, sp;	AIS_ISIMPLE	ldr r2, [fp, #−20];	AIS_MEM
stmdb sp, fp, ip, lr, pc;!	AIS_BMEM	ldr r3, [fp, #−16];	AIS_MEM
sub fp, ip, #4;	AIS_ISIMPLE	mul r3, r2, r3;	AIS_IMUL
sub sp, sp, #12;	AIS_ISIMPLE	str r3, [fp, #−24];	AIS_MEM
ldr r2, [fp, #−16];	AIS_MEM	ldr r2, [fp, #−16];	AIS_MEM
ldr r3, [fp, #−20];	AIS_MEM	ldr r3, [fp, #−24];	AIS_MEM
add r2, r2, r3;	AIS_ISIMPLE	add r2, r2, r3;	AIS_ISIMPLE
ldr r3, [fp, #−24];	AIS_MEM	ldr r3, [fp, #−20];	AIS_MEM
rsb r3, r3, r2;	AIS_ISIMPLE	mul r3, r2, r3;	AIS_IMUL
str r3, [fp, #−24];	AIS_MEM	str r3, [fp, #−16];	AIS_MEM
ldr r2, [fp, #−16];	AIS_MEM	sub sp, fp, #12;	AIS_ISIMPLE
ldr r3, [fp, #−20];	AIS_MEM	ldmia sp, {fp, sp, pc};	AIS_BMEM
add r2, r2, r3;	AIS_ISIMPLE	mov ip, sp;	AIS_ISIMPLE
ldr r3, [fp, #−24];	AIS_MEM	stmdb sp, fp, ip, lr, pc;!	AIS_BMEM
mul r3, r2, r3;	AIS_IMUL		

(c)

A signature of a Kahn process represents its computational requirements. These processes signatures describe the computational complexity at a high level of abstraction using an Abstract Instruction Set (AIS). Currently, our AIS consists of the small set of abstract instruction types as shown in Table 1(a)[1]. To construct a signature, the real machine instructions that embody the computation, derived from an Instruction Set Simulator (ISS), are first mapped onto the AIS, after which a compact execution profile is made. This means that the resulting signature is a *vector* containing the instruction counts of the different AIS instructions. The first column in Table 1(a) shows the signature (vector) index that each AIS instruction type corresponds to.

The high level of abstraction of the AIS makes it architecture independent and, as will become clear later on, makes the signatures relatively small and easy to handle. Nevertheless, the AIS could always be refined when needed (see also Section 6). Given the fact that our AIS only consists of a few instruction opcodes, many different real machine instructions will thus map onto the same AIS instruction. For example, all (single-element) load and store instructions will map onto AIS_MEM, integer

---

[1] In this paper, we focus on programmable cores as processor targets, but the AIS also contains a special "co-processor" instruction that can be used for modeling dedicated HW blocks.

multiplications and divisions onto AIS_MUL, and basic integer operations such as additions, subtractions and logical operations onto AIS_ISIMPLE. The AIS_UNKNOWN opcode is used when a machine instruction cannot be mapped onto any of the other AIS instruction types. Our experiments have demonstrated, however, that the influence of this AIS_UNKNOWN class of AIS instructions is negligible.

The computational (i.e., *execute*) events in the application event traces from a KPN application model together with the separate signatures of each of the associated computational operations determine the signature for each Kahn process. To illustrate this, consider Table 1(b) which shows an example event trace of Kahn process k_1. When deriving the signature of process k_1, only the *execute* events in its event trace are considered. Each *execute* event comes with an identifier of an operation, to indicate which operation was executed. The signature of k_1 is the sum of the signatures of the operations executed by k_1. In the example of Table 1(b), operations op_1 and op_2 have signatures that describe the computational requirements of these operations. Now, assume that an ISS generates the sequence of (in this case, ARM) instructions as shown in the first column of Table 1(c) for op_1. The next step is to classify these instructions (is it a basic integer instruction, or a memory operation, or a branch instruction, etc.). In other words, the assembly instructions have to be mapped to the AIS instructions defined for our signatures. The result of this classification is shown in the second column of Table 1(c). Then, a signature for op_1 can be generated based on the counts of the different AIS opcodes. For op_1, this gives

$$op_1.\text{signature} = [3, 15, 1, 0, 3, 9, 0, 0] \qquad (1)$$

with the AIS opcode counts ranked according to the first column of Table 1(a). Using the same method, a signature for op_2 can be generated. Assume that its signature is:

$$op_2.\text{signature} = [8, 17, 8, 0, 2, 29, 2, 0] \qquad (2)$$

Then, using these signatures we can answer the original question, that is, calculate the signature of process k_1 (i.e., α_{k_1}). According to the event trace of process k_1, op_1 was executed two times, op_2 one time. Thus,

$$k_1.\text{signature} = 2op_1.\text{signature} + op_2.\text{signature} = [14, 47, 10, 0, 8, 47, 2, 0] \qquad (3)$$

An important thing to note is that in practice, if an operation is executed more than once, the derived signatures for each execution of the operation may not be equal (due to data dependencies, or pseudo-random behaviour of the operation). In that case, the operation's signature becomes the average signature of all executions of that operation.

A signature of a FIFO channel describes the load induced by the channel on memory components (i.e., α_b and β_b from Section 2). This communication requirement of a FIFO channel depends on the size of the token (in bytes) sent via the channel, and the total number of tokens sent. In our application models, the size of the tokens sent via one particular FIFO channel is always fixed (although the token size between channels can vary). The number of tokens sent via a FIFO channel can be extracted from the Kahn process' event trace. Each *write*-event in an event trace contains data about to which communication port the token was sent. So, the signature of a FIFO channel f is a two-element vector containing the number of tokens sent via the channel and the size of each token:

$$f.\text{signature} = [n_{tokens}, n_{size}] \tag{4}$$

For example, assume the event trace of process k_1 in Table 1(b) and a token size for channel f_1 of $n_{size} = 12$ bytes. Since process k_1 writes four times a token of 12 bytes to f_1 (see Table 1(b)), the signature of f_1 thus becomes:

$$f_1.\text{signature} = [4, 12] \tag{5}$$

4   Architectural Capabilities

Previously, the computational and communication *requirements* of an application have been defined. In this section, the computational and communication *capabilities* of processors and memories will be defined. These capabilities will also be encoded as (vector-based) signatures.

If a Kahn process k_1 is mapped onto a processor p_1, then the number of cycles p_1 is busy processing k_1 (denoted as $\mathcal{T}(p_1)$) can be calculated as a function of the signatures of k_1 (the computational requirements) and p_1 (the processor capabilities):

$$\mathcal{T}(p_1) = f(k_1.\text{signature}, p_1.\text{signature}) \tag{6}$$

The aim is to find or define both p_1.signature and the function f in (6). With these, we can calculate the number of cycles a processor is busy processing the *execute* events emitted by Kahn processes mapped onto the processor.

Using an ISS, we can measure how many cycles a certain operation takes when executed on a specific processor (like an ARM). If this is repeated for many operations, a *training set* can be built. Using this training set, the computational capabilities of a processor (i.e., its signature) can be derived by, for example, linear regression, or techniques used in the field of machine learning.

Using the example from the previous section, a (very small) training set can be made. This training set consists of the signatures of op_1 and op_2 and the associated cycle counts. Let us assume that executing op_1 took 185 cycles, and that op_2 took 369 cycles when executed on an ARM processor. Since a training set consists of a list of vectors (operation signatures), and a list of cycle counts, this problem can be solved using the least-squares method. For example, let $\vec{S}$ be the matrix with the signatures of operations op_1 and op_2 as rows, p_1.signature be the weight vector we want to calculate for processor p_1, and $\vec{c}$ be the vector with cycle counts for each row in $\vec{S}$. Then, $\vec{S} \cdot p_1.\text{signature} = \vec{c}$ is solved using the least squares method.

$$\begin{pmatrix} 3 & 15 & 1 & 0 & 3 & 9 & 0 & 0 \\ 8 & 17 & 8 & 0 & 2 & 29 & 2 & 0 \end{pmatrix} \cdot p_1.\text{signature} = \begin{pmatrix} 185 \\ 369 \end{pmatrix} \tag{7}$$

The signature of p_1 is the vector consisting of weights for each AIS opcode. The unit of the elements in the vector is 'cycles per instruction'. Note that these weights can be adapted in order to perform high-level architectural design space exploration for the given processor (e.g., make multiplications more/less expensive, etc.).

$$p_1.\text{signature} = [2.19, 7.11, 1.62, 0.0, 1.19, 7.4, 0.33, 0.0] \tag{8}$$

$\mathcal{T}^c(p) \leftarrow 0$
foreach $k \in X_p$ **do**
    foreach $f \in FIFOChannels_{k,\text{ext}}$ **do**
        $b \leftarrow f.\text{signature}[n_{tokens}] \cdot f.\text{signature}[n_{size}]$
        $m \leftarrow \mathcal{M}(f)$
        if f *is an incoming channel of k* **then**
            $\mathcal{T}^c(p) \leftarrow \mathcal{T}^c(p) + b/m.\text{signature}[r_{read}]$
        end
        if f *is an outgoing channel of k* **then**
            $\mathcal{T}^c(p) \leftarrow \mathcal{T}^c(p) + b/m.\text{signature}[r_{write}]$
        end
    end
end

Algorithm 1. Calculation of $\mathcal{T}^c(p)$

Given an operation signature s that is not included in the training set, the estimated number of cycles on p_1 for that signature is simply the inner product of s and p_1.signature. As will be elaborated in Section 6, this allows us to perform (off-line) training of our signature-based performance models. To derive processor signatures in this case, we use operation signatures from a training set of selected benchmark applications which is representative for our multimedia application domain. Hereafter, the computational performance of operation signatures from any (multimedia) application can be estimated using the above inner product.

The signature (and thus the communication capability) of a memory component (i.e., c_m) is a two-element vector $[r_{read}, r_{write}]$ that only consists of the (average) read and write latencies. Evidently, our current memory model fully abstracts away the underlying memory architecture. Also, in contrast to processor signatures, we have not yet developed any methods to get reliable memory signatures. Instead, a designer may use values from memory data sheets to create a memory signature.

5   Analytical Performance Estimation

In the previous sections, portions of a (signature-based) analytical performance model were presented. In this section, these portions are forged together to get an analytical performance model for an MP-SoC architecture.

First, some definitions have to be made. The set X_p is the set of processes that are mapped onto processor p. A similar definition applies to X_m, the set of channels mapped onto memory m. $\mathcal{M}(f)$ denotes the memory onto which channel f is mapped and $FIFOChannels_{k,\text{ext}}$ is the set of channels of process k that are mapped onto an external memory. Thus, $FIFOChannels_{k,\text{ext}} \subseteq B_k$ (see Section 2).

The time $\mathcal{T}^e(p)$ a processor p is spending on executing computational operations is the inner product of the sum of the signatures of all processes mapped on p, with the signature of p.

$$\mathcal{T}^e(p) = \left\langle \left(\sum_{k \in X_p} k.\text{signature} \right), p.\text{signature} \right\rangle \qquad (9)$$

$b \leftarrow 0$
foreach $f \in X_m$ **do**
    $b \leftarrow b + f.\text{signature}[n_{tokens}] \cdot f.\text{signature}[n_{size}]$
end
$\mathcal{T}(m) \leftarrow b/m.\text{signature}[r_{read}] + b/m.\text{signature}[r_{write}]$

Algorithm 2. Calculation of $\mathcal{T}(m)$

The time $\mathcal{T}^c(p)$ the processor is communicating depends on the number of bytes sent and received via FIFO channels that are mapped on an external memory. This quantity can be calculated by Algorithm 1. This algorithm should be self-explanatory as it simply calculates $\mathcal{T}^c(p)$ by accumulating all access latencies of the memories used by processor p.

The total time processor p is busy processing *read*, *write*, and *execute* events is

$$\mathcal{T}(p) = \mathcal{T}^e(p) + \mathcal{T}^c(p) \tag{10}$$

The number of cycles $\mathcal{T}(m)$ a memory m is busy sending or receiving data is calculated in Algorithm 2, in a similar way as $\mathcal{T}^c(p)$. Here, for each byte stored in the memory we accumulate both its read and write latencies.

The processing time of an architecture with a certain mapping depends on the architecture component with the largest processing time. Therefore, optimizing for performance (i.e., minimizing processing time) during design space exploration thus leads to solving

$$\min \max \left(\max_{p \in P} \mathcal{T}(p), \max_{m \in M} \mathcal{T}(m) \right) \tag{11}$$

6 Experimental Results

In this section, we present a validation experiment using a Motion-JPEG (M-JPEG) encoder application in which mapping exploration results from our signature-based analytic performance model are compared to simulation results. Furthermore, we also discuss an experiment in which we perform off-line training of the signature-based performance models using the Mediabench benchmark suite [6] as an external training set.

6.1 Initial Validation

To validate our signature-based analytic performance model, we studied the mapping of a Motion-JPEG (M-JPEG) encoder application onto an MP-SoC architecture. This is illustrated in Figure 2. The target MP-SoC consists of four ARM processors with local memory, FIFO buffers for streaming data, and a crossbar interconnect. The design space we considered for this experiment consists of all possible mappings of the M-JPEG tasks (i.e. processes) on the processors in the MP-SoC platform.

Before the M-JPEG application model was mapped on the architecture model, the application was compiled using an ARM C++ compiler, and executed within the SimIt-ARM instruction set simulator environment [9]. The generated ARM instruction traces

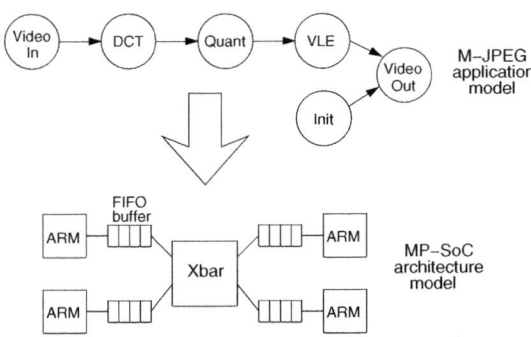

Fig. 2. Mapping an M-JPEG application to a crossbar-based MP-SoC architecture

were used to create the application *and* architecture signatures. These signatures were subsequently used for determining the parameters in our analytical performance model, as was previously explained. Note that this process is a one-time effort only.

Since the design space in our experiment is limited (consisting of 4096 mappings[2]), it was possible to quickly evaluate all of these mappings, both analytically as well as by simulation using our Sesame framework. In a first experiment, we applied the concept of signatures both in our analytical model *and* in the simulation model to which we compare. With respect to the latter, the processor components in our simulation model use the processor signatures to dynamically calculate computational latencies of incoming computational events (which are described using operation signatures) by means of the inner product as explained in Section 4. So, in this experiment we compare static (i.e. analytical) versus dynamic (i.e., simulative) performance estimation, both using signature-based models.

The analytical and simulation results are shown in Figure 3. Note that only the first fifty mappings are depicted due to space limitations (to avoid cluttering in the graph). Each mapping instance gets a certain index. The order of the mappings in Figure 3 is more or less arbitrary. Mappings with successive indices are not necessarily related to each other. In this experiment, we measured an average relative error of our analytical model compared to simulation of only 0.1%, with a standard deviation of 0.2. Evidently, these small errors with respect to the simulation-based estimates are promising results.

Although the above validation is a good sanity check, comparing against a simulation model that uses the same signature-based performance approximation provides good preconditions for obtaining small errors. Therefore, in a next experiment, we compare the results from our signature-based analytical model to the results from a more accurate simulation model that uses 'exact' latencies for the various computational events as directly obtained by ISS measurements (so, no latencies that are obtained using linear regression). In the remainder of this paper, we refer to this simulation model as our *reference model*. Figure 4 shows a scatter plot of the DSE results for both the signature-based analytical model and the reference model. The graph only shows the performance

---

[2] The number of unique mappings is even considerably less since the target platform is symmetrical.

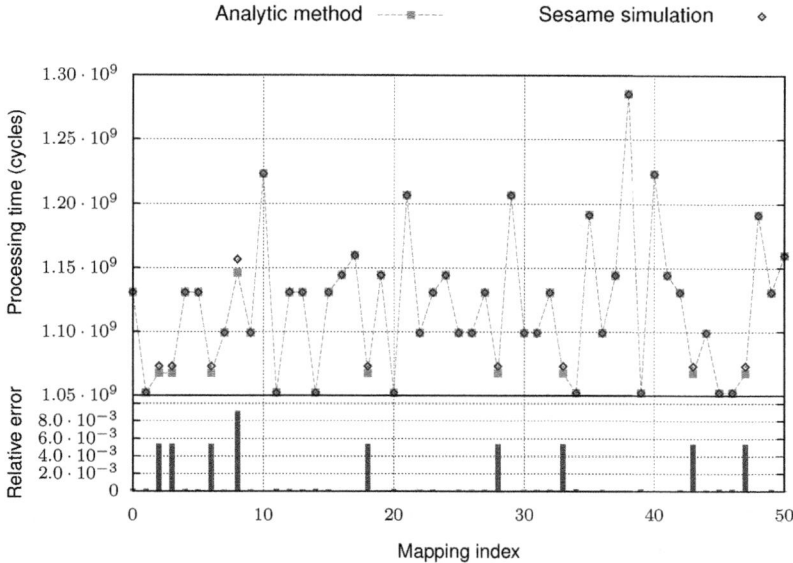

Fig. 3. Comparison between signature-based simulation and analytical models for M-JPEG mapping DSE on a crossbar-based multiprocessor architecture

results of *unique* mapping instances. Here, we have sorted all mapping instances based on the performance order of the mappings from the reference model.

The results from Figure 4 indicate that the estimates of our signature-based analytical model are fairly accurate, especially for the better-performing mappings (i.e. lower mapping indices in Figure 4). The overall average error is 9.2% with a standard deviation of 5.8. For the best 100 mappings, the average error only is 4.5% with a standard deviation of 2.1. But most importantly, our signature-based analytical model finds exactly the same optimal mappings as the reference model. Needless to say, this precision of finding the correct optimal mappings is of eminent importance to the process of design space pruning, helping the designer to decide which design points need to be studied in more detail using simulative methods. Another observation that can be made is that for the less optimal mappings (i.e., higher mapping indices), the error as well as the trend behavior deteriorate. This can be explained by the fact that in these less optimal mappings less concurrency is exploited, and therefore any errors in the signature-based latency calculations are more easily accumulated.

Besides accuracy, the efficiency of the performance evaluation is of great importance since the proposed performance models are targeted towards pruning large design spaces. Here, we would like to stress that the evaluation time of our signature-based analytical performance models is several orders of magnitude smaller as compared to Sesame's system-level simulations. This should allow us to study much larger design spaces, from which promising candidate designs can be selected that can then be further studied using system-level simulation.

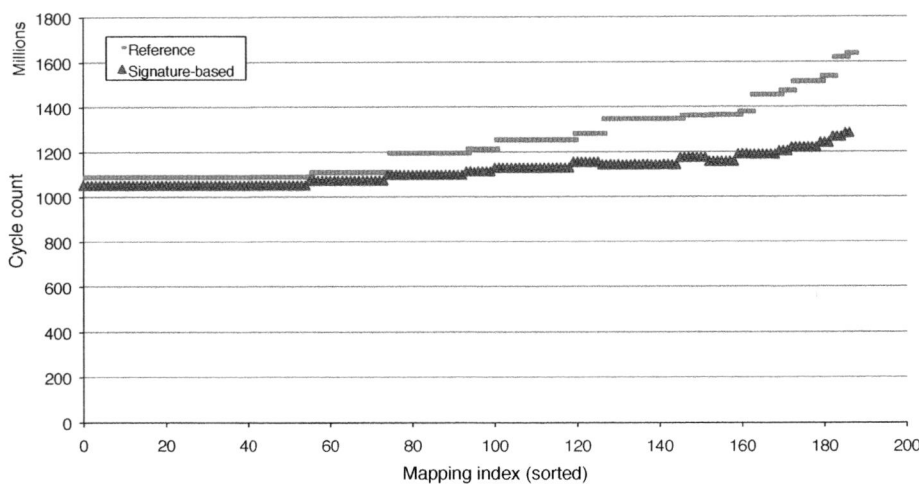

Fig. 4. Comparing the DSE results from our signature-based model against those from an ISS-calibrated reference simulation model

6.2 Off-Line Training of the Performance Model

In the previous section, we used the same application (M-JPEG) for both training of the signature-based analytical performance model (i.e., obtaining processor signatures for ARM processors) and the performance estimation itself. Since this may be less realistic, we also present several results from an experiment in which we perform off-line training of the signature-based performance model using the Mediabench benchmark suite [6], after which we again apply this externally calibrated performance model to the M-JPEG case study.

To train our performance model, we first constructed the (application) operation signatures for each separate Mediabench program[3] using the approach as discussed in Section 3. Since the execution time (in terms of simulated cycles) of the mpeg2enc program is quite high, we split up the execution of this program into four chunks, and generated a separate operation signature for each of these chunks (each representing different execution phases of the program). Figure 5 shows the histogram of the resulting AIS opcode counts for each Mediabench program. This graph clearly shows that most programs are dominated by AIS_ISIMPLE instructions, followed by AIS_MEM and AIS_BRANCH instructions respectively.

Similar to Figure 5, Figure 6 shows the AIS opcode histogram for the application processes in our target M-JPEG application. Here, we excluded the AIS opcodes with a zero or insignificant contribution. At first sight, the trends in both Figures 5 and 6 are similar, which thus appears to be confirming that Mediabench is a representative training set for M-JPEG.

---

[3] The pgp, ghostscript, and sphere benchmarks were excluded due to execution problems on the SimIt-ARM simulator.

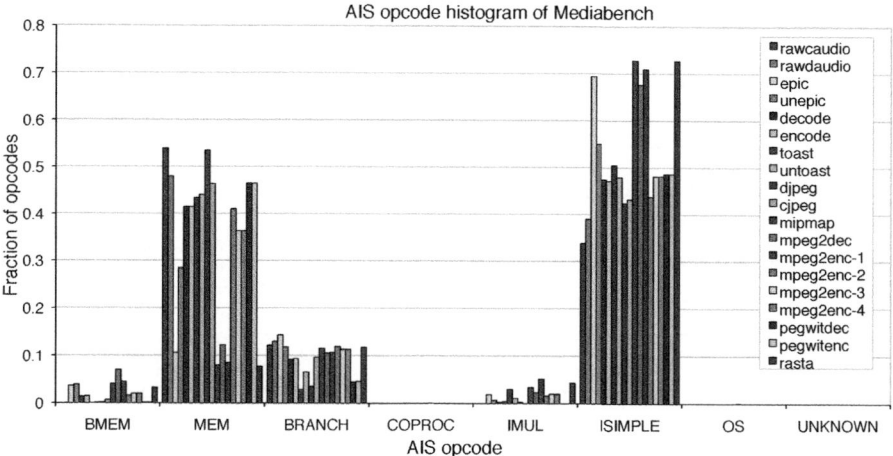

Fig. 5. Histogram with the various AIS opcode counts of the Mediabench training set

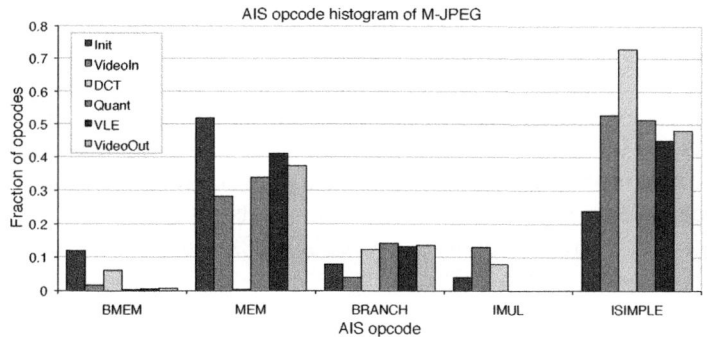

Fig. 6. Histogram with the various AIS opcode counts of M-JPEG

As a next step, we determined the processor signatures for our performance model using the Mediabench operation signatures. Using this Mediabench-trained performance model, we again performed the DSE experiment with the M-JPEG application. Figure 7 shows a comparison of the DSE results of the Mediabench-trained ("Full Mediabench" in the graph) and the reference simulation model from the previous section. Again, the graph only shows the performance results of unique mappings, and all mapping instances are sorted based on the performance order of the mappings from the reference model. Comparing the Mediabench-trained model ("Full Mediabench") to the reference model, it is clear that there is a significant absolute error between the results of these models (an average error of 29.6%, see Table 2). But, the trends of the graphs of the two models still are highly similar. This is especially true for the better-performing mapping instances (lower mapping indices). This again implies that both models find exactly the same optimal mappings.

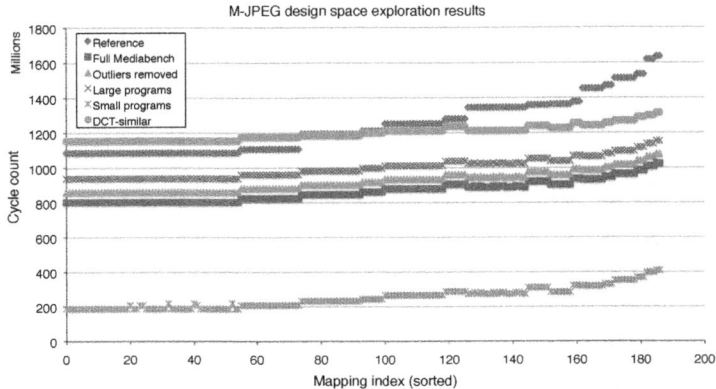

Fig. 7. Comparing the DSE results from our Mediabench-trained models against those from the reference model from Section 6.1

To study the sensitivity of the selected benchmark programs that are used for training, we performed a number of experiments in which we clustered the Mediabench programs according to some measure, after which we trained our performance model with the programs from such a cluster only. As a first experiment, we applied our performance model that was trained with all Mediabench programs to the operation signatures from the Mediabench programs themselves. Then, we clustered only those programs that show a good fit with the performance model (i.e., removing the outliers). Training the performance model again with this cluster, gives the results that are tagged with "Outliers removed" in Figure 7 and Table 2. The results of this new performance model are slightly better (average error of 24.9%, see Table 2) than the model that was trained with all Mediabench programs.

We selected the program size as the second means to cluster our Mediabench training set. Programs with more than 500 million executed instructions are clustered as "Large programs", while the remaining programs are clustered as "Small programs". Figure 7 again shows the DSE results when training our performance model with one of these clusters. The cluster with large programs again shows an accuracy improvement, lowering the average error to 18.6%. Clearly, the cluster with small programs only yields poor results, both in terms of average error (79.8%) and trend behavior. The latter can even be seen at the lower mapping indices where some optimal mappings (according to the reference model) are not considered optimal according to the model trained with small programs only.

Since the DCT process in the M-JPEG encoder is dominant in terms of computational intensity, our final clustering is based on similarity with the DCT process (in terms of AIS opcode distribution). We again trained our model with these DCT-similar programs. The DSE results of this cluster show again considerable improvement with an average error of only 7%, which is even slightly better than the result from the M-JPEG-trained model from the previous section. This can be explained by the fact that M-JPEG also contains processes that are dissimilar to the DCT process and which have a negative influence on the training of the model.

Table 2. Average error and standard deviation of the various trained models as compared to the reference model

	Full Mediabench	Outliers removed	Large programs	Small programs	DCT-similar programs
Av. error	29.6%	24.9%	18.6%	79.8%	7.0%
Std.dev.	3.8	4.4	5.1	2.1	4.5

6.3 Discussion

The results from the previous section show that Mediabench can be a suitable training set for our signature-based performance models, provided that a proper cluster of Mediabench programs is selected for training. The "Big programs" cluster already yields decent results whereas the "DCT-similar" cluster shows that fairly accurate results are possible with off-line training. Noteworthy, however, is the fact that almost all training sets / clusters, except for the cluster with small Mediabench programs, yield the same optimal design points. This indicates that, at least for the studied M-JPEG application, signature-based performance modeling is a relatively robust technique for quickly exploring and pruning the vast mapping design space. However, more study is needed in several directions. For example, we need to investigate additional types of clustering of Mediabench, where e.g. the granularity of the code sequences used for generating operation signatures also plays a role. That is, so far we have used entire Mediabench programs (except for `mpeg2enc`) to generate operation signatures. But, like we did for `mpeg2enc`, we can also study the splitting of other large programs in smaller chunks (representing different execution phases of these programs) to have more control on the size of the training set, which could e.g. open up new possibilities for clustering.

Moreover, and naturally following from the above clustering discussion, we also need to investigate the refinement of our AIS. Since most machine instructions map onto only three AIS opcodes (`AIS_ISIMPLE`, `AIS_MEM`, and `AIS_BRANCH`), these opcodes can be refined to improve the accuracy of our analytical models. To further increase accuracy of our signature-based models, we should also study the extension of our signatures to better capture micro-architectural behavior (such as cache behavior), but still at a high level of abstraction. Of course, such extensions may again affect the possibilities for clustering of the training set (e.g., clustering on different cache behavior).

7   Related Work

Much work has been performed in the area of software performance estimation [10], including methods that use profiling information, typically gathered at the instruction level. For example, in [11] a static software performance estimation technique is presented which uses profiling at the instruction level and which includes the modeling of pipeline hazards in the timing model. In [12], a source-based estimation technique is proposed using the concept of "virtual instructions". These are similar (albeit a bit more low level) to our AIS instructions, but are directly generated by a compiler framework.

Software performance is then calculated based on the accumulation of the performance estimates of these virtual instructions. The idea of convolving application and machine signatures, where the signatures contain coarse-grained system-level information, has also been applied in the domain of performance prediction for high-performance computer systems [13].

In [14], a workload modeling approach based on execution profiles is discussed for statistical micro-architectural simulation. Because the authors address simulation at the micro-architectural level, their profiles include much more details (such as pipeline and cache behavior), while we address system-level modeling at a higher level of abstraction. In [15], the authors suggest to derive a linear model from a small set of simulations. This method tries to model the performance of a processor at a mesoscopic level. For example, cache behaviour and pipeline characteristics are taken into account. The significance of all cache and pipeline related parameters is determined by simulation-based linear regression models. This may be comparable with the 'weight' vector discussed in Section 4. Another interesting approach is presented in [16], in which the CPI for in-order architectures is predicted using a Monte Carlo based model. The Milan framework [17] deploys a design pruning approach using symbolic (instead of analytic) analysis methods to reduce the design space that needs to be explored with simulation.

8   Conclusions

In this paper, we presented a technique for calibrating our analytical performance models used for system-level design space pruning. More specifically, we introduced the concept of application and architecture signatures, which can be related with each other to obtain performance estimates. Using a case study with a Motion-JPEG encoder application, we showed that our signature-based analytical performance model shows promising results with respect to accuracy. Moreover, we presented a number of experiments in which we performed so-called off-line training of our signature-based performance model using the Mediabench benchmark suite. These experiments indicate that such off-line training is a promising mechanism for obtaining trustworthy estimation models in the scope of early design space pruning.

Since the Motion-JPEG application used in our study still is relatively static in its behavior, and thus fairly well-suited for prediction, we need to extend our experiments in the future to also include more dynamic applications. Moreover, we need to further study the off-line training of our models, also in relationship to possible refinement and/or extension of our signatures to better capture both application as well as micro-architectural behavior.

References

1. Pimentel, A.D., Erbas, C., Polstra, S.: A systematic approach to exploring embedded system architectures at multiple abstraction levels. IEEE Trans. on Computers 55, 99–112 (2006)
2. Erbas, C., Pimentel, A.D., Thompson, M., Polstra, S.: A framework for system-level modeling and simulation of embedded systems architectures. EURASIP Journal on Embedded Systems (2007), doi:10.1155/2007/82123

3. Erbas, C., Cerav-Erbas, S., Pimentel, A.D.: A multiobjective optimization model for exploring multiprocessor mappings of process networks. In: Proc. of the Int. Conference on Hardware/Software Codesign & System Synthesis (CODES+ISSS), pp. 182–187 (2003)
4. Erbas, C., Cerav-Erbas, S., Pimentel, A.D.: Multiobjective optimization and evolutionary algorithms for the application mapping problem in multiprocessor system-on-chip design. IEEE Trans. on Evolutionary Computation 10, 358–374 (2006)
5. Jaddoe, S., Pimentel, A.D.: Signature-based calibration of analytical system-level performance models. In: Bereković, M., Dimopoulos, N., Wong, S. (eds.) SAMOS 2008. LNCS, vol. 5114, pp. 268–278. Springer, Heidelberg (2008)
6. Lee, C., Potkonjak, M., Mangione-Smith, W.H.: Mediabench: a tool for evaluating and synthesizing multimedia and communicatons systems. In: Proc. of the ACM/IEEE International Symposium on Microarchitecture (Micro), pp. 330–335 (1997)
7. Kahn, G.: The semantics of a simple language for parallel programming. Information Processing 74, 471–475 (1974)
8. Keutzer, K., Malik, S., Newton, A., Rabaey, J., Sangiovanni-Vincentelli, A.: System level design: Orthogonalization of concerns and platform-based design. IEEE Trans. on Computer-Aided Design of Integrated Circuits and Systems 19 (2000)
9. Qin, W., Malik, S.: Flexible and formal modeling of microprocessors with application to retargetable simulation. In: Design, Automation and Test in Europe (DATE) Conference, pp. 556–561 (2003)
10. Bammi, J.R., Harcoun, E., Kruijtzer, W., Lavagno, L., Lazarescu, M.: Software performance estimation strategies in a system level design tool. In: International Conference on Hardware Software Codesign (CODES), pp. 82–87 (2000)
11. Beltrame, G., Brandolese, C., Fornaciari, W., Salice, F., Sciuto, D., Trianni, V.: An assembly-level execution-time model for pipelined architectures. In: Proc. of Int. Conference on Computer Aided Design (ICCAD), pp. 195–200 (2001)
12. Giusto, P., Martin, G., Harcourt, E.: Reliable estimation of execution time of embedded software. In: Proc. of the Design, Automation, and Test in Europe (DATE) Conference, pp. 580–588 (2001)
13. Snavely, A., Carrington, L., Wolter, N.: Modeling application performance by convolving machine signatures with application profiles. In: Proc. of the IEEE Workshop on Workload Characterization, pp. 149–156 (2001)
14. Eeckhout, L., Nussbaum, S., Smith, J., De Bosschere, K.: Statistical simulation: adding efficiency to the computer designer's toolbox. IEEE Micro 23, 26–38 (2003)
15. Joseph, P., Vaswani, K., Thazhuthaveetil, M.: Construction and Use of Linear Regression Models for Processor Performance Analysis. In: Proc. of the Int. Symposium on High-Performance Computer Architecture, pp. 99–108 (2006)
16. Srinivasan, R., Cook, J., Lubeck, O.: Performance Modeling Using Monte Carlo Simulation. IEEE Computer Architecture Letters 5 (2006)
17. Mohanty, S., Prasanna, V.K.: Rapid system-level performance evaluation and optimization for application mapping onto SoC architectures. In: Proc. of the IEEE Int. ASIC/SOC Conference (2002)

Author Index

GPSR Compliance

The European Union's (EU) General Product Safety Regulation (GPSR)
is a set of rules that requires consumer products to be safe and our
obligations to ensure this.

If you have any concerns about our products, you can contact us on
ProductSafety@springernature.com

In case Publisher is established outside the EU, the EU authorized
representative is:

Springer Nature Customer Service Center GmbH
Europaplatz 3
69115 Heidelberg, Germany

Batch number: 09490872

Printed by Printforce, the Netherlands